# Introduction to Digital Control Systems

# INTRODUCTION TO DIGITAL CONTROL SYSTEMS

**Macmillan Publishing Company**

*New York*

**Collier Macmillan Publishers**

*London*

Macmillan Publishing Company
866 Third Avenue, New York, New York 10022

Collier Macmillan Canada, Inc.


Library of Congress Cataloging in Publication Data

VanLandingham, Hugh F.
  Introduction to digital control systems.

  Includes index.
  1. Digital control systems. I. Title.
TJ223.M53V36 1985          003          84-10031
ISBN 0-02-422610-6


Printing: 1 2 3 4 5 6 7 8     Year: 5 6 7 8 9 0 1 2



ISBN 0-02-422610-6

*In Memory of my Mother*

# PREFACE

For many years the study of control systems has implied a study of analysis and design techniques directed toward continuous-time systems; originally as frequency domain methods and more recently as state-variable methods. With the advent of inexpensive, reliable digital computation the emphasis is being shifted rapidly toward discrete-time systems and computer control. The material in this text is directed to this present and growing need for a comprehensive exposition of the current techniques in this area.

The level of this book is appropriate for senior or first-year graduate students in engineering. It is assumed that students using this book have had some applications of Laplace transforms and some familiarity with matrix operations, for example in the study of networks. It is also helpful if they have had an introduction to linear systems as, for instance, in a classical controls course. Advanced students may be able to overcome background deficiencies by reviewing the material in the appropriate appendix.

The basic material, including many of the present chapters, has been used in a first-year graduate controls sequence in the Electrical Engineering Department at Virginia Polytechnic Institute and State University, but Part I and portions of Part II could easily be used in an undergraduate controls option to supplement a standard introductory text in control theory. Some sections are marked with a star (★). These can be omitted without loss of continuity.

This text has been written on the premise that a better understanding of computer control methods is achieved by presenting a proper balance of transform and state-variable techniques. Many of the elementary procedures are introduced in the context of the $z$-domain (discrete-time system transform domain) and subsequently extended in scope by a translation into a state-variable format. An effort has been made to maintain the direction of the book toward practical system models at the expense of not being completely general. For instance, linear, constant-coefficient models are used whenever possible to simplify the development and understanding of techniques which may be suitable for a wider class of systems such as time-dependent or nonlinear systems.

Part I presents an introduction to discrete-time systems and some general techniques of analysis, including the $z$-transform approach and the basics of state-variable analysis. Part II contains the design oriented material, again both from an operational and from a state-variable approach. An effort was made to include some classical sampled-data design as well as the basic design methods of modern control theory. Both Part I and Part II deal primarily with deterministic signals, but in the latter part of Chapter 9 some of the design methods are extended to include stochastic signals. Optimal estimation is combined with optimal control to provide solutions to LQG-problems (Linear model, Quadratic performance measure and Gaussian disturbances). The material in this book may be used for a one-quarter or a one-semester course, but is more comfortably used over a longer period, particularly at the undergraduate level where the presentation is necessarily more detailed. The material divides well for one part per quarter at the senior level following a first course in classical control.

Chapters 1, 2, 3 and major portions of Chapters 6, 7 and 8 provide sufficient material for a one quarter introduction of discrete-time systems to students at the undergraduate level. To emphasize digital control with its quantization effects, the material of Chapter 5 should be included in place of some of the detail of Chapters 7 and 8. A semester course would allow ample time to cover all of these topics.

The modeling and analysis portion of the text can be given proper treatment in a one quarter course. The emphasis is on fundamental understanding and appreciation of digital effects. Students with some previous background in discrete-time systems, particularly at the graduate level, could easily devote most of their effort toward the design chapters after an appropriate selection of review material from the earlier chapters.

A number of programs are listed in Appendix D. These programs provide additional capability for certain sections of the text and are not meant to be inclusive of every possible need. For the most part the student is encouraged to develop his own programs as needed. The programs in Appendix D have been written in BASIC for the IBM PC, but may be translated to other machines relatively easily.

Since the end-of-chapter problems provide an integral part of the learning mechanism, an instructor's manual containing detailed solutions to the chapter problems will be available on request.

H.F.V.

# CONTENTS

## APPENDICES

## ANSWERS TO SELECTED PROBLEMS

## INDEX

# Introduction to Digital Control Systems

# PART I

# MODELING AND ANALYSIS OF DISCRETE-TIME SYSTEMS

## CHAPTER 1

# Introduction to Digital Control

This book is devoted to the study of techniques of analyzing and designing discrete-time control systems. Other terms frequently used interchangeably are discrete-data, sampled-data, and digital control systems. As we will see later in this chapter, the term ''digital'' usually implies a quantization of amplitude as well as of time due to finite binary word lengths. Also involved with digital control is signal coding; for instance, coding into binary number representations. However, the emphasis of the material in this text is mainly at a level higher than that of detailed binary coding or associated electronic circuitry. In this chapter the basic definitions and concepts of systems and control are presented along with a fundamental development of discrete-time system response via the method of convolution. Subsequent chapters introduce alternative approaches of working with discrete-time system models; in particular, $z$-transforms and state variables, with a much higher percentage of the effort on state variables since that formulation is directly applicable to the development of associated computer algorithms for multivariable systems.

## BASIC SYSTEM CONCEPTS AND CLASSIFICATION

The important concepts and techniques, which are presented later, are based on mathematical models. These mathematical models represent the formulation of prior information into analytic or numerical structure. Most engineering problems involve "modeling" as a first stage in the solution. Modeling is a difficult part of an analysis. It is here that the engineer must make a compromise between mathematical complexity and accuracy of representation, hence the need for engineering judgement. With complex problems a typical approach is to formulate simple models at first, followed by more realistic and, therefore, more complicated models.

The problem of modeling is unavoidably related to the formalism of system classification. For instance, a physical device whose behavior is represented by a set of ordinary differential equations is said to be a (finite) continuous-time, lumped-parameter system. However, if the device is described more exactly by a set of partial-differential equations, the system model is referred to as a distributed-parameter system. The following development establishes and illustrates different categories of analytical models. It will be evident that the basic laws of physics are the primary tools of modeling.

The system model of the physical process is then a description of an operation that processes the excitation into the system response. This cause and effect relation is illustrated in Fig. 1-1 and can be represented symbolically as

$$H[e] = r \tag{1-1}$$

This is the classical system "black-box" viewpoint. The significance of Fig. 1-1 is to focus attention on the external behavior of the system. The word "system" is used loosely to refer either to the physical abstraction being modeled or to a mathematical representation (model) of this physical abstraction. To be more precise, it becomes necessary to state explicitly what is meant by certain technical terms. For instance, a system could be defined very generally as any segment of our environment; however, for present purposes this definition is much too vague to be of any use. Let us, then, define a *physical system* as a collection of interacting component parts, usually with identified excitations and responses. From the physical system a mathematical model is derived. This *mathematical model*, or simply model, is an analytical description of the physical system.

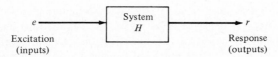

**FIGURE 1-1. Input-output block diagram.**

The inputs and outputs generally are "measurable" variations in time such as voltage, velocity, pressure, and so on. Physical variables exhibiting this time variation are called *signals*. Signals whose values are of interest over a continuum of time points are *continuous-time signals,* for example, sin $t$, $a + bt$, exp $(at)$ for values of $t$ greater than 0. It is frequently convenient to think of all physical variables as being intrinsically continuous-time signals. Practically, of course, there are many cases where measurements of signals are made at discrete points in time such as every second or twice a month. The resulting set of samples describes a *discrete-time signal* since it is a signal either defined at, or of interest only at, a discrete set of time values.

A system model whose signals are all continuous-time signals is called a *continuous-time system*. System models having only discrete-time signals are *discrete-time systems*. Typically, continuous-time systems are characterized by differential equations, whereas discrete-time systems are described by difference equations. Systems with both categories of signals are referred to as *hybrid systems*. See Section 1-7 for a discussion of difference equations.

### EXAMPLE 1-1 (A Continuous-Time System)

The physical model for this system is the network shown in Fig. 1-2. From Kirchhoff's voltage law and the elemental relations a mathematical model for the circuit is easily determined to be

$$L \frac{di(t)}{dt} + Ri(t) = e(t) \tag{1-2}$$

Equation (1-2) is a differential equation, which suggests that if $e(t)$ is a known forcing function (input), that $i(t)$, the network response (output), can be determined once the parameters $R$, $L$, and the initial current $i(0)$ are specified. Thus, a system description would be a black box with input signal $e(t)$ and output signal $i(t)$ with the cause and effect relationship represented analytically by Eq. (1-2). ∎

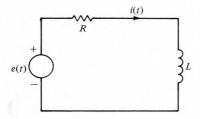

**FIGURE 1-2.   Electrical network for Example 1-1.**

### EXAMPLE 1-2 (A Discrete-Time System)

Suppose that the familiar process of compound interest is viewed as a discrete-time system. An initial sum of money $u(1)$ is invested in a savings account at time zero and an $r\%$ interest rate accrues annually. Additional deposits $u(k)$ are made at the beginning of year $k$ for $k = 2, 3, 4, \ldots$. If $p(k)$ represents the amount on deposit during year $k$, it can be shown that

$$p(k) = (1 + 0.01r)p(k - 1) + u(k), \quad p(0) = 0 \qquad (1\text{-}3)$$

From knowledge of the initial investment and subsequent yearly deposits the value $p(k)$ can be determined for $k = 1, 2, 3, \ldots$. Clearly, Eq. (1-3) represents a discrete-time system with input sequence $u(k)$ and output (response) $p(k)$ for $k = 1, 2, 3, \ldots$. ∎

Many other classifications for systems have proved useful. Among these are the concepts of being linear, stationary, random, or lumped. To develop these ideas, consider that with the notation of Eq. (1-1), $H$ is simply a correspondence between two collections of signal functions. Since the operator $H$ represents a mathematical model of the physical system in that $H$ describes implicitly the behavior of the model, it will be possible to classify systems from the properties of their $H$ operator.

Using the notation that $H[x]$ is the response of a system to the signal $x$, we make the following definitions:

A system is *homogeneous* whenever $H[ax] = aH[x]$, where $x$ represents a signal and $a$, a constant multiplier.
A system is *additive* whenever $H[x + y] = H[x] + H[y]$ for any two signals $x$ and $y$.
A system that is both additive and homogeneous is a *linear* system.

To illustrate the above definitions, consider the following simple electric circuit.

### EXAMPLE 1-3 (Interpretation of an Electric Network)

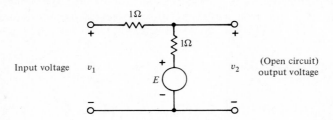

(a) Consider the voltage $v_1$ to be the excitation and $v_2$ to be the open-circuit response signal.

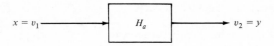

Then $y = v_2 = 0.5(v_1 + E) \equiv H_a[v_1] = H_a[x]$. Since $v_2 \neq 0$ when $v_1 = 0$, the system $H_a$ is not homogeneous and therefore *not* linear!
(b) Now, consider the voltage $E$ as a second excitation signal.

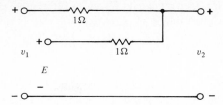

In the more conceptual form this system appears as follows.

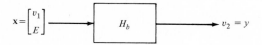

that is, the two inputs are grouped together as a vector input. The output can be written as $y = H_b[\mathbf{x}]$, where $H_b$ is a constant matrix.

$$y = v_2 = 0.5 \begin{bmatrix} 1 & 1 \end{bmatrix} \begin{bmatrix} v_1 \\ E \end{bmatrix} = 0.5 \begin{bmatrix} 1 & 1 \end{bmatrix} \mathbf{x} = H_b[\mathbf{x}] \qquad \blacksquare$$

The system described in this manner satisfies the definition of linearity. The property of linearity is sometimes referred to as the *superposition principle* since for a linear system $H$ with two excitation signals $x_1$ and $x_2$ having arbitrary magnitudes $a$ and $b$, the response is equivalent to superimposing the two response signals from the separate inputs, that is,

$$H[ax_1 + bx_2] = aH[x_1] + bH[x_2] \qquad (1\text{-}4)$$

In Example 1-3a the operator $H_a$ is simply a function of the input signal. Thus, the value of the output signal at time $t$ depends only on the value of the input signal at the same instant $t$. A system having this property will be called *instantaneous*. More generally, the response of a system at time $t$ will depend on some portion (possibly all) of the past history of the excitation(s), called a *dynamic* system. Typical descriptions of dynamic systems are differential equations (for continuous-time systems) and difference equations (for discrete-time systems).

The system is termed *deterministic* if for each input signal (vector), there corresponds a unique output signal (vector); that is, no random variations are present in the system.

Referring back to Example 1-3a again, it is easily seen that if $E$ is a function of time, the system description $H_a$ will change with time. That is, the response will be different for different times of inputting the same excitation signal. Such a system will be called *time-varying* or *nonstationary;* otherwise, time-invariant or stationary.

The mathematical model of a physical system may take various forms. Thus far, except for Examples 1-1 and 1-2 the operator $H$ has represented all the internal complexity of the model; but a more familiar and frequent characterization is a differential equation (or a set of simultaneous differential equations).

Suppose now that a certain system model is a single differential equation relating the response $y$ with the excitation $x$ as follows.

$$\frac{dy}{dt} + ay(t) = x(t) \tag{1-5}$$

Equation (1-5) could, for instance, be the mathematical model of a unit mass moving under the force $x(t)$ with friction present ($y$ being the velocity of the rigid mass). If it is further assumed [for a unique solution $y(t)$] that at time $t = 0$, $y$ has the value $y_0$, then an equivalent expression relating $x$ and $y$ is

$$y(t) = e^{-at}\left\{ y_0 + \int_0^t e^{aw} x(w)\, dw \right\} \tag{1-6}$$

Equations (1-5) and (1-6) illustrate two means of describing the same physical system. Both of these relations will satisfy the property of linearity when the initial velocity $y_0 = 0$. Indeed, Eq. (1-5) is a linear differential equation. Similar expressions reflecting nonlinearities of system behavior can, however, be extremely complicated.

Usually, the implicit form of Eq. (1-5) is the more convenient form to use; thus, the term *differential systems* describing such models is common.

There are many classifications for differential systems, most of which correspond to terminology used in the theory of differential equations per se and some are very natural extensions of that terminology.

An *ordinary scalar differential equation* is one that expresses a relation between an independent variable and a dependent variable together with derivatives of the dependent variable with respect to the independent variable. Equation (1-5) is such an equation, where $t$ is the independent variable representing the time continuum and $y(t)$ is the dependent variable. More generally, a single differential equation will involve several independent variables, for example, $x$, $y$, $z$, and $t$ representing the three Cartesian coordinates and the time variable. Such an equation is referred to as a *partial differential equation* since a notation is required to indicate with respect to which independent variable derivatives are taken, namely, partial derivatives. Another important classification is with regard to the order of the highest derivative, referred to as the *order* of the equation. When, in an ordinary or partial differential equation, the dependent variable and its derivatives occur to the first power, and not to other powers or products, the equation is said to be *linear*. Note that a linear differential equation, like Eq. (1-5), represents a linear system only if the initial conditions are zero, that is, only if the zero-input solution or response is zero.

From these concepts of differential equations let us further classify our system models. If the time-domain description of a system is a differential system involving partial differentials, that is, more than one independent variable, then the model will be referred to as a *distributed-parameter system*. If the differential system model involves only ordinary differential equations, the model is a *lumped-parameter system*.

These last two definitions are motivated from the descriptions of physical systems. For example, in analyzing the vibration of a spring-mass system, we may choose to regard the mass as a perfectly rigid body and the spring as being an inertialess device that relates a particular deformation to a particular force acting between its extremities. In this case, all the interaction between the mass and the spring occurs as if these were "point" elements, for example, as if the mass were "lumped" at one point located at its center of gravity.

In general, distributed-parameter systems are more difficult to analyze, and it is frequently possible to consider an equivalent "discretized" lumped-parameter system that is a reliable model for the system.

Clearly, if the mass is made small enough, the inertia of the spring itself will become appreciable. If this is the situation, the lumped-parameter model will require modification, and a more appropriate model would consider the "distributed" aspect of the mass in the spring.

More specific examples related to the modeling stage and how the choice of a model relates to predicted system performance will be given later. Whatever the problem, however, our approach will generally be to construct a linear discrete-time, deterministic, stationary model if at all feasible. A primary motivation is to obtain structures amenable to computer simulation and control without additional approximation.

**1-2**

## FEEDBACK SYSTEMS AND DIGITAL CONTROL

The word "control" can be used in various contexts to have different meanings. All of these meanings, however, have a common base: that "control" means influence in the cause-and-effect sense. Everyday situations present innumerable problems of this nature; to drive a car is to control the actions of the car. Light switches, thermostats, and so on exert control over illumination or temperature. Even walking combines intricate operations of muscles and nerves in some complex fashion to provide a sophisticated control mechanism. From the background of the previous section, any system with an excitation and a response (see Fig. 1-1) can be called a *control system* if the underlying design is such that the excitations produce some *desired* response.

The particular way in which the excitation is formed leads us to distinguish between two types of control systems. The first type is an *open-loop* control system, which derives its excitation completely independently of its response. Although open-loop control has some fundamental drawbacks, there are many useful systems that employ this mode of operation. For instance, the common washing machine could be considered a system whose excitations are soap, water, and number of wash cycles. Its sole response is to elicit the response of cleanliness of its contents. The normal operation is open-loop since all inputs are preset, relying only on the initial judgement of the operator, and not de-

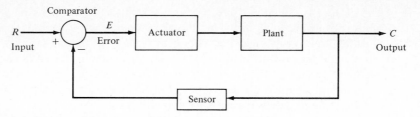

**FIGURE 1-3.   A basic feedback structure.**

pendent on the cleanliness of its contents at any time during the wash. The second general type of control is called closed-loop control. A *closed-loop* control system is one in which excitation in some suitable way depends on its response. Thus, the output is coupled back for comparison with the input to the system. This is called *feedback*. Nearly all sophisticated control systems involve feedback. A general feedback configuration is illustrated in Fig. 1-3. For many problems the input represents a "reference setting," for instance, a setting on a thermostat for temperature regulation. The reader will note that Fig. 1-3 shows an "error signal," which is the difference between the input (reference) and the (controlled) output. A key ingredient of feedback control is the ability of the system to generate this error signal. A classical example of feedback control is the mechanism of eye–hand coordination where the "feedback" is obtained visually. When the command (input) is given to reach for an object, the brain generates an "error" related to the distance between the hand and the object and continues to "actuate" the hand's motion until the error is zero. The superiority of feedback control over open-loop control is its ability to "adapt" to circumstances unforeseen by the open-loop system. Feedback provides additional benefits such as a reduced sensitivity to inaccuracies of the system model, random disturbances, and parameter variations. The specific advantages of feedback in controlling system response will be discussed in detail in later chapters.

The application of digital computers to feedback control is an exciting opportunity for today's engineers. Many industrial processes in paper mills, chemical plants, and such presently use computer feedback control only on certain specific processes for which a large financial return is possible with accurate control. The reason for this is the relatively large investment necessary in the past to implement such systems. With the present trend of small computers becoming more plentiful and less expensive, an increasing number of applications for digital control are being made economically feasible.

The basic feedback loop of Fig. 1-3 can be expanded to illustrate the use of a digital computer in the loop. The flexibility of the computer is used to adjust the signal to the actuator to provide acceptable system response. Note that Fig. 1-4 includes an *analog-to-digital converter* (ADC) and a *digital-to-analog converter* (DAC) to condition the signals into and out of the computer. The scheme shown in Fig 1-4 implies that the error signal is formed within the computer. Comparing Fig. 1-4 with Fig. 1-3, observe that the "fixed elements" consist of an *actuator* and *plant*. The actuator supplies the power required for control

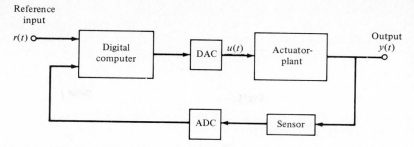

**FIGURE 1-4.   Direct digital control with output feedback.**

while the plant is usually taken to be the passive part of the fixed elements. The power of the actuator is applied to the plant under the stimulus of the error signal to produce the desired behavior of the output.

The reference signal of Fig. 1-4 is sometimes supplied by a supervisory computer that governs the operation of many such control loops. Let us now concentrate our efforts toward *direct digital control* (DDC) because of its great application potential. It is convenient to think of the controller's operation as that of exciting the actuator based on the (feedback) error. Perhaps the simplest control law is to provide "proportional" control, that is, a situation where the signal to the actuator is proportional to the error signal. This and other basic control laws that can be provided by the controller are (see Fig. 1-5)

Proportional Control $u(t) = k_p e(t)$

Integral Control $u(t) = k_i \int e(t)\, dt$

Proportional-Integral Control (PI) $u(t) = k_p e(t) + k_i \int e(t)\, dt$

Proportional-Integral-Derivative Control (PID)

$$u(t) = \mathrm{k}_p e(t) + k_i \int e(t)\, dt + k_d \frac{de(t)}{dt}$$

The error signal $e(t)$ represents the difference between the reference signal $r(t)$ and the controlled output $y(t)$. The controller output is $u(t)$, the actuator signal.

Although a digital controller cannot provide exact integration or differentiation, similar operations can be made. However, the design techniques presented in later chapters will be significantly more sophisticated than these basic control laws. These control laws are mentioned here because they provide some insight to the function of the controller, and in many situations acceptable control can

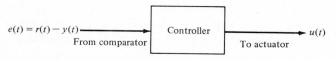

**FIGURE 1-5.   The controller block.**

be accomplished without a great deal of design effort using one of these laws. More will be said later regarding the use of these laws. The operation of the digital controller is to output the proper sequence to a DAC given the error sequence from the ADC (see Fig. 1-4). A typical expression might be

$$u(k) = k_p e(k) + T k_i e(k) + u(k - 1) \qquad (1\text{-}7)$$

where $T$ is the time interval between samples. Equation (1-7) represents a simple PI control. The reader should investigate that an approximate integration of $e(t)$ can be specified implicitly by

$$v(k) = v(k - 1) + T e(k) \qquad (1\text{-}8)$$

where $v(t)$ is the approximate integral of $e(t)$. One approach is to view $v(k)$ as the sum of error samples times the sample interval $T$. Hint: Work with Eq. (1-8) for $k = 0, 1, 2, \ldots$ with $v(-1) = 0$.

The control law represented in Eq. (1-8) would, of course, be implemented by a program in the control computer. Various techniques of programming a given control law will be discussed in a subsequent chapter.

★1-3

## SAMPLING AND RECONSTRUCTION OF SIGNALS

Nearly all engineering problems fall into the category of analog or continuous-time systems. Even logic circuits at the timing diagram level are necessarily considered to be analog systems; it is only under proper operation that logic circuits are taken to be discrete-time systems. The term "proper operation" used here refers to conditions whereby the signals reach steady "logic levels" prior to each clocked observation.

Discrete-time signals, which will be introduced in the next section, are familiar to us as sequences of numbers. The process of obtaining these sequence values to represent an analog signal is called *sampling*. In the simplest case the samples of $x(t)$ are taken to be the values of $x(t)$ at equispaced points in time. Thus, the sequence $\{x(kT)\}$, $k = 0, \pm 1, \pm 2, \ldots$, is a discrete-time signal "representing" $x(t)$; and because the sequence values are exact values of $x(t)$, they are called *ideal samples*. The reverse problem of obtaining the original analog signal from its samples is called *data reconstruction* or *interpolation*.

### 1-3.1 The Sampling Process

A natural method of sampling a continuous-time signal $x(t)$ is to observe it periodically by effectively switching it on and off at a regular rate. This procedure, illustrated in Fig. 1-6, is called *pulse-amplitude modulation* (PAM). If the pulse width of each pulse of $p(t)$ is $\tau$ seconds, the PAM signal pulses will generally have a variable amplitude over the $\tau$-second interval. As will be dis-

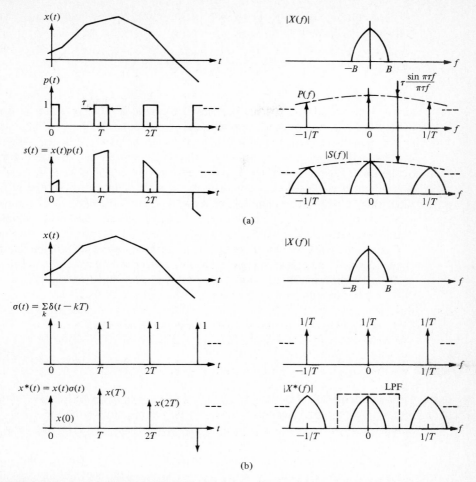

**FIGURE 1-6.** The sampling process: time and frequency descriptions for (a) pulse-amplitude modulation and (b) ideal (impulse) sampling.

cussed later, a holding device is frequently used (usually holding the leading-edge amplitude) to form a "flattopped" PAM signal. By reducing $\tau$, the pulse amplitudes of $s(t)$ [for reasonably smooth signals $x(t)$] become more nearly constant. The only problem that arises is that in the limit as $\tau$ approaches zero (for fixed $T$), the power of $s(t)$ also approaches zero.

Both the time and the frequency descriptions of the signals involved in the sampling process are presented in Fig. 1.6. In doing so, it is assumed, first, that $x(t)$ is "band-limited", that is, has no frequency component higher than some fixed frequency; and, second, that $\tau$ is small compared to the period of the highest frequency component of $x(t)$. With these assumptions the frequency description of $s(t)$, namely $S(f)$, is nearly a periodic replication of $X(f)$. The only difference is that the amplitudes of the pulse-type segments of $S(f)$ are modulated by the function

$$\frac{\tau \sin (\pi \tau f)}{(\pi \tau f)}$$

which is nearly constant for small $\tau f$, that is, for $f << 1/\tau$. The amplitude factor $\tau$ above indicates the need to boost the gain of $p(t)$ for small $\tau$. If the limit is taken as $\tau$ approaches zero with the amplitude of the pulses of $p(t)$ equal to $1/\tau$, then the sampling is called *ideal* or *impulse sampling*. Impulse sampling is illustrated in Fig. 1-6. Even though impulse sampling is an idealization, it is of the same type as many other useful engineering concepts in that it can be approximated as closely as desired by the sampling process illustrated in Fig. 1-6a, that is, when the sampling pulse widths are sufficiently small, but not zero, and the pulse amplitudes are large enough to ensure reasonable sampled-data signal levels.

Figure 1-6 requires some Fourier transform background for a complete understanding of the transform pairs shown, but primarily uses the result (in common with Laplace transform theory) that a product of signals in one domain corresponds to a convolution of the signals in the other domain (in this case either time or real frequency domains). For example, in Fig. 1-6b, $x^*(t) = x(t) \cdot \sigma(t)$, a product in the $t$-domain, becomes

$$X^*(f) = \int_{-\infty}^{\infty} X(p) \cdot \Sigma(f - p) \, dp$$

a convolution in the $f$-domain ($\Sigma(f) = \mathcal{F}\{\sigma(t)\}$). The result of this convolution is the periodic frequency function shown on the bottom line of Fig. 1-6b. An alternate development leading to the same result is presented in Appendix A, Section A-3.

There are two principal modes of using discrete-time signals. One mode occurs when the elements (numbers) of the signal sequences are processed on a number-by-number basis such as the processing which occurs internally to digital computers. In this case there is no conceptual difficulty with describing discrete-time signals as sequences of numbers. The second mode occurs when a discrete-time signal is used to drive or interface with a continuous-time system. In this case the impulse-sampled version is conceptually useful. Typically, the elements of the discrete-time signal that feed an analog system are held constant, sometimes referred to as "clamping" or "latching." In this situation it is convenient to model the clamp as a continuous-time system whose impulse-response function is a square pulse. The clamp serves as a digital-to-analog device; it is excited by each "pulse" of the impulse-sampled signal to form a step-type analog signal whose step amplitudes are the original discrete-time signal values. Again, there should be no conceptual difficulty with impulse sampling since it is but an intermediate signal model in the physical process of clamping amplitudes of a discrete-time signal. More discussion will be devoted to the clamping device in a subsequent section.

## 1-3.2 Signal Reconstruction

It should be recognized that the clamping operation mentioned above represents a crude effort at regenerating the original analog signal $x(t)$ from its equivalent sampled-data signal. As shown in Fig. 1-6, a device that has a transfer characteristic approximating the rectangular shape shown dashed in Fig. 1-6b is called a "low-pass" filter in that it passes the low and rejects the high frequencies. Thus, passing $x^*(t)$ through such a low-pass filter would select the single pulse segment that represents $X(f)$ from the periodic array of $X^*(f)$. Specifically, if $L(f)$ is the transfer function of the low-pass filter, then

$$X(f) = L(f) X^*(f)$$

This is the frequency domain equivalent of the *interpolation formula*

$$x(t) = \sum_{n=-\infty}^{\infty} x(nT) \frac{\sin \pi(t - nT)/T}{\pi(t - nT)}$$

where $T$ is the sample spacing and $x(t)$ satisfies the assumption of being band-limited, $|X(f)| = 0$ for $|f| > B$, with $1/T > 2B$ as illustrated in Fig. 1-6. When the sampling rate is too slow, or when $x(t)$ is not approximately band-limited, then overlap of separate "periods" of $X^*(f)$ will cause a distortion of the base spectrum representing $X(f)$. This distortion is due to overlapping segments of the spectrum, a folding over of frequencies called *aliasing*.

The interpolation formula is a type of convolution (which we will cover in more detail later in the chapter) between the two time-domain signals that correspond to $L(f)$ and $X^*(f)$. We already know that

$$\mathscr{F}^{-1}\{X^*(f)\} = \sum_{n=-\infty}^{\infty} x(nT)\, \delta(t - nT)$$

as illustrated on the bottom graph of Fig. 1-6b. The low-pass frequency function $L(f)$ was taken to be (ideally) rectangular (having an infinitely sharp cutoff between the "pass" and the "stop" frequencies). From Fourier transform theory, if $L(f) = \text{rect}(f/f_c)$, where $f_c = 1/T$, then $L(f)$ is unity for $|f| < 1/2T$ and zero elsewhere and corresponds to the time-domain signal

$$\mathscr{F}^{-1}\{L(f)\} = \frac{1}{T} \text{sinc}\left(\frac{t}{T}\right) = \frac{\sin(\pi t/T)}{\pi t}$$

Thus, although the interpolation formula has a formidable appearance, it is simply a linear sum of sinc functions which are centered about the sample values, having amplitudes equal to the samples. Using the interpolation formula, values of $x(t)$ between sample times can be obtained with arbitrary accuracy depending on the number of terms taken. (Since the amplitude of the sinc function decreases as $1/t$, relatively few terms near a particular sample will provide good results.)

Let us review the main ideas presented here. Under appropriate conditions of band-limiting (which may require "prefiltering") and sufficiently fast sampling, a sampled-data signal can represent the original analog signal faithfully and, moreover, can be used to reconstruct the analog signal at any step of the process by interpolating in time or low-pass filtering in frequency. Particularly when interacting with an analog system, the appropriate mathematical model for a discrete-time signal is a sequence of numbers $\{x(kT)\}$, which in turn can be represented in a continuous-time context as its time-density equivalent, namely, the ideal impulse-sampled signal

$$x^*(t) = \sum_{n=0}^{\infty} x(nT)\, \delta(t - nT) \qquad (1\text{-}9)$$

where $\delta$ is the Dirac delta (unit-impulse function). Note that the signal is assumed to be defined only for positive time. For control-oriented problems this is generally the most useful case, especially for initial-value related problems.

## 1-4

## COMPUTER INTERFACING

As shown in Fig. 1-4, signal conversion devices can be used to provide an interface between the digital computer and the analog control system. The ADC serves the purpose of translating a number, representing a single sample, into a binary code which can be understood by the digital computer. Similarly, the DAC produces an analog signal proportional to the digital signal present at its input.

### 1-4.1  Digital-to-Analog Conversion (DAC)

Referring to Fig. 1-7, the digital computer supplies the input to the DAC in the form of a binary word. Typical converters can handle binary word lengths varying from 4 to 18 bits. The purpose of the DAC is typically to decode the binary information into a usable sample amplitude value. Normally, the most significant bit (MSB) of a binary word is taken to represent the sign of the number. Many digital computers use the *2's complement representation* for negative numbers. A number $N$ might be represented as a binary word $N = b_n$

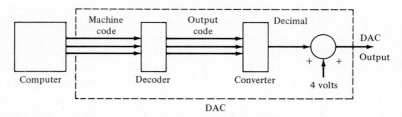

**FIGURE 1-7.  Block diagram for the example DAC.**

$\ldots b_2 b_1 b_0$, where each symbol $b_k$ is either a 1 or a 0. As mentioned above, $b_n$ would indicate the sign of the number, 0 for $+$ and 1 for $-$. The remaining symbols would follow the standard binary number system; that is, the magnitude

$$N = b_0 + b_1 2 + b_2 2^2 + b_3 2^3 + \cdots + b_{n-1} 2^{n-1}$$

For example, the binary word 0101 would correspond to $+(1 + 4) = +5$. Notice that the sign bit indicates a positive number. A *2's complement* of a binary number $+N$ will represent the corresponding negative number $-N$. To form the 2's complement of a binary word, each bit is "complemented" (a logic 1 changes to logic 0 and a logic 0 changes to a logic 1) *and* a 1 is added to the least significant bit (LSB). Thus, $-5$ would correspond to the binary word 1011. Notice that the sign bit now indicates a negative number. It is important to remember to first take the 2's complement of a negative number in order to convert it back to a readable magnitude, that is, 1011 does *not* represent $-3$, but does represent $-(2\text{'s complement of } 1011) = -5$.

To illustrate one possible arrangement for the binary code, consider that the encoded values from the computer correspond to voltage amplitudes between $-3$ and $+3$. Further suppose that our computer word length is only 3 bits to simplify the discussion. In this case only 2 bits are useable for magnitude information! Therefore, only $2^2 = 4$ distinct magnitudes can be represented. Table 1-1 shows the corresponding values and their binary codes. The output code is obtained from the machine code by complementing the MSB. Notice that the output code can be "translated" by its decimal equivalent given in the fourth column of Table 1-1. The DAC output is then simply a shift of 4 V to conform with the actual decimal numbers.

The purpose of the development here is to indicate some of the details involved in signal conversion, but not to provide an in depth study of such operations. However, when appropriate, simple electronic circuits that illustrate the different functions will be presented. For instance, the final voltage-shift operation is conveniently performed using an operational amplifier (Op Amp) circuit and can be incorporated with a "weighted resistor" implementation of the con-

**TABLE 1-1  Binary Code for Example DAC**

| Decimal | Machine Code† | Binary Output Code | Decimal Output | DAC Output |
|---------|---------------|--------------------|----------------|------------|
| 3 | 011 | 111 | 7 | 3 |
| 2 | 010 | 110 | 6 | 2 |
| 1 | 001 | 101 | 5 | 1 |
| 0 | 000 | 100 | 4 | 0 |
| $-1$ | 111 | 011 | 3 | $-1$ |
| $-2$ | 110 | 010 | 2 | $-2$ |
| $-3$ | 101 | 001 | 1 | $-3$ |

† Binary with 2's complement representation.

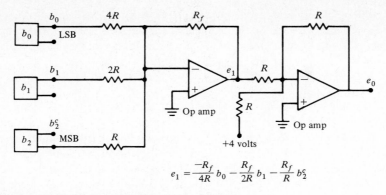

$$e_1 = \frac{-R_f}{4R} b_0 - \frac{R_f}{2R} b_1 - \frac{R_f}{R} b_2^c$$

**FIGURE 1-8.    Circuit diagram for example DAC.**

verter block. For the example above, Fig. 1-8 shows a possible circuit to implement the complete DAC.

Since each bit-place of a binary register corresponds to a digital flip-flop and assuming that logic levels are, say, $+5$ V for logic 1 and 0 V for logic 0, then, corresponding to decimal 3 V (the first entry in Table 1-1), $b_2 b_1 b_0 = 011$. This, in turn, implies that the ratio $R_f/R = 0.8$, which takes account of the 5-V logic level from the flip-flops. Note that the input from the MSB (sign bit) is the complement of the bit stored; this implements the Binary Output Code (Column 3 of Table 1-1). For a check consider decimal $-1$, that is, $b_2 b_1 b_0 = 111$. From the first Op Amp stage (refer to Fig. 1-8)

$$e_1 = -0.8(b_2^c + \tfrac{1}{2}b_1 + \tfrac{1}{4}b_0)\, 5 = -3\ \text{V}$$

where $b_2^c$ is the notation for the complement of $b_2$ and

$$e_0 = -e_1 - 4 = -1\ \text{V}$$

Notice that $b_2^c = 0$ since $b_2 = 1$.

An important consideration for DACs is the *resolution* they can provide. With the 3-bit DAC above, the resolution was limited to 1 V (the voltage output at $e_1$ corresponding to the LSB) out of a full-scale range of 7 V (see Fig. 1-9). Since there are only a finite number of decimal values that can be represented, there is a natural quantization of the analog values to the nearest digital level.

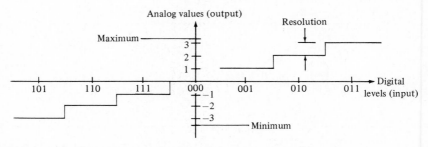

**FIGURE 1-9.    Graph of the quantization effect for the example.**

Figure 1-9 shows a rounding off of the analog numbers for the example above. For example, any analog value between $-0.5$ and $+0.5$ is quantized to level 0 (binary 000) and any analog value between 2.5 and 3.5 is interpreted as level 3 (full scale). Thus, for the present example the analog values may range from $-3.5$ to $+3.5$ V. Clearly, if more bits were available (and the range of analog values remained the same), more quantization levels could be made, thereby reducing the effect of quantization on the signal.

A natural effect of a DAC is to hold the output analog value as long as the digital input register remains the same. In this manner the DAC provides an analog signal that is piecewise constant between sample times. This effect is referred to as a zero-order hold.

## 1-4.2 Analog to Digital Conversion (ADC)

The process of converting an analog signal to a digital signal is the inverse operation of a DAC. There are several ways to implement ADC units, but only the *successive-approximation* type, the most widely used type, will be discussed here. The reason for the popularity of this type is its reasonable compromise between speed of conversion and complexity of equipment.

Referring to Fig. 1-10, the ADC is a feedback system in itself which, as part of its structure, incorporates a DAC. For simplicity only a 3-bit ADC is shown in Fig. 1-10.

The analog input is typically derived from a sample-and-hold device (to be discussed in Section 1-4.3) so that the analog input to the ADC does not change during the interval of conversion.

The operation can be easily understood by considering a particular analog input value as given in Fig. 1-11, showing 4-bit conversion with a maximum analog input of 4 V. The times $c_0$, $c_1$, $c_2$, . . . represent clock times (leading edges of clock pulses) and $s$ represents a start-conversion time (which also sets the status to "busy"). Shown in Fig. 1-11 is the analog input 2.9 V. When the

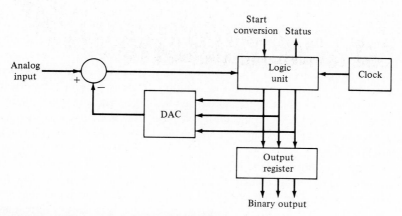

**FIGURE 1-10.  Block diagram of a 3-bit ADC.**

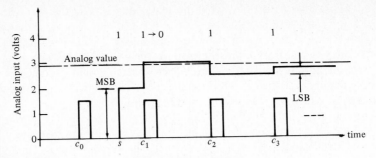

**FIGURE 1-11.  Diagram to illustrate ADC operation.**

conversion begins, the MSB is set high. By the next clock pulse the relatively fast DAC has fedback the value 2 V (corresponding to binary 1000). The comparator, in turn, indicates to the logic unit that the analog value is higher than 2 V. The logic then keeps the MSB high and turns on the next significant bit, thereby completing the cycle of operations. During the next cycle the comparator indicates that the analog value is less than 3 V, thereby requiring that the second most significant bit be reset to zero when the third MSB is set to one at time $c_2$, providing the level of 2.5 V shown in Fig. 1-11 prior to clock time $c_3$. After the least significant bit (LSB) has been set, the conversion is completed with the binary output being stored in the output register.

With $n$ bits the conversion time is approximately $n$/clock rate. In this example development the analog value of 2.9 V is quantized to the digital level 2.75 V, corresponding to the binary output 1011. This method of conversion leads to a signed-magnitude representation, that is, sign bit and standard binary magnitude. A subsequent encoding would be necessary if the computer was programmed for 2's complement negative numbers, but this will not be developed here.

### 1-4.3  Sample and Hold (S/H) Operation

For the ADC, which can have significant conversion time (typically 30–40 $\mu$ sec for 12 bits), a fast acting S/H device may be necessary to keep the ADC input from changing. A simple S/H unit is shown in Fig. 1-12a. This circuit simply stores (holds) a voltage value on the capacitor $C$ between sample pulses and "tracks" the input when the sampling pulse is present. The effect is accomplished with "buffer" amplifiers having large input and small output impedances (typical of op-amp circuits) and results in an inexpensive means of acquiring sample values of an analog signal and holding these values for subsequent processing.

Whether or not the ADC conversion time is significant enough to be included in the system's mathematical model depends on the conversion speed relative to sampling rate(s) of the system; in many cases it can be neglected. Similarly, the quantization involved in digitizing the signals is usually insignificant when

**INTRODUCTION TO DIGITAL CONTROL**

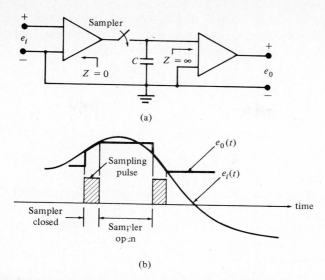

FIGURE 1-12.   S/H device; (a) circuit; (b) typical operation.

the binary words used to represent sample values in the computer have 12 bits
or more. Techniques for determining the effects of quantization will be presented
in a later chapter.

# DISCRETE-TIME SYSTEM RESPONSE

In this section some specific techniques for analyzing discrete-time systems will
be considered; however, no effects of amplitude quantization will be considered
here. Recall that all signals present in the discrete-time system are sequences of
sample values, that is, sampled-data or discrete-time signals. Thus, if a continuous-time signal $f(t)$ is sampled every $T$ seconds beginning at $t = 0$, the
corresponding sampled data is denoted as the sequence

$$\{f(kT)\} = f(0), f(T), f(2T), f(3T), \dots \qquad (1\text{-}10)$$

In the context of a discrete-time analysis the sequence notation, as well as the
explicit dependence on the parameter $T$, is sometimes omitted. As shown in Eq.
(1-10), signals will usually be taken to have zero value for negative time.

Various particular discrete-time signals are useful in analysis, and occasional
specially defined signals will be made as needed. In particular, the *unit function*
(unit pulse) is perhaps the most important of these special discrete-time signals
and is defined as (the Kronecker delta)

$$\delta(k - N) = \delta_{k-N} = \begin{array}{l} 1, \; k = N \\ 0, \; k \neq N \end{array}, \qquad (1\text{-}11)$$

where the signal is taken as a function of $k$. Note that the subscript notation is used interchangeably with the argument notation. If $f(k)$ represents an arbitrary sequence (signal), the unit function can be used to write

$$f(k) = \sum_{n=0}^{\infty} f(n) \, \delta(k - n) \tag{1-12}$$

Equation (1-12) is an identity since $f(k)$ is any discrete-time signal. The unit function is the counterpart of the Dirac impulse function used in continuous-time analysis.

## 1-5.1 The Unit-Pulse Response (Weighting Sequence)

A fundamental approach to the analysis of linear discrete-time systems is based on the unit-pulse response. Figure 1-13 illustrates that when an unenergized system is excited by a unit pulse at time $k = n$, a characteristic response called the *unit-pulse response* or *weighting sequence,* denoted by $h(k, n)$, occurs. The response sequence represents the response at time $k$ to the unit pulse applied at time $n$. If the system is stationary (time invariant), the unit-pulse response is a function only of the difference $(k - n)$, sometimes called the *age variable* since it is the time lapsed since the input was applied. The *causality property,* a property associated with physical cause-and-effect relationships, requires that $h(k, n) = 0$ for $k < n$, that is, a physical system cannot respond to an input before the occurence of the input.

The response to an arbitrary input sequence is developed as follows. If $x(k)$ is the input signal, then by Eq. (1-12)

$$x(k) = \sum_{n=0}^{\infty} x(n) \, \delta(k - n) \tag{1-13}$$

[Again $x(k)$ is taken to be zero for negative time.] Also, if $y(k)$ represents the output sequence, then using the operator notation of Eq. (1-1),

$$y(k) = H[x(k)] \tag{1-14}$$

where $y$ is the result of the linear operator $H$ operating on the input $x$. The key property is that of linearity. Equation (1-13) breaks the input into a sum of separate pulses. Therefore, since

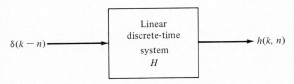

**FIGURE 1-13.  The unit-pulse response of a system.**

$$y(k) = H\left[\sum_{n=0}^{\infty} x(n)\,\delta(k-n)\right] \qquad (1\text{-}15)$$

then by linearity

$$y(k) = \sum_{n=0}^{\infty} x(n)\,H[\delta(k-n)] \qquad (1\text{-}16)$$

Inserting the unit-pulse response for the factor $H[\delta(k-n)]$ in Eq. (1-16),

$$y(k) = \sum_{n=0}^{\infty} x(n)\,h(k,\,n) \qquad (1\text{-}17)$$

Equation (1-17) is the important *convolution summation* relation between input and output sequences. An underlying assumption is that no initial energy be present in the system, or alternately that Eq. (1-17) is only the forced response of the system.

When the system is time invariant, the unit-pulse response is a function of a single variable, specifically the age variable $(k-n)$, and is written as $h(k)$. The convolution summation of Eq. (1-17) in this case is conveniently symbolized as a "star product," that is

$$y(k) = x(k) * h(k) = \sum_{n=0}^{\infty} x(n)\,h(k-n) \qquad (1\text{-}18)$$

It is easily shown that $x(k) * h(k) = h(k) * x(k)$ by a change of variables.

### EXAMPLE 1-4

Consider Example 1-2 as a discrete-time system where $r$ is 10%. The mathematical model, Eq. (1-3), becomes for $k = 0, 1, 2, 3, \ldots$

$$p_k = 1.10\,p_{k-1} + u_k,\ p_{-1} = 0 \qquad (1\text{-}19)$$

To find the unit-pulse sequence and use it to calculate the response: The system unit-pulse response sequence provides an alternate method for characterizing the system. For this example assume as before that $u_k$ is the input and $p_k$ is the resulting output sequence in Eq. (1-19). The unit-pulse response sequence $h_k$ is then the solution of Eq. (1-20), which corresponds to the system with a unit-pulse input:

$$h_k = 1.10\,h_{k-1} + \delta_k,\ h_{-1} = 0 \qquad (1\text{-}20)$$

**SOLUTION:** $h_{-1} = 0$ (Since the system is initially unenergized, all initial conditions are zero.) From Eq. (1-20), $(k = 0)$, $h_0 = 1$ from Eq. (1-11). For $k = 1$, $h_1 = 1.10$. For $k = 2$, $h_2 = (1.10)^2$, and so on, to obtain the general expression for the system unit-pulse response: $h_k = (1.10)^k$ for $k \geq 0$ ($h_k = 0$ for $k < 0$).

If, in addition, 100 dollars is placed on account at the beginning of each year, that is, $u_k = 100$ for $k = 0, 1, 2, \ldots$, then from Eq. (1-18) the amount on deposit during year $k + 1$ is $p_k = u_k * h_k$, that is,

$$p_k = \sum_{n=0}^{k} 100 \, (1.10)^{k-n}$$

Techniques for evaluating convolution products will be presented later.  ∎

## 1-5.2  Multiple-Input/Multiple-Output Systems

In many cases a system model is required that relates many inputs with many outputs such that any one input affects several outputs. This is particularly true of complex control systems where specific (output) variables are to be regulated in some manner by proper variations of the controlling inputs. The previous system characterization is easily extended to include such systems.

Since in a vector system each output can be related to each input (with all other inputs set to zero) in the same fashion as before, that is, by a convolution of its scalar unit-pulse response and input sequence, it is possible to write the matrix $\mathbf{H}(k, n)$ as the system unit-pulse response as follows. If $h_{ij}(k, n)$ represents the response at output $i$ at the $k$th instant ($t = kT$) to a unit function applied to input $j$ at the $n$th instant, then the vector output $\mathbf{y}(k)$ responds to the vector input sequence $\mathbf{u}(k)$ by the summation

$$\mathbf{y}(k) = \sum_{n=0}^{\infty} \mathbf{H}(k, n) \, \mathbf{u}(k) \tag{1-21}$$

where the $ij$ entry of the matrix $\mathbf{H}$ ($i$th row, $j$th column entry) is $h_{ij}$. Equation (1-21) is the vector generalization of Eq. (1-17). Note that when the system is causal [$\mathbf{H}(k, n) = 0$ for $n > k$], the upper limit becomes $k$.

The system pulse-response concept also implies a corresponding modeling procedure where the response of an unknown system to a unit-pulse input is actually measured to obtain the system response, as in Fig. 1-13.

## 1-6

## CONVOLUTION OF SEQUENCES

To more fully understand the process of convolution relating the output to the convolutional product of the input sequence and the system unit-pulse response, consider Eq. (1-18), repeated here for convenience:

$$y(k) = x(k) * h(k) = \sum_{n=0}^{\infty} x(n) \, h(k - n) \tag{1-18}$$

Since both convolutional factors are zero for negative $k$; $h(k - n) = 0$ for $n > k$ by causality; the first two terms of $y(k)$ are $y(0) = x(0)h(0)$ and $y(1) =$

**TABLE 1-2  Tabulation for Discrete Convolution**

|        | $x(0)$    | $x(1)$             | $x(2)$             | $x(3)$    |
|--------|-----------|--------------------|--------------------|-----------|
| $h(0)$ | $x(0)h(0)$ | $x(1)h(0)$         | $x(2)h(0)$         | $x(3)h(0)$ |
| $h(1)$ |           | $x(0)h(1)$         | $x(1)h(1)$         | $x(2)h(1)$ |
| $h(2)$ |           |                    | $x(0)h(2)$         | $x(1)h(2)$ |
| . . .  |           |                    |                    | . . .     |

$y(k) = \{x(0)h(0),\ x(1)h(0) + x(0)h(1),\ x(2)h(0) + x(1)h(1) + x(0)h(2),\ \ldots\}.$

$x(1)h(0) + x(0)h(1)$. Direct computation of Eq. (1-18) is feasible, but without a guide it is difficult to keep track of all the terms contributing to the higher sequence terms of $y(k)$. Table 1-2 is a useful intermediate step in the calculation of Eq. (1-18). The given sequences $x(k)$ and $h(k)$ are written as top row and left column. Products are formed in an upper triangular fashion as shown. The first column element is similarly multiplied by each top row element and, in addition, is shifted one place to the right. Continuing the indicated process, the table is filled. Finally, the output sequence values are simply the sums of the generated columns. Note that the roles of $x(k)$ and $h(k)$ could as well have been interchanged. Also, the shifting process can be omitted by remembering to add diagonally, as will be illustrated in the next example.

## EXAMPLE 1-5

In the previous example, the convolutional sum of $\{(1.10)^k\}$ with $\{100\}$ was developed, but was not carried out. Using the tabular formation given in Table 1-2, the convolutional product sequence $\{p_k\}$ from Example 1-4 can be calculated. Note that the row shifting was omitted in favor of adding diagonally to obtain the sequence values of $p_k$. The diagonal lines were added as an aid.

**TABLE 1-3  Convolution for Example 1-5**

|         | 100   | 100   | 100   | 100   | 100   | . . . |
|---------|-------|-------|-------|-------|-------|-------|
| 1       | 100   | 100   | 100   | 100   | 100   |       |
| 1.100   | 110   | 110   | 110   | 110   | 110   |       |
| 1.210   | 121   | 121   | 121   | 121   | 121   |       |
| 1.331   | 133.1 | 133.1 | 133.1 | 133.1 | 133.1 |       |
| . . .   | . . . |       |       |       |       |       |

$\{p_k\} = \{100,\ 210,\ 331,\ 464.1,\ \ldots\}.$

Convolution will be discussed in the context of transforms in the next chapter. ∎

## LINEAR DIFFERENCE EQUATIONS

As illustrated in Example 1-2, ordinary difference equations provide a useful method of describing the dynamics of discrete-time systems. The elementary difference equation

$$y(k + 1) = ay(k) \text{ for } k = 0, 1, 2, \ldots \tag{1-22}$$

represents a fixed relation between values of the dependent variable $y$ at different times, that is, at different values of the independent variable $k$. Alternatively, Eq. (1-22) can be viewed as an infinite set of simultaneous equations, one for each value of the index variable $k$. Although a large body of mathematical literature is available on the subject of difference equations, we will discuss only the special subset of those that are linear and have constant coefficients; these correspond to our time-invariant, linear, discrete-time systems.

The *order* of a difference equation is the difference between the highest and lowest indices. Thus, Eq. (1-22) is a first-order equation whereas

$$y(k + 3) - 6y(k) + y(k - 1) = 0 \text{ for } k = 0, 1, 2, 3, \ldots$$

is fourth order. The difference equation is linear if it can be put in the form

$$y(k) = \sum_{j=1}^{N} c_j y(k - j) + f(k) \text{ for } k = 0, 1, 2, \ldots \tag{1-23}$$

where $f(k)$ may contain various terms not related to $y(k)$. If, in addition, the coefficients $\{c_j\}$ do not depend on the index $k$, the system is time invariant.

Just as with linear differential equations, an $n$th-order difference equation, such as Eq. (1-23), will have one and only one solution [assuming the coefficients $\{c_j\}$ and forcing function $f(k)$ are specified] for each set of "initial conditions," $\{y(-1), y(-2), \ldots, y(-N)\}$. Difference equations are also called *recurrence formulas* since knowledge of the first $N$ values of $y$ permits all values of $y$ to be calculated in a sequential manner.

### 1-7.1 Shift-Operator Representation

A convenient discrete-time operator is the *shift-operator* $E$ defined for integer values $k$ by

$$E[y(k)] = y(k + 1) \tag{1-24}$$

Repeated application of $E$ can be used to generate different shifts of the signal $y(k)$. For example,

$$E^2[y(k)] = E[Ey(k)] = y(k + 2) \tag{1-25}$$

The reader may also be familiar with the *difference operator* $\Delta$, defined by

$$\Delta[y(k)] = y(k + 1) - y(k) \tag{1-26}$$

In terms of the shift operator, $\Delta$ is equivalent to $E - 1$, but we will not pursue further developments using the operator $\Delta$.

With an appropriate shift of the index variable and a redefining of the coefficients, Eq. (1-23) can be written as

$$[a_N E^N + a_{N-1} E^{N-1} + \cdots + a_1 E + a_0]y(k) = f(k) \tag{1-27}$$

And since the operation on $y(k)$ is a polynomial in $E$, the notation can be further simplified to

$$A(E)y(k) = f(k) \tag{1-28}$$

We will typically find it more convenient to use the shifted form of Eq. (1-27) so that the "initial (or boundary) conditions" are specified by the set $\{y(0),$ $y(1), y(2), \ldots, y(N - 1)\}$. In this way the signals can usually be taken as single sided, that is, $f(k)$ and $y(k)$ are zero for $k < 0$.

## 1-7.2  Classical Solution

In this introductory chapter we are trying to digest various topics related to computer control systems, and without being too formal, this section will summarize the classical approach to solving linear difference equations with constant coefficients. Later material will build on this development to give us more convenient methods of solution.

The classical approach to obtaining a solution to a linear difference equation is to solve two problems. The first is to find a general solution to the homogeneous equation, namely, the *homogeneous solution*, $y_H(k)$. If we refer to Eq. (1-28), the *homogeneous equation* is found by setting those terms not involving $y$, namely, $f(k)$, to zero. The form of the solution will be determined from the roots of the *characteristic equation*

$$A(z) = 0 \tag{1-29}$$

where $A$ is the same polynomial function as given in Eq. (1-28). The second part is a particular solution corresponding in some way to the form of the forcing function $f(k)$; this *particular solution* $y_P(k)$ must satisfy the original difference equation. Thus, the *total solution* $y(k)$ is given by

$$y(k) = y_H(k) + y_P(k) \tag{1-30}$$

The total solution given above will contain $N$ arbitrary constants (the order of the equation) associated with $y_H(k)$. The initial (or boundary) conditions may then be used to remove these constants, providing a unique solution.

*The Homogeneous Solution.*　If the polynomial $A(z)$ has distinct roots $r_1, r_2, \ldots, r_N$, then the form of the homogeneous solution is taken to be

$$y_H(k) = C_1 r_1^k + C_2 r_2^k + \cdots + C_N r_N^k \tag{1-31}$$

where $C_1, C_2, \ldots, C_N$ are the $N$ arbitrary constants mentioned previously. Variations on the form of $y_H$ occur when $A(z)$ has multiple roots; if, say, $r_1$ is repeated $M$ times, the first $M$ terms of $y_H$ would be

$$(C_1 + C_2 k + C_3 k^2 + \cdots + C_M k^{M-1}) r_1^k$$

Equation (1-31) is still appropriate when complex conjugate roots of the characteristic equation occur. Even though the solution will appear complex valued, proper manipulation of complex numbers will reveal that the solution sequence is real. For example, corresponding to, say, $r_1 = ae^{jb}$ and $r_2 = ae^{-jb}$, the terms in the solution could be put into the form

$$a^k(C_1 \cos bk + C_2 \sin bk)$$

***A Particular Solution.*** Any particular solution $y_P(k)$, that is, a nontrivial solution reducing the original equation to an identity, plus the general homogeneous solution give the total solution. In other words, any particular solution, $y_P(k)$, is related to any other particular solution, $y_P^*(k)$, by

$$y_P^*(k) = y_P(k) + w(k)$$

where $w(k)$ satisfies the homogeneous equation. A particular solution is directly related to the convolution methods studied earlier in the chapter since the basic problem is to determine a particular solution (output) sequence for a given forcing (input) sequence.

A classical method of obtaining $y_P(k)$ is the method of *Undetermined Coefficients*. This approach amounts to an educated guess for the form of $y_P(k)$. For simple forcing functions there are some guidelines for choosing $y_P(k)$. For instance, if $f(k) = q^k$; then, as long as $q$ is not a root of the characteristic equation,

$$y_P(k) = D_1 q^k$$

where $D_1$ is to be found by substituting $y_P(k)$ into the difference equation. More generally, $f(k)$ may be a polynomial, sinusoidal, or exponential function of $k$ or a product or linear combination of such functions. The assumed $y_P(k)$ must not contain terms of the same form as terms of $y_H(k)$. To avoid this, such terms of $y_P(k)$ are multiplied by the lowest power of $k$ to remove the duplication.

Specifically, if $f(k)$ in Eq. (1-28) has the form

$$\begin{aligned}
f(k) = a^k \cos (bk)(a_1 + a_2 k + \cdots a_m k^{m-1}) \\
+ a^k \sin (bk)(b_1 + b_2 k + \cdots + b_m k^{m-1})
\end{aligned} \tag{1-32}$$

where either $a_m$ or $b_m$ is not zero, but any of the other coefficients $\{a_i\}$ or $\{b_i\}$, $i = 1, 2, 3, \ldots, m$ may be zero, then the normal form for $y_P(k)$ is

$$\begin{aligned}
y_P(k) = a^k e^{jbk}(D_1 + D_2 k + \cdots + D_m k^{m-1}) \\
+ a^k e^{-jbk}(D_{m+1} + D_{m+2} k + \cdots + D_{2m} k^{m-1})
\end{aligned} \tag{1-33}$$

which has $2m$ undetermined coefficients. Furthermore, if $(ae^{jb})$ is a $p$th-order root of the characteristic equation, $A(z) = 0$, then the expression $y_P(k)$ in Eq. (1-33) must be multiplied by $k^p$.

## EXAMPLE 1-6

Given the difference equation

$$y(k + 2) + y(k + 1) = 12k^2 + 4k^3,$$

the characteristic equation, $z^2 + z = 0$, has roots $z = 0$ and $z = -1$. Consequently, the homogeneous solution has the form

$$y_H(k) = C_1 + C_2(-1)^k$$

Since $a = 1$ and $b = 0$ for the given forcing function $f(k)$, $ae^{jb} = 1$ is not a root of the characteristic equation; and

$$y_P(k) = (D_1 + D_2k + D_3k^2 + D_4k^3)$$ ∎

## EXAMPLE 1-7

For the forcing function $f(k) = k^2 3^k \sin 4k$, and assuming that $(3e^{j4})$ is not a root of the characteristic equation, then $y_P$ would be taken as

$$y_P(k) = (D_1k^2 + D_2k + D_3)3^k e^{j4k} + (D_4k^2 + D_5k + D_6)3^k e^{-j4k}$$

or, alternatively,

$$y_P(k) = (D_1k^2 + D_2k + D_3)3^k \cos 4k + (D_4k^2 + D_5k + D_6)3^k \sin 4k$$

To complete this section let us put the above information together to solve a second-order difference equation with initial conditions and forcing sequence. ∎

## EXAMPLE 1-8

Given the difference equation

$$y(k + 2) + 3y(k + 1) + 2y(k) = 4k(-2)^k$$

Solve for the sequence $y(k)$ that satisfies the difference equation *and* the initial conditions: $y(0) = 1$, $y(1) = 0$.

*SOLUTION:* The homogeneous equation is given by

$$(E^2 + 3E + 2)y(k) = y(k + 2) + 3y(k + 1) + 2y(k) = 0$$

The characteristic equation, $z^2 + 3z + 2 = 0$ has roots $-1$ and $-2$. Therefore,

$$y_H(k) = C_1(-1)^k + C_2(-2)^k$$

Since $f(k) = 4k(-2)^k$, $y_P(k)$ would normally be of the form $y_P(k) = (D_1 + D_2k)(-2)^k$; however, the first term duplicates the second term of $y_H(k)$; in other words, $-2$ is a first-order root of the characteristic equation, thus we take

$$y_P(k) = (-2)^k(D_1k + D_2k^2)$$

Substituting $y_P(k)$ into the difference equation yields, after simplifying,

$$[2D_1 + (10 + 4k)D_2](-2)^k = 4k(-2)^k$$

whence
$$D_1 = -5 \text{ and } D_2 = 1$$

The total solution is then

$$y(k) = (-2)^k(k^2 - 5k) + C_1(-1)^k + C_2(-2)^k$$

Using $y(0) = 1$ and $y(1) = 0$ permits solving for $C_1 = -6$ and $C_2 = 7$. The final (unique) solution is

$$y(k) = (k^2 - 5k + 7)(-2)^k - 6(-1)^k \qquad \blacksquare$$

It should be emphasized that if the forcing sequence $f(k)$ is not a sum of terms of the form given in Eq. (1-32), then the method of Undetermined Coefficients is not applicable; other methods, such as convolution, must be used. In the next chapter a more compact method of solving linear difference equations is developed through the $z$-transform.

## 1-8

---

## SOLVED PROBLEMS

In this section a few examples are discussed to supplement those given along with the theory.

### 1-8.1 Loan Amortization

This example develops a useful formula for calculating the amount of installment payments which are required to pay off (or amortize) a loan over a given time period.

Similar to the structure of Example 1-2 we can define:

$d(k)$ = debt at the end of the $k$th time period

$k$ = integer number of time periods; $k = 0, 1, 2, \ldots$

$r$ = interset rate on loan

$L$ = loan amount (initial debt, $d(0) = L$)

$P$ = payment made at the end of each time period (constant)

$n$ = loan period (total number of payment periods)

The discrete-time equation that incorporates the effects of interest increasing the debt and payments that reduce the debt is given by

$$d(k + 1) = (1 + r)d(k) - P \qquad (1\text{-}34)$$

Given that $d(0) = L$ is known and letting $(1 + r) = a$, we have, recursively,

$$d(1) = a\, d(0) - P$$

$$d(2) = a^2\, d(0) - aP - P$$

$$d(3) = a^3\, d(0) - a^2 P - aP - P \qquad\qquad (1\text{-}35)$$

$$\cdots$$

$$d(n) = a^n L - (a^{n-1} + a^{n-2} + \cdots + a + 1)\, P = 0$$

If we let

$$S = 1 + a + a^2 + \cdots + a^{n-1}$$

then multiplying by $a$ and subtracting from $S$

$$(1 - a)S = 1 - a^n$$

Using this result for $S$, and solving Eq. (1-35) for $P$,

$$P = \frac{rL}{1 - (1 + r)^{-n}} \qquad\qquad (1\text{-}36)$$

## EXAMPLE 1-9

Equation (1-36) would be used by your banker in determining the monthly payments to be made on your house mortgage. Consider borrowing $100,000 for 20 years at 12% per annum. The appropriate parameters are then

$$k = \text{integer number of months}$$

$$L = 100{,}000 \text{ dollars}$$

$$r = 0.01 \; (1\% \text{ per month}), \text{ and}$$

$$n = (20)(12) = 240 \text{ months}$$

The individual monthly payments are then calculated from Eq. (1-36) to be

$$P = \frac{1000}{1 - (1.01)^{-240}} = \$1101.09 \qquad\blacksquare$$

## 1-8.2 Periodic Structures

Most of our discrete-time models involve dynamics with time being the independent variable. In this section, however, the independent variable will refer to the $n$th identical structure cell. For exposition of the idea an electrical ladder network is used, but the method can be used to model other structures as well.

In Fig. 1-14 is shown a network whose structure can be thought of as composed of identical cells or loops. Taking the approach of solving for the circulating loop currents, the number of simultaneous equations can be quite large;

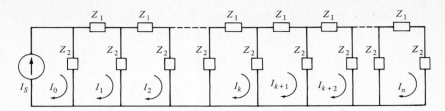

**FIGURE 1-14.** Ladder network with repetitive system structure.

but, if the symmetry is noted, the set of loop currents can be reduced to a single difference equation with boundary conditions.

***Analysis.*** Considering the general $(k + 1)$st-loop current

$$(Z_1 + 2Z_2)I_{k+1} - Z_2I_k - Z_2I_{k+2} = 0 \tag{1-37}$$

where $Z_1$ and $Z_2$ are the impedance values of the elements in the structure and the loop currents are taken to be in the Laplace transform domain (or equivalently the phasor domain). Equation (1-37) holds for $k = 0, 1, 2, \ldots, n - 2$ as can be seen from Fig. 1-14. The first and last cell represent the boundary conditions:

$$I_0 = I_s \quad \text{and} \quad (Z_1 + 2Z_2)I_n = Z_2I_{n-1} \tag{1-38}$$

Thus, the system is modeled by the difference equation

$$I_{k+2} - aI_{k+1} + I_k = 0, \, k = 0, 1, \ldots, n - 2 \tag{1-39}$$

where $a = 2 + Z_1/Z_2$, along with the boundary conditions of Eq. (1-38):

$$I_0 = I_s, I_n = \frac{1}{a}I_{n-1} \tag{1-40}$$

**EXAMPLE 1-10**

If $n = 12$, $I_s = 1A$ (constant), $Z_1 = 2\Omega$ and $Z_2 = 1\Omega$, that is, a network of resistors, then Eqs. (1-39) and (1-40) reduce to

$$I_{k+2} - 4I_{k+1} + I_k = 0, \, k = 0, 1, \ldots, 10$$

$$I_0 = 1, I_{12} = \frac{1}{4}I_{11}$$

Since the main dynamical equation has no independent input, we solve for the homogeneous solution:

$$\lambda^2 - 4\lambda + 1 = 0$$

$$\text{Roots} \quad \lambda_1 = 2 + \sqrt{3}, \lambda_2 = 2 - \sqrt{3}$$

$$I_k = C_1(2 + \sqrt{3})^k + C_2(2 - \sqrt{3})^k$$

Eliminating the arbitrary constants $C_1$ and $C_2$ with the boundary conditions,

$$I_0 = 1: C_1 + C_2 = 1$$

$$4I_{12} = I_{11}: 4C_1(2 + \sqrt{3})^{12} + 4C_2(2 - \sqrt{3})^{12}$$

$$= C_1(2 + \sqrt{3})^{11} + C_2(2 - \sqrt{3})^{11}$$

we find that

$$C_1 = -1.347 \times 10^{-15} \text{ and } C_2 = 1 - C_1 = 1$$

Since $C_1$ is approximately zero,

$$I_k = (2 - \sqrt{3})^k \text{ for small } k$$

However, for $k$ near 12 both terms are needed since the $C_1$ term will no longer be negligible with respect to the $C_2$ term. ∎

## 1-8.3  Archeological Dating

There are various methods by which ancient artifacts are dated. One interesting method involves an isotope of carbon, $^{14}C$. This isotope appears to be produced at a steady rate in the atmosphere through the action of cosmic radiation. Since it combines readily with oxygen, it is uniformly present in the atmosphere in a form of carbon dioxide. Since carbon dioxide is absorbed by plants and indirectly by animals eating plants or other animals, all living things have roughly the same concentration of this isotope in their body. The key idea is that at death the isotope is no longer consumed by the plant or animal and its natural disintegration (into nitrogen) takes over. The half-life of $^{14}C$ is known to be 5685 years, meaning that after a period of 5685 years the concentration of $^{14}C$ will be halved. The following example is used to illustrate the application of the method.

### EXAMPLE 1-11
Assuming that a preserved wooden artifact measures only 0.2 of the normal (living) radiation, what is the age of the artifact?

*SOLUTION:* Let $e(k)$ = emitted radiation after 5685 $k$ years. Then, since $e(k)$ decreases by half every integer $k$,

$$e(k + 1) = 0.5 \, e(k)$$

Solving

$$e(k) = (0.5)^k e(0)$$

Taking $e(0)$ as unity (normalized amount of radiation),

$$e(n) = (0.5)^n = 0.2$$

Therefore,

$$n = \frac{\log(0.2)}{\log(0.5)} = 2.32$$

and the age is $(2.32)(5685) = 13,200$ years. ■

## 1-8.4  Discrete Convolution

To better illustrate the mechanism involved when passing a signal through a linear system, consider a situation where the system response to a unit pulse is given by the (single-sided) sequence

$$h(k) = \{h_0, h_1, h_2, h_3, \ldots\}$$

and the input sequence is given by

$$u(k) = \{u_0, u_1, u_2, u_3, \ldots\}$$

In this section an alternative method to the previous tabular process is presented.

If we review the convolution summation formula, we find that the output sequence is calculated according to the following expression:

$$y(k) = \sum_{n=0}^{k} h(k - n)u(n) \tag{1-41}$$

When we study the above operation closely, it is observed that for a fixed $k$ the two sequences involved may be plotted as a function of $n$, the summation index. In particular, $u(n)$ is in its natural order, but the sequence $h(k - n)$ versus $n$ is both reversed (since $n$ has a negative sign in the argument of $h$) and shifted by an amount $k$. If we imagine that the sequence values are recorded on two strips of paper, $u(n)$ in forward order $h(n)$ in reverse order, then the process of convolving becomes one of sliding the $h$-strip relative to the $u$-strip and multiplying and adding the overlapping sequence values. Let us illustrate by an example.

### EXAMPLE 1-12 (Discrete Convolution)

Given that $h(k) = \{3, 2, 1\}$ and $u(k) = \{1, -2, 1\}$, we construct the corresponding sequence values on our conceptual strips of paper:

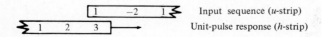

By "sliding" the second strip one interval at a time and multiplying and adding at each step, we arrive at the output sequence

$$y(k) = \{3, -4, 0, 0, 1\}.$$ ■

## SUMMARY

In this chapter some basic system concepts have been explained, and certain aspects of digital control, as it differs from analog feedback control, have been introduced. In particular, the notion of what sort of operations a digital controller performs was discussed, as well as the important problems of signal conversion used to interface the digital controller to the plant. These latter ideas were illustrated explicitly to provide the reader with some idea of the electronics needed for implementation.

The fundamental convolution property that describes the output of a discrete-time linear system in terms of its input and characteristic weighting sequence was developed and illustrated. Lastly, the classical solution to difference equations was investigated in some detail.

Each of the topics, although widely different, provides some insight into problems associated with digital control. In the following chapters of Part I the basic methods and tools necessary for modeling and analysis of the constituent parts of a digital control system are presented.

## REFERENCES

**Section 1-1** *State Variables for Engineers;* P. M. DeRusso, R. J. Roy, and C. M. Close; John Wiley and Sons, 1965.

**Section 1-2** *Modern Control Engineering;* K. Ogata; Prentice-Hall, 1970.
*Digital Computer Process Control;* C. L. Smith; Intext Educational Publishers, 1972.

**Section 1-3** *Digital Signal Processing;* W. D. Stanley; Prentice-Hall (Reston), 1975.
*The Fast Fourier Transform;* E. O. Brigham; Prentice-Hall, 1974.

**Section 1-4** *Computer System Architecture;* M. M. Mano; Prentice-Hall, 1976.
*Introduction to Feedback Control Systems;* P. Emanuel and E. Leff; McGraw-Hill, 1979.
*Digital Control Systems;* B. C. Kuo; Holt, Rinehart and Winston, 1980.

**Section 1-5** *Discrete-Time and Computer Control Systems;* J. A. Cadzow and H. R. Martens; Prentice-Hall, 1970.

**Section 1-7** *Operational Methods for Linear Systems;* W. Kaplan; Addison-Wesley, 1962.

## PROBLEMS

**1-1** Consider the following descriptions of systems with excitation $u$ and response $y$. Classify each as linear or nonlinear system models.

**(a)** $\ddot{y}(t) + 2y(t) = 3u(t)$

**(b)** $\ddot{y}(t) + \sin y(t) = u(t)$

**(c)** $\dot{y}(t) + a(t) y(t) = b(t)u(t)$

**(d)** $\dot{y}(t) + 3y^2(t) + a(t)y(t) = u(t)$

**1-2**    For each system model given in Problem 1-1 classify the system as a stationary (time-invariant) or nonstationary system.

**1-3**    An electrical transmission line and vibrating string are both examples of distributed systems. State qualitatively how the following system model might relate to each system.

$$\frac{\partial^2 z}{\partial t^2} - c^2 \frac{\partial^2 z}{\partial x^2} = u(x, t)$$

**1-4**    Determine the sequence $v(k)$, $k = 0, 1, 2, \ldots$ from Eq. (1-8) when $T = 1$ and $v(-1) = 0$ for an arbitrary excitation sequence $e(k)$. With a sketch show how $v(k)$ is related to the integral of $e(t)$.

**1-5**    Given that a signal $x(t) = \sin 2t + 3 \cos 10t$, determine the minimum sampling rate so that no aliasing errors would occur.

**1-6**    If the signal $x(t)$ in Problem 1-5 is sampled (ideally) at a uniform rate of 10 Hz, synchronized with $t = 0$, determine and plot the first five or six values of the corresponding discrete-time signal. How could the original continuous-time signal $x(t)$ be obtained from the samples $x(kT)$, $k = 0, 1, 2, \ldots$?

**1-7**    A 4-bit binary word can be used to represent integers from 0 to 15. Alternatively, using the most significant bit (MSB) as a sign bit, the 4-bit word might represent integers from $-7$ to $+7$.
(a) With ''zero'' as positive, construct a table of binary words representing the integers $-7$ to 7.
(b) Construct a second table similar to the first two columns of Table 1-1 illustrating the 2's complement representation.

**1-8**    A discrete-time signal $x(k)$ is presented as a sequence of values that occur at a rate of 100 values per second. Determine the ''period'' of the frequency spectrum $X(\omega)$ in radians per second.

**1-9**    Discuss the operation of the DAC shown in Figs. 1-7 and 1-8. For your discussion, assume that the computer is outputting a decimal $-2$ value.

**1-10**   A sample-and-hold device samples the signal $x(t) = \sin \frac{1}{4}\pi t$, starting at $t = 0$ with sample interval $T = 1$ second; see Fig. 1-12. Assuming a negligible width for the ''sampling pulse,'' sketch the output $y(t)$ showing exact values for the piecewise constant values of $y(t)$.

**1-11**   A sample-and-hold device is used to feed an analog input into a 12-bit ADC. Assume that the system sampling interval $T$ is 50 msec and that the ADC is a successive-approximation type, as illustrated in Figure 1-10. Discuss the conversion operation assuming that the ADC range is $-10$ to $+10$ V of analog input. Include any requirements on the ADC clock (which is not the same as the clock governing the system sampling rate) and specify the maximum quantization error in volts. As an example, determine the ADC output for a $+2.9$ V input.

**1-12** The dynamics of a savings account is a good example of a discrete-time system. For an initial deposit of $P_0$ dollars the principal in the account at the end of the $k$th interval is given by $P_k$ where

$$P_{k+1} = (1 + r)P_k, \, k = 0, 1, 2, \ldots$$

Determine the effective annual percentage rate (APR) corresponding o
**(a)** a 6% annual rate compounded quarterly.
**(b)** a 6% annual rate compounded monthly.

**1-13** Determine the unit-step response $c(k)$ for a discrete-time system whose unit-pulse response sequence is $h(k) = (0.5)^k, \, k = 0, 1, 2, \ldots$.

**1-14** Convolve $x(k)$ with $y(k)$:
**(a)** $x(k) = \{1, 1, -1, 1\}, \, y(k) = \{1, 0, 2, -1, -2\}$
**(b)** $x(k) = \{1, 1, 1, \ldots\}, \, y(k) = \{1, 2, 3, \ldots\}$
   where the sequences of part (a) are assumed to be zero outside the defined range and those of part (b) are infinite, continuing according to the pattern.

**1-15** Determine your monthly payments if you borrow $10,000 for a new car if you take the loan for 36 months at 12% per annum.

**1-16** Calculate the unit-step response for a discrete-time system having the (finite) unit-pulse response sequence: $h(k) = \{4, 3, 2, 1\}$. Use enough terms to find the steady-state response.

**1-17** Show that the discrete convolution between two sequences of length $M$ and $N$, respectively, is a sequence of length $(M + N - 1)$.

**1-18** Using classical methods, solve the following difference equations.
**(a)** $y(k + 1) + 2y(k) = 1, \, y(0) = -1$
**(b)** $y(k + 2) - 2y(k + 1) + y(k) = 2^k, \, y(0) = y(1) = 1$
**(c)** $y(k + 2) - 3y(k + 1) + 2y(k) = 2^k, \, y(0) = y(1) = 1$

## CHAPTER 2

# Transform Analysis

In Chapter 1 we learned to determine a discrete-time system response by convolving the system's input sequence with its unit-pulse response (weighting) sequence. This is a technique that will always be available to us; however, it can be cumbersome when dealing with higher-order systems. In this chapter input–output calculations will be performed in the short-hand notation of the $z$-transform. The reader will learn to appreciate the simplicity of the $z$-transform, particularly for its ease in performing input–output calculations on discrete-time systems; the difficulties of solving difference equations and those related to the convolution methods are "transformed" into elementary algebraic problems.

## 2-1

### INTRODUCTION TO $z$-TRANSFORMS

The discussion in this section will be limited to stationary, linear, discrete-time systems, thus limiting the utility of the transform method; but, within this restriction the $z$-transform provides a valuable analytic tool. There are two fundamental approaches to the analysis of linear constant-parameter systems. Since a linear, discrete-time system is describable by a set of difference equations, a direct approach (called the time-domain approach) is to manipulate the difference equations themselves. However, certain important concepts are lacking with this approach, principally those associated with the idea of transfer functions. The reader familiar with the analysis of continuous-time systems by Laplace transforms will recognize the benefits which accrue from a transform approach. Not surprisingly, an analogous transform exists for discrete-time signals. As motivation for the $z$-transform definition, we first reconsider the DAC problem discussed in Chapter 1.

*Data Reconstruction (Zero-Order Hold).* In Section 1-4 some details of digital-to-analog conversion were discussed. If, for present purposes, we neglect the quantization effects of the DAC due to finite (binary) word length, we can investigate the reconstruction of the digital signal when it is necessary to drive an analog device. Figure 2-1 shows a portion of a computer-controlled system. The block on which we wish to focus our attention is the Data Reconstruction Unit. The ideal reconstruction of a sampled-data signal was seen in Section 1-3 to be a low-pass filter; however, the principal purpose of reconstruction is to obtain a continuous-time signal from the sampled-data output of the DAC. Since ideal reconstruction is rarely necessary for control purposes, several approximate methods are typically preferred. The simplest reconstruction is to "hold" or "clamp" the discrete samples as shown in Fig. 2-2. This clamping action is known as a *Zero-Order Hold* (ZOH) and represents a crude method of interpolating between the points of the discrete-time signal. The samples are denoted by single point values occurring at regular intervals; the clamped signal is obtained from the samples by holding the current sample value until the subsequent sample arrives. These ideal sampler and ZOH operations are illustrated in Fig. 2-3 by a simplified block diagram representation of a digital controller with its interfacing devices.

Interestingly, an ADC device performs the same type of operations as a combination of sampling and clamping except that in the case of the ADC the stored result is typically in binary form, ready to be accessed by the digital computer. By not delving into computation at the binary level, in other words, by not considering the effects of quantization, the separate sampler switch can be used to represent an ideal ADC. Similarly, the clamp can be used to represent the ideal DAC, which would perform its operation instantly and without quantization. This is illustrated in Fig. 2-3b. The digital algorithm implemented by the computer in Fig. 2-3 manipulates the error sequence $e(kT)$ to provide an appropriate actuation signal $u(t)$, which is a continuous-time, piecewise-constant

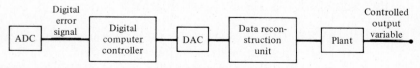

**FIGURE 2-1. Portion of a digital control system.**

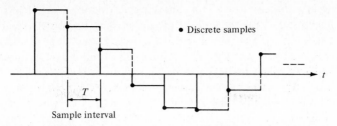

Sample interval

**FIGURE 2-2.** **Discrete samples and corresponding clamped signal.**

(staircase) function. For now we will content ourselves to investigate the ideal sampling and holding processes separately, even though physically, for example, in an actual DAC, they cannot be separated. Note that the symbolism of Fig. 2-3b is useful to indicate that at different points in the diagram the signal is either a continuous-time (argument $t$) or a discrete-time (argument $kT$) signal.

Let us reconsider the operation of sampling from a somewhat mathematical point of view. In Section 1-3 we considered briefly the operation of sampling as a multiplication of an analog signal by a train of unit amplitude pulses, each $\tau$-seconds in duration. Since we are interested in ideal samples, one way to achieve an approximate point sample is to take $\tau$ nearly zero. But as we let $\tau$ approach zero, the signal energy vanishes. In order to attribute some energy to the sampled signal, it is common to represent the discrete-time signal as a sum of weighted Dirac impulses. This is a "density" expression for the ideal sample points:

$$x^*(t) = \sum_{n=0}^{\infty} x(nT)\, \delta(t - nT) \tag{2-1}$$

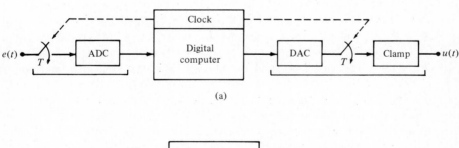

(a)

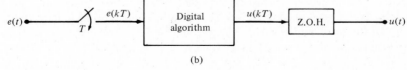

(b)

**FIGURE 2-3.** **Block diagram idealization of signal conversion devices: (a) hardware viewpoint; (b) operational viewpoint.**

The motivation for the expression in Eq. (2-1) is to associate with each sample pulse a unit area that occurs at a single instant of time—clearly an idealization! However, when the discrete-time signal is followed by a clamp, this ideal sampling becomes part of a realistic model since the clamp (or ZOH) output is a practical staircase-type function.

Alternatively, the reader can conceptually consider taking $p(t)/\tau$ as the pulse train signal used to multiply the analog signal in Fig. 1-3, which implies increasing the gain on the signal whenever $\tau$ is decreased. In practice we should have a satisfactory sampled signal without going to the limit of $\tau = 0$.

Working with the ideal impulse-sampled signal of Eq. (2-1), the Laplace transform of $x^*(t)$ is easily taken if the reader will recall that

$$\mathcal{L}\{\delta(t - nT\} = e^{-nTs} \tag{2-2}$$

where $s$ is the Laplace transform variable. Using capital letters to symbolize transform functions, $x^*(t)$ in Eq. (2-1) has the Laplace transform

$$X^*(s) = \sum_{n=0}^{\infty} x(nT)\, e^{-nTs} \tag{2-3}$$

The expression in Eq. (2-3) serves to motivate the following definition of the $z$-transform of a sequence.

**Definition 2-1:**  The *z-transform* of the sequence $\{x(kT)\}$ is

$$Z\{x(kT)\} \equiv X(z) \equiv \sum_{n=0}^{\infty} x(nT)\, z^{-n} \tag{2-4}$$

where $\equiv$ signifies "equal by definition." The symbol $z$ is the $z$-transform variable, and like its counterpart, the Laplace variable $s$, will in general be complex. We will refer to the function $X(z)$ as the *z-transform* of the sequence $\{x(kT)\}$, and the sequence $\{x(kT)\}$ as the *inverse tranform* of $X(z)$.

Before dealing further with the $z$-transform, it is important to emphasize that $X(z)$ was formed from a sequence and, as such, contains only the information of $x(t)$ at the discrete sampling points. Thus, from $X(z)$ we can say nothing about the values of the original function $x(t)$ at points other than the sample points! In a similar way, $X(z)$ and $\{x(kT)\}$ form a unique pair in that from either one, the other may be obtained; but, beware that $X(z)$ does correspond to *many* continuous-time functions $x(t)$! The reason is simple; namely, that there are many functions $x(t)$ that have the same set of samples $\{x(kT)\}$. For example, the set of samples $\{1\}$, that is, the value 1 at each sample, could have been derived from the function $x(t) = 1$ (constant) or it could have come from any one of the set of functions $(1 + \sin M\pi t)$ for $T = 1$ and $M = 1, 2, 3, \ldots$.

Comparing the structure of Definition 2-1 with Eq. (2-3), the $z$-transform could equivalently have been defined in terms of the Laplace transform with

$$z \equiv e^{sT} \tag{2-5}$$

This is an important relationship—one about which we will have more to say later. Thus, any signal that is Laplace transformable is also $z$-transformable. Later, when we talk of $z$-transforms of signals described by a Laplace transform it will imply the $z$-transform of the ideal-sampled version of the corresponding continuous-time (inverse Laplace transform) signal.

The fact that Eq. (2-4) is in the form of an infinite series (in powers of $z^{-1}$) implies that the mathematical techniques of infinite series can be used to investigate regions of the complex $z$-plane for which the series has meaning, that is to say, converges. The determination of the convergence of a particular $z$-transform will usually involve the concepts of geometric series. Here let it be said that only the fundamentals and most useful aspects of the $z$-transform technique will be studied in this chapter. The main reason for not going into more depth with the $z$-transform is to allot more space and effort to the more flexible methods of state variables. The reader will also find that much appreciation of $z$-transforms will come indirectly from the subsequent study of discrete-time state variables.

At the outset let us state that only single-sided signals will be considered here. In other words, any sequence $\{f(kT)\}$, as a sampled continuous-time function $f(t)$, or simply a sequence given as a set of numbers, such as $\{1, 2, 3, 4, \ldots\}$, will be taken to be zero for negative index values. Also, the elements of a sequential array will always be assumed to be in proper order, that is, the values given to correspond to the "time" index $k$, starting with $k = 0$ (from left to right).

Before returning to the development of the $z$-transform, recall that the infinite geometric series

$$S = 1 + a + a^2 + a^3 + a^4 + \cdots \qquad (2\text{-}6)$$

either has an infinite value (diverges) for $|a| > 1$, possibly an indefinite value, such as for $a = -1$; or a well-defined (finite) sum whenever $|a| < 1$. Forming $(S - aS)$, one can show that if defined, that is, for $|a| < 1$, the value of the infinite sum is

$$S = \frac{1}{1 - a} \qquad (2\text{-}7)$$

Drawing for the moment on the background of Laplace transforms, recall that for single-sided signals the Laplace transform typically converges in a region of the $s$-plane for which Real $\{s\} > \sigma_0$, where $\sigma_0$ depends on the signal being transformed. Recall, also, that in the practical manipulation of transformed signals, the convergence region at any step of the calculations is not usually considered important, the reason being that for transformable single-sided (positive-time) signals there is always a half-plane of convergence defined by some $\sigma_0$. Which particular $\sigma_0$ is of no interest except for certain methods of inversion. This discussion is all preliminary to saying that the actual region of convergence for $z$-transforms involved in our calculations will generally not be of interest, and will most often be omitted.

However, considering briefly the convergence of expressions of the form of Eq. (2-4), there are several methods discussed in the mathematics literature on determining regions, generally circles, of convergence of infinite series, and power series in particular. One method is to find a suitable geometric series $\{Kr^n\}$ which ''bounds'' the sequence $\{x(nT)\}$, that is, one which is larger on a term-by-term basis. If the $z$-transform were defined with positive powers of $z$, convergence would be inside some circle in the $z$-plane. But, since the definition is actually in terms of negative powers of $z$, convergence will be *outside* of some circle in the $z$-plane. Specifically, the infinite series in Eq. (2-4) will converge for $|z| > r$ when $|x(nT)| < Kr^n$ for some $K$ and $r > 0$. For those familiar with complex variable theory, $X(z)$ is an ''analytic function'' in this region of (absolute) convergence.

For now, let us become more acquainted with the $z$-transform by forming the transform of some commonly occurring signals. The unit pulse $\delta(k)$, defined in Eq. (1-11), is considered first.

### EXAMPLE 2-1 (The z-Transform of the Unit Pulse)

$$Z\{\delta(k)\} = \sum_{n=0}^{\infty} \delta(n) \, z^{-n} = 1(z^{-0}) = 1 \tag{2-8}$$

The convergence region here is the entire $z$-plane.

Next, the discrete-time unit-step signal will be considered. The reader is cautioned not to confuse ''unit pulse'' and ''unit step'' since they represent quite different signals. ∎

### EXAMPLE 2-2 (The z-Transform of the Discrete-Time Unit-Step Signal)

The unit step, denoted $1(k)$, is defined as having a value of 1 for $k \geq 0$ (and a value of 0 for $k < 0$, since it is ''single-sided''). Therefore, applying Eq. (2.4),

$$I(z) = \sum_{n=0}^{\infty} 1(n) \, z^{-n} = \sum_{n=0}^{\infty} z^{-n} = \frac{1}{1 - z^{-1}} \tag{2-9}$$

Here the region of convergence is determined to be $|z| > 1$ from the infinite geometric series result in Eq. (2-7). Since $I(z)$ is simply a function of the complex variable $z$, algebraic manipulations can be made. As with Laplace transforms the standard form for a transform function is a ratio of polynomials. It follows that we can write

$$I(z) = \frac{z}{z - 1} \tag{2-10}$$

that is, a ratio of polynomials in $z$ with the coefficient of the highest power of $z$ in the denominator taken as unity. ∎

### EXAMPLE 2-3 (The z-Transform of a Geometric Sequence)

For the sequence $f(k) = \{a^k\}$ for $k = 0, 1, 2, 3, \ldots$; $[f(k) = \{1, a, a^2, a^3, \ldots\}]$. The $z$-transform is

$$F(z) = \sum_{n=0}^{\infty} a^n z^{-n} = \sum_{n=0}^{\infty} (az^{-1})^n = \frac{1}{1 - az^{-1}} = \frac{z}{z - a}$$

which converges for $|az^{-1}| < 1$ or $|a| < |z|$. ■

### EXAMPLE 2-4 (The z-Transform of a Sampled Exponential Function)

For the continuous-time signal $f(t) = e^{-bt}$ and a uniform sampling rate of $T^{-1}$ hertz, the sampled signal becomes $f(kT) = \{e^{-bkT}\}$ for $k = 0, 1, 2, 3, \ldots$. (This sequence is bounded if $b > 0$ and unbounded if $b < 0$.) From the previous example the z-transform (recognizing that $e^{-bT} = a$) is

$$F(z) = \frac{z}{z - e^{-bT}}, \ |z| > e^{-bT}$$

Note that transforming sampled-data signals is basically no different than transforming ordinary sequences except that perhaps the parameter $T$, representing the sample interval, may be present in the expression.

Let us now examine a few of the fundamental properties of the z-transform. ■

## 2-2

## BASIC z-TRANSFORM PROPERTIES

*Linearity.* Both the direct and the inverse z-transform obey the key property of linearity. Thus, if $Z\{f(k)\}$ and $Z\{g(k)\}$ are denoted by $F(z)$ and $G(z)$, respectively, then

$$Z\{af(k) + bg(k)\} = aF(z) + bG(z) \tag{2-11}$$

where $a$ and $b$ are any constant multipliers. The validity of Eq. (2-11) follows directly from the definition of the z-transform for a sequence, that is, from the linearity of the summation operation.

### EXAMPLE 2-5

We wish to find the z-transform of $f(k) = 3 \, \delta(k) + 5 \, (-2)^k$. Referring back to Examples 2-1 and 2-3, we see that by linearity

$$F(z) = 3(1) + 5\left(\frac{z}{z + 2}\right) = \frac{8z + 6}{z + 2}$$

The next property provides us with the basis of solving linear difference equations by the transform method. ■

*Translation.* Frequently the terms of an equation involve a time-shifted signal of the form $f(k + 1)$, or more generally $f(k + N)$ for some integer $N$. We will first prove that

$$Z\{f(k + 1)\} = zF(z) - zf(0) \tag{2-12}$$

where $f(0)$ is to be interpreted as a given initial condition.

*Proof:*

$$Z\{f(k + 1)\} = \sum_{n=0}^{\infty} f(n + 1)z^{-n} \qquad \text{by Definition 2-1}$$

$$= \sum_{m=1}^{\infty} f(m)z^{-m+1} \qquad \text{for } m = n + 1$$

$$= z\left[\sum_{m=0}^{\infty} f(m)z^{-m} - f(0)\right] \qquad \text{by adding and subtracting } zf(0)$$

$$= zF(z) - zf(0) \qquad \text{since the summation is } F(z)$$

The result just proved is easily extended to higher-order time shifts. For example, if $g(k + 1) = f(k + 2)$, then [since $g(k) = f(k + 1)$]

$$Z\{f(k + 2)\} = Z\{g(k + 1)\} = zG(z) - zg(0)$$

$$= z[zF(z) - zf(0)] - zf(1) \qquad (2\text{-}13)$$

$$= z^2F(z) - z^2f(0) - zf(1)$$

In a similar manner the transform of the general $N$th-order time shift takes on the form

$$Z\{f(k + N)\} = z^N F(z) - z^N f(0) - z^{N-1} f(1) - \cdots - zf(N - 1) \quad (2\text{-}14)$$

or, a slightly different form,

$$Z\{f(k + N)\} = z^N F(z) - [z^N f(0) + z^{N-1} f(1) + \cdots + zf(N - 1)]$$

which emphasizes that except for the first term, all other terms are associated with the initial or boundary conditions for the shifted signal.

### EXAMPLE 2-6

Let us find $Y(z)$, the $z$-transform of $y(k)$, which satisfies the first-order difference equation

$$y(k + 1) - ay(k) = 1(k), a \neq 1, a > 0$$

where $1(k)$ denotes the unit-step sequence and the initial condition $y(0) = 0$.

*SOLUTION:* Taking $z$-transforms on both sides,

$$Z\{y(k + 1) - ay(k)\} = Z\{1(k)\}$$

By linearity on the left and from Example 2-2 on the right,

$$Z\{y(k + 1)\} - aZ\{y(k)\} = \frac{z}{z - 1}$$

Applying Eq. (2-12) with $y(0) = 0$,

$$zY(z) - aY(z) = \frac{z}{z - 1}$$

Solving for $Y(z)$,

$$Y(z) = \frac{z}{(z-1)(z-a)} \text{ for } |z| > \max\{1, a\} \qquad \blacksquare$$

Later we will be able to complete the solution of the difference equation by inverting $Y(z)$ to obtain $y(k)$. For higher-order difference equations Eq. (2-14) would have to be used; but otherwise, the procedure would be the same.

We will now develop the key "convolution property" of $z$-transforms. It is this property which enables us to use the concept of transfer functions with discrete-time systems. Section 2-4 will be devoted especially to this topic.

***Convolution.*** As we have seen in Chapter 1, the operation of discrete convolution is important in finding the response of a discrete-time system to an arbitrary input sequence. It is possible (by this property of the $z$-transform) to avoid the direct convolution process. In the $z$-domain the equivalent operation is a simple product of the corresponding transforms! Stated formally,

$$Z\{f(k) * g(k)\} = F(z)\, G(z) \qquad (2\text{-}15)$$

where $f(k)$ and $F(z)$, and $g(k)$ and $G(z)$ are transform pairs.

***Proof:***

$$Z\{f(k) * g(k)\} = Z\left\{ \sum_{k=0}^{\infty} f(k)\, g(n-k) \right\} \qquad \text{by the definition of convolution [Eq. (1-18)]}$$

$$= \sum_{n=0}^{\infty} \left[ \sum_{k=0}^{\infty} f(k)\, g(n-k) \right] z^{-n} \qquad \text{by Definition 2-1}$$

$$= \sum_{k=0}^{\infty} f(k) \sum_{m=-k}^{\infty} g(m)\, z^{-m-k} \qquad \text{by interchanging summations} \dagger \text{ and letting } m = n - k$$

$$= \left[ \sum_{k=0}^{\infty} f(k)\, z^{-k} \right]\left[ \sum_{m=0}^{\infty} g(m)\, z^{-m} \right] \qquad \text{since } g(m) = 0 \text{ for } m < 0, \text{ completing the proof}$$

### EXAMPLE 2-7

In Example 1-6 we performed a convolution by tabulation. Let us now use $z$-transforms to obtain $P(z)$ when

$$\{p_k\} = \{(1.10)^k\} * \{100\} \text{ for } k = 0, 1, 2, 3, \ldots$$

***SOLUTION:*** Applying Eq. (2-15),

$$P(z) = Z\{(1.10)^k\}\, Z\{100\}$$

that is,

$$P(z) = \frac{1}{1 - 1.1z^{-1}} \frac{100z}{z - 1} \text{ for } |z| > 1.10$$

---

$\dagger$ This assumes that the infinite series are uniformly convergent in some region of the $z$-plane.

Note that $\{100\}$ is interpreted as $100\ 1(k)$ since it is a single-sided, positive-time sequence. Therefore,

$$P(z) = \frac{100z^2}{(z - 1.1)(z - 1)} \text{ for } |z| > 1.10$$

Again we must defer checking our result, $\{p_k\}$, in Example 1-6. ■

*Time Delay.* Since we have assumed all signals to be single-sided, that is, $f(k) = 0$ for $k < 0$, the following (called the Time-Delay property) is a useful result:

$$Z\{f(k - n)\} = z^{-n} F(z) \tag{2-16}$$

Note that no initial conditions are involved.

*Proof:*

$$Z\{f(k - n)\} = \sum_{m=0}^{\infty} f(m - n) z^{-m} \quad \text{by Definition 2-1}$$

$$= \sum_{p=-n}^{\infty} f(p) z^{-p} z^{-n} \quad \text{by letting } p = m - n$$

$$= z^{-n} \sum_{p=0}^{\infty} f(p) z^{-p} \quad \text{since } f(p) = 0 \text{ for } p < 0$$

$$= z^{-n} F(z)$$

With the single-sided assumption the reader must remember to rewrite "delayed" signals as "advanced" signals and apply the translation property if nonzero initial conditions are present. Consider the following example.

### EXAMPLE 2-8

Given the discrete-time system description

$$y(k) + ay(k - 1) = bu(k) + cu(k - 1)$$

where $u(k)$ is the input sequence and $y(k)$ is the output sequence with the initial condition $y(0) = d$. To solve for $Y(z)$ using $z$-transforms, we first change variables so that no signals are time-delayed. Letting $m = k - 1$, the system description becomes

$$y(m + 1) + ay(m) = bu(m + 1) + cu(m)$$

with initial value $y(0) = d$. At this point applying the transform method will automatically incorporate the initial value via the Translation property. Note that $u(0)$ is needed also, but it will be known since the input sequence $\{u(k)\}$ will be given. ■

*Initial Value.* The initial sequence value $f(0)$ may be found without inversion by the expression

$$f(0) = \lim_{z \to \infty} F(z) \tag{2-17}$$

**Proof:**

$$F(z) = \sum_{n=0}^{\infty} f(n) \, z^{-n} \qquad \text{by Definition 2-1}$$

$$= f(0) + f(1)z^{-1} + f(2)z^{-2} + \cdots$$

Therefore, as $z \to \infty$, all terms vanish except for $f(0)$, completing the proof.

### EXAMPLE 2-9

In Example 2-5 the transform

$$F(z) = \frac{8z + 6}{z + 2} = \frac{8 + 6z^{-1}}{1 + 2z^{-1}}$$

was derived. From the Initial Value property $f(0) = 8$, which corresponds to the $\{f(k)\}$ in the example.  ∎

*Final Value.* In many control situations the final steady value of a sequence is desired. This may be obtained from the transform without inversion. Of course, the restriction must be made that a final value does exist. The complete statement is that

$$f(\infty) = \lim_{k \to \infty} f(k) = \lim_{z \to 1} (1 - z^{-1}) \, F(z) \qquad (2\text{-}18)$$

providing that $(1 - z^{-1}) \, F(z)$ is analytic for $|z| \geq 1$. (A rational function $H(z)$ is analytic in a region $R$ if $H(z)$ has no poles in $R$.) This condition on applying the Final Value property can also be stated that $(1 - z^{-1})F(z)$ must be asymptotically stable, a condition for which we will develop criteria and tests for in Section 2-6.

*Proof:*  From the sequence $f(k)$ define the first-difference sequence

$$\Delta f(k) = g(k) = f(k + 1) - f(k)$$

As $f(k)$ reaches a steady value, note that $g(k)$ will approach zero:

$$Z\{f(k + 1) - f(k)\} = \lim_{n \to \infty} \sum_{i=0}^{n} [f(i + 1) - f(i)]z^{-i} \quad \text{by Definition 2-1}$$

$$= Z\{f(k + 1)\} - Z\{f(k)\} \qquad \text{by linearity}$$

$$= z \, F(z) - z \, f(0) - F(z) \qquad \text{by Translation Property}$$

Thus, comparing with step 1 in the proof,

$$(1 - z^{-1}) \, F(z) - f(0) = \lim_{n \to \infty} \sum_{i=0}^{n} [f(i + 1) - f(i)] \, z^{-(i+1)}$$

Taking the limit as $z$ approaches 1, and interchanging limit operations (this interchange will be valid for a stable $(1 - z^{-1})F(z)$, ensuring that a final value exists),

$$\lim_{z \to 1} [(1 - z^{-1}) \, F(z) - f(0)] = \lim_{n \to \infty} [f(n + 1) - f(0)]$$

Finally, adding $f(0)$ to both sides,

$$f(\infty) = \lim_{n \to \infty} f(n + 1) = \lim_{z \to 1} (1 - z^{-1}) F(z)$$

completing the proof.

### EXAMPLE 2-10

Consider the transform $Y(z)$ in Example 2-6,

$$Y(z) = \frac{z}{(z - 1)(z - a)} \quad \text{for } |z| > \max\{1, a\}$$

Thus,

$$y(\infty) = \lim_{z \to 1} (1 - z^{-1}) Y(z) = \lim_{z \to 1} \left( \frac{z - 1}{z} \right) Y(z) = \lim_{z \to 1} \frac{1}{z - a} = \frac{1}{1 - a}$$

The final value (steady-state value) of the signal $y$ is $1/(1 - a)$ *when it exists!* The strict application of the Final-Value property requires first to check that $(1 - z^{-1})Y(z)$ is analytic for $|z| \ge 1$. In this example if $a < 1$, this is true and the final value calculated is correct; however, if $a > 1$, then no final value exists even though the formula, Eq. (2-18), indicates a finite value. Therefore, the reader must apply this property with care! Many times the "stability" methods of Section 2-6 are required to determine whether the Final-Value property can validly be applied. ∎

*Multiplication by $\alpha^k$.*  For a real constant $\alpha$

$$Z\{\alpha^k f(k)\} = F(z/\alpha) \tag{2-19}$$

In other words, the $z$-plane can be scaled by multiplication with an exponential sequence.

*Proof:*

$$Z\{\alpha^k f(k)\} = \sum_{n=0}^{\infty} \alpha^n f(n) z^{-n} = \sum_{n=0}^{\infty} f(n)(z/\alpha)^{-n} = F(z/\alpha)$$

This property can frequently be used to generate new transform pairs from known pairs.

### EXAMPLE 2-11

Since $Z\{1(k)\} = z/(z - 1)$, the transform of the unit-step sequence

$$Z\{a^k 1(k)\} = \frac{(z/a)}{(z/a) - 1} = \frac{z}{z - a}$$

which checks the result of Example 2-3. ∎

The properties of the $z$-transform discussed up to this point are not meant to be a complete compendium of properties, but only a selected number whose

## TABLE 2-1 Properties of the z-Transform

| Sequence Domain | z-Domain |
|---|---|
| $f(k)$ | $F(z)$ |
| $af(k)$ | $aF(z)$ |
| $f_1(k) + f_2(k)$ | $F_1(z) + F_2(z)$ |
| $f(k + 1)$ | $z\,F(z) - z\,f(0)$ |
| $f(k + 2)$ | $z^2F(z) - z^2f(0) - z\,f(1)$ |
| $f(k + N)$ | $z^NF(z) - z^Nf(0) - \cdots - z\,f(N - 1)$ |
| $a^kf(k)$ | $F(z/a)$ |
| $f(0)$ | $\displaystyle\lim_{z\to\infty} F(z)$† |
| $f(\infty)$ | $\displaystyle\lim_{z\to 1}(z - 1)F(z)$‡ |
| $\displaystyle\sum_{n=0}^{k} f(n)\,g(k - n)$ | $F(z)\,G(z)$ |
| $f(k - N)$ | $z^{-N}\,F(z)$ |

† If the limit exists.

‡ If $(1 - z^{-1})F(z)$ has all its poles in the region $|z| < 1$.

usefulness will be indicated in later application-oriented sections. For now we turn to a discussion of the inversion of z-transforms.

For future reference the properties that have been discussed are summarized in Table 2-1.

## 2-3

## INVERSE z-TRANSFORM TECHNIQUES

As we have seen in several of the previous examples, in order to complete the utility of the z-transform approach to the analysis of discrete-time systems, we must be able to invert a z-transform function. By this is meant to extract the unique sequence corresponding to the z-domain expression. Recall that since we have assumed that the sequences to be dealt with are single-sided, positive-time sequences, the transforms all exist outside some circle centered at the origin in the z-plane. Thus, it is not necessary to specify the exact region of convergence in order to perform the inversion.

There are three basic techniques used for translating z-domain functions into their corresponding sequences. These are (in the order that we will discuss them)

1. long division (expansion into power series)

2. partial fraction expansion and table look-up
3. complex integration

Since one of the attractions of the transform method is to obtain closed-form expressions for the sequences, the partial fraction technique, being conceptually easy, will be used almost exclusively. The long-division method is, however, useful for obtaining the first few terms of a sequence, but does not easily permit writing a closed-form sequence expression. The third method mentioned, that of complex integration, is not difficult, but does rely on some background in complex variable theory. This last inversion approach may be omitted without any loss of continuity.

## 2-3.1   Poles, Zeros, and Residues

Before developing the specific techniques for $z$-transform inversion we will establish certain key concepts and notation. First of all, the general form of $z$-domain function with which we are interested in working is called a *rational function*, that is, a ratio of two polynomials in $z$.

Consider then the following general $z$-domain function:

$$F(z) = \frac{q(z)}{p(z)} = \frac{b_0 z^M + b_1 z^{m-1} + \cdots + b_{M-2} z^2 + b_{M-1} z + b_M}{a_0 z^N + a_1 z^{N-1} + \cdots + a_{N-2} z^2 + a_{N-1} z + a_N} \quad (2\text{-}20)$$

or, in factored form,

$$F(z) = \frac{K(z - z_1)(z - z_2) \cdots (z - z_M)}{(z - p_1)(z - p_2) \cdots (z - p_N)} \quad (2\text{-}21)$$

The function $F(z)$ is a ratio of two polynomial expressions $q(z)$ and $p(z)$ as shown in Eq. (2-20). The *zeros* of $F(z)$ are the roots of $q(z) = 0$; and, the *poles* of $F(z)$ are the roots of $p(z) = 0$. Since Eq. (2-21) shows the function $F(z)$ in "factored form," it is easily seen that the zeros of $F(z)$ are $\{z_1, z_2, \ldots, z_M\}$, and similarly, the poles of $F(z)$ are $\{p_1, p_2, \ldots, p_N\}$. Note that the numerator, being $M$th order, has $M$ roots (zeros) and the denominator, being of order $N$, has $N$ roots (poles). These roots are not always distinct or different. When several of the roots are the same number, that value is said to be a *multiple root* (mutliple zero or multiple pole).

The term "residue" of a (complex-valued) function often arises in the context of transform techniques. For future reference we will define the *residue of $F(z)$ at the pole $p$* as follows:

Case 1. If $p$ is a simple pole, that is, a pole of multiplicity one, then the residue is

$$\text{Res}\{F(z); p\} = \{(z - p) F(z)|_{z=p}\} \quad (2\text{-}22)$$

Case 2. If $p$ is an $m$th-order pole, that is, a pole of multiplicity $m$, then the residue is

$$\text{Res}\{F(z); p\} = \frac{1}{(m - 1)!} \frac{d^{m-1}}{dz^{m-1}} \{(z - p)^m F(z)|_{z=p}\} \quad (2\text{-}23)$$

Although the above expressions indicate exactly how to calculate residues, we will not have a great amount of use for them. Residue calculations are used primarily with the complex integration technique, which will not be emphasized here.

## 2-3.2  Inverse z-Transform by Power Series Expansion

A conceptually simple, but somewhat tedious, technique for inverting a z-domain function $F(z) = q(z)/p(z)$, which is a ratio of two polynomials $q(z)$ and $p(z)$, is to divide the numerator polynomial by the denominator polynomial in a "long division" manner. They are divided in such a way as to obtain a series expansion in terms of negative powers of $z$, that is, a power series in the variable $z^{-1}$. Referring to the definition of the z-transform, we can see that $z^{-n}$ is an indicator that its coefficient is the $n$th element of the corresponding sequence. The procedure will be illustrated by generating the first two terms of the sequence corresponding to the general transform of Eq. (2-20):

$$a_0 z^N + a_1 z^{N-1} + \cdots + a_N \overline{)b_0 z^M + b_1 z^{M-1} + \cdots + b_M} \quad \frac{(b_0/a_0)z^{M-N} + [(a_0 b_1 - b_0 a_1)/a_0]z^{M-N-1} +}{}$$

$$(2\text{-}24)$$

The following is given for a specific numerical example.

### EXAMPLE 2-12

To calculate the first terms of the sequence corresponding to the transform

$$Y(z) = \frac{z^3 - 2z^2 + 2z}{z^3 - 3z^2 + 3z - 1}$$

Dividing numerator by denominator,

$$Y(z) = 1 + z^{-1} + 2z^{-2} + 4z^{-3} + \cdots$$

so that by Definition 2-1, Eq. (2-4),

$$y(k) = \{1, 1, 2, 4, \ldots\} \qquad \blacksquare$$

The fact that the power series expansion method does not result in a closed-form sequence detracts from its usefulness, but in some situations (such as inputs without analytical descriptions) it may not be possible, or even desirable, to obtain closed-form expressions. These cases will also be handled quite easily by the state variable techniques of the next chapter.

## 2-3.3  Inverse z-Transforms by the Partial Fraction Method

By far the most useful inversion technque for our purposes is the method to be developed here. This method is a combination of expanding the transform function, if necessary, into "partial-fractions" and using an available table of elementary transform pairs to write the inverse sequence. Table 2-2 presents some useful z-transform pairs, but is not intended to be other than a brief listing. For the purpose of interpreting Table 2-2, recall that a sequence may be simply a set of numbers, or it may be the result of sampling some continuous-time signal. The main distinction is whether or not the sampling-time interval $T$ enters the description explicitly. If the sequence domain is required, one simply assumes that $T = 1$ in the sampled-data formulation of Table 2.2.

Because no transform table can claim to contain all transforms that might be

**TABLE 2-2  A Table of Transforms**

| Time Domain | s Domain | z Domain† |
|---|---|---|
| 1. $1(t)$ | $\dfrac{1}{s}$ | $\dfrac{z}{z-1}$ |
| 2. $t$ | $\dfrac{1}{s^2}$ | $\dfrac{Tz}{(z-1)^2}$ |
| 3. $\dfrac{1}{2}t^2$ | $\dfrac{1}{s^3}$ | $\dfrac{T^2z(z+1)}{2(z-1)^3}$ |
| 4. $e^{-at}$ | $\dfrac{1}{s+a}$ | $\dfrac{z}{z-e^{-aT}}$ |
| 5. $t\,e^{-at}$ | $\dfrac{1}{(s+a)^2}$ | $\dfrac{Tze^{-aT}}{(z-e^{-aT})^2}$ |
| 6.‡ $e^{-at}\sin\omega t$ | $\dfrac{\omega}{(s+a)^2+\omega^2}$ | $\dfrac{ze^{-aT}\sin\omega T}{z^2-2ze^{-aT}\cos\omega T+e^{-2aT}}$ |
| 7.‡ $e^{-at}\cos\omega t$ | $\dfrac{s+a}{(s+a)^2+\omega^2}$ | $\dfrac{z^2-z\,e^{-aT}\cos\omega T}{z^2-2ze^{-aT}\cos\omega T+e^{-2aT}}$ |
| 8. $e^{-at}\cos(\omega t-\theta)$ | $\dfrac{\cos\theta(s+a)+\omega\sin\theta}{(s+a)^2+\omega^2}$ | $\dfrac{z\cos\theta(z-\alpha)-z\beta\sin\theta}{(z-\alpha)^2+\beta^2}$ |
| | where $\alpha = e^{-aT}\cos\omega T$ and $\beta = e^{-aT}\sin\omega T$ | |
| 9. $a^k$ | $\cdots$ | $\dfrac{z}{z-a}$ |
| 10. $ka^{k-1}$ | $\cdots$ | $\dfrac{z}{(z-a)^2}$ |
| 11. $\dfrac{1}{2}k(k-1)a^{k-2}$ | $\cdots$ | $\dfrac{z}{(z-a)^3}$ |
| 12. $\dfrac{1}{(M-1)!}\left[\displaystyle\prod_{i=0}^{M-2}(k-i)\right]a^{k-M+1}$ | $\cdots$ | $\dfrac{z}{(z-a)^M}$ |

† The time-domain function is assumed to be sampled at a uniform rate with sample period $T$ seconds for the purpose of obtaining the z-transform.

‡ Note that the undamped sinusoid is obtained by setting $a = 0$.

needed, it is necessary to have a method of subdividing complex transform functions into basic transforms that are tabularized. The process of partial fraction expansion, which is suitable for rational expressions, is the technique we will use to decompose complicated functions into simple ones.

Assume that $F(z)$ is expressed in the form of Eq. (2-21), that is, with its denominator in factored form and that $M \leq N$. Instead of expanding $F(z)$, we will expand $F(z)/z$; the reason for this will become clear later. In many cases there will be a zero of $F(z)$ at the origin which facilitates this expansion; but, if not, one may still divide both sides by $z$, which may introduce an additional pole at the origin. Then, for distinct poles, the *partial fraction* expansion becomes

$$\frac{F(z)}{z} = \frac{q(z)}{z(z - p_1)(z - p_2) \cdots (z - p_N)} = \sum_{n=0}^{N} \frac{A_n}{(z - p_n)} \quad (2\text{-}25)$$

where $p_0 = 0$ and $A_0$ may be zero due to the cancellation of a numerator and denominator factor $z$.

The values of each $A_n$ can be found by the residue formula of Eq. (2-22). Thus, for every distinct pole one term is generated in the partial fraction expansion. An $m$th-order pole, on the other hand, will generate $m$ separate terms of the expansion, as follows. If $F(z)$ has an $m$th-order pole at $z = p$, the $m$ terms associated with the pole $p$ are given by

$$\frac{q'(z)}{(z - p)^m} = \frac{B_m}{(z - p)^m} + \frac{B_{m-1}}{(z - p)^{m-1}} + \cdots + \frac{B_1}{(z - p)} \quad (2\text{-}26)$$

The partial fraction coefficients in Eq. (2-26) can be calculated using the following formula:

$$B_{m-n} = \frac{1}{n!} \frac{d^n}{dz^n} [q'(z)]\big|_{z=p}, \, n = 0, 1, \ldots, m - 1 \quad (2\text{-}27)$$

where $q'(z)$ is all of $F(z)$ except its denominator factor $(z - p)^m$.

Note that each of the $z$-transforms of Table 2-2 has a zero at the origin, that is, a factor of $z$ in the numerator. This, at least, gives some credence to the remarks made prior to Eq. (2-25) regarding the expansion of $F(z)/z$ rather than $F(z)$. After obtaining the partial-fraction expansion of $F(z)/z$ either in the form of Eq. (2-25) or, possibly, with additional terms such as given in Eq. (2-26), $F(z)$ is obtained by multiplying both sides by $z$. Each term of the $F(z)$ expansion is then invertible by looking up the corresponding form in Table 2-2.

## EXAMPLE 2-13

Let us consider the expression for $Y(z)$ obtained in Example 2-6. Recall that

$$Y(z) = \frac{z}{(z - 1)(z - a)}$$

was the $z$-domain version of the solution to the equation

$$y(k + 1) - a \, y(k) = 1(k), \, a \neq 1$$

Using the partial fraction method,

$$\frac{Y(z)}{z} = \frac{1}{(z - 1)(z - a)} = \frac{(1 - a)^{-1}}{z - 1} + \frac{(a - 1)^{-1}}{z - a}$$

Multiplying by $z$ to obtain $Y(z)$, the two terms are easily recognized as of the form of Table 2-2 entries 1 and 9, respectively. Thus,

$$y(k) = \frac{1}{1 - a} - \frac{1}{1 - a}(a)^k = \frac{1 - a^k}{1 - a}$$

is the desired solution sequence of Example 2-6. ∎

## EXAMPLE 2-14

Another transform obtained earlier is the convolution product from Example 2-7:

$$P(z) = \frac{100z^2}{(z - 1.1)(z - 1)}$$

Expanding,

$$\frac{P(z)}{z} = \frac{100 z}{(z - 1.1)(z - 1)} = \frac{-1000}{z - 1} + \frac{1100}{z - 1.1}$$

Therefore, after the proper table look-up,

$$p(k) = 1100(1.1)^k - 1000 = \{100, 210, 331, \ldots\}$$

which checks the results of Example 1.6. ∎

## EXAMPLE 2-15

As an example to illustrate the partial fraction method when the transform does not have a natural numerator factor of $z$, consider inverting

$$Y(z) = \frac{z + 4}{(z - 1)(z - 2)}$$

Thus,

$$\frac{Y(z)}{z} = \frac{z + 4}{z(z - 1)(z - 2)} = \frac{2}{z} + \frac{-5}{z - 1} + \frac{3}{z - 2}$$

and

$$y(k) = 2\,\delta(k) - 5 + 3(2)^k = \{0, 1, 7, 19, \ldots\}$$

Since the inverse transform of a constant is the unit pulse, the first term of $Y(z)$ inverts to the sequence $2\,\delta(k) = \{2, 0, 0, 0, \ldots\}$. ∎

## EXAMPLE 2-16 (Multiple Poles)

Since a major application of the $z$-transform is in solving difference equations, consider solving for $y(k)$ given

$$y(k + 1) - y(k) = k, \; y(0) = 1$$

**SOLUTION:** Taking $z$-transforms, (see entry 2 in Table 2-2)

$$zY(z) - zy(0) - Y(z) = Z\{k\} = \frac{z}{(z-1)^2}$$

$$(z-1)Y(z) = z + \frac{z}{(z-1)^2} = \frac{z^3 - 2z^2 + 2z}{(z-1)^2}$$

Expanding,

$$\frac{Y(z)}{z} = \frac{z^2 - 2z + 2}{(z-1)^3} = \frac{B_3}{(z-1)^3} + \frac{B_2}{(z-1)^2} + \frac{B_1}{(z-1)}$$

where the partial fraction coefficients are given by Eq. (2-27) as follows:

$$B_3 = (z^2 - 2z + 2)\big|_{z=1} = 1$$

$$B_2 = \frac{d}{dz}(z^2 - 2z + 2)\big|_{z=1} = (2z - 2)\big|_{z=1} = 0$$

$$B_1 = \frac{1}{2}\frac{d^2}{dz^2}(z^2 - 2z + 2)\big|_{z=1} = 1$$

Thus, the sequence for $y(k)$ is given by (entries 9 and 11 of Table 2-2)

$$y(k) = 1 + \tfrac{1}{2}k(k-1) = \{1, 1, 2, 4, 7, \ldots\}$$

The reader is invited to check a few terms of the sequence by the series expansion method. ■

**Complex-Conjugate Poles.**  In case the pole $p$ is complex, there will also be another pole at $p^*$ (the complex-conjugate value of $p$). It is possible to show in this situation that the partial fraction coefficients (residues) associated with $p$ and $p^*$ are themselves a complex-conjugate pair, and the two terms when inverted can be combined into a real-valued oscillatory sequence.

The use of a hand calculator simplifies the determination of residues for complex poles. For example, two such terms in an expansion are shown as follows:

$$Y(z) = \cdots + \frac{A_1}{z - \alpha - j\beta} + \frac{A_2}{z - \alpha + j\beta} + \cdots \qquad (2\text{-}28)$$

Since $A_1$ is the residue for $p_1 = \alpha + j\beta$, then $A_2 = A_1^*$ is the residue for $p_2 = p_1^* = \alpha - j\beta$. In particular, if

$$A_1 = (z - p_1)Y(z)\big|_{z=p_1} = M\, e^{j\theta} \qquad (2\text{-}29)$$

then

$$\frac{zMe^{j\theta}}{z - p_1} + \frac{zMe^{-j\theta}}{z - p_1^*} = \frac{2zM\cos\theta\,(z - \alpha) - 2z\beta M\sin\theta}{(z-\alpha)^2 + \beta^2} \qquad (2\text{-}30)$$

which may be inverted using transform pair number 8 in Table 2-2. Let us now touch on the third method of inversion.

## *2-3.4 Inverse z-Transform by Complex Integration

This inversion approach requires some understanding of complex variable theory. For present purposes it will suffice to present the method without explanation (for those readers with the proper background to understand the terms related to complex variable theory). Formally, the inverse sequence of $F(z)$ is given by

$$f(k) = \frac{1}{2\pi j} \oint_C F(z) \, z^{k-1} \, dz, \; k = 0, 1, \ldots \qquad (2\text{-}31)$$

where $C$ is a closed contour inside the region of convergence of the function $F(z)$. Equation (2-31) presents a general (but somewhat formidable) expression. Actual contour integration is, in practice, rarely carried out. Instead, the useful result from complex variable theory is that Eq. (2-31) can be evaluated by the method of residues. The following expression is equivalent to evaluating the integral in Eq. (2-31) for single-sided, positive-time sequences:

$$f(k) = \sum_{\{\text{poles in } C\}} \{\text{residues of } F(z) \, z^{k-1} \text{ at poles of } F(z) \text{ in } C\} \qquad (2\text{-}32)$$

To see this method in action, we will consider some examples.

### EXAMPLE 2-17

To compare the residue/complex integration method with the partial fraction approach, let us invert the $Y(z)$ of Example 2-13 with our new method:

$$Y(z) = \frac{z}{(z-1)(z-a)}, \; a \neq 1$$

By Eq. (2-32), using Eq. (2-22),

$$y(k) = \left. \frac{z^k}{z-a} \right|_{z=1} + \left. \frac{z^k}{z-1} \right|_{z=a}$$

$$y(k) = \frac{1}{1-a} + \frac{a^k}{a-1} = \frac{1-a^k}{1-a}, \; k = 0, 1, 2, 3, \ldots$$

This checks with the solution obtained in Example 2-13. ∎

### EXAMPLE 2-18

It is also of interest to see the residue method applied to invert a transform with multiple poles. For the $Y(z)$ of Example 2-16, namely,

$$Y(z) = \frac{z^3 - 2z^2 + 2z}{(z-1)^3}$$

Thus, applying Eq. (2-32) along with Eq. (2-23),

$$y(k) = \frac{1}{2} \frac{d^2}{dz^2} \left. (z^{k+2} - 2z^{k+1} + 2z^k) \right|_{z=1}$$

This reduces to

$$y(k) = \frac{1}{2}(k^2 - k + 2), \quad k = 0, 1, 2, 3, \ldots$$

which is but a rearrangement of the solution obtained in Example 2-16. ■

Now let us begin to apply our $z$-transform methods.

## PULSE TRANSFER FUNCTIONS

As we have seen, the $z$ transform plays an important role in the analysis of difference equations and discrete-time systems in general. Of particular interest to us is the area of sampled-data systems, the general study of systems involving both continuous-time and discrete-time processing. In this section we seek to exploit the convolution property of $z$-transforms.

Recall from Section 1-5.1 that the unit-pulse response sequence of a discrete-time system is somehow characteristic of that system in that it can be used to obtain the system response to any specified input sequence (with zero initial energy assumed in the system). The convolution summation of Eq. (1-18) can be used to calculate the response sequence $y(k)$ resulting from the input sequence $x(k)$ if the unit-pulse response $h(k)$ is known for the system. However, as was seen in Section 1-6, the convolution operation can be somewhat cumbersome when applying it directly. Fortunately, with the result of the convolution property of $z$-transforms the convolution summation is reduced to a simple product of $z$-domain functions.

Referring to Fig. 2-4, the response $y(k)$ is given by [see Eq. (1-18)]

$$y(k) = \sum_{n=0}^{\infty} h(k - n)\, u(n) \tag{2-33}$$

If the sequence $y(k)$ is to be obtained indirectly using $z$-transforms, then [from the convolution property, Eq. (2-15)]

$$Y(z) = H(z)U(z), \tag{2-34}$$

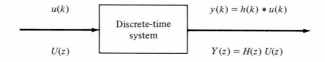

$h(k)$ = System unit-pulse response

$H(z) = Z\{h(k)\}$ = System pulse transfer function
(Also, $z$-domain transfer function, or discrete-time transfer function)

**FIGURE 2-4.  Pulse transfer function.**

where $Y(z)$ and $U(z)$ are the output and input transforms, respectively, and $H(z)$ is the $z$-transform of the unit-pulse response sequence. Since $H(z)$ can be used to describe the discrete-time system, we state the following.

**Definition 2-2:**   The (discrete-time) *pulse transfer function* is defined to be the $z$-transform of the unit-pulse response sequence.

As an example of a pulse transfer function consider the following application.

### EXAMPLE 2-19

Let us determine the equivalent pulse transfer function for the elementary discrete-time system whose output sequence is the summation of all its input sequence values:

$$y(k) = \sum_{n=0}^{k} u(n) \tag{2-35}$$

for an arbitrary sequence $u(k)$. A simple solution is to recognize that Eq. (2-35) is a particular form of the convolution summation of Eq. (2-33), where

$$h(k - n) = 1 \text{ for } n \leq k, \text{ and } 0 \text{ for } n > k$$

In other words, $h(k)$ is the unit-step sequence. Therefore,

$$H(z) = \frac{z}{z - 1}$$

is the system (pulse) transfer function. Also, if $U(z)$ is the $z$-transform of an arbitrary input sequence $u(k)$, the output is given by

$$Y(z) = \frac{z}{z - 1} U(z)$$

Suppose that the input sequence is a sampled version of $e^{-t}$ for $t = 0, T, 2T, \ldots$, that is,

$$u(k) = e^{-kT}, \quad k = 0, 1, 2, 3, \ldots$$

Therefore, using entry 4 of Table 2-2,

$$Y(z) = \frac{z^2}{(z - 1)(z - e^{-T})}$$

The reader may check that $Y(z)$ inverts to

$$y(k) = \frac{1 - e^{-(k+1)T}}{1 - e^{-T}}$$

which is also the sum of a finite geometric series. ∎

## 2-4.1   Impulse Sampling Revisited

In Section 1-3 impulse sampling was discussed as a limit operation as the sampling pulse widths approached zero. At that time it was mentioned that such ideal sampling is only to be considered as a mathematical model of the sampling process, not to be used alone, but always taken in the context of being followed with some type of digital-to-analog device such as a clamp. Again, earlier in this chapter, in particular, the discussion associated with Fig. 2-3, it was emphasized that the mathematical model of ideal sampling must be used with care.

To investigate more in detail what effects are incurred by a zero-order-hold (clamp) device, consider Fig. 2-5, showing a continuous-time signal ideally sampled and clamped. We are already acquainted with the overall effect of a clamp operation, namely, that of a staircase type of output as illustrated in Fig. 2-2. At this point we want to clarify when the impulse-sampling model for a discrete-time signal can be used.

Equation (2-1) gives the expression for an impulse-sampled signal $x(t)$. Repeating Eq. (2-1) here for convenience,

$$x^*(t) = \sum_{n=0}^{\infty} x(nT) \, \delta(t - nT) \qquad (2\text{-}36)$$

Since the output $u(t)$ in Fig. 2-5 is piecewise constant over the sample intervals, we can write that

$$u(t) = \sum_{n=0}^{\infty} x(nT)[1(t - nT) - 1(t - nT - T)] \qquad (2\text{-}37)$$

Recalling the time-delay property of Laplace transforms, the Laplace transform of $u(t)$ is given by

$$U(s) = \sum_{n=0}^{\infty} x(nT)\left[\frac{1}{s}(e^{-nTs} - e^{-(nT+T)s})\right] \qquad (2\text{-}38)$$

Extracting those factors which are independent of the summation index,

$$U(s) = \left[\frac{1}{s}(1 - e^{-sT})\right]\left[\sum_{n=0}^{\infty} x(nT)e^{-nTs}\right] \qquad (2\text{-}39)$$

Equation (2-39) is of the form of a product of two functions of $s$. The second factor is recognized as the Laplace transform of $x^*(t)$ of Eq. (2-36). Thus, the overall effect of clamping a discrete-time signal $x(kT)$ can be mathematically interpreted as the continuous-time response to a train of impulses weighted by the exact samples $x(kT)$, $k = 0, 1, 2, 3, \ldots$, where the clamp transfer function is given by

$$H_0(s) = \frac{1}{s}(1 - e^{-sT}) \qquad (2\text{-}40)$$

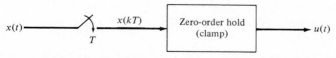

**FIGURE 2-5. Ideal sample/clamp operation.**

**2-4 PULSE TRANSFER FUNCTIONS**

We state once more for emphasis that the combination of the impulse-sampled signal and following continuous-time transfer function must go together as a package to be a realistic model of the operation.

Assuming that some reasonable type of DAC properly interfaces the discrete-time signal with the continuous-time processor, the previous discussion is applicable. Figure 2-6 shows a discrete-time signal $u(kT)$ as an input to the analog system $G(s)$. Using the previous method, $u(kT)$ can be modeled as $u^*(t)$, namely, that shown in Fig. 2-6.

Since $g(t)$, the inverse Laplace transform of $G(s)$, is the impulse response of the linear continuous-time system, we can write that

$$y(t) = \sum_{n=0}^{\infty} u(nT)\, g(t - nT) \tag{2-41}$$

and if $y(t)$ is sampled synchronously with the incoming samples, then

$$y(kT) = \sum_{n=0}^{\infty} u(nT)\, g(kT - nT) = u(kT) * g(kT) \tag{2-42}$$

which is the convolution summation between the discrete-time input sequence and the sampled impulse response of the continuous-time system. Therefore, in terms of $z$-transforms

$$Y(z) = G(z)\, U(z) \tag{2-43}$$

In other words, the pulse transfer function of an input/output-sampled continuous-time system is the $z$-transform of its $s$-domain transfer function.

In the next section we will work with the specific practical case where the continuous-time system is a combination of a zero-order-hold (clamp) device and an arbitrary analog plant.

## 2-4.2  Sampled-Data Equivalent Systems

Many of the applications for digital control involve interfacing discrete-time signals with continuous-time systems. As in the previous section, if we concern ourselves with signal values only at regular sampling intervals, then certain segments of sampled-data systems can be thought of as purely discrete-time systems. This may be the case even though the segment in question does involve

$$u^*(t) = \sum_{n=0}^{\infty} u(nT)\delta(t - nT)$$

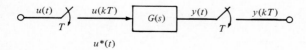

**FIGURE 2-6.  Sampled-data system.**

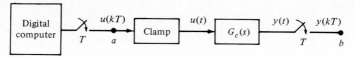

**FIGURE 2-7.   A segment of a sampled-data system.**

some continuous-time processing. Referring to Fig. 2-7, $u(kT)$ represents a discrete-time signal that is the result of some digital processing. The signal $u(kT)$ is being interfaced to an analog plant with transfer function $G_c(s)$. Subsequently, the response of the continuous-time system is being sampled in synchronism with the computer output; this sampling may, or may not, be physically implemented. That is to say, we may be interested in the plant output only at the sample times even though it is not being physically sampled. One may think of $y(kT)$ as the output of a conceptual, or fictitious sampler. Clearly, however, that portion of the system between $u(kT)$ and $y(kT)$ is a discrete-time system.

Our objective will now be to develop the equivalent discrete-time transfer function of the clamped-input, sampled-output plant. To do this, we first recall Eq. (2-40), which is the clamp (or ZOH) transfer function. Since the clamp is in cascade with the plant, the total effective continuous-time transfer function is the product $H_0(s)G_c(s)$.

From the discussion of the previous section the effective discrete-time system between $u(kT)$ and $y(kT)$ of Fig. 2-7 is the $z$-transform of $H_0(s)G_c(s)$. In other words, the equivalent discrete-time system pulse transfer function between points $a$ and $b$ of Fig. 2-7 is given by the $z$-transform

$$G_d(z) = Z\{H_0(s)G_c(s)\} = Z\left\{\frac{1 - e^{-sT}}{s} G_c(s)\right\} \qquad (2\text{-}44)$$

where $G_d(z)$ is the effective discrete-time system, or the ZOH equivalent system, corresponding to $G_c(s)$. Using linearity and the time-delay property (and noting that $e^{-sT} = z^{-1}$), Eq. (2-44) can be simplified to

$$G_d(z) = (1 - z^{-1}) Z\left\{\frac{G_c(s)}{s}\right\} \qquad (2\text{-}45)$$

### EXAMPLE 2-20 (Sampled-Data Equivalent System)

Given that $G_c(s) = 1/(s + 1)$ in Fig. 2-7, the effective discrete-time plant is [from Eq. (2-45)]

$$G_d(z) = (1 - z^{-1}) Z\left\{\frac{1}{s(s + 1)}\right\} = (1 - z^{-1}) Z\left\{\frac{1}{s} - \frac{1}{s + 1}\right\}$$

From Table 2-2, entries 1 and 4,

$$G_d(z) = (1 - z^{-1})\left(\frac{z}{z - 1} - \frac{z}{z - e^{-T}}\right)$$

Therefore,

$$G_d(z) = \frac{1 - e^{-T}}{z - e^{-T}}$$

The reader will become aware of a cancellation of $(z - 1)$ factors using this method. As will be made clear in later material, this is a natural effect that points out the discrete-time equivalent system $G_d(z)$ is the *same order* as the original continuous-time system $G_c(s)$. ∎

The effect of the clamp in Example 2-20 is easily demonstrated by omitting $H_0(s)$ in Eq. (2-44). In this case a different discrete-time system results. From Table 2-2

$$Z\left\{\frac{1}{s + 1}\right\} = \frac{z}{z - e^{-T}} \tag{2-46}$$

Compare the pulse transfer function of Eq. (2-46) with $G_d(z)$ in Example 2-20. Since the normal DAC contains an inherent clamping operation, Eq. (2-45) does give a suitable model to represent the system as an equivalent system for designing a digital controller.

In order to fully utilize the transfer function concept, it is necessary to have a method of interconnecting subsystems to achieve complex systems. Conversely, the modeling of a complex system can be simplified by describing the dynamics of separate parts and completing the system model by appropriately interconnecting these subsystem models. The next section provides the necessary background for interconnecting separate transfer functions.

**2-5**

## BLOCK DIAGRAMS AND SIGNAL-FLOW GRAPHS

Block diagrams have been used extensively in various developments of previous sections. To the engineer, block diagrams help to provide a conceptual picture of the interrelation of system equations. Usually each main block represents a system transfer function. Being in the transform domain, algebraic manipulations can be made to either expand the detail of the subsystems involved or to aggregate subsystems into an effective single system function.

### 2-5.1 Block Diagrams

The three basic elements of a block diagram are given in Fig. 2-8. Typically, the variables shown will be functions of $s$ or $z$, depending on whether they are continuous-time or discrete-time signals.

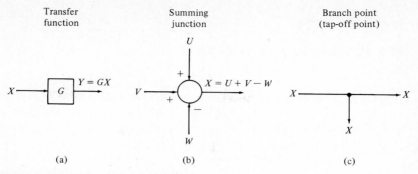

| Transfer function | Summing junction | Branch point (tap-off point) |
|---|---|---|

$Y = GX$

$X = U + V - W$

(a)         (b)         (c)

**FIGURE 2-8. Elements of a block diagram.**

A complicated system can be diagrammed by considering small subsystems and their interconnections. Since block diagrams represent the mathematical models used for the actual devices, the functional operation of the system can be better understood from a study of the block diagram than by studying the physical system. Note that the summing junction of Fig. 2-8 can be used to add or subtract any number of signals. One principal use of the summing junction is an error detector model which essentially forms the difference of two signals to obtain the "error" signal. Similarly, the branch point can be used to "supply" a variable to any number of other points in the diagram.

### EXAMPLE 2-21 (A Field-Controlled dc Motor)

With the assumption that a constant current $I_a$ is being supplied between terminals a and a' of Fig. 2-9, the torque $T$ provided by the motor is proportional to the field current $I$ with proportionality constant $K$. Writing the various equations describing the dynamics of different parts of the system, we have

$$E(s) = (R + sL)I(s)$$

where $R$ and $L$ are the field winding resistance and inductance, respectively. Also,

$$T(s) = KI(s) = (Js^2 + Bs)\theta(s),$$

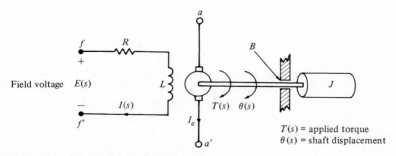

$T(s) = $ applied torque
$\theta(s) = $ shaft displacement

**FIGURE 2-9. A field-controlled DC motor.**

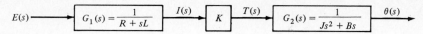

**FIGURE 2-10.** **Block diagram for Example 2-21.**

where $J$ is the inertia of the rotating mass and $B$ is the viscous friction associated with the bearings. The first equation is an application of Kirchhoff's voltage law around the field loop; the last equation describes the mechanical rotational dynamics. Working with the transfer function blocks (output over input) $I/E$, $T/I$, and $\theta/T$, the block diagram of the (open-loop) system is shown in Fig. 2-10.

Note that the block diagram provides a clear picture of the manner in which cause-and-effect relationships lead from one variable to the next.

**Block Diagram Reduction.**    Complicated block diagrams can be interpreted easily by using the defining elements of Fig. 2-8. For instance, from Fig. 2-10,

$$I = G_1 E$$

$$T = KI = KG_1 E$$

$$\theta = G_2 T = (G_2 K G_1) E$$

which tells us that the overall transfer function of Example 2-21 is

$$G(s) = K G_1(s) G_2(s) = \frac{K}{s(R + sL)(Js + B)} \tag{2-47}$$

In general, interpreting a block diagram is facilitated by defining signals where necessary and writing simultaneous equations for variables which are the outputs of summing junctions.

## 2-5.2   Signal-Flow Graphs (SFG)

Representation of a system's structure by signal-flow graphs is very similar to that of block diagrams. With a slight modification of notation the SFG becomes a short-hand notation for the more cumbersome block diagrams. As with block diagrams each of the three operations of Fig. 2-8 are provided in a SFG, but with certain notational changes. For instance, Fig. 2-11a illustrates a single branch of a SFG, corresponding to the block transfer function of Fig. 2-8a. An additional advantage of SFGs, other than abbreviated notation, is the ability to write by inspection the transfer function between any two access points (nodes) of the graph. This method, referred to as Mason's Gain Formula, will be discussed subsequently in detail.

A SFG is fundamentally a graphical representation of a set of linear simul-

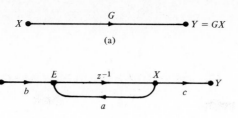

FIGURE 2-11. Signal-flow graphs: (a) single branch; (b) first-order difference equation.

taneous equations. As can be seen from the simple examples of Fig. 2-11, a SFG is made up of *nodes,* which represent system variables (signals), and *branches,* which are directed gains connecting two nodes. The SFG of Fig. 2-11b represents the scalar equations:

$$E = bU + aX \tag{2-48}$$

$$X = z^{-1}E \tag{2-49}$$

and

$$Y = cX \tag{2-50}$$

The last two equations are of the type of simple gain between input and output nodes. The direction of the branch is always from the input node toward the output node. Thus, each branch gain (also called a *transmittance*) can be thought of as a transfer function between the two signals corresponding to the two nodes connected to the branch. Equation (2-48) illustrates that a node serves a multipurpose; it both represents a signal ($E$), and can be used both as a tap-off point and as a summing junction. The set of equations represented by a SFG are exactly the set of equations taken from setting each node signal equal to the sum of the signals being directed into that node. The reader should review Eqs. (2-48)–(2-50) in light of this statement. The only node not used for an equation is the (source) node $U$; the signal $U$ is the system input and therefore has no branches directed into it, that is to say, it is independent of the other system variables. The system output signal is $Y$ and can be interpreted as an "output" (or sink) by virtue of having no branches directed away from it. Finally, combining Eqs. (2-48)–(2-50), and interpreting $z^{-1}$ as a unit-time delay, the system represented by the SFG of Fig. 2-11b is given by

$$x(k + 1) = ax(k) + bu(k) \tag{2-51}$$
$$y(k) = cx(k)$$

We have discussed the interpretation of a SFG as a set of equations. Conversely, given a set of equations, for instance,

$$(1 - a) x_1 + bx_2 = r_1 \tag{2-52}$$
$$cx_1 + (1 - d)x_2 = r_2$$

we can write

$$x_1 = ax_1 - bx_2 + r_1$$
$$x_2 = dx_2 - cx_1 + r_2$$

(2-53)

Clearly, Eqs. (2-53) are equivalent to those of Eqs. (2-52); but, they are now in the SFG form, namely, with the dependent signals isolated in separate equations. Noting that both $r_1$ and $r_2$ are independent inputs (sources), Eqs. (2-53) are illustrated graphically in the SFG of Fig. 2-12. A peculiarity of SFGs are the "self-loops" (at $x_1$ and $x_2$ of Fig. 2-12) that occasionally occur; they simply indicate that, for example, one of the terms of the equation for $x_1$ depends on $x_1$ itself.

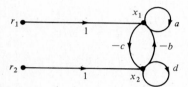

**FIGURE 2-12.  SFG of equations 2-53.**

*Mason's Gain Formula.*   Complicated SFGs may be reduced to a single gain expression between any source node and any other (nonsource) node by a recipe known as the (Mason's) Gain Formula (MGF). The gain formula is useful in determining overall transfer functions of systems whose structure involves many feedback and feedforward loops. Before stating the gain formula, we define a few terms:

A *forward path* is a directed path between source node and output node, crossing no node more than once. The direction of the path is always along the indicated signal direction of the branch. The *forward path gain* is the product of the individual branch gains in a forward path.

A *loop* is a directed path that begins and ends on the same node and encounters no other node more than once.

The *loop gain* is the product of the individual branch gains around the loop.

*Touching Segments:*   Two segments of a SFG are said to touch if they have a common node.

**The Gain Formula.**

$$G = \frac{\sum_k P_k \Delta_k}{\Delta}$$

(2-54)

where

$P_k = k$th forward path gain

$\Delta$ = graph determinant to be calculated as follows:

$$\Delta = 1 - \text{(sum of all different loop gains)}$$

$$+ \text{(sum of gain products of all nontouching pairs of loops)}$$

$$- \text{(sum of gain products of all nontouching sets of three loops)}$$

$$+ \cdots$$

$$\Delta = 1 - \sum_i L_i + \sum_{i,j} L_i L_j - \sum_{i,j,k} L_i L_j L_k + \cdots \qquad (2\text{-}55)$$

where

$$\sum_i L_i = \text{sum of all single loop gains}$$

$$\sum_{i,j} L_{ij} = \text{sum of all gain products of two nontouching loops}$$

$$\sum_{i,j,k} L_{ijk} = \text{sum of all gain products of three nontouching loops}$$

$\Delta_k$, the $k$th forward path cofactor, is calculated exactly the same way as $\Delta$ in Eq. (2-55) after first deleting any loops which touch the $k$th forward path

It is easy to be initially overwhelmed with the details of the gain formula, but rest assured that the generality of the method is hardly ever employed for most control structures. For instance, even though Eq. (2-55) is infinite in nature, many problems will not have a sufficient number of nontouching loops to advance beyond the first two or three terms. A few simple examples will help to see how the gain formula is applied.

### EXAMPLE 2-22

In Fig. 2-13 a system is represented both as a block diagram and as a SFG. By learning to translate a block diagram into a SFG, the Gain Formula will provide a method of block diagram reduction.

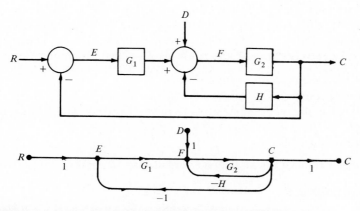

**FIGURE 2-13. Block diagram and SFG for Example 2-22.**

In this example there are two independent inputs to the system, $R$ and $D$, but only one signal, $C$, designated as an output (by extending the node C to an extra node having no branches directed away from it). Consequently, one could ask for the effective transfer function between $R$ and $C$, or between $D$ and $C$. Since the system is linear, we can use the superposition principle to state that

$$C = T_1 R + T_2 D \qquad (2\text{-}56)$$

where $T_1$ is the transfer function $C/R$ with $D = 0$, and $T_2$ is the transfer function $C/D$ with $R = 0$. Equation (2-56) displays the total effect on the output $C$, one part of which is the desired effect from the "reference" signal $R$ and the other, a perhaps undesired response resulting from the "disturbance" signal $D$.

Application of the gain formula must be done for one transfer function at a time.

For $T_1 = C/R$ there is only one forward path with gain

$$P_1 = G_1 G_2$$

The individual loop gains are

$$L_1 = -G_1 G_2, \; L_2 = -G_2 H$$

Therefore,

$$T = \frac{P_1 \Delta_1}{\Delta} = \frac{G_1 G_2 \,(1)}{1 - L_1 - L_2} = \frac{G_1 G_2}{1 + G_1 G_2 + G_2 H} \qquad (2\text{-}57)$$

where it is recognized that both loops touch the forward path ($\Delta_1 = 1$) and each other eliminating the higher order terms of $\Delta$.

Similarly, for $T_2 = C/D$, the only difference is the forward path gain $G_2$ from $D$ to $C$; therefore,

$$T_2 = \frac{G_2}{1 + G_1 G_2 + G_2 H} \qquad (2\text{-}58)$$

■

We conclude this section with a more involved example of the use of the gain formula. In all but the simplest of such problems it is recommended that the formula be applied very methodically. Once the input (source) and output (sink) nodes have been determined, the following procedure should be carried out:

1. List all possible forward path gains.
2. List all possible individual loop gains.
3. Determine all combinations of nontouching loop gain products for pairs of loops, triples of loops, and so on.
4. Evaluate the path cofactors.

From this preliminary work the gain formula can be applied with ease.

### EXAMPLE 2-23

For the system represented in the signal-flow graph below, we will determine the transfer function $G = C/R$ using the gain formula.

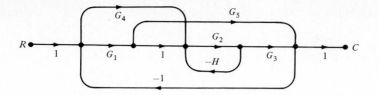

(1) Forward Path Gains:

$$P_1 = G_1G_2G_3, \quad P_2 = G_1G_5, \quad P_3 = G_4G_2G_3$$

(2) Individual Loop Gains:

$$L_1 = -G_2H, \quad L_2 = -G_1G_2G_3, \quad L_3 = -G_4G_2G_3, \quad L_4 = -G_1G_5$$

(3) Loops $L_1$ and $L_4$ are nontouching. All other loop pairs are touching. Thus, there are no terms of Eq. (2-55) beyond the second summation.

(4) Forward Path Cofactors:
Since all loops touch paths $P_1$ and $P_3$; $\Delta_1 = 1$ and $\Delta_3 = 1$.
Loop $L_1$ does not touch path $P_2$; $\Delta_2 = 1 - L_1$.

From Eq. (2-54)

$$G = \frac{P_1 + P_2(1 - L_1) + P_3}{1 - (L_1 + L_2 + L_3 + L_4) + L_1 L_4}$$

$$G = \frac{G_1G_2G_3 + G_1G_5 + G_1G_2G_5H + G_2G_3G_4}{1 + G_2H + G_1G_2G_3 + G_2G_3G_4 + G_1G_5 + G_1G_2G_5H} \quad \blacksquare$$

**2-6**

---

## RESPONSE FROM z-DOMAIN FUNCTIONS

This section is divided into three parts; the first part provides the relationship between the $s$-domain and the $z$-domain; the second part shows the basic sequence responses corresponding to various pole locations in the $z$-plane, while the third part illustrates the interpretation of a numerical algorithm from a SFG. For those readers with a good background in Laplace transforms the first development will help to translate various types of responses into the $z$-domain.

### 2-6.1 Relation between s-Domain and z-Domain

We are already familiar with the basic relation from Eq. (2-5) that

$$z = e^{sT} \tag{2-59}$$

Let us elaborate. If a general $s$-plane point is given by its rectangular coordinates

$$s = \sigma + j\omega \tag{2-60}$$

then from Eq. (2-59)

$$z = \exp\{\sigma T + j\omega T\} \qquad (2\text{-}61)$$

For convenience we define the normalized variables

$$\hat{\sigma} = \sigma T \text{ and } \hat{\omega} = \omega T \qquad (2\text{-}62)$$

Thus,

$$z = e^{\hat{\sigma}}e^{j\hat{\omega}} = e^{\hat{\sigma}}/\underline{\hat{\omega}} \qquad (2\text{-}63)$$

In other words the corresponding $z$-domain image point for the general $s$-plane point under the mapping $z = \exp(sT)$ is a complex number in polar coordinates with radius $\exp(\sigma T)$ and angle measured from the horizontal reference of $\omega T$ radians. Of course, the reader must keep in mind that all the points

$$s = \sigma + j\left(\omega + \frac{2\pi n}{T}\right), \, n = 0, \, \pm 1, \, \pm 2, \ldots \qquad (2\text{-}64)$$

map into the same $z$-plane image point. This phenomenon gives rise to the periodic nature of discrete-time signals when viewed in the frequency domain. For the present discussion it is assumed that the $s$-plane points are restricted to the *primary strip*

$$\left\{\omega : -\frac{\pi}{T} < \omega < \frac{\pi}{T}\right\} \qquad (2\text{-}65)$$

This is the infinite strip whose boundaries are shown in dashed lines in Fig. 2-14. We will discuss this effect further in a later section on sample-rate selection.

Figure 2-14 illustrates the mapping of Eq. (2-63) for rectangular grid lines in the $\hat{s}$-plane. Note that the unit circle in the $z$-plane is the locus of points on the imaginary axis of the $\hat{s}$-plane. Similarly, concentric circles in the $z$-domain correspond to lines of fixed real-part (vertical grid lines) in the $\hat{s}$-plane. Hori-

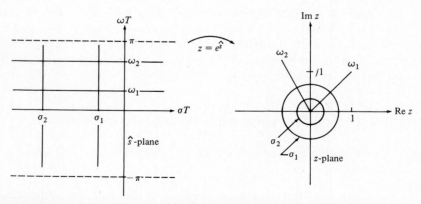

**FIGURE 2-14. Correspondence between normalized $s$-Plane and $z$-Plane.**

zontal grid lines or lines of fixed imaginary part in the $\hat{s}$-domain result in radial lines in the $z$-plane. The reader will recall that when dealing with sequences of numbers the parameter $T$ may not be important. In this case the $s$-plane and the normalized $\hat{s}$-plane are the same; that is, we can effectively let $T = 1$.

From Laplace transform we are familiar with the fact that an elementary signal with pole in the left-half plane corresponds to a time-domain signal that decays with increasing time, whereas an elementary signal with pole in the right-half $s$-plane represents a time-domain signal with unbounded amplitude; that is, an "unstable" response. As a consequence the *imaginary axis* of the $s$-plane may be called the *stability boundary* for continuous-time systems. From Fig. 2-14 we see that the *unit circle* in the $z$-plane would correspond to the *stability boundary* for discrete-time systems since it is the image of the $s$-plane stability boundary. In the same manner the general features of a time-domain signal can be studied from its transform representation whether $z$-domain or $s$-domain. We will take a closer look at this idea of signal stability in the next section; but, for example, the closer a pole to the origin of the $z$-plane, the faster the corresponding time sequence damps out. Also, the smaller the angle of a (complex) pole in the $z$-plane, the more samples per oscillation associated with the corresponding time sequence.

Before leaving this topic it is well to consider another locus on the $z$-plane, one that has some use in the design of controllers. The reader may recall that a basic second-order system transfer function is given by

$$T(s) = \frac{\omega_n^2}{s^2 + 2\,\zeta\,\omega_n s + \omega_n^2} \tag{2-66}$$

where $\omega_n$ is the *natural frequency* and $\zeta$ is the *damping ratio*. For $0 < \zeta < 1$ the poles of $T(s)$ are a complex-conjugate pair. A fixed value of $\zeta$ corresponds to a radial line in the $s$-plane (second quadrant for the upper pole).

Figure 2-15 on page 74 shows that a general line of constant damping ratio corresponds to a logarithmic spiral in the $z$-plane.

## 2-6.2 Elementary Discrete-Time Signals

In this section we investigate the correspondence of $s$-domain, $z$-domain, and time-domain at the elementary signal level. In the following development the effect of the function's pole location(s) is of primary importance, but in the discrete-time case a zero at $z = 0$ is necessary to avoid an extra unit-time delay affecting the response. The reader may want to refer back to Table 2-2 to see actual analytical expressions corresponding to the entries of Table 2-3, p. 75.

Table 2-3 illustrates corresponding descriptions of signals in the different domains which behave in the same characteristic manner with respect to their time responses. Normalized amplitudes are indicated where needed, and the variables $t$ and $k = t/T$ are used to distinguish between continuous- and discrete-time domains. The $z$-domain is represented with the unit circle to provide a scale on the axes.

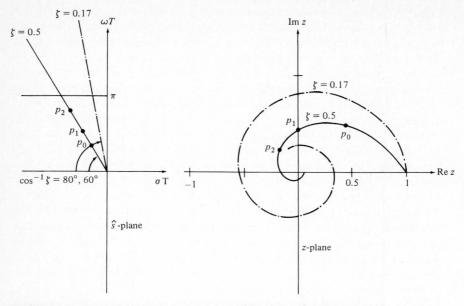

**FIGURE 2-15.** Image locus for a line of constant damping ratio.

The first three illustrations of Table 2-3 correspond to entries 1 and 4 (or 9) of Table 2-2 for various values of the parameter $a$. The remaining three illustrations are second-order and oscillatory in nature. Special attention should be paid to the angle of the poles in the $z$-plane and the corresponding number of samples per oscillation. In the following example illustration number 4 will be worked out in analytical detail.

### EXAMPLE 2-24 (Corresponding Descriptions of an Oscillating Signal)

Referring to Table 2-2, entry 6 (with $a = 0$),

$$\mathscr{L}\{\sin \omega_0 t\} = \frac{\omega_0}{s^2 + \omega_0^2}, \text{ poles at } \pm j\omega_0$$

If this sinusoid is now sampled at a rate $T^{-1}$ Hz, the corresponding description in the $z$-domain is given (from Table 2-2) by

$$\frac{z \sin \omega_0 T}{z^2 - 2z \cos \omega_0 T + 1}$$

Furthermore, if $\omega_0 T$ is $\pi/2$ (as shown in illustration 4 of Table 2-3), the $z$-transform reduces to

$$\frac{z}{z^2 + 1}, \text{ poles at } \pm j1$$

**TABLE 2-3  Comparison of Elementary Signals**

Neglecting the zero, we obtain by long division that

$$\frac{1}{z^2 + 1} = z^{-2} - z^{-4} + z^{-6} - z^{-8} + \cdots$$

The corresponding sequence is

$$\{0, 1, 0, -1, 0, 1, 0, \ldots\}$$

which is shown graphically in Table 2-3.  ∎

## 2-6.3 Digital Algorithms from Signal-Flow Graphs

The following development uses a simple example to present a method of using a programmable machine to generate system responses or inverse transform sequences. The method is easy to use and helps to eliminate some of the algebraic work involved in certain types of problems.

We begin by considering the second-order discrete-time system described by the set of equations

$$x_1(k + 1) = x_2(k) \tag{2-67}$$

$$x_2(k + 1) = bx_1(k) + ax_2(k) + u(k) \tag{2-68}$$

$$y(k) = (c + be) x_1(k) + (d + ae) x_2(k) + eu(k) \tag{2-69}$$

A SFG is easily constructed using $u(k)$ as input and $y(k)$ as output. The intermediate variables $x_1(k)$ and $x_2(k)$ are used with unit-time delay elements $z^{-1}$ to establish the first two equations. In the next chapter we will recognize this set of equations as a state-variable model. Obtaining such a model from either a difference equation or a pulse-transfer function will become second nature for us. Figure 2-16 shows the SFG. The purpose of this section is to show that a programmable machine can be made to simulate the system.

By considering Fig. 2-16, we reserve storage registers for temporary memory of $x_1(k)$, $x_2(k)$ (outputs of the unit-delay elements), and $u(k)$ as well as for permanent memory of the parameters $a, b, c, d,$ and $e$. Initially we start with the temporary registers containing $x_1(0)$, $x_2(0)$, and $u(0)$. The program then implements the output equation, Eq. (2-69), then resets the temporary registers according to Eq. (2-67) and Eq. (2-68). At this point $x_1(1)$, $x_2(1)$, and $y(0)$ are available. By entering $u(1)$ into the previous location of $u(0)$, the next cycle of the algorithm may be carried out, and so on cycle by cycle. In this simple process the results at the end of each cycle can be recorded to provide a complete output history.

### EXAMPLE 2-25
A useful sequence that appears in various patterns in nature is the Fibonacci sequence $f(k)$, $k = 0, 1, 2, \ldots$ . This sequence can be generated from the

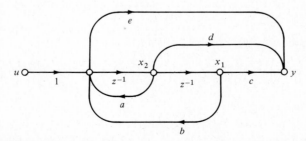

**FIGURE 2-16.  Signal-flow graph for an example system.**

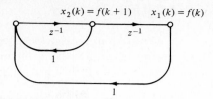

$$x_2(k) = f(k + 1) \qquad x_1(k) = f(k)$$

**FIGURE 2-17.  Diagram for example 2.25.**

difference equation

$$f(k + 2) - f(k + 1) - f(k) = 0, \, k \geq 0$$

with $f(0) = 1$ and $f(1) = 1$. We will generate a few of the terms of the sequence. First we define $x_1(k) = f(k)$ and $x_2(k) = f(k + 1)$. This leads us to a set of equations similar to Eqs. (2-67)–(2-69) and a SFG shown in Fig. 2-17. It is helpful to keep the system diagram of Fig. 2-17 in mind for the following algorithm.

*Algorithm: Steps:*
1. Store $x_1(0) = 1$, $x_2(0) = 1$
2. Record $f(0) = 1$
3. Calculate $x_2(1) = x_1(0) + x_2(0)$
4. Reset stored values $x_2(1)$ and $x_1(1) = x_2(0) = 1$
5. Record $f(1) = 1$
6. Calculate $x_2(2) = x_1(1) + x_2(1)$ and so on to obtain

$$f(k) = \{1, \, 1, \, 2, \, 3, \, 5, \, 8, \, 13, \, 21, \, 34, \, . \, . \, .\}$$

Of course, this simple algorithm does not require a computer since we just add the previous two sequence values to obtain the next, but a programmable machine will be convenient with more complicated problems. It is interesting that the Fibonacci sequence approaches a constant ratio $f(k)/f(k + 1)$ for large $k$. This constant, called the "golden mean," was thought by ancient Greek philosophers to be the most esthetically appealing value for the ratio of two sides of a rectangle. ∎

In the next chapter we will investigate in more depth the concept of system state and methods of modeling the system that are useful in simulations.

**2-7**

# A STABILITY TEST FOR LINEAR DISCRETE-TIME SYSTEMS

The question of system stability is the most important single consideration for a control system. Only after the system is guaranteed to be stable do the secondary problems of response time, overshoot, and so on, arise.

## 2-7.1 Bounded-Input/Bounded-Output Stability

The basic concept of stability involves a discussion of measurable signals and whether their values increase without bound, or not. We say a discrete-time signal $f(k)$ is *bounded* if there is some (finite) number $\beta$ such that

$$f(k) < \beta \text{ for all } k \geq 0 \tag{2-70}$$

In a typical work environment engineers study a device through testing in the sense of exciting the device with an appropriate signal and measuring its response. Systems, particularly those with feedback, can sometimes behave in an extremely undesirable fashion. One undesirable behavior might be a steady oscillation where none is wanted; another might involve signals that tend to be unbounded, that is signals whose value continually increases until some "red line" or design-limited condition on the system is exceeded.

The following definition incorporates the basic engineering concept of system stability.

*Definition 2-3:* A linear system is *stable* in the bounded-input/bounded-output (BIBO) sense if for every bounded input signal, the output response remains bounded.

The reader will recall that for a continuous-time system to be BIBO stable, the poles of the system transfer function must be in the open left-half $s$-plane. As we have also seen in Section 2-6.1, the corresponding statement for a discrete-time system would require its poles to be inside the $z$-plane unit circle. In a later chapter the whole concept of stability is investigated more thoroughly. For now we will accept the basic definition of system stability and proceed to discuss a method of testing whether a characteristic polynomial has any of its roots outside of the unit circle.

## 2-7.2 The Jury Stability Test

The Routh test for continuous-time systems provides a direct test on the coefficients of a polynomial to determine the number of roots of the polynomial that lie in the right-half complex plane. Clearly, this test is useful in determining the BIBO stability of a continuous-time system since it can be applied to the characteristic polynomial of the system. Unfortunately, the Routh test is not directly useful to determine the stability of discrete time systems. Another test, called the Jury stability test, was designed to indicate if any roots of a polynomial lie outside of the unit circle in the complex plane. The nature of the test is very similar to that of the Routh test in that various conditions are placed on an array generated from the original polynomial coefficients. The array is, however, constructed differently from the corresponding Routh array and, for this reason, may be initially confusing to those familiar with the Routh test. The Jury test does provide a set of *necessary* and *sufficient* conditions for the roots of the polynomial to lie within the unit circle, that is, in the region $|z| < 1$.

Let us assume that a discrete-time linear system has a characteristic polynomial (denominator of its pulse transfer function) given by

$$F(z) = a_n z^n + a_{n-1} z^{n-1} + \cdots + a_1 z + a_0 \qquad (2\text{-}71)$$

where $a_n > 0$. Usually, it is convenient to normalize the polynomial by dividing through by $a_n$ in which case the coefficient $z^n$ is unity. Before discussing the criterion, we first show how to construct the tabular array.

***Jury Array.*** From the (given) coefficients in Eq. (2-71) we construct the table of coefficients appearing in Table 2-4. Note that the required number of rows in the table is $(2n - 3)$. Thus, for $n = 2$ only one row is needed and if $n = 3$, only three rows. The first two rows require no calculation and are simply the original coefficients of $F(z)$ arranged first backwards, then forwards.

Beginning with row 3, each new entry is calculated as the determinant of a two-by-two array. For the entries of row 3

$$b_k = \begin{vmatrix} a_0 & a_{n-k} \\ a_n & a_k \end{vmatrix}, \ k = 0, 1, 2, \ldots, n - 1 \qquad (2\text{-}72)$$

These determinants are formed from the previous two rows of known entries. The first column stays fixed while the second column begins at the far right end with $k = 0$ and progresses to the left. Once the third row entries have been found, the fourth row is a reverse replication of these same values as shown in Table 2-4. The remaining rows follow this same pattern. Thus, for row 5

$$c_k = \begin{vmatrix} b_0 & b_{n-1-k} \\ b_{n-1} & b_k \end{vmatrix}, \ k = 0, 1, 2, \ldots, n - 2 \qquad (2\text{-}73)$$

By continuing on in like manner until the entries of the row $(2n - 3)$ have been determined, the table is completed. The actual test may now be stated in terms of the calculated values.

**TABLE 2-4  Construction for the Jury Test**

| Row | $z^0$ | $z^1$ | $z^2$ | $\cdots$ | $z^{n-k}$ | $\cdots$ | $z^{n-2}$ | $z^{n-1}$ | $z^n$ |
|---|---|---|---|---|---|---|---|---|---|
| 1 | $a_0$ | $a_1$ | $a_2$ | $\cdots$ | $a_{n-k}$ | $\cdots$ | $a_{n-2}$ | $a_{n-1}$ | $a_n$ |
| 2 | $a_n$ | $a_{n-1}$ | $a_{n-2}$ | $\cdots$ | $a_k$ | $\cdots$ | $a_2$ | $a_1$ | $a_0$ |
| 3 | $b_0$ | $b_1$ | $b_2$ | $\cdots$ | $b_{n-k}$ | $\cdots$ | $b_{n-2}$ | $b_{n-1}$ | |
| 4 | $b_{n-1}$ | $b_{n-2}$ | $b_{n-3}$ | $\cdots$ | $b_{k-1}$ | $\cdots$ | $b_1$ | $b_0$ | |
| 5 | $c_0$ | $c_1$ | $c_2$ | $\cdots$ | $c_{n-k}$ | $\cdots$ | $c_{n-2}$ | | |
| 6 | $c_{n-2}$ | $c_{n-3}$ | $c_{n-4}$ | $\cdots$ | $c_{k-2}$ | $\cdots$ | $c_0$ | | |
| $\cdots$ | | | | | | | | | |
| $2n - 5$ | $g_0$ | $g_1$ | $g_2$ | $g_3$ | | | | | |
| $2n - 4$ | $g_3$ | $g_2$ | $g_1$ | $g_0$ | | | | | |
| $2n - 3$ | $h_0$ | $h_1$ | $h_2$ | | | | | | |

***Stability Criterion.*** The discrete-time system with characteristic polynomial $F(z)$ of order $n$ in Eq. (2-71) is (BIBO) stable if and only if each and every one of the $(n + 1)$ conditions below is satisfied:

$$(1) \quad F(1) > 0$$

$$(2) \quad \begin{array}{l} F(-1) > 0, \ n \text{ even} \\ \phantom{F(-1)} < 0, \ n \text{ odd} \end{array}$$

$$(3) \quad |a_0| < a_n > 0$$

$$(4) \quad |b_0| > |b_{n-1}|$$

$$(5) \quad |c_0| > |c_{n-2}| \tag{2-74}$$

$$(6) \quad |d_0| > |d_{n-3}|$$

.

.

.

$$(n + 1) \ |h_0| > |h_2|$$

It is worth noting that the previous set of conditions must *all* be satisfied for a stable system; and, if even *one* condition fails, the system is unstable. Since the first three conditions do not require the Jury table, it is useful to check these conditions before troubling to construct the table. Conditions 4 and higher do involve the Jury table and in each case call for the magnitude of the first entry in a row to be greater than the magnitude of the last entry in the row, these rows being the "calculated" elements of rows 3, 5, 7, . . . , $(2n - 3)$. An example will help to illustrate how the test can be applied.

### EXAMPLE 2-26

$F(z) = z^2 + z + 0.2 \ (n = 2)$

$(1) \quad F(1) = 2.2 > 0 \ \checkmark$

$(2) \quad F(-1) = 0.2 > 0 \ \checkmark$ (since $n = 2$ is even)

$(3) \quad |a_0| = 0.2 < a_2 = 1 \ \checkmark$

Only $(2n - 3) = 1$ row was required rendering any table calculations unnecessary. The polynomial $F(z)$ has all of its roots inside the unit circle since every condition was satisfied. ∎

## 2-8

## SOLVED PROBLEMS

Several example solutions are presented to aid the reader in assimilating the theory of this chapter.

## 2-8.1 Solving Difference Equations

The first example illustrates the equivalence of a difference equation and its shifted version.

### EXAMPLE 2-27

We wish to solve the equation

$$y(m) = 2\,y(m - 1) + u(m)$$

where $u(m)$ is a unit-step forcing sequence, and the boundary condition on $y$ is $y(-1) = 1$.

Using the natural recursion,

$$
\begin{aligned}
m &= 0 &\quad y(0) &= 2 + 1 = 3 \\
m &= 1 &\quad y(1) &= 6 + 1 = 7 \\
m &= 2 &\quad y(2) &= 14 + 1 = 15
\end{aligned}
$$

To solve by $z$-transforms, let $m \to k + 1$. (In general, we would shift so that no delayed signals are present in the dependent variable $y$.)

$$y(k + 1) = 2\,y(k) + u(k + 1),\ y(0) = 1$$

Note that the boundary condition at $m = -1$ advances to $k = 0$. Taking the transform of both sides, we have

$$zY(z) - z = 2\,Y(z) + z\,U(z) - z$$

Note that in taking the transform of $u(k + 1)$, the translation property of Eq. (2-12) can be applied, knowing that $u(0) = 1$ from the definition of the unit step. Since $U(z) = z/(z - 1)$, the expression for $Y(z)$ reduces to

$$Y(z) = \frac{z^2}{(z - 1)(z - 2)}$$

Expanding in partial fractions

$$\frac{Y(z)}{z} = \frac{-1}{z - 1} + \frac{2}{z - 2}$$

$$y(k) = 2(2)^k - 1,\ k = 0, 1, 2, \ldots$$

the first few terms of which are

$$y(k) = \{1, 3, 7, \ldots\}$$

This checks with the original recursion showing us that a convenient shift of the time axis may be made before taking transforms. ∎

This next example illustrates the use of the partial-fraction inversion method for a function with complex-conjugate poles and includes two useful transform pairs.

### EXAMPLE 2-28 (Complex Conjugate Poles)

We wish to invert $F(z)$ into a closed-form sequence $f(k)$ when

$$F(z) = \frac{z^3 - 8z^2 + 2z}{(z + 2)^2(z^2 + 2z + 2)}$$

The expansion is

$$\frac{F(z)}{z} = \frac{A}{(z + 2)^2} + \frac{B}{z + 2} + \frac{Cz + D}{z^2 + 2z + 2}$$

Note that the actual complex poles of the last fraction are avoided by assuming a first-order numerator. Using Eq. (2-27),

$$A = \frac{z^2 - 8z + 2}{z^2 + 2z + 2}\bigg|_{z = -2} = 6$$

$$B = \frac{d}{dz}\frac{z^2 - 8z + 2}{z^2 + 2z + 2}\bigg|_{z = -2} = \frac{5}{2}$$

Taking the first two terms of the expression to the left side and combining,

$$\frac{Cz + D}{z^2 + 2z + 2} = \frac{-2.5z - 5}{z^2 + 2z + 2}$$

A useful variation on entries 6 and 7 of Table 2-2 is given by

$$Z\{b^k \sin ak\} = \frac{bz \sin a}{z^2 - 2bz \cos a + b^2} \tag{2-75}$$

$$Z\{b^k \cos ak\} = \frac{z^2 - bz \cos a}{z^2 - 2bz \cos a + b^2} \tag{2-76}$$

By comparing with our derived fraction, we have

$$\frac{-2.5z - 5}{z^2 + 2z + 2} = \frac{\alpha(z - b \cos a) + \beta(b \sin a)}{z^2 - 2bz \cos a + b^2}$$

The factor $z$ in the numerator was removed because the original expansion is for $F(z)/z$. This factor will be replaced at the final step. From the denominator of the previous expression

$$a = \frac{3\pi}{4}, \quad b = \sqrt{2}$$

Knowing $a$ and $b$, the numerator coefficients match with

$$\alpha = -2.5, \quad \beta = 1$$

Thus, the final step is to return to the expansion of $F(z)/z$, multiply by $z$, incorporate the calculated coefficients, and look up the individual terms in Table 2-2, including Eq. (2-75) and Eq. (2-76). The end result is the desired sequence

$$f(k) = (-2)^k\left(\frac{5}{2} - 3k\right) + (\sqrt{2})^k\left(\sin\frac{3\pi k}{4} - \frac{5}{2}\cos\frac{3\pi k}{4}\right)$$

for $k = 0, 1, 2, \ldots$ ∎

As a final example of this subsection, consider the problem of handling an initial condition on the output of a system specified by a pulse-transfer function.

### EXAMPLE 2-29
Given the system with transfer function

$$\frac{Y(z)}{X(z)} = \frac{1}{z - a}$$

Solve for the closed-form output sequence $y(k)$ that corresponds to the input sequence $x(k)$ = unit step and the initial condition $y(0) = 2$.

***SOLUTION:*** Using the transfer relation

$$(z - a)Y(z) = X(z)$$

we obtain,

$$y(k + 1) - ay(k) = x(k)$$

Now taking $z$-transforms allows us to incorporate the initial condition automatically

$$zY(z) - 2z - aY(z) = \frac{z}{z - 1}$$

Thus,

$$\frac{Y(z)}{z} = \frac{2z - 1}{(z - 1)(z - a)} = \frac{1/(1 - a)}{z - 1} + \frac{(2a - 1)/(a - 1)}{z - a}$$

and

$$y(k) = \frac{2a - 1}{a - 1}(a)^k + \frac{1}{1 - a}; \quad k = 0, 1, 2, \ldots.$$

As a check,

$$y(0) = \frac{2a - 1}{a - 1} - \frac{1}{a - 1} = 2$$

∎

## 2-8.2 Deconvolution of Sequences

In Chapter 1 we discussed convolution of two sequences. In particular, recall that the forced part of the output response is the convolution between the input sequence and the unit-pulse or weighting sequence for the (linear) system. Occasionally a problem arises where the output sequence and input sequence are known, and one would like to construct the unit-pulse sequence for the system: in other words, using the convolution notation, given that

$$y(k) = h(k) * x(k) = \sum_{n=0}^{k} h(n) \, x(k - n) \tag{2-77}$$

where $y(k)$ and $x(k)$ are known sequences, to find the appropriate sequence $h(k)$.

The convolution property of $z$-transforms is particularly useful for unscrambling a convolutional sum. From Table 2-1 (last entry)

$$Y(z) = H(z)X(z) \tag{2-78}$$

Therefore, at least formally

$$H(z) = \frac{Y(z)}{X(z)} \tag{2-79}$$

If the sequences have finite length, say $x(k)$ has length $N$ and $h(k)$ has length $M$, and then $y(k)$ will have length $N + M - 1$. Thus, given the corresponding data on $x(k)$ and $y(k)$, we can interpret the appropriate length of the weighting sequence. The following example illustrates the method.

### EXAMPLE 2-30 (System Identification by Deconvolution)

Suppose that a team of ecologists have measured the average rainfall over a certain watershed that feeds a river as follows. The measurements are taken hourly on rainfall and riverflow, which are both translated into the same units, for instance, cubic meters per second:

| River Flow | 100 | 101 | 102 | 106 | 109 | 108 | 105 | 103 | 102 | 101 | 100 |
|---|---|---|---|---|---|---|---|---|---|---|---|
| Rainfall | | 0 | 10 | 12 | 6 | 2 | 0 | 0 | 0 | 0 | 0 | 0 |

Using deconvolution, the team thereby calculates the (linearized) equivalent system unit-pulse response, which can be used to predict flooding, time-to-crest, and so on, after excessive rain. Clearly, the deconvolution is carried out only on the incremental response of the river to the rain, that is, the normal flow of 100 is subtracted from each term, giving the input–output sequences:

$$x(k) = \{10, 12, 6, 2\}$$

$$y(k) = \{1, 2, 6, 9, 8, 5, 3, 2, 1\}$$

In this problem $N = 4$ and $N + M - 1 = 9$ so that the desired system sequence is of length $M = 6$. Performing the necessary division (synthetically)

$$\frac{0.10 \; 0.08 \; 0.44 \; 0.30 \; 0.16 \; 0.04 \; 0.10 \; 0.03 \; 0 \; -0.04 \cdots}{10 \; 12 \; 6 \; 2 \; ) \quad 1 \quad 2 \quad 6 \quad 9 \quad 8 \quad 5 \quad 3 \quad 2 \quad 1 \quad 0}$$

By carrying out more terms than necessary, we can see that round-off errors and measurement inaccuracies can lead to meaningless terms of $h(k)$. Therefore, stopping at the required 6 terms,

$$h(k) = \{0.10, \; 0.08, \; 0.44, \; 0.30, \; 0.16, \; 0.04\}$$

The interpretation is given as the linear equivalent system:

$$\text{Rainfall} \longrightarrow \boxed{h(k)} \longrightarrow \text{Riverflow}$$

For a unit amount of rainfall on the watershed over a single hour the approximate incremental change in the riverflow is described by $h(k)$. Since the largest element of $h(k)$ is $h(2) = 0.44$, there is about a 2 hour delay in the effect of the rainfall. Thus, knowing the height of the river banks and the actual rainfall as a function of time, this characterization of the effect on the river could be used to predict flooding. ∎

### 2-8.3 Using Signal-Flow Graphs

#### EXAMPLE 2-31 (Block Diagram Reduction by the SFG Method)
The system shown in Fig. 2-18 is complicated enough that the standard diagram reduction of modification and combination would be very tedious. Instead, we elect to use the SFG gain formula to solve for the effective transfer function $C/R$. Normally, with experience comes the ability to apply the gain formula directly from the block diagram; however, for convenience the SFG corresponding to the system block diagram of Fig. 2-18 is provided in Fig. 2-19. The gain formula from Eq. (2-54) is

$$G = \frac{C}{R} = \frac{1}{\Delta} \sum_k P_k \Delta_k$$

From Fig. 2-19, we have the following:
The forward path gains:

$$P_1 = G_1 G_2 G_3 G_4, \quad P_2 = G_5 G_3 G_4, \quad P_3 = G_1 G_6$$

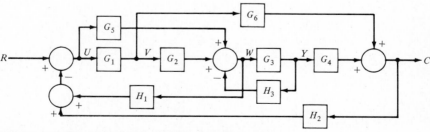

**FIGURE 2-18.   System block diagram for Example 2.31.**

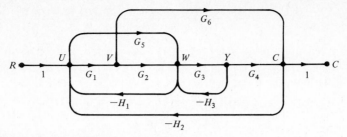

**FIGURE 2-19. SFG for example system.**

The individual loop gains:

$$L_1 = -G_1 G_2 H_1 \quad L_4 = -G_1 G_2 G_3 G_4 H_2$$

$$L_2 = -G_5 H_1 \quad L_5 = -G_5 G_3 G_4 H_2$$

$$L_3 = -G_3 H_3 \quad L_6 = -G_1 G_6 H_2$$

The graph determinant:

$$\Delta = 1 - \sum_k L_k + L_3 L_6$$

The forward path cofactors:

$$\Delta_1 = \Delta_2 = 1, \Delta_3 = 1 - L_3$$

Combining these calculations in the formula,

$$\frac{C}{R} = \frac{G_1 G_2 G_3 G_4 + G_3 G_4 G_5 + G_1 G_6 (1 + G_3 H_3)}{1 + G_1 G_2 H_1 + G_5 H_1 + G_3 H_3 + G_1 G_2 G_3 G_4 H_2 + G_3 G_4 G_5 H_2 + G_1 G_6 H_2 + G_1 G_3 G_6 H_2 H_3} \quad \blacksquare$$

### EXAMPLE 2-32 (Closed-Loop Sampled-Data Transfer Function)

Consider the system in Fig. 2-20. As a first step toward finding the closed-loop transfer function for the system, let us apply Eq. (2-45) to obtain the effective open-loop discrete-time plant model.

$$G(z) = (1 - z^{-1}) Z \left\{ \frac{1}{s(s + 1)} \right\}$$

$$G(z) = \frac{z - 1}{z} Z \left\{ \frac{1}{s} - \frac{1}{s + 1} \right\}$$

$$G(z) = \frac{1 - e^{-T}}{z - e^{-T}}$$

Assuming that the digital controller implements the "integration" operation

$$x(kT) = x(kT - T) + e(kT)$$

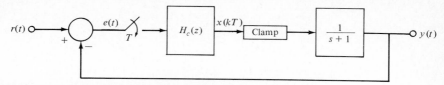

**FIGURE 2-20.  Sampled-data system for Example 2-32.**

it is easily found by taking $z$-transforms that

$$H_c(z) = \frac{X(z)}{E(z)} = \frac{z}{z - 1}$$

Finally, if we are interested in the output only at the sampling times, then the complete discrete-time model can be described as in Fig. 2-21. Applying the gain formula, the closed-loop transfer function is

$$\frac{Y(z)}{R(z)} = \frac{(1 - e^{-T}) z}{z^2 - 2e^{-T} z + e^{-T}} \tag{2-80}$$

This transfer function shows explicitly the effect of sampling time $T$ on the system coefficients. The stability can be investigated using the Jury Test. ∎

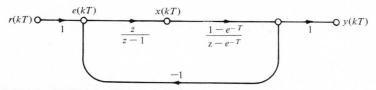

**FIGURE 2-21.  SFG for Example 2.32**

## 2-8.4  Using the Jury Test

In Section 2-7 the Jury stability test was discussed. Our most important use of the test would involve system parameters since it is usually a fairly routine matter to determine whether a low-order polynomial with numerical coefficients has its roots inside the unit circle. In the following example the stability region for a second-order system is found for the parameter plane whose coordinates consist of the polynomial coefficients.

### EXAMPLE 2-33
Given the polynomial

$$F(z) = z^2 + az + b$$

we want to determine the region in the parameter plane, that is, the $(a, b)$ plane, such that the roots of $F(z)$ both have magnitude less than unity; thus, the stability

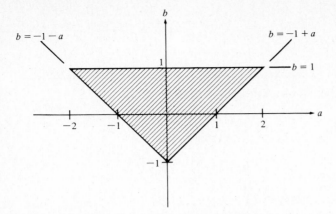

**FIGURE 2-22. Stability region for Example 2.33.**

region for a second-order discrete-time system with characteristic polynomial $F(z)$.

**SOLUTION:** Employing the Jury test, the three conditions to be met are

(i)   $F(1) > 0$;   $1 + a + b > 0$

(ii)  $F(-1) > 0$;  $1 - a + b > 0$

(iii) $|b| < 1$

Figure 2-22 illustrates the open triangular region that satisfies these three conditions simultaneously. For any parameter set within the cross-hatched region the roots of $F(z)$ will lie inside the unit circle. ∎

## 2-9

### SUMMARY

This chapter has been devoted to establishing the $z$-transform as a reliable tool with which to analyze discrete-time system problems. In Sections 2-1 and 2-2 the definition and basic properties of the transform were presented and applied to simple examples. Several methods of transform inversion were discussed in Section 2-3. The principal method for our use was that of partial-fraction expansion and table look-up. The important concept of a transfer function for a discrete-time system was developed in Section 2-4, followed by a discussion of interconnected systems. In particular, the use of block diagrams and (more conveniently) signal-flow graphs provides a means of interconnecting constituent parts in the forming of a complex system. This idea and basic reduction techniques were developed and illustrated in Section 2-5.

The remainder of the chapter presented peripherally related topics. In Section 2-6 the relation between $s$-plane and $z$-plane was discussed, followed by specific discrete-time signals and their corresponding pole-zero patterns both in the $z$-plane and the $s$-plane. In addition, the $z$-domain flowgraph was used to generate an algorithm for calculating corresponding response sequences; for instance, when used with a programmable calculator.

Lastly, a discussion of BIBO stability motivated having a test that will determine from the coefficients of a polynomial, for example, the system characteristic polynomial, whether any roots are outside the unit circle. (In the next chapter the interior of the unit circle in the $z$-plane is established as the stability region for discrete-time systems.) The Jury test described in Section 2-7 was demonstrated as one such test that is convenient to use; it is particularly useful for describing the system stability in terms of system parameters.

# REFERENCES

**Section 2-3**  *Digital Control Systems;* B. C. Kuo; Holt, Rinehart and Winston, 1980.
**Section 2-4**  *Introduction to Continuous and Digital Control Systems;* R. Saucedo and E. E. Schiring; Macmillan, 1968.
**Section 2-5**  *State Space and Linear Systems;* D. M. Wiberg; McGraw-Hill, (Shaum), 1971.
**Section 2-6**  *Introduction to Continuous and Digital Control Systems;* R. Saucedo and E. E. Schiring; Macmillan, 1968.
**Section 2-7**  *Digital Control Systems;* B. C. Kuo; Holt, Rinehart and Winston, 1980.

# PROBLEMS

**2-1**    Show that the sum

$$S_n = 1 + a + a^2 + \cdots + a^n = \frac{1 - a^{n+1}}{1 - a}$$

Hint: Form $S_n - a S_n$

**2-2**    Calculate a closed form $z$-transform for the infinite discrete-time signal

$$x(k) = \{0, 1, 2, 3, 3, 3, 3, \ldots\}$$

**2-3**    Use the convolution property of $z$-transforms to determine the sequence $c(k) = x(k) * y(k)$, where
   **(a)** $x(k) = \{1, 2, 1\}$, $y(k) = 1(k)$, a unit step
   **(b)** $x(k)$ as given in Problem 2-2, $y(k) = \{1, -1, 1, -1, 1, -1, \ldots\}$

**2-4**    Solve for the first three terms by recursion, then check your result by using $z$-transforms to solve the following.
   **(a)** $y(k + 1) + 2 y(k) = 0$, $y(0) = 1$
   **(b)** $y(k + 1) - a y(k) = r(k - 1)$, $y(0) = 0$, $r(k) = 1(k)$, a unit-step sequence

**2-5**     Find the unit-pulse response sequence $h(k)$ in closed form for a discrete-time
system whose pulse transfer function is given by

$$H(z) = \frac{5z^2 + 2z + 1}{z^2 + 3z + 2}$$

**2-6**     The "backward difference operator" $\Delta$ is defined as $\Delta f(k) = f(k) - f(k-1)$.
**(a)** Determine the discrete-time transfer function for the system which performs
a $\Delta^2$ operation on the input sequence.
**(b)** For the signal $f(k) = \{1, 4, 9, 16, 25, \ldots, (k+1)^2, \ldots\}$, derive the
transform $F(z)$ by first forming $\Delta^2 f(k)$ and using the result of part (a).

**2-7**     Using deconvolution, determine the discrete-time system transfer function $D(z)$
if the system excitation $\{1, 0.6\}$ produces the infinite response $\{3.8, 0.2, 1, 1,
1, \ldots\}$.

**2-8**     Determine the system unit-pulse response and unit-step response if the input
sequence

$$x(k) = \{1, 1, -1, 1\}$$

produces the finite response

$$y(k) = \{1, 1, 1, 2, -5, 1, 1, -2\}$$

Of what length is the unit-pulse response sequence?

**2-9**     Find the transfer function $H(z)$ associated with a causal system whose output
$y(k)$ is related to its input $u(k)$ by the difference equation

$$y(k+2) - y(k+1) - 2\,y(k) = 6\,u(k+2) - 2\,u(k+1)$$

Provide a pole-zero plot of the system in the $z$-plane.

**2-10**    A discrete-time system is said to have an infinite impulse response (IIR) if its
characteristic unit-pulse response sequence has an infinite number of nonzero
elements. Otherwise, the system has a finite inpulse response (FIR). Characterize
the following causal discrete-time systems as either IIR or FIR and provide a
pole-zero plot for each.

**(a)** $H_a(z) = \dfrac{1}{z-1}$

**(b)** $H_b(z) = 1 - 2\,z^{-1} + z^{-2}$

**(c)** $H_c(z) = \dfrac{1 - z^{-4}}{1 - z^{-1}}$

**2-11**    The transfer function $H(z) = z/(z-1)^2$ is an IIR system whose unit-pulse
response is a ramp sequence,

$$h(k) = k, \quad k = 0, 1, 2, \ldots$$

Design a FIR system in cascade with $H(z)$ as shown in Fig. P2-11 so that the overall system has the given triangular shaped unit-pulse response.

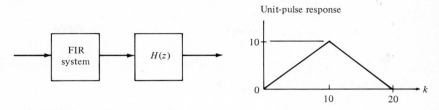

**FIGURE P2-11.**

**2-12** Explain why a discrete-time transfer function whose numerator is of higher order than its denominator describes a noncausal system, that is, one which does not satisfy the causality property: $h(k) = 0$ for $k < 0$, and therefore would not be representative of a physical system.

**2-13** Determine the transfer function $D(z)$ for a discrete-time system whose response to a unit-step input is

$$y(k) = 2 - (1/2)^k \quad \text{for} \quad k = 0, 1, 2, \ldots$$

**2-14** Calculate the response sequence $y(k)$ in closed-form for the system shown in Fig. P2-14 if the initial output $y(0) = 3$ and the input is a unit-step sequence.

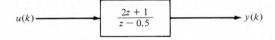

**FIGURE P2-14.**

**2-15** From the signal-flow graph provided in Fig. P2-15 determine the discrete-time transfer function
**(a)** from $R(z)$ to $Y(z)$
**(b)** from $R(z)$ to $C(z)$

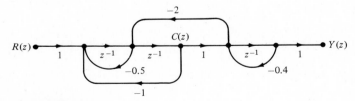

**FIGURE P2-15.**

**2-16** Reduce the given signal-flow graph of Fig. P2-16 to a single transfer between indicated input and output.

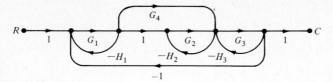

**FIGURE P2-16.**

**2-17** Determine the sequences in closed form that correspond to the following.

**(a)** $Y_a(z) = \dfrac{z^3 - 4z^2 + 5}{(z - 1)^3}$

**(b)** $Y_b(z) = \dfrac{3z^3 - 3z^2 + z}{(z - 1)(z^2 - 2z + 2)}$

**2-18** Solve for $x(k)$ in closed form

$$x(k + 1) + 2\,x(k) + x(k - 1) = 0; \; x(-1) = 2, \; x(0) = 1$$

**2-19** Years ago it was not uncommon to receive in the mail a ''chain letter,'' which instructed you to send a certain amount of money to the first name on an included list of names, then delete that name and add your name at the bottom of the list and send copies of the revised letter to several friends. Included in the text of the letter was usually some allusion to a ''curse for breaking the chain'' as well as pointing out the expected revenue. How much would you receive if the list includes seven names and you must send one dollar to the top name and send the revised letter to four friends? Assume that everyone follows instructions and no one receives more than one letter.

Hint: Let $N(k)$ be the number of letters in the $k$th generation with your letter corresponding to $N(0) = 1$.

**2-20** Superimpose on rectangular graph paper a mapping from the $\hat{s}$-plane to the $z$-plane of

$$\sigma T = \frac{-k}{2}, \; k = 0, 1, 2, \ldots, 5 \text{ and } \omega T = \pm \frac{\pi}{8} k, \; k = 0, 1, 2, \ldots, 8$$

to obtain a coordinate mapping. Describe qualitatively what occurs in the $z$-plane for a fixed pole at $s = -1$ as the sampling interval is varied.

**2-21** Use entry 6 in Table 2-2 to plot the discrete-time signal whose $z$-transform has a zero at $z = 0$ and poles $z = 0.5 \pm j\,0.5$. What is the effect of $T$?

**2-22** Determine the discrete-time equivalent transfer function for the following continuous-time systems which are sampled and clamped as shown in Fig. 2-7.

**(a)** $G_a(s) = \dfrac{1}{s^2}$

**(b)** $G_b(s) = \dfrac{2}{s(s + 2)}$

**(c)** $G_c(s) = \dfrac{2}{s(s + 1)(s + 2)}$

**2-23** Simpson's rule for integration approximates

$$I(t) = \int_0^t u(t)\, dt$$

**(a)** Draw a signal-flow graph of $H(z)$ below using unit delay elements as in Fig. 2-16.

$$H(z) = \frac{T(z^2 + 4z + 1)}{3(z^2 - 1)}$$

**(b)** Assume $T = 1$ and plot the response from $H(z)$ to a sampled version of $u(t)$ shown in Fig. P2-23.

**(c)** Evaluate the integral of $u(t)$ and compare the samples with the results of part $b$.

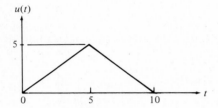

**FIGURE P2-23.**

**2-24** Plot the stability region on the $(a, b)$ parameter plane for a discrete-time system with characteristic equation given by

$$P(z) = z^3 - az + b$$

**2-25** Determine the range of the parameter $\alpha$, if any, for which a discrete-time system with characteristic polynomial $P(z)$ is stable.
**(a)** $P_a(z) = z^3 + z^2 + \alpha z - 0.5$
**(b)** $P_b(z) = z^4 + z^3 - z^2 - z + \alpha$
**(c)** $P_c(z) = z^3 + (2 - 2\alpha)z^2 + (\alpha^2 - 1.5\alpha - 0.25)z - (0.5\alpha^2 - 1.25\alpha + 0.5)$

**2-26** Solve for $y(k)$ in closed form if $y(k + 2) - 9y(k + 1) + 20\, y(k) = 12\, r(k)$ where $y(0) = 6$, $y(1) = 24$, and $r(k) = 1(k)$ (unit step).

**2-27** Determine the unit-ramp response $y(k)$ in closed form for a causal system with unit-pulse response sequence $h(k) = a^k$. Assume that $y(0) = 0$ and $a \neq 1$.

**2-28** Demonstrate with a general second-order system $H(z)$ that the forced response $y(k)$ to an input $c^k$ is given by $H(c) \, c^k$ whenever $c$ is not a system pole.

**2-29** For the closed-loop system shown in Fig. P2-29 determine the discrete-time transfer function $Y(z)/U(z)$ if $G_c(s) = 1/s^2$. Use Fig. 2-22 to determine if there is any sample value $T$ for which the system is stable.

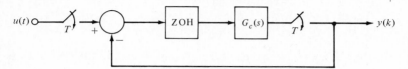

**FIGURE P2-29.**

**2-30** Repeat the exercise of Problem 2-29 if $G_c(s) = \dfrac{1}{(s+1)(s+2)}$

**2-31** Assume a general third-order, rational $z$-transform

$$F(z) = \frac{b_3 z^3 + b_2 z^2 + b_1 z + b_0}{z^3 + a_2 z^2 + a_1 z + a_0} = \frac{N(z)}{D(z)}$$

Since $F(z) = f(0) + f(1)z^{-1} + f(2)z^{-2} + \cdots$ , it follows that $N(z) = D(z) \, F(z)$. Expand the right-hand side and equate coefficients with the left-hand side to show that

$$f(k+3) + a_2 f(k+2) + a_1 f(k+1) + a_0 f(k) = 0 \text{ for } k > 0$$

(It can be shown that a necessary and sufficient condition for $f(k)$, $k = 0, 1, 2, \ldots$ to have a rational $z$-transform $F(z)$ of order $n$ is that

$$\sum_{i=0}^{n} a_i f(k+i) = 0 \text{ (with } a_n = 1) \text{ for all } k > 0$$

**2-32** A discrete-time function

$$H(z) = \frac{b_0 + b_1 z^{-1} + \cdots + b_m z^{-m}}{1 + a_1 z^{-1} + \cdots + a_n z^{-n}} = \frac{N(z)}{D(z)}$$

is sometimes referred to as an *ARMA model* (auto-regressive, moving average model), where $N(z)$ is the transfer function of the moving average (MA) part and $1/D(z)$ is the transfer function of the autoregressive (AR) part. Determine the AR and MA parts of the models represented in Problem 2-10.

## CHAPTER 3

# State-Variable Analysis for Discrete-Time Systems

In working with discrete-time systems it is important to have as many analytical tools as possible. At this point the reader has gained some valuable insight into discrete-time systems with discrete convolution and $z$-transforms, but by far the most versatile analytical tool will be through state-variable formulations. With state-variable methods we can extend our capabilities to time-varying, and even nonlinear, multi-input–output systems, although the majority of our work will continue to be with linear, constant-parameter and single-input–output systems. Most modern control design techniques involve state-variable modeling to the extent that lack of familiarity with the state-variable method would prohibit an engineer from utilizing the important computer-aided design techniques that are now standard design approaches.

The material in this chapter is critical to the initial phase of design, namely, obtaining a suitable mathematical model with which to represent the plant. Since our approach will be to use the state-variable model as a basis upon which to design a digital controller, we indicate initially how linear models are obtained from the more fundamental laws of physics, for example, those of Newton and Kirchhoff. To accomplish this modeling stage, it is expected that the reader may fill in any gaps of knowledge between the given examples, as it is not our purpose to treat the mechanics part in any depth.

## INTRODUCTION TO DISCRETE-TIME STATE VARIABLES

The principal drawback of the transform approach to the analysis and design of systems is its inherent lack of flexibility in the transition from simple linear stationary systems to complex multivariable, time-varying, or nonlinear models. The state-variable formulation of system descriptions provides a structure that *can* make such a transition without a great deal of change in the basic system procedures. Of perhaps equal importance is that the mathematical framework of state-variable models provides a more complete description of the system. The general *state (variable) model* for a discrete-time system incorporates the input–output behavior of the system as well as the internal variations of the "state of the system" with two sets of (vector) equations. The following equations represent general nonlinear and time-varying dynamics:

$$\text{State Model} \quad \mathbf{x}(k + 1) = \mathbf{f}(\mathbf{x}(k), \mathbf{u}(k), k) \tag{3-1}$$

$$\mathbf{y}(k) = \mathbf{g}(\mathbf{x}(k), \mathbf{u}(k), k) \tag{3-2}$$

where $\mathbf{x}(k)$ is the state vector (vector of state variables), $\mathbf{u}(k)$ is the input vector, $\mathbf{y}(k)$ is the output vector, and the vector functions $\mathbf{f}$ and $\mathbf{g}$ specify the nonlinear system dynamics.

The general state model above is simply a set of difference equations in first-order form, Eq. (3-1), plus a set of algebraic equations, Eq. (3-2), defining the outputs of the system. Figure 3-1 illustrates the system "black box" diagram with the new ingredient being the internal state vector.

Although Eqs. (3-1) and (3-2) are given as nonlinear, time-dependent equations, most design and computational procedures are based on linear models. *Linear state models* are of the form

$$\mathbf{x}(k + 1) = A\mathbf{x}(k) + B\mathbf{u}(k) \tag{3-3}$$

$$\mathbf{y}(k) = C\mathbf{x}(k) + D\mathbf{u}(k) \tag{3-4}$$

where $A$, $B$, $C$, and $D$ are appropriately dimensioned matrices (possibly time dependent, but for present purposes, usually constant).

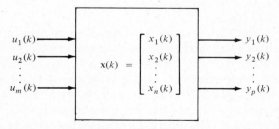

**FIGURE 3-1. System diagram showing internal state vector.**

The output vector sequence $\mathbf{y}(k)$ in Eq. (3-4) can readily be determined once the vector difference equation, Eq. (3-3), has been solved [since $\mathbf{u}(k)$ is assumed to be a known vector sequence]. Thus, implicit in the description of Eq. (3-3) is some "initial condition vector" $\mathbf{x}(0)$, which would be required for a unique solution sequence $\mathbf{x}(k)$.

The very concept of the state vector is closely related to this set of initial conditions. To solve an $n$th-order (scalar) difference equation, for instance, $n$ initial conditions are required. The specific number of initial conditions is related in this natural way to the degree of complexity of the model. The state of the system is a generalization of the set of initial conditions to a kind of running set of conditions that could initialize the system at any time. Alternatively, one can think of the state of a system as an instantaneous "memory" of past influences.

**Definition 3-1:** The *state* of a discrete-time system is the minimum amount of information necessary, together with the input, to determine the future variables of the system.

### EXAMPLE 3-1
In Section 1-8.1, Eq. (1-34), a discrete-time system was presented. The structure of Eq. (3-3) is obtained by considering that $u(k) = -P$:

$$d(k + 1) = (1 + r)d(k) + u(k) \tag{3-5}$$

Comparing with Eq. (3-3) shows that $A = (1 + r)$ and $B = 1$. The system is time invariant unless $r$, the interest rate, changes with time. The absence of an output equation in the form of Eq. (3-4) is taken to imply that the "output" or desired variable is the state itself. In this case, $d(k)$ is the state variable and output for our model; this is reinforced in Section 1-8.1 where it is necessary to specify $d(0)$, as well as the input sequence, $u(k) = -P$, to solve for the "output" sequence $d(k)$. ■

Readers familiar with state-variable analysis of continuous-time systems are aware that the selection of state variables for a given system is most conveniently based on those variables most naturally specified for initial conditions. For example, the state vector of an electric network is usually taken to be the collection of capacitor voltages and inductor currents. The state of a rigid body moving in space could, in the same manner, be taken as the collection of its position and velocity variables (both rectilinear and angular if the body's attitude is important). In the future, we will refer to the initial condition vector $\mathbf{x}(0)$ of Eq. (3-3) as the *initial state* of the system since it is the initial value of the evolving vector $\mathbf{x}(k)$.

The concept of state can be utilized in a fashion that aids our understanding of dynamic systems. Although it is inconvenient to sketch dimensions higher than two, we can visualize the evolving state vector when $\mathbf{x}$ is a two-dimensional vector as shown in Fig. 3-2. The vector space containing the state vectors $\mathbf{x}(k)$ is called the *state space*. In addition, we refer to the set of points traced out by

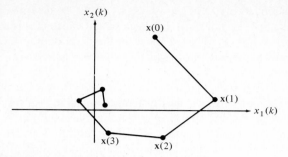

**FIGURE 3-2.  A trajectory in state space.**

$\mathbf{x}(k)$, $k = 0, 1, 2, \ldots$ as the *state trajectory*. Usually, the state trajectory is depicted as the separate plot of the components of $\mathbf{x}(k)$ versus the time index $k$ for convenience in dealing with higher-order systems.

*Linearization.*    A common situation which arises when dealing with non-linear descriptions such as Eqs. (3-1) and (3-2) is the desire to obtain linear variational equations. In fact, many linear models are derived from more realistic nonlinear models in just this way.

If we assume from Eq. (3-1) that

$$\mathbf{x}_0(k + 1) = \mathbf{f}(\mathbf{x}_0(k), \mathbf{u}_0(k), k) \tag{3-6}$$

representing a specific solution or trajectory $\mathbf{x}_0(k)$ in response to a particular input sequence $\mathbf{u}_0(k)$, then the *linear* terms of a Taylor series expansion of Eq. (3-1) are given by

$$\mathbf{x}(k + 1) \doteq \mathbf{f}(\mathbf{x}_0, \mathbf{u}_0) + \frac{\partial \mathbf{f}}{\partial \mathbf{x}}\bigg|_{\{\mathbf{x}_0, \mathbf{u}_0\}} (\mathbf{x} - \mathbf{x}_0) + \frac{\partial \mathbf{f}}{\partial \mathbf{u}}\bigg|_{\{\mathbf{x}_0, \mathbf{u}_0\}} (\mathbf{u} - \mathbf{u}_0) \tag{3-7}$$

where the dependence of the right-side terms on $k$ has been dropped for simplicity. Similar manipulations on Eq. (3-2) yield

$$\mathbf{y} \doteq \mathbf{g}\bigg|_{\{\mathbf{x}_0, \mathbf{u}_0\}} + \frac{\partial \mathbf{g}}{\partial \mathbf{x}}\bigg|_{\{\mathbf{x}_0, \mathbf{u}_0\}} (\mathbf{x} - \mathbf{x}_0) + \frac{\partial \mathbf{g}}{\partial \mathbf{u}}\bigg|_{\{\mathbf{x}_0, \mathbf{u}_0\}} (\mathbf{u} - \mathbf{u}_0) \tag{3-8}$$

If we define $\mathbf{y}_0(k) = \mathbf{g}(\mathbf{x}_0(k), \mathbf{u}_0(k), k)$ and the incremental variables $\delta \mathbf{x} = \mathbf{x} - \mathbf{x}_0$, $\delta \mathbf{u} = \mathbf{u} - \mathbf{u}_0$, and $\delta \mathbf{y} = \mathbf{y} - \mathbf{y}_0$, then the resulting linearized equations become

$$\delta \mathbf{x}(k + 1) = A \, \delta \mathbf{x}(k) + B \, \delta \mathbf{u}(k) \tag{3-9}$$

$$\delta \mathbf{y}(k) = C \, \delta \mathbf{x}(k) + D \, \delta \mathbf{u}(k) \tag{3-10}$$

where the matrix

$$A = \frac{\partial \mathbf{f}}{\partial \mathbf{x}}(\mathbf{x}_0(k), \mathbf{u}_0(k), k), \; B = \frac{\partial \mathbf{f}}{\partial \mathbf{u}}(\mathbf{x}_0(k), \mathbf{u}_0(k), k)$$

$$C = \frac{\partial \mathbf{g}}{\partial \mathbf{x}}(\mathbf{x}_0(k), \ \mathbf{u}_0(k), \ k), \ D = \frac{\partial \mathbf{g}}{\partial \mathbf{u}}(\mathbf{x}_0(k), \ \mathbf{u}_0(k), \ k)$$

Note that Eqs. (3-9) and (3-10) are of the same form as Eqs. (3-3) and (3-4), respectively.

Perhaps the easiest technique for obtaining state (variable) models is to develop methods for transcribing ordinary difference equations or discrete-time transfer function models into state-variable form. The approach taken in a later section to make this transition to state models uses simulation diagrams. For those readers familiar with programming differential equations on analog computers, these techniques will seem familiar with the exception that a pure time-delay (of one sample interval, that is, $z^{-1}$) replaces the pure integration $s^{-1}$.

**3-2**

---

## STATE VARIABLES FOR CONTINUOUS-TIME SYSTEMS

Although our primary interest is in studying discrete-time systems, particularly as they relate to digital control, most applications can be viewed as controlling a continuous-time plant. In this section we devote some time to describing our plant in the state-variable form. A linear, continuous-time state model will be of the form

$$\dot{\mathbf{x}}(t) = A\mathbf{x}(t) + B\mathbf{u}(t) \tag{3-11}$$

$$\mathbf{y}(t) = C\mathbf{x}(t) + D\mathbf{u}(t) \tag{3-12}$$

The continuous-time state model has the same structure as Eqs. (3-3) and (3-4). Later, when we are converting continuous-time system models to equivalent discrete-time models, we will have to take care not to confuse the continuous-time $A$, $B$, $C$, $D$ matrices with the corresponding discrete-time $A$, $B$, $C$, $D$ matrices since they are generally different matrices.

Most all of the concepts and manipulations of state models apply equally well to both continuously and discretely varying systems. For example, the linearization method previously discussed in the context of discrete-time state models can be used with continuous-time state models as well.

A basic method of establishing a state model for a continuous-time plant is to develop the model first as a set of simultaneous differential equations, then to define a natural set of state variables. Let us illustrate the method with an example.

### EXAMPLE 3-2

In Chapter 2 a field-controlled dc motor was modeled. From Fig. 2-10 one can derive the following differential equations:

$$L \frac{di}{dt} + R \ i(t) = e(t)$$

$$J \frac{d^2\theta}{dt^2} + B \frac{d\theta}{dt} = K\,i(t)$$

For the first equation $x_1 = i$ is a natural state variable. In the second equation we let $x_2 = \theta$ and $x_3 = \dot\theta$, resulting in the following state model:

$$\begin{bmatrix} \dot{x}_1 \\ \dot{x}_2 \\ \dot{x}_3 \end{bmatrix} = \begin{bmatrix} -L^{-1}R & 0 & 0 \\ 0 & 0 & 1 \\ J^{-1}K & 0 & -J^{-1}B \end{bmatrix} \begin{bmatrix} x_1 \\ x_2 \\ x_3 \end{bmatrix} + \begin{bmatrix} L^{-1} \\ 0 \\ 0 \end{bmatrix} e(t)$$

$$\theta(t) = \begin{bmatrix} 0 & 1 & 0 \end{bmatrix} \mathbf{x}$$

Note that the highest derivative of each original equation became one of the state equations. ∎

*Phase Variables.*  The so-called "natural" state variables for a scalar differential equation given by

$$y^{(n)}(t) + a_{n-1}y^{(n-1)}(t) + \cdots + a_1 y^{(1)}(t) + a_0 y(t) = u(t) \qquad (3\text{-}13)$$

are the *phase variables* for the system, namely,

$$x_1 = y, \; x_2 = y^{(1)}, \ldots, \; x_n = y^{(n-1)}$$

where $y^{(j)} = d^j y/dt^j$. The state model for Eq. (3-13) is then given by

$$\dot{\mathbf{x}}(t) = \begin{bmatrix} 0 & 1 & 0 & \cdots & 0 \\ 0 & 0 & 1 & \cdots & 0 \\ & & \cdots & & \\ 0 & 0 & 0 & \cdots & 1 \\ -a_0 & -a_1 & -a_2 & \cdots & -a_{n-1} \end{bmatrix} \mathbf{x}(t) + \begin{bmatrix} 0 \\ 0 \\ \vdots \\ 1 \end{bmatrix} u(t) \qquad (3\text{-}14)$$

$$y(t) = \begin{bmatrix} 1 & 0 & 0 & \cdots & 0 \end{bmatrix} \mathbf{x}(t)$$

With this method all of the coefficients of the differential equation are in the final state equation, which is $\dot{x}_n = y^{(n)}$, that is, the expression obtained from Eq. (3-13) for the highest derivative of $y$. The phase variables are associated with a natural set of state variables since they are exactly those variables that are most conveniently specified for initial conditions on the system.

The phase-variable method also applies to forming state models from difference equations, the only change being that

$$x_{j+1}(k) = x_j(k+1) \text{ for } j = 1, 2, \ldots, n$$

### EXAMPLE 3-3 (Discrete-Time Phase-Variable Model)

For

$$y(k+2) + 2y(k+1) + 3y(k) = u(k)$$

define

$$x_1(k) = y(k), \; x_2(k) = x_1(k+1) = y(k+1)$$

Thus, the state model is

$$\mathbf{x}(k + 1) = \begin{bmatrix} 0 & 1 \\ -3 & -2 \end{bmatrix} \mathbf{x}(k) + \begin{bmatrix} 0 \\ 1 \end{bmatrix} u(k)$$

$$y(k) = [1 \quad 0] \mathbf{x}(k)$$

∎

In a later section we will learn to deal with derivatives (or shifts) of the input signals as well as multiple inputs and outputs.

## 3-3

## GENERAL SOLUTION FOR THE CONTINUOUS-TIME STATE MODEL

Before continuing our consideration of state models for discrete-time systems, let us first develop the solution for continuous-time systems. This is necessary since in most cases the plants to which we apply digital control techniques are continuous-time systems. Thus, given the model

$$\dot{\mathbf{x}}(t) = A\mathbf{x}(t) + B\mathbf{u}(t), \mathbf{x}(t_0) \tag{3-15}$$
$$\mathbf{y}(t) = C\mathbf{x}(t) + D\mathbf{u}(t)$$

we seek a form for the general solution to $\mathbf{x}(t)$ [and $\mathbf{y}(t)$]. For present purposes we consider only linear, time-invariant systems.

By analogy to the scalar equation

$$\dot{x} = ax, x(0) \tag{3-16}$$

whose solution is

$$x(t) = e^{at}x(0) \tag{3-17}$$

we introduce (for $A$ an $n \times n$ constant matrix) the notation $e^{At}$ or exp $(At)$ and define this exponential function of a square matrix by the well known series representation for an exponential function, that is, we define

$$\exp (At) \triangleq I + At + A^2 \frac{t^2}{2!} + \cdots + A^k \frac{t^k}{k!} + \cdots \tag{3-18}$$

It is important to recognize that exp $(At)$ has meaning *only* through Eq. (3-18), which itself is a well-defined matrix series since $A^k$ is simply $A$ times itself $k$ times. The series Eq. (3-18) is absolutely convergent for any finite matrix $At$, thereby allowing us to manipulate the series on a term-by-term basis. For instance, using Eq. (3-18),

$$\frac{d}{dt} \exp (At) = A + A^2t + \cdots A^k \frac{t^{k-1}}{(k-1)!} + \cdots$$

Since $A$ can be factored out as a pre- or a postmultiplier,

$$\frac{d}{dt} \exp (At) = A \exp (At) = \exp (At) A \tag{3-19}$$

showing that $A$ and $\exp (At)$ commute. Similarly, we can prove other important attributes of the matrix exponential function.

Again working with the defining series,

$$e^{A(t-\tau)} = I + (t-\tau)A + \frac{(t-\tau)^2}{2!} A + \cdots + \frac{(t-\tau)^k}{k!} A^k + \cdots \tag{3-20}$$

By multiplying out the two series and collecting like powers of $A$, we arrive at the familiar property of exponential functions given in Eq. (3-21):

$$e^{At}e^{A(-\tau)} = \left( I + tA + \frac{t^2}{2!} A^2 + \cdots \right)\left( I - \tau A + \frac{\tau^2}{2!} A^2 - \cdots \right)$$

$$e^{At}e^{-A\tau} = \left( I + (t-\tau)A + \frac{(t-\tau)^2}{2!} A^2 + \cdots \right) = e^{A(t-\tau)} \tag{3-21}$$

Since from Eq. (3-18) it is clear that

$$e^{A(0)} = I \tag{3-22}$$

we readily deduce that

$$e^{-At} = [e^{At}]^{-1} \tag{3-23}$$

by letting $\tau = t$ in Eq. (3-21) $e^{At}e^{-At} = I$).

We are now ready to present the general solution to the continuous-time linear state model of Eq. (3-15).

From Eq. (3-15)

$$\dot{\mathbf{x}}(t) - A\mathbf{x}(t) = B\mathbf{u}(t)$$

Premultiplying by $\exp (-At)$, the left side is recognized as an exact derivative. The reader can easily check this using the relation that for $C = AB$, then $\dot{C} = \dot{A}B + A\dot{B}$. Integrating from $t_0$ to $t$,

$$\int_{t_0}^{t} \frac{d}{d\tau} [e^{-A\tau}\mathbf{x}(\tau)] \, d\tau = \int_{t_0}^{t} e^{-A\tau}B\mathbf{u}(\tau) \, d\tau \tag{3-24}$$

$$e^{-At}\mathbf{x}(t) - e^{-At_0}\mathbf{x}(t_0) = \int_{t_0}^{t} e^{-A\tau}B\mathbf{u}(\tau) \, d\tau \tag{3-25}$$

Finally,

$$\mathbf{x}(t) = e^{A(t-t_0)} \mathbf{x}(t_0) + \int_{t_0}^{t} e^{A(t-\tau)}B\mathbf{u}(\tau) \, d\tau \tag{3-26}$$

is the *general solution* to the state equation of Eq. (3-15); the first term is the *zero-input solution* and the second term is the *zero-state solution*. The output

$y(t)$ is simply a combination of the solution $x(t)$ and the input $u(t)$. Equation (3-26) is an important theoretical result to which we will return many times in future developments, but it is also a practical method of solving for the state vector of the system.

*Transition Matrix.* A special name (and notation) is sometimes used for our exponential matrix:

$$\Phi(t, \tau) = e^{A(t-\tau)} \tag{3-27}$$

The matrix $\Phi$ is called the *(state) transition matrix* for the system in Eq. (3-15). Since we are already aware of the basic properties of exp $(At)$, the corresponding properties of $\Phi$ will be listed with only a brief discussion.

With $u(t) = 0$, the zero-input solution from Eq. (3-26) is

$$x(t) = \Phi(t, t_0) x(t_0) \tag{3-28}$$

which illustrates that $\Phi$ provides a "transition" between the state vector at time $t_0$ and the state vector at time $t$. Note that for a time-invariant system $\Phi(t, \tau)$ is a function of only one variable, $(t - \tau)$ in Eq. (3-27), and is sometimes denoted $\Phi(t - \tau)$, or simply $\Phi(t)$, to emphasize this fact.

*Properties of $\Phi(t - \tau)$.*

1. $\dot{\Phi}(t) = A\Phi(t),\ \Phi(0) = I$ \hfill (3-29)

2. $\Phi(t_2 - t_0) = \Phi(t_2 - t_1)\,\Phi(t_1 - t_0)$ \hfill (3-30)

This property is called the *group property* and is easily proved by considering Eq. (3-28); namely,

$$x(t_1) = \Phi(t_1 - t_0)x(t_0)$$

$$x(t_2) = \Phi(t_2 - t_1)x(t_1)$$

$$x(t_2) = \Phi(t_2 - t_1)[\Phi(t_1 - t_0)x(t_0)]$$

Comparing the first expression to the last, completes the proof.

3. $\Phi(t_1 - t_2) = \Phi^{-1}(t_2 - t_1)$ \hfill (3-31)

These three properties of the transition matrix are of course those properties we already know to apply to the matrix exponential function.

**3-4**

## DISCRETE-TIME STATE MODELS
## FOR SAMPLED-DATA SYSTEMS

In many applications of digital control the plant information is given in the form of a continuous-time state model and the only problem is to discretize the con-

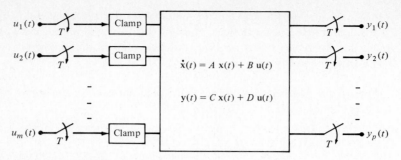

**FIGURE 3-3. Sampled-data system.**

tinuous-time system in some realistic manner. As has been discussed in Section 2-4, the sample-and-hold equivalent is one of the more convenient techniques. Figure 3-3 presents the problem of sampled/clamped inputs to a continuous-time state modeled system.

Assuming the linear system is time invariant and $\mathbf{x}(t_0)$ is known, the solution for $\mathbf{x}(t)$ as developed in the previous section is

$$\mathbf{x}(t) = e^{A(t-t_0)}\mathbf{x}(t_0) + \int_{t_0}^{t} e^{A(t-\tau)}B\mathbf{u}(\tau) \, d\tau$$

If we are interested in $\mathbf{x}(t)$ only at the sample times, consider evaluating $\mathbf{x}$ at time $(kT + T)$ with $t_0$ taken to be $kT$,

$$\mathbf{x}(kT + T) = e^{AT}\mathbf{x}(kT) + \int_{kT}^{kT+T} e^{A(kT+T-\tau)}B\mathbf{u}(\tau) \, d\tau \qquad (3\text{-}32)$$

If, as indicated in Fig. 3-3, $\mathbf{u}(t)$ into the plant is clamped, then

$$\mathbf{u}(t) = \mathbf{u}(kT) \text{ for } kT \le t < kT + T \qquad (3\text{-}33)$$

for integer $k$. Letting $t = kT + T - \tau$, Eq. (3-32) becomes

$$\mathbf{x}(kT + T) = \{e^{AT}\} \mathbf{x}(kT) + \left\{ \int_{0}^{T} e^{At}B \, dt \right\} \mathbf{u}(kT)$$

$$\mathbf{x}(kT + T) = \Phi(T) \mathbf{x}(kT) + \Gamma(T)\mathbf{u}(kT) \qquad (3\text{-}34)$$

Also, by considering the outputs only at the same sample times (even though they may not be actually sampled),

$$\mathbf{y}(kT) = C\mathbf{x}(kT) + D\mathbf{u}(kT) \qquad (3\text{-}35)$$

To simplify the notation, the $T$ factors are usually left out.

Equations (3-34) and (3-35) together comprise an *equivalent discrete-time state model* for the system of Fig. 3-3. In a later section we will show how the coefficient matrices of Eq. (3-34) can be machine calculated.

**STATE-VARIABLE ANALYSIS**

## EXAMPLE 3-4

Given the open-loop sampled-data system in Fig. 3-4a, the simplest technique for applying the results in Eq. (3-34) is to expand the continuous-time transfer function into partial fractions:

$$\frac{3s + 7}{s^2 + 5s + 6} = \frac{1}{s + 2} + \frac{2}{s + 3}$$

The partial-fraction expansion permits (via the diagram of Fig. 3-4b) us to write down the continuous-time state equation:

$$\dot{\mathbf{x}}(t) = \begin{bmatrix} -2 & 0 \\ 0 & -3 \end{bmatrix} \mathbf{x}(t) + \begin{bmatrix} 1 \\ 1 \end{bmatrix} u(t)$$

Therefore, implementing Eqs. (3-34) and (3-35), the resulting discrete-time model is given below. Note that formulating $A$ as a diagonal matrix greatly simplifies calculating exp $\{AT\}$, (exp $\{$diag $[\lambda_i]\}$ = diag $[\exp \{\lambda_i\}]$):

$$\mathbf{x}(kT + T) = \begin{bmatrix} e^{-2T} & 0 \\ 0 & e^{-3T} \end{bmatrix} \mathbf{x}(kT) + \begin{bmatrix} (1 - e^{-2T})/2 \\ (1 - e^{-3T})/3 \end{bmatrix} e(kT)$$

$$y(kT) = \begin{bmatrix} 1 & 2 \end{bmatrix} \mathbf{x}(kT) \qquad\blacksquare$$

An approach for calculating $\Phi(T)$ and $\Gamma(T)$ in Eq. (3-34) for low-order systems is given next.

***Calculation of $\Phi(T)$ and $\Gamma(T)$ (See also Section 3-9.4).*** In our equivalent model Eq. (3-34)

$$\Phi(T) = e^{AT}, \quad \Gamma(T) = \int_0^T e^{AT}B \; dt \qquad (3\text{-}36)$$

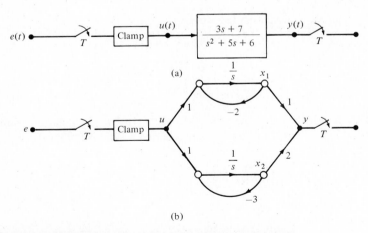

(a)

(b)

**FIGURE 3-4.  Diagrams of sampled-data system example.**

Note that $\Phi(T)$ is the state transition matrix. There are several matrix techniques for calculating $e^{AT}$ from a (constant, square) matrix $A$. For second- and even third- or fourth-order systems a closed form can be obtained as follows:

$$\Phi(t) = \mathcal{L}^{-1}\{[sI - A]^{-1}\} \tag{3-37}$$

**Proof:** Consider $\dot{x}(t) = Ax(t)$, $x(0)$ given and $A$ constant. Thus, from Eq. (3-26)

$$x(t) = e^{At} x(0)$$

However, by Laplace transforms,

$$sX(s) - x(0) = AX(s)$$

$$[sI - A]X(s) = x(0)$$

$$X(s) = [sI - A]^{-1}x(0)$$

Therefore [uniqueness property of Laplace transforms and uniqueness of the solution $x(t)$],

$$\mathcal{L}\{e^{At}\} = [sI - A]^{-1}$$

The $n \times n$ matrix $[sI - A]$ is called a *matricant* or *resolvent* matrix of $A$.

For high-order systems a more convenient approach is to use the basic defining series

$$e^{At} = I + At + \frac{t^2}{2!}A^2 + \cdots + \frac{t^k}{k!}A^k + \cdots \tag{3-38}$$

More will be said later concerning Eq. (3-38) and machine-based calculations.


### EXAMPLE 3-5

Consider the continuous-time system

$$\dot{x} = \begin{bmatrix} 0 & -2 \\ 1 & -3 \end{bmatrix} x + \begin{bmatrix} 2 & -2 \\ 0 & -3 \end{bmatrix} u$$

$$y = \begin{bmatrix} 1 & 0 \\ 1 & -3 \end{bmatrix} x + \begin{bmatrix} 0 & 0 \\ 1 & -3 \end{bmatrix} u \tag{3-39}$$

Find the equivalent discrete-time state model if the input $u(t)$ is sampled at $t = 0, 1, 2, \ldots$ seconds and clamped between sample instants.

*SOLUTION:* Using Eq. (3-37)

$$[sI - A]^{-1} = \begin{bmatrix} s & 2 \\ -1 & s+3 \end{bmatrix}^{-1} = \frac{\begin{bmatrix} s+3 & -2 \\ 1 & s \end{bmatrix}}{s^2 + 3s + 2}$$

Therefore,

$$\Phi(t) = \mathscr{L}^{-1} \begin{bmatrix} \dfrac{2}{s+1} - \dfrac{1}{s+2}, & \dfrac{-2}{s+1} + \dfrac{2}{s+2} \\[3mm] \dfrac{1}{s+1} - \dfrac{1}{s+2}, & \dfrac{-1}{s+1} + \dfrac{2}{s+2} \end{bmatrix}$$

(3-40)

$$\Phi(t) = \begin{bmatrix} (2e^{-t} - e^{-2t}) & (2e^{-2t} - 2e^{-t}) \\ (e^{-t} - e^{-2t}) & (2e^{-2t} - e^{-t}) \end{bmatrix}$$

For $T = 1$ second (sample interval)

$$\Phi(1) = \begin{bmatrix} 0.600 & -0.465 \\ 0.233 & -0.097 \end{bmatrix}$$

(3-41)

By integrating Eq. (3-40) from 0 to $T$ seconds according to Eq. (3-36), and evaluating at $T = 1$,

$$\Gamma(1) = \begin{bmatrix} 1.664 & -0.465 \\ 0.400 & -1.097 \end{bmatrix}$$

(3-42)

Matrices $\Phi(1)$ and $\Gamma(1)$ together with the output matrices in Eq. (3-39) complete our discrete-time model [see Eqs. (3-34) and (3-35)]. ∎

## 3-5

## SYSTEM RESPONSE BY RECURSION

Once a discrete-time state model has been obtained by some means or other, the solution is a simple recursion process, easily implemented on a digital computer. This section presents, first of all, the general solution of a discrete-time state model, and, secondly, an alternate form to the recursive solution that is useful in open-loop control.

Consider the linear, stationary-state model with specified initial state:

$$\mathbf{x}(k + 1) = A\mathbf{x}(k) + B\mathbf{u}(k), \ \mathbf{x}(0)$$
$$\mathbf{y}(k) = C\mathbf{x}(k) + D\mathbf{u}(k)$$

(3-43)

Note that to simplify the notations, matrices $A$ and $B$ are now used in the context of the discrete-time coefficient matrices. Indeed, $A$ and $B$ of Eq. (3-43) are the $\Phi$ and $\Gamma$ of Eq. (3-36).

***Recursive Solution.*** Beginning with the known vectors $\mathbf{x}(0)$; $\mathbf{u}(0)$, $\mathbf{u}(1)$, . . .

$$\mathbf{x}(1) = A\mathbf{x}(0) + B\mathbf{u}(0) \tag{3-44}$$
$$\mathbf{x}(2) = A\mathbf{x}(1) + B\mathbf{u}(1) = A^2\mathbf{x}(0) + AB\mathbf{u}(0) + B\mathbf{u}(1)$$

.
.
.

$$\mathbf{x}(k) = A^k\mathbf{x}(0) + \sum_{n=0}^{k-1} A^{k-n-1}B\mathbf{u}(n) \tag{3-45}$$

Equation (3-45) represents the *general solution* $\mathbf{x}(k)$ for the discrete-time state model. The reader will recognize the second term as a convolutional sum. In practice, the procedure indicated in the first step, Eq. (3-44), is more convenient for calculations, that is, as new values of $\mathbf{x}$ are calculated they are used to update the old values. Program 1 in Appendix D uses this approach.

Similarly, the output vector is

$$\mathbf{y}(k) = CA^k\mathbf{x}(0) + \sum_{n=0}^{k-1} CA^{k-n-1}B\mathbf{u}(n) + D\mathbf{u}(k) \tag{3-46}$$

Since $\mathbf{y}(k)$ can be determined from $\mathbf{x}(k)$ and $\mathbf{u}(k)$, the recursive approach for $\mathbf{x}(k)$ also applies for calculating the output sequence $\mathbf{y}(k)$. As in the continuous-time case, the first term of Eq. (3-45) or Eq. (3-46) is called the *zero-input response* while the remaining terms of either equation form the *zero-state response*.

As a special case, consider formulating the unit-pulse response $h(k)$ for a single-input, single-output system in terms of the state model. From Eq. (3-46) $h(k)$ is the zero-state output sequence in response to an input $u(k) = \delta(k)$, $[\mathbf{x}(0) = \mathbf{0}]$. Thus (see Section 1-5.1),

$$h(k) = \sum_{n=0}^{k-1} CA^{k-n-1} B\delta(n) + D\delta(k)$$

The first few terms of the characteristic sequence are easily calculated to be

$$h(k) = \{D, CB, CAB, CA^2B, \ldots\} \tag{3-47}$$

Note that the input feedthrough term $D$ provides the undelayed sequence value.

### EXAMPLE 3-6
From the previous example we use the model

$$\mathbf{x}(k + 1) = \begin{bmatrix} 0.600 & -0.465 \\ 0.233 & -0.097 \end{bmatrix} \mathbf{x}(k) + \begin{bmatrix} -0.465 \\ -1.097 \end{bmatrix} u(k)$$
$$y(k) = [\ 1 \qquad -3\ ] \mathbf{x}(k) + [-3] u(k) \tag{3-48}$$

This discrete-time model corresponds to the sampled/clamped-input equivalent of the system in Eq. (3-39) using the second input variable and second output variable to form a single-input, single-output plant model. The unit-pulse response can be calculated directly from Eq. (3-48) using Eq. (3-47),

$$h(k) = \{-3, 2.83, 2.36, -0.0222, \ldots\} \qquad \blacksquare$$

A useful alternate form of the recursive solution can be developed from Eq. (3-45) by rearranging terms to obtain

$$S_k \mathbf{U} = \mathbf{x}(k) - A^k \mathbf{x}(0) \qquad (3\text{-}49)$$

where

$$\mathbf{U} = [\mathbf{u}^T(0), \mathbf{u}^T(1), \ldots, \mathbf{u}^T(k-1)]^T$$

and

$$S_k = [A^{k-1}B, A^{k-2}B, \ldots, B]$$

Both Eqs. (3-45) and (3-49) represent the same transition of the state vector at $t = 0$ to the state vector at $t = kT$ under the "control" of the input sequence $\{\mathbf{u}(0), \mathbf{u}(1), \mathbf{u}(2), \ldots, \mathbf{u}(k-1)\}$. The utility of Eq. (3-49) is found in calculating an appropriate open-loop sequence to accomplish a certain state transition. For instance, to calculate the sequence $u(0), u(1)$, that would drive a single-input, second-order plant from an arbitrary initial state $\mathbf{x}(0)$ to the origin $\mathbf{0}$ in two steps, Eq. (3-49) is established for $k = 2$, and $\mathbf{x}(k) = \mathbf{0}$:

$$[AB, A] \begin{bmatrix} u(0) \\ u(1) \end{bmatrix} = -A^2 \begin{bmatrix} x_1(0) \\ x_2(0) \end{bmatrix} \qquad (3\text{-}50)$$

The vector $\mathbf{U} = [u(0), u(1)]^T$ can be determined by solving Eq. (3-50) as a set of simultaneous equations.

From the expression in Eq. (3-49) the notion of state "reachability" can be introduced. For instance, it is possible to determine for a given system that set of states which may be reached from the origin (zero state) in $k$ time-steps. An unexpected and useful result is that for an $n$th-order system: if $S_n$ has rank $n$, then the *entire* state-space is reachable in at most $n$ *steps!* We will prove this statement and provide further discussion on the subject when we develop the important concept of state controllability. For now our main concern is becoming better acquainted with state models.

## 3-6

---

## STATE MODELS FROM DIFFERENCE EQUATIONS

In this section the background previously developed in $z$-domain techniques will be of use in translating difference equations into state-variable form. Three principal methods will be presented. The developments will be based on the following third-order scalar difference equation,

$$y(k + 3) + a_2 y(k + 2) + a_1 y(k + 1) + a_0 y(k)$$
$$= b_3 u(k + 3) + b_2 u(k + 2) + b_1 u(k + 1) + b_0 u(k) \qquad (3\text{-}51)$$

Although Eq. (3-51) is not completely general, the extension to higher-order equations will be clear from our developments on this third-order system. Another form of Eq. (3-51) is

$$y(k) = \sum_{m=0}^{3} b_{3-m}u(k-m) - \sum_{m=1}^{3} a_{3-m}y(k-m) \qquad (3\text{-}52)$$

This latter form illustrates more directly that the present value of output $y(k)$ may depend on present input $u(k)$ and past values of both input and output.

Recall that in the context of transfer functions all initial energy in the system is zero. Thus, when the $z$-transform of Eq. (3-51) is taken (with zero initial conditions) each time-advanced signal results in a multiplication by $z$ as follows [see Eq. (2-12)]:

$$(z^3 + a_2z^2 + a_1z + a_0)Y(z) = (b_3z^3 + b_2z^2 + b_1z + b_0)U(z) \qquad (3\text{-}53)$$

Hence the transfer function (always the output-to-input transform ratio) becomes

$$\frac{Y(z)}{U(z)} = \frac{b_3z^3 + b_2z^2 + b_1z + b_0}{z^3 + a_2z^2 + a_1z + a_0} \qquad (3\text{-}54)$$

Also,

$$\frac{Y(z)}{U(z)} = \frac{b_3 + b_2z^{-1} + b_1z^{-2} + b_0z^{-3}}{1 + a_2z^{-1} + a_1z^{-2} + a_0z^{-3}} \qquad (3\text{-}55)$$

since algebraic manipulations are allowed in the transform domain.

### 3-6.1   The Controllable Canonical Form

The first method to be presented is a basic state model based on a natural extension of the phase variables to include systems with numerator dynamics.

From Eq. (3-55) we solve for $Y(z)$ in the following way:

$$Y = (b_3 + b_2z^{-1} + b_1z^{-2} + b_0z^{-3})E \qquad (3\text{-}56)$$

where

$$E = \frac{U}{1 + a_2z^{-1} + a_1z^{-2} + a_0z^{-3}}$$

An equivalent expression for $E$ is obtained by cross-multiplying and solving for $E$ in terms of itself and $U$:

$$E = U - (a_2z^{-1} + a_1z^{-2} + a_0z^{-3})E \qquad (3\text{-}57)$$

The diagram for Eq. (3-57) is shown in Fig. 3-5 using solid lines. From Eq. (3-57) the sequence $e(k)$ is the sum

$$e(k) = u(k) - a_2e(k-1) - a_1e(k-2) - a_0e(k-3)$$

The feedback configuration of Fig. 3-5 accomplishes this with a cascade connection of unit delay elements. From $e(k)$ and its delayed versions indicated in Eq. (3-56) the output is developed, and that portion of Fig. 3-5 is shown as dashed lines. Extension of the above development is facilitated by the symmetry seen in Fig. 3-5.

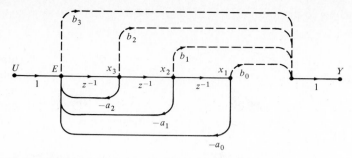

**FIGURE 3-5.  Signal flow diagram for equation 3-56.**

By labeling the outputs of the unit-time delay elements as state variables as shown in Fig. 3-5, the following equations are derived from the diagram:

$$x_1(k + 1) = x_2(k)$$

$$x_2(k + 1) = x_3(k)$$

$$x_3(k + 1) = -a_0 x_1(k) - a_1 x_2(k) - a_2 x_3(k) + u(k)$$

$$y(k) = (b_0 - a_0 b_3) x_1(k) + (b_1 - a_1 b_3) x_2(k)$$

$$+ (b_2 - a_2 b_3) x_3(k) + b_3 u(k)$$

When these equations are put into vector-matrix form, the following structure of the state model, Eqs. (3-3) and (3-4), is obtained.

$$\begin{bmatrix} x_1(k + 1) \\ x_2(k + 1) \\ x_3(k + 1) \end{bmatrix} = \begin{bmatrix} 0 & 1 & 0 \\ 0 & 0 & 1 \\ -a_0 & -a_1 & -a_2 \end{bmatrix} \begin{bmatrix} x_1(k) \\ x_2(k) \\ x_3(k) \end{bmatrix} + \begin{bmatrix} 0 \\ 0 \\ 1 \end{bmatrix} u(k) \qquad (3\text{-}58)$$

$$y(k) = [b_0 - a_0 b_3,\ b_1 - a_1 b_3,\ b_2 - a_2 b_3] \begin{bmatrix} x_1(k) \\ x_2(k) \\ x_3(k) \end{bmatrix} + b_3 u(k) \qquad (3\text{-}59)$$

Equations (3-58) and (3-59) together represent the *controllable form* of the state model.

### EXAMPLE 3-7

We wish to find the controllable form state model for the difference equation

$$y(k) = u(k) + 2u(k - 1) + u(k - 2) - 5y(k - 1) - 6y(k - 2)$$

**SOLUTION:** Taking the $z$-transform as a preliminary step, the transfer function expression is

$$\frac{Y(z)}{U(z)} = \frac{1 + 2z^{-1} + z^{-2}}{1 + 5z^{-1} + 6z^{-2}}$$

corresponding to the form of Eq. (3-55); the diagram for the system is given as follows:

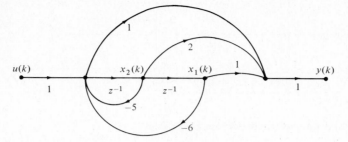

From the diagram the state model

$$\begin{bmatrix} x_1(k + 1) \\ x_2(k + 1) \end{bmatrix} = \begin{bmatrix} 0 & 1 \\ -6 & -5 \end{bmatrix} \begin{bmatrix} x_1(k) \\ x_2(k) \end{bmatrix} + \begin{bmatrix} 0 \\ 1 \end{bmatrix} u(k)$$

$$y(k) = [-5 \quad -3] \begin{bmatrix} x_1(k) \\ x_2(k) \end{bmatrix} + u(k)$$

is obtained. ∎

The controllable canonical form just presented provides an extremely useful method of obtaining a set of state equations from a given transfer function. With sufficient practice the reader will be able to skip the intermediary diagram and fill in the state model directly from the transfer function. For instance, it will be noted that the system coefficient matrix consists of a shifted identity matrix above the last row, which has an orderly correspondence with the denominator coefficients of the transfer function. The input distribution matrix is all zero except for the last entry, which is unity. The output matrix and feedthrough element incorporate the numerator coefficients in a specific manner. Note that the absence of the $b_3$ (feedthrough) element greatly simplifies the output matrix.

A second canonical form that will be useful to us later is the observable form. We present this next as an alternate state model (different state variables) for the same third-order system used here. The development is slightly different, but again the proof is presented via a signal-flow diagram.

## 3-6.2   The Observable Canonical Form

Our second method of representing a system in state-variable form is developed in this section. Both this and the previous controllable form will play an important role in the design of feedback controllers.

From Eq. (3-55) let us solve for $Y$ and group terms to obtain

$$Y = b_3U + z^{-1}(b_2U - a_2Y) + z^{-2}(b_1U - a_1Y) + z^{-3}(b_0U - a_0Y)$$

$$(3\text{-}60)$$

The diagram for Eq. (3-60) is given in Fig. 3-6. Equation (3-60) has terms

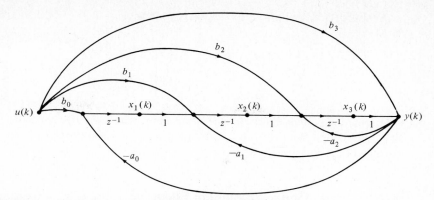

**FIGURE 3-6.  Signal-flow diagram for equation 3-60.**

which are associated with no delay, one unit-time delay, and so on. The reader should be able to follow the contribution of each term to the output sequence. For instance, the one-step-delay term $z^{-1}(b_2 U - a_2 Y)$ is incorporated into the diagram of Fig. 3-6 by feeding the signals $b_2 u(k)$ and $-a_2 y(k)$ into the final delay element.

As in the previous case, the state variables are assigned to the outputs of the delay elements (a standard policy) as shown in Fig. 3-6. The resulting state model, called the *observable form* state model, is given by the following structured equations:

$$\begin{bmatrix} x_1(k+1) \\ x_2(k+1) \\ x_3(k+1) \end{bmatrix} = \begin{bmatrix} 0 & 0 & -a_0 \\ 1 & 0 & -a_1 \\ 0 & 1 & -a_2 \end{bmatrix} \begin{bmatrix} x_1(k) \\ x_2(k) \\ x_3(k) \end{bmatrix} + \begin{bmatrix} b_0 - a_0 b_3 \\ b_1 - a_1 b_3 \\ b_2 - a_2 b_2 \end{bmatrix} u(k) \quad (3\text{-}61)$$

$$y(k) = [0 \quad 0 \quad 1] \begin{bmatrix} x_1(k) \\ x_2(k) \\ x_3(k) \end{bmatrix} + b_3 u(k) \quad (3\text{-}62)$$

**EXAMPLE 3-8**

To construct the observable form state model for the system of Eq. (3-59) the transfer function is repeated here for convenience:

$$T(z) = \frac{z^2 + 2z + 1}{z^2 + 5z + 6}$$

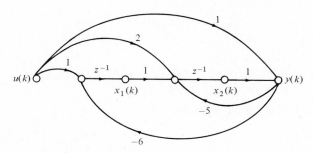

**SOLUTION:** Following the above procedure

$$\begin{bmatrix} x_1(k+1) \\ x_2(k+1) \end{bmatrix} = \begin{bmatrix} 0 & -6 \\ 1 & -5 \end{bmatrix} \begin{bmatrix} x_1(k) \\ x_2(k) \end{bmatrix} + \begin{bmatrix} -5 \\ -3 \end{bmatrix} u(k)$$

$$y(k) = \begin{bmatrix} 0 & 1 \end{bmatrix} \begin{bmatrix} x_1(k) \\ x_2(k) \end{bmatrix} + u(k)$$

Note that the system matrix for the observable form is the transpose of that for the controllable form and, in addition, the input and output matrices are interchanged (and transposed). ■

### 3-6.3 The Jordan Canonical Form

The final specific form of state model to be discussed corresponds to a diagonal or block-diagonal coefficient matrix, which greatly facilitates solving the equation. This method is referred to as the Jordan canonical form since the final structure of the coefficient matrix is that of a Jordan canonical matrix. To begin with, we assume a factored form for the transfer function denominator. Assuming distinct roots, we first expand into partial fractions:

$$\frac{Y}{U} = \frac{b_3 z^3 + b_2 z^2 + b_1 z + b_0}{(z - \lambda_1)(z - \lambda_2)(z - \lambda_3)} = b_3 + \frac{R_1}{z - \lambda_1} + \frac{R_2}{z - \lambda_2} + \frac{R_3}{z - \lambda_3} \tag{3-63}$$

If the roots are not distinct, for instance, if $\lambda_1 = \lambda_2$, then the partial fraction expansion becomes

$$\frac{Y}{U} = b_3 + \frac{Q_1}{(z - \lambda_1)^2} + \frac{R_1}{z - \lambda_1} + \frac{R_3}{z - \lambda_3} \tag{3-64}$$

The diagrams for Eqs. (3-63) and (3-64) are given in Figs. 3-7 and 3-8, respectively.

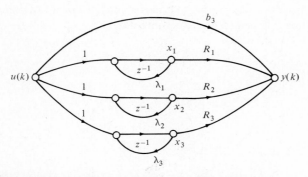

**FIGURE 3-7.** Signal-flow diagram for equation 3-63.

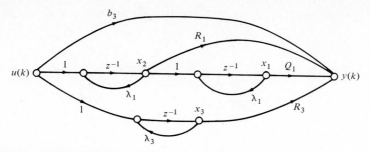

**FIGURE 3-8.** Signal-flow diagram for equation 3-64.

The state models from Figs. 3-7 and 3-8 are given in Eqs. (3-65) and (3-66) below, respectively:

$$\begin{bmatrix} x_1(k+1) \\ x_2(k+1) \\ x_3(k+1) \end{bmatrix} = \begin{bmatrix} \lambda_1 & 0 & 0 \\ 0 & \lambda_2 & 0 \\ 0 & 0 & \lambda_3 \end{bmatrix} \begin{bmatrix} x_1(k) \\ x_2(k) \\ x_3(k) \end{bmatrix} + \begin{bmatrix} 1 \\ 1 \\ 1 \end{bmatrix} u(k)$$

$$y(k) = [R_1 \quad R_2 \quad R_3] \begin{bmatrix} x_1(k) \\ x_2(k) \\ x_3(k) \end{bmatrix} + b_3\, u(k)$$

(3-65)

$$\begin{bmatrix} x_1(k+1) \\ x_2(k+1) \\ x_3(k+1) \end{bmatrix} = \begin{bmatrix} \lambda_1 & 1 & 0 \\ 0 & \lambda_1 & 0 \\ 0 & 0 & \lambda_3 \end{bmatrix} \begin{bmatrix} x_1(k) \\ x_2(k) \\ x_3(k) \end{bmatrix} + \begin{bmatrix} 0 \\ 1 \\ 1 \end{bmatrix} u(k)$$

$$y(k) = [Q_1 \quad R_1 \quad R_3] \begin{bmatrix} x_1(k) \\ x_2(k) \\ x_3(k) \end{bmatrix} + b_3\, u(k)$$

(3-66)

Note that this "parallel" type structure results in a state equation that is either fully decoupled, as in Eq. (3-65), or partially decoupled, as in Eq. (3-66); that is, Eq. (3-65), in particular, is simply three scalar difference equations which can be solved independently.

### EXAMPLE 3-9

We want to construct the Jordan form state model for the system of Example 3-6. Expanding into partial fractions, first divide numerator by denominator (since they are of the same order) to obtain

$$T(z) = 1 + \frac{-3z - 5}{(z+2)(z+3)}$$

Therefore, the completed partial fraction expansion is

$$T(z) = 1 + \frac{1}{z+2} + \frac{-4}{z+3}$$

Similar to the structure of Fig. 3-7, the diagram follows:

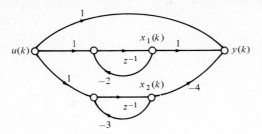

From the diagram the state model is derived

$$\begin{bmatrix} x_1(k+1) \\ x_2(k+1) \end{bmatrix} = \begin{bmatrix} -2 & 0 \\ 0 & -3 \end{bmatrix} \begin{bmatrix} x_1(k) \\ x_2(k) \end{bmatrix} + \begin{bmatrix} 1 \\ 1 \end{bmatrix} u(k)$$

$$y(k) = \begin{bmatrix} 1 & -4 \end{bmatrix} \begin{bmatrix} x_1(k) \\ x_2(k) \end{bmatrix} + u(k)$$

∎

In this section we have developed three basic canonical state models. We shall see in the next section that for each state model representing a particular system there is a unique transformation on the state vector, which changes the description from one state model to another. The reader should note that although the same x-vector notation was used for each of the three derivations, each description corresponds to a *different* set of internal state variables. However, the input and output signals remain the same for each realization.

**3-7**

## EQUIVALENT STATE MODELS
## AND MULTIVARIABLE SYSTEMS

We are already familiar with the fact that the choice of state variables for a system is not unique from our different methods of simulation. For instance, a system may usually be described by any one of its canonical forms.

### 3-7.1 Transformation of State Vector

Consider now a typical linear time-invariant system model [repeated here from Eq. (3-3) and Eq. (3-4)]:

$$\begin{aligned} \mathbf{x}(k+1) &= A\mathbf{x}(k) + B\mathbf{u}(k) \\ \mathbf{y}(k) &= C\mathbf{x}(k) + D\mathbf{u}(k) \end{aligned}$$
$$\text{S1} \qquad\qquad\qquad\qquad\qquad (3\text{-}67)$$

Let us refer to this set of equations as system description S1, as labeled above. Any equivalent system description is derivable from S1 by a change of state variables, say,

$$\mathbf{x} = P\boldsymbol{\xi} \tag{3-68}$$

where $P$ is an invertible (constant) *transformation* matrix. The system description in terms of the new state vector $\boldsymbol{\xi}$ is

$$S2 \qquad \begin{aligned} \boldsymbol{\xi}(k + 1) &= (P^{-1}AP)\boldsymbol{\xi}(k) + (P^{-1}B)\mathbf{u}(k) \\ \mathbf{y}(k) &= (CP)\,\boldsymbol{\xi}(k) + D\mathbf{u}(k) \end{aligned} \tag{3-69}$$

The important thing to note is that descriptions S1 and S2 describe the *same* system having the same inputs and outputs, therefore the same transfer function, which means, in particular, that the characteristic polynomial is invariant under such a change of variables.

To demonstrate the relation between the Jordan form state model of the previous section and this transformation of state vectors, we will assume that the eigenvalues of $A$ are distinct. The reader will recall the results from matrix theory that under the assumption of distinct eigenvalues, the modal matrix $P$ whose columns are the eigenvalues of $A$ diagonalizes $A$, that is,

$$P^{-1}AP = \text{diag } \{\lambda_1, \lambda_2, \ldots, \lambda_n\}$$

where $\lambda_i$, $i = 1, 2, \ldots, n$ are the distinct eigenvalues of $A$. The assumption that the eigenvalues are distinct simplifies the forthcoming results, but does not restrict the generality of the remarks. More generally, $P^{-1}AP$ is the Jordan form matrix of $A$.

If we rewrite Eq. (3-69) as if $P^{-1}AP = \Lambda$, a diagonal matrix, then

$$\begin{aligned} \boldsymbol{\xi}(k + 1) &= \Lambda\boldsymbol{\xi}(k) + B'\mathbf{u}(k) \\ \mathbf{y}(k) &= C'\boldsymbol{\xi}(k) + D\mathbf{u}(k) \end{aligned} \tag{3-70}$$

Equation (3-70) will be similar to the form shown in Eq. (3-65). Since $\Lambda$ is diagonal, the dynamic equations are decoupled, thereby providing advantages in obtaining solutions as well as for implementation of the system.

## 3-7.2 State Models of Matrix Transfer Functions

When the system of interest has more than one input or output variable, the transfer function characterization becomes a matrix of scalar transfer functions. Let us extend our modeling techniques to this case. A particular problem with two inputs and two outputs will be considered as a background for our general remarks.

Our first development describes a method of constructing a state model from a transfer matrix. The development is brief and intended only to introduce some of the ideas of multivariable systems that do not occur with purely scalar input/output systems. In this section a simple 2-input/2-output system is used as an example of the conversion method. The reader should be able to use the procedure on more complicated systems after studying the following step-by-step development.

**Step 1.** Given a transfer matrix, expand each element into its partial fractions and combine the array of partial fractions into numerical matrices associated with the different system poles. For our example,

$$H(z) = \begin{bmatrix} \dfrac{3z+1}{z(z+1)} & \dfrac{z}{z+1} \\[3mm] \dfrac{5z+1}{z(z+1)} & \dfrac{3z}{z+1} \end{bmatrix} = \underbrace{\begin{bmatrix} 0 & 1 \\ 0 & 3 \end{bmatrix}}_{\text{T1}} + \underbrace{\begin{bmatrix} 1 & 0 \\ 1 & 0 \end{bmatrix}\dfrac{1}{z}}_{\text{T2}} + \underbrace{\begin{bmatrix} 2 & -1 \\ 4 & -3 \end{bmatrix}\dfrac{1}{z+1}}_{\text{T3}}$$

(3-71)

Note that this appears as an ordinary partial-fraction expansion except that the residues are now matrices multiplying their associated transfer fractions.

**Step 2.** Observe the rank of the residue matrices. The rank of a residue matrix tells us the number of separate realizations of the associated transfer fraction necessary to implement that term.

Term T1 is a direct connection from input to output with no dynamics. Remember that each term of $H(z)$ behaves as a separate transfer matrix in the form $\mathbf{Y} = H\mathbf{U}$, each contribution to be summed at the output.

Term T2 is associated with a pure delay $z^{-1}$. The rank of the residue matrix is *one*. This tells us that the entire term can be realized (diagrammed) by *one* unit delay.

Term T3 is associated with the transfer block $(z+1)^{-1}$. The rank of the residue matrix is *two*, indicating a need for *two* such blocks in our diagram. As an aid we decompose the residue matrices of Eq. (3-71) into outer products as follows:

$$H(z) = \begin{bmatrix} 0 & 1 \\ 0 & 3 \end{bmatrix} + \begin{bmatrix} 1 \\ 1 \end{bmatrix}[1 \quad 0]\dfrac{1}{z} + \begin{bmatrix} 2 \\ 4 \end{bmatrix}[1 \quad 0]\dfrac{1}{z+1}$$
$$+ \begin{bmatrix} -1 \\ -3 \end{bmatrix}[0 \quad 1]\dfrac{1}{z+1}$$

(3-72)

**Step 3.** Construct the signal-flow diagram. From Eq. (3-72) and step 2 we have determined the need for a simple delay and two $(z+1)^{-1}$ blocks. This is the beginning of the diagram shown in Fig. 3-9. The dimensions of $H$, in this case, require two inputs and two outputs. The term T1 is easily incorporated as a contribution of $y_1 = u_2$ and of $y_2 = 3u_2$ directly. Term T2 requires the contributions $y_1 = x_1$ and $y_2 = x_1$, and term T3 requires the contributions $y_1 = 2x_2 - x_3$ and $y_2 = 4x_2 - 3x_3$.

For simplicity some of the connections are only indicated in Fig. 3-9.

**Step 4.** Using the delay outputs as state variables, construct the state model. Note that this procedure yields a minimal-order state model, that is, order three for the present example instead of the sixth-order system which results by realizing each term of $H(z)$ separately.

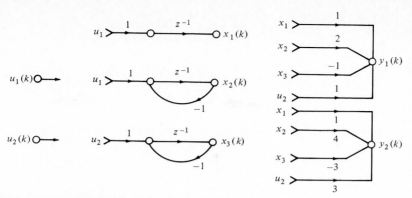

**FIGURE 3-9.** Diagram for a multivariate system.

$$
\begin{bmatrix} x_1(k+1) \\ x_2(k+1) \\ x_3(k+1) \end{bmatrix} = \begin{bmatrix} 0 & 0 & 0 \\ 0 & -1 & 0 \\ 0 & 0 & -1 \end{bmatrix} \begin{bmatrix} x_1(k) \\ x_2(k) \\ x_3(k) \end{bmatrix} + \begin{bmatrix} 1 & 0 \\ 1 & 0 \\ 0 & 1 \end{bmatrix} \begin{bmatrix} u_1(k) \\ u_2(k) \end{bmatrix}
$$

$$
\begin{bmatrix} y_1(k) \\ y_2(k) \end{bmatrix} = \begin{bmatrix} 1 & 2 & -1 \\ 1 & 4 & -3 \end{bmatrix} \begin{bmatrix} x_1(k) \\ x_2(k) \\ x_3(k) \end{bmatrix} + \begin{bmatrix} 0 & 1 \\ 0 & 3 \end{bmatrix} \begin{bmatrix} u_1(k) \\ u_2(k) \end{bmatrix}
$$

(3-73)

This development has been a recipe for converting a matrix transfer function into a (minimal) state model. The system is characterized in the Jordan canonical form. Although we can work with multivariable systems, our primary focus will still be on single-input/output systems.

As part of our repertoire, we now have three separate structures of state models available to us from (scalar) transfer functions. Suppose, now, that the reverse process is desired, that of translating a state model into a transfer function characterization.

### 3-7.3 Transfer Matrices from State Models

In this section the conversion is in the reverse direction of obtaining a transfer function from a state model. Note that the development is applicable both to single input/output systems and multi-input/output systems.

We begin with the basic state model structure:

$$\mathbf{x}(k+1) = A\mathbf{x}(k) + B\mathbf{u}(k)$$

$$\mathbf{y}(k) = C\mathbf{x}(k) + D\mathbf{u}(k)$$

where $A$, $B$, $C$, and $D$ are taken as constant matrices, and seek $H(z)$, where

$$\mathbf{Y}(z) = H(z)\mathbf{U}(z)$$

Taking $z$-transforms [with $\mathbf{x}(0) = \mathbf{0}$], we have

$$z\mathbf{X}(z) = A\mathbf{X}(z) + B\mathbf{U}(z) \tag{3-74}$$
$$\mathbf{Y}(z) = C\mathbf{X}(z) + D\mathbf{U}(z)$$

Solving for $\mathbf{Y}$ in terms of $\mathbf{U}$,

$$\mathbf{Y}(z) = [C(zI - A)^{-1}B + D]\mathbf{U}(z) \tag{3-75}$$

where $\mathbf{X}(z) = (zI - A)^{-1}B\mathbf{U}(z)$ was obtained from the first equation. Hence, the term in brackets in Eq. (3-75) is the *transfer matrix* $H(z)$. Note that it is improper to write $\mathbf{Y}(z)/\mathbf{U}(z)$ in the vector case. We conclude this section with two examples.

## EXAMPLE 3-10

As a check on our previous development for multivariable systems, consider applying Eq. (3-75) to Eq. (3-73):

$$(zI - A)^{-1} = \begin{bmatrix} z & 0 & 0 \\ 0 & z+1 & 0 \\ 0 & 0 & z+1 \end{bmatrix}^{-1} = \begin{bmatrix} z^{-1} & 0 & 0 \\ 0 & (z+1)^{-1} & 0 \\ 0 & 0 & (z+1)^{-1} \end{bmatrix}$$

$$C(zI - A)^{-1} = \begin{bmatrix} 1 & 2 & -1 \\ 1 & 4 & -3 \end{bmatrix} \begin{bmatrix} \dfrac{1}{z} & 0 & 0 \\ 0 & \dfrac{1}{z+1} & 0 \\ 0 & 0 & \dfrac{1}{z+1} \end{bmatrix}$$

$$= \begin{bmatrix} \dfrac{1}{z} & \dfrac{2}{z+1} & \dfrac{-1}{z+1} \\ \dfrac{1}{z} & \dfrac{4}{z+1} & \dfrac{-3}{z+1} \end{bmatrix}$$

$$H(z) = C(zI - A)^{-1}B + D = \begin{bmatrix} \dfrac{1}{z} & \dfrac{2}{z+1} & \dfrac{-1}{z+1} \\ \dfrac{1}{z} & \dfrac{4}{z+1} & \dfrac{-3}{z+1} \end{bmatrix} \begin{bmatrix} 1 & 0 \\ 1 & 0 \\ 0 & 1 \end{bmatrix} + \begin{bmatrix} 0 & 1 \\ 0 & 3 \end{bmatrix}$$

Therefore,

$$H(z) = \begin{bmatrix} \left( \dfrac{1}{z} + \dfrac{2}{z+1} \right) & \left( 1 - \dfrac{1}{z+1} \right) \\ \left( \dfrac{1}{z} + \dfrac{4}{z+1} \right) & \left( 3 - \dfrac{3}{z+1} \right) \end{bmatrix}$$

which is the original partial-fraction form of $H(z)$ from Eq. (3-71), thereby checking our development. ∎

## EXAMPLE 3-11

Given the discrete system determined by the state matrices

$$A = \begin{bmatrix} 0.601 & -0.466 \\ 0.233 & -0.098 \end{bmatrix}, \; B = \begin{bmatrix} 1.664 & -0.466 \\ 0.400 & -1.099 \end{bmatrix}$$

$$C = \begin{bmatrix} 1 & 0 \\ 1 & -3 \end{bmatrix}, \qquad D = \begin{bmatrix} 0 & 0 \\ 0 & -3 \end{bmatrix}$$

to find $y_1(k)$ if $u_2 = 0$, $\mathbf{x}(0) = \mathbf{0}$ and

$$u_1(k) = 1, \; k \text{ even}$$
$$0, \; k \text{ odd}$$

***SOLUTION:*** Using Eq. (3-74),

$$H(z) = \frac{\begin{bmatrix} 1 & 0 \\ 1 & -3 \end{bmatrix} \begin{bmatrix} z + 0.098 & -0.466 \\ 0.233 & z - 0.601 \end{bmatrix} \begin{bmatrix} 1.664 & -0.466 \\ 0.400 & -1.099 \end{bmatrix}}{z^2 - 0.503z + 0.0497} + \begin{bmatrix} 0 & 0 \\ 0 & -3 \end{bmatrix}$$

$$H(z) = \frac{\begin{bmatrix} 1.664\,z - 0.023 & -0.466\,z + 0.466 \\ 0.464\,z - 0.465 & -3z^2 + 4.34z - 1.338 \end{bmatrix}}{z^2 - 0.503\,z + 0.0497}$$

Thus,

$$Y_1(z) = H_{11}(z)\,U_1(z) = \frac{1.664z^3 - 0.0233z^2}{z^4 - 0.503z^3 - 0.950z^2 + 0.503z - 0.0497}$$

since

$$U_1(z) = 1 + 0\,z^{-1} + 1\,z^{-2} + 0\,z^{-3} + \cdots = \frac{1}{1 - z^{-2}}$$

Expanding into partial-fraction form,

$$Y_1(z) = \frac{-0.396}{z - 0.368} + \frac{0.016}{z - 0.135} + \frac{1.500}{z - 1} + \frac{0.543}{z + 1}$$

Inverting the partial fractions,

$$y_1(k) = -1.076(0.368)^k + 0.119(0.135)^k + 1.500 - 0.543(-1)^k$$

The first few terms of the sequence are

$$y_1(k) = \{0, 1.664, 0.813, 1.989, 0.936, 2.034, 0.953, \ldots\}$$

This example illustrates the use of the transform method to solve a problem specified in state-variable form. The main advantage is ending up with a closed-form sequence for $y_1(k)$; otherwise the recursion method of Section 3-5 is more convenient for the given problem. ∎

## DISCRETE-TIME SYSTEM STABILITY

In Section 2-7 a stability test was presented to be used to determine if the characteristic polynomial of a discrete-time system has all its roots inside the unit circle of the complex plane. In this section we present, more formally, the requirements for a linear, discrete-time system to be BIBO stable and some concepts of stability in the sense of Liapunov. Liapunov stability pertains to the equilibrium points of a dynamic system. The problem of determining the stability of an equilibrium point of a nonlinear system can be a difficult problem; however, we will limit our discussion in this section to the corresponding problem for linear systems only.

For the case of a linear system described by the state model

$$\mathbf{x}(k + 1) = A\mathbf{x}(k) + B\mathbf{u}(k) \qquad (3\text{-}76)$$
$$\mathbf{y}(k) = C\mathbf{x}(k) + D\mathbf{u}(k)$$

the fundamental stability question discussed earlier in Section 2-7, namely, that of bounded-input/bounded-output (BIBO) stability, is: Does the state (or output) vector remain bounded whenever the inputs are all bounded? Let us consider this question in some detail.

### 3-8.1 Implications of the BIBO Criterion

The general solution for the state of a discrete-time state model was given by Eq. (3-45). This general expression is repeated here for convenience:

$$\mathbf{x}(k) = A^k\mathbf{x}(0) + \sum_{n=0}^{k-1} A^{k-n-1}B\mathbf{u}(n) \qquad (3\text{-}77)$$

From Eq. (3-77) the state vector will remain bounded when the input is bounded if and only if $A^k$ is bounded for any positive integer $k$.

Since $A^k$ is an analytic function of the matrix $A$, some results of matrix theory may be applied. The *Jordan Canonical Form* of $A$ can be obtained from a similarity transformation $P$, that is, $A = PJP^{-1}$, where $J$ is the Jordan form for $A$. Thus,

$$A^k = PJ^kP^{-1} \qquad (3\text{-}78)$$

the matrix $J^k = \text{diag }\{J_i^k\}$, where $J_i$ are the diagonal blocks of $J$ having the form (where $\lambda$ may be complex)

$$
J_i = \begin{bmatrix}
\lambda & 1 & 0 & \cdots & 0 & 0 \\
0 & \lambda & 1 & \cdots & 0 & 0 \\
& & \cdots & & & \\
0 & 0 & 0 & & \lambda & 1 \\
0 & 0 & 0 & \cdots & 0 & \lambda
\end{bmatrix}
$$

Therefore, for each diagonal block of $J^k$, (associated with a particular $\lambda$),

$$J_i^k = \begin{bmatrix} \lambda^k, & k\lambda^{k-1}, & \frac{1}{2}k(k-1)\lambda^{k-2}, & \cdots \\ 0, & \lambda^k, & k\,\lambda^{k-1}, & \cdots \\ & \cdots & & \\ 0, & 0, & \cdots & , \lambda^k \end{bmatrix} \qquad (3\text{-}79)$$

From Eq. (3-79) it is observed that each entry of $J_i^k$ (and so of $J^k$) remains bounded if for each eigenvalue of $A(\lambda_j, j = 1, 2, \ldots, r)$, $\lambda_j^k$ remains bounded in magnitude for arbitrarily large integers $k$.

In summary the basic criterion for the *stability* of a *linear discrete-time system* is that the eigenvalues of the system satisfy

$$|\lambda_j| < 1 \qquad \text{for } j = 1, 2, \ldots, r \qquad (3\text{-}80)$$

the integer $r$ being the number of distinct eigenvalues.

**Remark:** The region of stability for a linear discrete-time system is the interior of the unit circle (of the complex plane). This corresponds to the left-half plane for the region of stability of continuous-time systems.

### EXAMPLE 3-12
We wish to test the stability of the system given below:

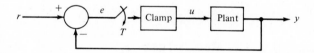

Plant Model:

$$\dot{\mathbf{x}}(t) = \begin{bmatrix} -1 & 0 \\ 1 & 0 \end{bmatrix} \mathbf{x}(t) + \begin{bmatrix} 1 \\ 0 \end{bmatrix} u(t)$$

$$y(t) = \begin{bmatrix} 0 & 1 \end{bmatrix} \mathbf{x}(t)$$

To illustrate the effect of sampling rate, we will carry out the test for $T = 1$ and $T = 5$ (seconds).

**SOLUTION:** The transition matrix for the equivalent closed-loop discrete-time system is obtained from the open-loop system using the relation that $e = r - x_2$ and collecting terms. The final result is given by

$$A(T) = \begin{bmatrix} e^{-T} & (e^{-T} - 1) \\ (1 - e^{-T}) & (2 - T - e^{-T}) \end{bmatrix} \quad \text{for } A_{\text{open}}(T) = \begin{bmatrix} e^{-T} & 0 \\ 1 - e^{-T} & 1 \end{bmatrix}$$

For $T = 1$ sec:

$$A(1) = \begin{bmatrix} 0.368 & -0.632 \\ 0.632 & 0.632 \end{bmatrix}$$

$$\det(A - \lambda I) = \lambda^2 - \lambda + 0.632 = 0$$

$$\lambda_{1,2} = 0.5 \pm j0.625$$

$$|\lambda_1| = |\lambda_2| = 0.796 < 1, \textit{ stable}$$

For $T = 5$ sec:

$$A(5) = \begin{bmatrix} 0.0067 & -0.9933 \\ 0.9933 & -3.0067 \end{bmatrix}$$

$$\det (A - \lambda I) = \lambda^2 - 3\lambda + 0.9665 = 0$$

Since $-3 = -(\lambda_1 + \lambda_2)$, at least one eigenvalue has a magnitude $> 1$, and the *system* is *unstable*. As a check we can apply the Jury test of Section 2-7 to the general characteristic polynomial:

$$\det [A(T) - \lambda I] = \lambda^2 + (T - 2)\lambda + (1 - Te^{-T}) = 0$$

$$\text{Jury Test: (1) } F(1) = T(1 - e^{-T}) > 0 \qquad \checkmark$$

$$\text{(2) } F(-1) = 4 - T - Te^{-T} > 0$$

$$\text{(3) } |(1 - Te^{-T})| < 1 \qquad \checkmark$$

Condition (1) holds for $T > 0$. Condition (2) is true only for $T < 3.922$. And condition (3) is valid for all $T > 0$. Therefore, from condition (2), the system is stable only for $T < 3.922$, and $T = 5$ sec clearly corresponds to an unstable system, which checks our earlier result. ■

## 3-8.2 Extension of the Routh Test

The Routh criterion is used to determine if a polynomial has any right-half complex plane roots. By using a suitable mapping, the unit circle of the $z$-plane may be transformed into the left-half $s$-plane. One mapping that does this is given by

$$z = \frac{s + 1}{s - 1} \tag{3-81}$$

Thus, a discrete-time system characteristic polynomial in $z$ can be changed to a corresponding polynomial in $s$ with the substitution of Eq. (3-81). Since the interior of the unit circle in the $z$-plane is now represented by the left-half $s$-plane, the Routh test can be used on a new polynomial to determine system stability. The obvious drawback of this method is the algebra involved in simplifying the polynomial expression after substitution, particularly for polynomials higher than third or fourth order.

### EXAMPLE 3-13

Using the polynomial of Example 2-26,

$$F_1(z) = z^2 + z + 0.2$$

substituting

$$z = \frac{s + 1}{s - 1}$$

we obtain (after simplification)

$$F_2(s) = 2.2s^2 + 1.6s + 0.2$$

The Routh test on a second-order polynomial reduces to the requirement that each coefficient have the same sign. Thus, the roots of $F_2(s)$ are in the LHP, and it follows that the roots of $F_1(z)$ are inside the unit circle. ∎

In general, the original polynomial in $z$ is a stable system polynomial if and only if the derived polynomial in $s$ is a stable system polynomial in the context of a continuous-time system.

### 3-8.3 Stability in the Sense of Liapunov

We have found that a necessary and sufficient condition for the BIBO stability of the zero-input ($\mathbf{u} = \mathbf{0}$) solution $\mathbf{x}(kT)$ of the system in Eq. (3-76) can be stated that all eigenvalues of $A$ have magnitudes less than unity. Since finding the eigenvalues of $A$ can be difficult for a high-order system, we consider the Liapunov approach to determine system stability which is algebraic and does not require a factoring of the characteristic polynomial. In addition, this approach will be useful in introducing optimal design of controllers in a later chapter.

When $\mathbf{u} = \mathbf{0}$ in the state equation of Eq. (3-76), the origin $\mathbf{x} \equiv \mathbf{0}$ is a system solution (trajectory), also called an *equilibrium state*. Liapunov stability generalizes the basic notion that a dynamic system is stable if its total energy decreases with time until an equilibrium state is reached. Thus, for a given mathematical model, if a *Liapunov function*, a fictitious energy function, can be found and shown to decrease with time, then the system is stable.

Consider the homogeneous system

$$\mathbf{x}(k + 1) = A\mathbf{x}(k) \tag{3-82}$$

We now investigate the stability of $\mathbf{x} = \mathbf{0}$ in the sense of Liapunov that if the system is perturbed away from its equilibrium point at the origin, does the trajectory return to equilibrium (stable) or diverge (unstable)?

As a possible Liapunov function we choose

$$V[\mathbf{x}(k)] = \mathbf{x}^T(k)P\mathbf{x}(k) \tag{3-83}$$

and hope that we can select $P$ appropriately as a positive definite matrix (so that $V$ has the characteristics of energy of the system).

By construction we form $\Delta V$ as follows:

$$\Delta V[\mathbf{x}(k)] = V[\mathbf{x}(k + 1)] - V[\mathbf{x}(k)] \tag{3-84}$$

Substituting from Eq. (3-82) and Eq. (3-83) and collecting terms, we obtain

$$\Delta V[\mathbf{x}(k)] = \mathbf{x}^T(k)[A^TPA - P]\mathbf{x}(k) \tag{3-85}$$

If $\Delta V$ is negative definite, the system will be asymptotically stable since its "energy" $V$ continually decreases with time.

Thus, if

$$\Delta V[\mathbf{x}(k)] = -\mathbf{x}^T(k)Q\mathbf{x}(k) \tag{3-86}$$

for

$$Q = -(A^TPA - P) \tag{3-87}$$

positive definite, the system is stable.

Usually the test for stability is more conveniently handled in a reverse order; namely, we specify a positive definite matrix $Q$ and determine whether the solution $P$ from

$$P - A^TPA = Q \tag{3-88}$$

is positive definite. We summarize with the following test.

***Liapunov Stability Test:*** A necessary and sufficient condition for the origin of the system in Eq. (3-76) to be stable: Given *any* positive definite (symmetric) matrix $Q$, there is a positive definite matrix $P$ which satisfies Eq. (3-88).

If the system in Eq. (3-82) passes the test, $V = \mathbf{x}^T P \mathbf{x}$ is a Liapunov function for the system.

### EXAMPLE 3-14

Given the system

$$\mathbf{x}(k + 1) = \begin{bmatrix} 1 & 3 \\ -3 & -2 \end{bmatrix} \mathbf{x}(k)$$

(a) Determine the stability of the origin by the Liapunov Test.
(b) Determine the system stability using the Jury Test.

***SOLUTION:*** (a) Assume $Q = I$. From Eq. (3-88)

$$\begin{bmatrix} a & b \\ b & c \end{bmatrix} - \begin{bmatrix} 1 & -3 \\ 3 & -2 \end{bmatrix} \begin{bmatrix} a & b \\ b & c \end{bmatrix} \begin{bmatrix} 1 & 3 \\ -3 & -2 \end{bmatrix} = \begin{bmatrix} 1 & 0 \\ 0 & 1 \end{bmatrix}$$

$$\begin{bmatrix} 6b - 9c & -3a + 12b - 6c \\ -3a + 12b - 6c & -9a + 12b - 3c \end{bmatrix} = \begin{bmatrix} 1 & 0 \\ 0 & 1 \end{bmatrix}$$

The three equations (for $a$, $b$, and $c$) are

$$6b - 9c = 1$$

$$-3a + 12b - 6c = 0$$

$$-9a + 12b - 3c = 1$$

from which

$$a = \frac{-4}{21}, \quad b = \frac{-1}{14}, \quad c = \frac{-1}{21}$$

$$P = \begin{bmatrix} \dfrac{-4}{21} & \dfrac{-1}{14} \\ \dfrac{-1}{14} & \dfrac{-1}{21} \end{bmatrix} \text{ is } \textit{not} \text{ positive definite}$$

Therefore, the origin is an *unstable* equilibrium point.

(b) To use the Jury test, we construct the characteristic equation:

$$F(z) = \det [zI - A] = z^2 + z + 7 = 0$$

(1)  $F(1) = 9 > 0$  ✓

(2)  $F(-1) = 7 > 0$  ✓

(3)  $|a_0| = 7 < 1$  × Fails!

which checks part (a) that the linear system is unstable.  ∎

***Remark:*** The fact that the Liapunov test provides a test of system stability is due to the fact that for the linear discrete-time system the origin can be unstable only when the system has a pole outside the unit circle. But this is exactly what the Jury test determines, so that for linear systems either test will work.

## 3-9

## SOLVED PROBLEMS

The following selected problems are intended to offer helpful extensions and applications to the methods described earlier in this chapter.

### 3-9.1  Linearization and Equilibrium Points

A typical application of linearization is to reduce the dynamics of a nonlinear system to a linear model, for instance, in controlling a nonlinear plant about some equilibrium condition. The design of surface controls for aircraft is a case in point since the equations describing the aircraft dynamics are very nonlinear. Even simple nonlinear systems may have several "equilibrium" conditions. For example, a pendulum has two natural equilibrium conditions: one in a vertically up (balanced) position and the other vertically down, at rest.

If the dynamics of a nonlinear system are given by

$$\dot{\mathbf{x}}(t) = \mathbf{f}[\mathbf{x}(t)] \tag{3-89}$$

then its *equilibrium points* are defined as the solutions $\mathbf{x}_e$ to the vector equation

$$\mathbf{f}(\mathbf{x}_e) = \mathbf{0} \tag{3-90}$$

To illustrate, consider the following example.

### EXAMPLE 3-15

For the nonlinear oscillator equation (van der Pol's equation),

$$\ddot{x} - (1 - x^2)\dot{x} + x = 0$$

we first write a nonlinear state model. With

$$\dot{x} = y, \quad \mathbf{x} = [x, y]^T = [x_1, x_2]^T$$

$$\dot{\mathbf{x}} = \begin{bmatrix} y \\ -x + (1 - x^2)y \end{bmatrix} = \mathbf{f}(\mathbf{x})$$

It is readily seen that setting $\mathbf{f} = \mathbf{0}$ results in the single equilibrium point $\mathbf{x}_e = \mathbf{0}$.

Applying the technique of Section 3-1, linearization about the origin, Eq. (3-7),

$$\dot{\mathbf{x}} = \begin{bmatrix} \dfrac{\partial f_1}{\partial x_1} & \dfrac{\partial f_1}{\partial x_2} \\ \dfrac{\partial f_2}{\partial x_1} & \dfrac{\partial f_2}{\partial x_2} \end{bmatrix}\Bigg|_{\mathbf{x}=\mathbf{0}} \mathbf{x} = \begin{bmatrix} 0 & 1 \\ -1 - 2xy & 1 - x^2 \end{bmatrix}\Bigg|_{x=y=0} \mathbf{x} = \begin{bmatrix} 0 & 1 \\ -1 & 1 \end{bmatrix} \mathbf{x}$$

This linear description will be valid near the origin and we can determine the stability of the system at the origin by investigating the eigenvalues of the system coefficient matrix. (The origin is, in fact, an unstable equilibrium.) ∎

In the next example we consider an "input" force for use as a possible control input to the system. The system itself is an inverted pendulum/cart assembly.

### EXAMPLE 3-16 (Dynamic Equations for Cart/Pendulum System)

For the system shown below we will use standard methods to arrive at the (nonlinear) equation that relates the pendulum deflection to the cart position.

From the free-body diagrams we obtain:

1. $\Sigma$ horizontal forces on cart: $MD^2x = f - H$, where $D^2 = d^2/dt^2$

2. $\Sigma$ horizontal forces on rod: $mD^2(x + l \sin \theta) = H$

3. $\Sigma$ vertical forces on rod: $mD^2(l \cos \theta) = V - mg$

4. $\Sigma$ moments about rod c.g.: $(JD^2 + BD)\theta = Vl \sin \theta - Hl \cos \theta$

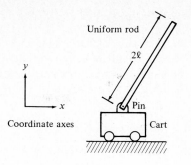

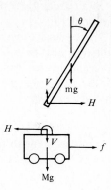

Uniform rod

$2\ell$

y

x

Coordinate axes

Pin

Cart

Cart c.g. at $(x, -a)$
Rod c.g. at $(x + \ell\sin\theta, \ell\cos\theta)$
c.g. = center of gravity.
$\ell$ = one-half of the length of the rod.
$x$ = the position of the cart c.g. relative to
    the origin of the coordinate axes.
$\theta$ = the deflection of the rod from vertical (balance position).
$m$ = the mass of the rod.
$M$ = the mass of the cart.
$g$ = the acceleration of gravity.
$H$ = the horizontal pin reaction force.
$V$ = the vertical pin reaction force.
$f$ = the control force.

where

$$J = \frac{1}{3} ml^2 = \text{ the inertia of the rod about its c.g.}$$

$B$ = the viscous friction coefficient due to friction at the pin connection

Expanding 2 and 3 above, we obtain

$$H = m\ddot{x} + ml\ddot{\theta} \cos \theta - ml(\dot{\theta})^2 \sin \theta$$

$$V = mg - ml\ddot{\theta} \sin \theta - ml(\dot{\theta})^2 \cos \theta$$

Introducing these expressions for $H$ and $V$ into 4, we obtain

$$\frac{1}{3} ml^2 \ddot{\theta} + B\dot{\theta} = mgl \sin \theta - ml^2\ddot{\theta} - ml\ddot{x} \cos \theta$$

Notice that the nonlinearities involve only the sine and cosine functions of $\theta$. If we assume that $\theta$ is near 0, for instance, kept there by the action of the control force $f$ on the cart; then we can use $\sin \theta = \theta$ and $\cos \theta = 1$ as good approximations for $\theta$ near zero. Thus,

$$\ddot{\theta} + \frac{3B}{4ml^2} \dot{\theta} - \frac{3g}{4l} \theta = \frac{-3}{4l} \ddot{x} \qquad (3\text{-}91)$$

This equation is the desired linearized relation between the pendulum deflection and the motion of the cart. We will return to this equation later in the text when we are concerned about designing a feedback controller to stabilize the equilibrium point $\theta = 0$.

To emphasize the fact that the construction of state-variable models as presented in Section 3-6 apply equally well to continuous-time (differential) equations and discrete-time (difference) equations, consider obtaining the state model for the system having to input $x(t)$ and output $\theta(t)$ described by Eq. (3-91). For convenience we write

$$\ddot{\theta} + a\dot{\theta} - b\theta = -c\ddot{x}$$

To correspond with the development of subsection 3-6.1, the transfer function $T(s) = \theta/X$ is given by

$$T(s) = \frac{-cs^2}{s^2 + as - b}$$

This is a second-order system as seen from the denominator polynomial. Therefore, it requires two integrators (represented by $1/s = s^{-1}$). Following Fig. 3-5, we have the diagram

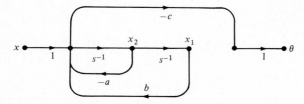

where the outputs of the integrators have been designated as state variables $x_1$ and $x_2$, not to be confused with the input signal $x$. Using the vector $\mathbf{x} = [x_1 \ x_2]$, the state model is given by

$$\dot{\mathbf{x}} = \begin{bmatrix} 0 & 1 \\ b & -a \end{bmatrix} \mathbf{x} + \begin{bmatrix} 0 \\ 1 \end{bmatrix} x$$

$$\theta = [-bc \quad ac] \, \mathbf{x} - cx$$

where $\mathbf{x}$ is the state vector, $x$ is the input, and $\theta$ is the output. ∎

## 3-9.2 Using the General State Model Solution

Given a state-variable description of the system, it is sometimes convenient to use that description to find response signals, that is, using Eq. (3-26) directly.

### EXAMPLE 3-17

For the system described by

$$\dot{\mathbf{x}}(t) = \begin{bmatrix} 0 & 1 \\ -8 & -4 \end{bmatrix} \mathbf{x}(t) + \begin{bmatrix} 0 \\ 1 \end{bmatrix} u(t)$$

$$y(t) = [8 \quad 0] \, \mathbf{x}(t)$$

where $u(t)$, the input, is given as a unit-step function and the initial state $\mathbf{x}(0) = [1, 1]^T$. To solve for the output $y(t)$, $0 \leq t$.

**SOLUTION:** As required by Eq. (3-26), the transition matrix $\Phi(t) = \exp\{At\}$ must first be determined. Using Eq. (3-37),

$$\Phi(t) = \mathcal{L}^{-1}\{[sI - A]^{-1}\}$$

$$\Phi(s) = [sI - A]^{-1} = \begin{bmatrix} s & -1 \\ 8 & s+4 \end{bmatrix}^{-1} = \frac{\begin{bmatrix} s+4 & 1 \\ -8 & s \end{bmatrix}}{s^2 + 4s + 8}$$

$$\Phi(s) = \begin{bmatrix} \dfrac{s+4}{(s+2)^2 + 2^2} & \dfrac{1}{(s+2)^2 + 2^2} \\[3mm] \dfrac{-8}{(s+2)^2 + 2^2} & \dfrac{s}{(s+2)^2 + 2^2} \end{bmatrix}$$

Inverting each element,

$$\Phi(t) = \begin{bmatrix} e^{-2t}(\cos 2t + \sin 2t) & \frac{1}{2}e^{-2t} \sin 2t \\ -4e^{-2t} \sin 2t & e^{-2t}(\cos 2t - \sin 2t) \end{bmatrix}$$

Applying Eq. (3-37),

$$\mathbf{x}(t) = \Phi(t)\mathbf{x}(0) + \int_0^t \Phi(t - \tau)\begin{bmatrix} 0 \\ 1 \end{bmatrix} d\tau$$

Noting that $y(t)$ depends on only the first component of $\mathbf{x}(t)$,

$$y(t) = 8e^{-2t}\left(\cos 2t + \frac{3}{2} \sin 2t\right) + 8\int_0^t \frac{1}{2} e^{-2(t-\tau)} \sin 2(t - \tau)\, d\tau$$

Changing variables of integration ($x = t - \tau$),

$$y(t) = 8e^{-2t}\left(\cos 2t + \frac{3}{2} \sin 2t\right) + 4\int_0^t e^{-2x} \sin 2x\, dx$$

Finally, we obtain the response $y(t)$ for $t \geq 0$,

$$y(t) = 1 + e^{-2t}(7 \cos 2t + 11 \sin 2t), \quad t \geq 0 \qquad \blacksquare$$

This next example will obtain the zero-order-hold equivalent system for the same continuous-time system.

### EXAMPLE 3-18 (Discrete-Time Model)

For the system described in the previous example, we assume that the input $u(t)$ is a sampled-clamped signal. Under this condition the system may be reduced to a discrete-time model giving the state and output at the sample times. Following the technique of Secion 3-4, we calculate $\Phi(T)$ and $\Gamma(T)$ of Eq. (3-34). The first matrix is available from Example 3-17:

$$\Phi(T) = \begin{bmatrix} e^{-2T}(\cos 2T + \sin 2T) & \tfrac{1}{2}e^{-2T}(\sin 2T) \\ -4e^{-2T}(\sin 2T) & e^{-2T}(\cos 2T - \sin 2T) \end{bmatrix}$$

The second matrix is obtained starting from the expression from Eq. (3-34) that

$$\Gamma(T) = \int_0^T \Phi(t)B \, dt, \text{ where } B = \begin{bmatrix} 0 \\ 1 \end{bmatrix}$$

therefore,

$$\Gamma(T) = \int_0^T \begin{bmatrix} \tfrac{1}{2}e^{-2t}\sin 2t \\ e^{-2t}(\cos 2t - \sin 2t) \end{bmatrix} dt$$

$$\Gamma(T) = \begin{bmatrix} \tfrac{1}{8}\{1 - e^{-2T}(\cos 2T + \sin 2T)\} \\ \tfrac{1}{2}e^{-2T}\sin 2T \end{bmatrix}$$

As discussed briefly in Section 1-3 the sampling rate should be at least twice the highest frequency of the signal to represent the analog signal well. In practice it is better to use a sampling frequency of 10 or more times the highest signal frequency. Although the expressions for $\Phi(T)$ and $\Gamma(T)$ above are exact, the expressions themselves indicate that $T$ should be chosen small enough so that $2T$ is a small part of the period of the sinusoidal terms. Thus, for $T = 0.1$, $2T = 0.2$ is significantly less than the period $\pi = 3.14$.

Discrete-time model ($T = 0.1$ sec):

$$\mathbf{x}(k + 1) = \begin{bmatrix} 0.9651 & 0.0813 \\ -0.6506 & 0.6398 \end{bmatrix} \mathbf{x}(k) + \begin{bmatrix} 0.0044 \\ 0.0813 \end{bmatrix} u(k)$$

$$y(k) = [8 \quad 0] \, \mathbf{x}(k)$$

Now, given the same conditions as in Example 3-17, we can use recursion to obtain the corresponding output values at the sample times. For instance, since $\mathbf{x}(0) = [1, 1]^T$, $y(0) = 8$. Note that this checks with $y(0)$ from the $y(t)$ expression of Example 3-17. Similarly, at $t = T = 0.1$

$$y(t)|_{t=T} = 8.406$$

whereas from the discrete-time model, with $u(k)$ a unit-step sequence and $\mathbf{x}(0) = [1, 1]^T$

$$\mathbf{x}(1) = \mathbf{x}(T) = \begin{bmatrix} 1.0508 \\ 0.0705 \end{bmatrix}$$

and

$$y(1) = 8(1.0508) = 8.406$$

as expected.

These calculations exemplify the exact nature of the discrete model when the input is of the form of a sampled-clamped signal such as the unit step in this case. Thus, the output sequence $y(kT)(k = 0, 1, 2, \ldots)$ can also be represented by Eq. (3-46), where the $(A, B, C, D)$ matrices are taken from the discrete-time state model. The values should match the continuous-time solution $y(t)$ with $t = kT(k = 0, 1, 2, \ldots)$ from Example 3-17 since a sampled-clamped version of the unit-step input signal is again a unit-step signal. ∎

### 3-9.3 Multiple Input/Multiple Output Systems (MIMO)

A major interest in using the state-variable models is the ability to make the transition from single input/single output (SISO) systems to MIMO systems with comparative ease. In Section 3-7.1 we discussed the general change of state variables, which, of course, is valid for MIMO systems as well as SISO systems. The following example demonstrates that with such a change of variables the characteristic polynomial is invariant, that is, equivalent models have the same characteristic equations.

#### EXAMPLE 3-19 (Characteristic Polynomials)
From S1 in Eq. (3-67) the characteristic polynomial is given by

$$p_1(z) = \det\{zI - A\}$$

and that of S2 in Eq. (3-69) is

$$p_2(z) = \det\{zI - P^{-1}AP\} = \det\{zP^{-1}IP - P^{-1}AP\}$$

Thus,

$$p_2(z) = \det\{P^{-1}(zI - A)P\} = \det\{P^{-1}\} \det\{zI - A\} \det\{P\}$$

Here we have used the fact that the determinant of a product is equal to the product of the determinants. Furthermore, since

$$\det\{P^{-1}\} = \frac{1}{\det\{P\}}$$

$$p_2(z) = \det\{zI - A\} = p_1(z)$$

thus completing the proof. ∎

More generally, as mentioned in Section 3-7.1, the transfer matrix of a system is invariant under a change of state vector. This is easily demonstrated by manipulating the $(A', B', C', D)$ matrices of Eq. (3-69) as in the next example.

#### EXAMPLE 3-20 (Transfer Matrices)
The system description S1 and S2 in Section 3-7.1 are related by the state transformation $\mathbf{x} = P\boldsymbol{\xi}$. By Eq. (3-75) the transfer matrix of S1 is

$$H(z) = C(zI - A)^{-1}B + D$$

We now show that the transfer matrix for S2 is the same as that for S1. Noting that $(A', B', C', D) = (P^{-1}AP, P^{-1}A, CP, D)$ from Eq. (3-69),

$$H'(z) = CP[zI - P^{-1}AP]^{-1}P^{-1}B + D$$

$$= CP[P^{-1}(zI - A)P]^{-1}P^{-1}B + D$$

$$= (CP)P^{-1}(zI - A)^{-1}P(P^{-1}B) + D$$

$$= C(zI - A)^{-1}B + D = H(z)$$

Thus, the input–output description of a system does not change under a transformation of state vector. ∎

Many times a MIMO system will be described in terms of simultaneous difference (or differential) equations. Special care must be taken in obtaining the poles and zeros of such a system. Consider the following example.

### EXAMPLE 3-21 (Further Characterizations of MIMO Systems)

A system with inputs $u_1$, $u_2$ and outputs $y_1$, $y_2$ is given by the simultaneous equations:

$$y_1(k + 2) + y_2(k) + y_2(k - 1) = u_1(k) + u_1(k + 1) + 2u_2(k)$$

$$-y_1(k + 1) + y_2(k) - 3y_2(k - 1) = -3u_1(k) - u_2(k)$$

Another representation for the system can be obtained in the transform domain as

$$z^2Y_1(z) + (1 + z^{-1})Y_2(z) = (1 + z)U_1(z) + 2U_2(z)$$

$$-zY_1(z) + (1 - 3z^{-1})Y_2(z) = -3U_1(z) + (-1)U_2(z)$$

In matrix form,

$$\begin{bmatrix} z^2 & 1 + z^{-1} \\ -z & 1 - 3z^{-1} \end{bmatrix} \mathbf{Y}(z) = \begin{bmatrix} 1 + z & 2 \\ -3 & -1 \end{bmatrix} \mathbf{U}(z) \tag{3-92}$$

In this form the coefficient matrix of $\mathbf{Y}(z)$ is the *characteristic matrix* for the system. To obtain the characteristic equation, one must set the determinant of the characteristic matrix times $z^{m_1 + m_2}$ equal to zero, where $m_1$ and $m_2$ are the largest integers such that $z^{-m_1}Y_1(z)$ and $z^{-m_2}Y_2(z)$ appear in the characteristic matrix. In this case,

$$p(z) = z \begin{vmatrix} z^2 & 1 + z^{-1} \\ -z & 1 - 3z^{-1} \end{vmatrix} = z^3 - 2z^2 + z$$

with eigenvalues at $z = 1, 1, 0$.

The *transfer matrix* is obtained by solving Eq. (3-92) for $\mathbf{Y}(z)$:

$$H(z) = \begin{bmatrix} \dfrac{z - 3}{z(z - 1)^2} & \dfrac{-z - 1}{z(z - 1)^2} \\ \dfrac{z}{(z - 1)^2} & \dfrac{z^2}{(z - 1)^2} \end{bmatrix} \begin{bmatrix} z + 1 & 2 \\ -3 & -1 \end{bmatrix}$$

$$H(z) = \frac{\begin{bmatrix} z^2 + z & 3z - 5 \\ -2z^3 + z^2 & -z^3 + 2z^2 \end{bmatrix}}{z(z - 1)^2}$$

The *Matrix Factor Description* for the system is of the form

$$H(z) = M^{-1}(z)N(z) \tag{3-93}$$

where both $M(z)$ and $N(z)$ are matrices whose entries are polynomials of $z$ (polynomial matrices). In the previous example if $y_2(k)$ is redefined to be $y_2'(k + 1)$, then

$$H'(z) = \begin{bmatrix} z^2 & z + 1 \\ -z & z - 3 \end{bmatrix}^{-1} \begin{bmatrix} z + 1 & 2 \\ -3 & -1 \end{bmatrix}$$

would be a matrix factor description for the modified system. ∎


### 3-9.4 Leverrier's Algorithm (Program 2 in Appendix D is based on Leverrier's algorithm)

This is a method for numerically calculating the resolvent matrix $(sI - A)^{-1}$. The characteristic polynomial will be represented as follows:

$$p(s) = s^n - \alpha_1 s^{n-1} - \alpha_2 s^{n-2} - \cdots - \alpha_{n-1} s - \alpha_n \tag{3-94}$$

Since, formally, the inverse of $(sI - A)$ can be written

$$(sI - A)^{-1} = \frac{\text{Adj } (sI - A)}{\det (sI - A)} \tag{3-95}$$

then

$$\text{Adj } (sI - A) \cdot (sI - A) = \det (sI - A)I = p(s)I \tag{3-96}$$

The adjoint matrix can be expanded as

$$\text{Adj } (sI - A) = Is^{n-1} + (A - \alpha_1 I)s^{n-2} + (A^2 - \alpha_1 A - \alpha_2 I)s^{n-3}$$
$$+ \cdots + (A^{n-1} - \alpha_1 A^{n-2} - \cdots - \alpha_{n-1}I) \tag{3-97}$$

To see that this expansion is valid, the reader should take time to multiply Eq. (3-97) by $(sI - A)$, thereby checking Eq. (3-96). By writing

$$(sI - A)^{-1} = \frac{1}{p(s)} [R_1 s^{n-1} + R_2 s^{n-2} + \cdots + R_n] \tag{3-98}$$

where the matrix $R_i$ is the $i$th coefficient matrix in Eq. (3-97) ($i = 1, \ldots, n$), we observe that

$$R_1 = I, \quad R_2 = R_1 A - \alpha_1 I, \quad R_3 = R_2 A - \alpha_2 I$$

and so on until
$$R_n = R_{n-1}A - \alpha_{n-1}I$$

Also, since the matrix $A$ satisfies its own characteristic equation, $p(A) = 0$,

$$R_nA - \alpha_nI = 0 \qquad (3\text{-}99)$$

Leverrier's algorithm is a recursive method that simultaneously calculates the coefficients of the characteristic polynomial in Eq. (3-94) as well as the matrix coefficients of adj $(sI - A)$ shown in Eq. (3-98). The recursion steps begin with a matrix result that the coefficient $\alpha_1$ in Eq. (3-94) is the sum of the eigenvalues of $A$, which, in turn, is equal to the trace (sum of the main diagonal elements) of $A$:

$$R_1 = I, \qquad\qquad \alpha_1 = \text{Tr }(A)$$

$$R_2 = R_1A - \alpha_1I, \qquad \alpha_2 = \frac{1}{2}\text{Tr }(R_2A)$$

$$R_3 = R_2A - \alpha_2I, \qquad a_3 = \frac{1}{3}\text{Tr }(R_3A)$$

$$\cdot$$
$$\cdot$$
$$\cdot$$

$$R_n = R_{n-1}A - \alpha_{n-1}I, \quad \alpha_n = \frac{1}{n}\text{Tr }(R_nA)$$

Equation (3-99) can be used as a numerical check on the above calculations.

## EXAMPLE 3-22 (Leverrier's Algorithm)

The system used in Example 3-5 had the following $A$ matrix:

$$A = \begin{bmatrix} 0 & -2 \\ 1 & -3 \end{bmatrix}$$

We will calculate $(sI - A)^{-1}$ with the above algorithm and check the result both with Eq. (3-99) and that obtained in Example 3-5.

*SOLUTION:* Following the recursion steps listed above,

$$R_1 = \begin{bmatrix} 1 & 0 \\ 0 & 1 \end{bmatrix}, \alpha_1 = -3$$

$$R_2 = A + 3I = \begin{bmatrix} 3 & -2 \\ 1 & 0 \end{bmatrix}$$

$$R_2A = \begin{bmatrix} -2 & 0 \\ 0 & -2 \end{bmatrix}, \alpha_2 = -2$$

From Eq. (3-99)

$$R_2A + 2I = 0$$

which checks our computations. Therefore, from Eq. (3-98)

$$(sI - A)^{-1} = \frac{\begin{bmatrix} 1 & 0 \\ 0 & 1 \end{bmatrix} s + \begin{bmatrix} 3 & -2 \\ 1 & 0 \end{bmatrix}}{s^2 + 3s + 2}$$

This result is also confirmed by the first step in the solution of Example 3-5.


## 3-10

## SUMMARY

In this chapter we established the concept of state (as a minimum collection of variables that describes the current status of the system) and the associated methods of analysis. In Section 3-1 the method of linearization (determining the incremental model) about a particular state was developed. The modeling of continuous-time state models was briefly discussed, along with the development of the general solution for the state vector at any time, given in Eq. (3-26). This important equation, in turn, provided the basis of constructing the ZOH equivalent discrete-time model of an analog plant to be controlled digitally. Similarly, in Section 3-5 a general solution was generated for the discrete-time state model.

Although there are other standard state-variable structures, we choose to describe only three forms, which we label as the *controllable, observable,* or *Jordan* canonical forms. Each of these description forms will be helpful to us later. These were explained in Section 3-6. In the more general context of MIMO systems the relationship between transfer matrices and state models was discussed and illustrated in Section 3-7.

In the last portion of the chapter the topic of discrete-time system stability was reintroduced from Chapter 2, this time with a more rigorous approach to show that the interior of the unit circle in the complex $z$-plane is the stability region for discrete-time systems. Stability in the sense of Liapunov was introduced as an alternate method of investigating the stability of a linear (discrete-time) system, as well as to give us a different perspective of the concept of stability, namely, that of the stability of an equilibrium point of the system.


## REFERENCES

**Section 3-1** *Modern Control Theory;* W. L. Brogan; Quantum Publishers, 1974.
**Section 3-2** *Automatic Control Systems* (4th Ed.); B. C. Kuo; Prentice-Hall, 1982.
**Section 3-3** *State Variables for Engineers;* P. M. DeRusso, R. J. Roy, and C. M. Close; John Wiley and Sons, 1966.
**Section 3-6** *Discrete-Time and Computer Control Systems;* J. A. Cadzow and H. R. Martens; Prentice-Hall, 1970.
**Section 3-7** *Modern Control Theory;* W. L. Brogan; Quantum Publishers, 1974.
**Section 3-8** *Modern Control Engineering;* K. Ogata; Prentice-Hall, 1970.

## PROBLEMS

**3-1**  For the given discrete-time state equation

$$\mathbf{x}(k + 1) = \begin{bmatrix} -1 & 1 \\ 0 & -1 \end{bmatrix} \mathbf{x}(k) + \begin{bmatrix} 1 \\ 2 \end{bmatrix} u(k)$$

plot the system state as shown in Fig. 3-2 when $u(k) = 1$ for $k \geq 0$ and
**(a)** $\mathbf{x}(0) = [0, 2]^T$
**(b)** $\mathbf{x}(0) = [1, 1]^T$
Explain the results of part (b).

**3-2**  In Fig. P3-2 is shown a "double pendulum" constrained to oscillate in the plane of the paper. By using the angles $\theta$ and $\phi$ as generalized coordinates, the equations of motion can be found to be (with lengths $l$ normalized to have the value $g$)

$$(3 + 2c\phi)\ddot{\theta} + (1 + c\phi)\ddot{\phi} - s\phi(\dot{\phi}^2 + 2\dot{\theta}\dot{\phi}) + 2s\theta + s(\theta + \phi) = 0$$

$$(1 + c\phi)\ddot{\theta} + \ddot{\phi} + \dot{\theta}^2 s\phi + s(\theta + \phi) = 0$$

where $cx$ and $sx$ represent $\cos x$ and $\sin x$, respectively.

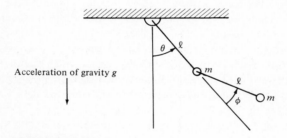

Acceleration of gravity $g$

**FIGURE P3-2.**

**(a)** Assume that the angles and their derivatives are small and write a set of linearized equations (using $\sin x = x$ and $\cos x = 1$ for small $x$ and neglecting products of small quantities) in the form of

$$\ddot{\mathbf{x}} = M\mathbf{x}$$

where $\mathbf{x} = [\theta, \phi]^T$ and $M$ is a constant matrix.
**(b)** Investigate the two modes of vibration by calculating the eigenvalues (mode frequencies) and eigenvectors of $M$. Show that for the lower frequency mode the relation between $\theta$ and $\phi$ is

$$\phi = (\sqrt{2} - 1)\theta$$

and for the higher frequency mode

$$\phi = -(1 + \sqrt{2})\theta$$

**138**

**3-3**    Figure P3-3 shows a container with two adjacent chambers each filled with a fluid. Since the thermal energy stored in a fluid is proportional to its temperature in degrees Kelvin, we assume that the energy in chamber 1 is $W_1 = 2T_1$ (joules) and the energy in chamber 2 is $W_2 = 6T_2$ (joules). In addition, the heat transfer rate $q$ through the walls is proportional to the temperature difference.

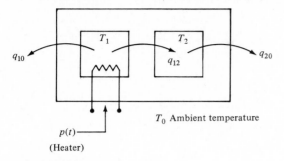

**FIGURE P3-3.**

Chamber 1 to chamber 2: $q_{12} = 6(T_1 - T_2)$ joules/sec

Chamber 1 to ambient:   $q_{10} = 2(T_1 - T_0)$ joules/sec

Chamber 2 to ambient:   $q_{20} = 6(T_2 - T_0)$ joules/sec

The resistance heater is capable of supplying a power $p(t)$.

**(a)** Determine a set of state equations with $T_1$ and $T_2$ as state variables by first writing a power balance equation for each chamber.

**(b)** Find the steady power $p_s$ that would be required to maintain a steady value of $T_2$ at 40° above the ambient temperature $T_0$.

**(c)** Develop the "incremental" state equations in terms of **x** by defining $x_1 = T_1 - T_{1s}$, $x_2 = T_2 - T_{2s}$, and $u = p - p_s$, where, for instance, $T_{2s}$ is the steady value of $T_2(T_{2s} = T_0 + 40)$ used in part (b).

**3-4**    A mass–spring combination (with negligible friction) moves on a horizontal track as shown in Fig. P3-4. The position $x(t)$ is measured with $x = 0$ when the spring is unstretched and the external force $f(t) = 0$.

**(a)** Determine the state model using $x$ and $\dot{x}$ as state variables by first writing the equation of motion for the mass. Use $M = 1$ kg and $K = 4$ N/m. Include an output equation for the measurement.

**(b)** Calculate the discrete-time state model (for the same state variables) if the force $f(t)$ is the output of a sample-and-clamp (zero-order-hold) operation.

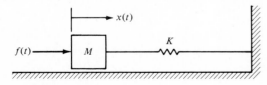

**FIGURE P3-4.**

**3-5** Develop a state model for the permanent-magnet dc motor and load shown in Fig. P3-5. You may assume the following characteristics for the dc motor:

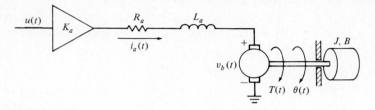

**FIGURE P3-5.**

- Torque is proportional to armature current
  $T = K_m i_a$
- Back-emf is proportional to shaft angular velocity
  $v_b = K_b \dot\theta$ (see remark below)
- Neglect the armature winding inductance
  $L_a = 0$

The input $u(t)$ is a control voltage, and the output is $\theta(t)$, the shaft angular position.

    **Remark:**  The parameters $K_m$ and $K_b$ differ numerically only by a constant factor that depends on the units used. This can be shown by setting the instantaneous (electrical) input power to the armature, $p_e(t) = v_b(t)i_a(t)$, equal to the instantaneous output (mechanical) power, $p_m(t) = T(t)\dot\theta(t)$. In particular,

$$p_e(t) = k_b\dot\theta(t)K_m^{-1}T(t) \overset{\text{set}}{=} p_m(t) = T(t)\dot\theta(t)$$

and we see that nominally $K_b = K_m$. However, if, for example, the English system of units are used, $p_e(t)$ in watts becomes

$$p_e(t) = \frac{v_b(t)i_a(t)}{745.7} \text{ (hp)}$$

$$p_m(t) = \frac{T(t)\dot\theta(t)}{550} \text{ (hp)}$$

when $T$ is in (ft-lb) and $\dot\theta$ is in (rad/sec). In this case

$$\frac{K_b}{K_m} = \frac{745.7}{550.0} = 1.356$$

Thus, although the constants $K_b$ and $K_m$ may differ, it is important to recognize their close physical relationship.

**3-6** Determine the response of the system of Fig. P3-6 to a unit-step input using a phase-variable state model of the system with an initial state of
(a) $\mathbf{x}(0) = \mathbf{0}$
(b) $\mathbf{x}(0) = [0 \quad -1]^T$

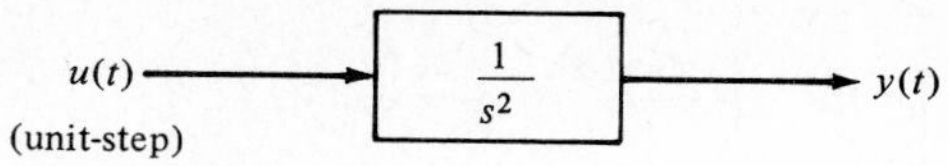

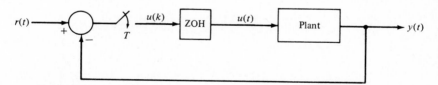

$u(t)$ ————→ [ $\frac{1}{s^2}$ ] ————→ $y(t)$
(unit-step)

**FIGURE P3-6.**

**3-7** Repeat Problem 3-6 for a system whose transfer function is given by

$$G(s) = \frac{2}{s(s + 2)}$$

**3-8** Calculate the sampled-data (ZOH) equivalent discrete-time system transfer functions for the continuous-time systems

**(a)** $G_a(s) = \frac{1}{s^2}$

**(b)** $G_b(s) = \frac{2}{s(s + 2)}$

**3-9** **(a)** Find the ZOH equivalent discrete-time (state) model for the plant

$$\dot{\mathbf{x}}(t) = \begin{bmatrix} 0 & 1 \\ -2 & -3 \end{bmatrix} \mathbf{x}(t) + \begin{bmatrix} 0 \\ 1 \end{bmatrix} u(t)$$

$$y(t) = [1 \quad 0] \, \mathbf{x}(t)$$

**(b)** Determine the equivalent closed-loop (discrete-time) state model when the plant has feedback as shown in Fig. P3-9 by using the constraint that $u(k) = r(k) - y(k)$.

$r(t)$ ———→⊕———/ —— $u(k)$ → [ZOH] — $u(t)$ → [ Plant ] ———→ $y(t)$
        +  −    $T$

**FIGURE P3-9.**

**3-10** Calculate the zero-state response of the system

$$\dot{\mathbf{x}}(t) = \begin{bmatrix} 0 & 1 \\ 0 & -2 \end{bmatrix} \mathbf{x}(t) + \begin{bmatrix} 0 \\ 2 \end{bmatrix} u(t)$$

$$y(t) = [1 \quad 0] \, \mathbf{x}(t)$$

to the input $u(t) = 1(t) - 1(t - 0.5)$, where $1(t)$ is the notation for a unit-step function.

**3-11** **(a)** Write the phase-variable form for the state model of the continuous-time plant $1/s^2$.

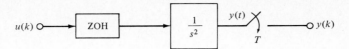

**FIGURE P3-11.**

**(b)** Using the state model of part (a), calculate the state model for the discrete-time system shown in Fig. P3-11 as a function of $T$.
**(c)** Use recursion to establish the first four terms of the zero-state response to a unit step.

**3-12**   Determine the unit-pulse response $h(k)$ for the system given in Fig. P3-11.

**3-13**   For the discrete-time system described by

$$\mathbf{x}(k + 1) = \begin{bmatrix} 1 & 0 \\ 0 & 2 \end{bmatrix} \mathbf{x}(k) + \begin{bmatrix} 1 \\ 1 \end{bmatrix} u(k)$$

$$y(k) = [\, 2 \quad 3\,]\ \mathbf{x}(k) + [1]\ u(k)$$

**(a)** Calculate the first five terms of the unit-pulse response sequence $h(k)$.
**(b)** Use $h(k)$ to determine the first five terms of the (zero-state) unit-step response by convolution.
**(c)** Check your result of part (b) by using recursion on the original state model.

**3-14**   A continuous-time system is represented by the state model

$$\dot{\mathbf{x}}(t) = \begin{bmatrix} 0 & 0 & 0 \\ 0 & 1 & 0 \\ 0 & 0 & 2 \end{bmatrix} \mathbf{x}(t) + \begin{bmatrix} 1 \\ 1 \\ 1 \end{bmatrix} u(t)$$

$$y(t) = [\, -1 \quad -2 \quad 3\,]\ \mathbf{x}(t)$$

If it is known that the input $u(t)$ is piecewise constant with changes that occur only at instants $t_k = 0.1k$ sec with $k = 0, 1, 2, \ldots$, calculate an equivalent discrete-time model with which to obtain values of $\mathbf{x}$ or $y$ at times $t = t_k$.

**3-15**   For the system in Fig. P3-15
**(a)** Determine the (zero-state) unit-step discrete-time response $c(k)$
**(b)** Calculate the continuous response $c(t)$ for $0 < t < 0.3$ sec using the knowledge of $u(t)$ from part $a$.

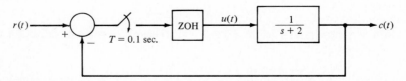

**FIGURE P3-15.**

**STATE-VARIABLE ANALYSIS**

**3-16**   A two-input, two-output discrete-time system is shown in Fig. P3-16.
   **(a)** Use the variables which are outputs of the unit-time delay elements as state
   variables and construct the vector state equations.
   **(b)** Calculate the $2 \times 2$ transfer matrix $H(z)$.

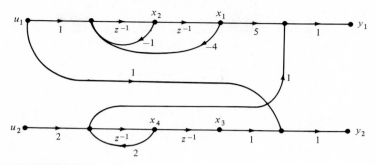

**FIGURE P3-16.**

**3-17**   For a plant described by

$$G(s) = \frac{Y(s)}{U(s)} = \frac{4s + 2}{s(s + 1)(s + 2)}$$

   **(a)** Write the state equations in each of the three canonical forms of Section
   3-6.
   **(b)** For any one of the forms of part (a) construct the ZOH discrete-time equivalent state model (equations) for an arbitrary sample interval $T$.

**3-18**   Describe the feedback system in Fig. P3-18 by an equivalent set of discrete-
   time state model equations (as if every signal were of interest only at the sample
   instants).

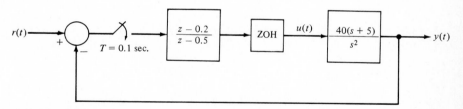

**FIGURE P3-18.**

**3-19**   Derive a minimal order state variable model for the system whose transfer matrix
   is

$$H(z) = \begin{bmatrix} \dfrac{1}{z + 1} - \dfrac{1}{z + 2}, & \dfrac{-10}{z + 1}, & \dfrac{3}{z + 2} \\[3mm] \dfrac{-8}{z + 2}, & \dfrac{1}{z + 1} + \dfrac{2}{(z + 1)^2}, & \dfrac{5/2}{z} - \dfrac{5/2}{z + 2} \end{bmatrix}$$

   Your answer should be a sixth-order set of state equations.

**3-20**  A discrete-time system is described by

$$\mathbf{x}(k + 1) = \begin{bmatrix} 1 & 0.5 \\ 0.2 & 1 \end{bmatrix} \mathbf{x}(k) + \begin{bmatrix} 1.2 \\ 0.5 \end{bmatrix} u(k)$$

$$y(k) = [1 \quad 0] \, \mathbf{x}(k)$$

(a) Calculate the pulse transfer function $G(z) = Y(z)/U(z)$

(b) Derive a new state model to describe the system using a new state $\mathbf{v}$:

$$\mathbf{x}(k) = \begin{bmatrix} 1 & -1 \\ 1 & 1 \end{bmatrix} \mathbf{v}(k)$$

(c) Calculate $G(z)$ from the new state model as a check on the result of part (a).

**3-21**  Use Leverrier's algorithm to obtain the matricant $(sI - A)^{-1}$ for the following $A$ matrices. In each case determine the same result in a direct manner as a check.

(a) $\begin{bmatrix} 0 & 1 \\ 0 & -2 \end{bmatrix}$ 
(b) $\begin{bmatrix} -1 & 0 \\ 0 & -2 \end{bmatrix}$

(c) $\begin{bmatrix} 0 & 1 & 0 \\ 0 & 0 & 1 \\ -12 & -19 & -8 \end{bmatrix}$ 
(d) $\begin{bmatrix} -1 & 1 & 0 \\ 0 & -1 & 1 \\ 0 & 0 & -1 \end{bmatrix}$

## CHAPTER 4

# System Simulation Techniques

One of the most useful aspects of digital computers is the ability to provide accurate simulation capabilities for a wide class of system models. The area of system simulation and numerical analysis, in general, is far too wide for present purposes. Consequently, we will consider only a few specific techniques. In this chapter we will build onto our background of discrete-time systems to the extent of examining various methods by which a discrete-time algorithm can approximate a continuous-time system response. Included in our study will be simple programmable methods of evaluating sampled-data system responses, at sample times and between sample times. With a slight modification of these methods we will be able to incorporate the effects of system nonlinearities, even though the main thrust of this text is not in this direction.

## MACHINE CALCULATION
## OF THE TRANSITION MATRICES

This section deals with the important zero-order-hold (ZOH) model for a sample-clamped, continuous-time system, which was discussed in Section 3-4. Repeating briefly, given a continuous-time system described in state variable form, we have

$$\dot{\mathbf{x}}(t) = F\mathbf{x}(t) + G\mathbf{u}(t) \tag{4-1}$$

where $F$ and $G$ are constant matrices.

To avoid confusion between continuous- and discrete-time models, we will use the $F$, $G$ notation as in Eq. (4-1) for continuous-time and keep the $A$, $B$ notation to describe the corresponding discrete-time model.

If the inputs $\mathbf{u}(t)$ in Eq. (4-1) satisfy that

$$\mathbf{u}(t) = \mathbf{u}(kT) \qquad \text{for } kT \leq t < kT + T \tag{4-2}$$

as would be the case of a uniformly sampled and clamped (ZOH) inputs, then from Chapter 3 we know that the exact values of $\mathbf{x}$ in Eq. (4-1) at $t = kT$, $k = 0, 1, 2, \ldots$ can be obtained from the discrete-time model

$$\mathbf{x}(k + 1) = A(T)\mathbf{x}(k) + B(T)\mathbf{u}(k) \tag{4-3}$$

where

$$A(T) = e^{FT}, \, B(T) = \int_0^T e^{Ft}G \, dt$$

The reader may want to review the development leading up to Eq. (3-34) to refresh his/her memory.

The matrix $A(T)$ is defined through the infinite series (see Eq. (3-38)),

$$A(t) = I + tF + (t^2/2!) F^2 + \cdots + (t^k/k!) F^k + \cdots \tag{4-4}$$

For low-order systems $A(t)$ can be calculated analytically using Eq. (3-37). The emphasis in this section is to provide a method for numerically calculating $A(T)$ for a given sample interval $T$, which is useful for higher-order systems.

It is fortunate that the series in Eq. (4-4) is very well behaved; it converges for all finite constant matrices $tF$ and usually does so with amazingly few terms. That is to say, within 10 or 15 terms the series of Eq. (4-4) has typically converged to the numerical matrix $A(t)$ with four or five place accuracy.

A similar series can be developed for $B(T)$ by integrating Eq. (4-4) term by term to get

$$B(t) = [tI + (t^2/2!)F + (t^3/3!)F^2 + \cdots + (t^k/k!)F^{k-1} + \cdots]G \tag{4-5}$$

With an eye toward approximating $A$ and $B$ for a particular $t$, $F$, and $G$, we note that the digital computer is ideally suited to performing the indicated operations of Eq. (4-4) or Eq. (4-5). Both series have the useful property that the next term is a good estimate of the accuracy obtained for a given truncation. Rather than work out both series, we define

$$E(t) = tI + (t^2/2!)F + (t^3/3!)F^2 + \cdots \qquad (4\text{-}6)$$

If $E(t)$ is first computed to a specified accuracy for a given $t = T$ and $F$, then

$$A(T) = I + FE(T), \qquad B(T) = E(T)G \qquad (4\text{-}7)$$

The computation of $E$ from the series of Eq. (4-6) requires a truncation after $r$ terms. As was mentioned, 15 terms will typically suffice. A simple convergence test (to determine when a sufficient number of terms of Eq. (4-6) has been taken) is to compare the next (matrix) term entry-by-entry with the cal-

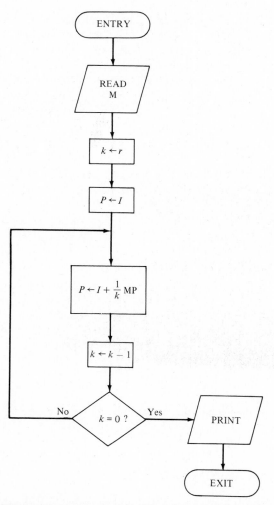

**FIGURE 4-1. Flow chart for implementing equation 4–8.**

culated partial sum so that the entries of the partial sum are changed by less than some percent error by the addition of the next term.

If for the accuracy desired, the number of terms can be decided in advance, then the series we have discussed can be put into a "nested" form for programming convenience. For instance, if we let $M = tF$ in Eq. (4-4) for some fixed value of $t$, the partial sum which includes $M^r$, that is, the first $(r + 1)$ terms, can be written as

$$\sum_{k=0}^{r} \frac{M^k}{k!} = \left\{ I + M\left[ I + \frac{M}{2}\left( I + \cdots + \frac{M}{r - 2}\left[ I + \right. \right.\right.\right.$$
$$\left.\left.\left.\left. \frac{M}{r - 1}\left( I + \frac{M}{r} \right) \right] \cdots \right) \right] \right\} \quad (4\text{-}8)$$

In this form a program can be set up to perform the calculations from the inside out. The flowchart in Fig. 4-1 on page 147 illustrates a possible structure. Program 3 in Appendix D is based on Eq. (4-8). The factorial in the denominator of the series terms helps to provide rapid convergence. For example, division by 25! is a denominator factor in excess of $10^{25}$. Thus, if the truncation error is too high after 25 terms, the problem may require reformulation based on a smaller transition time, $T$.

## EXAMPLE 4-1

We wish to determine the transition matrix for the given system: (a) analytically, and (b) numerically to investigate the convergence of the series of Eq. (4-4):

$$\dot{\mathbf{x}} = \begin{bmatrix} 0 & 1 \\ 0 & -2 \end{bmatrix} \mathbf{x}$$

*SOLUTION:* (a) From Eq. (3-37) the matricant

$$[sI - F]^{-1} = \begin{bmatrix} s & -1 \\ 0 & s + 2 \end{bmatrix}^{-1} = \frac{\begin{bmatrix} s + 2 & 1 \\ 0 & s \end{bmatrix}}{s(s + 2)}$$

Inverse-transforming each entry,

$$A(t) = \begin{bmatrix} 1 & (1 - e^{-2t})/2 \\ 0 & e^{-2t} \end{bmatrix}$$

Taking $T = 0.1$ second, then to six-place accuracy,

$$A(0.1) = \begin{bmatrix} 1 & 0.090635 \\ 0 & 0.818731 \end{bmatrix}$$

(b) The matrix series of Eq. (4-4) begins with

$$\begin{bmatrix} 1 & 0 \\ 0 & 1 \end{bmatrix} + \begin{bmatrix} 0 & 0.1 \\ 0 & -0.2 \end{bmatrix} + \begin{bmatrix} 0 & -0.01 \\ 0 & 0.02 \end{bmatrix} + \begin{bmatrix} 0 & 0.00066 \\ 0 & -0.00133 \end{bmatrix} + \cdots$$

Since the first column of $A(0.1)$ is determined by the first term and does not change thereafter, we will concentrate on elements $a_{12}$ and $a_{22}$ of the second column. After four terms we already have four-place accuracy:

$$\begin{bmatrix} a_{12} \\ a_{22} \end{bmatrix} = \begin{bmatrix} 0.09067 \\ 0.81867 \end{bmatrix}$$

The fifth term's second column is

$$\begin{bmatrix} -0.000033 \\ 0.000066 \end{bmatrix}$$

Note that the amount to be "added" on to the partial sum of four terms is zero to within the four-place accuracy already attained. ∎

Admittedly, the ZOH equivalent is a simple model of the continuous-time input signals and may be somewhat inaccurate unless, as in a digital control system, the effect of the DAC closely resembles the ZOH model. A straight simulation of a continuous-time input driving a continuous-time system where the input is described only by its uniform samples can easily be improved. One method is to linearly interpolate between input samples to reconstruct the driving signals; this is illustrated in Fig. 4-2. From Fig. 4-2 we write the straight-line relation

$$\mathbf{u}(t) = [(t - kT)/T]\mathbf{u}(kT + T) + [(kT + T - t)/T]\mathbf{u}(kT) \qquad (4\text{-}9)$$

With this more elaborate model of the inputs the general solution to the state equation, given by Eq. (3-26), can be used (in much the same manner as was done in Section 3-4 for the ZOH model) to arrive at the "extended" discrete-time model

$$\mathbf{x}(k + 1) = \Phi(T)\mathbf{x}(k) + \theta(T)\mathbf{u}(k) + \Psi(T)\mathbf{u}(k + 1) \qquad (4\text{-}10)$$

where the $T$ factor has been dropped from the signal arguments to simplify notation and

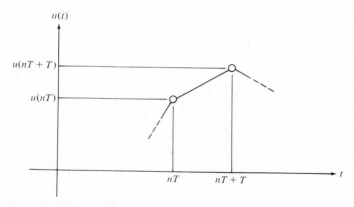

**FIGURE 4-2. Linearly interpolated input sequence.**

$$\Phi(T) = \sum_{k=0}^{\infty} (T^k/k!)F^k$$

$$\theta(T) = \sum_{k=0}^{\infty} [(k + 1)/(k + 2)!]T^{k+1}F^kG$$

$$\Psi(T) = \sum_{k=0}^{\infty} [T^{k+1}/(k + 2)!]F^kG$$

Equation (4-10) evaluates the present state as a weighted sum of present input, past input, and past state. The coefficient matrices would have to be handled numerically as was discussed for $A$ and $B$ of Eq. (4-3). We will not pursue higher-order developments along this line.

**4-2**

## DIGITAL FILTER TECHNIQUES

In the previous section we were primarily interested in exact calculations of systems with approximate inputs; that is to say, our model was based on the type of interpolation made on the input samples. This section deals with a slightly different approach conceptually—one which has been typical for modeling continuous-time systems in the literature on digital filters.

A simple definition for a digital filter (for our purposes) is a digital algorithm that in some way mimicks the effect of an analog device. We will not delve beyond the very elementary considerations of digital filters. The principal reason for including this section is to gain a feel for "digital redesign"; that is, conversion of an analog (controller) design into a digital controller with similar performance.

The particular techniques which we will consider in this section are

1. Impulse Response Matching
2. Numerical Integration
3. Pole–Zero Mapping

### 4-2.1 Impulse Response Matching

With this approach we are trying to determine a discrete-time filter (or transfer function) whose unit-pulse response matches the samples of the continuous-time-system unit-impulse response function $h(t)$. Recall that a linear system may be described by its unit-impulse response function $h(t)$ in that the output $y(t)$ can be written in terms of the input $u(t)$ by the convolution integral

$$y(t) = \int_{-\infty}^{t} h(t - \lambda)u(\lambda)\, d\lambda \tag{4-11}$$

Note that $C \exp [At]B$ is the unit-impulse response for the state model; see Eq. (3-26).

To develop the digital filter corresponding to a given (scalar) $h(t)$ we conceptually sample to obtain $\{h(kT), k = 0, 1, 2, \ldots\}$ and view the sequence as being the unit-pulse response of the digital filter. Actually, to preserve the proper amplitudes, the $h(kT)$ sequence must be scaled by a factor of $T$. But, aside from the factor of $T$, this is simply a discrete-time transfer function given by the $z$-transform of $h(t)$. In particular,

$$D(z) = Z\{Th(kT)\} \qquad (4\text{-}12)$$

Variations of this expression arise when it is recognized that the transfer function $H(s)$ is the Laplace transform of $h(t)$. A later expression (following the discussion of Fig. 4-3) will supersede Eq. (4-12) whenever $h(t)$ has discontinuities.

### EXAMPLE 4-2

For the simple "low-pass" filter given by the $RC$ network shown, derive a discrete-time algorithm which will approximate the filter's effect by using impulse response matching. Assume ideal source and measurement for the network.

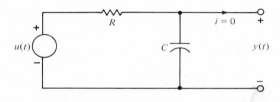

*SOLUTION:* The voltage-to-voltage transfer function for the above-mentioned network is easily obtained (using, for instance, a single mesh equation) to be

$$H(s) = 1/(\tau s + 1), \quad \tau = RC$$

Thus,

$$h(t) = (1/\tau)e^{-t/\tau}, \qquad t \geq 0$$
$$= 0, \qquad t < 0$$

Applying Eq. (4-12),

$$D(z) = Z\{(T/\tau)e^{-kT/\tau}\}$$

From Table 2-2 (entry 4)

$$D(z) = az/(z - e^{-a}) = Y(z)/U(z), \quad a = T/\tau$$

The corresponding "algorithm" between input and output signal samples could be obtained by first cross-multiplying to get

$$(z - e^{-a})Y(z) = azU(z)$$

Thus,

$$y(k) = au(k) + e^{-a}y(k - 1)$$

could be easily programmed on a digital computer to provide the low-pass filter effect on the samples of input voltage $u$. In the next section we will see a minor modification of the above result. ∎

## 4-2.2 Frequency Response of Digital Filters

Our need for transform domains has until now been limited to $s$- and $z$-planes. Often, however, it is more convenient to make arguments in the domain of real (radian) frequency, $\omega$. This parameter is closely associated with the $s$-domain variable. In particular, a continuous-time transform $H(s)$ may be described by its values along $s = j\omega$ as $\omega$ varies from 0 to $\infty$. Since $H(j\omega)$ is generally complex-valued, the description typically takes the form of two real-valued graphs:

1. $|H(j\omega)|$ versus $\omega$
2. Arg $H(j\omega)$ [or angle of $H(j\omega)$ versus $\omega$]

In a similar manner we can describe the *frequency response* of a digital filter, $D(z)$, to be the complex-valued function $D(e^{j\omega T})$. The reason for this argument stems from the ideas of Section 2-6.1 and Section A-3.

In the study of digital filters the real frequency domain plays a key role in comparing the quality of one filter versus another. We can use the concept to compare the frequency responses of the continuous-time system with that of approximating discrete-time systems. This is a useful approach since both types of systems will have a continuous frequency response.

### EXAMPLE 4-3
For a comparison of our result of Example 4-2, we will plot the two filter response magnitudes for $\tau = 1$ and $T = 0.2$, 0.4, and 0.8 sec. Thus,

$$H(j\omega) = \frac{1}{1 + j\omega}, \quad D(e^{j\omega T}) = \frac{T\,e^{j\omega T}}{e^{j\omega T} - e^{-T}}$$

Figure 4-3 shows $|H|$ and $|D|$ plotted versus $\omega$. In checking these results it is convenient to use Euler's identity for reducing $D$, namely, $e^{j\omega T} = \cos \omega T + j \sin \omega T$. ∎

Program 4 in Appendix D is a useful aid in obtaining the frequency response of a discrete-time transfer function once the fundamental idea has been mastered.

Let us now examine the results presented in Fig. 4-3. The lower curve represents the desired frequency response curve. The upper three curves are the achieved responses of the digital filters designed according to Eq. (4-12). We see good correspondence for small frequencies, except for a vertical displacement of the curves. We also know that the frequency response of a digital filter is periodic in $\omega$ with period $2\pi/T$. Note that the period of the upper curve is

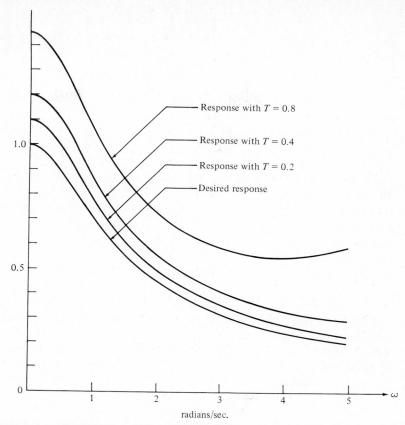

**FIGURE 4-3.** Comparison of digital filter designs by impulse response matching; plots of magnitude frequency response for example 4—3.

$2\pi/0.8 = 7.85$, which shows up as even symmetry around 3.93. The vertical displacements are caused by sampling $h(t)$ at $t = 0$ to get 1. To eliminate this problem, the samples at discontinuities of a function must be taken at the midpoint of the step. Thus, for Example 4.3 the samples to be used in Eq. (4-4) should have been as illustrated in Fig. 4-4. Thus, if the samples of $h(t)$ fall at discontinuous points of $h$, then the samples are placed at

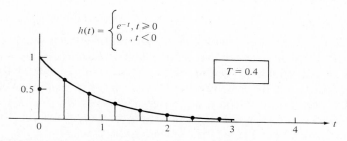

**FIGURE 4-4.** Proper sampling at a discontinuity.

$$\tfrac{1}{2}[h(kT^+) + h(kT^-)] \qquad (4\text{-}13)$$

where the superscript $+$ and $-$ mean the limit of $h(kT)$ from the right and from the left, respectively. Thus, Eq. (4-12) should read

$$D(z) = Z\{(T/2)[h(kT^+) + h(kT^-)]\} \qquad (4\text{-}14)$$

Note that expression (4-13) reduces to $h(kT)$ when $kT$ is a continuous point of $h(t)$.

In Example 4-3 the correct $D(z)$ is

$$D(z) = az/(z - e^{-a}) - a/2 \qquad (4\text{-}15)$$

The term subtracted off will eliminate the vertical displacements of the digital filter responses shown in Fig. 4-3.

In the next section we will investigate some numerical methods of representing continuous-time systems.

## 4-2.3  Numerical Integration

As we have seen in Chapter 3, it is possible to represent linear continuous-time transfer functions in terms of ideal integrators, $s^{-1}$ blocks, plus gains and summing junctions. Not to wander too far into the density of numerical analysis, we will concentrate on the basic operation of (scalar) integration and its approximations. In particular, consider the (ideal) integration of a continuous function $f$,

$$i(t) = \int_0^t f(\tau)\, d\tau \qquad (4\text{-}16)$$

Our problem will be to calculate approximate values for $i(t)$ in some reasonable way given samples of the integrand $f(t)$. The numerical evaluation of $i(t)$ from the sample points of $f(t)$ is the alternative to a closed-form solution and is indispensable when $f(t)$ is not in some convenient analytical form. As we shall see, the key step in evaluating $i(t)$ is the method of approximating $f(t)$ from its sample values, $f(kT)$, $k = 0, 1, 2, \ldots$. Once the approximation for $f(t)$ has been obtained, that for $i(t)$ follows routinely. The present discussion will be limited to considering polynomial curve fits for approximating $f(t)$. For example, the notation $f_0(t)$ might be used to represent the piecewise *constant* function

$$f_0(t) = f(kT), \quad kT \le t < kT + T \qquad (4\text{-}17)$$

and $f_1(t)$, to represent a piecewise *linear* approximation which simply approximates $f(t)$ by linearly interpolating between sample values (see Fig. 4-2).

Let us first determine $i_0(t)$ using Eq. (4-17) to evaluate Eq. (4-16). Our procedure will be to (conceptually) differentiate $f_0(t)$ once to obtain a sequence of impulses whose values represent the step amplitudes of $f_0(t)$. The idea is illustrated in Fig. 4-5. If $f(-T)$ is taken to be zero, we note that the derivative ''amplitudes'' correspond to a discrete-time sequence given by

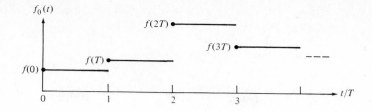

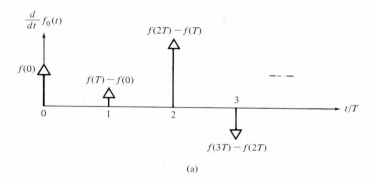

(a)

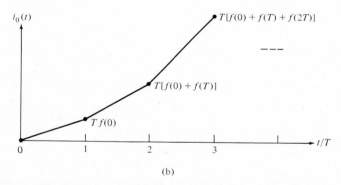

(b)

**FIGURE 4-5.** (a) Approximation of f(t) and its derivative; (b) $i_0(t)$, the Integral of $f_0(t)$.

$$\frac{d}{dt} f_0(t) = \sum_{k=0}^{\infty} [f(kT) - f(kT - T)] \, \delta(t - kT) \qquad (4\text{-}18)$$

where the right-hand side is interpreted as an ideal impulse-sampled signal; see Eq. (1-9). In the (Laplace) transform domain

$$I_0(s) = \left(\frac{1}{s}\right) F_0(s) = \left(\frac{1}{s^2}\right) \mathscr{L}\left\{\left(\frac{d}{dt}\right) f_0(t)\right\} \qquad (4\text{-}19)$$

where the extra $s^{-1}$ factor is the inverse of the differentiation of $f_0$. Recalling Eq. (2-2), we obtain from Eqs. (4-18) and (4-19) that

$$I_0(s) = \frac{1}{s^2} \sum_{k=0}^{\infty} [f(kT) - f(kT - T)]e^{-kTs}$$

The similarity to the $z$-transform notation, see Eq. (2-3) and Eq. (2-4), leads us to write

$$I_0(z) = Z[I_0(s)] = Z[s^{-2}] \sum_{k=0}^{\infty} [f(kT) - f(kT - T)]z^{-k}$$

or

$$I_0(z) = Z[s^{-2}] F(z)(1 - z^{-1}) \tag{4-20}$$

Finally, we recognize that $(1 - z^{-1}) = (Z[s^{-1}])^{-1}$ from entry 1 of Table 2-2 and write that the transform of the (sampled) output $i_0$ in terms of the transform of the sampled input $f_0$ is

$$I_0(z) = \frac{Z[s^{-2}]}{Z[s^{-1}]} F(z) \tag{4-21}$$

Notice that $F(z)$ is the $z$-transform of the original set of samples and no subscript is required. It is a simple matter to refer to Table 2-2 to find that the equivalent discrete-time transfer function (approximating the original continuous-time transfer function of $s^{-1}$) is

$$\frac{I_0(z)}{F(z)} = \frac{T}{z - 1} \tag{4-22}$$

Check the result of Fig. 4-5 to see that it conforms to this analytical result. This numerical approximation corresponds to a "forward rectangular rule" of integration.

For the *linearly* interpolated approximation to $f(t)$, namely, $f_1(t)$, we could repeat the process by first differentiating *twice* to obtain a series of impulses whence, corresponding to Eq. (4-19)

$$I_1(s) = (1/s)F_1(s) = (1/s^3)\mathcal{L}\{(d^2/dt^2)f_1(t)\}$$

leading to

$$I_1(z) = Z[s^{-3}]F(z)\{T^{-1}z^{-1}(z - 1)^2\}$$

where the factor in the braces arrives from the fact that the amplitudes of the impulses in Eq. (4-18) would be of the form [after two derivatives of $f_1(t)$]

$$T^{-1}[f(kT + T) - 2f(kT) + f(kT - T)]$$

Finally, after consulting Table 4-1, we find that the next higher approximation to $s^{-1}$ is the discrete-time transfer function

$$\frac{I_1(z)}{F(z)} = \frac{Z[s^{-3}]}{Z[s^{-2}]} = \frac{T(z + 1)}{2(z - 1)} \tag{4-23}$$

**TABLE 4-1** *z*-Domain Equivalents of Pure Integrations

| *s*-Domain | *z*-Domain |
|---|---|
| $s^{-1}$ | $z(z - 1)^{-1}$ |
| $s^{-2}$ | $Tz(z - 1)^{-2}$ |
| $s^{-3}$ | $(1/2) T^2 z(z + 1)(z - 1)^{-3}$ |
| $s^{-4}$ | $(1/6) T^3 z(z^2 + 4z + 1)(z - 1)^{-4}$ |
| $s^{-5}$ | $(1/24) T^4 z(z^3 + 11z^2 + 11z + 1)(z - 1)^{-5}$ |
| $s^{-6}$ | $(1/120) T^5 z(z^4 + 26z^3 + 66z^2 + 26z + 1)(z - 1)^{-6}$ |

where the subscript 1 indicates that the approximation to $f(t)$ was the linearly interpolated function $f_1(t)$. In this case one more derivative is required to reduce $f_1(t)$ to a sequence of impulse functions. Equation (4-23) corresponds to the trapezoidal rule of integration. Similarly, Simpson's rule is given by

$$\frac{I_2(z)}{F(z)} = \frac{Z[s^{-4}]}{Z[s^{-3}]} = \frac{T(z^2 + 4z + 1)}{3(z^2 - 1)} \tag{4-24}$$

where $I_2$ indicates that a quadratic fit of the integrand data was made. It can be shown that the generalization to higher- and higher-order (more accurate) approximations follows the same pattern:

$$\frac{I_N(z)}{F(z)} = \frac{Z[s^{-(N+2)}]}{Z[s^{-(N+1)}]}, \qquad \text{for } N = 0, 1, 2, \ldots \tag{4-25}$$

Table 4-1 is provided for use in developing particular *z*-domain transfer functions associated with Eq. (4-25).

*Numerical Differentiation.* In like manner we can define various approximations for

$$d(t) = (d/dt)f(t) \tag{4-26}$$

From the previous development, the reciprocal of Eq. (4-22) gives us

$$D_0(z) = T^{-1}(z - 1)F(z)$$

or

$$D_0(z) = Z[s^{-1}]/Z[s^{-2}]F(z) \tag{4-27}$$

In its generalization, the *N*th-order approximation for $s$, when needed, is given by

$$\frac{D_N(z)}{F(z)} = \frac{Z[s^{-(N+1)}]}{Z[s^{-(N+2)}]} \qquad \text{for } N = 0, 1, 2, \ldots \tag{4-28}$$

Note that the approximations for $s$ are reciprocals of the corresponding approximations for $s^{-1}$. To illustrate an application of the previous developments, we will use Eq. (4-23) to create a digital filter to represent a simple first-order filter in the following example. This particular approach has been called Tustin's method and, more generally, is a "bilinear transformation" from the $s$-plane to the $z$-plane.

### EXAMPLE 4-4 (Tustin's Method)

To develop a discrete-time transfer function to correspond to the analog filter

$$H(s) = 1/(\tau s + 1)$$

*SOLUTION:* We may directly substitute, from Eq. (4-28) with $N = 2$,

$$s = (2/T)[(z - 1)/(z + 1)] \tag{4-29}$$

or, in some cases, it may be more convenient to write

$$H(s) = (s^{-1})/(\tau + s^{-1})$$

and substitute for $s^{-1}$, from Eq. (4-23). The result is, of course, the same either way, namely that

$$\hat{H}(z) = \frac{T(z + 1)}{(T + 2\tau)z + (T - 2\tau)} \tag{4-30}$$

In comparing $H(s)$ with $\hat{H}(z)$, two approaches will be taken:

1. A time-domain unit-step response
2. A magnitude frequency response

Both will be calculated with $\tau = 1$ and $T = 0.8$ sec; thus,

$$\hat{H}(z) = (2z + 2)/(7z - 3) \tag{4-31}$$

Comparison:

(1) The result of the step-response calculations are

$$h(t) = 1 - e^{-t}, \qquad t \geq 0$$
$$\hat{h}(k) = 1 - (5/7)(3/7)^k, \qquad k \geq 0$$

These are shown in Fig. 4-6a. Except for a large initial discrepancy which decays with time, the two responses are quite similar.

*Remark:* In dealing with control systems it may be reasonable to use a step-input as a test situation; but, as has been mentioned previously, a more meaningful test between two *filters* is a comparison of their frequency responses.

(2) The plots of magnitude frequency response are shown in Fig. 4-6b. Again $\tau = 1$ and $T = 0.8$ sec:

$$H(j\omega) = 1/(1 + j\omega)$$
$$\hat{H}(e^{j0.8\omega}) = \frac{2 e^{j0.8\omega} + 2}{7 e^{j0.8\omega} - 3}$$

Using Euler's identity

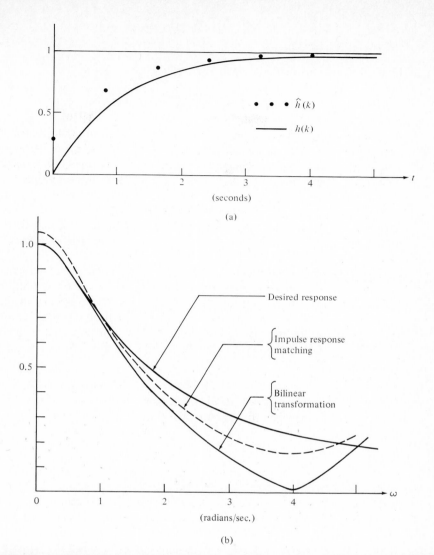

**FIGURE 4-6.** Comparisons for example 4-4: (a) unit-step responses; (b) magnitude frequency responses.

$$\hat{H}(e^{j0.8\omega}) = \frac{(2c + 2) + j2s}{(7c - 3) + j7s}$$

where

$$c = \cos (0.8\omega), \quad s = \sin (0.8\omega)$$

In addition to plots of $|H|$ and $|\hat{H}|$, a third response is included in Fig. 4-6b, that of $|D|$, where $D$, given in Eq. (4-15), is the corrected version of the digital filter designed by impulse response matching. Thus, with $a = T = 0.8$,

$$D(e^{j0.8\omega}) = \frac{0.8e^{j0.8\omega}}{e^{j0.8\omega} - e^{-0.8}} - \frac{0.8}{2}$$

Using the previous notation $c$ and $s$, $D$ reduces to

$$D(e^{j0.8\omega}) = \frac{0.4[c + e^{-0.8}) + js]}{(c - e^{-0.8}) + js}$$

the magnitude of which is presented as a dashed curve in Fig. 4-6b. The reader should take the time to compare $|D|$ in Fig. 4-6b with the upper curve of Fig. 4-3. In particular, note that the vertical shift has been virtually eliminated with the corrected sampling. As expected, both digital filters begin to repeat periodically near $\omega = 4$ radians per second. Also, both offer reasonable reproductions of the desired frequency response at low frequencies.

*Remark:* A more detailed comparison would take into account both magnitude and phase (or real and imaginary parts) of the frequency functions. ∎

*Frequency Prewarping.* The bilinear transformation (or Tustin's method) has a nice feature in that the transformation, Eq. (4-29), maps the stability region (left-half plane) of the $s$-plane into the stability region of the $z$-plane (the interior of the unit circle). In other words, using this method on a stable continuous-time filter $H(s)$ ensures that the resulting $\hat{H}(z)$ will also be stable. This is a property that not all numerical transformations possess. To test a particular transformation, say,

$$s = f(z) \quad \text{or} \quad z = f^{-1}(s) \tag{4-32}$$

one would calculate how the stability boundary, the $j\omega$ axis, of the $s$-plane is mapped into the $z$-plane. For example, the "forward rectangular rule" given in Eq. (4-22)

$$s = (z - 1)/T \quad \text{or} \quad z = 1 + Ts \tag{4-33}$$

clearly maps the $s = j\omega$ axis into the $z = 1$ axis, $(z = 1 + j\omega T$ as $\omega$ varies from $-\infty$ to $\infty)$. For most of the transformations implied by Eq. (4-25), the mapping of the left-half $s$-plane is much more difficult to determine.

One undesirable property of the bilinear transformation is that in mapping the infinite $\omega$ axis into the $2\pi$ length of circumference of the unit circle a severe "warping" of frequency points occurs. To be specific, since the bilinear transformation implies that

$$z = (2 + Ts)/(2 - Ts) \tag{4-34}$$

which is not the true relation between $s$ and $z$ $(z = e^{sT})$, there is a natural distortion of the frequencies in using this design method. In particular, if $s = j\omega_0$, where $\omega_0$ is a critical design frequency such as a cutoff frequency for a low-pass filter or the 180° phase-shift frequency of a compensator, then from Eq. (4-29)

$$j\omega_0 = \frac{2(e^{j\omega T} - 1)}{T(e^{j\omega T} + 1)} \tag{4-35}$$

where $\omega_0$ is the true frequency value and $\omega$ (unsubscripted) is the achieved value. By first writing Eq. (4-35) in the form

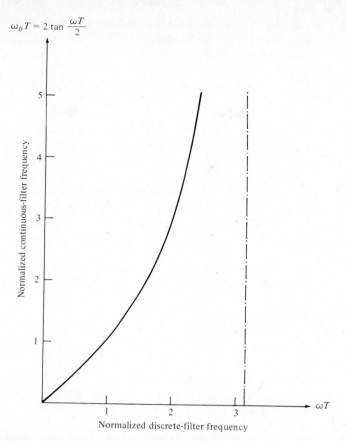

$\omega_0 T = 2 \tan \dfrac{\omega T}{2}$

Normalized continuous-filter frequency

5 —

4 —

3 —

2 —

1 —

1       2       3     $\omega T$

Normalized discrete-filter frequency

**FIGURE 4-7.** **Curve showing frequency distortion incurred with the bilinear tranformation.**

$$j\omega_0 = \frac{2}{T} \frac{e^{j(\omega T/2)}(e^{j(\omega T/2)} - e^{-j(\omega T/2)})}{e^{j(\omega T/2)}(e^{j(\omega T/2)} + e^{-j(\omega T/2)})} \tag{4-36}$$

we easily arrive at the frequency relation

$$\omega_0 = (2/T) \tan(\omega T/2) \tag{4-37}$$

that is, a true frequency $\omega_0$ will be naturally warped into $\omega < \omega_0$. This relation is graphed in Fig. 4-7. Note the severity of the distortions as the curve approaches the asymptotic line at $\omega T = \pi$. Fortunately, most control situations fall in the low-frequency range, where the graph is nearly linear.

The idea of "prewarping" is simply to adjust the original $s$-plane design so that after application of the transformation, repeated here from Eq. (4-29),

$$s = (2/T)(z - 1)/(z + 1) \tag{4-38}$$

the critical frequencies will be at the desired locations. The following sequence of operations will help to establish the technique.

**Step 1.** Prewarp critical frequencies of specifications using Eq. (4-37) or Fig. 4-7, that is, convert to higher frequencies initially so that the subsequent design will warp back to the desired values.

**Step 2.** Design a continuous-time filter $H(s)$ to meet the specifications at the prewarped frequencies.

**Step 3.** Transform $H(s)$ to the designed digital filter $\hat{H}(z)$ using Eq. (4-38).

We will conclude this discussion with a simple example to illustrate the technique of prewarping.

### EXAMPLE 4-5 (Bilinear Transformation with Prewarping)

Using a sampling frequency of 10 Hz ($T = 0.1$ sec), we wish to perform a "digital redesign" of the compensator filter function

$$H(s) = \omega_0/(s + \omega_0)$$

where

$$\omega_0 = 16.$$

*SOLUTION:* First we rewrite the desired filter as

$$H(j\omega) = \frac{1}{1 + j(\omega/\omega_0)} = \frac{1}{1 + j(\omega/16)} \tag{4-39}$$

1. Prewarping: Instead of immediately substituting for $s$ according to Eq. (4-38), recognizing that natural warping would cause the desired value of 16 to be reduced to about 13.5 (from Fig. 4-7), we first calculate a prewarped parameter, from Eq. (4-37),

$$\omega_0' = (2/0.1) \tan [16(0.1)/2] = 20.6$$

Keep in mind the prewarped frequencies will be larger than the original desired frequencies.

2. Now Tustin's method can be applied:

$$\hat{H}(z) = \frac{20.6}{\dfrac{20(z - 1)}{z + 1} + 20.6} = \frac{0.5074(z + 1)}{z + 0.0148} \tag{4-40}$$

This is the final digital filter design. As a check we note that $|H(j16)| = 0.7071$ in Eq. (4-39). Calculating from Eq. (4-40),

$$\hat{H}(e^{j1.6}) = 0.7072$$

The difference in the fourth decimal place is due to a lack of precision in determining $\omega_0'$. ∎

We will now conclude our brief study of digital filter techniques by considering a very natural means of designing a digital filter from a known continuous-time transfer function.

## 4-2.4 Pole–Zero Mapping

As control engineers we are aware that a rational function is completely described by the locations of its poles and zeros plus a gain parameter. In addition, we know the exact relation between the continuous-time $s$-plane and the discrete-time $z$-plane. So it should not be surprising that a simple translation of critical frequencies from $s$-plane to $z$-plane via

$$z = e^{sT} \tag{4-41}$$

would provide a good digital redesign method. One minor problem is that a continuous-time transfer function $H(s)$ will usually possess more poles than zeros; thus, it must be determined how these ''zeros at infinity'' are handled. Of the various methods that have been used, the approach that places a zero at $z = -1$ for each excess pole of $H(s)$ appears to be favored. Lastly, the gain of the digital filter function $\hat{H}(z)$ can be matched to that of $H(s)$ at some appropriate frequency, for instance, at $dc$ ($s = 0$ and $z = 1$) for a low-pass function. As a summary, the pole–zero mapping technique requires the following, given a rational $H(s)$:

1. Each pole and (finite) zero of $H(s)$ is calculated and transformed into a $z$-plane value according to Eq. (4-41).
2. Each zero of $H(s)$ at $s = \infty$ is mapped into $z = -1$.
3. The filter gains are matched at an appropriate frequency, for instance at dc,

$$H(0) = \hat{H}(1) \tag{4-42}$$

As an illustration of this technique, consider the following example.

### EXAMPLE 4-6 (Pole–Zero Mapping)
Given the controller (compensator) transfer function

$$H(s) = \frac{10(s + 1)}{(s + 5)(s + 10)}$$

we wish to determine an approximate digital filter function $\hat{H}(z)$ using the pole–zero mapping technique and a sampling rate of 10 Hz.

*SOLUTION:* Following step 1:

- the zero at $s = -1$ is mapped into $z = e^{-T} = e^{-0.1} = 0.905$.
- the pole at $s = -5$ is mapped into $z = e^{-0.5} = 0.607$.
- the pole at $s = -10$ is mapped into $z = e^{-1} = 0.368$.

Thus,

$$\hat{H}(z) = \frac{K(z + 1)(z - 0.905)}{(z - 0.607)(z - 0.368)}$$

where the $(z + 1)$ factor has been added for the zero at $s = \infty$. From step 3:

$$H(0) = 0.2 \stackrel{\text{set}}{=} \hat{H}(1) = 0.765K$$

Thus,

$$K = 0.261$$

and

$$\hat{H}(z) = \frac{0.261(z + 1)(z - 0.905)}{(z - 0.607)(z - 0.368)}$$

is the final design. ∎

In connection with pole–zero mapping, we mention one extension to the basic problem of modeling a rational (continuous-time) transfer function into the $z$-domain.

***Transport Delay.*** It is not unusual for a plant or process to have a non-negligible pure time delay as part of its description. In particular, the time delay caused by physical motion such as fluid traveling in a pipe is a typical factor in transfer functions of chemical processes. We know from Laplace theory (Appendix B) that a pure delay of $\tau$ seconds in time can be represented as an $s$-domain factor of $e^{-s\tau}$. Thus, a continuous-time model of the form

$$G(s) = H(s)e^{-s\tau} \tag{4-43}$$

will be a nonrational function of $s$. The pure delay term is called *transport delay*, also *transportation lag* or *dead time*.

The modeling of transport delay can be handled in several ways; however, we will limit our consideration to pole–zero mapping. Recall the basic property of $z$-transformations from Eq. (2-16) that

$$Z\{f(k - n)\} = z^{-n}F(z) \tag{4-44}$$

If the time delay in Eq. (4-43) is an integer multiple of the sampling interval $T$, say, $\tau = nT$, then the transport delay factor $e^{-s\tau}$ can be mapped into $z^{-n}$ ($n$ poles at $z = 0$). More generally, we will assume that

$$\tau = nT + \Delta \tag{4-45}$$

where $\Delta$ is the amount of time (delay) that $\tau$ exceeds an integer ($n$) number of sample intervals. Since

$$e^{-s\tau} = (e^{-sT})^n e^{-\Delta s} \tag{4-46}$$

the problem of mapping $e^{-s\tau}$ becomes a problem of mapping $e^{-\Delta s}$ where $\Delta$ is now "small." In achieving our result, we write that

$$e^{-\Delta s} = \frac{e^{(-\Delta s/2)}}{e^{(\Delta s/2)}} \cong \frac{1 - (\Delta/2)s}{1 + (\Delta/2)s} \tag{4-47}$$

where the final expression represents a ratio of the truncated exponential series. This is our desired rational approximation for $\exp(-\Delta s)$. The approximation of Eq. (4-47) can be included with the rational part of $G(s)$ in Eq. (4-43) when applying the pole–zero mapping technique.

## EXAMPLE 4-7 (Transport Delay)

We wish to determine a digital filter equivalent to the analog transfer function

$$G(s) = [2/(s + 2)]e^{-0.85s}$$

using the pole–zero mapping approach if the sample rate is 4 Hz.

**SOLUTION:** Since $T = 1/4$ sec,

$$e^{-0.85s} = e^{-3Ts} e^{-0.10s}, \quad (\Delta = 0.10 \text{ sec})$$

From Eq. (4-47)

$$e^{-0.1s} \cong \frac{1 - 0.05s}{1 + 0.05s} = -\frac{s - 20}{s + 20}$$

Pole–zero mapping: From the continuous-time system

$$G(s) = \frac{-2(s - 20)}{(s + 2)(s + 20)} e^{-3Ts}$$

we obtain

$$\hat{G}(z) = \frac{K(z + 1)(z - 148)}{z^3(z - 0.607)(z - 0.007)} \tag{4-48}$$

Note that the unit-pulse response of the resulting digital filter $\hat{G}(z)$ starts off with a pure delay of three sample steps due to the $z^3$ in the denominator. ∎

The general technique of modeling transport delay presented above can be used in obtaining other models such as a ZOH equivalent discrete-time system; see Section 2-4.2 and Eq. (2-45), in particular, to review the details. Using the notation of Eqs. (4-43) and (4-46), Eq. (2-45) becomes

$$G_d(z) = (1 - z^{-1})z^{-n}Z\left\{s^{-1}H(s)\frac{1 - (\Delta/2)s}{1 + (\Delta/2)s}\right\} \tag{4-49}$$

In many situations, $\tau$ may be rounded to the nearest integer multiple of $T$ to simplify the calculations. Alternatively, the ZOH equivalent can be approximated by writing, instead of Eq. (4-45),

$$\tau = (n + 1)T - \delta \tag{4-50}$$

where $\delta$ is the time needed to extend $\tau$ to the next integer multiple of $T$. Thus, the ZOH calculation becomes

$$\hat{G}_d(z) = (1 - z^{-1})z^{-(n+1)}Z\{(1/s)H(s)e^{\delta s}\} \tag{4-51}$$

The difference comes in the evaluation of the z-transform. For example, in the case of the previous example,

$$\hat{G}_d(z) = (1 - z^{-1})z^{-4} Z\left\{\frac{2e^{0.15s}}{s(s + 2)}\right\}$$

$$\hat{G}_d(z) = (z^{-4} - z^{-5}) Z\left\{\frac{1}{s} + \frac{-e^{-0.3}}{s + 2}\right\} \tag{4-52}$$

$$\hat{G}_d(z) = \frac{0.259z + 0.134}{z^4(z - 0.607)}$$

Compare results obtained in Eqs. (4-48) and (4-52) to see that a variety of different forms may be used to approximate a given analog function. This concludes our discussion of "digital filter techniques" as such, although the whole chapter is devoted to digitizing techniques of one kind or another. In the next section the simple ZOH method is extended to form a useful *ad hoc* simulation tool; that is, one which can be adapted quickly to a particular control system to evaluate its performance.

**4-3**

## HOMOGENEOUS EQUIVALENT SYSTEMS

For the control engineer, simulation work is usually of a very specific type. In particular, his dealings with system simulation typically fall into the category of a preliminary test of the effect of a newly designed controller on system performance. The engineer recognizes the fact that his design almost always incorporates various approximations related to plant model and disturbance inputs as well as idealizations of sampling and signal conversion. The simulation phase is thus a necessary part of any control system design—to verify, as nearly as possible, whether the design will achieve the required specifications and, if not, provide some indication of where the problems lie.

In keeping with the motivation of "testing a control system," command inputs will be restricted to the form of (piecewise) polynomial time functions or damped sinusoidal functions in the following development. Note that the classical "test" functions of steps, ramps, and sinusoids are included in this set of functions.

The basic ideas of the present approach to simulation can be presented in terms of simulating a system given by the following state model:

$$\dot{\mathbf{x}}(t) = A\mathbf{x}(t) + B\mathbf{r}(t) \tag{4-53}$$

$$\mathbf{y}(t) = C\mathbf{x}(t) + D\mathbf{r}(t) \tag{4-54}$$

For simplicity the coefficient matrices will be taken to be constant. It is assumed that the system inputs $\mathbf{r}(t)$ can be generated as outputs of a homogeneous linear system; that is, one having no independent forcing functions. The "input generator" system then could, in turn, be represented as a state model without an input vector:

$$\dot{\mathbf{z}}(t) = R\mathbf{z}(t) \tag{4-55}$$

$$\mathbf{r}(t) = Q\mathbf{z}(t) \tag{4-56}$$

where the (constant) matrices $R$ and $Q$ are constructed according to a method to be discussed subsequently.

By combining the system model of Eqs. (4-53) and (4-54) with the input generator of Eqs. (4-55) and (4-56), we arrive at the *homogeneous equivalent system*

$$\dot{\mathbf{v}}(t) = G\mathbf{v}(t) \qquad (4\text{-}57)$$

$$\mathbf{y}(t) = H\mathbf{v}(t) \qquad (4\text{-}58)$$

where

$$\mathbf{v} = \begin{bmatrix} \mathbf{x} \\ \mathbf{z} \end{bmatrix}, \; G = \begin{bmatrix} A & BQ \\ 0 & R \end{bmatrix}, \; H = [C \quad DQ]$$

and the simulation problem has been reduced to one of obtaining a zero-input state response.

Once a sample interval $T$ has been chosen, the transition matrix $\Phi(T) = \exp\{GT\}$ [see Eq. (4-4)] can be calculated numerically, thereby converting the continuous-time model of Eq. (4-57) to a discrete-time model that is equivalent at the sample instants; namely,

$$\mathbf{v}(kT + T) = \Phi(T)\,\mathbf{v}(kT), \quad k = 0, 1, 2, \ldots \qquad (4\text{-}59)$$

It follows from Eq. (4-58) that

$$\mathbf{y}(kT) = H\mathbf{v}(kT) \qquad (4\text{-}60)$$

Thus, we first need to construct the matrix $G$ of Eq. (4-57) and the initial vector $\mathbf{v}(0)$, then calculate $\Phi$ and use recursion on Eq. (4-59):

$$\mathbf{v}(T) = \Phi\mathbf{v}(0)$$

$$\mathbf{v}(2T) = \Phi\mathbf{v}(T) = \Phi^2\mathbf{v}(0)$$

$$\mathbf{v}(kT) = \Phi^k\mathbf{v}(0)$$

The output is determined from EQ. (4-60). An example is presented to help clarify the procedure.

### EXAMPLE 4-8 (Simulation of a Continuous-Time System)

We wish to simulate the zero-state unit-step response of a position control system with transfer function

$$T(s) = \frac{15}{s^2 + 4s + 15}$$

Using an integrator with initial condition equal to one, but no input, for generating the unit-step test function, the system flow graph is given below.

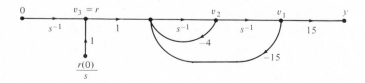

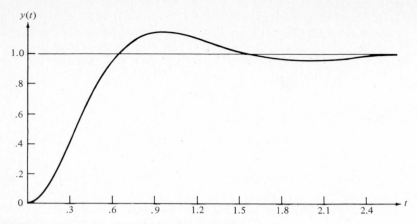

**FIGURE 4-8.  Unit step-response for example 4-8.**

Corresponding to Eqs. (4-57) and (4-58) we have

$$\dot{\mathbf{v}} = \begin{bmatrix} 0 & 1 & 0 \\ -15 & -4 & 1 \\ 0 & 0 & 0 \end{bmatrix} \mathbf{v}, \ \mathbf{v}(0) = \begin{bmatrix} 0 \\ 0 \\ 1 \end{bmatrix}$$

$$y = [\quad 15 \quad 0 \quad 0] \ \mathbf{v}$$

Note that $R = 0$ (scalar) and that $\mathbf{v}(0)$ is established from the desire that the plant be initially unenergized with a *unit* step input.

Using $T = 0.05$ sec and 15 terms of the exponential series, we find that

$$\Phi = \begin{bmatrix} 0.982494 & 0.045035 & 0.001167 \\ -0.675522 & 0.802355 & 0.045035 \\ 0 & 0 & 1 \end{bmatrix}$$

The transition matrix solution solves for $\mathbf{v}(kT)$ with better than five-place accuracy, and a plot of the output $y(t)$ is the unit step response shown in Fig. 4-8. It may be noted that a plot which is linearly interpolated between points spaced at 0.05 sec apart would appear virtually smooth to the eye, thus a simple plot program to connect the calculated output points $\{y(kT); k = 0, 1, 2, \ldots\}$ by straight lines is adequate. ∎

**4-4**

## DISCRETE-TIME SYSTEM SIMULATION

We are already well aware of the basic recursion equations of Section 3-5 and need not repeat that development here. However, to facilitate the simulation of mixed or hybrid systems containing both digital and analog processing, consider the following interpretation of a discrete-time system.

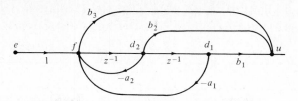

**FIGURE 4-9. Controller model for discussion.**

Given a system, say, a digital controller, with transfer function $D(z)$ given by

$$D(z) = \frac{U(z)}{E(z)} = \frac{b_3 z^2 + b_2 z + b_1}{z^2 + a_2 z + a_1} \tag{4-61}$$

relating its input $e(k)$ to its output $u(k)$, we can generate the signal-flow diagram shown in Fig. 4-9, where $d_1$ and $d_2$ are the state variables for the system.

We may have some idea of the intricate details that take place inside the computer when it is implementing the $D(z)$ algorithm of Eq. (4-61). However, from the *exterior* of our system we see the $e(k)$ sequence being clocked in and $u(k)$ being clocked out. What we want to do is to "model" the internal process that makes this happen, even though it may differ from the actual internal processes of the computer! Once this hurdle is passed, we can picture the system as operating in continuous time and assume that (for purposes of simulating exterior results) all internal changes occur *instantaneously* at the sample instants

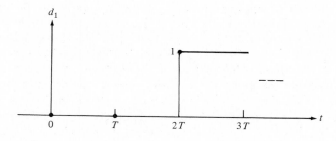

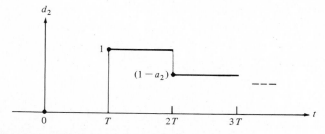

**FIGURE 4-10. Model of discrete-time states.**

and are constant otherwise. Thus, for instance, if $d_1(0) = d_2(0) = 0$ and $e(k)$ is a constant unit input, we can construct the following values by recursion from Fig. 4-9:

| k | e(k) | f(k) | d₂(k) | d₁(k) | u(k) |
|---|------|------|-------|-------|------|
| 0 | 1 | 1 | 0 | 0 | $b_3$ |
| 1 | 1 | $1 - a_2$ | 1 | 0 | $b_3f + b_2$ |
| 2 | 1 | $1 - a_1 - a_2 + a_2^2$ | $1 - a_2$ | 1 | $b_3f + b_2d_2 + b_1$ |
| | . . . | | | | |

From these values we "imagine" that the states in continuous-time appear as in Fig. 4-10 on page 169. In other words, all resetting of registers and such, for our purposes, occurs exactly at the sampling instants. In the next section we will see where this fits in.

## SIMULATION OF DIGITAL CONTROL SYSTEMS

The previous artifice of generating test functions as zero-input responses of linear systems can also be used in the context of testing sampled-data systems in which some signals are discrete and others continuous.

We will, however, not concern ourselves, at least initially, with nonlinear effects such as quantization and saturation. Using the specific structure of Fig. 4-11 as being typical, we will assume that external inputs (reference inputs) are continuous in nature, but that the control system itself contains both discrete-time dynamics as well as an analog part fed with clamped (actuator) inputs.

To establish the notation for the following development, we assume the plant is a continuous-time system described by

$$\dot{\mathbf{x}}(t) = A\mathbf{x}(t) + B\mathbf{u}(t) \qquad (4\text{-}62)$$

$$\mathbf{y}(t) = C\mathbf{x}(t) + D\mathbf{u}(t) \qquad (4\text{-}63)$$

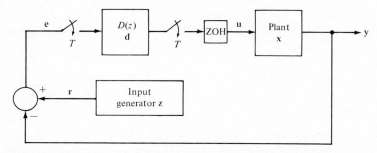

FIGURE 4-11.  Assumed direct digital control (DDC) structure.

and the inputs $\mathbf{u}(t)$ are (clamped) held constant between sample times. Since $\mathbf{u}$ is a vector, there may be many clamping or ZOH devices in the system. As before, the input generator will be taken as

$$\dot{\mathbf{z}}(t) = R\mathbf{z}(t) \tag{4-64}$$

$$\mathbf{r}(t) = Q\mathbf{z}(t) \tag{4-65}$$

The digital controller $D(z)$ will be in the form of, or will be converted to, the discrete-time state model

$$\mathbf{d}(k + 1) = E\mathbf{d}(k) + F\mathbf{e}(k) \tag{4-66}$$

$$\mathbf{u}(k) = L\mathbf{d}(k) + M\mathbf{e}(k) \tag{4-67}$$

The "total state" vector for the system will be defined as

$$\mathbf{v} = \begin{bmatrix} \mathbf{x} \\ \mathbf{u} \\ \mathbf{d} \\ \mathbf{z} \end{bmatrix} \begin{array}{l} \text{Plant states} \\ \text{Clamp outputs} \\ \text{Controller states} \\ \text{Input generator states} \end{array} \tag{4-68}$$

It should not be too surprising that $\mathbf{u}$ is included in this set since the clamp (ZOH) operation, when restricted to a sample interval, behaves as an ideal integration.

Combining our Eqs. (4-62) to (4-68), we have the following dynamics describing variation *during* the sample interval:

$$\dot{\mathbf{v}}(t) = \begin{bmatrix} A & B & 0 & 0 \\ 0 & 0 & 0 & 0 \\ 0 & 0 & 0 & 0 \\ 0 & 0 & 0 & R \end{bmatrix} \mathbf{v}(t), \quad kT < t < kT + T \tag{4-69}$$

The second and third row of zeros indicate that the elements are assumed to be constant between sample instants. (Recall the discussion of Section 4-4.) the partitioned matrix of Eq. (4-69) corresponds to the $G$ matrix used in Eq. (4-57). The procedure of producing the evolving state $\mathbf{v}(t)$ is the same as in our earlier discussion.

In particular, if $\mathbf{v}(kT)$ is known (following some sample instant), we can select a time increment $\Delta$ as shown in Fig. 4-12, calculate the transition matrix $\Phi(\Delta)$ for the system in Eq. (4-69) and determine recursively the values of $\mathbf{v}$ at

**FIGURE 4-12.** Partition of sample interval.

the times $kT + \Delta, kT + 2\Delta, \ldots, kT + N\Delta$, where we assume that the sample interval $T$ is an integer multiple of $\Delta$, $(T = N\Delta)$ for convenience.

Let us back up to find $\mathbf{v}(kT)$, which was assumed in the previous paragraph. We will denote values just prior to the sample instants and just following them with a superscript $-$ or $+$, respectively. The question at hand then is how to deal with the changes right at the sample instants. For this we define a "jump matrix" $J$ such that

$$\mathbf{v}(kT^+) = J\mathbf{v}(kT^-) \tag{4-70}$$

Note that Eq. (4-70) represents only an instantaneous change when various registers become reset to new values. Returning to Eqs. (4-62) through (4-68), the $J$ matrix for the DDC structure of Fig. 4-11 can be written as

$$\begin{bmatrix} \mathbf{x} \\ \mathbf{u} \\ \mathbf{d} \\ \mathbf{z} \end{bmatrix}_{t=kT^+} = \begin{bmatrix} I & 0 & 0 & 0 \\ -MC & -MD & L & MQ \\ -FC & -FD & E & FQ \\ 0 & 0 & 0 & I \end{bmatrix} \begin{bmatrix} \mathbf{x} \\ \mathbf{u} \\ \mathbf{d} \\ \mathbf{z} \end{bmatrix}_{t=kT^-} \tag{4-71}$$

The fact that the integrators cannot change instantaneously shows up in the first and last rows. The remaining entries are taken directly from the various equations that were assumed for the structure. Specifically, all updated values are based on the associated equations using nonupdated values. For instance, from Eq. (4-66),

$$\mathbf{d}(kT^+) = E\mathbf{d}(kT^-) + F[\mathbf{r}(kT^-) - \mathbf{y}(kT^-)] \tag{4-72}$$

Incorporating Eqs. (4-65) and (4-63), we determine that

$$\mathbf{d}(kT^+) = E\mathbf{d}(kT^-) + FQ\mathbf{z}(kT^-) - FC\mathbf{x}(kT^-) - FD\mathbf{u}(kT^-) \tag{4-73}$$

which is represented by row 3 of Eq. (4-71).

To summarize, for a given system we can through diagramming techniques or from algebraic manipulations obtain the two principal equations:

1. $\dot{\mathbf{v}}(t) = G\mathbf{v}$, which is valid for
   $kT < t < kT + T, k = 0, 1, 2, \ldots$ ; and
2. $\mathbf{v}(kT^+) = J\mathbf{v}(kT^-)$, which provides the information for resetting the states at the sample instants.

The procedure for simulating the system can now be stated. From (1) an *inter-sample response increment* $\Delta$ and the corresponding transition matrix $\Phi$ are established according to the discussion for Fig. 4-12. Having, in addition, obtained the $J$ matrix which provides the information on resetting the discrete-time states (including the clamp outputs), the algorithm begins with the initial vector $\mathbf{v}(0^-)$. The flowchart of Fig. 4-13 will help to organize our summary.

- System information consists of the matrices $G$ and $J$, the initial vector $\mathbf{v}(0^-)$ and the sampling interval $T$.
- For the specific solution, the total solution interval will be taken as $MT$ seconds, where $M$ is an integer to be given by the engineer, and the intersample

interval is chosen so that $T = N\Delta$ for some integer $N$. (The higher the value of $N$ the more refined will the intersample information be.)

- The transition matrix $\Phi = e^{G\Delta}$ is calculated. (See the discussion on this topic in Section 4-1.)
- In Fig. 4-13 $Q$ is established as the "time" variable.
- The outer loop uses the jump matrix $J$ at intervals of $T$ seconds (actual sample interval).
- The inner loop uses the transition matrix $\Phi$ at intervals of $\Delta$ seconds (the intersample interval).

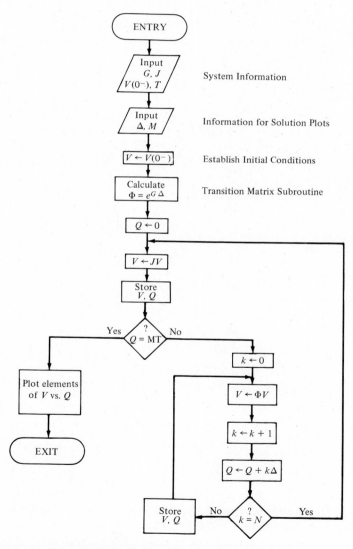

**FIGURE 4-13.  Flow chart for simulation procedure.**

- After each loop the vector $V = \mathbf{v}$ and the corresponding time $Q$ are stored.
- When the program has completed the calculations through the desired solution interval of $MT$ seconds, selected (or all) elements of the vector $V$ can be recalled for plotting versus time ($Q$).

A simple example will now be considered for purposes of illustrating the above simulation algorithm.

### EXAMPLE 4-9 (Digital Control System Simulation)

We wish to provide a plot of the response $c(t)$ for the system shown in Fig. 4-14 when $r(t)$ is a unit-step input and $c(0) = 0.2$.

*SOLUTION:* As a preliminary step toward generating the $G$ and $J$ matrices, we first draw a "hybrid" signal flow graph including the input generator (single integrator for a step input). From the SFG the vector $\mathbf{v}$ is established as the collection of signals which are outputs of integrators, delay elements or ZOHs.

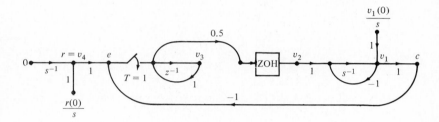

Using the SFG, we can write

$$(1) \quad \dot{\mathbf{v}}(t) = \begin{bmatrix} -1 & 1 & 0 & 0 \\ 0 & 0 & 0 & 0 \\ 0 & 0 & 0 & 0 \\ 0 & 0 & 0 & 0 \end{bmatrix} \mathbf{v}(t) \qquad \text{for } kT < t < kT + T$$

and

$$(2) \quad \mathbf{v}(kT^+) = \begin{bmatrix} 1 & 0 & 0 & 0 \\ -0.5 & 0 & 0.5 & 0.5 \\ -1 & 0 & 1 & 1 \\ 0 & 0 & 0 & 1 \end{bmatrix} \mathbf{v}(kT^-)$$

These correspond to Eqs. (4-69) and (4-71), respectively. Incorporating the initial condition information, the initial vector $\mathbf{v}(0^-) = [0.2, 0, 0, 1]^T$. We will choose a solution interval of 8 sec ($= 8T$) and an intersample spacing of $\Delta = 0.2$ sec. To simplify the formal procedure, only the first two state variables need be used for the intersample transitions (since the other two remain constant and do not affect the first two). Similarly, only $v_2$ and $v_3$ require updating at the sampling instants since $v_1$ and $v_4$ cannot change instantaneously.

Following the algorithm of Fig. 4-13,

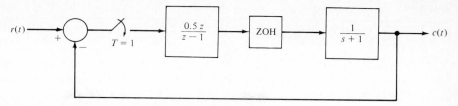

**FIGURE 4-14.** Example system for simulation.

$$\mathbf{v}(0^+) = J\mathbf{v}(0^-) = [0.2, 0.4, 0.8, 1]^T$$

$$\mathbf{v}(0.2) = \Phi\mathbf{v}(0^+) = [0.236, 0.4, 0.8, 1]^T$$

$$\mathbf{v}(0.4) = \Phi\mathbf{v}(0.2) = [0.266, 0.4, 0.8, 1]^T$$

$$\mathbf{v}(0.6) = \Phi\mathbf{v}(0.4) = [0.290, 0.4, 0.8, 1]^T$$

$$\mathbf{v}(0.8) = \Phi\mathbf{v}(0.6) = [0.310, 0.4, 0.8, 1]^T$$

$$\mathbf{v}(1.0) = J\Phi\mathbf{v}(0.8) = [0.326, 0.737, 1.474, 1]^T$$

and so on. See Fig. 4-15 for a plot of $v_1(t)$ versus $t$. Note that the $J$ matrix is used only at the sample instants. The continuous output $v_1(t)$ and the stepwise input $v_2(t)$ are shown in Fig. 4-15. Note the expected exponential behavior of the first-order plant between sample instants in response to the step inputs. Both $v_1$ and $v_2$ will settle to the constant value of $v_4$ (unity). ■

*Remarks:*
- With higher-order plants it is important to be able to investigate the continuous-time variables between sample instants as we have done. This is particularly true when sample intervals are on the order of some system time constants.
- The simulation method presented can be extended to include systems with nonuniform and multiple-rate sampling.

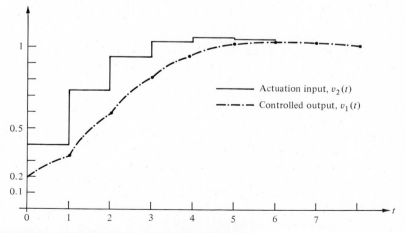

**FIGURE 4-15.** Simulation results for example 4-9.

## SOLVED PROBLEMS

In this section we try to exercise certain aspects of the chapter material in such a way as to show a comparison of related methods or to indicate extra flexibility of the approaches presented. The first general problem is one of simulating a system actuated by a "pulse-width modulated" signal.

### 4-6.1 Pulse-Width Modulated (PWM) Actuation

There are many ways in which the digital information from a computer controller can be conveyed to a plant. For instance, we are familiar with "amplitude-modulated" signals in which the amplitude of the computer word is clamped and fed into the (continuous-time) plant as a step input. Another form that has been found useful in practice is that of "pulse-width modulation." With this type of modulation the (actuation) signal is binary, that is, takes only two values. Typically, the signal is high (say, unity for convenience) following a sample instant and at some point drops to zero for the remainder of the sample interval. The "value" of the sample depends on its duration at unity. Usually a small sample will correspond to a short duration and vice versa. Figure 4-16 illustrates a pulse-width modulated (PWM) signal. Ideally, the pulse widths could take on a continuum of values, but when representing words from a digital controller, the widths would be limited to a finite number of possible values.

Consider a continuous-time plant with state dynamics described by

$$\dot{\mathbf{x}}(t) = A\mathbf{x}(t) + Bu(t) \tag{4-74}$$

where $A$ and $B$ are constant coefficient matrices. Further, let us assume that $u(t)$ is a PWM signal of the form given in Fig. 4-16 with known widths $\{w_0, w_1, w_2, \ldots\}$.

In order to develop a specific form of the solution for $\mathbf{x}(t)$, we will limit our interest in $\mathbf{x}(t)$ to its values at the sample instants only. From the general solution of Eq. (3-26), assuming $\mathbf{x}(kT)$ is known, we write that

$$\mathbf{x}(kT + w_k) = \Phi(w_k)\mathbf{x}(kT) + \Gamma(w_k) \tag{4-75}$$

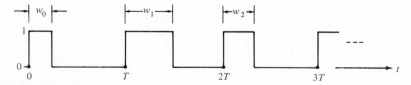

**FIGURE 4-16.  A pulse-width modulated signal.**

where $\Phi(\ )$ and $\Gamma(\ )$ are the state and input transition matrices defined in Eq. (3-34). Note that the input $u(t)$ does not show explicitly in Eq. (4-75) since its value is 1 over the interval in question. Also, we can write that

$$\mathbf{x}(kT + T) = \Phi(T - w_k)\mathbf{x}(kT + w_k) \qquad (4\text{-}76)$$

since $u(t) = 0$ for $kT + w_k < t < kT + T$. Using the properties of $\Phi$ (see Section 3-3), Eqs. (4-75) and (4-76) can be combined to give

$$\mathbf{x}(kT + T) = \Phi(T)\{\mathbf{x}(kT) + \Phi(-w_k)\Gamma(w_k)\} \qquad (4\text{-}77)$$

Let us now illustrate the use of this result.

### EXAMPLE 4-10 (dc Motor with SCR Control)

Figure 4-17 shows a dc motor with a silicon-controlled rectifier (SCR) actuator. SCR controllers are used in industrial settings where large amounts of power need to be controlled. A well-designed and fabricated SCR package is compact, robust (unaffected by vibration and shock), and reliable (no inherent failure mechanisms) and can provide a virtually limitless operating life even in a harsh environment. Basically, an SCR is a three-terminal electronic device that acts as a voltage-controlled switch, similar to a mechanical relay. The gate drive to control the SCR requires only nominal power (in the range of 5 V and 10–20 mA), but the SCR can be used to switch hundreds of amperes!

For purposes of illustrating the effect of PWM actuation, we assume that the (armature-controlled) dc motor–load combination can be modeled by the transfer function

$$\frac{\theta(s)}{U(s)} = \frac{1}{s(s + 1)}$$

and that the control signal $u(t)$ is of the PWM form as shown in Fig. 4-16 with

$$\{w_0, w_1, w_2\} = \{0.1, 0.3, 0.2\}.$$

**SOLUTION:** To calculate the response $\theta(t)$, we first write a state model for the plant as

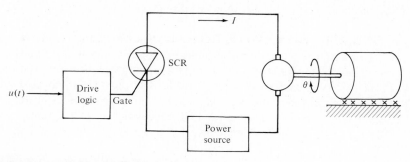

**FIGURE 4-17.   SCR controlled dc motor.**

$$\dot{\mathbf{x}}(t) = \begin{bmatrix} 0 & 1 \\ 0 & -1 \end{bmatrix} \mathbf{x}(t) + \begin{bmatrix} 0 \\ 1 \end{bmatrix} u(t)$$

$$\theta(t) = \begin{bmatrix} 1 & 0 \end{bmatrix} \mathbf{x}(t)$$

Calcultion of $\Phi(t)$ and $\Gamma(t)$ according to Eq. (3-34) yields

$$\Phi(t) = \begin{bmatrix} 1 & 1 - e^{-t} \\ 0 & e^{-t} \end{bmatrix}, \Gamma(t) = \begin{bmatrix} t - 1 + e^{-t} \\ 1 - e^{-t} \end{bmatrix}$$

With these matrices, $T = 1$, and the given pulse widths, Eq. (4-77) reduces to (after multiplication and collection of terms)

$$x_1(k + 1) = x_1(k) + (1 - e^{-1})x_2(k) + (w_k + e^{-1} - e^{w_k - 1})$$

$$x_2(k + 1) = e^{-1}x_2(k) + (e^{w_k - 1} - e^{-1})$$

Therefore, since $\theta(t) = x_1(t)$, we can calculate that with $\mathbf{x}(0) = \mathbf{0}$,

$$\theta(k) = \{0, 0.0613, 0.2571, 0.4660\}$$ ∎

### Remarks:
- If all additional input values are zero, the stored energy in the system will drive $\theta$ to a steady-state value of 0.600.
- Intersample values could have been obtained as well by using a smaller transition interval, say $\Delta = 0.1$ sec.

The reader should begin to realize soon, if not already, that the state-variable formulation is both a flexible and efficient approach to solve any type of hybrid linear system problem.

### 4-6.2  Digital Redesign

When we speak of "digital redesign," we mean a conversion from an existing analog controller to one that mimicks the analog operation, but is implemented on a digital computer. In this chapter in Section 4-2 in particular, we have discussed various methods by which a digital redesign could be carried out. Let us consider bringing into focus on one problem all of the appropriate techniques.

### EXAMPLE 4-11 (Digital Redesign of an Analog Compensator)
The transfer function below is an analog "lag" compensator, typically introduced into the forward path of a control loop to improve the steady-state behavior of the system. The particular function specified provides a gain of 10 (20 dB) for low frequencies ($\omega < 0.01$ sec$^{-1}$). For the purpose of evaluating the approximating digital designs we would like the gain at $\omega = 1$ to remain the same ($|G_c(j1)| = 1.4072$), and for convenience we take $T = 1$ sec, sampling at 1 Hz):

$$G(s) = (s + 1)/(s + 0.1)$$

We will construct digital equivalents using the following methods:

(a) ZOH equivalent
(b) Numerical integration—order zero
(c) Numerical integration—order two (Tustin)
(d) Bilinear transformation (Tustin with prewarping)
(e) Pole–zero mapping

**SOLUTION:** Given $G(s) = (s + 1)(s + 0.1)^{-1}$:

(a)

$$G_a(z) = (1 - z^{-1})Z\{s^{-1}G(s)\}$$

$$G_a(z) = \frac{z - (10e^{-0.1} - 9)}{z - e^{-0.1}}$$

$$G_a(z) = \frac{z - 0.0484}{z - 0.9048}$$

(b)

$$G_b(z) = G(s)|_{s=T^{-1}(z-1)}$$

$$G_b(z) = \frac{z}{z - 0.9}$$

(c)

$$G_c(z) = G(s)|_{s=2T^{-1}(z-1)(z+1)^{-1}}$$

$$G_c(z) = \frac{30z - 10}{21z - 19}$$

$$G_c(z) = \frac{1.4286(z - 0.3333)}{z - 0.9048}$$

(d) Since we want the gain at $\omega = 1$ to match that of the analog function, we will prewarp $\omega T = 1$ to $\omega_0 T = 1.0926$ using Eq. (4-37). We could, in fact, prewarp each "corner" frequency, but $\omega T = 0.1$ is barely affected. Consequently, we have

$$G_d(z) = [(s + 1.0926)(s + 0.1)^{-1}]|_{s=2T^{-1}(z-1)(z+1)^{-1}}$$

$$G_d(z) = \frac{1.4727(z - 0.2934)}{z - 0.9048}$$

(e)

$$G_e(z) = \frac{K(z - e^{-1})}{z - e^{-0.1}}$$

$$G_e(z) = \frac{K(z - 0.3679)}{z - 0.9048}$$

Evaluating $K$ so that $G_e(z)$ will be 1.4072 at $\omega = 1$,

$$G_e(z) = \frac{1.5024(z - 0.3679)}{z - 0.9048}$$

Comparison:

|  | Pole | Zero | Gain at $\omega = 1$ |
|---|---|---|---|
| (a) ZOH equivalent: | 0.90484 | 0.0484 | 1.0629 |
| (b) Forward rectangular: | 0.90000 | 0 | 1.0928 |
| (c) Trapezoidal: | 0.90476 | 0.3333 | 1.3500 |
| (d) Bilinear transform: | 0.90476 | 0.2934 | 1.4083 |
| (e) Pole–zero map: | 0.90484 | 0.3679 | 1.4072 |

From the above comparison table one notes a close correspondence among the pole locations, but a relatively wide variation for the zero location. As far as maintaining a specific gain at a certain frequency, the pole–zero map and bilinear transform approaches are far superior to the others, primarily because these methods allow for such special considerations.

*Remark:* The impulse response matching technique, noticeable by its absence, is not suitable for this problem or any problem with an improper transfer function (since the corresponding impulse response will have impulsive components).

### 4-6.3 Simulation of Nonlinear Elements

In Section 4-5 we discussed a method of simulating linear control systems with both discrete-time and continuous-time subsystems. There, any sampling operation was to represent an actual system sampling (ADC) process. In this section the method will be extended to allow nonlinear, memoryless elements in the system. Such nonlinearities as amplifier saturation, deadzone (as in a loose gear train), and even the quantization inherent in digitizing a signal fall into our category of nonlinear elements.

If a memoryless nonlinearity, as shown in Fig. 4-18a, occurs in the system structure, an artifical sampler and clamp can be introduced as in Fig. 4-18b. We will refer to these extra samplers (and clamps) as *induced samplers* (and clamps) (existing only because of the nonlinear element) to distinguish them from actual samplers (and clamps) in the system. It is easily demonstrated that the variation $y_c$ in Fig. 4-18b follows that of $y$ in Fig. 4-18a as a piecewise constant approximation and that, in fact,

$$\lim_{\Delta \to 0} |y_c(t) - y(t)| = 0 \qquad (4\text{-}78)$$

uniformly with $\Delta$.

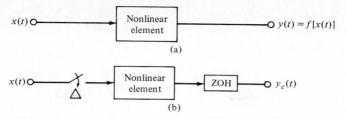

(a)

(b)

**FIGURE 4-18.** (a) nonlinear memoryless device; (b) induced sampler and clamp for the nonlinearity.

As in our previous simulation procedure, the clamp outputs (including these induced clamps) are taken as part of the total state vector **v**. The only modification of the technique shows up in the resetting of the induced clamps at the instants $k\Delta$, $k = 0, 1, 2, \ldots$, where $\Delta$ may differ from the system sample interval $T$. [From Eq. (4-78) one can see that a faster sampling (shorter time intervals $\Delta$) for the nonlinearity will improve the approximation.] This modification amounts to using the nonlinear function to determine the reset value for the induced clamp. The reader will be able to see how this works from the following illustrative example. One result is that the $J$ matrix of Section 4-5 is no longer a linear matrix, but a combination of linear and nonlinear relationships used to reset the clamp outputs.

### EXAMPLE 4-12 (Nonlinear System Simulation)

Figure 4-19a shows a system with nonlinear damping. We will establish the continuous-time equations ($G$ matrix) valid between samples, and the update

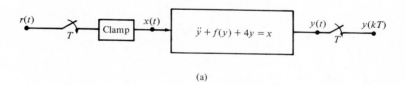

(a)

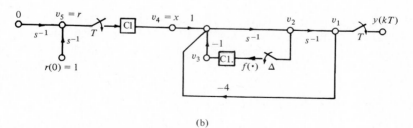

(b)

**FIGURE 4-19.** (a) nonlinear sampled-data system; (b) simulation diagram for system.

equations required at the sample instants that would be used to obtain the unit-step response for the system. The remainder of the simulation would follow the algorithm of Fig. 4-13 except that the induced clamp should be updated at each interval. In other words, just prior to multiplication by $\Phi$, the induced clamp is updated. To illustrate, we first redraw the system as shown in Fig. 4-19b, where the state variables for the vector $\mathbf{v}$ have been labeled. The reader will note that since $v_5$ is always unity, the $v_4$ clamp is not necessary: it is included only to indicate a more general procedure.

**SOLUTION:** Since only $v_1$ to $v_4$ are involved in the continuous-time dynamics, we write

$$d/dt \begin{bmatrix} v_1 \\ v_2 \\ v_3 \\ v_4 \end{bmatrix} = \begin{bmatrix} 0 & 1 & 0 & 0 \\ -4 & 0 & -1 & 1 \\ 0 & 0 & 0 & 0 \\ 0 & 0 & 0 & 0 \end{bmatrix} \begin{bmatrix} v_1 \\ v_2 \\ v_3 \\ v_4 \end{bmatrix} \tag{4-79}$$

for $kT < t < kT + T$. The coefficient matrix above is the $G$ matrix for the system. In the simulation procedure $\Phi = \exp(G\Delta)$ is calculated for the inter-sample interval $\Delta$; see Fig. 4-12. Prior to multiplying by $\Phi$ at each $\Delta$ interval the nonlinear update is made

$$v_3(k\Delta^+) = f[v_2(k\Delta^-)] \tag{4-80}$$

The system clamp would be reset according to

$$v_4(kT^+) = v_5(kT^-) \tag{4-81}$$

Let us choose the nonlinearity to be

$$f(\dot{y}) = \dot{y}|\dot{y}|$$

representing a square-law damping or drag term. The transition matrix for the vector $\mathbf{v}$ can be determined analytically to be ($v_5 = v_4$ and is not included)

$$\Phi(t) = \begin{bmatrix} a & b & c & -c \\ -4b & a & -b & b \\ 0 & 0 & 1 & 0 \\ 0 & 0 & 0 & 1 \end{bmatrix}$$

where $a = \cos 2t$, $b = (1/2) \sin 2t$, $c = (1/4)[(\cos 2t) - 1]$.

To ensure that the nonlinearity is being simulated accurately, one method would be to "run" the simulation for an initial value of $\Delta$, then repeat for a reduced (smaller) value of $\Delta$. If there is no significant change in the accuracy, then the chosen $\Delta$ is small enough. Otherwise, one must try again with a further reduced value.

To illustrate, we will evaluate the initial 1 sec portion of the zero-state unit-step response. The results are tabulated below for $v_1$ and $v_2$ for the desired times $t = 0, 0.25, 0.50, 0.75,$ and $1.00$:

| Δ | t | $v_1$ | $v_2$ |
|---|---|---|---|
| 0.2500 | 0.25 | 0.03060 | 0.23971 |
| | 0.50 | 0.11317 | 0.40696 |
| | 0.75 | 0.22240 | 0.44864 |
| | 1.00 | 0.32717 | 0.37194 |
| 0.0125 | 0.25 | 0.03033 | 0.23526 |
| | 0.50 | 0.11095 | 0.39200 |
| | 0.75 | 0.21667 | 0.43454 |
| | 1.00 | 0.31945 | 0.37253 |
| 0.0100 | 0.25 | 0.03032 | 0.23520 |
| | 0.50 | 0.11091 | 0.39185 |
| | 0.75 | 0.21660 | 0.43443 |
| | 1.00 | 0.31937 | ˋ0.37257 |

■

From the comparison table above one can see that if three-place accuracy were required, $\Delta = 0.25$ would not be small enough, whereas with $\Delta = 0.01$, four-place accuracy is achieved, the only difference being the accuracy of approximating the nonlinearity. Of course, higher accuracy is needed for longer solution intervals since errors tend to "propagate" with time.

## 4-7

## SUMMARY

Two principal problems were investigated in this chapter: One is the problem of translating an analog controller (transfer function) into an equivalent digital controller (algorithm or z-domain transfer function). Such an operation has been termed "digital redesign" and is widely employed where older control systems are being replaced by computer control systems. The other problem studied is that of simulating a completed control system design. This is a necessary phase of the design process—to demonstrate that the design is within required specifications and to indicate whether the design is tolerant of small parameter variations.

Particular solutions for the digital redesign problem that were discussed include

- impulse response matching
- bilinear transformation
- pole–zero mapping

in addition to our principal technique of ZOH equivalent, which was presented in both Chapters 2 and 3. The approach taken for the problem of system simulation was to restrict inputs to typical test functions such as steps, ramps, and sinusoids and to generate a "homogeneous equivalent" model for the system.

This method has the flexibility to work with hybrid systems (containing both analog and digital parts) and extends easily to allow nonlinearities in the system model. This approach to system simulation demonstrates the utility of the state-variable method when numerical computation is required.

## REFERENCES

**Section 4-1**  *Discrete-Time and Computer Control Systems:* J. A. Cadzow and H. R. Martens; Prentice Hall, 1970.
**Section 4-2**  *Digital Signal Processing;* W. D. Stanley; Reston, 1975.
*Modern Digital Control Systems;* R. G. Jacquot; Marcell Dekker, 1981.
*Digital Control;* G. F. Franklin and J. D. Powell; Addison-Wesley, 1980.
**Section 4-6**  *Digital Control Systems;* B. C. Kuo, Holt, Rinehart and Winston, 1980.

## PROBLEMS

**4-1**  For the matrix $F$ used in Example 4-1 tabulate the error in the (2, 2) term of the partial sum of Eq. (4-4) versus the number of terms in the series expansion of $e^{0.1F}$ up to seven terms. [The largest absolute error occurs in the (2, 2) term for any partial sum.] For instance, the error with but a single term is $|1 - 0.8187| = 0.1813$.

**4-2**  Expand Eq. (4-8) with $r = 5$ to show that the nested form is equivalent to a truncated standard series.

**4-3**  For the system

$$\dot{\mathbf{x}} = \begin{bmatrix} 0 & 1 \\ 0 & -2 \end{bmatrix} \mathbf{x} + \begin{bmatrix} 0 \\ 1 \end{bmatrix} u(t)$$

with $u(t) = u(kT)$ for $kT \le t < kT + T$, $(T = 0.1 \text{ sec})$:
**(a)** Calculate the ZOH equivalent discrete-time model using an exact analytical method.
**(b)** Determine $E(T)$ using four terms of Eq. (4-6) and subsequently $A(T)$ and $B(T)$ from Eqs. (4-7).
**(c)** Compare the approximate results of (b) with the analytical results of (a).

**4-4**  Derive Eq. (4-10).

**4-5**  A zero-order-hold equivalent introduces an additional phase delay of approximately $0.5T$. In some simulations this extra phase delay is unacceptable. In contrast a first-order-hold device has a much reduced delay. If the input sequence to the holding device is given by

$$u(k) = \{u(0), u(1), u(2), \ldots\}$$

then the *first-order-hold* (FOH) provides the continuous-time output:

$$m(t) = u(n) + \frac{u(n) - u(n - 1)}{T} (t - nT) \qquad \text{for } nT \leq t < nT + T$$

**(a)** Sketch the FOH output for an input sequence

$$u(k) = \{1, 0.5, 0.2, -0.1, 0, \ldots, 0\}$$

**(b)** Compare the ZOH and the FOH outputs for $T = 1$ and

$$u(k) = \left\{ \sin \frac{\pi k}{4}; k = 0, 1, 2, \ldots \right\}$$

by plotting the outputs together for a full cycle of the input.

**4-6**   Obtain a digital filter that approximates an analog filter with the following unit-impulse response functions. Use the method of Impulse Response Matching and the given sampling rate.
**(a)** $t e^{-t}, t \geq 0; T^{-1} = 1/3$ Hz
**(b)** $e^{-t} \sin 2t, t \geq 0; T^{-1} = 8/\pi$ Hz
**(c)** $e^{-t} \cos 2t, t \geq 0; T^{-1} = 8/\pi$ Hz

**4-7**   Compare the frequency responses of the designs of Problem 4-6 with that of the "true" analog filter. Calculate enough points to provide a smooth graph of each for frequencies less than one-half the sampling rate.

**4-8**   For the function $f(x) = 3x^2$
**(a)** Calculate (analytically) the true value of

$$I = \int_0^1 f(x) \, dx$$

**(b)** Using samples $f(0.2k)$ for $k = 0, 1, 2, \ldots, 5$ approximate $I$ by $I_0$, $I_1$, and $I_2$ from Eqs. (4-22), (4-23), and (4-24), respectively.
**(c)** Tabulate the results with percent errors.

**4-9**   Repeat Problem 4-8 with the function $f(x) = \sin (\pi x/8)$ and

$$I = \int_0^8 f(t) \, dt$$

For the approximations use $f(k)$ for $k = 0, 1, \ldots, 8$.

**4-10**   Demonstrate that for linearly interpolated samples $f(kT)$ of a smooth function $f(t)$, namely, $f_1(t)$, that

$$\frac{d^2}{dt^2} f_1(t) = \sum_{k=0}^{\infty} \frac{1}{T} [f(kT + T) - 2f(kT) + f(kT - T)] \delta(t - kT)$$

for $k = 0, 1, 2, \ldots$.

**4-11**   Using the function $f$ from Problem 4-8 (and the same samples) plot $d_0(k)$, $d_1(k)$, and $d(k)$, the true derivative, on the same graph, where $d(t) = \dot{f}(t)$ and $d_0$ and $d_1$ are defined through Eq. (4-28). Use $d_1(0) = d(0)$ to provide a starting point for $d_1(k)$.

**4-12**   Repeat Problem 4-11 using the function $f$ from Problem 4-9.

**4-13**   For the discrete-time transfer function with $a = T = 1$

$$H(z) = \frac{az}{z - e^{-aT}} = \frac{Y(z)}{U(z)}$$

sketch the system frequency response (magnitude and phase) over a complete cycle. Use a minimum of 16 points to obtain accurate plots.

**4-14**   A Butterworth filter is defined as a low-pass filter having a maximally flat amplitude response:

$$|G(j\omega)|^2 = \frac{1}{1 + (\omega/\omega_c)^{2n}}$$

for an $n$th-order filter.
**(a)** Show that the poles of $|G(s)|^2$ are equally spaced on a circle $|s| = \omega_c$ in the $s$-plane.
**(b)** For $n = 3$ plot the poles of $|G(s)|^2$.

**4-15**   The left-half plane poles of

$$|H(s)|^2 = \frac{1}{1 - s^6}$$

correspond to the poles of $H(s)$. Assuming that this $H(s)$ represents an analog controller, develop a digital redesign with $T = 0.5$ sec using
**(a)** impulse invariance
**(b)** Tustin's method
**(c)** pole–zero mapping
Specify your designs as $z$-domain transfer functions.

**4-16**   **(a)** Use $T = 0.2$ sec and pole–zero mapping to determine an equivalent $\hat{H}(z)$ for

$$H(s) = \frac{6}{(s + 2)(s + 3)}$$

Match gains at dc.
**(b)** Compare $|H|$ and $|\hat{H}|$ versus $\omega$ for $\omega < 5\pi$.

**4-17**   Repeat Problem 4-16 for the analog function

$$H(s) = \frac{1}{s+1} e^{-0.4s}$$

**4-18**  Use the bilinear transformation with prewarping to obtain an approximate discrete-time compensator for the following analog compensators:

(a) $G_a(s) = \dfrac{1}{1 + 0.1s}$ with $T = 0.2$ sec

and prewarping the corner frequency $\omega_0 = 10$.

(b) $G_b(s) = \dfrac{1}{(1 + 0.05s)(1 + 0.01s)}$ with $T = 0.02$ sec

Prewarp both corner frequencies.

**4-19**  For the phase-lead compensator

$$H(s) = \frac{100\, s + 1}{10\, s + 1}$$

Tabulate the pole–zero configurations and the gain at $\omega = 3$ with $T = 0.25$ using

(1) ZOH equivalent
(2) $N = 0$ integration [see Eq. (4-25)]
(3) $N = 1$ integration
(4) Bilinear with prewarping for $\omega = 3$
(5) Pole–zero mapping (with gain matching at $\omega = 3$)

**4-20**  Simulate the (zero-state) unit-step response for the continuous-time system

$$G(s) = \frac{4}{s(s+2)}$$

(a) Use the transition technique described in Section 4-3 with the interval between transitions given by $T = 0.05$ sec and a solution interval of 2 sec.
(b) Check your numerical simulation analytically using Laplace transforms and evaluating a few points on the graph.
(c) Assume that $G(s)$ is the forward gain function of a unity negative feedback loop and repeat parts (a) and (b).

**4-21**  Repeat Problem 4-20 with $G(s) = s^{-2}$.

**4-22**  A digital system is required to provide an actuation sequence $m(k)$ in response to an error sequence $e(k)$ so that

$$m(k) = m(k - 1) + 2m(k - 2) + 3e(k) - e(k - 1)$$

(a) Provide a $z$-domain diagram using unit delay elements.
(b) Simulate the zero-state unit-step response using a tabular format as developed in Section 4-4. Carry out your calculations to obtain five output sequence values.
(c) Check your solution using $z$-transforms.

**4-23**    Repeat Problem 4-22 using the digital compensator

$$D(z) = \frac{az + b}{z - c}$$

where $a$, $b$, and $c$ are arbitrary real parameters.

**4-24**    Simpson's rule for integration is given by

$$\int_0^a f(t)\, dt \doteq \frac{T}{3} (f_0 + 4f_1 + 2f_2 + 4f_3 + \cdots + 2f_{2n-2} + 4f_{2n-1} + f_{2n})$$

where $f_k = f(kT)$ and $a = 2nT$.
Take $n = 3$, $T = 1$ and compare Simson's rule results with the output of the following system to the input sequence $\{f_0, f_1, f_2, \ldots, f_6\}$:

$$H(z) = \frac{z^2 + 4z + 1}{3(z^2 - 1)}$$

**4-25**    A discrete-time system is described by its pulse-transfer function $D(z)$, given by

$$D(z) = \frac{16z^2 + 26z + 9}{16z^3 + 34z^2 + 26z + 9}$$

**(a)** Find the first five terms of the unit-pulse response.
**(b)** Simulate the zero-state unit-step response.

**4-26**    Given the sampled-data control system in Fig. P4-26. Calculate the response $c(t)$ to the pulse input:

$$r(t) = 1, \qquad 0 \le t < 5 \text{ sec}$$

$$= 0, \qquad \text{other } t$$

Assume that no initial energy is present in the system. Plot the output $c(t)$ at 0.25-sec intervals from $0 \le t \le 10$ sec.

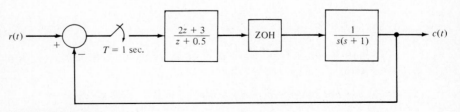

**FIGURE P4-26.**

**4-27**    A plant is described by the state model:

$$\dot{\mathbf{x}}(t) = \begin{bmatrix} 0 & -2 \\ 1 & -3 \end{bmatrix} \mathbf{x}(t) + \begin{bmatrix} -2 \\ -3 \end{bmatrix} u(t)$$

$$y(t) = \begin{bmatrix} 1 & -3 \end{bmatrix} \mathbf{x}(t)$$

If the input $u(t)$ is the output of a sample-and-hold device, determine the first five terms of the unit-pulse response for the equivalent discrete-time system [as if $y(t)$ were sampled along with the input at the rate $T^{-1}$ Hz].

**4-28**  Figure P4-28 shows a signal-flow diagram that attempts to model the economic cycle between corn and hogs. From the diagram one can see that a large number of hogs or a large amount of corn on the market will (instantaneously) drive the respective prices down (both $-c$ and $-d$ are negative constants), whereas there is a year delay to produce hogs or corn (indicated by the positive constants $a$ and $b$ multiplying the unit-delay operator). In addition, hogs consume corn and a high price on corn discourages hog production (so that $-e$ is negative and $f$ is positive).

**(a)** Determine the characteristic equation for this discrete-time system.

**(b)** For $a = b = c = d = e = 1$ and $f = 0.5$ simulate the system response ($X$ and $Y$) if $X(0) = 0$ and $Y(0) = 1$.

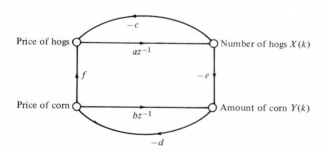

**FIGURE P4-28.**

**4-29**  Simulate the unit-pulse response for the open-loop system shown in Fig. P4-29 using 0.2 sec between calculations for a solution interval of 4 sec. Assume zero initial energy in the system.

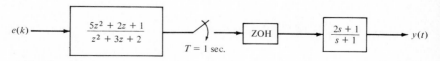

**FIGURE P4-29.**

**4-30**    Simulate the (zero-state) unit-step response of the closed-loop system in Fig. P4-30 using an intersample calculation interval of 0.25 sec and a solution interval of 5 sec.

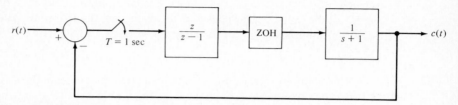

**FIGURE P4-30.**

**4-31**    Repeat Problem 4-30 for a unit-ramp response.

**4-32**    Show that the transfer function for a first-order hold (FOH) as described in Problem 4-5, is given by

$$H_1(s) = \frac{1 - sT}{Ts^2}(1 - e^{-sT})^2$$

in the same way that $H_0(s)$ in Eq. (2-40) represents the transfer function of a zero-order hold device.

## CHAPTER 5

# Digital Implementation

Before we discuss design techniques in detail it is perhaps worthwhile mentioning that a great deal of the motivation for studying digital control is the availability of inexpensive computational power in the form of microcomputers. And although it is outside the scope of this text to dwell on the innumerable variations of computer hardware structure, it is useful to make some general remarks concerning digital implementation.

## 5-1

### DIGITAL QUANTIZATION

In any computer realization we must concern ourselves with the quantization effects of having finite register lengths, and particularly so with fixed-point arithmetic and small word length machines. The ADC signal conversion mentioned in Chapter 1 illustrates quantization of an analog signal into a finite number of possible digital values. Another example of quantization occurs during a multiplication of one digital word with another inside the computer; the reason for this is that a binary word of length $N$ times another binary word of length $N$ can generate a binary product of length up to $2N$, the least significant $N$ bits of which are typically lost. Yet another example is the quantization of system parameters into a binary word. One principal effect of quantization is to generate errors within the system. We will interpret these errors as "noise" (undesirable signal variations) and show in this chapter (along with Appendix C) how to analyze its effect on system response.

There are two basic types of quantization:

1. *Rounding*. Values are approximated by the nearest quantization level.
2. *Truncation*. Values are approximated by the nearest quantization level whose magnitude is less than the sample magnitude.

Figure 5-1 illustrates the effect of rounding as a nonlinear mapping from a signal with continuous amplitude to a signal with discrete amplitudes.

We will use the convention that if the analog value is precisely in the middle of two adjacent quantization levels, the quantized value is the larger magnitude.

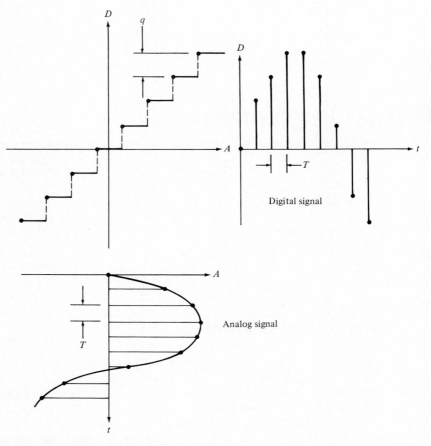

**FIGURE 5-1. Signal quantization.**

**DIGITAL IMPLEMENTATION**

Note that the quantization levels are separated by $q$ units, which corresponds to the least significant bit (LSB) of the computer register. The error of the digital approximation obviously depends on whether rounding or truncation is used. The quantization level spacing will depend on both the range of the signal and the length of the register at the output of the ADC unit. For instance, if fixed-point arithmetic is used, then a register of length $N$ bits (including a sign bit) will have $(2^N - 1)$ discrete levels to be distributed (linearly) over the signal range. Before proceeding with the following development, the reader is advised to read the material presented in Appendix C.

Consider an analog signal $x(t)$ to be digitized (sampled at $t = kT$, $k = 0, 1, 2, \ldots$ and quantized to amplitude levels $q_n$, $n = 0, \pm 1, \pm 2, \ldots, \pm N$). The *quantization error* at the $k$th sample is

$$e(k) = x(kT) - q_i \tag{5-1}$$

where $q_i$ is the appropriate amplitude level. In most practical situations there will be a large number of quantization levels, so that for different samples, it is reasonable to assume that $e(n)$ and $e(k)$ are uncorrelated random variables whenever $n \neq k$ since $x(nT)$ and $x(kT)$ will tend to vary over many levels. If we then consider the distribution of error, we find that both round-off and truncation policies have uniform distributions as presented in Fig. 5-2.

With the interpretation that $e(k)$ is an additive "noise" component, we can write that

$$x(kT) = x_0(kT) + e(k) \tag{5-2}$$

where $x_0(kT)$ represents an error-free sampled signal and $e(k)$ is the quantization error (for either round-off or truncation). We will now somewhat arbitrarily restrict our attention to the use of round-off since this error distribution has zero mean. The variance of $e$ can be calculated (See Appendix C) as follows:

$$\sigma^2 = \int_{-\infty}^{\infty} x^2 p(x)\, dx = \int_{-q/2}^{q/2} q^{-1} x^2\, dx = q^2/12 \tag{5-3}$$

Knowing the "noise" statistics, we can calculate the effects of the noise on the system response, and by being able to predict noise effects on the system, we can search for control algorithms that minimize these effects. As mentioned earlier, multiplying two binary words also generates quantization errors. This is illustrated in the next example.

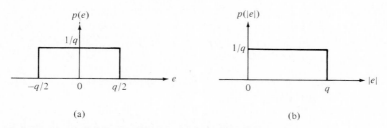

(a)                                (b)

**FIGURE 5-2.   Pdf of (a) round-off and (b) truncation errors.**

### EXAMPLE 5-1 (Multiplier Noise)

Consider the multiplication of two binary words that might, for instance, be a stored coefficient and an input signal sample. Assuming a fixed-point form, with $A = 1110$ and $B = 1011$ representing a fixed register length, then $C = AB = 10011010$. Thus, the stored product (by quantizing to 4 bits) would be $C = 1001$ using truncation and $C = 1010$ by rounding to the nearest level. This, of course, assumes that all values are represented by the same binary word length. ∎

From Example 5-1 it follows that every multiplication generates a quantization error source similar to that generated by an ADC unit. Parameter quantization, however, can have a more profound effect on system response than adding a small amount of noise. To show this, let us consider a particular control algorithm.

### EXAMPLE 5-2 (Parameter Quantization)

Consider a simple control algorithm given by the discrete-time transfer function between $E(z)$, the error signal from the comparator, and $U(z)$, the actuation signal:

$$G(z) = \frac{U(z)}{E(z)} = \frac{z}{z - p} \tag{5-4}$$

where $p$ is a (quantized) parameter.

The quantization of $p$ causes an error $\Delta p$ in the parameter. In this example the error translates into a direct shift of the designed pole of $G(z)$. This may or may not have a large effect. For instance, if $\Delta p/p$ is $0.1$ (a large quantization) and the nominal (designed) value $p$ is $0.5$, then the effect on the system would probably not be great. However, if the nominal $p$ is $0.9$, the effect may be more severe. A method of investigating small parametric variations (due to quantization) is given next. ∎

## 5-2

## SENSITIVITY ANALYSIS

In this section we will review the classical definition of sensitivity functions. Typically, we want to know the fractional change that occurs in some discrete-time transfer function in response to a small fractional change of a system parameter.

**Definition:** The sensitivity of $T(z, p)$ to the parameter $p$ is the *sensitivity function* $S_p^T$, defined as

$$S_p^T = \lim_{\Delta p \to 0} \frac{\Delta T/T}{\Delta p/p} = \frac{\partial T/T}{\partial p/p} = \frac{\partial T}{\partial p} \frac{p}{T} \tag{5-5}$$

An alternate form is given by

$$S_p^T = \frac{\partial T/T}{\partial p/p} = \frac{\partial \ln T}{\partial \ln p} \tag{5-6}$$

from the calculus relation that $d \ln x = dx/x$. Since $T$ is typically a rational expression, that is,

$$T(z, p) = N(z, p)/D(z, p) \tag{5-7}$$

the form of Eq. (5-6) may be used as follows:

$$S_p^T = \frac{\partial \ln N}{\partial \ln p} - \frac{\partial \ln D}{\partial \ln p} = S_p^N - S_p^D \tag{5-8}$$

The sensitivity function $S_p^T$ is evaluated at the nominal value of the parameter $p$, but will generally be a function of $z$. Consider the following example.

### EXAMPLE 5-3 (Parameter Sensitivity)

From Example 5-2, $G(z) = z/(z - p)$, we wish to determine $S_p^G$ for a nominal parameter $p_0$.

*SOLUTION:* From Eq. (5-5)

$$S_p^G = \frac{\partial G}{\partial p} \frac{p}{G}$$

$$S_p^G = \left. \frac{+z}{(z - p)^2} \frac{p(z - p)}{z} \right|_{p = p_0} = \frac{p_0}{z - p_0} \tag{5-9}$$

∎

Although sensitivity functions are valid only for small parameter deviations, they are often helpful in determining weak points in a controller design where a particular parameter variation may lead to unacceptably large transfer function changes. Sensitivity functions may be interpreted as functions of real frequency using $z = e^{j\omega T}$, and one useful point is $\omega = 0$(dc) or $z = 1$, which pertains to the effect on steady-state values.

### EXAMPLE 5-4 (Interpretation of Sensitivity Function)

In Example 5-3, consider a nominal value $p_0 = 0.5$ and a constant unity input to $G(z)$; then a quick calculation tells us that the steady output has a value of $(1 - p_0)^{-1} = 2$. Now, assuming a 5% increase in $p$, $\Delta p = +0.025$, then by direct calculation the steady output value increases to 2.105.

Equation (5-9) indicates that $S = 1$; therefore, if $p$ increases by 5%, then $G$ also increases by the same 5%. In this instance, the steady output increased 5.26% through the change in $G$. The reason for the slight discrepancy is that a 5% change in $p$ was not sufficiently small to represent an infinitessimal change. ∎

The effect of feedback can greatly reduce the sensitivity to parameter variations. This is one of the rewards of using feedback. Suppose for simplicity a single-loop unity feedback system whose transfer function is given by

$$T = G/(1 + G) \tag{5-10}$$

where $G = G(z, p)$. Applying Eq. (5-5)

$$S_G^T = \frac{\partial T}{\partial G} \frac{G}{T} = \frac{1}{1 + G} \tag{5-11}$$

In words, some parametric change that causes a change in the open-loop function $G$ in turn causes a change in $T$. The ratio of percent change in $T$ to percent change in $G$ is given by Eq. (5-11). It is to be noted that typically $G \gg 1$ in the frequency band of the control loop so that the effect on the response from any change in $G$ is small. Thus, a well-designed feedback system will have a natural reduction to parameter variations of any kind and parameter quantization, in particular. Let us now consider in more detail the system effects of quantization in signal conversion and product operations.

## 5-3

## RESPONSE OF DISCRETE-TIME SYSTEMS TO WHITE NOISE

In order to evaluate the system effects of quantization noise, we must first determine how a general noise is propagated through a linear system. Consider the linear system of Fig. 5-3 with input consisting of signal $s_i(k)$ plus noise $n_i(k)$. Furthermore, assume that the noise $n_i(k)$ has zero mean and is an uncorrelated stationary sequence with known variance.

We know from linearity that the output signal $s_o(k)$ is that part of the response due to $s_i(k)$ and that the output noise $n_o(k)$ is the response to the excitation $n_i(k)$. Since we know how to determine $s_o(k)$, let us assume for a moment that only the noise input $n_i(k)$ is present. We know that $E[n_i(k)] = 0$ and that $E[n_i^2(k)] = \sigma_i^2$ (by our previous assumption). Consequently, we may deduce that $E[n_o(k)] = 0$ from Eq. (C-17) and that

$$\sigma_o^2 = \frac{\sigma_i^2}{2\pi j} \oint_C H(z)H(z^{-1})z^{-1} \, dz \tag{5-12}$$

from Eq. (C-29). Alternately, since

**FIGURE 5-3. A linear system with a noisy input.**

$$n_o(k) = \sum_{m=0}^{\infty} h(m)n_i(k - m) \qquad (5\text{-}13)$$

then

$$\sigma_o^2 = E[n_o^2(k)] = E\left[\sum_{m=0}^{k} h(m)n_i(k - m) \sum_{q=0}^{k} h(q)n_i(k - q)\right] \qquad (5\text{-}14)$$

Taking the averaging operator $E$ inside the summations,

$$\sigma_o^2 = \sum_{m=0}^{k} h(m) \sum_{q=0}^{k} h(q)E[n_i(k - m)n_i(k - q)] \qquad (5\text{-}15)$$

The fact that $n_i(k)$ is a white sequence tells us that

$$E[n_i(r)n_i(p)] = \sigma^2 \qquad \text{if } r = p$$
$$= 0 \qquad \text{if } r \neq p \qquad (5\text{-}16)$$

Therefore, Eq. (5-15) reduces to

$$\sigma_o^2 = \sum_{m=0}^{k} h^2(m) \, \sigma_i^2 \qquad (5\text{-}17)$$

By comparing Eqs. (5-17) and (5-12), we see that in the limit as $k \rightarrow \infty$,

$$\sum_{m=0}^{\infty} h^2(m) = \frac{1}{2\pi j} \oint_C H(z)H(z^{-1})z^{-1} \, dz \qquad (5\text{-}18)$$

### EXAMPLE 5-5 (A Noise Excited Linear System)
Consider a simple first-order system with transfer function

$$H(z) = \frac{z}{z - a} = \frac{U(z)}{E(z)}$$

and suppose a zero-mean white noise sequence with a (constant) variance of $\sigma_e^2$ is applied as an input. Describe the output signal.

*SOLUTION:* To begin with we know that the output will be a zero-mean noise. To determine the variance of the response sequence, we can recognize that the weighting sequence corresponding to the given $H(z)$ is

$$h(k) = a^k, \quad k \geq 0$$

Applying Eq. (5-17)

$$\sigma_u^2(k) = \sum_{m=0}^{k} a^{2m} \, \sigma_e^2$$

$$\sigma_u^2(k) = \sigma_e^2 \left[\frac{1 - a^{2k+2}}{1 - a^2}\right] \rightarrow \sigma_e^2 \left[\frac{1}{1 - a^2}\right]$$

Also, we can say something about the correlation of the output signal. For instance, Eq. (C-21) may be applied. But for now, let us investigate the requirements on register length to meet a 40-dB signal-to-noise amplitude as well as a 40-dB signal range if the noise comes from ADC quantization with $a = 0.95$.

Since the ADC quantization noise is uniformly distributed as shown in Fig. 5-2a, $\sigma_e^2 = q^2/12$. It follows from the above development that

$$\sigma_u = 0.9245q$$

With 40 dB of signal-to-noise amplitude and dynamic range, the output register must have a range of $10^4 \sigma_u = 9245q$, which is 14 bits (13 bits is not sufficient since $2^{13} = 8192$). Note that $\sigma_u^2$ becomes increasingly large as the parameter $a$ approaches unity, so that the register requirement may vary from one system to another. ∎

The most useful information about the response signal is to specify its autocorrelation function or equivalently its $z$-transform, as in Eq. (C-21). One difference we encounter over ordinary signal representations is that the autocorrelation is not a single-sided sequence, but an even symmetric, double-sided sequence. The even symmetry property allows us to effectively consider it as single-sided, however.

### EXAMPLE 5-6 (Output Autocorrelation)

In the previous example, $H(z) = z/(z - a) = U(z)/E(z)$. Thus, if the input $e(k)$ is a stationary, zero-mean, white noise with a unit variance, then $R_e(k) = \delta(k)$ and $S_e(z) = 1$. The output spectral density is given by Eq. (C-21) as

$$S_u(z) = \frac{z}{z - a} \frac{z^{-1}}{z^{-1} - a} = \frac{z}{(z - a)(1 - az)}$$

To find $R_u(k)$, we can use Eq. (2-32) (where C is the unit circle). Only those poles of $S_u(z)$ that are in the circle contribute to the positive $k$ values of $R_u(k)$. Therefore,

$$R_u(k) = \left. \frac{z^k}{1 - az} \right|_{z = a} = a^k/(1 - a^2)$$

for $k = 0, 1, 2, \ldots$, and by symmetry, $R_u(-k) = R_u(k)$. ∎

In the next section we investigate the total quantization noise effect at the output of a given transfer function for different realizations. The results may be unexpected.

## COMPARISON OF PROGRAM REALIZATIONS

The general approach taken here is that in any digital realization (hardware or software) the algorithm of concern will have various quantization noise sources. For each of these noise sources we will determine the transmittance (or transfer function) between noise source and output. From this transmittance we can calculate the noise variance at the output contributed from the corresponding source. This must be done for each source in the realization. By assuming that each contribution is statistically unrelated to any other, the total noise variance can be established as the sum of all contributing noise variances:

$$\sigma_T^2 = \sigma_1^2 + \sigma_2^2 + \cdots + \sigma_N^2 \tag{5-19}$$

where $\sigma_i^2$ is the $i$th source variance transferred to the output according to Eqs. (5-17) and (5-18).

Following Eq. (5-2) the ADC unit and each multiplication operation within the realization is taken to be an exact, noise-free operation with an additive quantization noise with zero mean and variance $q^2/12$, as determined in Eq. (5-3).

As a generic problem for discussion (not meant to be completely general), let us consider a digital control algorithm of the form

$$H(z) = \frac{U(z)}{E(z)} = \frac{(c + d)z^2 - (ad + bc)z}{z^2 - (a + b)z + ab} \tag{5-20}$$

Alternate forms of $H(z)$ are given by

$$H(z) = \frac{cz}{z - a} + \frac{dz}{z - b} \tag{5-21}$$

a parallel realization, and

$$H(z) = \frac{z[(c + d)z - (ad + bc)]}{(z - a)(z - b)} \tag{5-22}$$

where this last form will be considered as a cascade structure.

Without exhausting all of the possibilities, we present three structural forms for realizing $H(z)$. The first is the controllable canonical form (from Chapter 3), the second is a parallel form (which by itself has many variations by interchanging gain terms in the parallel branches), and the third is a cascade form based on Eq. (5-22). These three realizations are presented in Fig. 5-4. In each instance the number of quantization noise sources are shown (circled) entering the system following an ADC or a product operation.

To illustrate the procedure of determining the total output noise variance (from quantization), note that three sources pass through the whole system, $H(z)$, and two sources contribute directly to the output in the controllable form of Fig. 5-4a. Consequently, the output quantization noise variance is

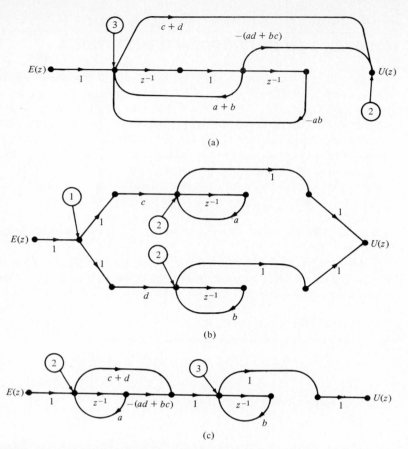

**FIGURE 5-4. Three distinct realizations of the same digital algorithm: (a) controllable form, (b) parallel or Jordan form, and (c) cascade form.**

$$\sigma_1^2 = 3(q^2/12) \sum_{m=0}^{\infty} h^2(m) + 2(q^2/12) \tag{5-23}$$

where the subscript refers to the realization for later comparison. The summation can be calculated according to Eq. (5-18), or as illustrated in Example 5-6. In particular, using Eq. (2-32) for $k = 0$,

$$F = \sum_{m=0}^{\infty} h^2(m) = \sum_{\text{(poles } a,b)} \text{Res} \left[ \frac{(Az - B)(A - Bz)}{(z - a)(z - b)(1 - az)(1 - bz)} \right] \tag{5-24}$$

where $A = (c + d)$ and $B = (ad + bc)$. Thus, in this case,

$$F = \frac{(Aa - B)(A - Ba)}{(a - b)(1 - a^2)(1 - ab)} + \frac{(Ab - B)(A - Bb)}{(b - a)(1 - ab)(1 - b^2)} \tag{5-25}$$

Moving to the second realization of Fig. 5-4b, the output variance is given by

$$\sigma_2^2 = (q^2/12)[F + 2T_a + 2T_b] \tag{5-26}$$

where $T_a$ and $T_b$ correspond to the transmittances between the double noise sources and output in Fig. 5-4b. Since $T_a$ corresponds to a transmittance of $z/(z - a)$, we can use the result of Example 5-6 to write that (for $k = 0$)

$$T_a = a/(1 - a^2) \tag{5-27}$$

and similarly for $T_b$ that

$$T_b = b/(1 - b^2) \tag{5-28}$$

thereby completing the needed expressions to calculate $\sigma_2^2$.

For the third realization of Fig. 5-4c, we write the output variance as

$$\sigma_3^2 = (q^2/12)[2F + 3T_b] \tag{5-29}$$

To show more clearly the differences in the effects of the quantization noise at the output of the digital controller, let us consider a particular numerical example.

### EXAMPLE 5-7 (Quantization Noise Levels for Different Realizations)

For some quantitative results let $H(z)$, the controller algorithm, be of the form in Eq. (5-20) with the parameter values $c = d = 1$, $a = 0.9$, $b = 0.5$:

$$H(z) = \frac{2z^2 - 1.4z}{(z - 0.5)(z - 0.9)}$$

Then, corresponding to the three realizations of Fig. 5-4, the following table shows the results of the calculations of Eqs. (5-23), (5-26), and (5-29):

| Realization Number | Output Variance × $12/q^2$ |
| --- | --- |
| 1 | 32.7 |
| 2 | 21.1 |
| 3 | 22.5 |

Clearly, from noise considerations, it pays to investigate the possible realizations when quantization is significant. ∎

The previous example would indicate that a significant amount of effort may be needed to determine an optimal configuration to minimize quantization noise for higher-order controllers; however, these effects pale into insignificance when word lengths are 16 bits or higher; (32 bit microcomputers may soon be readily available for control applications at reasonable price levels).

Other effects of quantization are to create deadbands, zones where the state is insensitive to inputs; and small oscillation conditions. In the following chapters we will look at techniques for handling small biases in a controlled variable.

## 5-5

## MICROPROCESSOR IMPLEMENTATION

In Chapter 1 we discussed very briefly some concepts of signal conversion, changing signal information from analog form to digital form and back. Earlier in this chapter some methods of modeling quantization effects on a digital algorithm were considered. In this section we will look at the basic computer structure used in microcomputers.

In simple terms there are three main components to a digital computer, although individual computers will vary greatly in the details of these components. Figure 5-5 illustrates a typical interconnection of the three microcomputer components:

1. the microprocessor unit (MPU)
2. the memory (MEM) unit
3. the input/output (I/O) devices

The interconnection lines are shown to have the different functions of controlling the information traffic and providing paths for data transfer and addressing specific locations in memory. Let us consider each of these major components separately. The heart of the computer is the MPU, which has a very complex detailed structure. We will concern ourselves only with the basic characteristics of the MPU.

*The Microprocessor Unit.* The MPU, also known as the central processing unit (CPU), is a device that performs all the arithmetic and logic manipulations, transfers data between certain registers, and provides the timing and control signals which interface with the external blocks. Figure 5-6 shows the MPU as being functionally composed of an arithmetic/logic unit (ALU), some

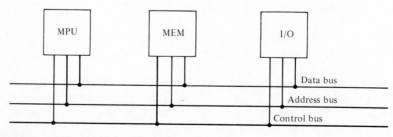

**FIGURE 5-5. A microcomputer diagram.**

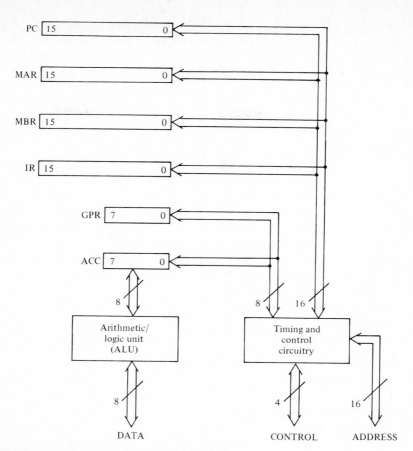

**FIGURE 5-6. The microprocessor Unit (MPU).**

specific registers, and control circuitry. For convenience in describing the computer functions, an 8-bit computer has been assumed.

Since the MPU performs almost all of the data processing operations in the computer, there are several general purpose registers (GPR) used to provide temporary storage of binary data. The accumulator (AC) register is typically interfaced with logic devices that enable it to perform various arithmetic and logic operations. Usually there are several "processor" registers for more efficient operation. For example, a multiplier–quotient (MQ) register can be used to store the multiplier and partial product during a multiplication operation.

The interaction between ALU and memory requires several registers: Index registers (IR) that store current values of counters and return addresses; Program counter (PC) registers and others such as the Memory Address Register (MAR); the Memory Buffer Register (MBR) and an Instruction Register (IR) whose functions are connected with accessing the memory unit.

An MPU with a large number of registers may have its own internal bus lines as shown in Fig. 5-6. The external connections to the MPU consist of the power supply and ground wires in addition to the three sets of binary channels shown in Fig. 5-6. The data bus passes 8 bits of binary data (one byte of information) between I/O devices, memory and the MPU, whereas the memory address bus is 16-bits (or 2 bytes) wide. With 16 bits we can specify uniquely $2^{16} = 65536$ different I/O devices or memory locations; this is referred to as "64K" bytes. The control bus is shown with 4 bits, but this varies from one MPU to another. As indicated in Fig. 5-5, the three busses all connect memory and the I/O devices with the MPU.

*The Memory Unit.*    Memory is an indispensable component of a computer. The data and program steps that instruct the computer are stored in memory. The memory unit can be thought of as a large array of (8-bit) storage registers, each one with its own unique (16-bit) address code. There are three types of memory:

1. Random Access Memory (RAM)
2. Read-Only Memory (ROM)
3. Bulk Memory

RAM is like a scratch pad, which can be accessed by the computer at any (random) time. Information can be read from RAM or written (stored) into RAM. RAM, however, is a volatile memory and its contents are lost when the power is turned off. ROM is a permanent form of memory present when the computer is turned on. ROM typically contains programs which can check out the computer functions and provide programs that allow new programs to be loaded into RAM. The third category, bulk memory, can be external devices such as magnetic tapes or disks, which can provide permanent memory for large amounts of data.

*Input/Output Devices.*    Without any means of getting information into or out of the computer it would be of little use. The I/O devices provide this function. As we have seen in Chapter 1, ADC and DAC devices provide input and output interfaces between the computer and analog systems. Other I/O devices are keyboards, magnetic disk drives, teletypewriters, and CRT monitors, to mention a few.

All I/O devices have access to the bus lines at any time. A typical method of providing the connection of a particular device is to "enable" an electronic switch to one of the control lines. This procedure allows only one device to transmit information at any one time. The control signals for transferring information come from the "timing and control" section of the MPU.

*Microcomputer Operation.*    As discussed previously, various hardware devices properly connected provide the necessary timing and control to permit the computer to access memory and I/O devices, store information in temporary registers of the ALU and perform arithmetic and/or logic operations on the contents of these registers.

Suppose that with an understanding of the set of instructions (at the assembly language level) we have loaded a program into RAM that implements some control law; that is, some $z$-domain transfer function, $G(z)$. The general structure of the program would then follow a certain pattern. The main steps might be as follows:

1. Input the current loop error $e(k)$ from the ADC.
2. Perform the calculations indicated by $G(z)$ to obtain the corresponding response $u(k)$.
3. Output $u(k)$ to the DAC.

These steps necessarily omit the details of step (2) since we have not stated what control law we are working with. To provide a little more detail let us consider the following example.

### EXAMPLE 5-8 (Implementing G(z) on a Computer)
Given that

$$G(z) = \frac{fz^2 + dz + c}{z^2 - az - b} = \frac{U(z)}{E(z)}$$

represents a digital control law whose input is the error sequence values $\{e(k)\}$, $k = 0, 1, 2, \ldots$ and whose output is the plant actuation sequence $\{u(k)\}$, $k = 0, 1, 2, \ldots$, write the sequence of operations that must be taken by the computer to process each new error sample.

*SOLUTION:* We will assume that the program is to implement $G(z)$ from its controllable form, and that special registers are set aside to store the current input and the corresponding state variables. Thus, initially R1 and R2 have states $x_1(0)$ and $x_2(0)$, respectively, and R3 is clear. One cycle of the algorithm is

Step 1: Read in $e$ from the ADC to register R3.
Step 2: Calculate

$$u = fe + (c + bf)x_1 + (d + af)x_2$$

Step 3: Output $u$ to the DAC.
Step 4: Calculate

$$w = bx_1 + ax_2$$

Step 5: Transfer $x_2$ from register R2 to register R1 and the result $w$ of Step 4 from its (temporary) register to R2.
Step 6: Return to Step 1.

These six steps form the outline of the required program. During the first cycle the $e$ in steps 1 and 2 will be $e(0)$ and the $x_1$ and $x_2$ of step 2 will be $x_1(0)$ and $x_2(0)$. The $u$ of step 3 is the initial output $u(0)$. Step 4 calculates $w$, which is $x_2(1)$, and step 5 updates the states to $x_1(1) = x_2(0)$ and $x_2(1)$ as calculated in step 4. Returning to step 1, the first cycle is complete. The next input would be $e(1)$. ■

The sample interval (governed by some submultiple of the MPU clock) must be long enough to allow one cycle of calculations before entering the next sample. This constraint puts a limit on the allowable complexity of the control algorithm for a given sample period and microcomputer.

In the next section we will look at some problems associated with quantization.

## 5-6

---

## SOLVED PROBLEMS

In keeping with the spirit of the "solved problems" section we will use some examples to amplify certain concepts previously discussed. The first problem illustrates the effects mentioned at the end of Section 5-4 using a simple first-order system.

### 5-6.1  Quantization Effects on Steady State Response

We will assume that quantization effects result from rounding and that the quantizing levels are uniformly placed on the interval $-M$ to $M$, centered about 0; $M$ is the maximum expected signal amplitude. If we are working with an $N$-bit register, we will have $(2^N - 1)$ levels, for example see Table 1-1. Since one bit is used for sign information there are $2^{N-1}$ positive levels (including 0). Figure 5-1 illustrates round-off quantization. From Fig. 5-1 we can determine that the maximum signal amplitude $M$ is related to the maximum round-off error $(q/2)$ by

$$M = (2^N - 1)(q/2) \qquad (5\text{-}30)$$

Consequently, given the maximum signal amplitude and quantization error, one can find the minimum required binary-word length $N$.

#### EXAMPLE 5-9 (Quantization Effect on Steady State Response)
Consider the digital control algorithm given by

$$\frac{U(z)}{E(z)} = \frac{1}{z - a}$$

Without an input $e(k)$, the output $u(k)$ from an initial value $u(0)$ is

$$u(k) = a^k u(0)$$

For $|a| < 1$, $u(k)$ will approach a steady value of zero using precise arithmetic (no quantization).

Assume now $|u(0)| < 1$ ($M = 1$) and that a 3-bit (register length) quantization is used. Describe the quantization levels and calculate the steady state value for $u$ if $u(0) = 0.571$ and $a = 0.857$ using quantized values. Here, it is assumed that the parameter $a$ must satisfy the same quantization levels.

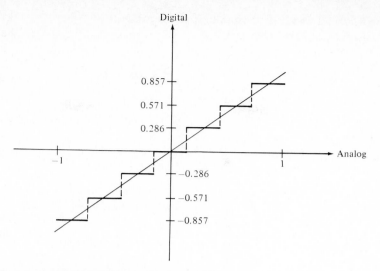

**FIGURE 5-7.  Quantization for Example 5-9.**

**SOLUTION:** There are $(2^N - 1) = (2^3 - 1) = 7$ quantization levels. Each level is, solving for $q$ in Eq. (5-30),

$$q = 2M/7 = 2/7 = 0.2857 \text{ units}$$

Figure 5-7 shows the 7 quantization levels between $-1$ and $1$. Since $u(0) = 0.571$ is a quantization level, it is unaffected by quantization. Therefore,

$$u(1) = au(0) = (0.857)(0.571) = 0.489$$

But this value is rounded to the nearest quantization level of $0.571$. Since this calculation repeats for $u(2)$, $u(3)$, and so on, the steady state value is $0.571$ (not zero!). ∎

**Remark:**  If the parameter $a$ was taken to be $-0.857$, the system instead of decaying to zero as one would expect with precise arithmetic would oscillate between $0.571$ and $-0.571$. Both phenomena are undesirable effects of quantization and are best handled using as small a quantization as possible, that is to say, large register lengths. In the next example this same quantization is applied to the parameters of a second-order digital algorithm.

## 5-6.2  Effects of Parameter Quantization

It was mentioned in an earlier section that parameter quantization has a potentially more disastrous effect on system behavior than simple additive noise. Let us consider a problem with two parameters, both of which are represented as 3-bit binary words quantizing the interval $-1$ to $+1$. This is the same quantization as depicted in Fig. 5-7.

**EXAMPLE 5-10 (Parameter Quantization)**

Consider the digital algorithm

$$G(z) = \frac{U(z)}{E(z)} = \frac{z^2}{z^2 + az + b}$$

To investigate the limitations imposed by quantization:

(a) Plot the allowable parameter plane points under quantization that, in addition, maintain a stable system.
(b) Plot both the unit-pulse response with precise arithmetic and using the (coarse) quantization specified when $a = -0.9$ and $b = 0.2$.

*SOLUTION:* (a) Recalling the stability results of Fig. 2-22 and using Fig. 5-7 as an aid, the allowable points on the parameter plane are shown in Fig. 5-8.

(b) For the given nominal parameters and precise arithmetic:

$$G(z) = \frac{z^2}{z^2 - 0.9z + 0.2} = \frac{-4z}{z - 0.4} + \frac{5z}{z - 0.5}$$

Therefore the unit-pulse response (or weighting sequence) is

$$g(k) = 5(0.5)^k - 4(0.4)^k = \{1, 0.9, 0.369, 0.2101, \ldots\}$$

When the parameters are quantized, the corresponding function is

$$G_q(z) = \frac{z^2}{z^2 - 0.857z + 0.286}$$

Factoring the denominator of $G_q(z)$ indicates complex-conjugate roots!

$$G_q(z) = \frac{z^2}{(z - 0.429)^2 + (0.319)^2}$$

Using Eqs. (2-75) and (2-76), we find that

$$g_q(k) = (0.535)^k(\cos 0.641k + 1.341 \sin 0.641k), \quad k = 0, 1, 2, \ldots$$

$$g_q(k) = \{1, 0.858, 0.449, 0.140, \ldots\}$$

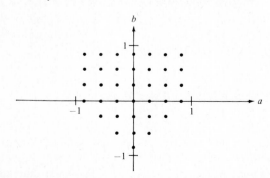

**FIGURE 5-8.   Allowable quantized parameters for Example 5-10.**

Note that except for the first couple of terms the quantized-parameter response is quite different from the nominal response; even the oscillatory form is different. ∎

Although most quantization is not as severe as that used in this problem, this example indicates the possible troubles that might arise.

## 5-6.3  A Case Study

As a summary to this chapter, let us consider the simulation of a particular system using a relatively severe degree of quantization on the digital controller, corresponding to a short computer word length.

The plant will be taken as

$$G_p(s) = \frac{8}{s(s + 2)} \tag{5-31}$$

We will assume that this model is exact, and in the simulation whatever input signals are supplied by the digital controller will be processed faithfully according to this transfer function. The design we are testing out is illustrated in detail in Fig. 5-9. A digital compensation algorithm (one that will be formulated in the next chapter) based on a sampling period $T = 0.1$ sec is given by

$$G_c(z) = z^{-2}(2.5044z - 2.0504) \tag{5-32}$$

As can be seen from Fig. 5-9, the controllable form is used in the simulation of $G_c(z)$. There is one quantizer shown with the ADC and each of the two gains of $G_c(z)$ is similarly quantized.

To calculate the unit-step response, let us assume that fixed-point arithmetic is used and that all parameter and signal values are in the numerical range $-3.75$ to $3.75$ units.

*Quantization: A 4-Bit Word Length is Used.*  From Eq. (5-30), with $M = 3.75$ and $N = 4$, $q = 0.5$. This establishes the quantization levels:

$$\{q_i\} = \{0, \pm 0.5, \pm 1, \pm 1.5, \ldots, \pm 3.5\} \tag{5-33}$$

Note that the gains in Fig. 5-9 are shown as quantized values. Applying the methods of Chapter 4, we use $\Delta = 0.05$ sec and the plant representation:

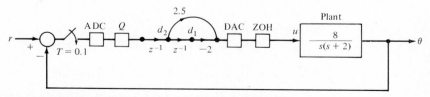

**FIGURE 5-9.  Simulation diagram for the case study.**

$$\dot{x}(t) = \frac{d}{dt}\begin{bmatrix} \theta \\ \dot{\theta} \\ u \end{bmatrix} = \begin{bmatrix} 0 & 1 & 0 \\ 0 & -2 & 8 \\ 0 & 0 & 0 \end{bmatrix}\begin{bmatrix} \theta \\ \dot{\theta} \\ u \end{bmatrix}, \quad kT < t \leq kT + T \quad (5\text{-}34)$$

Evaluating $e^{A\Delta}$,

$$x(k\Delta + \Delta) = \begin{bmatrix} 1 & 0.0476 & 0.0097 \\ 0 & 0.9048 & 0.3807 \\ 0 & 0 & 1 \end{bmatrix}x(k\Delta) \quad (5\text{-}35)$$

The update equations (for a unit-step input) are

$$u(kT^+) = 2.5\, d_2(kT^-) - 2\, d_1(kT^-)$$

$$d_1(kT^+) = d_2(kT^-) \quad (5\text{-}36)$$

$$d_2(kT^+) = 1 - x_1(kT^-)$$

Keep in mind that each of the signals $d_1$, $d_2$, and $u$ are allowed to take on only the quantized values in Eq. (5-33)! For a few sample calculations, suppose that $v(0^-) = 0$, where

$$v = [\theta, \dot{\theta}, u, d_1, d_2]^T$$

Step 1: Since $t = 0$ is a sampling instant, we use the update equations, Eq. (5-36), to obtain

$$v(0^+) = [0 \quad 0 \quad 0 \quad 0 \quad 1]^T$$

Step 2: The transition equation, Eq. (5-35), is now used twice before incurring the next sample instant ($t = 0.1$):

$$v(0.05) = v(0.01^-) = v(0^+) \quad \text{(unchanged)}$$

Step 3: Using the update equations,

$$v(0.1^-) = [0 \quad 0 \quad 0 \quad 0 \quad 1]^T$$

becomes

$$v(0.1^+) = [0 \quad 0 \quad 2.5 \quad 1 \quad 1]^T$$

(These values are all quantization levels.)

Step 4: Transitioning:

$$v(0.15) = [0.024 \quad 0.952 \quad 2.5 \quad 1 \quad 1]^T$$
$$v(0.2^-) = [0.094 \quad 1.813 \quad 2.5 \quad 1 \quad 1]^T$$

Step 5: Updating:

$$v(0.2^+) = [0.094 \quad 1.813 \quad 0.500 \quad 1 \quad 0.906]^T$$

which (last three elements only) must be quantized to

$$v(0.2^+) = [0.094 \quad 1.813 \quad 0.5 \quad 1 \quad 1]^T$$

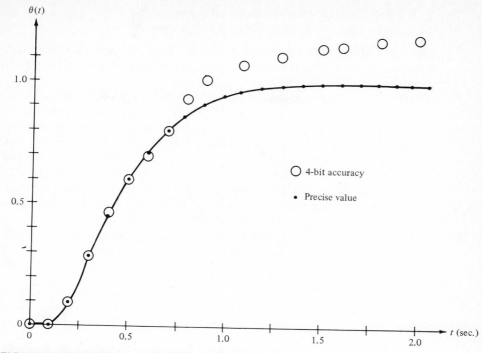

**FIGURE 5-10. Step-response for the case study.**

The steps continue by transitioning twice, updating, quantizing, and repeating. Figure 5-10 presents the resulting step response. The results are plotted for 3 sec, showing both the precise values (large word length) and the 4-bit-quantization values.

*Remarks:*
- The limited accuracy curve is nearly the same as the ideal curve initially, except for slight variations that appear as superimposed noise.
- The steady state value increases to about 1.20, 20% higher than the ideal curve!

Both of these effects would be expected from our earlier discussions.

This study is readily adapted to a laboratory exercise where the digital controller is implemented on a microcomputer and the plant is implemented on an analog computer.

## 5-7

## SUMMARY

In this chapter we have discussed the basic concept of amplitude quantization, which is a necessary evil associated with digital computers. We saw that there are two major effects of quantization on system performance:

1. It introduces noise (undesirable signal fluctuations).
2. It causes a general deterioration in dynamic response.

This latter effect can show up as either an altered transient or steady state response, or both. The principal effect on the transient response is typically caused by parameter quantization.

Methods were presented for the purpose of analyzing and predicting the effects of quantization. Parameter sensitivity calculations can be made to determine if the quantization may have a disastrous effect such as destabilizing the system. Similarly, one can anticipate having different noise levels in the response due simply to the structure of the realization. Probabilistic methods were developed to estimate the output noise level for a given realization; however, perhaps the most useful technique for determining the system effects for a given structure and quantization is to apply the simulation method of Chapter 4, as was illustrated in the previous case study of Section 5-6.3.

With the next chapter we begin to look at design procedures—ways in which we can "engineer" a digital control system to behave in a particular (desirable) manner.

## REFERENCES

**Section 5-1** *Digital Processing of Signals;* B. Gold and C. M. Rader; McGraw-Hill, 1969.
*Digital Signal Processing;* A. V. Oppeheim and R. W. Schafer; Prentice-Hall, 1975.

**Section 5-2** *Modern Control Systems;* R. C. Dorf; Addison-Wesley, 3rd. ed., 1980.

**Section 5-3** *Random Signal Analysis,* D. F. Mix; Addison-Wesley, 1969.
*Probabilistic Systems Analysis;* A. M. Breipohl; John Wiley and Sons, 1970.

**Section 5-4** *Digital Processing of Signals;* B. Gold and C. M. Rader; McGraw-Hill, 1969.
*Digital Control System Analysis and Design;* C. L. Phillips and H. T. Nagle; Jr.; Prentice-Hall, 1984.

**Section 5-5** *Programming Microprocessor Interfaces for Control and Instrumentation;* M. Andrews; Prentice-Hall, 1982.

**Section 5-6** *Digital Control Systems;* B. C. Kuo; Holt, Rinehart and Winston, 1980

## PROBLEMS

**5-1** Calculate and plot the sampled, quantized, and clamped version of the following signals:

(a) $x_a(t) = \sin 2\pi t$

(b) $x_b(t) = t, 0 \leq t < 1$
$\qquad = 2 - t, 1 \leq t < 2$

Use a sampling interval of $T = 0.1$ sec and round-off quantization with quantized values at $0.2k$, $k = 0, \pm 1, \pm 2, \ldots, \pm 5$.

**DIGITAL IMPLEMENTATION**

**5-2**     Repeat the exercise of Problem 5-1 with the two signals specified there, but use a sampling interval of $T = 0.2$ sec and quantization levels of $0.25k$; $k = 0$, $\pm 1, \pm 2, \ldots, \pm 5$, with
  **(a)** round-off quantization
  **(b)** truncation quantization

**5-3**     Apply the resulting digital version of the signals in Problem 5-1 to
  **(a)** an ideal integrator with an initial output of zero.
  **(b)** an analog system with transfer function $(s + 1)^{-1}$

**5-4**     Assume that the sinusoidal signal

$$x(t) = \sin t$$

is sampled at a rate of 1 Hz ($T = 1$ sec) and clamped at quantization levels $\{q_i\} = \{k/5$ for $k = 0, \pm 1, \pm 2, \ldots\}$ using round-off. Calculate the sequence of round-off errors and plot their occurrences on the error axis. All errors should fall in the interval $-0.1$ to $0.1$. After collecting 10 to 20 error samples, create a bar graph of errors by dividing the error interval into 10 subintervals of 0.02 units and plotting a constant value over each subinterval whose value is the number of error samples to fall into that subinterval. Do your results compare favorably with the assumption of uniform error distribution indicated in Fig. 4-5a? If not, why not?

**5-5**     Parameter quantization effects can be evaluated using the real frequency plots of $z$-domain transfer functions. For the following pulse-transfer functions, first plot the magnitude and phase functions using precise arithmetic, and second, with the parameters quantized (using round-off) to levels $\{q_i\} = \{k/4$ for $k = 0, \pm 1, \pm 2, \ldots\}$:

**(a)** $F_a(z) = \dfrac{0.32z}{z - 0.65}$

**(b)** $F_b(z) = \dfrac{z}{z^2 - 0.9z + 0.2}$

Use $\omega T$ intervals of 0.5 radians for your plots.

**5-6**     **(a)** Convert the sampled-data system of Fig. P5-6 into an equivalent $z$-domain system.

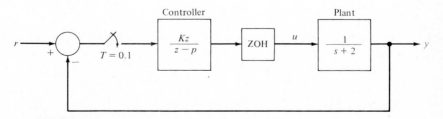

FIGURE P5-6.

(b) Determine the sensitivity of the closed-loop transfer function $T(z)$ to the parameter $K$ if the nominal value of $K$ is 0.2 and $p = 0.9$.

(c) By how much is the steady state value of the unit-step response changed for a 5% increase in $K$?

**5-7** Repeat the exercise of Problem 5-6 for the parameter $p$, instead of $K$; that is, following part (a), determine the sensitivity of $T(z)$ with respect to $p$ using the nominal values given in Problem 5-6 and, finally, the percent change of the final value of the unit-step response for a 5% increase in $p$.

**5-8** Using the results of Problems 5-6 and 5-7, estimate the final value of the unit-step response when both $K$ and $p$ are rounded-off to the nearest level of the set $\{q_i\} = \{\pm 5k/4 \text{ for } k = 0, 1, 2, \ldots\}$. Assume that the two effects act independently and determine the combined effect by calculating the root-mean-squared value of the two separate predictions. Check your estimate by finding the true steady state responses before and after quantization.

**5-9** Consider the problem of implementing the control algorithm

$$D(z) = \frac{1.582z - 0.582}{z + 0.418} = \frac{U(z)}{E(z)}$$

(a) Diagram $D(z)$ in both the controllable and the observable canonical forms (see Section 3-6).

(b) Approximate the total quantization noise at the output using the methods presented in Sections 5-3 and 5-4 if $q = \frac{1}{4}$ for both canonical structures.

**5-10** (a) Repeat the exercise of Problem 5-9 for the control law

$$D(z) = \frac{0.60z^2 - 0.28z}{z^2 - 0.80z + 0.12}$$

(b) Diagram $D(z)$ as a Jordan canonical structure and as a cascade of two first-order sections. Calculate the corresponding output noise and tabulate the four noise levels, that is, including those calculated in part (a).

**5-11** In a unity feedback system structure similar to that shown in Fig. P5-6 the plant is described by the state model

$$\dot{\mathbf{x}}(t) = \begin{bmatrix} 0 & 1 \\ 0 & -1 \end{bmatrix} \mathbf{x}(t) + \begin{bmatrix} 0 \\ 1 \end{bmatrix} u(t)$$

$$y(t) = [1 \quad 0] \mathbf{x}(t)$$

A digital controller has been designed having the form

$$D(z) = \frac{1.582z - 0.582}{z + 0.418}$$

Calculate the unit-step response of the equivalent discrete-time (closed-loop) system using

**(a)** precise arithmetic

**(b)** round-off quantization for both digital signals and digital parameters with the quantization levels specified in Eq. (5-33)

**5-12** For the general configuration of Fig. P5-6 assume that the plant is given by the transfer function

$$\frac{Y(s)}{U(s)} = \frac{0.048}{s^3 + 0.80s^2 + 0.12s}$$

Digital control laws have been designed for two possible sampling rates:

$$D_1(z) = \frac{0.154(z - 0.523)}{z - 0.425}$$

for $T = 0.15$ sec, and

$$D_2(z) = \frac{0.339(z - 0.926)}{z - 0.976}$$

for $T = 0.04$ sec.

Use the simulation technique illustrated in Section 5-6.3 to obtain the system unit-step response for both designs with

**(a)** precise arithmetic

**(b)** round-off quantization in the digital control law with quantization levels established by a 4-bit word length ($N = 4$) and a maximum analog level of $M = 1.875$

**(c)** round-off quantization in the ADC unit *only* (same quantization levels of part b); all other calculations performed with no quantization

**(d)** round-off quantization in ADC and DAC units only

**(e)** Repeat parts (b), (c), and (d) with quantization levels established by an 8-bit word length

PART **II**

# DESIGN TECHNIQUES FOR DISCRETE-TIME SYSTEMS

## CHAPTER 6

# Design in the *z*-Domain

In this chapter we begin our study of design methods. To achieve "control system design" various aspects of system performance, such as stability, transient, and steady state responses must be considered. As we know, problems of stability can arise whenever feedback is used; this is the price we must pay to obtain the benefits of feedback. In addition to stability, we generally want to be able to specify particular types of responses in terms of accuracy and speed. More recently we also see requirements with regard to robustness and parameter sensitivity—so that the system may perform adequately even in the face of unforeseen disturbances and parameter changes. The first design approach that will be presented is the classic second-order system design, followed by a discussion of higher-order system design by this method.

## 6-1

## SECOND-ORDER SYSTEM DESIGN

In Chapter 4 we briefly discussed the redesign or translation from an *s*-domain transfer function to an "equivalent" *z*-domain transfer function. Since our experience is usually greater with continuous-time systems, we might well consider the standard second-order system described by the transfer function

$$T(s) = \frac{\omega_n^2}{s^2 + 2\zeta\omega_n s + \omega_n^2} \tag{6-1}$$

where $\zeta$ is the damping ratio and $\omega_n$ is the natural frequency. A large portion of classical design methods is, in fact, based on the assumption that the closed-loop system can be made to behave in a way that closely matches that of the system function of Eq. (6-1) for some $\zeta$ and $\omega_n$. Using the developments of Section 2-6.1, one can "map" the system of Eq. (6-1) into the $z$-plane to determine "equivalent" pole locations as well as contours of constant damping ratio for design purposes (see Figure 2-15).

However, rather than take the approach of "redesign" from a continuous-time system, we will adjust our thinking in terms of direct design with discrete-time systems. Let us define a *standard second-order discrete-time system* as one with a pulse transfer function given by

$$T(z) = \frac{C(z)}{R(z)} = \frac{(1 - b\cos a)z + b^2 - b\cos a}{z^2 - (2b\cos a)z + b^2} \tag{6-2}$$

where $b$ and $a$ represent the two defining parameters for the system. As we shall see, the above "ideal" system has several useful features, not the least being that we can generate such things as the general unit-step response in terms of the two system parameters $b$ and $a$.

A step input test provides a good deal of insight into the responsive nature of the system. To demonstrate this fact, the unit-step response will be obtained for the "standard system" of Eq. (6-2). Although the detailed development is not presented, the procedure is a straightforward application of the $z$-transform method. Thus, for $R(z)$, a unit-step sequence in Eq. (6-2)

$$\frac{C(z)}{z} = \frac{T(z)}{(z - 1)} \tag{6-3}$$

Employing the transform pair of Eq. (2-76), we invert Eq. (6-3) to find the response sequence $c(k)$; the reader is encouraged to fill in the omitted steps. The result is the "ideal second-order step response"

$$c(k) = 1 - b^k \cos ak \tag{6-4}$$

The parameters $b$ and $a$ are exactly the polar coordinates of the system poles, as shown in Figure 6-1. It is interesting to note that the gain and zero of $T(z)$ are

$$K = 1 - x, \quad z_1 = -(b^2 - x)(1 - x)^{-1} \tag{6-5}$$

where $x = b\cos a$ is the real part of the pole location and $b$ is the radial distance of the pole location. The end result is that the gain and zero location are *locked* to the pole locations through relations in Eqs. (6-5).

From the general form of the step response in Eq. (6-4) we note that $b$ must be less than one for stability. Furthermore, $a$ will typically represent a small angle to provide several "samples" during the cosine cycle (see Table 2-3). If the system is stable, then the steady state value of $c(k)$ will be unity, or in other words, the system responds in a Type 1 manner. (We will be discussing system

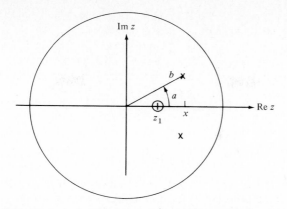

**FIGURE 6-1.    Pole-zero plot for standard second-order system.**

type in Section 6-3.) Another important ingredient for time response is the "settling time." In keeping with standard practice we will refer to the *settling time* of a system as the time required for the response to reach its steady state value within a tolerance of 2%. Figure 6-2 illustrates a typical step response (presented as if the response were continuous for convenience), showing the key parameters likely to be the object of performance specifications.

Variations on our definitions of the step-response parameters will be found in the literature. For example, settling time can be specified for other percent tolerances about the steady state value and a more standard definition of rise time is the time required for the response to go from 10% to 90% of the steady state value. However, for present purposes the values corresponding to those in Figure 6-2 will be adequate.

Returning now to the desired step response $c(k)$ of Eq. (6-4), we will investigate some particular responses. Although our "ideal" step response lacks complete generality, it has the advantage of simplicity. From the form of Eq. (6-4) we can quickly pick out some particular features:

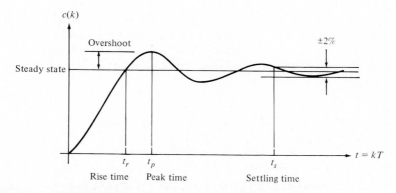

**FIGURE 6-2.    Illustration of step-response parameters.**

1. Steady state: The error, $e(k) = r(k) - c(k)$, is zero in steady state for $b < 1$, when the reference input $r(k)$ is a step function.
2. Settling time: The 2% settling time is approximated by setting $b^N = 0.02$, and solving for $N$, whence $t_s = NT$, where $T$ is the sample interval.
3. Peak time: An estimate for the time at which the peak overshoot occurs is $t_p = (\pi T / a)$, or $k_p = (\pi / a)$. An exact value, if needed, could be determined.
4. Percent overshoot (P.O.): Evaluating $c(k)$ at $k_p$,

$$\text{P.O.} = 100[c(k_p) - 1] = 100b^{k_p} \tag{6-6}$$

Let us now proceed to construct a design method built around this second-order response.

First, we will assume that we have a second-order system with adequate pole locations, but lacking the proper zero location required by Eq. (6-5).

## 6-1.1  Feedforward Control

Figure 6-3 illustrates a compensator system whose purpose is to provide zeros with the proper locations related to the desired pole positions to achieve the controlled standard response of Eq. (6-4). At this point let us assume that the plant transfer function is given by

$$G_p(z) = \frac{k(z - z_1)(z - z_2)}{z^2 - 2bz \cos a + b^2} \tag{6-7}$$

where $z_1$ and $z_2$ are undesirable zero locations, but the pole locations are satisfactory. If the zeros $z_1$ and $z_2$ are inside the unit circle, $G_p(z)$ is said to be a *minimum-phase* (transfer) *function*. Assuming this to be the case, the zero-compensator system $G_c(z)$ of Fig. 6-3 can be designed to have the transfer function

$$G_c(z) = \frac{(1 - b \cos a)z + (b^2 - b \cos a)}{(z - z_1)(z - z_2)} \tag{6-8}$$

Note that the overall compensator/plant transfer function is now given by $T(z)$ in Eq. (6-2).

As we will see shortly both in this chapter and the next, *feedback* control will provide the mechanism for altering the pole locations; consequently, the zero compensator is sometimes referred to as a *feedforward* controller. Also, feedforward control plays an important role in disturbance rejection in the manner

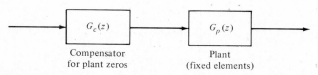

**FIGURE 6-3.**  Diagram showing feedforward (zero) compensator.

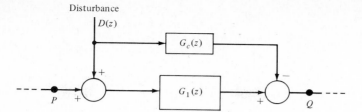

Disturbance $D(z)$

**FIGURE 6-4.** Portion of system illustrating disturbance cancellation.

presented in Fig. 6-4. That is, if a disturbance can be measured, its effect can be processed and fed forward to achieve a cancellation. In this situation the key is having a good model for $G_1(z)$ so that the compensator $G_c(z)$ can be designed to match $G_1(z)$, thereby cancelling the disturbance at point $Q$ without otherwise affecting the transmission between $P$ and $Q$ in Fig. 6-4. An access point such as the summing junction $Q$ is, of course, a necessity for this type of disturbance rejection.

Thus, we are able to use feedforward control to alter the system zero locations as well as cancelling certain (measurable) types of disturbance signals. Let us consider a simple example before continuing the discussion.

### EXAMPLE 6-1 (System Zero Relocation)

We assume that the process of finding a ZOH equivalent system for a certain (continuous-time) plant with input sampled at a rate of 10 Hz has led to the following discrete-time model:

$$G_p(z) = \frac{0.5750(z^2 - z + 0.5000)}{z^2 - 1.3858z + 0.5625}$$

and further that the system response to a unit step must have less than 15% peak overshoot, a maximum settling time of 2 sec and a zero error in steady state. We are to design a feedforward compensator $G_c(z)$ so that the cascade system $G_c(z)G_p(z)$ will satisfy the specifications.

**SOLUTION:** Since $T = 0.1$ sec and $b = 0.7500$ (from $b^2 = 0.5625$, the denominator constant term), we find that

$$(0.75)^N \leq 0.02$$

requires $N \geq 14$. Therefore, the settling time $t_s < 1.4$ sec. Also from the denominator, $(2b \cos a = 1.3858)$, $a = 0.3927$; and estimating the percent overshoot, $k_p = 8$,

$$\text{P.O.} = 100(0.75)^8 = 10.01\%$$

These estimates indicate that the system poles are adequate to meet the design specifications if the zero can be located (relative to these pole locations) according to Eq. (6-5). We can calculate from $G_p$ that the actual plant zeros have

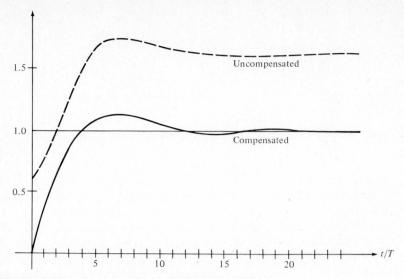

**FIGURE 6-5.   Unit-step responses for Example 6-1.**

the complex locations $z_{1,2} = 0.5 \pm j0.5$; thus, the plant is a minimum phase system, and we may use the compensator of Eq. (6-8) to obtain

$$G_c(z) = \frac{0.5341(z - 0.4246)}{(z^2 - z + 0.5)}$$

The zero of $G_c$ conforms to Eq. (6-5), and the gain of $G_c$ includes the reciprocal of the gain in $G_p$ so that the product $G_cG_p$ results in the standard second-order form as given in Eq. (6-2) (with gain constant 0.3071). Figure 6-5 presents the unit-step responses for both $G_p(z)$ and $G_c(z)G_p(z)$ for comparison. ■

We note from the results in Fig. 6-5 that the main advantage of controlling the system zeros shows up in the improved steady state response; the steady value of the original plant respresents a 63% error. Let us contrast this "numerator" effect with a corresponding "denominator" effect.

## 6-1.2   Feedback Control

In the previous development we found that a feedforward compensator could alter the zero locations without affecting the system poles. With unity (negative) feedback, as illustrated in Fig. 6-6, just the reverse situation occurs.

Consider that

$$G(z) = N(z)/D(z) \tag{6-9}$$

where both $N$ and $D$ are polynomials without common factors. By calculating $T(z) = C(z)/R(z)$,

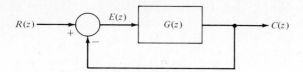

**FIGURE 6-6. Unity (negative) feedback.**

$$T(z) = \frac{G(z)}{1 + G(z)} = \frac{N/D}{1 + (N/D)} = \frac{N(z)}{N(z) + D(z)} \qquad (6\text{-}10)$$

and we see that *feedback affects only the pole locations!* In terms of a step response, the pole locations determine the type of "transient" response that evolves to the steady state, or in the case of any pole(s) outside the unit circle, the instability of the system. In Section 6-4 we will study a useful technique for parameter design that permits us to sketch the location of all possible pole positions as a function of the parameter.

## 6-2

## DOMINANT SECOND-ORDER SYSTEMS

If we are to capitalize on our knowledge of second-order systems, we must find a way to design a controller that would force a (higher-order) system to behave (approximately) as a standard second-order system. The combination of feed-forward and feedback control can be used to alter both the zero and the pole locations of the system, but what are the criteria for relocating these poles and zeros?

To establish the basis for design, consider the step-response of a system with transfer function

$$T(z) = \frac{C(z)}{R(z)} = \frac{K(z - z_1)(z - z_2) \cdots (z - z_m)}{(z - p_1)(z - p_2) \cdots (z - p_n)} \qquad (6\text{-}11)$$

where $m < n$ and the poles are assumed to be distinct and not equal to 1 (although they may occur in complex conjugate pairs). Consequently, to find the unit-step response, we form

$$\frac{C(z)}{z} = \frac{K(z - z_1)(z - z_2) \cdots (z - z_m)}{(z - 1)(z - p_1)(z - p_2) \cdots (z - p_n)} \qquad (6\text{-}12)$$

Assuming that $p_1 = p_2^*$ is the desired second-order pole location and that $z_1$ is the associated zero in Eq. (6-2), then the partial fraction expansion of $C(z)$ becomes

$$\frac{C(z)}{z} = \left( \frac{A}{z - 1} + \frac{B}{z - p_1} + \frac{B^*}{z - p_2} \right) + \sum_{i=3}^{n} \frac{R_i}{z - p_i} \qquad (6\text{-}13)$$

where (with the proper gain and steady state design, $A = 1$) the first three terms should invert to the ideal (designed) second-order step-response sequence of Eq. (6-4). The $R_i$ (residue) coefficients in Eq. (6-13) are given by

$$R_i = (z - p_i)z^{-1}C(z)\big|_{z=p_i} \tag{6-14}$$

or

$$R_i = \frac{K(p_i - z_1)(p_i - z_2) \cdots (p_i - z_m)}{(p_i - 1)(p_i - p_1) \cdots (p_i - p_{i-1})(p_i - p_{i+1}) \cdots (p_i - p_n)} \tag{6-15}$$

In order to approximate the ideal step response with the higher-order system, the summation term in Eq. (6-13) must have a negligible effect. This can happen in two ways:

1. $R_i \cong 0$
2. $p_i \cong 0$

The residue $R_i$ in Eq. (6-15) can be made (nearly) zero by adjusting pole locations so that $p_i$ is (nearly) equal to some zero (other than the design zero $z_1$). In this case the term involving $p_i$ will be (nearly) identically zero. In the second case $p_i$ has a negligibly small magnitude; we are left with a unit delay factor in Eq. (6-12) that has only a minor effect on the transient response. Let us summarize the results with the following design procedure.

*Design Procedure.*   We wish to design a control system to meet time-domain specifications:

1. Determine an acceptable (second-order) system of the form in Eq. (6-2).
2. Adjust the zeros of the system to achieve the required zero of Eq. (6-5) and any others to cancel undesired plant poles using feedforward compensation.
3. Locate two poles to match the design poles of Eq. (6-2) and the remainder to either an undesirable zero location or to the origin.

This third part assumes that we can control pole positions; this will be the topic of much consideration both in this chapter and in the next.

### EXAMPLE 6-2 (Second-Order Design)

Using a plant with a pole–zero plot as given below, we wish to determine the pole–zero plot of the feedforward compensator and the closed-loop pole positions obtained by feedback.

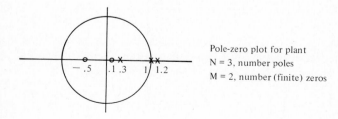

Pole-zero plot for plant
N = 3, number poles
M = 2, number (finite) zeros

We will assume that the parameters $b = 0.750$, and $a = 0.393$ are sufficient to meet the specification requirements; see Eq. (6-2).

### SOLUTION:

1. Since $b$ and $a$ are given, we know that the design is toward a closed-loop system with poles at $0.693 \pm j0.287$ and a zero at $+0.425$ from Eq. (6-2)
2. The feedforward compensator must add a zero at 0.425 and cancel out those at 0.1 and $-0.5$. In addition it is convenient to add a zero at 0.3 to cancel one pole.*

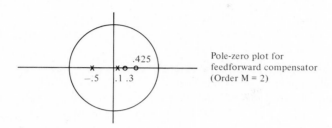

Pole-zero plot for feedforward compensator (Order M = 2)

If the number of plant poles is $N$ and the number of (finite) plant zeros is $M$, then the feedforward compensator must be of order $M$. Also, since only one zero must be placed for the second-order design, $(M - 1)$ poles can be cancelled, leaving only $(N - M + 1)$ poles to be dealt with using feedback techniques.

3. In this case feedback is used to obtain pole locations at $0.693 \pm j0.287$ (since only $N - M + 1 = 2$ poles remain). ∎

### Remarks:

- This method will work only for plants that are *minimum phase* (no zeros (or poles) outside the unit circle), for no matter how accurate the model there will always be a slight error in cancellation that will lead to system instability.
- In Chapter 7 we will discuss state-variable feedback, which gives complete freedom in pole placement; however, a simple parameter design can sometimes be sufficient, as we will see in Section 6-4.

## 6-3

## DESIGN FOR STEADY STATE ERROR RESPONSE

We already know that feedforward control can be used to improve steady state behavior. In this section we further investigate special conditions of an open-loop system used in a unity feedback context. Thus, although a restricted class of problems, single-loop feedback occurs quite often in practice. The simple

---

* Later we will see that feedback can provide an even better solution than pole–zero cancellation.

configuration of Fig. 6-6 can many times be used to achieve an acceptable system design. It is for this classical design problem that the definition of system "Type" was introduced.

**Definition 6-1:** An open-loop discrete-time transfer function $G(z)$ (shown in Fig. 6-6) is said to be a *Type N* system if $G(z)$ possesses (after removal of a common numerator and denominator factors) exactly $N$ poles at $z = 1$.

The utility of the above definition shows up in the calculation of steady state errors for various test inputs. From Fig. 6-6 we can see that the error signal $E(z)$ is given by

$$E(z) = R(z) - C(z) = \frac{R(z)}{1 + G(z)} \tag{6-16}$$

From this basic form we can investigate the steady state value of error using the Final Value property of $z$-transforms, Eq. (2-18). Of course, stability of $(1 - z^{-1})E(z)$ must be determined *before* we can guarantee that such a steady value exists! Consider $R(z) = (1 - z^{-1})^{-1}$, a unit-step input, then the *steady state error to a unit step* is

$$e_{ss} = \lim_{k \to \infty} e(k) = \lim_{z \to 1} (1 - z^{-1})E(z) = \frac{1}{1 + G(1)} \tag{6-17}$$

In the classical "servomechanism" problem the controlled variable was usually a mechanical position variable. Consequently, when the reference $R(z)$ is a step, the command is for a change in "position." Similarly, if $R(z)$ is a ramp input, the command corresponds to a rate of change of "position" or, in other words, a change in "velocity." The result is that the inputs of steps, ramps, and parabolas are referred to as position, velocity, and acceleration inputs, respectively, regardless of the fact that the actual system may be a temperature regulating system or an inventory control system.

As was done in Eq. (6-17) for a step (position) input, let us assume a unit-ramp (velocity) input and find an expression for $e_{ss}$.

The *steady state error to a unit ramp* is

$$e_{ss} = \lim_{z \to 1} (1 - z^{-1}) \frac{Tz(z - 1)^{-2}}{1 + G(z)} = \lim_{z \to 1} \frac{1}{T^{-1}(z - 1)G(z)} \tag{6-18}$$

Similarly, the *steady state error to a unit parabola* input is

$$e_{ss} = \lim_{z \to 1} \frac{(1 - z^{-1})(1/2)T^2 z(z + 1)}{(z - 1)^3[1 + G(z)]} = \lim_{z \to 1} \frac{1}{T^{-2}(z - 1)^2 G(z)} \tag{6-19}$$

See Table 2-2 for the $z$-domain expressions for the inputs. The steady state error expressions of Eqs. (6-17), (6-18), and (6-19) will now be used to define the steady state error constants.

**Steady State Error Constants.** As an intermediate step to finding the steady state error for a certain reference input, let us define the following:

1. The *Position Error Constant, $K_p$*:

$$K_p = \lim_{z \to 1} G(z) = G(1) \qquad (6\text{-}20)$$

2. The *Velocity Error Constant, $K_v$*:

$$K_v = \frac{1}{T} \lim_{z \to 1} (z - 1)G(z) \qquad (6\text{-}21)$$

3. The *Acceleration Error Constant, $K_a$*:

$$K_a = \frac{1}{T^2} \lim_{z \to 1} (z - 1)^2 G(z) \qquad (6\text{-}22)$$

And we could continue on to the rate of change of acceleration (known as "jerk") as well as higher "polynomial inputs," but these we have defined are typically the only error constants used to state system specifications.

By combining the error results with the defined error constants we find that

$$e_{ss}\big|_{\text{unit step}} = \frac{1}{1 + K_p} \qquad (6\text{-}23a)$$

$$e_{ss}\big|_{\text{unit ramp}} = \frac{1}{K_v} \qquad (6\text{-}23b)$$

$$e_{ss}\big|_{\text{unit parabola}} = \frac{1}{K_a} \qquad (6\text{-}23c)$$

Thus, designers experienced with their use often employ some design specification in terms of an error constant (instead of on the steady state error directly).

Let us now return to the idea of system type. A Type 0 system has no pole at $z = 1$ and consequently will have a finite, nonzero value for $K_p$ and zero values for both $K_v$ and $K_a$, whereas a Type 1 system will have an infinite $K_p$, a

**TABLE 6-1   Steady State Errors**

| System Type | Reference Input | | |
|---|---|---|---|
| | Unit Step | Unit Ramp | Unit Parabola |
| 0 | $\dfrac{1}{1 + K_a}$ | $\infty$ | $\infty$ |
| 1 | 0 | $\dfrac{1}{K_v}$ | $\infty$ |
| 2 | 0 | 0 | $\dfrac{1}{K_a}$ |
| 3 | 0 | 0 | 0 |

finite, nonzero $K_v$, and a zero $K_a$, and so on, for higher types. These results are summarized in Table 6-1 in terms of the resulting steady state errors. The reader should check the table entries using the previous definitions and results.

It is clear from Table 6-1 that the higher the system type, the better the steady state error response. Thus, a feedforward compensator could, for instance, be used to place an extra pole at $z = 1$ to increase the system type of an open-loop system.

### EXAMPLE 6-3 (Steady State Error Calculation)

Given a stable unity feedback system as shown in Fig. 6-6 with a Type 2 $G(z)$ having $K_a = 5$, determine the steady state error to an input sequence

$$r(k) = 10 + 2k + 0.1k^2$$

**SOLUTION:** Since the system is Type 2 any constant or ramp inputs will have a zero error in steady state. Referring to entry 3 of Table 2-2, we find that a unit parabolic sequence is $(\frac{1}{2})k^2$. Therefore, the "amplitude" of the parabolic component of $r(k)$ is 0.2, and the steady state error is

$$e_{ss} = \frac{0.2}{K_a} = 0.04$$

∎

*Remark:* A system is said to *track* any signal for which the steady state error is zero. In the previous example the system will track any piecewise linear input.

### EXAMPLE 6-4 (Compensation for Steady State Response)

Given the Type 1 plant

$$G_p(z) = \frac{K(z - 0.9)}{(z - 1)(z + 0.2)}$$

it is desired to improve the system steady state behavior to ramp inputs by adding an "integral" compensator $G_c(z)$.

**SOLUTION:** The complete open-loop system will be given by $G(z) = G_c(z)G_p(z)$. We choose the compensator to be

$$G_c(z) = \frac{z}{z - 1}$$

The additional pole at $z = 1$ makes $G(z)$ a Type 2 system, so that if we operate the system as in Fig. 6-6 with gain $K$ at a suitable value for stability, the closed-loop system will track ramp inputs. The actual transient performance depends on the closed-loop pole locations, which in turn depend on the value of the gain $K$ of the open-loop system. ∎

*Remarks:*
• Example 6-4 can also be viewed as a feedforward compensation with a particular type of feedback, that of unity (negative) feedback.

- The effect of changing the parameter $K$ on the poles of the closed-loop system is the topic of the next section.

## PARAMETER DESIGN BY THE ROOT-LOCUS METHOD

In the previous sections we saw that the numerator dynamics of the closed-loop transfer function determines the appropriate steady state behavior, while the denominator dynamics affects the transient response. Feedforward compensation was discussed as a method for establishing the appropriate numerator function for acceptable steady state response. Subsequently the important concept of system type was introduced along with the discrete-time steady state error constants. These constants serve as an aid to satisfying steady state response specifications for standard unity (negative) feedback systems from considerations of the open-loop function. In this section we again consider the basic single-loop design, but now for the purpose of controlling the locations of the system poles. The process of establishing the proper pole locations (or eigenvalues) for the system is the main reason for incorporating feedback into the design.

### 6-4.1  The Root-Locus Method

An important aspect of the root-locus method is the visualization of possible closed-loop system behavior as a function of a key parameter. Consequently, the method, being graphical in nature, is primarily for a qualitative study rather than one with which high precision design values are obtained. The basic method assumes that the characteristic equation of the system can be written as

$$1 + KG(z) = 0 \qquad (6\text{-}24)$$

where $K$ is a positive system parameter whose value is to be obtained. The particular form in Eq. (6-24) naturally occurs with a single-loop system such as that shown in Fig. 6-6; however, it is well to note that even a multiloop system can have its characteristic equation in that form also. For example, Eq. (2-55) presents a very general form where $KG(z)$ could represent the sum of all the terms except the first; more will be presented on this later.

To proceed with the development, we have from Eq. (6-24) that

$$KG(z) = -1 \qquad (6\text{-}25)$$

Also, since Eq. (6-25) is generally complex valued, it may be written as the two real equations:

$$|G(z)| = 1/K \qquad (6\text{-}26)$$

$$\underline{/G(z)} = 180° \qquad (6\text{-}27)$$

where we have assumed that $K$ is positive. These equations will be referred to as the *magnitude* and *angle requirements*, respectively. However, before pre-

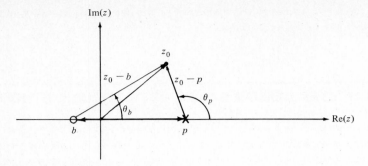

**FIGURE 6-7.** Graphical evaluation.

senting the details of root-locus construction, let us review the useful method of graphical evaluation.

Suppose that we need to determine the value of a function $G(z)$ at $z = z_0$. Furthermore, assume that the poles and zeros of $G(z)$ are known. Algebraically, $G(z_0)$ is obtained by direct substitution and simplification of the resulting complex numbers. Graphically, we may use the correspondence between complex numbers and two-dimensional vectors. Figure 6-7 illustrates the idea with one pole and one zero of $G(z)$.

From Fig. 6-7 $z_0$ is considered as a "test point" (or point of evaluation), $p$ is a pole of $G$, and $b$ is a zero of $G$. Thus,

$$G(z_0) = \frac{\prod_{i=1}^{m} (z_0 - z_i)}{\prod_{i=1}^{n} (z_0 - p_i)} = \frac{\cdots (z_0 - b) \cdots}{\cdots (z_0 - p) \cdots} \tag{6-28}$$

or in terms of magnitude and angle,

$$|G(z_0)| = \frac{\cdots |(z_0 - b)| \cdots}{\cdots |(z_0 - p)| \cdots} \tag{6-29}$$

$$\underline{/G(z_0)} = (\cdots + \theta_b) - (\theta_p + \cdots) \tag{6-30}$$

The key idea is that the factors occurring in the numerator or denominator of $G(z_0)$ show up graphically as "vectors" between the pole or zero and the point of elevation; see Fig. 6-7. Consequently, the magnitudes and angles in Eqs. (6-29) and (6-30) are available graphically as lengths of the lines from pole or zero to the test point and the angles which these lines make with respect to the horizontal reference. An example may help clarify the procedure.

### EXAMPLE 6-5 (Graphical Evaluation)

Given the function $G(z)$ having the poles and zeros shown and a gain constant of unity, determine (a) $|G(0.5)|$ and (b) $\underline{/G(j0.5)}$.

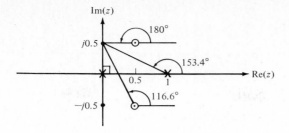

**SOLUTION:** Using the graphical method,

$$|G(0.5)| = \frac{1(0.5)(0.5)}{(0.5)(0.5)} = 1$$

and

$$\underline{/G(j0.5)} = (180° + 116.6°) - (90° + 153.4°) = 53.2° \qquad \blacksquare$$

To continue with the main development, we define the *root loci* of a function $G(z)$ as the locus of those points in the $z$-plane for which the angle requirement, Eq. (6-27), is satisfied. Note that for any point $z$ for which the angle requirement is satisfied, if the gain $K$ was set equal to $|G(z)|^{-1}$, then $z$ would be a closed-loop system pole location. Thus, the root-locus plot for a function $G(z)$ illustrates all possible closed-loop pole locations as a function of the parameter $K$. Fortunately, rather than an exhaustive search for the points in the plane that satisfy the angle requirement, there are a few simple concepts that allow root-locus sketches to be made quite easily. First, let us illustrate the root loci for a simple function. Consider

$$KG(z) = K/z^N \qquad (6\text{-}31)$$

where $N$ can take on integer values. The characteristic equation is therefore

$$z^N + K = 0 \qquad (6\text{-}32)$$

Alternately, we have

$$z = (-K)^{1/N} \qquad (6\text{-}33)$$

Using complex notation,

$$z = [Ke^{j(180° + q360°)}]^{1/N} \qquad (6\text{-}34)$$

where $q = 0, 1, 2, \ldots, N - 1$. Thus, considering only the angle requirement, Eq. (6-27), the loci are described by straight lines with angles from reference given by

$$\frac{180° + q360°}{N} = \frac{(1 + 2q)180°}{N} \qquad (6\text{-}35)$$

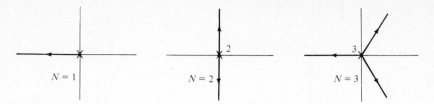

**FIGURE 6-8. Loci for *G(z)* in Eq. (6-31).**

for $q = 0, 1, 2, \ldots, N - 1$. Figure 6-8 illustrates the loci for $G(z)$ in Eq. (6-31) for $N = 1, 2,$ and 3. The angle configurations of $180°(N = 1)$, $\pm 90°(N = 2)$, $180°$, and $\pm 60°(N = 3)$ will occur several times in our discussion of root-locus construction rules.

**Remark:** It is worthwhile to note that whereas the loci in Fig. 6-8 intersect at the origin, the loci for

$$KG(z) = K/(z - \sigma)^N \tag{6-36}$$

would have the same angles, but intersect at $z = \sigma$. We will make use of this special case later.

### 6-4.2  Root-Locus Construction Rules

The construction rules will be divided into two sets: rules for sketches and rules for accurate plots, the former being by far the easier to apply. The following rules are based on the parameter $K$ varying between zero and infinity (positively).

**Primary Rules (Suitable for Qualitative Information).** For each value of the parameter $K$ there will be $n$ roots of $1 + KG(z) = 0$, that is to say, $n$ poles of the closed-loop system. If the value of $K$ is changed, then generally all $n$ roots will also change. A plot of how each of the $n$ roots changes as $K$ increases positively from zero to infinity is the complete *root-locus plot* for $G(z)$.

Let us assume that $G(z)$ is in factored form so that the basic root-locus equation is given by

$$1 + K \frac{(z - z_1) \cdots (z - z_m)}{(z - p_1) \cdots (z - p_n)} = 0 \tag{6-37}$$

Alternatively,

$$[(z - p_1) \cdots (z - p_n)] + K[(z - z_1) \cdots (z - z_m)] = 0 \tag{6-38}$$

Note that for $K = 0$ the closed-loop poles are exactly the *poles* of the open-loop gain function. Also, by dividing Eq. (6-38) by $K$, one can see that the closed-loop poles are the *zeros* of the open-loop function when $K$ goes to infinity. Thus, we have the first important principle.

**Rule 1:** There are $n$-branches corresponding to the number of open-loop poles (since there are usually more finite poles than zeros). Each open-loop pole serves as a beginning ($K = 0$) and each open-loop zero, as an end ($K = \infty$) of a continuous path (branch) traversed by a closed-loop pole.

If we think of these continuous paths requiring specific end points, we are led to the concept of zeros at infinity. That is, with more poles, say, $n$, than zeros, say $m$, there will be $(n - m)$ "zeros at infinity." Also, since zeros are termination points for the loci, $(n - m)$ paths must approach infinity. In the complex plane "infinity" is any "point" infinitely distant from the origin, regardless of direction. Thus, we must investigate more closely the concept of asymptotes. In particular, these "asymptotes" can be determined by approximating Eq. (6-37) to

$$1 + K/(z - \sigma)^{n-m}, \tag{6-39}$$

where

$$(z - \sigma)^{n-m} \cong [G(z)]^{-1} \text{ for very large } z.$$

Thus, retaining only the higher powers of $z$, we have from Eq. (6-39)

$$(z - \sigma)^{n-m} = z^{n-m} - (n - m)\sigma z^{n-m-1} + \cdots \tag{6-40}$$

and from Eq. (6-37)

$$[G(z)]^{-1} = \frac{z^n - (p_1 + p_2 + \cdots + p_n)z^{n-1} + \cdots}{z^m - (z_1 + z_2 + \cdots + z_m)z^{m-1} + \cdots} \tag{6-41}$$

From Eq. (6-41), by long division,

$$G(z) = z^{n-m} - \left( \sum_{i=1}^{n} p_i - \sum_{i=1}^{m} z_i \right) z^{n-m-1} + \cdots \tag{6-42}$$

Also, by comparing Eqs. (6-42) with (6-40), we arrive at

$$\sigma = \frac{\sum_{i=1}^{n} p_i - \sum_{i=1}^{m} z_i}{n - m} \tag{6-43}$$

To complete this development recall from Eq. (6-36) that the loci associated with Eq. (6-39) are straight lines intersecting at $z = \sigma$ and having directions given by the angles of Eq. (6-35). Since Eq. (6-39) matches Eq. (6-37) for large $z$ with $\sigma$ given in Eq. (6-43), we have a description of the asymptote lines directed towards the zeros at infinity. Let us summarize with Rule 2.

**Rule 2:** As $K$ becomes large, $(n - m)$ branches become asymptotic to straight lines that intersect at $z = \sigma$, given in Eq. (6-43), and whose angles with respect to reference are given by

$$\frac{(1 + 2q)180°}{n - m}, \quad q = 0, 1, 2, \ldots, \quad n - m - 1 \tag{6-44}$$

where $n$ and $m$ are the number of poles and (finite) zeros of $G(z)$, respectively.

A third rule usually provides a great deal of information about the structure of the root-locus plot with a minimal effort. The proof of this rule rests simply on the application of the angle requirement to points on the real axis.

**Rule 3:**   The root-locus plot includes those portions of the real axis which lie to the left of an odd number of real poles plus real zeros of $G(z)$.

The fact that a complex-conjugate pair of poles (or zeros) does not affect the angle contribution at a real-axis point is easily seen; equal and opposite angles have a canceling affect.

These first three rules comprise the basic set, and often they suffice to provide a sketch of the root-locus diagram. Let us consider some simple examples.

### EXAMPLE 6-6

We wish to construct the root-locus plot for a system whose characteristic equation is given by Eq. (6-24) with
(a)

$$G_a(z) = \frac{z(z - 0.5)}{(z - 1)(z + 1)}$$

(b)

$$G_b(z) = \frac{(z - 0.3)}{z(z - 1)(z - 0.5)}$$

(c)

$$G_c(z) = \frac{z(z - 0.8)}{(z - 1)^2(z - 0.3)}$$

**SOLUTION:** (a) From the pole–zero plot of the loop-gain function let us first apply Rule 3 because of its simplicity. Thus, real-axis segments of the root-locus occur as shown. The arrows indicate the direction of increasing gain $K$.

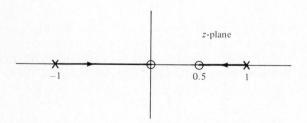

Note that only two branches are expected and that the ends of each branch are well-defined points (according to Rule 1). Since there are no zeros of $G_a$ at $z = \infty$, Rule 2 does not apply.

(b) Again applying Rules 1 and 3 first, we have one complete branch and the other branches starting at the right-hand poles. Since there are two excess poles ($n = 3$ and $m = 1$), we expect two branches to approach asymptotes.

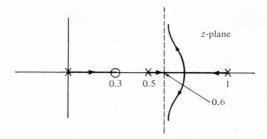

Applying Rule 2,

$$\sigma = (1/2)(1 + 0.5 - 0.3) = 0.6$$

is the intersection of the two asymptotes that are at $\pm 90°$ since $(n - m) = N = 2$. We reason that the two branches in question must come together at some point to form a double pole before "breaking away" as a pair of complex-conjugate poles. Without worrying about the exact point at which this happens (usually near the middle of the real-axis segment) we complete the sketch as shown with the two branches approaching the asymptotic lines. Note that by symmetry only the upper half plane need be drawn.

(c) Following the same procedure by determining the real-axis loci, we have a complete branch and a termination for a second branch. In addition, there should be a single (180°) asymptotic line by Rule 2.

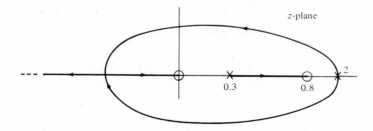

Just as occurred in part (b) for some value of $K$ we have a double pole (here, for $K = 0$). Since no real-axis segments surround the double pole, the branches must become a complex-conjugate pair. Without knowing the exact path followed by these two branches, we do know that one must eventually arrive at $z = 0$ and the other must "go west" to follow the asymptote line. Thus, we reason that a "break-in" point must exist on the negative real axis as shown. Although just a sketch, the plot gives us some pictorial insight into the variation of the closed-loop poles. ∎

***Remarks:*** Before discussing the remaining rules of construction, it is worthwhile to point out that the loci are very "regular" curves in that they generally consist of smooth arcs or lines. A single branch cannot cross itself; and when two or more branches meet, a multiple root is indicated.

An analogy that often helps to visualize the direction of a particular branch is to think of each open-loop pole as a "positively charged particle" fixed in the plane and each (finite) open-loop zero as a corresponding "negatively charged particle" also fixed in the plane. The branch direction at any point is that taken by a small positively charged test particle. Thus, one would not expect any exceedingly complicated paths for the loci.

Calculation of the gain $K$ at a point on the locus can be accomplished from the basic equation.

$$K = -[G(z)]^{-1} \tag{6-45}$$

Algebraically, the point $z$ can be read from the graph and used in Eq. (6-45) to obtain $K$. Alternately, from Eq. (6-37), $K$ is the following ratio of magnitudes:

$$K = \frac{|z - p_1| \cdots |z - p_n|}{|z - z_1| \cdots |z - z_n|} \tag{6-46}$$

which can be found graphically, since each factor is the distance from an open-loop pole or zero to the point $z$ on the locus.

### EXAMPLE 6-7 (Calculation of Gain on the Locus)

To illustrate the gain calculation, consider the loop-gain function given by

$$KG(z) = \frac{K(z^2 + 0.16)}{z(z - 1)}$$

The root-locus plot, as shown below, indicates that $z = 0.3$ is a point on the locus.

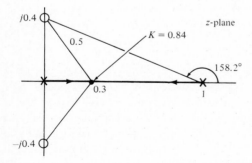

The gain $K$ is the product of the distances to the poles divided by the distances to the zeros:

$$K = \frac{(0.3)(0.7)}{(0.5)(0.5)} = 0.84$$

The inverse problem of finding a point on the locus that corresponds to a certain value of gain requires some "trial and error," usually with linear interpolation between two points. ■

**Secondary Rules (for More Accurate Plots).**   A few additional rules are worthwhile considering. These rules will help to add detail to the root-locus plots. For instance, in Example 6-6b it might be important to know where the "breakaway" point occurs, particularly if the design called for critical damping.

**Rule 4:**   Breakaway points on the real axis occur at real values $z$ for which $K$ is a local maximum. Thus, using Eq. (6-45), one can differentiate $K$ with respect to $z$, set to zero, and solve for the extremum points, or (perhaps more useful) simply calculate values of $K$ for real $z$ in the vicinity of a possible interval containing a breakaway point until a maximum value of $K$ is found—the break-away point is the corresponding $z$ value. Similarly, a "break in" point on the real axis (such as occurs in Example 6-6c) corresponds to a local minimum value of $K$ for real $z$.

Another detail of the root-locus plot is to determine angles of departure (or arrival) for complex poles (or zeros). Such an instance is seem in Example 6-7, where the loci must "arrive" at the complex zeros.

**Rule 5:**   Angles of arrival (or departure) for complex poles (or zeros) are obtained from the angle requirement by assuming an unknown angle $\theta$ for the angle in question and summing (algebraically) the total angle contribution to a point just off the pole or zero. Let us illustrate Rules 4 and 5 with the root-locus plot for the loop-gain function given in Example 6-7.

### EXAMPLE 6-8 (Breakaway Point and Angle of Arrival)
Redrawing the pole–zero plot from the previous example, we reason that there must be a breakaway point in the interval from 0 to 1 on the real axis. Using Rule 4, we write

$$K = \frac{-z(z - 1)}{(z^2 + 0.16)}$$

and calculate the following values:

| $z$ | 0.1 | 0.2 | 0.3 | 0.4 |
|-----|-----|-----|-----|-----|
| $K$ | 0.53 | 0.80 | 0.84 | 0.75 |

For more accuracy,

| $z$ | 0.25 | 0.26 | 0.27 | 0.28 |
|-----|------|------|------|------|
| $K$ | 0.8427 | 0.8453 | 0.8463 | 0.8456 |

Thus, $z = 0.27$ corresponds to the maximum $K$ and is the breakaway point on the graph.

If we assume that a point on the locus, extremely close to the zero at $z = j0.4$ makes an angle $\theta$ with the zero we can write that

$$(\theta + 90°) - (90° + 158.2°) = -180°$$

Therefore, $\theta = -21.8°$. The resulting root-locus plot is shown below. ■

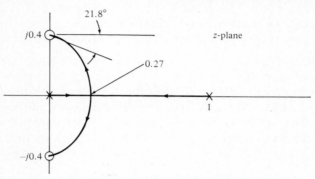

**Parameter Design.**   The main use of a root-locus plot, as has already been mentioned, is to determine the effect of a key parameter on the closed-loop system behavior by visualizing graphically all possible closed-loop pole locations as a function of that parameter. In the discussion thus far it has been assumed that the parameter of concern is an open-loop gain $K$; however, more generally, the parameter can be any system parameter such as sampling rate or a critical time constant.

The procedure for "isolating" a parameter $\alpha$ is to expand the characteristic equation of the closed-loop system and group those terms that are independent of $\alpha$ separately from those that depend on $\alpha$. We assume that the parameter enters "linearly" (as a simple coefficient of terms) so that the result of the above procedure is a characteristic equation of the form

$$P(z) + \alpha Q(z) = 0 \qquad\qquad (6\text{-}47)$$

where $P$ and $Q$ are polynomial functions of $z$. To obtain the "root-locus form" from Eq. (6-47), the two terms are divided by $P(z)$,

$$1 + \alpha \frac{Q(z)}{P(z)} = 0 \qquad\qquad (6\text{-}48)$$

Compare with Eq. (6-24). Let us illustrate the procedure.

### EXAMPLE 6-9 (Isolating a Parameter for Root Locus)

Consider a sampled-data control system as shown below.

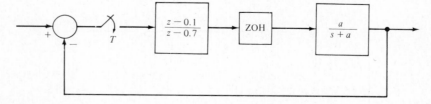

The effective discrete time plant is given by [See Eq. (2-45)]

$$(1 - z^{-1})Z\left\{\frac{a}{s(s + a)}\right\} = \frac{1 - e^{-aT}}{z - e^{-aT}}, \quad a > 0$$

Thus, the characteristic equation is

$$1 + \frac{(z - 0.1)(1 - \alpha)}{(z - 0.7)(z - \alpha)} = 0$$

where $\alpha = e^{-aT}$ is the parameter of concern. In order to isolate $\alpha$ for root-locus considerations, we must expand the characteristic equation as follows:

$$(z - 0.7)(z - \alpha) + (z - 0.1)(1 - \alpha) = 0$$

$$(z^2 + 0.3z - 0.1) - \alpha(2z - 0.8) = 0$$

Finally, in factored form, we have

$$1 + K \frac{(z - 0.4)}{(z - 0.2)(z + 0.5)} = 0$$

where $K = -2\alpha$. Note that the effect of positive $\alpha$ on this system leads us to consider root-locus for "negative gain." ∎

## 6-4.3  Modifications for Zero-Degree Locus

The angle requirement with which we have been working, Eq. (6-27), namely that the contribution of the open-loop gain function should be 180° at each point of the root locus, included the assumption that the gain parameter $K$ was positive. If the gain is negative, the angle requirement changes to 0° at each point of the root locus.

There are several ways in which the modification to a "zero-degree locus" may come about:

1. We might be interested in the root-locus plot for negative values of the parameter in a standard root-locus context.
2. The feedback (see Figure 6-6) may itself be positive, which changes the characteristic equation to

$$1 - KG(z) = 0 \qquad (6-49)$$

which would require a 0° locus for positive $K$.
3. Lastly, for a general parameter the effect of isolating the parameter for a root-locus plot may require a 0° locus as seen in Example 6-9.

Only those construction rules that depend directly on the angle requirement change; these are listed below.

### Root-Locus Construction Rules for 0° Locus

**Rule 1:**  (Unchanged)

***Rule 2:*** The asymptote angles are given by

$$\frac{q360°}{n - m}, \quad q = 0, 1, 2, \ldots, \quad n - m - 1 \tag{6-50}$$

***Rule 3:*** The root-locus plot includes those portions of the real axis that lie to the left of an *even* number of poles plus zeros of $G(z)$. (No poles and zeros are included as an even number so that the positive real axis beyond any poles or zeros is part of the locus.)

***Rule 4:*** Breakaway and break-in points on the real axis still correspond to extremum values of $K$ as a function of real $z$.

***Rule 5:*** The method of calculating the angle of arrival (angle of departure) for a complex zero (pole) is the same except that the total angle contribution is $0°$, instead of $180°$.

To illustrate the differences let us return to Example 6-9.

### EXAMPLE 6-10 (Zero-Degree Root Locus)

From the result of Example 6-9 the characteristic equation for the system of interest is

$$1 + K \frac{(z - 0.4)}{(z - 0.2)(z + 0.5)} = 0$$

where $K = -2\alpha$ varies between 0 and $-\infty$ (since $\alpha$ must be positive).

From the pole–zero plot of the equivalent open-loop gain function, the real-axis rule indicates a single $0°$ asymptote and a breakaway point between $z = -0.5$ and $z = 0.2$. Working with Rule 4, we find that the breakaway point on the real axis is $z = -0.024$ and the break-in point is $z = 0.824$.

To find the value of $\alpha$ for which the system becomes unstable, we first calculate that

$$-K = \frac{(0.8)(1.5)}{(0.6)} = 2$$

so that $\alpha = 1$, but this cannot happen since $a > 0$. ∎

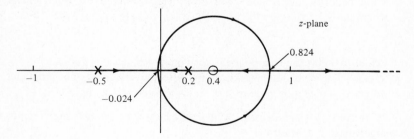

In the next section we investigate the important consideration of parameter sensitivity.

## PARAMETER SENSITIVITY

Many control systems do not achieve their full potential because of sensitivity problems. For instance, if the performance of a system depends on very close tolerances for its parameters (amplifier gains, resistance, capacitance values, spring constants, and so on), then it is not likely that the system will function well outside of a laboratory environment. Consequently, users will generally be dissatisfied with the product.

As control system designers, we must have ways of constructing the system to be forgiving of slight parameter mismatches. When a completed design has this property, we can refer to the system as being *robust*.

The fundamental idea of a sensitivity function, as introduced in Section 5-2, is one that provides a measure of performance change given a small change in a particular parameter, typically a ratio of percentage change in performance to percentage change in parameter. This can be written as

$$S_p^T \cong \frac{\Delta T/T_0}{\Delta p/p_0} \tag{6-51}$$

where $p_0$ and $T_0$ are the nominal values of parameter and response function, respectively. The function $T$ often represents a system transfer function that depends on the parameter $p$. Using Eq. (6-51) as motivation, let us define the *sensitivity of T(z, p) with respect to p* as

$$S_p^T = \frac{\partial T/T}{\partial p/p} = \frac{d(\ln T)}{d(\ln p)} \tag{6-52}$$

where the second form is a result of the fact that

$$\frac{d(\ln x)}{dx} = \frac{1}{x} \tag{6-53}$$

In practice, a convenient method of analytical calculation is to use the first form of Eq. (6-52) as follows:

$$S_p^T = \frac{\partial T}{\partial p} \frac{p}{T} \tag{6-54}$$

### EXAMPLE 6-11 (Parameter Sensitivity Calculation)

Consider a unity feedback system with an equivalent open-loop gain of $KG(z)$, and determine the effect of a small change in amplifier gain $K$ on the closed-loop transfer function $T(z)$.

*SOLUTION:* Since

$$T(z, K) = \frac{KG(z)}{1 + KG(z)}$$

$$S_K^T = \frac{\partial T}{\partial K} \frac{K}{T} = \frac{(1 + KG)G - (KG)G}{(1 + KG)^2} \frac{1 + KG}{G}$$

Therefore,

$$S_K^T = \frac{1}{1 + KG(z)}$$

which indicates that a small change in $K$ will cause an even smaller change in $T$ when the nominal loop gain $KG(z)$ is high.

Noting also that for "open-loop sensitivity"

$$S_K^{KG} = \frac{\partial(KG)}{\partial K} \frac{K}{KG} = 1$$

points out a distinct advantage of feedback. ∎

Since pole locations define to a great extent what the system performance will be, it is reasonable to consider more specifically pole sensitivity.

Pole sensitivity with respect to a parameter $\alpha$ can be determined from a root-locus plot as a function of the parameter $\alpha$. In particular, if the pole locations are known for a nominal value of the parameter, say, $\alpha_0$, then the sensitivity of a given pole $p$ can be found by perturbing the pole slightly on the locus, calculating the resulting change in $\alpha$ and taking the proper ratio of fractional changes. More formally,

$$S_\alpha^p = \frac{(p - p_0)/p_0}{(\alpha - \alpha_0)/\alpha_0} \tag{6-55}$$

where $p_0$ and $\alpha_0$ are the nominal pole and parameter values, respectively. An interesting point to note from our root-locus plots is that if a closed-loop pole is located near an open-loop zero, the pole value is relatively insensitive to small changes in the parameter, whereas the pole value may be quite sensitive to a parameter change if the branch is approaching an asymptote line. This observation will be useful to us in the next chapter for capitalizing on the potential robustness of state-variable feedback.

An analytic formulation of pole sensitivity can be obtained by assuming a characteristic equation

$$F(z, \alpha) = 0 \tag{6-56}$$

and expanding $F$ in a Taylor series about $z = p_0$ and $\alpha = \alpha_0$

$$F(z, \alpha) \cong F(p_0, \alpha_0) + \frac{\partial F(p_0, \alpha_0)}{\partial z} (p - p_0) + \frac{\partial F(p_0, \alpha_0)}{\partial \alpha} (\alpha - \alpha_0) \tag{6-57}$$

Since $F(p_0, \alpha_0) = 0$ and $F(z, \alpha) = 0$ by definition of a pole being a root of the characteristic equation,

$$\frac{p - p_0}{\alpha - \alpha_0} = -\left(\frac{\partial F}{\partial \alpha}\right)\left(\frac{\partial F}{\partial p}\right)^{-1} \tag{6-58}$$

where the partial derivatives are evaluated at the nominal values $p_0$ and $\alpha_0$. The linear approximation of Eq. (6-58) can be combined with Eq. (6-55) to determine pole sensitivity information. To illustrate the calculation of pole sensitivity, consider the following example.

### EXAMPLE 6-12 (Pole Sensitivity Calculation)

To make use of previous calculations, let us assume that a particular design calls for second-order closed-loop poles at $z = 0.27$ for the system of Examples 6-7 and 6-8. Thus, from Example 6-8 the nominal gain $K_0 = 0.846$. Also, if the actual gain is $K = 0.840$, we know that one pole lies at $z = 0.3$ from Example 6-7. To find the pole sensitivity, we simply introduce the root-locus values already obtained into Eq. (6-55)

$$S_K^p = \frac{(0.3 - 0.27)/0.27}{(0.840 - 0.846)/0.846} = -15.7$$

For this pole change, an increase in the parameter $K$ caused a decrease in the (real) pole location and therefore a negative sensitivity. Typically, it is the magnitude of $S$ that is most relevant, and such a large sensitivity would not indicate a good design. ∎

## 6-6

## A SECOND-ORDER TRACKING FILTER

To illustrate some of the design elements discussed so far, we will consider the design of a second-order filter that could be used to track a noisy data signal. We will assume that the incoming signal is in discrete-time form such as might occur if it were generated by a radar system. A typical pulse radar provides a naturally sampled signal due to its operation of sending out a train of pulses that, when reflected back from the "target," generates the sampled data. This information must be processed and used to control the antenna position if its purpose is to track the target.

If we are concerned with a single axis, say, target bearing, then the filter should be able to "smooth-out" the noisy bearing angle data. For our present purpose we assume that the filter must track ramp inputs (which correspond to linear changes in bearing angle).

As a first step, then, let us hypothesize a structure for our filter as shown in Fig. 6-9. Since the open-loop function $G(z)$ in Fig. 6-9 is Type 2 (See Section

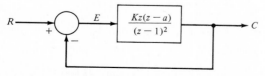

**FIGURE 6-9. Tracking filter structure.**

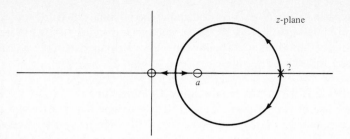

**FIGURE 6-10.    Root-locus plot for the system in Fig. 6-9.**

6-3), we know that the response will have a zero steady state error $E = R - C$ whenever $R$ corresponds to a linear variation in time.

A second step might be to investigate the system pole locations as a function of the parameter $K$. To do this, we have but to apply our root-locus rules to derive the plot of Fig. 6-10. The numerator was taken as second order to avoid any delay to the response, and the two adjustable parameters will be used to adjust the specific filter response. The resulting closed-loop transfer function is given by

$$F(z) = \frac{Kz(z - a)}{(1 + K)z^2 - (Ka + 2)z + 1}$$  (6-59)

Variations on the pole locations can come from a change in the zero location $a$ or the gain $K$. To simplify the situation, it has been determined that good filtering performance can be obtained by fixing the relation between $a$ and $K$ to be

$$\frac{K}{K + 1} = \frac{2a - 2}{a - 2}$$  (6-60)

thereby reducing the filter to a single parameter design. In terms of the parameter $a$,

$$F(z) = \frac{2(a - 1)z(z - a)}{(a - 2)z^2 - 2a(a - 2)z - a}$$  (6-61)

The parameter $a$ determines how rapidly the filter output will track the input data. When the data are "noisy," the parameter $a$ provides a basis of compromise between rapid data tracking and noise rejection: lower values for faster response (and therefore less noise rejection).

It is instructive to write a set of state equations to describe the filter $F(z)$.
The following set is referred to as an *alpha–beta filter:*

$$p(k + 1) = \hat{x}(k) + T\hat{v}(k)$$  (6-62)

$$\hat{x}(k + 1) = p(k + 1) + \alpha[z(k + 1) - p(k + 1)]$$  (6-63)

$$\hat{v}(k + 1) = \hat{v}(k) + (\beta/T)[z(k + 1) - p(k + 1)]$$  (6-64)

where $\hat{x}$ and $\hat{v}$ are the estimated position and velocity, respectively, z is the input data that contain noisy position information, and $p$ is the one-step predicted position.

In terms of the filter $F(z)$ in Eq. (6-61)

$$\alpha = \frac{2a - 2}{a - 2}, \quad \beta = \frac{\alpha^2}{2 - \alpha} \tag{6-65}$$

make the alpha–beta filter equivalent to $F(z) = \hat{X}(z)/Z(z)$. It is interesting to note that $F(z)$ is independent of $T$. In fact, by z-transforming (with zero initial conditions) and combining Eqs. (6-62)–(6-64),

$$\frac{\hat{X}(z)}{Z(z)} = \frac{\alpha z^2 + (\beta - \alpha)z}{z^2 + (\alpha + \beta - 2)z + (1 - \alpha)} \tag{6-66}$$

To illustrate the filtering effect of $F(z)$ in Eq. (6-61), we will generate the input data $z(k)$ as some random variations (noise) superimposed onto a deterministic ramp with slope of 0.5; these data are illustrated in Fig. 6-11.

Using the data of Fig. 6-11, we will run the filter for two different values of the parameter $a$. For $a = 0.3$ we find from Eq. (6-61) that

$$F_{0.3}(z) = \frac{0.82z^2 - 0.25z}{z^2 - 0.60z + 0.18} \tag{6-67}$$

For $a = 0.7$ we find that

$$F_{0.7}(z) = \frac{0.46z^2 - 0.32z}{z^2 - 1.40z + 0.54} \tag{6-68}$$

To compare the responses, we will assume that the true signal is the ramp $0.5k$. A plot of the error or deviation from the true signal is given in Fig. 6-12. The results in Fig. 6-12 indicate that the filter response is fast enough to track the noise when $a = 0.3$, whereas some smoothing effect is achieved when $a = 0.7$. As the filter response speed is further reduced, the filter will show

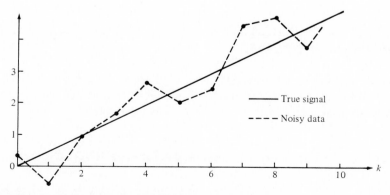

**FIGURE 6-11.   Input data for the filter of Eq. (6-61).**

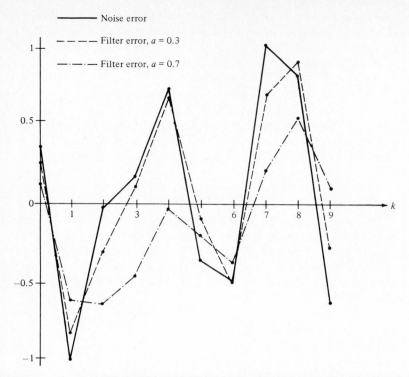

**FIGURE 6-12.** Comparison of filter tracking errors (lines connecting the points are present only for ease of display and do not imply continuous-time error signals).

less effect to noise "spikes"; however, it will also be more sluggish in tracking a changing true signal. Thus, the particular filter design will always be a compromise between noise rejection and signal tracking.

## 6-7

## SOLVED PROBLEMS

In this section we will elaborate on the methods of this chapter to obtain digital controller designs. The first method is that of a prestructured controller used to a great extent in the chemical industry for process control.

### 6-7.1 Proportional-Integral-Derivative (PID) Control

Classical control theory tells us that rich rewards can be gained in terms of reduced parameter sensitivity, disturbance rejection, and so on, with the basic use of feedback. The simplest feedback law is to generate an actuation signal that is proportional to the error between reference and controlled output; this is called *proportional* control. However, in many applications, particularly those for which the plant model is not well known, an extra measure of control is needed to provide an additional margin of stability for the system. For this purpose part of the actuation signal is made to be proportional to the derivative of the error signal; this is known as *derivative* control. Similarly, as a result of modeling errors and slight nonlinear effects, a situation can arise within the system that causes little or no actuation to take place even when an error exists between reference and output signals. In this case the error can be forced to zero by establishing a part of the actuation signal to be proportional to the integral of the error; this is *integral* (also known as *reset*) control. All different combinations of proportional, derivative, and integral control can be used on a system, the most general being PID control.

In place of the three proportionality constants $k_p$, $k_i$, and $k_d$ given in Section 1-2 for the corresponding continuous-time PID control law we will present a digital PID controller that uses an elementary discrete-time equivalent for the integral and derivative operation. More sophisticated digital PID control can be obtained by using the higher-order approximations of Section 4-2.3.

A simple $z$-transform version of the PID algorithm is given by

$$D(z) = U(z)/E(z) = K_p + K_i Tz/(z - 1) + K_d(z - 1)/Tz \quad (6\text{-}69)$$

where $E(z)$ and $U(z)$ are the transformed error and actuation signals, respectively. Equation (6-69) corresponds to the sequence operation

$$u(k) = K_p e(k) + K_i T \sum_{n=0}^{k} e(n) + K_d T^{-1}[e(k) - e(k - 1)] \quad (6\text{-}70)$$

An alternate algorithm that is also used calculates the change in the actuation variable at each sample time, $\Delta u(k) = u(k) - u(k - 1)$. After collecting terms this expression is

$$\Delta u(k) = K_p[e(k) - e(k - 1)] + K_i Te(k) + K_d T^{-1}$$
$$[e(k) - 2e(k - 1) + e(k - 2)] \quad (6\text{-}71)$$

The PID algorithm is simple enough to state some general "tuning" rules without exact knowledge of the plant and yet sufficiently effective to achieve reasonable system control; these qualities have made it attractive for process control applications. Typically, other controller designs perform better, but at the expense of requiring more information about the plant.

The classic tuning procedure, known as the Ziegler–Nichols method, is to increase $K_p$ (with $K_i = K_d = 0$) until a sustained oscillation occurs (with $K_p = K_{max}$) in the measured variable. Then, if the period of oscillation is $T_0$ seconds, the PID parameters are

$$K_p = 0.6 K_{max}$$
$$K_i \leq 2 K_p T_0^{-1} \quad (6\text{-}72)$$
$$K_d \geq 0.125 K_p T_0$$

If only PI control is used,

$$K_p = 0.45K_{max}, \quad K_i \leq 1.2K_pT_0^{-1} \tag{6-73}$$

For proportional control only,

$$K_p = 0.5K_{max} \tag{6-74}$$

To illustrate the tuning procedure we will assume an analytical model that is typical of a chemical process.

### EXAMPLE 6-13 (Digital PID Controller Tuning)

The sampling rate is assumed to be 10 Hz and the plant model

$$G_p(s) = (e^{-0.3s})/(s + 1) = Y(s)/U(s)$$

is to be controlled using a digital PID algorithm.

**SOLUTION:** In order to accommodate for the ZOH conversion between digital controller and continuous-time plant, we first determine the ZOH equivalent plant model:

$$\hat{G}_p(z) = (1 - z^{-1})Z\left\{\frac{e^{-0.3s}}{s(s + 1)}\right\}$$

Noting that $e^{-0.3s}$ represents an exact delay of three time steps,

$$\hat{G}_p(z) = \frac{z - 1}{z^4}Z\left\{\frac{1}{s(s + 1)}\right\}$$

$$\hat{G}_p(z) = \frac{1 - e^{-0.1}}{z^3(z - e^{-0.1})} = \frac{0.0952}{z^3(z - 0.9048)}$$

There are several acceptable analytical methods with which to calculate the maximum proportional gain $K_{max}$. One is to calculate the limiting gain using the Jury stability test, but this could be quite tedious since the system is fourth order. Another is to find the gain and phase of $\hat{G}_p$ versus the radian frequency; the maximum gain $K_{max}$ would then be the gain margin of the system. Taking the latter approach,

$$\hat{G}_p(e^{j0.1\omega}) = \frac{0.0952}{(\cos 0.3\omega + j \sin 0.3\omega)(\cos 0.1\omega - 0.9048 + j \sin 0.1\omega)}$$

For $\omega = 5.0362$ radians/second,

$$\hat{G}_p = 0.197 \underline{/-180°}$$

Therefore, the maximum proportional gain is

$$K_{max} = (0.197)^{-1} = 5.078$$

Since $\omega = 5.0362$, $T_0 = 2\pi/\omega = 1.248$ sec. Applying the relations of Eq. (6-72),

$$K_p = 3.05, \quad K_i \leq 4.88, \quad K_d \geq 0.475$$

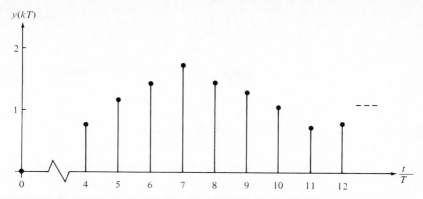

**FIGURE 6-13. Step-response of PID controlled plant of Example 6-13.**

To investigate the resulting step response, let us choose $K_p = 3.05$, $K_i = 4.50$, and $K_d = 0.50$. Introducing these values and $T = 0.1$ into Eq. (6-69) and collecting terms, we obtain the controller transfer function

$$D(z) = \frac{8.50z^2 - 13.05z + 5}{z(z - 1)}$$

Combining $D(z)$ with $\hat{G}_p(z)$ and closing the (unity) feedback loop, the overall system function is

$$T(z) = \frac{0.809z^2 - 1.242z + 0.476}{z^6 - 1.905z^5 + 0.905z^4 + 0.809z^2 - 1.242z + 0.476}$$

The first few terms of the (discrete-time) unit-step response obtained by long division are shown in Fig. 6-13. Note the three-step deadtime as expected. Although the response appears to be settling down, there is a large overshoot with these gain settings. To provide a more stable response the $K_d$ could be increased. However, the response is reasonable in light of the fact that only the natural frequency of oscillation and maximum gain under proportional-only control were used in the design; that is to say, the exact dynamics of the plant were assumed to be unknown, including the transport lag, which adds considerable difficulty to the control problem. ∎

In the next design approach it is assumed that the plant model is known to the design engineer.

## 6-7.2 Feedforward/Root-Locus Design

In this section we will utilize the second-order system design approach. To outline the procedure, we begin with an equivalent discrete-time plant and a set of performance specifications and follow the general procedure:

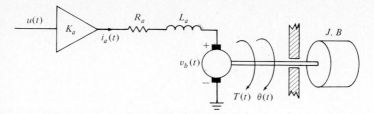

**FIGURE 6-14.   DC motor and load for Example 6-14.**

Step 1: Using the specifications, derive an appropriate (desired) closed-loop transfer function such as given in Eq. (6-2).

Step 2: From the desired pole and zero locations establish a suitable feed-forward compensator to supply the desired zeros and provide for the root-locus angle requirement to be satisfied at the desired pole locations.

Step 3: Establish the proper loop gain.

Step 4: Investigate the response of the system under typical test inputs.

Let us illustrate the approach with an example of controlling a permanent magnet servomotor as shown in Fig. 6-14.

### EXAMPLE 6-14 (Application of Root-Locus to dc Motor Control)

To establish the plant model, we derive the continuous-time transfer function

$$G_p(s) = \frac{8}{s(s + 2)}$$

from the relations that the motor torque $T = K_m i_a$ and the "back emf" $v_b = \omega K_b$, plus the other electrical and mechanical constraints we can derive the following signal-flow diagram. (See the remark following Problem 3-5.)

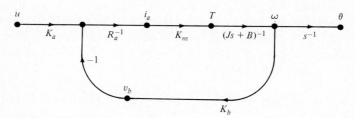

Defining the parameters $K = 4$ and $\tau = 0.5$ sec, where

$$K = \frac{K_a K_m}{R_a B + K_b K_m}$$

and

$$\tau = \frac{R_a J}{R_a B + K_b K_m}$$

we obtain $G_p(s)$ given above. Assuming that we will measure only $\theta$, a state-variable model for $G_p(s)$ is (with $\dot{\theta} = \omega$)

$$\frac{d}{dt}\begin{bmatrix} \theta \\ \dot{\theta} \end{bmatrix} = \begin{bmatrix} 0 & 1 \\ 0 & -2 \end{bmatrix}\begin{bmatrix} \theta \\ \dot{\theta} \end{bmatrix} + \begin{bmatrix} 0 \\ 8 \end{bmatrix} u(t)$$

$$y(t) = \begin{bmatrix} 1 & 0 \end{bmatrix}\begin{bmatrix} \theta \\ \dot{\theta} \end{bmatrix}$$

The following are desired performance attributes (*Specifications*). Based on a step-input command $r$, there should be

1. No overshoot to the step response
2. A zero steady state error ($e = r - \theta$)
3. A (2%) settling time of 1.75 sec or less

    *SOLUTION:* (Trial Design) From the state model we can determine that

$$\hat{G}_p(z) = \frac{0.2131(z + 0.8467)}{(z - 1)(z - 0.6065)}$$

where $T = 0.25$ sec has been assumed. This is now the starting point for our design. From Step 1 above we find that for a critically damped response Eq. (6-2) reduces to

$$T(z) = (1 - b)/(z - b)$$

which automatically satisfies specifications (1) and (2). And since 1.75 sec = 7 sample intervals, specification (3) will be satisfied if $b^7 \le 0.02$ or $b \le 0.57$. For a conservative design we select $b = 0.5$.

    For Step 2 we desire a pole at $z = 0.5$ and no finite zeros. We now select

$$G_c(z) = \frac{K_c(z - 0.6065)}{(z + 0.8467)}$$

to provide the proper compensation for plant. The gain $K_c$ is selected to provide the overall gain of 0.5 realizing that the numerator dynamics will show up as numerator dynamics for the closed-loop system. The total open-loop function is then $0.2131K_c/(z - 1)$, which clearly has a root-locus branch along the real axis to the left of $z = 1$, and a pole location at $z = 0.5$ for $0.2131K_c = 0.5$, so that $K_c = 2.346$ for Step 3.

    Figure 6.15 shows the complete system.

    For Step 4 we will employ the simulation method discussed in Section 4-5 to obtain the continuous-time step response.

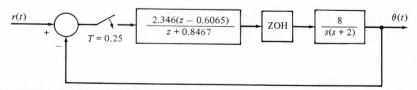

**FIGURE 6-15.** Trial design for a dc motor controller.

With the original state model representing the continuous-time plant and the simple first-order model

$$d(k + 1) = -0.8467 \, d(k) + e(k)$$

$$u(k) = -3.409 \, d(k) + 2.346e(k)$$

to represent the controller, we write that

$$\frac{d}{dt}\begin{bmatrix} \theta \\ \dot{\theta} \\ u \end{bmatrix} = \begin{bmatrix} 0 & 1 & 0 \\ 0 & -2 & 8 \\ 0 & 0 & 0 \end{bmatrix}\begin{bmatrix} \theta \\ \dot{\theta} \\ u \end{bmatrix}, \quad \begin{array}{l} kT < t < kT + T \\ (T = 0.25) \end{array} \quad (6\text{-}75)$$

$$u(kT^+) = 2.346 - 3.409 \, d(kT^-) - 2.346 \, \theta(kT^-) \quad (6\text{-}76)$$

$$d(kT^+) = 1 - 0.8467 \, d(kT^-) - \theta(kT^-)$$

From Eqs. (6-75) we find the transition equations (for $\Delta = 0.05$ seconds)

$$\mathbf{x}(k\Delta + \Delta) = \begin{bmatrix} 1 & 0.0476 & 0.0097 \\ 0 & 0.9048 & 0.3807 \\ 0 & 0 & 1 \end{bmatrix} \mathbf{x}(k\Delta), \quad (6\text{-}77)$$

where $\mathbf{x} = [\theta \quad \dot{\theta} \quad u]^T$.

Following the procedure outlined in Fig. 4-13, we obtain the unit-step response as plotted in Fig. 6-16.

The response is clearly not acceptable because of the intersample oscillation. Note that the discrete-time response, however, meets the specifications. The

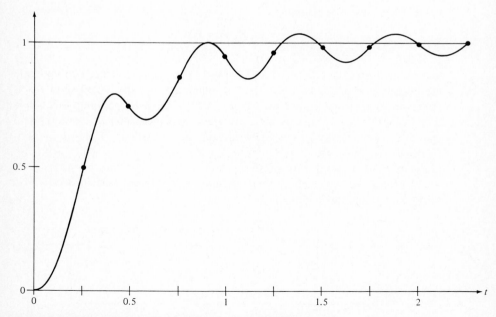

**FIGURE 6-16. Step-response for trial controller design.**

problem here is a combination of too low a sampling rate and a compensator with a pole on the negative real axis, causing the actuation signal to oscillate between positive and negative values. This and other considerations related to the selection of a suitable sample rate are presented in the next section (where a redesign of this dc motor controller is made). ∎

## 6-7.3  Sample Period Selection

There are several points to consider regarding the selection of a sample period $T$ for a control system. First and foremost is cost. As $T$ is reduced (that is, sample rate $T^{-1}$ increased), the cost generally becomes larger because faster signal converters and computers are necessary for a given algorithm. The actual computation time is the total time required for the computer to fetch the most recent error conversion, perform the control law calculations and output the result to a DAC. The reader may want to reflect back on the development of Section 4-4; one cycle of the simulation of $D(z)$ corresponds to the control calculation. Thus, for a given computer program the calculation time is the sum of all the detailed times for the multiplications, additions, and register transfers involved. This time plus the sum of the conversion times should be less than $T$.

Another consideration of primary importance is that of response smoothness, one that shows up very clearly in Example 6-14. From this aspect the sample interval $T$ should be small compared with the smallest time constant in the plant model, usually by a factor of 5 to 10 minimum. (In Example 6-14 the time-constant is 0.5 sec so that $T$ should be less than 0.1, and preferably much smaller since the output of the ZOH will excite all the plant modes at each actuation instant.)

A well-known result from Fourier transforms, used extensively in communication systems, is that a continuous-time (band-limited) signal must be sampled at a rate corresponding to at least twice its highest frequency in order to be able to reconstruct the signal from its samples (or, in other words, to capture all the information present in the signal). It follows that if a digital control system is to track a (continuous-time) reference input, the sample rate must be at least double the highest frequency of the reference signal since only the samples of the reference are used in the controller. In practice, signals are not band-limited and the sampling is made at a rate which is 10 to 20 times the highest (significant) input frequency to relieve the problem of aliasing.

Other aspects of the performance of a digital control system that are impacted by the selection of $T$ are parameter sensitivity and disturbance rejection. Although it is very involved and problem dependent to predict the exact effects, both of these performance measures deteriorate with increasing $T$. In some sense it should be evident that the general performance should get worse as $T$ increases since the system runs open-loop between sampling instants, and the less frequent the feedback updates, the poorer the performance of the system.

To illustrate the improvement of reducing $T$, let us rework the design example of the previous section with $T = 0.1$ sec.

## EXAMPLE 6-15 (Redesign Controller in Example 6-14)

The revised ZOH equivalent discrete-time plant model with $T = 0.1$ sec is given by

$$G_p(z) = \frac{z - 1}{z} Z\left\{\frac{8}{s^2(s + 2)}\right\}$$

The result for $T = 0.1$ is the plant model

$$G_p(z) = \frac{0.0375(z + 0.9355)}{(z - 1)(z - 0.8187)}$$

**SOLUTION:** (Second Approach) This time we elect to use a compensator of the form

$$G_c(z) = K_c z^{-2}(z - 0.8187)$$

the purpose being to avoid a pole on the negative real axis which causes an oscillatory actuating signal and corresponding intersample response (similar to that exhibited in Fig. 6-16). The root locus for $G_c(z) G_p(z)$ is shown below.

The compensator gain is chosen to be $K_c = 2.504$ in order to operate the system with a double pole at $z = 0.616$.

To simulate the step response, we note that the structure of the system is identical to that shown in Fig. 6-15 with $T$ now equal to 0.1 sec and

$$G_c(z) = z^{-2}(2.504z - 2.050)$$

Again we use $\Delta = 0.05$ sec and Eq. (6-77) along with the new update equations:

$$u(kT^+) = 2.5044\, d_2(kT^-) - 2.0504\, d_1(kT^-)$$

$$d_1(kT^+) = d_2(kT^-)$$

$$d_2(kT^+) = 1 - x_1(kT^-)$$

The resulting step response is presented in Fig. 6-17 using the same scale as Fig. 6-16. Compare the improved design.

The design is well within the desired specifications with a settling time of less than 1.5 sec. The one time-step deadtime is caused by the compensator having one excess pole, but with $T = 0.1$ sec it would typically not be a problem. Consequently, we may look on this design as being entirely satisfactory! ∎

In the next chapter we will introduce the more powerful design methods of state variable feedback.

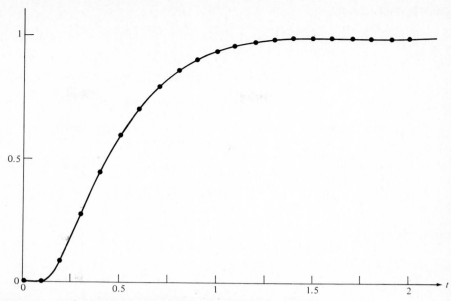

**FIGURE 6-17. Step-response of redesigned control system.**

## SUMMARY

In this chapter we first considered a general second-order design technique that uses a combination of feedforward and feedback control to implement a desired closed-loop transfer function. It was found that the feedforward component primarily determined the steady state behavior of the system while the feedback portion controlled the pole locations and therefore the system's transient behavior.

The steady state response was related to the steady state error constants and the useful concept of system type (for control systems with unity feedback) in Section 6-3. Following this, a presentation of the basic construction rules for obtaining a root-locus plot was given in Section 6-4; and in Section 6-5, a brief discussion of parameter sensitivity.

The material in Sections 6-6 and 6-7 relate to applications of the root-locus design procedures, including

1. A tracking filter design
2. Proportional-Integral-Derivative (PID) Control
3. Two dc motor controller designs

Considerations of sample period selection and the liability of a controller with a negative-real pole were discussed in connection with the designs in item (3) above.

# REFERENCES

**Section 6-1**  *Digital Control:* G. F. Franklin and J. D. Powell; Addison-Wesley, 1980.
*Modern Control Systems:* R. C. Dorf; 3rd ed. Addison-Wesley, 1980.

**Sections 6-2–6-4**
*Automatic Control;* S. C. Gupta and L. Hasdorff; John Wiley and Sons, 1970.
*Modern Control Engineering;* Ogata; Prentice-Hall, 1970.
*Automatic Control Systems;* B. C. Kuo; 3rd ed. Prentice-Hall, 1975.

**Section 6-5**  *Modern Digital Control Systems;* R. G. Jacquot; Marcell Dekker, 1981.

**Section 6-6**  *Discrete-Time and Computer Control;* J. A. Cadzow and H. R. Martens; Prentice-Hall, 1970.

**Section 6-7**  *Digital Computer Process Control;* C. L. Smith; Intext Educational Publishers, 1972.
*Digital Control;* G. F. Franklin and J. D. Powell; Addison-Wesley, 1980.

# PROBLEMS

**6-1**  A plant transfer function is given by

$$T(s) = \frac{K}{s^2 + s + K}$$

Determine
**(a)** the natural frequency $\omega_n$ in radians/second.
**(b)** the damping ratio $\zeta$.

**6-2**  Repeat Problem 6-1 for the closed-loop system shown in Fig. P6-2.

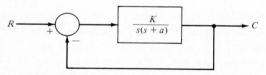

**FIGURE P6-2.**

**6-3**  Determine the standard second-order discrete-time system transfer function of Eq. (6-2) to satisfy the following specifications.
**(a)** A 5% peak overshoot and a 10 sample-step settling time.
**(b)** A 10% peak overshoot and a 12 sample-step settling time.
**(c)** A 20% peak overshoot and a 15 sample-step settling time.
Assume a 2% settling time.

**6-4**  Calculate the poles, zero, and gain values for the transfer functions derived in Problem 6-3.

**6-5**  Plot the poles and zero of $T(z)$ in Eq. (6-2) as a function of peak overshoot for a constant settling time of 10 sample periods.

**6-6**   Plot the poles and zero of $T(s)$ in Eq. (6-2) as a function of settling time (in sampling periods) for a fixed 10% peak overshoot.

**6-7**   What requirements are there on a feedforward compensator $G_c(z)$ for $G_c(z)$ to be a causal (realizable) system?

**6-8**   Which of the following discrete-time compensators are realizable?

(a) $G_a(z) = \dfrac{10(z + 0.4)}{z(z - 1)}$

(b) $G_b(z) = \dfrac{z^2(z - 0.1)}{z^2 - 2z + 1}$

(c) $G_c(z) = \dfrac{5(z - 2)}{z - 1.5}$

**6-9**   Given a plant with ZOH equivalent given by

$$G(z) = \frac{1.6z(z - 0.5)}{(z - 0.9)(z - 1.5)}$$

Determine a first-order compensator that might be helpful in controlling the plant.

**6-10**   For the plant described in Problem 6-9, specify the form of compensator that would guarantee a Type 1 system response with unity feedback.

**6-11**   Sketch the root-locus plots for the following loop-gain functions as the gain $K$ varies (positively) from zero to infinity.

(a) $G_a(z) = \dfrac{Kz^2}{(z - 1)(z - 0.5)}$

(b) $G_b(z) = \dfrac{K(z - 0.8)}{z^3(z - 1)}$

**6-12**   Work with the discrete-time equivalent model of the system in Fig. P6-12 and sketch the root locus as a function of the parameter $T$.

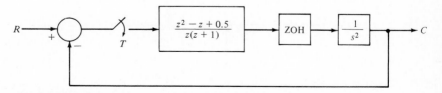

**FIGURE P6-12.**

**6-13** An equivalent discrete-time forward gain function is given by $G_c(z)G_p(z)$, where the compensator and plant functions are

$$G_c(z) = \frac{K(z - q)}{(z - p)}, \quad G_p(z) = \frac{0.25(z - 0.2)}{(z - 1)(z - 0.5)}$$

(a) Assume a unity feedback system and determine if it is possible to realize a closed-loop system with a transfer function of the form given in Eq. (6-2) with parameters

$$a = 0.4, \quad b = 0.5$$

(b) Use root-locus methods to specify $K$, $q$, and $p$ that will best approximate the desired transfer function of part (a).

**6-14** Consider the sampled-data system shown in Fig. P6-14 as a discrete-time system. Use root-locus techniques to
(a) determine the locus of closed-loop poles as a function of the sample period $T$.
(b) determine the (upper) limiting value of $T$ for a stable system.

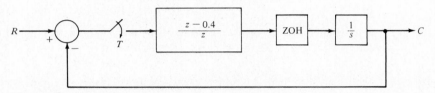

**FIGURE P6-14.**

**6-15** The digital computer in the system shown in Fig. P6-15 is used to provide a proportional control ($K$ is a constant gain).
(a) Using root-locus techniques as an aid, calculate the gain $K$ so that the system has a critically damped (double real pole) step response.
(b) Determine the 2% settling time to a step command.

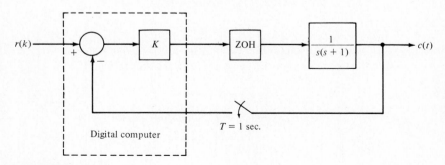

**FIGURE P6-15.**

**6-16**   A discrete-time control system model is shown in Fig. P6-16. Assume that the input $r(k)$ is a unit-ramp sequence, $r(k) = k$, $k = 0, 1, 2, \ldots$, and sketch a plot of the steady state error, $e_{ss}$, as a function of the gain parameter $K$ for $0 < K < 10$.

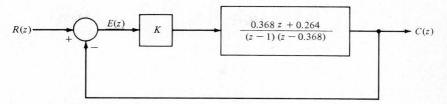

**FIGURE P6-16.**

## CHAPTER 7

# Controllability and State-Variable Feedback

In this chapter we will build onto the background of Chapter 3 with the goal of acquiring the principal design technique of state-variable theory, state-variable feedback. From our point of view state-variable design methods should be used in conjunction with the frequency-response methods of the previous chapter whenever possible, and the control designer should be aware of the capabilities and limitations of each approach. Unfortunately, this blend of the two methods is usually somewhat limited since the approaches are inherently so different. State-variable methods are almost exclusively used when the plant under consideration has multiple inputs or outputs, and most of the subsequent discussion will assume a multiple-input, multiple-outout (MIMO) system. We begin with an investigation of the fundamental concept of controllability.

## 7-1

### STATE CONTROLLABILITY

By "controlling" a plant, we mean to use its available dynamic inputs and specify their time variations, in order to obtain some desired response. We begin our discussion with the assumption that the modeling phase has been completed, that is to say, a basic discrete-time state model has been established given by the following pair of equations:

$$\mathbf{x}(k + 1) = A\mathbf{x}(k) + B\mathbf{u}(k) \tag{7-1}$$

$$\mathbf{y}(k) = C\mathbf{x}(k) + D\mathbf{u}(k) \tag{7-2}$$

where $\mathbf{x}$ is an $n$-vector, $\mathbf{u}$ is an $m$-vector, and $\mathbf{y}$ is a $p$-vector. As a fundamental consideration, we are interested to know under what circumstances can we be assured of being able to influence the state of the system using the inputs $\mathbf{u}(k)$. Also, in particular, is it possible to specify a certain state that, after an appropriate sequence of inputs, can be achieved? We view the state itself as the important consideration, not just the output, since the state of the system can affect the output directly and is, at the same time, more general. The following definition will help to formalize the idea.

**Definition 7-1:** The discrete-time system of Eq. (7-1) is (*completely state*) *controllable* if it is possible to force the state from any initial state $\mathbf{x}_0$ to an arbitrary "target" state $\mathbf{x}_f$ in a finite number of steps.

We will use this definition to derive a simple rank calculation to test for the property of controllability in a linear system. Unfortunately, there is no such easy test to apply to nonlinear systems.

Other authors use variations of this concept of controllability that apply to either a *subset* of the state variables or directly to the *output* variables, but for convenience we will use the simple word "controllable" to mean "completely state controllable" as defined above.

For linear systems the question of controllability can be restated as either a transfer from an arbitrary initial state $\mathbf{x}_0$ to the origin or as a transfer from the origin to an arbitrary final state $\mathbf{x}_f$. This latter perspective is often used to define "reachability," that is, certain sets of states may be reachable after one, two, or more steps. If a system is controllable, any state may be reached in a finite number of steps. We will demonstrate as follows. Recall from Section 3-5 that after $k$ steps the state $\mathbf{x}(k)$ of Eq. (7-1) is given by

$$\mathbf{x}(k) = A^k\mathbf{x}_0 + \sum_{j=0}^{k-1} A^{k-j-1} B\mathbf{u}(j) \tag{7-3}$$

Thus, if $\mathbf{x}(k) = \mathbf{x}_f$ and $A$ is nonsingular, Eq. (7-3) can be rewritten as

$$\mathbf{0} = [A^k(\mathbf{x}_0 - A^{-k}\mathbf{x}_f)] + \sum_{j=0}^{k-1} A^{k-j-1} B\mathbf{u}(j) \tag{7-4}$$

In this form the final state is the origin and the equivalent initial state is $(\mathbf{x}_0 - A^{-k}\mathbf{x}_f)$. Alternatively, we can shift the term in brackets to the left side of Eq. (7-4) and obtain the interpretation of "reachability," where the initial state is the origin and the equivalent final state is (negative of) the term in brackets.

We intuitively feel that if we can drive a system from one state to any other, then we can control the system in some more complicated manner. To investigate further, let us expand Eq. (7-3) to obtain

$$\mathbf{x}(k) - A^k\mathbf{x}(0) = B\mathbf{u}(k-1) + AB\mathbf{u}(k-2) + \cdots + A^{k-1}B\mathbf{u}(0) \quad (7\text{-}5)$$

More compactly, the final state after $k$-steps can be expressed as

$$\mathbf{x}_f - A^k\mathbf{x}(0) = [B \quad AB \quad A^2B \quad \cdots \quad A^{k-1}B]\begin{bmatrix} \mathbf{u}(k-1) \\ \mathbf{u}(k-2) \\ \ldots \\ \mathbf{u}(0) \end{bmatrix} \quad (7\text{-}6)$$

where the coefficient matrix is a partitioned matrix of the various products and the compound vector is the corresponding partition of the individual input vectors (in reverse order to their sequential application). It is to be emphasized that Eq. (7-6) is equivalent to Eq. (7-3) with $\mathbf{x}_0 = \mathbf{x}(0)$. The form of Eq. (7-6) is, however, more suggestive of solving for the set of inputs $\mathbf{u}(0), \mathbf{u}(1), \ldots,$ $\mathbf{u}(k-1)$ which, when applied to the system, will cause the state to end up at $\mathbf{x}_f$ after $k$ steps. The question of controllability can now be rephrased in terms of Eq. (7-6): Given the system matrices $A$ and $B$, does there exist a solution vector $\mathbf{U}$ for Eq. (7-6) for an arbitrary $\mathbf{x}_f$ where

$$\mathbf{U} = \begin{bmatrix} \mathbf{u}(k-1) \\ \mathbf{u}(k-2) \\ \ldots \\ \mathbf{u}(0) \end{bmatrix} \quad (7\text{-}7)$$

From Appendix B we know that a basic set of linear equations can be written in vector form as

$$A\mathbf{x} = \mathbf{y} \quad (7\text{-}8)$$

where the vector $\mathbf{x}$ is an unknown $n$-vector, $\mathbf{y}$ is a known $m$-vector, and $A$ is a known $m \times n$ matrix. Furthermore, there exists a solution $\mathbf{x}$ (possibly more than one) if and only if $\mathbf{y}$ can be expressed as a linear combination of the columns of $A$; that is to say, $\mathbf{y}$ is in the range space of $A$. An equivalent rank calculation for the existence of a solution $\mathbf{x}$ is given as

$$\text{rank } [A \mid \mathbf{y}] = \text{rank } [A] \quad (7\text{-}9)$$

In our problem, Eq. (7-6), we are assuming that $\mathbf{x}_f$ is any state in $n$-space. Thus, a solution $\mathbf{U}$ exists if and only if the partitioned matrix has rank $n$, that is, has an $n$-dimensional range space. Alternatively, there must be $n$ linearly independent columns out of

$$\mathscr{C}(k) = [B \quad AB \quad A^2B \quad \cdots \quad A^{k-1}B] \quad (7\text{-}10)$$

However, we have not, as yet, specified $k$. Suppose we continue the partitions $A^{k-1}B$ indefinitely; is it possible to continue generating linearly independent columns? No, the fact that a matrix satisfies its own characteristic equation (Cayley-Hamilton Theorem) tells us that $A^n$, where $A$ is an $n \times n$ matrix, can be written as a linear combination of $A^0 = I, A, A^2, \ldots, A^{n-1}$ and therefore that the partitions $A^nB$ and higher provide no new independent columns. For the special case where $k = n$, the order of the system, we drop the argument notation of Eq. (7-10) and define the *controllability matrix*

$$\mathscr{C} = [B \quad AB \quad A^2B \quad \cdots \quad A^{n-1}B] \qquad (7\text{-}11)$$

We summarize the present discussion with the following test.

***Controllability Test:*** A discrete-time system with state equation given by Eq. (7-1) is controllable if and only if its controllability matrix $\mathscr{C}$ of Eq. (7-11) has rank $n$, where $n$ is the order of the system.

Controllability is an inherent structural property of a system model, and equivalent systems will exhibit the same test results. The simple knowledge of whether a system is controllable or not is crucial to the subsequent state-variable feedback methods. Without controllability not all of the states can be "guided" by input manipulation. Unfortunately, the question of controllability gives rise to a yes or no answer—either the controllability matrix has rank $n$ or it does not! In some cases it is important to know the "degree of controllability," a measure of how close the system is to being uncontrollable. Since a fundamental method of testing the rank of a matrix involves finding the largest dimension nonzero determinant from the rows and columns of the matrix, one can imagine situations where the determinant becomes close to zero, but not actually zero. We will return to this discussion in a later section.

## EXAMPLE 7-1
For the following discrete-time system, determine if the system is controllable. If so, calculate the shortest input sequence that drives the system state to zero:

$$\mathbf{x}(k + 1) = \begin{bmatrix} 0 & 1 \\ 0 & 2 \end{bmatrix} \mathbf{x}(k) + \begin{bmatrix} 0 \\ 3 \end{bmatrix} u(k), \quad \mathbf{x}(0) = \begin{bmatrix} 6 \\ 3 \end{bmatrix}$$

*SOLUTION:* Forming the controllability matrix,

$$\mathscr{C} = \begin{bmatrix} 0 & 3 \\ 3 & 6 \end{bmatrix}; \quad \text{and rank } \mathscr{C} = 2$$

Therefore, the system is controllable. From Eq. (7-3) we try one step ($k = 1$),

$$\mathbf{0} = A\mathbf{x}(0) + Bu(0)$$

By substituting in the proper values, we find that no solution exists for $u(0)$ to satisfy the equation. For two steps ($k = 2$),

$$\mathbf{0} = A^2\mathbf{x}(0) + Bu(1) + ABu(0)$$

or in the form of Eq. (7-6)

$$\begin{bmatrix} 0 & 3 \\ 3 & 6 \end{bmatrix} \begin{bmatrix} u(1) \\ u(0) \end{bmatrix} = -\begin{bmatrix} 0 & 2 \\ 0 & 4 \end{bmatrix} \begin{bmatrix} 6 \\ 3 \end{bmatrix} = \begin{bmatrix} -6 \\ -12 \end{bmatrix}$$

Solving, we obtain

$$u(0) = -2, \quad u(1) = 0$$

Using a two-step recursion with this input sequence checks that the state at $k = 2$ is at the origin, $\mathbf{x}(2) = \mathbf{0}$. ∎

## 7-2

# MINIMUM-NORM SOLUTIONS

In the context of Eq. (7-6) we may at times be interested in solving sets of simultaneous equations that are either under- or overspecified, even solving for a closest solution in cases where no exact solution exists. There are two solution forms that we will consider here; each form represents a solution to Eq. (7-8), repeated here for convenience:

$$A\mathbf{x} = \mathbf{y} \tag{7-12}$$

where $A$ is a known $m \times n$ matrix and $\mathbf{y}$ is a known vector. Each form reduces $\mathbf{x} = A^{-1}\mathbf{y}$ whenever $A^{-1}$ exists, and consequently, they are sometimes referred to as *pseudoinverse* solutions.

**Case 1: Overspecified Equations; $m > n$.** The first form assumes that there are more equations than unknowns. This situation may arise, for instance, when multiple measurements are taken to overcome measurement inaccuracies. Typically, this set of equations may even be contradictory in that $\mathbf{y}$ is not contained in the range space of $A$.

However, a minimum-norm solution is obtained by premultiplying Eq. (7-12) by $A^T$ and inverting $A^TA$. This assumes that $A$ is full rank, that is to say, has at least $n$ independent columns, in which case the $n \times n$ matrix $A^TA$ is nonsingular. This first form of solution is given by

$$\hat{\mathbf{x}} = [(A^TA)^{-1}A^T]\,\mathbf{y} \tag{7-13}$$

Here, since there is normally no exact solution, $\hat{\mathbf{x}}$ is "minimum norm" in that it satisfies

$$\min_{\mathbf{x}}\|A\mathbf{x} - \mathbf{y}\| = \|A\hat{\mathbf{x}} - \mathbf{y}\| \tag{7-14}$$

where $\mathbf{e} = A\mathbf{x} - \mathbf{y}$ is the equation error and $\|\mathbf{e}\| = (\Sigma\, e_i^2)^{1/2}$, the Euclidian norm. Thus, $\hat{\mathbf{x}}$ is the "solution" that most nearly reduces Eq. (7-12) to an equality, even though no $\mathbf{x}$ will do it exactly. This solution is also known as a "least-squares error" solution because $\hat{\mathbf{x}}$ minimizes the sum of squares of the components of the error $\mathbf{e}$. Notice that the factor in brackets in Eq. (7-13) serves as $A^{-1}$ and is called a pseudoinverse of $A$.

## EXAMPLE 7-2 (Linear Least-Squares Error Curve Fit)

We are given the three data points presented graphically below.

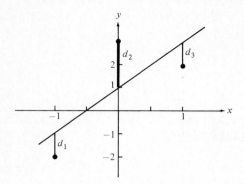

These data points may, for instance, represent the results of some noisy measurements. From this information we are to formulate a linear relation between $y$ and $x$ so that the sum of the squared errors from the points is minimized.

**SOLUTION:** Assume that

$$y(x) = \alpha_1 x + \alpha_2$$

where $\alpha_1$ and $\alpha_2$ are unknown parameters of the linear function. Evaluate the expression at the three points:

$$2 = \alpha_1 + \alpha_2$$

$$-2 = -\alpha_1 + \alpha_2$$

$$3 = \alpha_2$$

In matrix form we obtain

$$\begin{bmatrix} 1 & 0 \\ -1 & 1 \\ 0 & 1 \end{bmatrix} \begin{bmatrix} \alpha_1 \\ \alpha_2 \end{bmatrix} = \begin{bmatrix} 2 \\ -2 \\ 3 \end{bmatrix}$$

which is an overspecified set of equations ($m > n$). Applying Eq. (7-13), we first find that

$$A^T A = \begin{bmatrix} 2 & 0 \\ 0 & 3 \end{bmatrix}$$

confirming that it is invertible. Completing the operation, we have that

$$\begin{bmatrix} \hat{\alpha}_1 \\ \hat{\alpha}_2 \end{bmatrix} = \begin{bmatrix} 2 \\ 1 \end{bmatrix}$$

which implies that the best linear fit is a line with slope 2 and $y$ intercept 1, as shown in the previous figure.

This approach to the problem emphasized our minimum-norm solution. There is, of course, a direct approach that begins with the actual expression to be minimized, namely (from the figure),

$$J = d_1^2 + d_2^2 + d_3^2$$

with the assumed linear equation for $y$, for instance,

$$d_1 = -2 - y(-1) = -2 + \alpha_1 - \alpha_2$$

$J$ is then minimized by setting the partial derivatives with respect to $\alpha_1$ and $\alpha_2$ to zero and solving simultaneously the two resulting equations. ∎

**Case 2: Underspecified Equations; $m < n$.** The second class of problems represents one in which the number of unknowns exceeds the number of equations. Again we will assume that the coefficient matrix $A$ of Eq. (7-12) is of full rank, that is, rank $A = m$ (its smallest dimension). This means that all dependent equations have been eliminated at this point.

We now assume an arbitrary vector

$$\mathbf{x} = \mathbf{x}_1 + \mathbf{x}_2 \tag{7-15}$$

where $\mathbf{x}_1$ is in the range space of $A^T$ and $\mathbf{x}_2$ is in the null space of $A$, that is, $A\mathbf{x}_2 = \mathbf{0}$. In particular, if $r_j$ is a $1 \times n$ array representing the $j$th row of $A$, then $r_j\mathbf{x}_2 = \mathbf{0}$ for $j = 1, 2, 3, \ldots, m$; and $\mathbf{x}_1$ is some linear combination of the rows taken as vectors ($\mathbf{x}_1$ being in the range space of $A$)

$$\mathbf{x} = \sum_{j=1}^{m} v_j r_j^T = A^T\mathbf{v} \tag{7-16}$$

Thus, if

$$A\mathbf{x}_1 = \mathbf{y}$$

then

$$AA^T\mathbf{v} = \mathbf{y} \quad \text{or} \quad \mathbf{v} = (AA^T)^{-1}\mathbf{y}$$

and

$$\mathbf{x}_1 = [A^T(AA^T)^{-1}]\,\mathbf{y} \tag{7-17}$$

Equation (7-17) is the second form of solution we desired. In this case $\mathbf{x}_1$ is the (unique) orthogonal projection of $\mathbf{x}$ onto the range space of $A$ and thereby represents the minimum-norm vector that satisfies Eq. (7-12). In other words, there are *many* exact solutions and we are specifying by $\mathbf{x}_1$ in Eq. (7-17) that particular one which has a minimum length.

### EXAMPLE 7-3 (Underspecified Equations)
Given the set of two equations in four unknowns

$$x_1 - x_2 + x_3 - 2x_4 = 1$$

$$2x_2 + x_3 - x_4 = 2$$

(a) Solve for $x_1$ and $x_2$ in terms of $x_3$ and $x_4$.

(b) Find the minimum-norm solution.

**SOLUTION:** Performing the algebraic manipulations required for part (a), we obtain

$$x_1 = \tfrac{1}{2}(4 - 3x_3 + 5x_4)$$

$$x_2 = \tfrac{1}{2}(2 - x_3 + x_4)$$

For part (b) we rewrite the original equations in vector form:

$$\begin{bmatrix} 1 & -1 & 1 & -2 \\ 0 & 2 & 1 & -1 \end{bmatrix} \mathbf{x} = \begin{bmatrix} 1 \\ 2 \end{bmatrix}$$

Applying Eq. (7-17), we first calculate

$$AA^T = \begin{bmatrix} 7 & 1 \\ 1 & 6 \end{bmatrix}$$

Completing the indicated operations, the minimum-norm solution is

$$\hat{\mathbf{x}} = \frac{1}{41} [4 \quad 22 \quad 17 \quad -21]^T$$

The norm or length of this vector is

$$\|\hat{\mathbf{x}}\| = 0.855$$

and any other of the many solutions will be longer. For instance, setting $x_3 = x_4 = 0$, we obtain

$$\mathbf{x}' = [2 \quad 1 \quad 0 \quad 0]^T$$

whose norm $\|\mathbf{x}'\| = 2.236$. ∎

**7-3**

## OPEN-LOOP REGULATION

The purpose of this section is to develop a method for controlling a system in an open-loop mode. We will emphasize the problem of finite-time regulation using a minimum energy control sequence. First, we define some terms.

***Definition 7-2:*** A system is said to be *regulated* if its control inputs force any nonzero state of the system to the origin.

A typical situation where regulation is involved is in damping out unwanted vibrations in a dynamic system. Note that "regulation" has a more narrow meaning here than in general use. The process of regulating a system may be thought of as reducing the energy of the system (corresponding to the initial state) to zero.

CONTROLLABILITY AND STATE-VARIABLE FEEDBACK

With our discrete-time systems we assume a sequential input of the form

$$\{\mathbf{u}(k)\} = \{\mathbf{u}(0), \mathbf{u}(1), \mathbf{u}(2), \ldots\} \qquad (7\text{-}18)$$

**Definition 7-3:** The (*normalized*) *energy* of the sequence of $m$-vectors $\{\mathbf{u}(k)\}$ is given by

$$E_u = \sum_{k=0}^{\infty} \|\mathbf{u}(k)\|^2 \qquad (7\text{-}19)$$

where the norm-squared of each vector is the sum of squares of its components,

$$\|\mathbf{u}\|^2 = \sum_{i=1}^{m} u_i^2$$

For the special case where there is a single (scalar) control input the energy is the sum of the sequence values squared. The word "normalized" is usually omitted, and signal energy is understood from context to mean a normalized energy in the sense of the definition. If we have a finite sequence of inputs, and they are represented in the compact notation of Section 7-1, Eq. (7-7), then the energy of the sequence can be written as

$$E_u = \mathbf{U}^T\mathbf{U} = \|\mathbf{U}\|^2 \qquad (7\text{-}20)$$

Thus, solving Eq. (7-6) as a minimum-norm problem provides us with the *minimum energy control* sequence directly.

One of the important implications of Section 7-1 is that the entire state space is either reachable or controllable in $n$-steps for a linear system whose controllability matrix has rank $n$. Consequently, the minimum time required for regulating an $n$th-order system is $n$ sample steps. In Example 7-1 we found that a two-step control could provide regulation for the given conditions. In the next example the degree of control effort is considered.

### EXAMPLE 7-4 (Control Effort in Regulation)

Consider the sampled-data system depicted below.

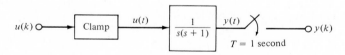

Following Section 3-4, we describe the continuous time plant as

$$\dot{\mathbf{x}}(t) = \begin{bmatrix} 0 & 1 \\ 0 & -1 \end{bmatrix} \mathbf{x}(t) + \begin{bmatrix} 0 \\ 1 \end{bmatrix} u(t)$$

$$y(t) = [\,1 \quad 0\,]\ \mathbf{x}(t)$$

The ZOH equivalent is given by

$$\mathbf{x}(k+1) = \begin{bmatrix} 1 & 1 - e^{-T} \\ 0 & e^{-T} \end{bmatrix} \mathbf{x}(k) + \begin{bmatrix} T + e^{-T} - 1 \\ 1 - e^{-T} \end{bmatrix} u(k)$$

or since $T = 1$ sec,

$$\mathbf{x}(k + 1) = \begin{bmatrix} 1 & 0.632 \\ 0 & 0.368 \end{bmatrix} \mathbf{x}(k) + \begin{bmatrix} 0.368 \\ 0.632 \end{bmatrix} u(k)$$

Assuming an arbitrary initial state $\mathbf{x}(0)$, we calculate the required input sequence to regulate the system in minimum time (two time steps). From Eq. (7-6) we calculate that

$$\begin{bmatrix} 0.368 & 0.767 \\ 0.632 & 0.233 \end{bmatrix} \begin{bmatrix} u(1) \\ u(0) \end{bmatrix} = - \begin{bmatrix} 1 & 0.865 \\ 0 & 0.135 \end{bmatrix} \mathbf{x}(0)$$

$$\begin{bmatrix} u(1) \\ u(0) \end{bmatrix} = \begin{bmatrix} 0.584 & 0.246 \\ -1.584 & -1.246 \end{bmatrix} \begin{bmatrix} x_1(0) \\ x_2(0) \end{bmatrix} \qquad (7\text{-}21)$$

Similarly, if we relax the regulation time requirement from two to three steps, we find using Eq. (7-6) that

$$\begin{bmatrix} 0.368 & 0.767 & 0.914 \\ 0.632 & 0.233 & 0.086 \end{bmatrix} \begin{bmatrix} u(2) \\ u(1) \\ u(0) \end{bmatrix} = - \begin{bmatrix} 1 & 0.950 \\ 0 & 0.050 \end{bmatrix} \mathbf{x}(0)$$

Using the minimum-norm solution of Eq. (7-17),

$$\mathbf{U} = - \mathscr{C}^T(3)[\mathscr{C}(3)\mathscr{C}^T(3)]^{-1}A^3\mathbf{x}(0)$$

where $\mathscr{C}(3)$ is the previous coefficient matrix, we obtain

$$\begin{bmatrix} u(2) \\ u(1) \\ u(0) \end{bmatrix} = \begin{bmatrix} 0.292 & 0.194 \\ -0.500 & -0.474 \\ -0.792 & -0.720 \end{bmatrix} \begin{bmatrix} x_1(0) \\ x_2(0) \end{bmatrix} \qquad (7\text{-}22)$$

We now assume a specific initial state of

$$\mathbf{x}(0) = [1 \quad 0]^T$$

and calculate from Eq. (7-21) that

$$u(0) = -1.58, \quad u(1) = 0.58$$

The minimum-time control energy is, then,

$$E_u = 2.85$$

Let us now illustrate that the price paid for speed of response is high control energy. Performing the above calculations for the three-step regulation solution of Eq. (7-22), using the same initial state,

$$u(0) = -0.792, \quad u(1) = -0.500, \quad u(2) = 0.292$$

Calculating the new control energy, we find that

$$E_u = 0.96$$

Note the drastic reduction of effort by allowing a 3-sec regulation, rather than 2 sec. ∎

The previous example shows that as the speed of response is increased, the control amplitudes tend to increase drastically. In most practical cases there are fixed limits on control amplitudes due primarily to limited actuation resources, for instance, a motor with a fixed power capability. Thus there is usually a practical limit on how fast a system may be made to respond. However, design for minimum-time response has always held a fascination for designers, and in the next section we discuss a method of feedback control that, although it has some practical drawbacks, is nevertheless an interesting basic design approach.

## 7-4

## DESIGN FOR DEADBEAT RESPONSE

The terminology "deadbeat response" refers to the special type of response, usually associated with sampled-data systems, in which the system responds to set-point commands in minimum time with no intersample oscillation. Thus, a system with deadbeat response will reach (and maintain) its steady state as quickly as possible. Strictly speaking, the approach is not limited to step inputs and can be extended to cover arbitrary order polynomial inputs. The present discussion will, however, be restricted to systems with piecewise constant command signals.

Figure 7-1 illustrates the sampled-data structure to be considered in this design approach. We are familiar with the ZOH equivalent discrete-time plant, which is represented by the clamped-input continuous-time plant, in particular that the order of the system is maintained. For a discrete-time plant of order $n$ the minimum time response is $nT$ seconds. Thus, for each new (constant) command input $r$ the system will require $nT$ seconds in which $y(t)$ will make a transition from the previous set-point to the new set-point. In order to ensure no additional variation in $y(t)$ between samples after steady state has been reached, we will work with the requirement that $\dot{\mathbf{x}} = \mathbf{0}$. The actual design, then, uses both the continuous-time model for the plant and its clamped equivalent. At the completion of the design we will have a digital controller, specified by its pulse transfer function, which implements the correct actuation sequence to the plant.

For this development we consider a SISO state model

$$\dot{\mathbf{x}}(t) = A\mathbf{x}(t) + Bu(t)$$
$$y(t) = C\mathbf{x}(t)$$

(7-23)

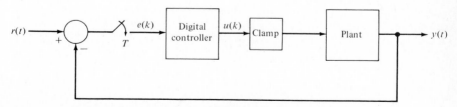

**FIGURE 7-1.  Digital control system structure.**

The first step is to assume a constant reference $r(t) = r_0$ and establish the requirements for steady state, namely,

$$y(t) = C\mathbf{x}(t) = r_0 \tag{7-24}$$

$$\dot{y}(t) = 0 \qquad \text{for } t \geq nT$$

As part of the steady state condition the correct constant input sequence must also be determined, although in most cases it will be zero. This can be calculated from the discrete-time equivalent for the system. If we write

$$\mathbf{x}(k + 1) = A_d\mathbf{x}(k) + B_d u(k) \tag{7-25}$$

for the clamped-equivalent system, where $A_d$ and $B_d$ are calculated according to Eq. (3-36), then at steady state

$$\mathbf{x}(n) = A_d\mathbf{x}(n) + b_d u_{ss} \tag{7-26}$$

the constant $u_{ss}$ may be found to satisfy Eq. (7-26). Finally, the required $n$-step sequence of inputs can be obtained by solving Eq. (7-6) for $k = n$, $\mathbf{x}_f = \mathbf{x}(n)$ and $\mathbf{x}(0) = \mathbf{0}$ (to simplify the calculations), using $A_d$ and $B_d$ from the discrete-time model.

If we imagine that we have calculated the values $u(0), u(1), \ldots, u(n - 1)$, then we would be able to generate the corresponding sequence of errors $e(0)$, $e(1), e(2), \ldots, e(n - 1)$ by applying $u(k)$ to the discrete-time model and feeding back $y(k)$ to determine $e(k)$ as in Fig. 7-1 for each $k$. From these calculations and the definition of $D(z)$, we have

$$D(z) = \frac{U(z)}{E(z)} = \frac{u(0) + u(1)z^{-1} + \cdots + u(n - 1)z^{-n-1}}{e(0) + e(1)z^{-1} + \cdots + e(n - 1)z^{-n-1}} \tag{7-27}$$

an $(n - 1)$th-order digital controller. Here it has been assumed that $u_{ss} = 0$. If $u_{ss} \neq 0$, a closed-form expression for $D(z)$ may still be obtained (by summing the steady state part as a shifted step function). We conclude this section with an example that follows the previous development in detail.

### EXAMPLE 7-5 (Deadbeat Control)

Given the second-order plant of Example 7-4 ($n = 2$),

$$\dot{\mathbf{x}}(t) = \begin{bmatrix} 0 & 1 \\ 0 & -1 \end{bmatrix} \mathbf{x}(t) + \begin{bmatrix} 0 \\ 1 \end{bmatrix} u(t)$$

$$y(t) = \begin{bmatrix} 1 & 0 \end{bmatrix} \mathbf{x}(t)$$

and using the same sample rate of 1 Hz, the discrete-time equivalent state equation is given by

$$\mathbf{x}(k + 1) = \begin{bmatrix} 1 & 0.632 \\ 0 & 0.368 \end{bmatrix} \mathbf{x}(k) + \begin{bmatrix} 0.368 \\ 0.632 \end{bmatrix} u(k)$$

For steady state,

$$y(t) = x_1(t) = r_0$$

$$\dot{y}(t) = \dot{x}_1(t) = x_2(t) = 0, \quad t \geq n$$

Thus, at $t = 2$ the steady state is $[r_0 \quad 0]^T$, and

$$\begin{bmatrix} r_0 \\ 0 \end{bmatrix} = \begin{bmatrix} 1 & 0.632 \\ 0 & 0.368 \end{bmatrix} \begin{bmatrix} r_0 \\ 0 \end{bmatrix} + \begin{bmatrix} 0.368 \\ 0.632 \end{bmatrix} u_{ss}$$

From the above equation $u_{ss} = 0$, that is, $u(k) = 0$ for $k \geq 2$ to maintain the steady state condition.

Using Eq. (7-6) with $k = 2$, and assuming $\mathbf{x}(0) = \mathbf{0}$

$$\begin{bmatrix} 0.368 & 0.767 \\ 0.632 & 0.233 \end{bmatrix} \begin{bmatrix} u(1) \\ u(0) \end{bmatrix} = \begin{bmatrix} r_0 \\ 0 \end{bmatrix}$$

From this

$$u(0) = 1.584r_0 \quad u(1) = -0.584r_0$$

The initial error (see Fig. 7-1) $e(0) = r_0 - y(0) = r_0$ since $\mathbf{x}(0) = \mathbf{0}$, and $e(k) = 0$ for $k \geq 2$. to find $e(1)$, $u(0)$ above is used to step the plant through one recursion as follows:

$$\mathbf{x}(1) = \mathbf{0} + B_d u(0)$$

$$y(1) = x_1(1) = 0.584r_0$$

$$e(1) = r_0 - y(1) = 0.416r_0$$

Therefore, from Eq. (7-26)

$$D(z) = \frac{1.584 - 0.584z^{-1}}{1 + 0.416z^{-1}} = \frac{1.584(z - 0.368)}{z + 0.416}$$

This is the desired controller. With this controller the closed-loop system of Fig. 7-1 will follow step inputs with a two-step deadbeat response for the given plant. Figure 7-2 illustrates the response $y(t)$ to a particular command $r(t)$ along with the actuation signal $u(t)$ generated from the controller. The calculations for these results may be done in discrete-time initially followed by solving for $y(t)$ using the original continuous-time plant with its ''initial'' state and step input found from the discrete-time analysis. ■

*Remarks:* The deadbeat control law requires the actuator input to be very precise. For instance, in the previous second-order example the actuator drives the system hard with the first pulse and must stop the motion at the exact set-point condition with the second pulse. Thus, intuitively, we can understand why deadbeat control is so very sensitive to parameter inaccuracies and such ''uncontrollables'' as are always found in a practical system.

If there is an effective amplitude limit on the actuation, a modified deadbeat control may still be possible. For example, if $|u| \leq 1$ in the previous problem, the desired vaue $u(0) = 1.584$ would saturate at 1.0. This value leads to the state $\mathbf{x}(1) = [0.368 \quad 0.632]^T$. As it turns out one can calculate that the three-step sequence

$$\{u(k)\} = \{1, 0.215, -0.215\}$$

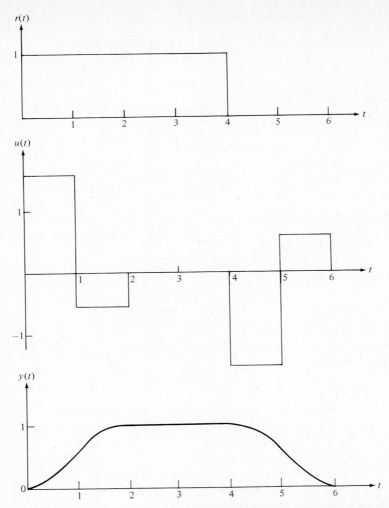

**FIGURE 7-2.** **Simulation results for Example 7-5: command *r(t)*; actuation *u(t)* and response *y(t)*.**

will work assuming a unit-step input. The corresponding controller found by calculating the error sequence involved, similar to that carried out in the previous example, is given by

$$D(z) = \frac{z^2 + 0.215z - 0.215}{z^2 + 0.632z + 0.153}$$

Unfortunately, this controller will work properly only for step inputs smaller than or equal to one. The saturation effect, being a nonlinear phenomenon, makes the design amplitude dependent.

In the next two sections we investigate the more general design technique known as state-variable feedback.

## TRANSFORMATION TO CONTROLLABLE FORM

Certain of the state-variable canonical forms of Chapter 3 have their use in design techniques. The controllable form finds its use in simplifying the calculations for state-variable feedback. In Section 3-7 the general transformation of state was discussed, while in this section we restrict our interest to finding the particular transformation

$$\mathbf{x} = P_c \mathbf{x}_c \tag{7-28}$$

which will take an arbitrary single-input, controllable plant described by the state $\mathbf{x}$ into an equivalent plant (with state $\mathbf{x}_c$) in controllable form. Thus, given a system state model

$$\begin{aligned} \mathbf{x}(k + 1) &= A\mathbf{x}(k) + Bu(k) \\ \mathbf{y}(k) &= C\mathbf{x}(k) + Du(k) \end{aligned} \tag{7-29}$$

we want to find the invertible matrix $P_c$ such that the transformed system

$$\begin{aligned} \mathbf{x}_c(k + 1) &= P_c^{-1}AP_c\mathbf{x}_c(k) + P_c^{-1}Bu(k) \\ \mathbf{y}(k) &= CP_c\mathbf{x}_c(k) + Du(k) \end{aligned} \tag{7-30}$$

is in controllable form. For simpler notation we write the controllable form system as

$$\begin{aligned} \mathbf{x}_c(k + 1) &= A_c\mathbf{x}_c(k) + B_cu(k) \\ \mathbf{y}(k) &= C_c\mathbf{x}_c(k) + Du(k) \end{aligned} \tag{7-31}$$

where the subscripts $c$ stand for controllable form. Recall from Section 3-6 the structure of the controllable form state model. Note that the system coefficient matrix $A_c$ is determined by the system characteristic equation, the (negatives of the) coefficients of which form the last row of the matrix.

Since a transformation of state does not change the system characteristic equation, we may calculate the characteristic equation from the given state model, Eqs. (7-29), and use its coefficients to fill out the matrix $A_c$. In addition, we know that the input distribution matrix $B_c$ is a vector of all zeros, except for unity as the last entry.

Knowing the pairs $(A, B)$ and $(A_c, B_c)$ allows us to construct the corresponding controllability matrices. For the original system model

$$\mathcal{C} = [B \quad AB \quad A^2B \quad \cdots \quad A^{n-1}B] \tag{7-32}$$

For the controllable form model

$$\mathcal{C}_c = [B_c \quad A_cB_c \quad A_c^2B_c \quad \cdots \quad A_c^{n-1}B_c] \tag{7-33}$$

We also know that controllability is an intrinsic property of a system; that is to say, assuming the original model is controllable ensures that any equivalent system is controllable.

For the single-input case at hand the controllability matrices $\mathcal{C}$ and $\mathcal{C}_c$ are both dimension $n \times n$. Since they both must have rank $n$, they are invertible. Introducing the notation of Eqs. (7-30), we obtain

$$\mathscr{C}_c = P_c^{-1} [B \quad AB \quad \cdots \quad A^{n-1}B] = P_c^{-1} \mathscr{C} \qquad (7\text{-}34)$$

From Eq. (7-34) we find the explicit form for $P_c$,

$$P_c = \mathscr{C} \mathscr{C}_c^{-1} \qquad (7\text{-}35)$$

To summarize, given the original system model, Eqs. (7-29), we can calculate $P_c$ and, therefore, the complete controllable form model of Eqs. (7-31). Let us consider an example which does this.

### EXAMPLE 7-6 (Controllable Form)

We wish to find the controllable form state model of the (controllable) system

$$\mathbf{x}(k + 1) = \begin{bmatrix} 1 & 2 & 0 \\ 3 & -1 & 1 \\ 0 & 2 & 0 \end{bmatrix} \mathbf{x}(k) + \begin{bmatrix} 2 \\ 1 \\ 1 \end{bmatrix} u(k)$$

$$y(k) = [\,0 \quad 0 \quad 1\,] \; \mathbf{x}(k)$$

Since the characteristic polynomial

$$p(z) = \det [zI - A] = z^3 + a_3 z^2 + a_2 z + a_1$$

(where $a_1 = 2$, $a_2 = -9$, and $a_3 = 0$ in this case) is invariant under a change of state variables, the first part of the controllable form state model can be written as

$$\mathbf{x}_c(k + 1) = \begin{bmatrix} 0 & 1 & 0 \\ 0 & 0 & 1 \\ -2 & 9 & 0 \end{bmatrix} \mathbf{x}_c(k) + \begin{bmatrix} 0 \\ 0 \\ 1 \end{bmatrix} u(k)$$

We now calculate $\mathscr{C}$ and $\mathscr{C}_c$ using Eq. (7-32) and Eq. (7-33), respectively,

$$\mathscr{C} = \begin{bmatrix} 2 & 4 & 16 \\ 1 & 6 & 8 \\ 1 & 2 & 12 \end{bmatrix}, \quad \mathscr{C}_c = \begin{bmatrix} 0 & 0 & 1 \\ 0 & 1 & 0 \\ 1 & 0 & 9 \end{bmatrix}$$

Thus, from Eq. (7-35)

$$P_c = \mathscr{C} \mathscr{C}_c^{-1} = \begin{bmatrix} -2 & 4 & 2 \\ -1 & 6 & 1 \\ 3 & 2 & 1 \end{bmatrix}$$

and we complete the controllable form state model by calculating the output equation

$$y(k) = [\,0 \quad 0 \quad 1\,] P_c \mathbf{x}_c(k) = [\,3 \quad 2 \quad 1\,] \, \mathbf{x}_c(k) \qquad \blacksquare$$

The previous development, unfortunately, requires a matrix inversion, which can be tedious when working by hand and somewhat inefficient in a computer-aided mode. A simpler recursive procedure for constructing $P_c$ that is based on the specific form of $\mathcal{C}_c$ is available. The proof will not be included, although it is a simple matter to show that the method is valid for low-order systems (up to third or fourth order). To present this method, let us consider a notation for the coefficients of $A_c$ that is slightly modified from that used in the developments of Chapter 3, namely,

$$
A_c = \begin{bmatrix}
0 & 1 & 0 & \cdots & 0 & 0 \\
0 & 0 & 1 & \cdots & 0 & 0 \\
& & \cdots & & & \\
0 & 0 & 0 & \cdots & 0 & 1 \\
a_1 & a_2 & a_3 & \cdots & a_{n-1} & a_n
\end{bmatrix}
\tag{7-36}
$$

In terms of this new notation the characteristic equation for the system becomes

$$
p(z) = z^n - a_n z^{n-1} - a_{n-1} a^{n-2} - \cdots - a_2 z - a_1
\tag{7-37}
$$

Note the differences between $A_c$ in Eq. (7-36) and the system coefficient matrix of Eq. (3-15).

Again assuming a single-input system, let us express $P_c$ in terms of its columns. In particular,

$$
P_c = [\mathbf{p}_1 \quad \mathbf{p}_2 \quad \mathbf{p}_3 \quad \cdots \quad \mathbf{p}_n]
\tag{7-38}
$$

where $\mathbf{p}_i$ denotes the $i$th column of $P_c$. Since the input distribution matrix $B$ is $n \times 1$, the vector aspect will be emphasized by letting $B = \mathbf{b}$ in the subsequent development. Recall from Eq. (7-35) that

$$
P_c \mathcal{C}_c = \mathcal{C} = [\mathbf{b} \quad A\mathbf{b} \quad \cdots \quad A^{n-1}\mathbf{b}]
\tag{7-39}
$$

By expanding the left-hand side of Eq. (7-39), taking full advantage of the special structure of $\mathcal{C}_c$ and equating columns, we obtain the following set of equations:

$$
\mathbf{p}_n = \mathbf{b}
$$

$$
\mathbf{p}_{n-1} = A\mathbf{p}_n - a_n\mathbf{p}_n
$$

$$
\mathbf{p}_{n-2} = A\mathbf{p}_{n-1} - a_{n-1}\mathbf{p}_n
$$

$$
\mathbf{p}_{n-3} = A\mathbf{p}_{n-2} - a_{n-2}\mathbf{p}_n
\tag{7-40}
$$

$$
\cdots
$$

$$
\mathbf{p}_1 = A\mathbf{p}_2 - a_2\mathbf{p}_n
$$

The set of Eqs. (7-40) is sequential and may be solved from top down. The next example will illustrate their use.

### EXAMPLE 7-7

From the previous example we have the following SISO system to change to controllable form:

$$\mathbf{x}(k + 1) = \begin{bmatrix} 1 & 2 & 0 \\ 3 & -1 & 1 \\ 0 & 2 & 0 \end{bmatrix} \mathbf{x}(k) + \begin{bmatrix} 2 \\ 1 \\ 1 \end{bmatrix} u(k)$$

$$y(k) = [\, 0 \quad 0 \quad 1\,] \; \mathbf{x}(k)$$

The characteristic polynomial is

$$\det\,(zI - A) = z^3 + 0z^2 - 9z + 2$$

so that with the notation of Eq. (7-37)

$$a_1 = -2, \quad a_2 = 9, \quad a_3 = 0$$

Using Eqs. (7-40),

$$\mathbf{p}_3 = \begin{bmatrix} 2 \\ 1 \\ 1 \end{bmatrix}, \qquad \mathbf{p}_2 = A\mathbf{p}_3 - 0\mathbf{p}_3 = \begin{bmatrix} 4 \\ 6 \\ 2 \end{bmatrix}$$

$$\mathbf{p}_1 = A\mathbf{p}_2 - 9\mathbf{p}_3 = \begin{bmatrix} -2 \\ -1 \\ 3 \end{bmatrix}$$

Therefore, the desired transformation matrix is

$$P_c = \begin{bmatrix} -2 & 4 & 2 \\ -1 & 6 & 1 \\ 3 & 2 & 1 \end{bmatrix}$$

Finally, knowing $P_c$, we obtain from Eqs. (7-30) the controllable form model

$$\mathbf{x}_c(k + 1) = \begin{bmatrix} 0 & 1 & 0 \\ 0 & 0 & 1 \\ -2 & 9 & 0 \end{bmatrix} \mathbf{x}_c(k) + \begin{bmatrix} 0 \\ 0 \\ 1 \end{bmatrix} u(k)$$

$$y(k) = [\quad 3 \quad 2 \quad 1]\; \mathbf{x}_c(k) \qquad\qquad \blacksquare$$

Now that a reasonably efficient method is available for transforming a given state model into its controllable form, presuming the system to be controllable, the design of a state feedback matrix presented in the next section will seem routine.

## 7-6

## STATE-VARIABLE FEEDBACK DESIGN

One of the most fundamental results of state-variable theory is that a suitable linear combination of the states fed back to augment the control input can be used to establish *any* desired degree of stability for the system. In particular, it will be shown that for any controllable system

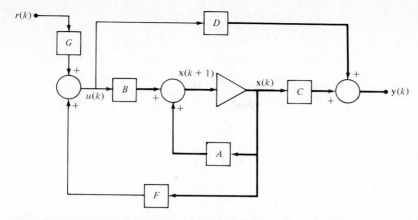

FIGURE 7-3.  System structure with state variable feedback.

$$\mathbf{x}(k + 1) = A\mathbf{x}(k) + Bu(k)$$
$$y(k) = C\mathbf{x}(k) + Du(k)$$

(7-41)

a feedback gain matrix $F$ exists such that with

$$u(k) = F\mathbf{x}(k) + Gr(k)$$

(7-42)

the "closed-loop" system matrix $(A + BF)$ eigenvalues may be specified arbitrarily. Figure 7-3 illustrates state feedback using a "vector block diagram"; each block represents either a scalar or matrix gain depending on whether its input is a scalar or vector signal, respectively. The triangular element of Fig. 7-3 is interpreted as a vector of unit-time delays, and heavy lines are used to represent paths of (possibly) vector valued signals.

Clearly, Fig. 7-3 is a graphical display of Eqs. (7-41) and Eq. (7-42) taken together. The matrices $A$, $B$, $C$, and $D$ are assumed known from the plant model, and, consequently, the design calls for a method of determining the gain $G$ and matrix $F$ to satisfy a specified system performance.

## 7-6.1  State Feedback Matrix

Let us first consider the feedback matrix $F$. Introducing $u(k)$ of Eq. (7-42) into the plant description, we obtain

$$\mathbf{x}(k + 1) = (A + BF)\mathbf{x}(k) + BGr(k)$$
$$y(k) = (C + DF)\mathbf{x}(k) + DGr(k)$$

(7-43)

This is called the *closed-loop state model*. Note that the stability of the system is determined from the system coefficient matrix $(A + BF)$.

Since we know that a controllable system can always be described in its controllable form, let us assume that matrices $A$ and $B$ above correspond to this form. Thus, with our modified notation, $A$ of Eqs. (7-43) has the form of $A_c$ in Eq. (7-36) and $B$ is a vector with unity in the last position, all other entries being zero. The dimensions of $F$ are $1 \times n$. Writing out the closed-loop coefficient matrix under these assumptions, we have

$$A_c + B_c F_c = \begin{bmatrix} 0 & 1 & 0 & \cdots & 0 & 0 \\ 0 & 0 & 1 & \cdots & 0 & 0 \\ & & \cdots & & & \\ 0 & 0 & 0 & \cdots & 0 & 1 \\ a_1 & a_2 & a_3 & \cdots & a_{n-1} & a_n \end{bmatrix} + \begin{bmatrix} 0 \\ 0 \\ \\ 0 \\ 1 \end{bmatrix} [f_1 f_2 \cdots f_n]$$

(7-44)

Therefore,

$$A_c + B_c F_c = \begin{bmatrix} 0 & 1 & 0 & \cdots & 0 \\ 0 & 0 & 1 & \cdots & 0 \\ & & \cdots & & \\ 0 & 0 & 0 & \cdots & 1 \\ a_1 + f_1 & a_2 + f_2 & a_3 + f_3 & & a_n + f_n \end{bmatrix}$$

(7-45)

With feedback we have changed the characteristic equation of the system. Using the notation above, the *closed-loop characteristic equation* is given by

$$p_{\text{CL}}(z) = z^n - (a_n + f_n)z^{n-1} - \cdots - (a_2 + f_2)z - (a_1 + f_1) \quad (7\text{-}46)$$

Note that each and every coefficient may be adjusted independently by one of the entries of $F_c$. This development proves that the designer can specify any desired set of system poles (with the exception that nonreal poles must have their complex-conjugate values present also).

Typically, the closed-loop pole locations $\{p_j\}$, $j = 1, 2, \ldots, n$ are determined by the designer (based on the desired system response and the experience of the designer) as an initial step. The actual feedback matrix $F_c$ can be found by equating corresponding terms of the polynomial $p_{\text{CL}}(z)$ of Eq. (7-46) with the "desired" polynomial

$$p_d(z) = \prod_{j=1}^{n} (z - p_j) \tag{7-47}$$

where $\{p_j\}$, $j = 1, 2, \ldots, n$ are the desired pole locations. Each coefficient determines one entry in $F_c$. Thus, finding $F_c$ given the system in controllable form and given the desired closed-loop locations is a straightforward problem.

Let us now backtrack and assume that the plant model is *not* in controllable form. Then, assuming that the desired poles of Eq. (7-47) are known, the design of the state feedback matrix may be summarized by the following steps:

1. Determine $P_c$ using Eqs. (7-40).
2. Write the plant description in controllable form using the method of Section 7-5.
3. Form the desired polynomial $p_d(z)$ in Eq. (7-47)

4. Calculate $F_c$ by setting $p_d(z)$ equal to $p_{CL}(z)$ of Eq. (7-46).
5. Transform $F_c$ for the original state description: $F = F_c P_c^{-1}$.

Step 5 follows since the feedback signal

$$F_c \mathbf{x}_c(k) = F_c[P_c^{-1}\mathbf{x}(k)] = [F_c P_c^{-1}]\mathbf{x}(k) = F\mathbf{x}(k) \qquad (7\text{-}48)$$

This procedure is referred to as *pole placement;* the design aspect enters in deciding the desired pole locations. One approach to the design is to interpret the desired performance of the system into an equivalent second-order system design as discussed in Chapter 6. With this approach two pole locations are used to establish the dominant poles, and the remaining pole locations are positioned either close to the origin or at undesired zero locations.

A major drawback of this method of state feedback is that *all* states are required for feedback, in general. That is to say, all state variables of the system must be measured to implement the scheme. In many practical situations this is not feasible, usually because of not having adequate sensors for each and every state variable. This deficiency will be removed in the next chapter by using additional dynamics to regenerate any inaccessible states.

Let us conclude this section with an example that illustrates the pole placement procedure. No claim is made for the given pole locations; they were chosen mainly for their numerical simplicity.

### EXAMPLE 7-8 (Pole Placement)

We wish to construct a feedback matrix $F$ for the system of Example 7-7 such that with $u(k) = F\mathbf{x}(k)$ the closed-loop poles are at $z = 0.5$ and $z = 0.5 \pm j0.5$.

***SOLUTION:*** In Example 7-7 we found that with $\mathbf{x}(k) = P_c \mathbf{x}_c(k)$, where

$$P_c = \begin{bmatrix} -2 & 4 & 2 \\ -1 & 6 & 1 \\ 3 & 2 & 1 \end{bmatrix}$$

the system was transformed into the controllable form

$$\mathbf{x}_c(k + 1) = \begin{bmatrix} 0 & 1 & 0 \\ 0 & 0 & 1 \\ -2 & 9 & 0 \end{bmatrix} \mathbf{x}_c(k) + \begin{bmatrix} 0 \\ 0 \\ 1 \end{bmatrix} u(k)$$

$$y(k) = \begin{bmatrix} 3 & 2 & 1 \end{bmatrix} \mathbf{x}_c(k)$$

From step 3 of our procedure we have

$$p_d(z) = (z - 0.5)(z - 0.5 - j0.5)(z - 0.5 + j0.5)$$

$$p_d(z) = z^3 - 1.5z^2 + 1.0z - 0.25$$

Matching coefficients with $p_{CL}(z)$ of Eq. (7-46) ($a_1 = -2$, $a_2 = 9$, $a_3 = 0$),

$$a_1 + f_1 = -2 + f_1 = 0.25$$

$$a_2 + f_2 = 9 + f_2 = -1.0$$

$$a_3 + f_3 = 0 + f_3 = 1.5$$

Therefore,

$$F_c = [2.25 \quad -10.0 \quad 1.5]$$

For the final step we find that

$$u(k) = F_c \mathbf{x}_c(k) = [F_c P_c^{-1}] \, \mathbf{x}(k) = F\mathbf{x}(k)$$

where

$$F = F_c P_c^{-1} = \frac{[2.25 \quad -10 \quad 1.5]}{8} \begin{bmatrix} -1 & 0 & 2 \\ -1 & 2 & 0 \\ 5 & -4 & 2 \end{bmatrix} = \frac{1}{32} \begin{bmatrix} 61 \\ -104 \\ 30 \end{bmatrix}^T$$

$$F = [1.91 \quad -3.25 \quad 0.94] \qquad \blacksquare$$

## 7-6.2 Input Gain

In Fig. 7-3 the gain block $G$ can be used to provide an overall dc gain of unity so that the steady output will match a constant reference input. From the closed-loop system, Eqs. (7-43), we can find the transfer function from $r(k)$ to any output.

$$H(z) = \hat{C}(zI - \hat{A})^{-1}\hat{B} + \hat{D} \qquad (7\text{-}49)$$

where $\hat{A} = A + BF$, $\hat{B} = BG$, $\hat{C} = C + DF$, and $\hat{D} = DG$. If there is only one output, then $H(z)$ will be a scalar transfer function, and we know from the steady state discussion of Chapter 6 that the *dc gain* of the system is given by

$$\text{dc gain} = \frac{\text{steady state response}}{\text{amplitude of step input}} = H(z)\Big|_{z=1} \qquad (7\text{-}50)$$

Therefore, the expression for $G$ can be determined from Eq. (7-49):

$$H(1) = [(C + DF)(I - A - BF)^{-1}B + D]G = 1 \qquad (7\text{-}51)$$

$$G = [(C + DF)(I - A - BF)^{-1}B + D]^{-1}$$

Although Eq. (7-51) appears complicated, at least $G$ is a scalar. Let us illustrate the calculation of $G$ in the next example.

### EXAMPLE 7-9 (Input Gain Calculation)

We first want to determine the transfer function for the closed-loop system of Example 7-7 with the feedback as calculated in Example 7-8, then evaluate at $z = 1$.

**SOLUTION:** Since the transfer function of a system is invariant under a change of state, let us use the controllable form from the previous example.

$$H(z) = C_c(zI - A_c - B_cF_c)^{-1}B_cG$$

$$H(z) = [3 \quad 2 \quad 1] \begin{bmatrix} z & -1 & 0 \\ 0 & z & -1 \\ -0.25 & 1 & z-1.5 \end{bmatrix}^{-1} \begin{bmatrix} 0 \\ 0 \\ 1 \end{bmatrix} G$$

$$H(z) = \frac{z^2 + 2z + 3}{z^3 - 1.5z^2 + z - 0.25} G$$

Therefore,

$$H(1) = 24G, \quad G = \tfrac{1}{24} = 0.0417 \qquad \blacksquare$$

## 7-7

## SOLVED PROBLEMS

In this section we will isolate certain specific problems of practical interest and/or extensions of the main chapter material. The first development will provide us additional understanding of the controllability concept.

### 7-7.1  Discrete-Time System Modes

From Chapter 3 we are already aware that a system with distinct eigenvalues is equivalent to a system whose $A$ matrix is diagonal. The matrix $M$ such that

$$\mathbf{x}(k) = M\boldsymbol{\xi}(k) \tag{7-52}$$

transforms the $\mathbf{x}$ system with coefficient matrices $A$, $B$, $C$, and $D$, into the $\boldsymbol{\xi}$ system with corresponding matrices $\Lambda$, $B'$, $C'$, and $D$, where $\Lambda$ is a diagonal matrix, is called the *model matrix*. For details the reader is referred back to Section 3-7.1. In the $\boldsymbol{\xi}$ description the dynamic equations are uncoupled and may be written as the set of scalar equations

$$\xi_i(k+1) = \lambda_i\xi_i(k) + q_i(k) \tag{7-53}$$

for $i = 1, 2, \ldots, n$, where $\lambda_i$ is the $i$th diagonal element of $\Lambda$ and $q_i(k)$, the *i*th *modal input*, is the $i$th entry of $B'\mathbf{u}(k) = M^{-1}B\mathbf{u}(k)$. If we expand Eq. (7-52), we obtain the expression

$$\mathbf{x}(k) = \mathbf{m}_1\xi_1(k) + \mathbf{m}_2\xi_2(k) + \cdots + \mathbf{m}_n\xi_n(k) \tag{7-54}$$

where $\mathbf{m}_i$ is the $i$th eigenvector of $A$ (corresponding to the distinct eigenvalue $\lambda_i$) and $\xi_i(k)$ is the solution of Eq. (7-53) for each $i$. The terms of Eq. (7-54) are called the *modes* of the system. In the following example we will perform a modal expansion of a system which is uncontrollable.

## EXAMPLE 7-10 (Modal Expansion)

Consider the system

$$\mathbf{x}(k + 1) = \begin{bmatrix} 1 & 4 \\ -2 & 7 \end{bmatrix} \mathbf{x}(k) + \begin{bmatrix} 2 \\ 1 \end{bmatrix} u(k)$$

$$y(k) = \begin{bmatrix} 0 & 1 \end{bmatrix} \mathbf{x}(k)$$

Checking controllability, we have

$$\mathscr{C} = \begin{bmatrix} 2 & 6 \\ 1 & 3 \end{bmatrix}, \quad \text{rank } \mathscr{C} = 1$$

(System is *not* controllable.)

Using the given $A$ matrix, the eigenvalues are determined to be $\lambda_1 = 3$ and $\lambda_2 = 5$. The corresponding eigenvectors are given by

$$\mathbf{m}_1 = \begin{bmatrix} 2 \\ 1 \end{bmatrix}, \quad \mathbf{m}_2 = \begin{bmatrix} 1 \\ 1 \end{bmatrix}$$

With the change of state of Eq. (7-52), the matrix $M$ made up of the columns $\mathbf{m}_1$ and $\mathbf{m}_2$ above, we obtain the decoupled system

$$\boldsymbol{\xi}(k + 1) = \begin{bmatrix} 3 & 0 \\ 0 & 5 \end{bmatrix} \boldsymbol{\xi}(k) + \begin{bmatrix} 1 \\ 0 \end{bmatrix} u(k)$$

$$y(k) = \begin{bmatrix} 1 & 1 \end{bmatrix} \boldsymbol{\xi}(k)$$

Figure 7-4 illustrates this uncontrollable system in block diagram form. In this modal form it is easy to see why the system is uncontrollable, namely, that the control input has influence over only one of the system modes. Note that in this instance the uncontrolled mode is unstable and would, in practice, become excited by random noise in the system, leading to an unbounded mode. (Of course, some sort of saturating nonlinearity would keep the state from actually increasing without bound.) It only takes one unstable mode to be disastrous for the system. For instance, in the example, even if $\xi_1(k)$ were stabilized by feedback, $\xi_2(k)$ and therefore the entire set of states $\mathbf{x}(k)$ would be unstable by Eq. (7-54). A system is said to be *stabilizable* if its uncontrollable modes are stable. Thus, the system of Fig. 7-4 is unstabilizable. ■

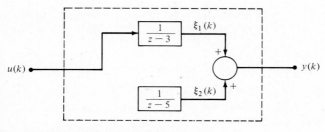

**FIGURE 7-4.  An uncontrollable system.**

*Left and Right Eigenvectors.* From the previous development, in particular Eq. (7-54), we know that the ordinary or right eigenvectors of a system specify certain directions in the state space that are important to that system. Whereas *right eigenvectors* of a matrix $A$ are defined in the natural form

$$A\mathbf{r}_i = \lambda_i \mathbf{r}_i \tag{7-55}$$

*left eigenvectors* of $A$ are defined as satisfying

$$\mathbf{l}_i^T A = \lambda_i \mathbf{l}_i^T \tag{7-56}$$

where $\mathbf{r}_i$ and $\mathbf{l}_i$ are the right and left eigenvectors corresponding to the eigenvalue $\lambda_i$ for each $i = 1, 2, \ldots, n$.

When we are dealing with a state-variable model, the eigenvalues of the coefficient matrix $A$ are identical to the system poles. To give an interpretation to left eigenvectors, let us assume an unforced system

$$\mathbf{x}(k + 1) = A\mathbf{x}(k) \tag{7-57}$$

and define a particular scalar function as a special linear combination of the state variables,

$$\xi_i(k) = \mathbf{l}_i^T \mathbf{x}(k) \tag{7-58}$$

where $\mathbf{l}_i$ satisfies Eq. (7-56) for $i = 1, 2, \ldots, n$.

Then, combining Eq. (7-57) and Eq. (7-58), we find that

$$\xi_i(k + 1) = \mathbf{l}_i^T \mathbf{x}(k + 1) = \mathbf{l}_i^T A\mathbf{x}(k) = \lambda_i \mathbf{l}_i^T \mathbf{x}(k) = \lambda_i \xi_i(k) \tag{7-59}$$

In other words, a left eigenvector determines a special scalar-valued function of the states that satisfies its own scalar dynamics. In the case of an unforced system as in Eq. (7-57) these scalar functions relate directly to the mode variations described in Eq. (7-54). In the next subsection the important problem of decoupling a MIMO system is addressed.

## 7-7.2 Multiple-Input System Design

The methods of Sections 7-5 and 7-6 pertain only to single-input systems. For multiple-input systems the corresponding techniques are much more involved. Yet, when it is required, one must be able to design feedback controls for multiple-input systems also. Of course, if the system is controllable from one of its scalar inputs, then the methods previously presented apply, and the proper feedback may be designed for that particular input as if it were a single-input system. More generally, the system may be controllable, but not from any single input. If this is the situation, an artificial "single input" can usually be constructed. One example of this would be to feed the identical feedback signal to all inputs, in which case the artificial input is equivalent to all of the inputs connected together. More generally, consider the scalar feedback signal $u_s(k)$ to be distributed over the $m$ inputs as follows

$$\mathbf{u}(k) = \boldsymbol{\alpha} u_s(k) \tag{7-60}$$

where $\boldsymbol{\alpha}$ is a constant vector to be determined. For instance, if $\boldsymbol{\alpha}$ is a vector of all ones, Eq. (7-60) corresponds to tying the inputs together.

To be useful, $\boldsymbol{\alpha}$ of Eq. (7-60) must be chosen so that $A$ and $B\boldsymbol{\alpha}$ form a controllable pair. In other words, the system must be controllable from the feedback signal $\alpha u_s(k)$. If controllability is satisfied, state feedback may be designed for the system using the system matrices $A$ and $B_s = B\boldsymbol{\alpha}$. Since the matrix $B_s$ is of dimension $n \times 1$, the methods of single-input systems can be applied. Furthermore, if it is determined that

$$u_s(k) = F_s\mathbf{x}(k) \tag{7-61}$$

then the actual feedback for the system is given by

$$\mathbf{u}(k) = \boldsymbol{\alpha}u_s(k) = [\boldsymbol{\alpha}F_s]\mathbf{x}(k) = F\mathbf{x}(k) \tag{7-62}$$

Let us illustrate the procedure.

### EXAMPLE 7-11 (State Feedback for a Multiple-Input System)

We wish to design a state variable feedback matrix $F$ for the following system

$$\mathbf{x}(k + 1) = \begin{bmatrix} 1 & 0 & 0 \\ 0 & -1 & 0 \\ 0 & 0 & 0 \end{bmatrix} \mathbf{x}(k) + \begin{bmatrix} 1 & 1 \\ 1 & 0 \\ 0 & 1 \end{bmatrix} \mathbf{u}(k) \tag{7-63}$$

such that with $\mathbf{u}(k) = F\mathbf{x}(k) + \mathbf{r}(k)$, the closed-loop pole locations are

$$z = -0.5, \quad z = 0.5 \pm j0.5$$

For these poles the characteristic equation is

$$p_d(z) = z^3 - 0.5z^2 + 0.25$$

Application of the controllability test indicates that, while the system is controllable, it is not controllable from either single input. However, with $\boldsymbol{\alpha} = [1 \quad 1]^T$, $A$ and $B_s = B\boldsymbol{\alpha}$ make a controllable pair. For the calculation of $F_s$ the system dynamic equation becomes effectively

$$\mathbf{x}(k + 1) = \begin{bmatrix} 1 & 0 & 0 \\ 0 & -1 & 0 \\ 0 & 0 & 0 \end{bmatrix} \mathbf{x}(k) + \begin{bmatrix} 2 \\ 1 \\ 1 \end{bmatrix} u_s(k)$$

Without resorting to a conversion to controllable form, since the problem is relatively easy, the characteristic equation of

$$A + B_sF_s = \begin{bmatrix} 1 + 2a & 2b & 2c \\ a & b - 1 & c \\ a & b & c \end{bmatrix}$$

where $F_s = [a \quad b \quad c]$, can be determined to be

$$z^3 - (2a + b + c)z^2 + (b - 2a - 1)z + c = 0$$

Comparing with $p_d(z)$ above, and solving we obtain

$$F_s = \frac{1}{16} [-3 \quad 10 \quad 4]$$

Therefore, from Eq. (7-62) the original two-input system of Eq. (7-63) has the state feedback matrix

$$F = \frac{1}{16} \begin{bmatrix} -3 & 10 & 4 \\ -3 & 10 & 4 \end{bmatrix}$$

■

With the above procedure we have the ability to calculate feedback matrices for MIMO systems for pole positioning. Note that the elements of $\boldsymbol{\alpha}$ provide relative weights to the inputs. In practice this may be useful, for instance, to allow particular actuators to carry more or less of the total control load.

***An Alternative Method for Pole Placement.*** The previous technique of creating an "equivalent single-input" system for feedback construction will occasionally *not* work. The reason for this is that in some instances, even though the system is controllable, there may be no vector $\boldsymbol{\alpha}$ as in Eq. (7-60) for which $A$ and $B\boldsymbol{\alpha}$ are a controllable pair. The method presented here requires its own amount of tedious calculation, but it has the great redeeming feature of being applicable to any controllable system. The technique calls for the designer to specify the $n$ pole positions $p_1, p_2, \ldots, p_n$ that are desired for the closed-loop system. From Fig. 7-3 it can be seen that the desired characteristic equation is

$$p_{\mathrm{CL}}(z) = \det (zI - A - BF) = 0 \qquad (7\text{-}64)$$

Since, by assumption, the system is controllable, there must exist a matrix $F$ that satisfies Eq. (7-64) for $z = p_1, p_2, \ldots, p_n$. (We assume that the desired poles are distinct.)

Factoring out the open-loop characteristic polynomial,

$$p_{\mathrm{CL}}(z) = \det \{(zI - A)[I - (zI - A)^{-1}BF]\}$$

$$p_{\mathrm{CL}}(z) = \det (zI - A) \det [I - T(z)F]$$

$$p_{\mathrm{CL}}(z) = p_{\mathrm{OL}}(z) \det [I - T(z)F]$$

where $T(z) = (zI - A)^{-1}B$ is the transfer matrix from inputs $\mathbf{u}$ to states. To satisfy Eq. (7-64), $F$ is chosen so that

$$\det [I - T(p_i)F] = 0 \qquad (7\text{-}65)$$

for $i = 1, 2, \ldots, n$. Alternatively, from Appendix B we can reverse the factors and work with

$$\det [I - FT(p_i)] = 0 \qquad (7\text{-}66)$$

The advantage of Eq. (7-66) over Eq. (7-65) is that the dimension of the determinant is usually smaller, namely, the number of inputs is typically smaller than the number of states.

Since Eq. (7-66) can be satisfied by selecting a particular column of the determinant to be zero, there is a great deal of flexibility available when actually applying the procedure and a corresponding nonuniqueness of the resulting $F$ matrix. Specifically, if the $j$th column is selected,

$$F\mathbf{t}_j(p_i) = \mathbf{e}_j \tag{7-67}$$

where $\mathbf{t}_j$ and $\mathbf{e}_j$ are the $j$th columns of $T$ and $I$, respectively. The complete $F$ matrix is then determined from $n$ independent equations of the above form:

$$F = E[\mathbf{t}_{j_1}(p_1)\ \mathbf{t}_{j_2}(p_2) \cdots \mathbf{t}_{j_n}(p_n)]^{-1} \tag{7-68}$$

where $E$ is the matrix of columns from an identity matrix corresponding to those selected for each of the desired pole positions. The procedure is illustrated in the following example.

### EXAMPLE 7-12 (MIMO System Pole Placement)
Given the 2-input, 2-output system

$$\mathbf{x}(k + 1) = \begin{bmatrix} 0 & 0 & 0 \\ 0 & -1 & 0 \\ 0 & 0 & 1 \end{bmatrix} \mathbf{x}(k) + \begin{bmatrix} 1 & 0 \\ 1 & 0 \\ 0 & 1 \end{bmatrix} \mathbf{u}(k)$$

$$\mathbf{y}(k) = \begin{bmatrix} 1 & 2 & -1 \\ 1 & 4 & -3 \end{bmatrix} \mathbf{x}(k) + \begin{bmatrix} 0 & 1 \\ 0 & 3 \end{bmatrix} \mathbf{u}(k)$$

let us use feedback to locate the poles at $z = 0.1$, $z = 0.2$, and $z = 0.3$. Applying the above method, we first need to calculate that

$$T(z) = (zI - A)^{-1}B = \begin{bmatrix} z^{-1} & 0 \\ (z + 1)^{-1} & 0 \\ 0 & (z - 1)^{-1} \end{bmatrix}$$

For $p_1 = 0.1$ and $p_2 = 0.2$ column one will be used and for $p_3 = 0.3$ column two will be used. Thus, after evaluation, Eq. (7-68) appears as follows:

$$F = \begin{bmatrix} 1 & 1 & 0 \\ 0 & 0 & 1 \end{bmatrix} \begin{bmatrix} 10 & 5 & 0 \\ \frac{10}{11} & \frac{5}{6} & 0 \\ 0 & 0 & -\frac{10}{7} \end{bmatrix}^{-1}$$

and the resulting feedback matrix

$$F = \frac{1}{50} \begin{bmatrix} -1 & 66 & 0 \\ 0 & 0 & -35 \end{bmatrix}$$ ∎

The reader should keep in mind that in the previous discussions all of the state variables are assumed to be accessible. In the next chapter this assumption is *not* made, resulting in a dynamic controller rather than the constant gains we have seen here.

## 7-7.3 System Decoupling

In Fig. 7-5 a MIMO system is illustrated. In the following development the number of control inputs is assumed to equal the number of controlled outputs as indicated in the figure.

The system of Fig. 7-5 may be characterized by a (square) transfer matrix $H(z)$ of dimension $m \times m$. Decoupling of the system has as its objective to use feedback to diagonalize $H(z)$ so that each input would affect one and only one output, thereby making the control of such a system much easier. An alternate method of describing the system is given by the state model

$$\mathbf{x}(k + 1) = A\mathbf{x}(k) + B\mathbf{u}(k) \tag{7-69}$$
$$\mathbf{y}(k) = C\mathbf{x}(k) + D\mathbf{u}(k)$$

If it is assumed that the states of the system are accessible for feedback, then we may consider that

$$\mathbf{u}(k) = F\mathbf{x}(k) + G\mathbf{r}(k) \tag{7-70}$$

To begin with, let us define

$$\mathbf{v}(k) = \mathbf{y}(k) - D\mathbf{u}(k) \tag{7-71}$$

as new "outputs," from which the true outputs may be easily found. This effectively eliminates the $D$ matrix in Eqs. (7-69). Thus, the modified transfer matrix from $\mathbf{r}$ to $\mathbf{v}$ becomes

$$H'(z) = C(zI - A - BF)^{-1}BG \tag{7-72}$$

For $H'(z)$ to be diagonal we must have $C(A + BF)^i BG$ diagonal for $i = 0, 1, 2, \ldots, n - 1$ from consideration of the inverse relation. The reader is referred to the zero-state portion of the response given in Eq. (3-46).

Corresponding to the $j$th output $v_j$, a set of $m$ integers is defined by

$$d_j = \text{the minimum } i \text{ such that} \tag{7-73}$$
$$\{C_j A^i B \neq \mathbf{0}, \quad i = 0, 1, 2, \ldots, n - 1\}$$

where $C_j$ is the $j$th row of the matrix $C$. If $C_j A^i B = \mathbf{0}$ for all $i$, then $d_j \overset{\triangle}{=} n - 1$. These integers relate to the following test.

**Test:** The system of Eqs. (7-69) (with $D = 0$) can be decoupled (non-

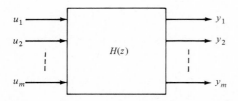

$u_1$     $y_1$

$u_2$     $y_2$

$H(z)$

$u_m$     $y_m$

**FIGURE 7-5.  A multiple-input multiple-output (MIMO) system.**

interactive controls) by the state feedback of Eq. (7-70) if and only if the $m \times m$ matrix

$$N = \begin{bmatrix} C_1 & A^{d_1} & B \\ C_2 & A^{d_2} & B \\ & \cdots & \\ C_m & A^{d_m} & B \end{bmatrix} \tag{7-74}$$

is nonsingular.

If $N$ is invertible, the system will be decoupled by

$$F = -N^{-1} \begin{bmatrix} C_1 & A^{d_1+1} \\ & \cdots & \\ C_m & A^{d_m+1} \end{bmatrix}, \qquad G = N^{-1} \tag{7-75}$$

in Eq. (7-70). This particular decoupling results in all the poles of the system at the origin and is called *delay decoupling*. The following example will illustrate the technique.


## EXAMPLE 7-13 (System Decoupling)

For this example we recall the system of Eqs. (3-73), which was modeled from the 2-input, 2-output transfer matrix of Eq. (3-71). Using the modified outputs $\mathbf{v}$ from Eq. (7-71),

$$\mathbf{x}(k+1) = \begin{bmatrix} 0 & 0 & 0 \\ 0 & -1 & 0 \\ 0 & 0 & -1 \end{bmatrix} \mathbf{x}(k) + \begin{bmatrix} 1 & 0 \\ 1 & 0 \\ 0 & 1 \end{bmatrix} \mathbf{u}(k)$$

$$\mathbf{v}(k) = \begin{bmatrix} 1 & 2 & -1 \\ 1 & 4 & -3 \end{bmatrix} \mathbf{x}(k) \tag{7-76}$$

From Eq. (7-73) $d_1$ and $d_2$ are both found to equal zero. Thus, $N$ is easily found from Eq. (7-74),

$$N = \begin{bmatrix} 3 & -1 \\ 5 & -3 \end{bmatrix}$$

Following Eqs. (7-75), $F$ and $G$ are obtained:

$$G = \frac{1}{4} \begin{bmatrix} 3 & -1 \\ 5 & -3 \end{bmatrix}, \qquad F = \frac{1}{2} \begin{bmatrix} 0 & 1 & 0 \\ 0 & -1 & 2 \end{bmatrix}$$

See Eq. (7-80) for the resulting state model between $\mathbf{r}(k)$ and $\mathbf{v}(k)$. As a check, let us form $H'(z)$ in Eq. (7-72):

$$A + BF = \frac{1}{2} \begin{bmatrix} 0 & 1 & 0 \\ 0 & -1 & 0 \\ 0 & -1 & 0 \end{bmatrix}$$

$$R = [zI - (A + BF)]^{-1} = \begin{bmatrix} \dfrac{1}{z} & \dfrac{1}{2z(z + \frac{1}{2})} & 0 \\ 0 & \dfrac{1}{(z + \frac{1}{2})} & 0 \\ 0 & \dfrac{-1}{2z(z + \frac{1}{2})} & \dfrac{1}{z} \end{bmatrix}$$

$$H'(z) = (CR)(BG) = \frac{1}{z}\begin{bmatrix} 1 & 2 & -1 \\ 1 & 4 & -3 \end{bmatrix} \frac{1}{4}\begin{bmatrix} 3 & -1 \\ 3 & -1 \\ 5 & -3 \end{bmatrix}$$

$$H'(z) = \begin{bmatrix} z^{-1} & 0 \\ 0 & z^{-1} \end{bmatrix}, \text{ diagonal delay elements} \quad \blacksquare$$

In most cases the resulting transfer matrix will *not* provide appropriate responses, and it is only natural to ask if it is possible to use additional feedback for pole placement *without* destroying the decoupled nature of the system. Unfortunately, the answer to this question is not always "yes," but it can be shown that at least

$$\left( m + \sum_{1}^{m} d_i \right)$$

poles can be placed.

If the previous procedure is first taken to establish the noninteractive nature of the controls, placement of the poles would require a second loop such as

$$\mathbf{r}(k) = L\mathbf{x}(k) + M\mathbf{c}(k) \tag{7-77}$$

Figure 7-6 illustrates the structure of the complete design. The new signal $\mathbf{c}(k)$ is the vector of noninteracting control commands. For instance, the components of $\mathbf{c}$ may be set-point commands for the corresponding outputs. Backsubstituting the expressions for $\mathbf{u}$ and $\mathbf{r}$ into the state equation yields

$$\mathbf{x}(k + 1) = [A + B(F + GL)]\,\mathbf{x}(k) + BGM\mathbf{c}(k) \tag{7-78}$$

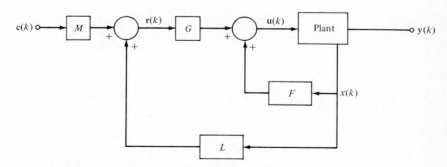

**FIGURE 7-6.   Double-loop feedback for decoupling and pole placement.**

Consequently, the overall (equivalent) feedback matrix is given by

$$F_{eq} = F + GL \tag{7-79}$$

The input matrix $M$ could be used for scaling the individual transfer function gains as discussed in Section 7-6.2. In the next example we investigate the possibilities of pole placement on a decoupled system.

### EXAMPLE 7-14 (Pole Placement on a Decoupled System)

From Example 7-13 the completed system is of the form in Fig. 7-3 with a state feedback matrix already incorporated. The resulting transfer matrix is diagonal with unit delays. However, from the original third-order system and the calculated $F$ matrix, the system poles are found to be at $z = 0$ (double pole) and $z = -\frac{1}{2}$. Recalling the results of the previous example, the new "open-loop" system is given by

$$\mathbf{x}(k + 1) = \frac{1}{2} \begin{bmatrix} 0 & 1 & 0 \\ 0 & -1 & 0 \\ 0 & -1 & 0 \end{bmatrix} \mathbf{x}(k) + \frac{1}{4} \begin{bmatrix} 3 & -1 \\ 3 & -1 \\ 5 & -3 \end{bmatrix} \mathbf{r}(k)$$

$$\mathbf{v}(k) = \begin{bmatrix} 1 & 2 & -1 \\ 1 & 4 & -3 \end{bmatrix} \mathbf{x}(k) \tag{7-80}$$

From the first equation the new $A$ and $B$ matrices will be used to place the system poles at

$$z = 0.3, \quad z = 0.4, \quad z = 0.5$$

A preliminary check indicates that the system is controllable, but not from either single input. In an effort to match the desired pole positions, we might try the method of Section 7-7.2; however, one quickly finds that this system is not amenable to that approach and requires more flexibility from the $2 \times 3$ feedback matrix in Eq. (7-77). For arbitrary entries assumed for $L$, the characteristic equation of $A + BL$ containing these six parameters results in a very complicated expression. Thus, we fall back to the alternative method associated with Eq. (7-68).

First, constructing $T(z) = (zI - A)^{-1}B$, we obtain

$$T(z) = \frac{\begin{bmatrix} 3(z + 1) & -(z + 1) \\ 3z & -z \\ 5z + 1 & -(3z + 1) \end{bmatrix}}{4z(z + 1/2)} \tag{7-81}$$

For $z = 0.3, 0.4,$ and $0.5$, columns 1, 2, and 1 are arbitrarily chosen, respectively, leading to

$$L = \begin{bmatrix} 1 & 0 & 1 \\ 0 & 1 & 0 \end{bmatrix} \begin{bmatrix} 4.06250 & -0.97\overline{2} & 2.25 \\ 0.93750 & -0.27\overline{7} & 0.75 \\ 2.604\overline{16} & -1.52\overline{7} & 1.75 \end{bmatrix}^{-1}$$

$$L = \begin{bmatrix} 1 & 0 & 1 \\ 0 & 1 & 0 \end{bmatrix} \begin{bmatrix} 0.844\overline{4} & -2.22\overline{2} & -0.1\overline{3} \\ 0.4000 & 1.600 & -1.20 \\ -0.90\overline{74} & 4.\overline{703} & -0.2\overline{7} \end{bmatrix}$$

$$L = \begin{bmatrix} -0.0630 & 2.4815 & -0.4111 \\ 0.4000 & 1.6000 & -1.2000 \end{bmatrix}$$

However, as mentioned earlier, there is no guarantee that $C(zI - A - BL)^{-1}B$ is a diagonal transfer matrix.

If the third pole is to be at $-0.5$, instead of $0.5$, there appears to be a problem evaluating $T(-0.5)$. This difficulty can in most cases be handled by carrying a parameter

$$\varepsilon = \lim_{z \to -0.5} (z + 1/2)^{-1}$$

which will eventually cancel out. For instance, in the preceding example if we desired the poles $0.3$, $0.4$, and $-0.5$, we could evaluate column 1 of Eq. (7-81) in terms of the above. Thus, the required feedback matrix is

$$L = \begin{bmatrix} 1 & 0 & 1 \\ 0 & 1 & 0 \end{bmatrix} \begin{bmatrix} 4.06250 & -0.97\overline{2} & -0.75\varepsilon \\ 0.93750 & -0.27\overline{7} & 0.75\varepsilon \\ 2.6041\overline{6} & -1.52\overline{7} & 0.75\varepsilon \end{bmatrix}^{-1}$$

Since the determinant of the right matrix has a factor $\varepsilon$ and each entry of the adjoint matrix is at most first order in $\varepsilon$, the matrix $L$ is finite. All terms of the form of constants divided by $\varepsilon$ are zero. ∎

Another important practical problem related to the previous problem of decoupling is that of isolating *undesired* inputs, usually referred to as disturbances. In a control system these disturbances may be in the form of a power supply signal "leaking" into the control channels, external forces such as wind gusts on a radar antenna being position controlled, or simply "crosstalk" with other channels. In any case such disturbances should be included in the basic system model as "disturbance inputs." Let us assume a basic discrete-time state model given by

$$\mathbf{x}(k + 1) = A\mathbf{x}(k) + B_1\mathbf{u}(k) + B_2\mathbf{w}(k)$$
$$\mathbf{y}(k) = C\mathbf{x}(k) + D\mathbf{u}(k)$$

(7-82)

where $\mathbf{u}$ is a vector of control inputs, $\mathbf{w}$ is a vector of disturbance inputs, and $\mathbf{y}$ is the vector response.

The fundamental problem, called *disturbance rejection*, is to find matrices $F$ and $G$ such that with

$$\mathbf{u}(k) = F\mathbf{x}(k) + G\mathbf{r}(k)$$

(7-83)

the effect of $\mathbf{w}(k)$ on $\mathbf{v}(k) = \mathbf{y}(k) - D\mathbf{u}(k)$ is eliminated, or at least minimized. One approach is to define an extraneous output vector $\mathbf{z}(k)$ and decouple the system so that $\mathbf{r}$ affects $\mathbf{y}$ and only $\mathbf{y}$, and $\mathbf{w}$ affects only $\mathbf{z}$. In this way we have reduced the problem of disturbance rejection to that of the previous problem of system decoupling—*if* the system can be decoupled! More discussion on this problem will be presented in the next chapter.

## 7-7.4 Output Feedback

In a situation where one is constrained to use only the measured outputs, and not the entire set of states, for feedback, techniques have been developed for designing *dynamic* feedback controllers, which we shall study in the next chapter. In some cases, however, it may be possible to achieve pole placement with only *constant* gains applied to the outputs. The following development is similar to the alternate method of pole placement discussed in Section 7-7.2. Consider the system described by

$$\mathbf{x}(k + 1) = A\mathbf{x}(k) + B\mathbf{u}(k)$$
$$\mathbf{y}(k) = C\mathbf{x}(k) + D\mathbf{u}(k) \qquad (7\text{-}84)$$

with output feedback given by

$$\mathbf{u}(k) = F\mathbf{y}(k) + G\mathbf{r}(k) \qquad (7\text{-}85)$$

Introducing the output equation into Eq. (7-85) and solving for $\mathbf{u}(k)$ yields the expression

$$\mathbf{u}(k) = (I - FD)^{-1}[FC\mathbf{x}(k) + G\mathbf{r}(k)] \qquad (7\text{-}86)$$

The closed-loop state equation then becomes

$$\mathbf{x}(k + 1) = [A + B(I - FD)^{-1}FC]\mathbf{x}(k) + B(I - FD)^{-1}G\mathbf{r}(k) \qquad (7\text{-}87)$$

Following the development leading up to Eq. (7-65), the closed-loop characteristic equation is written as

$$p_{\text{CL}}(z) = \det \{(zI - A)[I - (zI - A)^{-1}B(I - FD)^{-1}FC]\}$$

$$p_{\text{CL}}(z) = p_{\text{OL}}(z) \det [I - (zI - A)^{-1}B(I - FD)^{-1}FC]\}$$

Reversing factors as was done to obtain Eq. (7-66),

$$p_{\text{CL}}(z) = p_{\text{OL}}(z) \det [I - (I - FD)^{-1}FH(z)] \qquad (7\text{-}88)$$

where $H(z) = C(zI - A)^{-1}B$ is the transfer matrix between $\mathbf{u}$ and $\mathbf{v} = \mathbf{y} - D\mathbf{u}$ in Eqs. (7-84).

The approach is to set $p_{\text{CL}}(p_i) = 0$ for any desired closed-loop pole position $p_i$. If the number of outputs is $p \le n$, then the maximum rank of $C$ is $p$. The rank of $C$ determines the number of pole placements that can be made.

Suppose that $\mathbf{h}_{j_1}(p_i)$, $\mathbf{h}_{j_2}(p_2)$, . . . , $\mathbf{h}_{j_p}(p_p)$ are independent columns chosen from $H(z)$ evaluated at the desired pole locations $p_i$, $i = 1, 2, \ldots, p$. Then, from setting the determinant in Eq. (7-88) to zero for $z$ equal to each pole location [see Eq. (7-68)],

$$(I - FD)^{-1}F\hat{H} = E \qquad (7\text{-}89)$$

where $\hat{H}$ is the matrix of columns $\mathbf{h}_j$ and $E$ is the matrix of columns from an identity matrix corresponding to those columns of $H(z)$ picked to form $\hat{H}$. Solving for $F$ in Eq. (7-89),

$$F = E(\hat{H} + DE)^{-1} \tag{7-90}$$

The inverse matrix factor above is a square matrix of dimension $p$, the number of system outputs. The feedback matrix $F$ is, of course, of dimension $m \times p$, where $m$ is the number of inputs.

### EXAMPLE 7-15 (Proportional Output Feedback)
Given the following system

$$\mathbf{x}(k + 1) = \begin{bmatrix} 0 & 0 & 0 \\ 0 & -1 & 0 \\ 0 & 0 & 1 \end{bmatrix} \mathbf{x}(k) + \begin{bmatrix} 1 & 0 \\ 1 & 0 \\ 0 & 1 \end{bmatrix} \mathbf{u}(k)$$

$$\mathbf{y}(k) = \begin{bmatrix} 1 & 0 & -1 \\ 1 & 1 & 0 \end{bmatrix} \mathbf{x}(k)$$

place two poles at $z = 0.5$ and $z = 0.2$.

**SOLUTION:** From Eq. (7-88) we first determine $H(z)$:

$$H(z) = C(zI - A)^{-1}B$$

$$H(z) = \begin{bmatrix} 1 & 0 & -1 \\ 1 & 1 & 0 \end{bmatrix} \begin{bmatrix} z^{-1} & 0 & 0 \\ 0 & (z + 1)^{-1} & 0 \\ 0 & 0 & (z - 1)^{-1} \end{bmatrix} \begin{bmatrix} 1 & 0 \\ 1 & 0 \\ 0 & 1 \end{bmatrix}$$

$$H(z) = \begin{bmatrix} \dfrac{1}{z} & \dfrac{-1}{z - 1} \\ \dfrac{2z + 1}{z(z + 1)} & 0 \end{bmatrix}$$

For $p_1 = 0.5$ and $p_2 = 0.2$ we choose columns 1 and 2, respectively, in Eq. (7-89):

$$F \begin{bmatrix} 2 & \dfrac{5}{4} \\ \dfrac{8}{3} & 0 \end{bmatrix} = \begin{bmatrix} 1 & 0 \\ 0 & 1 \end{bmatrix}$$

Thus,

$$F = \begin{bmatrix} 0 & 0.375 \\ 0.800 & -0.600 \end{bmatrix}$$

Checking this result,

$$\overline{A} = A + BFC = \frac{1}{40} \begin{bmatrix} 15 & 15 & 0 \\ 15 & -25 & 0 \\ 8 & -24 & 8 \end{bmatrix}$$

with closed-loop poles (after solving det $[zI - \overline{A}] = 0$) located at

$$z = 0.20, \ 0.50, \ -0.75$$

Note that, although our result checks, there was no way of knowing in advance where the third root might appear. With certain pole specifications the required feedback may, in fact, cause the system to be unstable. Thus, this method must be used with great care. ∎

## 7-8

## SUMMARY

In this chapter the important system property of controllability was developed. The implications of controllability on both open-loop and closed-loop regulation were discussed, the latter specifically for the case of deadbeat response.

The main thrust of the chapter, however, was to establish techniques for designing feedback matrices for both SISO and MIMO systems. Single-input systems were considered in detail, including the methods of transformation to controllable form. In most cases the methods of SISO feedback calculation can be used for multiple-input systems as demonstrated in Section 7-7. However, for MIMO systems there are considerations for using feedback other than the basic pole location for obtaining proper transient behavior. In particular, there are the problems of system decoupling and disturbance rejection, which were introduced.

In the next chapter the dual concept of observability is studied and feedback design methods stemming from this study are linked back to the techniques learned in this chapter.

## REFERENCES

Section 7-1    *Digital Control Systems;* B. C. Kuo; Holt, Rinehart and Winston, 1980.
Section 7-4    *Discrete-Time and Computer Control Systems;* J. A. Cadzow and H. R. Martens; Prentice-Hall, 1970.
Section 7-5    *Intro. to Linear System Theory;* C. T. Chen; Holt, Rinehart and Winston, 1970.
Section 7-6    *Digital Control;* G. F. Franklin and J. D. Powell; Addison-Wesley, 1980.
Section 7-7    *Modern Control Theory;* W. L. Brogan; Quantum Pub., 1974.
              *Intro. to Dynamic Systems;* D. G. Luenberger; John Wiley and Sons, 1979.

# PROBLEMS

**7-1**   Determine if the following systems are controllable.

(a) $\mathbf{x}(k + 1) = \begin{bmatrix} 1 & 2 \\ 0 & 3 \end{bmatrix} \mathbf{x}(k) + \begin{bmatrix} 0 \\ 1 \end{bmatrix} u(k)$

$y(k) = \begin{bmatrix} 1 & 0 \end{bmatrix} \mathbf{x}(k)$

(b) $\mathbf{x}(k + 1) = \begin{bmatrix} -1 & 1 & 0 \\ 0 & -1 & 0 \\ 0 & 0 & 1 \end{bmatrix} \mathbf{x}(k) + \begin{bmatrix} 0 & 0 \\ 1 & 0 \\ 0 & 1 \end{bmatrix} \mathbf{u}(k)$

$\mathbf{y}(k) = \begin{bmatrix} 1 & 0 & 0 \\ 0 & 1 & 0 \end{bmatrix} \mathbf{x}(k)$

**7-2**   Calculate the transfer matrix (or function) for the systems given in Problem 7-1. What is the effect of an uncontrollable mode on a transfer function?

**7-3**   For the system given below, establish a Jordan form state model and determine the values of the parameter $p$ for which the system may not be controllable.

$$\frac{Y(z)}{U(z)} = \frac{z^2 + (p + 1)z + p}{z^3 - 6z^2 + 11z - 6}$$

**7-4**   For a general $n$th-order discrete-time system with zero initial state,

$$\mathbf{x}(k + 1) = A\mathbf{x}(k) + B\mathbf{u}(k), \quad \mathbf{x}(0) = \mathbf{0}$$

we define the reachability subspaces $\{R_i \text{ for } i = 1, 2, \ldots, n\}$ as follows:

$$R_i = \{\mathbf{x} : \mathbf{x} = \mathbf{x}(i) \text{ for some } \mathbf{u}(0), \mathbf{u}(1), \ldots, \mathbf{u}(i - 1)\}$$

In other words, $R_i$ is that portion of the state space that may be "reached" from the origin in $i$ steps. Describe the reachability subspaces of this particular system with

$$A = \begin{bmatrix} 1 & 2 & 3 & 4 \\ 1 & 0 & 0 & 0 \\ 0 & 1 & 0 & 0 \\ 0 & 0 & 1 & 0 \end{bmatrix}, \quad B = \begin{bmatrix} 1 \\ 0 \\ 0 \\ 0 \end{bmatrix}$$

A convenient way to describe these subspaces is to write them as the span of certain vectors.

**7-5**   Consider the discrete-time ZOH equivalent of the plant $G(s)$ shown in Fig. P7-5. Determine the values of $T$ for which the ZOH equivalent system is not controllable. Start with the continuous-time controllable form.

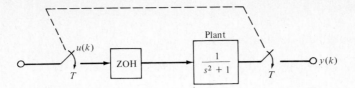

**FIGURE P7-5.**

**7-6** Given that the system

$$\mathbf{x}(k + 1) = A\mathbf{x}(k) + B\mathbf{u}(k)$$

is controllable, show that the system with state feedback $[\mathbf{u}(k) = F\mathbf{x}(k) + G\mathbf{v}(k)]$ is controllable.

*Hint:* Argue the result from the definition of controllability.

**7-7** Two systems $S_1$ and $S_2$ are described by

$$\mathbf{x}(k + 1) = \begin{bmatrix} 0 & 1 \\ -1 & -2 \end{bmatrix} \mathbf{x}(k) + \begin{bmatrix} 1 \\ p \end{bmatrix} u(k)$$

$$S_1$$

$$y(k) = [\ 1 \quad 0]\ \mathbf{x}(k)$$

$$S_2 \quad \begin{aligned} w(k + 1) &= w(k) + v(k) \\ z(k) &= w(k) - v(k) \end{aligned}$$

**(a)** Determine if each system is controllable. Specify the value(s) of $p$ for which $S_1$ is uncontrollable.

**(b)** For the interconnected system of Fig. P7-7 investigate possible values of $p$ for which the closed-loop system is uncontrollable.

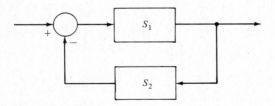

**FIGURE P7-7.**

**7-8** To determine the best linear least-squared error fit to the data:

| $y(t)$ | 3 | 4 | 2 | 1 |
|--------|---|---|---|---|
| $t$    | 0 | 1 | 2 | 3 |

Find $p_1$ and $p_2$ for the approximation

$$\hat{y}(t) = p_1 t + p_2$$

so that

$$\sum_{t=0}^{3} [y(t) - \hat{y}(t)]^2$$

is minimized.

*Hint:* Set the problem up as a set of linear equations in

$$\mathbf{p} = \begin{bmatrix} p_1 \\ p_2 \end{bmatrix}$$

**7-9** For a given sampling rate, $(1/T)$ Hz, determine the amplitude of the (single) pulse that will drive the (known) initial state of the system in Fig. P7-9 to the origin such that $c(t) = 0$, $t \geq T$.

**FIGURE P7-9.**

**7-10** Find a sequence of inputs that will drive the state of the following system to the origin in
(a) two time steps
(b) three time steps

$$\mathbf{x}(k + 1) = \begin{bmatrix} 0 & 1 \\ -2 & -1 \end{bmatrix} \mathbf{x}(k) + \begin{bmatrix} 0 \\ 1 \end{bmatrix} u(k)$$

**7-11** Using the results of Problem 7-10, compare the relative control energy of regulation between two and three steps.

**7-12** For the system shown in Fig. P7-9 let the parameter $a = 2$ and $T = 1$ second.
(a) Determine the equivalent discrete-time system and repeat the exercise of Problem 7-10 on this system.
(b) Using these results, compare the relative control energy of regulation between two and three steps.

**7-13** Repeat the exercise of Problem 7-12 using $T = 0.1$ sec. What sacrifice is made to regulate a system rapidly?

**7-14** A position control system (plant) has a transfer function given by

$$G(s) = \frac{\theta_c(s)}{V_c(s)} = \frac{50}{s(s + 34.5)}$$

**(a)** Design a digital controller, $D(z)$, so that the output $\theta_c(t)$ follows reference input step commands in a deadbeat manner. Use $T = 0.01$ sec.

**(b)** Calculate $v_c(t)$ and $\theta_c(t)$ for $r(t) = 1(t) - 1(t - 0.05)$. See Fig. P7-14.

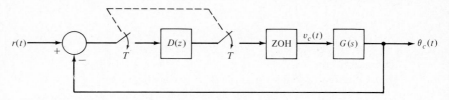

**FIGURE P7-14.**

**7-15** For the system shown in Fig. P7-15 construct an $F$ matrix so that with

$$u(k) = F\mathbf{x}(k) + r(k)$$

the system poles will be located at

$$z = -0.5 \pm j0.5$$

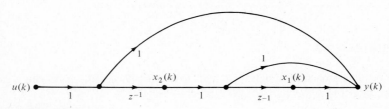

**FIGURE P7-15.**

**7-16** Given the following plant model:

$$\mathbf{x}(k + 1) = \begin{bmatrix} 1 & 0 & 1 \\ 0 & 2 & -1 \\ -1 & 1 & 0 \end{bmatrix} \mathbf{x}(k) + \begin{bmatrix} 1 & 1 \\ 1 & 0 \\ 0 & -1 \end{bmatrix} \mathbf{u}(k)$$

$$y(k) = \begin{bmatrix} 1 & 1 & 0 \end{bmatrix} \mathbf{x}(k)$$

**(a)** Determine if the system is controllable.

**(b)** Determine if the system is controllable from individual inputs.

**7-17** Calculate a SVF matrix $F$ for the following system so that with

$$\mathbf{u}(k) = F\mathbf{x}(k) + \mathbf{r}(k)$$

the closed-loop characteristic polynomial is

$$p(z) = z^3 - 0.5z^2 + 0.25$$

$$\mathbf{x}(k + 1) = \begin{bmatrix} 1 & 0 & 0 \\ 0 & 0 & 0 \\ 0 & 0 & -1 \end{bmatrix} \mathbf{x}(k) + \begin{bmatrix} 2 & 1 \\ 1 & 0 \\ 0 & 4 \end{bmatrix} \mathbf{u}(k)$$

**7-18**    Construct the controllable form state model for the following systems:

(a) $\mathbf{x}(k + 1) = \begin{bmatrix} 0 & 0 & 0 \\ 1 & 0 & -2 \\ 0 & 1 & -3 \end{bmatrix} \mathbf{x}(k) + \begin{bmatrix} 2 \\ 4 \\ 0 \end{bmatrix} u(k)$

$y(k) = [\, 0 \quad 0 \quad 1 \,] \, \mathbf{x}(k)$

(b) $\mathbf{x}(k + 1) = \begin{bmatrix} 1 & 0 & 1 \\ 0 & 2 & -1 \\ -1 & 1 & 0 \end{bmatrix} \mathbf{x}(k) + \begin{bmatrix} 1 \\ 1 \\ 0 \end{bmatrix} u(k)$

$\mathbf{y}(k) = \begin{bmatrix} 1 & 1 & 0 \\ 1 & 0 & -1 \end{bmatrix} \mathbf{x}(k)$

**7-19**    For each plant in Fig. P7-19
(a) Write the state equations (in matrix form).
(b) Construct a matrix $F$ so that with

$$u(k) = F\mathbf{x}(k) + r(k)$$

the system poles will be located at

$$z = 0.5987 \pm j0.2531$$

$$y(k + 2) - y(k) = 2u(k + 1) + u(k), \quad x_1(k) = y(k), \quad x_2(k) = y(k + 1)$$

(a)

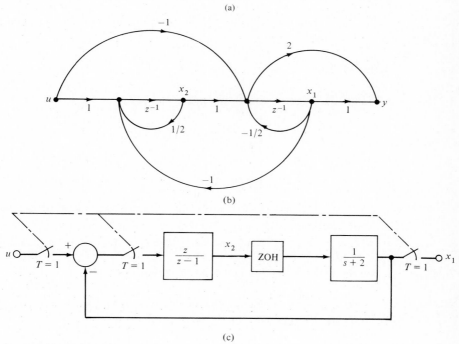

(b)

(c)

**FIGURE P7-19.**

**7-20** **(a)** Develop a deadbeat feedback system for the system in Fig. P7-9 if $a = 1$ and $T = 1$ second.

**(b)** Sketch the continuous-time response $c(t)$ to a unit-step input.

**7-21** Repeat the exercise of Problem 7-20 for the system presented in Fig. P7-5 using $T = 1$ second.

**7-22** For the system in Fig. P7-22

**(a)** Write a state model using the state variables $x_1$, $x_2$ and $x_3$ shown

**(b)** Design a SVF control law $u(k) = F\mathbf{x}(k) + r(k)$ so that the system will have one pole at $z = 0$ and the other two chosen for a settling time of 10 time steps with no overshoot to step inputs.

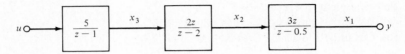

**FIGURE P7-22.**

**7-23** Determine the (scalar) gain $G$ in Fig. P7-23 so that the overall system behaves in Type 1 manner, that is, the steady-state output will equal any constant input.

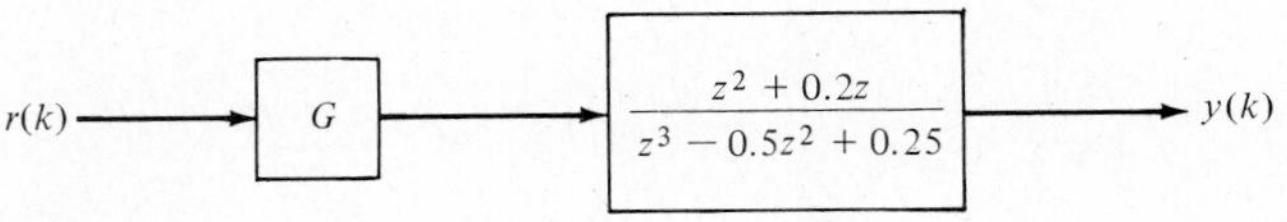

$r(k) \longrightarrow \boxed{G} \longrightarrow \boxed{\dfrac{z^2 + 0.2z}{z^3 - 0.5z^2 + 0.25}} \longrightarrow y(k)$

**FIGURE P7-23.**

**7-24** In a 2-input, 2-output system with transfer matrix

$$T(z) = \begin{bmatrix} \dfrac{z}{z - 0.1} & \dfrac{-2}{z - 0.5} \\[2mm] \dfrac{z - 0.2}{z - 0.5} & \dfrac{z^2 - 0.4z}{(z - 0.1)(z - 0.5)} \end{bmatrix}$$

Determine a $2 \times 2$ gain matrix $G$ such that the cascade system $T(z)G$ is a system that is *statically decoupled*, that is, $T_{11}(z)$ and $T_{22}(z)$ are Type 1 transfer functions whereas $T_{12}(z)$ and $T_{21}(z)$ have zero steady state response to any constant inputs.

**7-25** Describe the dynamic modes of the system given in Problem 7-1a.

**7-26** Expand the system of Problem 7-16 into its modal representation as given in Eqs. (7-52) and (7-53).

**7-27** Write the modal representation of the system in Fig. P7-22.

**7-28** For the system in Problem 7-1a calculate the left eigenvectors of the matrix $A$.

**7-29** For the system $x(k + 1) = Ax(k) + Bu(k)$ where

$$A = \begin{bmatrix} 0.1 & 0 & 0 \\ 0 & 0.2 & 0 \\ 0 & 0 & 0.3 \end{bmatrix}, \quad B = \begin{bmatrix} 1 & 0 \\ 0 & 1 \\ 1 & 0 \end{bmatrix}$$

design a SVF law so that the closed-loop system exhibits deadbeat response (all poles at the origin). Use the method of Eq. (7-62).

**7-30** Repeat the exercise of Problem 7-29 using the alternate method of Eq. (7-68).

**7-31** Determine if the system $T(z)$ in Problem 7-24 can be decoupled. If so, decouple the system using the results of Eqs. (7-75).

**7-32** Repeat the exercise of Problem 7-31 using the system of Problem 7-29 along with the output equation

$$y(k) = \begin{bmatrix} 1 & -1 & 0 \\ 1 & 0 & -1 \end{bmatrix} x(k)$$

**7-33** Can output feedback be used to locate the poles of the system in Problem 7-32 at the origin? If the answer is yes, design the feedback law.

## CHAPTER 8

# Observability and State Estimator Design

In the previous chapter the principal techniques of state feedback calculation were presented. In most cases state feedback requires access to each and every state variable; that is to say, each physical state variable must be measured whether it is pressure, voltage, velocity, temperature, or any other of the many possible physical variables in the system. Often it is inconvenient to measure every system state from considerations such as availability of sensors, economics, or simply the particular physical structure of the system. Yet, it would still be desirable to use the concept of state feedback if it were possible to "generate" the state variations in some indirect way. The main effort of this chapter is to show that given a certain system property, called observability, the state vector can be obtained, at least approximately, by incorporating feedback dynamics. Following this development, the general method of output feedback is presented.

## 8-1

### STATE OBSERVABILITY

For this discussion it is assumed that a known system model is available for the system under consideration, given by the following pair of equations:

$$\mathbf{x}(k + 1) = A\mathbf{x}(k) + B\mathbf{u}(k) \qquad (8\text{-}1)$$

$$\mathbf{y}(k) = C\mathbf{x}(k) + D\mathbf{u}(k) \qquad (8\text{-}2)$$

where $\mathbf{x}$ is an $n$-vector, $\mathbf{u}$ is an $m$-vector, and $\mathbf{y}$ is a $p$-vector. The matrices $A$, $B$, $C$, and $D$ are assumed to be known constant matrices.

The key idea of observability is that of being able to determine an initial state vector $\mathbf{x}(t_0)$ by "observing" the output and input sequences of the system for a finite period of time $[t_0, t_1]$. Recall that from Eq. (3-46)

$$\mathbf{y}(k) = CA^k\mathbf{x}(0) + \sum_{n=0}^{k-1} CA^{k-n-1}B\mathbf{u}(n) + D\mathbf{u}(k) \qquad (8\text{-}3)$$

so that if $\mathbf{u}(k)$ is known, the terms involving $\mathbf{u}$ can be calculated. Once calculated, the input terms (zero-state response) can be subtracted from $\mathbf{y}(k)$ leaving only the initial-state term (zero-input response). This point is made solely to simplify the following development.

***Definition 8-1:*** The discrete-time system of Eqs. (8-1) and (8-2) is *(completely state) observable* if it is possible to determine $\mathbf{x}(0)$ from knowledge of $\mathbf{u}(k)$ and $\mathbf{y}(k)$ over a finite number of steps $k = 0, 1, 2, \ldots, q$.

As in the presentation for controllability in Section 7-1, this definition will be used to develop a simple rank test for the property of observability in a system. Also, in keeping with previous usage we shall use the simple word "observable" to mean "completely state observable" as defined above.

Since the effect of a known input sequence $\mathbf{u}(k)$ on the system response can be subtracted out, we can assume without loss of generality that the system is unforced, $\mathbf{u}(k) = \mathbf{0}$. Thus,

$$\mathbf{y}(k) = CA^k\mathbf{x}(0) \qquad (8\text{-}4)$$

for $k = 0, 1, 2, \ldots q$. The question of observability is reduced to a question of whether or not $\mathbf{x}(0)$ can be calculated from Eq. (8-4) given the sequence of outputs. In vector equation form

$$\begin{bmatrix} C \\ CA \\ CA^2 \\ \cdots \\ CA^q \end{bmatrix} \mathbf{x}(0) = \begin{bmatrix} \mathbf{y}(0) \\ \mathbf{y}(1) \\ \mathbf{y}(2) \\ \cdots \\ \mathbf{y}(q) \end{bmatrix} \qquad (8\text{-}5)$$

We can solve for $\mathbf{x}(0)$ given the known vector on the right-hand side if and only if the $n$-columns of the coefficient matrix on the left-hand side are linearly independent. We note also (see Appendix B) that the number of linearly independent columns of a matrix equals the number of independent rows. Thus, as we add on partitions $CA^i$, $i = 1, 2, \ldots, q$ in Eq. (8-5) we tend to increase the rank of the coefficient matrix on the left. However, since we already know from the discussion leading up to the controllability matrix defined in Eq.

(7-11) that $A^n$ can be written as a linear combination of its lesser powers, it is clear that the rank of the coefficient matrix in Eq. (8-5) will not increase beyond $q = n - 1$.

For the special case where $q = n - 1$ we define the *observability matrix* for the system in Eqs. (8-1) and (8-2) as

$$\mathbb{O} = \begin{bmatrix} C \\ CA \\ CA^2 \\ \cdots \\ CA^{n-1} \end{bmatrix} \tag{8-6}$$

Since $\mathbb{O}$ represents the coefficient matrix in Eq. (8-5) that has maximal rank, and since we already know that for an arbitrary right-hand vector we can solve for $\mathbf{x}(0)$ if and only if the $n$-columns of $\mathbb{O}$ are linearly independent, a test for observability can be stated as follows.

**Observability Test:** A discrete-time system with its model given by Eqs. (8-1) and (8-2) is observable if and only if its observability matrix $\mathbb{O}$ of Eq. (8-6) has rank $n$, where $n$ is the order of the system.

Like controllability, observability is an intrinsic property of a system, and equivalent state models will exhibit identical test results. As we shall soon see, the property of observability is crucial to the development of state observer (also known as state estimator or state reconstructor) system. Again the basic question (like controllability) of observability leads to a yes, or no, answer—either the observability matrix has rank $n$ or it does not! In the problem section a measure of the "degree of observability" is defined, which could be of use in determining how close a system is to being unobservable in situations where it might be important to know, so that, for instance, corresponding numerical problems could be avoided.

## EXAMPLE 8-1

(a) Determine if the following system is observable.
(b) Draw the block diagram.

$$\mathbf{x}(k + 1) = \begin{bmatrix} 0.3 & 0 \\ 0 & 0.5 \end{bmatrix} \mathbf{x}(k) + \begin{bmatrix} 1 \\ 1 \end{bmatrix} u(k)$$

$$y(k) = [\; 1 \quad 0\;]\, \mathbf{x}(k)$$

**SOLUTION:** Using the observability test,

$$\mathbb{O} = \begin{bmatrix} 1 & 0 \\ 0.3 & 0 \end{bmatrix}, \text{ rank } \mathbb{O} \neq 2 \text{ (unobservable)}$$

The system structure shows us that the output is not observing both modes of the system.

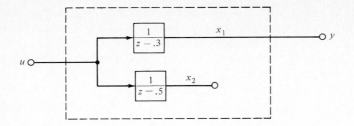

Notice that no variation of $x_2$ can be determined from $y$. ∎

**Remarks:**
- When the $A$ matrix is *diagonal;* a zero row of $B$ indicates an uncontrollable system, and zero column of $C$ indicates an unobservable system.
- A transfer function always represents the controllable and observable part of a system.

## 8-2

## TRANSFORMATION TO OBSERVABLE FORM

Another of the state-variable canonical forms which were introduced in Chapter 3 can be of future use to us, as designers. Following closely the approach presented in Section 7-5, we perform a change of state variables through the particular (nonsingular) transformation matrix $P_o$:

$$\mathbf{x} = P_o\mathbf{x}_o \tag{8-7}$$

where the subscript indicates "observable form." More formally, we want to be able to start with an observable single-output but otherwise arbitrary, system of the form

$$\mathbf{x}(k + 1) = A\mathbf{x}(k) + B\mathbf{u}(k)$$
$$y(k) = C\mathbf{x}(k) + D\mathbf{u}(k) \tag{8-8}$$

and use Eq. (8-7) to obtain

$$\mathbf{x}_o(k + 1) = A_o\mathbf{x}(k) + B_o\mathbf{u}(k)$$
$$y(k) = C_o\mathbf{x}_o(k) + D\mathbf{u}(k) \tag{8-9}$$

where $A_o = P_o^{-1}AP_o$, $B_o = P_o^{-1}B$, and $C_o = CP_o$ all have the special structure associated with the observable form presented in Section 3-6.2. In particular, from the coefficients of the characteristic equation of the system (which is invariant to a change of state vector) $A_o$ and $C_o$ are known. The reader is referred back to Eqs. (3-61) and (3-62) to recall the forms of these matrices.

Since the model of Eqs. (8-8) was given and $A_o$ and $C_o$ can easily be constructed, we may write the two observability matrices from Eq. (8-6):

$$O = \begin{bmatrix} C \\ CA \\ \cdots \\ CA^{n-1} \end{bmatrix}, \quad O_o = \begin{bmatrix} C_o \\ C_oA_o \\ \cdots \\ C_oA_o^{n-1} \end{bmatrix} \tag{8-10}$$

For the single-output case under consideration both of the above matrices are $n \times n$ matrices. Furthermore, if the system is observable, both matrices are invertible (they have rank $n$). Now, all we need to do is to introduce the expressions for $C_o$ and $A_o$ following Eqs. (8-9) and write

$$O_o = \begin{bmatrix} CP_o \\ CAP_o \\ \cdots \\ CA^{n-1}P_o \end{bmatrix} = OP_o \tag{8-11}$$

where $P_oP_o^{-1}$ factors have all canceled out. Finally, we have that the desired transformation matrix is

$$P_o = O^{-1}O_o \tag{8-12}$$

Since $P_o$ can be found, we can determine the complete observable form model given in Eqs. (8-9).

### EXAMPLE 8-2

We wish to determine the observable form state model of the (observable) system

$$\mathbf{x}(k + 1) = \begin{bmatrix} 1 & 2 & 0 \\ 3 & -1 & 1 \\ 0 & 2 & 0 \end{bmatrix} \mathbf{x}(k) + \begin{bmatrix} 2 \\ 1 \\ 1 \end{bmatrix} u(k)$$

$$y(k) = \begin{bmatrix} 0 & 0 & 1 \end{bmatrix} \mathbf{x}(k)$$

Step 1: Calculate the characteristic polynomial:

$$p(z) = \det [zI - A] = z^3 + 0z^2 - 9z + 2$$

Step 3: Construct $A_o$ and $C_o$ matrices:

$$A_o = \begin{bmatrix} 0 & 0 & -2 \\ 1 & 0 & 9 \\ 0 & 1 & 0 \end{bmatrix}, \quad C_o = \begin{bmatrix} 0 & 0 & 1 \end{bmatrix}$$

Step 3: Determine the observability matrices $O$ and $O_o$:

$$O = \begin{bmatrix} 0 & 0 & 1 \\ 0 & 2 & 0 \\ 6 & -2 & 2 \end{bmatrix}, \quad O_o = \begin{bmatrix} 0 & 0 & 1 \\ 0 & 1 & 0 \\ 1 & 0 & 9 \end{bmatrix}$$

Step 4: Calculate the required transformation matrix:

$$P_o = \mathbb{O}^{-1}\mathbb{O}_o = \frac{1}{6}\begin{bmatrix} 1 & 1 & 7 \\ 0 & 3 & 0 \\ 0 & 0 & 6 \end{bmatrix}$$

Step 5: Complete the observable form model by finding $B_o$:

$$B_o = P_o^{-1}B = \begin{bmatrix} 3 \\ 2 \\ 1 \end{bmatrix}$$

■

In the above step-by-step procedure a matrix inverse was required to find $P_o$, Eq. (8-12). An alternate method for determining $P_o$ that depends on the structure of $\mathbb{O}_o$ is recursive in nature and therefore more convenient to use for higher-order systems.

***Alternate Method for Determining $P_o$.*** We begin with Eq. (8-11) and define

$$Q_o = (P_o^T)^{-1} \tag{8-13}$$

Note that $(P_o^T)^{-1} = (P_o^{-1})^T$ and to simplify the notation $Q_o = P_o^{-T}$. The modified Eq. (8-11) becomes

$$Q_o\mathbb{O}_o^T = \mathbb{O}^T \tag{8-14}$$

If we let $\mathbf{q}_i$ denote the $i$th column of $Q_o$ and expand Eq. (8-14), we obtain

$$[\mathbf{q}_1 \; \mathbf{q}_2 \; \cdots \; \mathbf{q}_n]\mathbb{O}_o^T = [C^T \mid A^TC^T \mid (A^T)^2C^T \; \cdots] \tag{8-15}$$

By utilizing the triangular structure of $\mathbb{O}_o^T$, we can relate the columns of $Q_o$ to the right-hand side. The following equations presume a characteristic polynomial of the form

$$p(z) = z^n - a_n z^{n-1} - a_{n-1}z^{n-2} - \cdots - a_2 z - a_1 \tag{8-16}$$

Expanding Eq. (8-15)

$$\mathbf{q}_n = C^T$$

$$\mathbf{q}_{n-1} = A^T\mathbf{q}_n - a_n\mathbf{q}_n$$

$$\mathbf{q}_{n-2} = A^T\mathbf{q}_{n-1} - a_{n-1}\mathbf{q}_n$$

$$\mathbf{q}_{n-3} = A^T\mathbf{q}_{n-2} - a_{n-2}\mathbf{q}_n \tag{8-16'}$$

$$\cdots$$

$$\mathbf{q}_1 = A^T\mathbf{q}_2 - a_2\mathbf{q}_n$$

Compare with Eqs. (7-40). The above development will not be proved formally, but the reader is invited to ascertain the validity of the expansion for a third-order system. As can easily be seen, the columns of $Q_o$ can be calculated recursively, beginning with the last column $\mathbf{q}_n$. For comparison we will partially work the previous example using this method.

## EXAMPLE 8-3

For the system given in Example 8-2 calculate the transformation $P_o$ which takes the system into its observable form. From Eqs. (8-16)

$$\mathbf{q}_3 = [\, 0 \quad 0 \quad 1 \,]^T$$

$$\mathbf{q}_2 = \begin{bmatrix} 1 & 3 & 0 \\ 2 & -1 & 2 \\ 0 & 1 & 0 \end{bmatrix} \mathbf{q}_3 - 0\mathbf{q}_3 = \begin{bmatrix} 0 \\ 2 \\ 0 \end{bmatrix}$$

$$\mathbf{q}_1 = \begin{bmatrix} 1 & 3 & 0 \\ 2 & -1 & 2 \\ 0 & 1 & 0 \end{bmatrix} \mathbf{q}_2 - 9\mathbf{q}_3 = \begin{bmatrix} 6 \\ -2 \\ -7 \end{bmatrix}$$

Therefore,

$$Q_o^T = \begin{bmatrix} 6 & -2 & -7 \\ 0 & 2 & 0 \\ 0 & 0 & 1 \end{bmatrix}$$

$$P_o = (Q_o^T)^{-1} = \frac{1}{6} \begin{bmatrix} 1 & 1 & 7 \\ 0 & 3 & 0 \\ 0 & 0 & 6 \end{bmatrix}$$

which checks our previous result.  ∎

## 8-3

---

## STATE ESTIMATOR DESIGN

In our previous development of state-variable feedback (Section 7-6) we found it necessary to have access (that is, to measure) each state variable in the system in order to design the proper feedback gains. As this point without feeding back each state, we cannot guarantee the ability to place the closed-loop poles at designated locations. It is to avoid this problem of having to measure each state variable that the theory of state estimators (also commonly referred to as observers) was developed. No knowledge of statistics is required in this chapter, but will be in Chapter 9, where we account for randomness in our system model.

### 8-3.1 The State Estimation Problem

For the following development we assume that we have a system model described by

$$\begin{aligned} \mathbf{x}(k + 1) &= A\mathbf{x}(k) + B\mathbf{u}(k) \\ \mathbf{y}(k) &= C\mathbf{x}(k) + D\mathbf{u}(k) \end{aligned} \qquad (8\text{-}17)$$

In addition, we will require that the system be observable. We will see where this requirement comes into the development later. For present purposes we consider the vector **y** of outputs to be, specifically, measured outputs that can be used as inputs to other devices. In particular, since the dimension of **y** is perhaps much less than the number of states of the system, we will hypothesize a new (linear) dynamic system of the form

$$\mathbf{w}(k + 1) = G\mathbf{w}(k) + H\mathbf{u}(k) + K\mathbf{y}(k) \tag{8-18}$$

where, as yet, the matrices $G$, $H$, and $K$ are unspecified. Note that this new system has two sets of inputs: **u**, the original system inputs, and **y**, the measured outputs from the system. We now pose the problem.

***The State Estimation Problem:*** To construct a system of equations whose inputs are **u** and **y** and whose state **w** approximates the original system state **x** in the sense that the error vector $\mathbf{e} = \mathbf{x} - \mathbf{w}$, the difference between **x** and **w**, goes asymptotically to zero.

***SOLUTION:*** We begin the construction with the assumed system in Eqs. (8-17) and the assumed form of the estimator in Eq. (8-18). The first step is to write an equation for the error vector $\mathbf{e}(k)$. For simplification we write the modified output

$$\mathbf{v}(k) = \mathbf{y}(k) - D\mathbf{u}(k) \tag{8-19}$$

in order to eliminate the $D$ matrix, the direct feedthrough term in our model. From the definition

$$\mathbf{e}(k + 1) = \mathbf{x}(k + 1) - \mathbf{w}(k + 1)$$

Substituting on the right for the system equations,

$$\mathbf{e}(k + 1) = [A\mathbf{x}(k) + B\mathbf{u}(k)] - [G\mathbf{w}(k) + H'\mathbf{u}(k) + K\mathbf{v}(k)]$$

where the modified outputs have replaced **y** in Eq. (8-18). Next, we collect terms to obtain

$$\mathbf{e}(k + 1) = (A - KC)\mathbf{x}(k) - G\mathbf{w}(k) + (B - H')\mathbf{u}(k) \tag{8-20}$$

Note that the output equation from the system model has been used to eliminate the explicit dependence on **v**.

To further simplify the error equation, we will begin to assign matrix values to our estimator model in Eq. (8-18). Since $G$, $H$, and $K$ are at our disposal, we choose

(1) $$H' = B \tag{8-21}$$

(2) $$G = A - KC \tag{8-22}$$

The first assignment eliminates the input terms in Eq. (8-20); the second allows $G = A - KC$ to be factored out, leading to the error equation

$$\mathbf{e}(k + 1) = (A - KC)\mathbf{e}(k) \tag{8-23}$$

The reader will note that the error vector equation has no forcing terms. Consequently, for a given initial error vector $\mathbf{e}(0)$, $\mathbf{e}(k)$ will approach zero asymptotically if and only if the coefficient matrix $(A - KC)$ is "stable"; that is, has all its eigenvalues inside the unit circle. Fortunately, we are in a position to specify $K$ so that $(A - KC)$ is such a stable system matrix.

Figure 8-1 illustrates the vector block diagram of the state estimator system that is summarized as

$$\mathbf{w}(k + 1) = (A - KC)\mathbf{w}(k) + B\mathbf{u}(k) + K\mathbf{v}(k) \tag{8-24}$$

An alternate form, which we shall refer to as the Kalman form, is given by

$$\mathbf{w}(k + 1) = A\mathbf{w}(k) + B\mathbf{u}(k) + K[\mathbf{v}(k) - C\mathbf{w}(k)] \tag{8-25}$$

Both Eqs. (8-24) and (8-25) are equivalent, but the latter equation demonstrates how closely the estimator system matches the structure of the original system. The last term of Eq. (8-25) is sometimes interpreted as a "correcting" term based on the difference between the measurements $\mathbf{v}(k)$ and their expected values $C\mathbf{w}(k)$. The matrix gain $K$ will be called equivalently estimator gain, observer gain, Kalman gain, or filter gain. Figure 8-1 emphasizes that the estimator system has two vector inputs and one vector output. The detailed vector block diagram realizes the state estimator system in the form of Eq. (8-25) and, in addition, incorporates the modified outputs from Eq. (8-19).

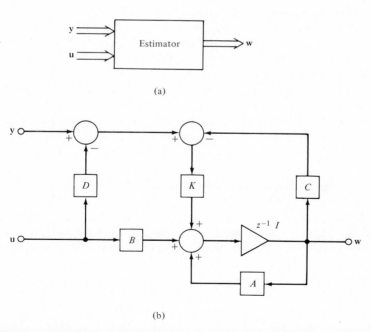

(a)

(b)

**FIGURE 8-1.** Full-order state estimator: (a) basic structure; (b) detailed vector-block diagram.

Lest the reader think that the gain matrix $K$ was forgotten, we have but saved the best till last. It is clear that once we specify the matrix $K$, the state estimator system will be complete. Returning to the vector error equation of Eq. (8-23), let us investigate the possibility of placing the estimator poles so that the error decay is rapid. Repeating the error equation with $G$ representing $(A - KC)$,

$$\mathbf{e}(k + 1) = G\mathbf{e}(k), \quad \mathbf{e}(0) = \mathbf{x}(0) - \mathbf{w}(0) \tag{8-26}$$

The solution of this is [see Eq. (3-45)]

$$\mathbf{e}(k) = G^k\mathbf{e}(0) \tag{8-27}$$

Also, from our study of stability in Section 3-8 we know that the smaller the magnitudes of the eigenvalues, the faster the decay.

Also, we know that the eigenvalues of $G^T$ and those of $G$ are the same. Pursuing this idea, consider

$$G^T = (A - KC)^T = (A^T - C^TK^T) \tag{8-28}$$

Note that with the correspondence $A^T \to A$, $C^T \to B$, and $K^T \to -F$, the matrix

$$(A^T - C^TK^T) \to (A + BF) \tag{8-29}$$

The point is that in Chapter 7 we developed several methods for placing the eigenvalues of $(A + BF)$ using the $F$ matrix. And this appears to be the same problem as using $K$ (or $-K^T$) to place the eigenvalues of $(A^T - C^TK^T)$. Recall that the assigned locations are completely arbitrary if the matrix pair $(A, B)$ is controllable. Here we anticipate the concept of duality by remarking that if $(A^T, C^T)$ form a controllable pair, then the pair $(A, C)$ is observable. This statement follows from the tests of controllability and observability previously discussed; see Section 8-6 for more details.

To summarize, if $A$ and $C$ form an observable pair, then the eigenvalues of $(A - KC)$ can be assigned arbitrary locations (as long as complex eigenvalues occur in complex-conjugate pairs) by appropriately evaluating $K$. In the next subsection we investigate the details of determining the gain matrix $K$.

## 8-3.2  The Estimator Gain Matrix

It should be evident that the coefficient matrix $(A - KC)$ of the error equation (8-23) has a key role in our achieving a state estimator system design. We will begin by assuming our original system is in observable canonical form and that the system has a single output. Thus,

$$(A_o - K_oC_o) = \begin{bmatrix} 0 & 0 & & 0 & a_1 \\ 1 & 0 & \cdots & 0 & a_2 \\ 0 & 1 & & 0 & a_3 \\ & & \cdots & & \\ 0 & 0 & \cdots & 0 & a_{n-1} \\ 0 & 0 & & 1 & a_n \end{bmatrix} - \begin{bmatrix} k_1 \\ k_2 \\ k_3 \\ \cdots \\ k_{n-1} \\ k_n \end{bmatrix}\begin{bmatrix} 0 \\ 0 \\ 0 \\ \cdots \\ 0 \\ 1 \end{bmatrix}^T \tag{8-30}$$

Combining into one array,

$$A_o - K_o C_o = \begin{bmatrix} 0 & 0 & & 0 & (a_1 - k_1) \\ 1 & 0 & \cdots & 0 & (a_2 - k_2) \\ 0 & 1 & & 0 & (a_3 - k_3) \\ & & \cdots & & \\ 0 & 0 & \cdots & 0 & (a_{n-1} - k_{n-1}) \\ 0 & 0 & & 1 & (a_n - k_n) \end{bmatrix} \qquad (8\text{-}31)$$

The characteristic polynomial of the original system is easily seen from $A_o$ to be

$$p(z) = z^n - a_n z^{n-1} - \cdots - a_2 z - a_1$$

and, similarly, the characteristic polynomial of the estimator is

$$p_o(z) = z^n - (a_n - k_n)z^{n-1} - \cdots - (a_2 - k_2)z - (a_1 - k_1) \qquad (8\text{-}32)$$

The elements of $K$ are then determined by matching the coefficients of $p_o(z)$ to a desired characteristic polynomial for the estimator system. The desired characteristic polynomial may be formed from the specified locations of the estimator eigenvalues. Thus, if $\lambda_1, \lambda_2, \ldots, \lambda_n$ are specified eigenvalues,

$$p_o(z) = (z - \lambda_1)(z - \lambda_2) \ldots (z - \lambda_n) \qquad (8\text{-}33)$$

Once Eq. (8-33) is expanded, the coefficients are compared to those of Eq. (8-32), and since the $a$ parameters are known from the original system, the $k$ parameters can be found.

## EXAMPLE 8-4

We wish to design a state estimator for the system

$$\mathbf{x}(k + 1) = \begin{bmatrix} 1 & 2 & 0 \\ 3 & -1 & 1 \\ 0 & 2 & 0 \end{bmatrix} \mathbf{x}(k) + \begin{bmatrix} 2 \\ 1 \\ 1 \end{bmatrix} u(k)$$

$$y(k) = \begin{bmatrix} 0 & 0 & 1 \end{bmatrix} \mathbf{x}(k)$$

with eigenvalues at $z = 0.5$ and $z = \pm j0.5$.

**SOLUTION:** Our approach will be to put the system into its observable form to begin with. The following results werre derived in Example 8-2:
With

$$\mathbf{x}(k) = \frac{1}{6} \begin{bmatrix} 1 & 1 & 7 \\ 0 & 3 & 0 \\ 0 & 0 & 6 \end{bmatrix} \mathbf{x}_o(k)$$

then

$$\mathbf{x}_o(k + 1) = \begin{bmatrix} 0 & 0 & -2 \\ 1 & 0 & 9 \\ 0 & 1 & 0 \end{bmatrix} \mathbf{x}_o(k) + \begin{bmatrix} 3 \\ 2 \\ 1 \end{bmatrix} u(k)$$

$$y(k) = \begin{bmatrix} 0 & 0 & 1 \end{bmatrix} \mathbf{x}_o(k)$$

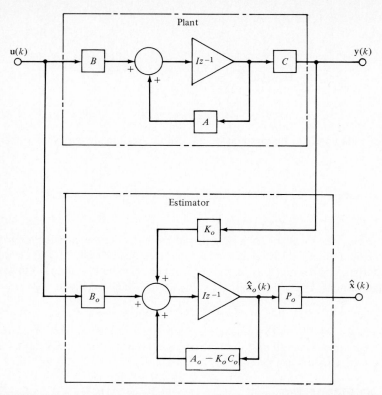

**FIGURE 8-2.** Vector block diagram for estimator structure based on the observable form model.

The desired characteristic polynomial for the estimator system is constructed from the specified eigenvalues:

$$p_o(z) = (z + 0.5)(z + j0.5)(z - j0.5)$$

$$p_o(z) = z^3 + 0.5z^2 + 0.25z + 0.125$$

From Eq. (8-32), $k_3 = 0.5$, $k_2 - 9 = 0.25$, and $k_1 + 2 = 0.125$ leading to the result that

$$K_o = \begin{bmatrix} -1.875 \\ 9.250 \\ 0.500 \end{bmatrix}$$

To complete the estimator, one could either translate the entire estimator system description back into the original **x** formulation using the known transformation matrix $P_o$, or simply use the $\mathbf{x}_o$ formulation followed by an "output" equation $\hat{\mathbf{x}}(t) = P_o \hat{\mathbf{x}}_o(t)$. We will take the second approach, where the estimated state for $\mathbf{x}_o(t)$ is labeled $\hat{\mathbf{x}}_o(t)$, instead of $\mathbf{w}(t)$ used in Eq. (8-25): the *estimator system*, in the form of Eq. (8-24),

$$\hat{\mathbf{x}}_o(k + 1) = \begin{bmatrix} 0 & 0 & -0.125 \\ 1 & 0 & -0.250 \\ 0 & 1 & -0.500 \end{bmatrix} \hat{\mathbf{x}}_o(k) + \begin{bmatrix} 3 \\ 2 \\ 1 \end{bmatrix} u(k) + \begin{bmatrix} -1.875 \\ 9.250 \\ 0.500 \end{bmatrix} y(k)$$

$$\hat{\mathbf{x}}(k) = \frac{1}{6} \begin{bmatrix} 1 & 1 & 7 \\ 0 & 3 & 0 \\ 0 & 0 & 6 \end{bmatrix} \hat{\mathbf{x}}_o(k)$$

Notice that the measured output $y(k)$ is taken from the original plant and that the $\hat{\mathbf{x}}(k)$ vector will approximate the original plant vector $\mathbf{x}(k)$. Figure 8-2 summarizes this approach; the subscripted matrices refer to the corresponding matrices for the observable canonical form. ∎

Thus far, the order of the estimator system dynamics is the same as that of the original system model. For this case the estimator is called a *full-order* estimator. There are occasions where dynamics of a lesser order is required as discussed in the next section.

### 8-3.3 Reduced-Order Estimator Design

If we take a closer look at the estimator problem, we see that the measurements $y(k)$ [or $v(k)$ if a $D$ matrix is present] represent $p$ linear combinations of the states. Assuming that these measurements are essentially error free, then the estimator system should only have to "regenerate" $(n - p)$ states. This argument is true whenever the $p$ measurements are linearly independent, but it is easier to comprehend when the measured variables are states of the system. Consider the system

$$\mathbf{x}(k + 1) = A\mathbf{x}(k) + B\mathbf{u}(k) \qquad (8\text{-}34)$$

$$\mathbf{y}(k) = C\mathbf{x}(k) \qquad (8\text{-}35)$$

where $\mathbf{x}$ is an $n$-vector, $\mathbf{u}$ is an $m$-vector, and $\mathbf{y}$ is a $p$-vector ($p < n$). Here, it is assumed that the $p \times n$ matrix $C$ has rank $p$, meaning that the measurements are linearly independent. (If this is not true, we eliminate the nonindependent measurements.)

Conceptually, we can make a change of state variables defined by

$$\mathbf{x}(t) = P \begin{bmatrix} \mathbf{y}(t) \\ \mathbf{x}_u(t) \end{bmatrix} \qquad (8\text{-}36)$$

where the new state vector consists of the actual measured outputs $\mathbf{y}$ and a remaining set of "unmeasured" states $\mathbf{x}_u$. With the system described in terms of the new states and partitioned appropriately, we have

$$\begin{bmatrix} \mathbf{y}(k + 1) \\ \mathbf{x}_u(k + 1) \end{bmatrix} = \begin{bmatrix} A_{11} & A_{12} \\ A_{21} & A_{22} \end{bmatrix} \begin{bmatrix} \mathbf{y}(k) \\ \mathbf{x}_u(k) \end{bmatrix} + \begin{bmatrix} B_1 \\ B_2 \end{bmatrix} \mathbf{u}(k) \qquad (8\text{-}37)$$

$$\mathbf{y}(k) = \begin{bmatrix} I & 0 \end{bmatrix} \begin{bmatrix} \mathbf{y}(k) \\ \mathbf{x}_u(k) \end{bmatrix} \qquad (8\text{-}38)$$

It is more easily seen now that only the $(n - p)$ states of $\mathbf{x}_u$ need be reconstructed by the estimator. The following development will confirm this.

Writing the first of the partitioned equations in Eq. (8-37),

$$\mathbf{y}(k + 1) = A_{11}\mathbf{y}(k) + A_{12}\mathbf{x}_u(k) + B_1\mathbf{u}(k) \tag{8-39}$$

From this equation we can extract that

$$A_{12}\mathbf{x}_u(k) = [\mathbf{y}(k + 1) - A_{11}\mathbf{y}(k) - B_1\mathbf{u}(k)] \tag{8-40}$$

where the right-hand side will be considered as a "measurement" term later. The second partitioned equation from Eq. (8-37) is

$$\mathbf{x}_u(k + 1) = A_{22}\mathbf{x}_u(k) + [A_{21}\mathbf{y}(k) + B_2\mathbf{u}(k)] \tag{8-41}$$

where the term in brackets will be taken as an "input" term.

Recall that from the general system model

$$\mathbf{x}(k + 1) = A\mathbf{x}(k) + [B\mathbf{u}(k)] \tag{8-42}$$

$$[\mathbf{y}(k)] = C\mathbf{x}(k) \tag{8-43}$$

we have developed the state estimator system of Eq. (8-25)

$$\hat{\mathbf{x}}(k + 1) = A\hat{\mathbf{x}}(k) + [B\mathbf{u}(k)] + K\{[\mathbf{y}(k)] - C\hat{\mathbf{x}}(k)\} \tag{8-44}$$

Note that the "input" term, $B\mathbf{u}$, of Eq. (8-42) and the "measurement" term, $\mathbf{y}(k)$, of Eq. (8-43) play particular roles in the estimator system, as indicated by the terms in brackets in Eq. (8-44).

Returning to the problem at hand, we associate Eq. (8-41) with Eq. (8-42) as the "dynamic equation" of the system, and Eq. (8-40) with Eq. (8-43) as the "output equation" for the system. In making this correspondence, we can write the estimator system as

$$\hat{\mathbf{x}}_u(k + 1) = A_{22}\hat{\mathbf{x}}_u(k) + [A_{21}\mathbf{y}(k) + B_2\mathbf{u}(k)]$$
$$+ K\{[\mathbf{y}(k + 1) - A_{11}\mathbf{y}(k) - B_1\mathbf{u}(k)] - A_{12}\hat{\mathbf{x}}_u(k)\} \tag{8-45}$$

Regrouping terms,

$$\hat{\mathbf{x}}_u(k + 1) - K\mathbf{y}(k + 1) = (A_{22} - KA_{12})\hat{\mathbf{x}}_u(k)$$
$$+ (B_2 - KB_1)\mathbf{u}(k) \tag{8-46}$$
$$+ (A_{21} - KA_{11})\mathbf{y}(k)$$

Introducing the variable $\mathbf{w}(k) = \hat{\mathbf{x}}_u(k) - K\mathbf{y}(k)$, we reduce Eq. (8-46) to the final *reduced-order estimator* with state vector $\mathbf{w}$, given by

$$\mathbf{w}(k + 1) = (A_{22} - KA_{12})\mathbf{w}(k) + (B_2 - KB_1)\mathbf{u}(k)$$
$$+ (A_{22}K - KA_{12}K + A_{21} - KA_{11})\mathbf{y}(k) \tag{8-47}$$

$$\hat{\mathbf{x}}_u(k) = \mathbf{w}(k) + K\mathbf{y}(k) \tag{8-48}$$

Just as in the case of the full-order estimator, the gain matrix $K$ is used to adjust

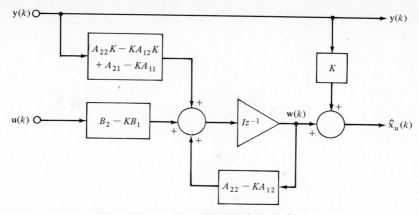

**FIGURE 8-3.** Reduced-order estimator vector-block diagram.

the speed of response. Equation (8-47) provides the estimator dynamics of order $(n - p)$, the dimension of $\mathbf{w}$, and Eq. (8-48) is the estimator output equation. Note that when $K$ is specified all of the matrices are known.

To have complete flexibility on placing the poles of the estimator system, the matrices $A_{22}$ and $A_{12}$ must form an observable pair. Figure 8-3 illustrates the overall structure of the reduced-order state estimator based on Eqs. (8-47) and (8-48). There is no difference in structure between estimators for continuous-time systems and estimators for discrete-time systems, as we will show by example.

### EXAMPLE 8-5 (Discrete-Time Estimator)

We wish to design a reduced-order estimator with poles each at $z = 0.5$ for the system

$$\mathbf{x}(k + 1) = \left[\begin{array}{c|cc} 0 & 1 & 0 \\ \hline 0 & -2 & 1 \\ -1 & 0 & -1 \end{array}\right] \mathbf{x}(k) + \left[\begin{array}{c} 0 \\ 0 \\ 1 \end{array}\right] u(k)$$

$$y(k) = [\quad 1 \mid 0 \quad 0] \; \mathbf{x}(k)$$

*SOLUTION:* From Eq. (8-47)

$$\hat{A} = (A_{22} - KA_{12}) = \begin{bmatrix} -(k_1 + 2) & 1 \\ -k_2 & -1 \end{bmatrix}$$

where $A_{22}$ and $A_{12}$ were taken from the partition shown above and $K = [k_1 \quad k_2]^T$. Since the desired characteristic polynomial for the estimator is

$$p_o(z) = (z - 0.5)^2 = z^2 - z + 0.25$$

therefore

$$\det (zI - \hat{A}) = z^2 + (k_1 + 3)z + (k_1 + k_2 + 2) \overset{\text{set}}{=} p_o(z)$$

Equating coefficients and solving, we obtain that

$$K = \begin{bmatrix} -4 \\ 2.25 \end{bmatrix}$$

With this gain matrix determined, it is a simple matter of calculating the remaining coefficient matrices of Eq. (8-47) to obtain estimator equations

$$\mathbf{w}(k+1) = \begin{bmatrix} 2 & 1 \\ -2.25 & -1 \end{bmatrix} \mathbf{w}(k) + \begin{bmatrix} 0 \\ 1 \end{bmatrix} u(k) + \begin{bmatrix} -5.75 \\ 5.75 \end{bmatrix} y(k)$$

$$\begin{bmatrix} \hat{x}_2(k) \\ \hat{x}_3(k) \end{bmatrix} = \begin{bmatrix} 1 & 0 \\ 0 & 1 \end{bmatrix} \mathbf{w}(k) + \begin{bmatrix} -4 \\ 2.25 \end{bmatrix} y(k)$$

■

### EXAMPLE 8-6 (Continuous-Time Estimator)

To design a reduced-order estimator with poles each at $s = -30$ for the system

$$u(t) \longrightarrow \boxed{\dfrac{3}{s(s+30)}} \xrightarrow{p(t)} \boxed{\dfrac{-5.1s^2}{s^2+10s-50}} \longrightarrow \theta(t)$$

where the state vector is taken to be

$$\mathbf{x}(k) = [p(t),\ \theta(t),\ \dot{p}(t),\ \dot{\theta}(t)]^T$$

Both $p(t)$ and $\theta(t)$ are measured variables. Thus,

$$\dot{\mathbf{x}} = \begin{bmatrix} 0 & 0 & 1 & 0 \\ 0 & 0 & 0 & 1 \\ 0 & 0 & -30 & 0 \\ 0 & 50 & 153 & -10 \end{bmatrix} \mathbf{x} + \begin{bmatrix} 0 \\ 0 \\ 3 \\ -15.3 \end{bmatrix} u$$

$$\mathbf{y} = \begin{bmatrix} 1 & 0 & 0 & 0 \\ 0 & 1 & 0 & 0 \end{bmatrix} \mathbf{x}$$

This model represents the cart/pendulum system described in Example 3-14 with nominal parameter values.

**SOLUTION:** Constructing $\det(sI - A_{22} + KA_{12})$, where $K$ is a $2 \times 2$ matrix of estimator gains,

$$\begin{vmatrix} s + k_{11} + 30 & k_{12} \\ k_{21} - 153 & s + k_{22} + 10 \end{vmatrix} \overset{\text{set}}{=} (s+30)^2$$

we find, after simplification, that a suitable solution is given by

$$K = \begin{bmatrix} 0 & 0 \\ 0 & 20 \end{bmatrix}$$

Therefore, the reduced-order estimator is

$$\dot{\mathbf{w}} = \begin{bmatrix} -30 & 0 \\ 153 & -30 \end{bmatrix} \mathbf{w} + \begin{bmatrix} 3 \\ -15.3 \end{bmatrix} u + \begin{bmatrix} 0 & 0 \\ 0 & -550 \end{bmatrix} \begin{bmatrix} x \\ \theta \end{bmatrix}$$

$$\begin{bmatrix} \hat{v} \\ \hat{\alpha} \end{bmatrix} = \begin{bmatrix} 1 & 0 \\ 0 & 1 \end{bmatrix} \mathbf{w} + \begin{bmatrix} 0 & 0 \\ 0 & 20 \end{bmatrix} \begin{bmatrix} x \\ \theta \end{bmatrix}$$

where $v = \dot{x}$ and $\alpha = \dot{\theta}$. These four estimator equations appear even simpler written as scalar equations. Note that the design procedure was the same for this continuous-time problem as for the previous discrete-time problem. ∎

In the next section we begin to tie together the concepts of state-variable feedback and state estimators.

## 8-4

## THE SEPARATION PRINCIPLE

With the necessity of accessing each and every state variable to implement state variable feedback (SVF), as we have seen in Chapter 7, and the ability to regenerate unmeasured states using state estimator theory, it should be clear that we need to look at the possibility of combining the two procedures in order to be able to use SVF even in cases where not all states are measured. At this point, however, it is not clear that everything will work out smoothly!

The idea is to have a control signal that is based on the estimator outputs rather than on the actual states. This appears promising since the estimator state $\mathbf{w} = \hat{\mathbf{x}}$ asymptotically approaches the actual system state $\mathbf{x}$ and, in addition, we generally have control over the speed with which $\hat{\mathbf{x}}$ approaches $\mathbf{x}$.

Consider the system (plant) model

$$\mathbf{x}(k + 1) = A\mathbf{x}(k) + B\mathbf{u}(k) \tag{8-49}$$

$$\mathbf{y}(k) = C\mathbf{x}(k) + D\mathbf{u}(k) \tag{8-50}$$

The state estimator system will be written in the form of Eq. (8-24) with Eq. (8-19) included; that is,

$$\hat{\mathbf{x}}(k + 1) = (A - KC)\hat{\mathbf{x}}(k) + (B - KD)\mathbf{u}(k) + K\mathbf{y}(k) \tag{8-51}$$

where it is assumed that $K$ has been chosen so that the estimator has the specific set of eigenvalues $\Lambda_o = \{\lambda: \det(\lambda I - A + KC) = 0\}$.

The feedback law is taken to be

$$\mathbf{u}(k) = F\hat{\mathbf{x}}(k) + Gr(k) \tag{8-52}$$

where the matrix $F$ is chosen so that the closed-loop system has its own specific set of eigenvalues $\Lambda_c = \{\lambda: \det(\lambda I - A - BF) = 0\}$. Although $F$ is the coefficient matrix for $\hat{\mathbf{x}}$ in Eq. (8-52), we assume that the calculation of $F$ is completely independent of the estimator system! The matrix $G$ is included for

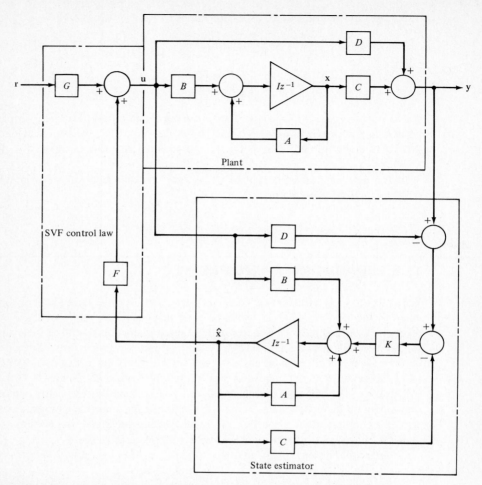

**FIGURE 8-4. Vector block diagram for estimator based SVF Conrol.**

completeness; it corresponds to the input gains of Eq. (7-51), which may be required for a Type 1 system design. The reference input $\mathbf{r}(k)$ is an independent set of input commands for the system. The complete structure comprising Eq. (8-49) through (8-52) is illustrated in Fig. 8-4. We will refer to this combination as estimator-based SVF. In Fig. 8-4 the plant, estimator, and control law are sectioned off. The estimator and control law taken together form the (feedback) *controller*.

**The Separation Principle.** The problems of SVF and estimator design are noninteracting for linear systems:

(a) The use of $\hat{\mathbf{x}}$ (in place of $\mathbf{x}$) in Eq. (8-52) does not alter the pole locations chosen for the closed-loop system $\Lambda_c$.

(b) A change of feedback ($F$) does not alter the estimator pole locations $\Lambda_o$.

To prove the separation principle, we first combine the states of plant and estimator to obtain

$$\begin{bmatrix} \mathbf{x}(k+1) \\ \hat{\mathbf{x}}(k+1) \end{bmatrix} = \begin{bmatrix} A & BF \\ KC & A-KC+BF \end{bmatrix} \begin{bmatrix} \mathbf{x}(k) \\ \hat{\mathbf{x}}(k) \end{bmatrix} + \begin{bmatrix} BG \\ BG \end{bmatrix} \mathbf{r}(k) \quad (8\text{-}53)$$

Next, we modify Eq. (8-53) by writing the dynamics in terms of $\mathbf{e}(k) = \mathbf{x}(k) - \hat{\mathbf{x}}(k)$ instead of $\hat{\mathbf{x}}(k)$. Thus,

$$\mathbf{e}(k+1) = \mathbf{x}(k+1) - \hat{\mathbf{x}}(k+1)$$

$$\mathbf{e}(k+1) = A\mathbf{x}(k) + BF\hat{\mathbf{x}}(k) - KC\mathbf{x}(k)$$
$$- (A - KC)\hat{\mathbf{x}}(k) - BF\hat{\mathbf{x}}(k) \quad (8\text{-}54)$$

$$\mathbf{e}(k+1) = (A - KC)[\mathbf{x}(k) - \hat{\mathbf{x}}(k)]$$

$$\mathbf{e}(k+1) = (A - KC)\mathbf{e}(k)$$

Thus, the total system dynamics can be written as

$$\begin{bmatrix} \mathbf{x}(k+1) \\ \mathbf{e}(k+1) \end{bmatrix} = \begin{bmatrix} A+BF & -BF \\ 0 & A-KC \end{bmatrix} \begin{bmatrix} \mathbf{x}(k) \\ \mathbf{e}(k) \end{bmatrix} + \begin{bmatrix} BG \\ 0 \end{bmatrix} \mathbf{r}(k) \quad (8\text{-}55)$$

The form of the coefficient matrix, being triangular, implies that the eigenvalues of the total system

$$\det (\lambda I - \overline{A}) = \det (\lambda I - A - BF) \det (\lambda I - A + KC) \quad (8\text{-}56)$$

where $\overline{A}$ is the coefficient matrix in Eq. (8-55). We have made use of the fact that the determinant of a triangular matrix is a product of the determinants of the diagonal partitions. Equation (8-56) is the result we need; it tells us that the total set of eigenvalues for the system are exactly the set of closed-loop eigenvalues $\Lambda_c$ plus the set of estimator eigenvalues $\Lambda_o$. Furthermore, there is no influence on $\Lambda_o$ by $F$, nor any on $\Lambda_c$ by $K$. Consequently, the property of separation exists between the SVF design for the matrix $F$ and the estimator design for the matrix $K$! That is to say, the procedures already discussed are appropriate (fortunately!) for determining the complete controller design, and the problem divides naturally into two separate problems. In a later section we will see that these problems have a degree of similarity called "duality."

**8-5**

# OUTPUT FEEDBACK CONTROLLER DESIGN

In Section 7-7.4, a procedure for nondynamic output feedback control was presented. The limitation of that approach lay in the fact that the rank of the output matrix determined the number of pole placements that could be made. This approach might work well, of course, if your particular system called for a generous supply of sensors. In the more general design problem, estimator theory must be used to reconstruct unmeasured state variations; that is, the "software" approach is still more typical than the "hardware" approach to gathering state information.

With the proof of the separation principle in the previous section, the general (dynamic) output feedback controller illustrated in Fig. 8-4 has been validated. In this section we apply our output feedback controller design to various systems.

## EXAMPLE 8-7

We wish to design a digital controller algorithm of the form of Eqs. (8-51) and (8-52) to control the response of the chemical process given by the plant transfer function

$$G(s) = \frac{3}{4s + 1} = \frac{Y(s)}{U(s)} \tag{8-57}$$

Figure 8-5 illustrates the structure to be used for digital control. The plant is interfaced with the computer through an ADC, which provides accurate samples of the output $y(t)$ at regular sample intervals of 1 sec and a DAC, which is effectively modeled as a zero-order-hold (ZOH) device. The reference signal is applied as a digital input.

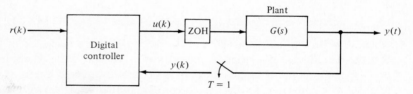

**FIGURE 8-5. Structure for problem of Example 8-7.**

The specifications for the problem are as follows:

(a) No steady state error ($e = r - y$) to constant reference inputs.
(b) A settling-time to within 2% of the final value should occur in less than 10 sec following a set-point command.

**SOLUTION:** For the plant in Eq. (8-57)

$$\dot{x}(t) = -0.25x(t) + u(t)$$

$$y(t) = 0.75x(t)$$

The ZOH equivalent model (see Section 3-4) for $T = 1$ sec is

$$x(k + 1) = 0.7788x(k) + 0.8848u(k)$$

$$y(k) = 0.75x(k)$$

***SVF Design.*** For a settling-time of 10 sec the closed-loop pole should be approximately $z = 0.67$. We will choose $z = 0.65$ so that the settling time is well within the 10-sec specification. Thus, for the (scalar) $F$

$$A + BF = 0.7788 + 0.8848F \overset{\text{set}}{=} 0.6500$$

$$F = -0.1456$$

Using Eq. (7-51), the scalar $G$ is found to be

$$G = [0.75(1 - 0.65)^{-1}0.8848]^{-1}$$

$$G = 0.5274$$

***Estimator Design.*** Since measured output is proportional to the (scalar) state of the system, we could determine $x(k)$ directly without an estimator, but to illustrate the general approach of estimator-based feedback, we will formally include the estimator design.

From Eq. (8-51) our estimator is given by

$$\hat{x}(k + 1) = (0.7788 - 0.75K)\hat{x}(k) + 0.8848u(k) + Ky(k)$$

As a rule-of-thumb we want the estimator to be faster (by a factor of 2 or more) than the closed-loop response. Consequently, we will choose the estimator eigenvalue at $z < 0.3$; for numerical convenience we take $K = 0.7$ corresponding to $z = 0.2538$. Thus, the controller design is

$$\hat{x}(k + 1) = 0.2538\hat{x}(k) + 0.8848u(k) + 0.7y(k)$$

$$u(k) = -0.1456\hat{x}(k) + 0.5274r(k)$$

To simulate our design, that is, to check its performance against the specifications; we combine the dynamics as was done in Eq. (8-53):

$$\begin{bmatrix} x(k + 1) \\ \hat{x}(k + 1) \end{bmatrix} = \begin{bmatrix} 0.7788 & -0.1288 \\ 0.5250 & 0.1250 \end{bmatrix} \begin{bmatrix} x(k) \\ \hat{x}(k) \end{bmatrix} + \begin{bmatrix} 0.4666 \\ 0.4666 \end{bmatrix} r(k)$$

$$y(k) = 0.75x(k)$$

*Simulations*

Case 1. $x(0) = \hat{x}(0) = 0$, $r(k) =$ unit step
Case 2. $x(0) = 0.3$, $\hat{x}(0) = 0$, $r(k) =$ unit step
Case 3. $x(0) = -0.3$, $\hat{x}(0) = 0$, $r(k) =$ unit step

In all three cases the reference command is a unit step, and, according to our design, the output $y$ should reach the commanded level (unity) within 10 sec (to within 2%). The results of the three simulations are presented in Fig. 8-6. In addition to the output, the estimation error, $e = x - \hat{x}$, is included for cases 2 and 3 (for case 1 the error is identically zero). Keep in mind that the plots of Fig. 8-6 are in discrete time and therefore are valid only at the sample times. The "continuous" plot is for clarity only. ∎

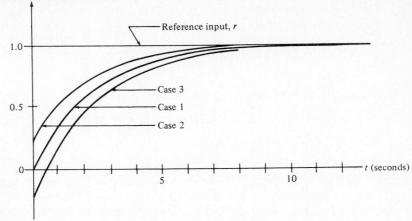

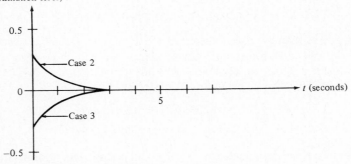

**FIGURE 8-6.   Simulation results for Example 8.7.**

*Remarks:*
- Slight variations in the output are caused by initial conditions on $x$ that either aid or hinder the output step response. In all cases, however, the settling-time requirement was met.
- The discrepancy between $x(0)$ and $\hat{x}(0)$ in cases 2 and 3 led to a nonzero estimation error. The error decay appears to be within the design (pole at 0.2538).

**8-6**

## DUALITY

In this chapter we have studied the problem of estimation and estimator design, and in the previous chapter that of state-variable feedback. The reader has no doubt sensed a certain similarity between the two chapters in that the mathematical manipulations involved tend to follow the same general pattern. With our background, then, we are in a good position to understand and appreciate the concept of "duality." As we shall see, duality arises in several different contexts. First, we will define when two systems are duals of each other and then relate particular items that we have already discussed to duality.

**Definition 8-2:**  A discrete-time system described by

$$S \qquad \begin{aligned} \mathbf{x}(k + 1) &= A\mathbf{x}(k) + B\mathbf{u}(k) \\ \mathbf{y}(k) &= C\mathbf{x}(k) + D\mathbf{u}(k) \end{aligned} \qquad (8\text{-}58)$$

is said to be the *dual* of the system

$$S' \qquad \begin{aligned} \mathbf{x}'(k + 1) &= A^T\mathbf{x}'(k) + C^T\mathbf{u}'(k) \\ \mathbf{y}'(k) &= B^T\mathbf{x}'(k) + D^T\mathbf{u}'(k) \end{aligned} \qquad (8\text{-}59)$$

It is easy to see that the relationship of duality is "reflexive"; that is to say, if a system $S$ is the dual of a system $S'$, then $S'$ is also the dual of $S$. Looking back to the canonical forms of Chapter 3, we recognize that the controllable form and the observable form are *dual* representations of the same system. Following this idea and recalling the rank tests for controllability and observability, we find the following:

- A system is controllable (observable) if and only if its dual system is observable (controllable).

### *Relation Between State Feedback and Estimator Design.*  Consider

again the *state variable feedback (SVF) problem* of pole placement: For the system $S$ of Eq. (8-58) a matrix $F$ must be constructed so that the eigenvalues of $(A + BF)$ take on the specified values $\{\lambda_1, \lambda_2, \ldots, \lambda_n\}$. In Chapter 7 we investigated several approaches to constructing the desired $F$ matrix. Similarly, in Section 8-3.1 we discussed the *estimator design problem,* which reduced to the following basic problem of pole placement: To construct a matrix $K$ so that the eigenvalues of $(A - KC)$ have the specified values $\{\lambda_1', \lambda_2', \ldots, \lambda_n'\}$. Recall that in Section 8-3.1 mention was made of the duality concept on which we elaborate here.

Repeating those comments given in Section 8-3.1 that relate to duality, the eigenvalues of a matrix $G$ are the same as those of its transpose $G^T$. Consequently,

$$\lambda\{(A - KC)\} = \lambda\{(A^T - C^T K^T)\} \qquad (8\text{-}60)$$

where $\lambda\{M\}$ is an abbreviated notation for "the set of eigenvalues of the matrix $M$." With our new insight of dual systems, we see that the estimator design problem of constructing $K$ is of the same form as that of constructing $F$ for the SVF problem. In particular, the construction of $F$ for the system $S$ of Eqs. (8-58) requires placement of the eigenvalues of $(A + BF)$, and the construction of $K$ for the system $S'$ of Eqs. (8-59) requires placement of the eigenvalues of $(A^T - KB^T)$, the transpose of which is $(A - BK^T)$. By comparison, we find the following:

* The calculation of the SVF matrix $F$ for a system to have a specified set of closed-loop pole locations is *identical* to the calculation of the gain matrix $K$ for the estimator of the dual system to have the same pole locations with the correspondence that

$$F = -K^T \tag{8-61}$$

This important result says that if we have a good algorithm for computing feedback gains $F$, then when we need to design an estimator system with gains $K$, we can *instead* calculate the feedback gains for the dual system, $F'$, and use Eq. (8-61) to determine that $K = -(F')^T$. (See also Section 8-7.3.)

We have discussed the result of Eq. (8-61) based on pole placement, but the result is the same for any other design method, such as an "optimal" design, where some cost function is minimized. Let us illustrate the basic result with an example.

### EXAMPLE 8-8 (Use of Duality)
For the system

$$\mathbf{x}(k + 1) = \begin{bmatrix} 1 & 3 & 0 \\ 2 & -1 & 2 \\ 0 & 1 & 0 \end{bmatrix} \mathbf{x}(k) + \begin{bmatrix} 0 \\ 0 \\ 1 \end{bmatrix} u(k)$$

$$y(k) = \begin{bmatrix} 2 & 1 & 1 \end{bmatrix} \mathbf{x}(k)$$

we wish to design a full order estimator system having pole locations at $z = 0.5$ and $z = 0.5 \pm j0.5$.

*SOLUTION:* Noting that the given system is dual to the one used in Example 7-7 for which the corresponding SVF matrix $F$ was determined (in Example 7-8) to be

$$F = [1.91 \quad -3.25 \quad 0.94]$$

the required gain matrix $K$ is

$$K = [-1.91 \quad 3.25 \quad -0.94]^T$$

The required estimator system is then given by either Eq. (8-24) or Eq. (8-25). ∎

## 8-7

## SOLVED PROBLEMS

In keeping with the previous chapters, this section will attempt to draw together the main points of the chapter as well as to offer extensions of some of the previous work.

## 8-7.1 Estimator-Based State Feedback Control

The methods of this and the previous chapter combine to form what is known as state-variable control, or more specifically, state feedback control. It is, perhaps, an opportune time to present a complete design that could help to clear up any remnant difficulties.

### EXAMPLE 8-9

We wish to design a digital state feedback controller for the continuous-time plant described by

$$\dot{\mathbf{x}}(t) = \begin{bmatrix} 0 & 1 \\ 0 & -2 \end{bmatrix} \mathbf{x}(t) + \begin{bmatrix} 0 \\ 1 \end{bmatrix} u(t)$$

$$y(t) = [1 \quad 0] \, \mathbf{x}(t)$$

The sampling rate is to be 10 Hz, and the system is to have a Type 1 behavior with a "2% settling time" of less than 2.5 sec and a peak overshoot to a step input of less than 10%.

**SOLUTION:** For the design we will choose to mimic a continuous-time system with closed-loop poles at $(-2 \pm j2)$, using an estimator with poles at the digital equivalent of $(-4 \pm j4)$ for continuous-time.

- Calculating the transition matrices, the ZOH equivalent for the plant with $T = 0.1$ sec is

$$\mathbf{x}(k + 1) = \begin{bmatrix} 1 & 0.09063 \\ 0 & 0.81873 \end{bmatrix} \mathbf{x}(k) + \begin{bmatrix} 0.00468 \\ 0.09063 \end{bmatrix} u(k)$$

$$y(k) = [1 \quad 0] \, \mathbf{x}(k)$$

- To match the continuous-time poles $-2 \pm j2$, we find that the required discrete-time pole locations are (from $z = e^{sT}$)

$$p_{1,2} = 0.80241 \pm j0.16266$$

- If $\overline{A} = A + BF$, where $F = [f_1 \quad f_2]$, then

$$\det (zI - \overline{A}) \overset{\text{set}}{=} (z - p_1)(z - p_2)$$

Equating coefficients of powers of $z$, we solve for $f_1$ and $f_2$:

$$F = [-7.22806 \quad -1.98677]$$

- Similarly, translating $-4 \pm j4$ to the desired discrete-time estimator pole locations, $p_{3,4} = 0.61741 \pm j0.26103$; and setting $\det (zI - \hat{A})$ to $(z - p_3)(z - p_4)$, where $\hat{A} = A - KC$, we find that

$$K = \begin{bmatrix} 0.58392 \\ 1.19908 \end{bmatrix}$$

- To check out the design, it is desirable to run a unit-step response. For this purpose we write from Eq. (8-55)

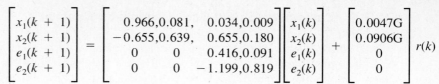

$$\begin{bmatrix} x_1(k+1) \\ x_2(k+1) \\ e_1(k+1) \\ e_2(k+1) \end{bmatrix} = \begin{bmatrix} 0.966, 0.081, & 0.034, 0.009 \\ -0.655, 0.639, & 0.655, 0.180 \\ 0 & 0 & 0.416, 0.091 \\ 0 & 0 & -1.199, 0.819 \end{bmatrix} \begin{bmatrix} x_1(k) \\ x_2(k) \\ e_1(k) \\ e_2(k) \end{bmatrix} + \begin{bmatrix} 0.0047G \\ 0.0906G \\ 0 \\ 0 \end{bmatrix} r(k)$$

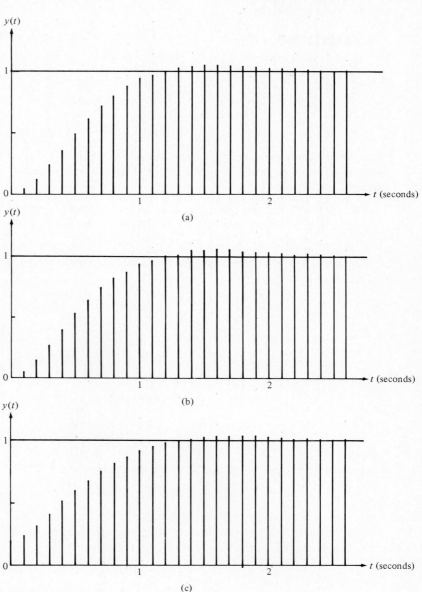

FIGURE 8-7. Step responses for Example 8-9 with initial states $[x_1 \ x_2 \ e_1 \ e_2] =$ (a) $O$; (b) $[0 \ 0 \ 0.2 \ 0.2]^T$ and (c) $[0.2 \ 0 \ 0.2 \ 0]^T$.

where $r(k)$ has been assumed to be unity and the gain $G$ is to be determined so that the steady state value of $y = x_1$ is also unity for the Type 1 system specification.

- First, with all initial states equal to zero (thereby effectively removing the estimator from the loop) the response is run to steady state of 0.138. Therefore, the value of $G$ is 7.25 (the reciprocal of the steady state value), so that the steady state error is zero. Figure 8-7 illustrates several step responses with different initial conditions. In each case the design is within the specifications. In Fig. 8-8 the error history is shown for $e(k) = x(k) - \hat{x}(k)$ when the initial error vector is $[0.2 \quad 0.2]^T$. The rate of error decrease could, of course, be made faster by starting with continuous-time estimator poles, which are further in the left-hand plane, that is, which have larger negative real parts. ■

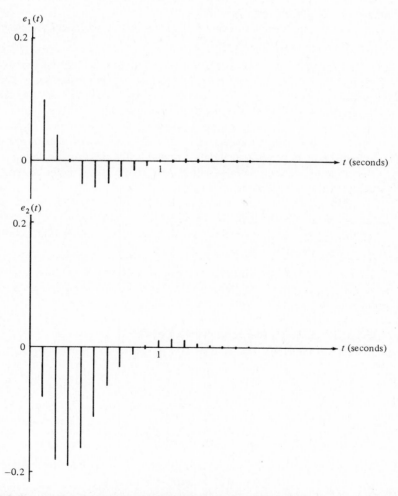

**FIGURE 8-8. Error decay for Example 8-9 for the initial error $e(0) = [0.2\ 0.2]^T$.**

*Remark:* Using an estimator in the loop will generally increase the settling time by as much as the settling time of the error. Thus, one must take this extra delay into account when establishing the original design from the given specifications.

In the next section we extend our techniques to the controller design for a multiple-input–output system.

## 8-7.2  Multivariable Feedback Control

In this section we want to apply estimator-based state feedback control methods to a vector-input–output system (sometimes called multivariable systems or multiple-input–output systems). The procedure is simply a combination of the techniques of this and the previous chapter.

To motivate the concept of multivariable systems, we mention certain applications that fall into this category:

1. Chemical processes: An example of a multiple-input–output process might be a chemical process requiring the mixture of several solutions. The inputs would typically be the flow rates of the various solutions, and the states (outputs), the relative amounts of each ingredient.
2. Temperature regulation: Another example of a vector input–output process might be one in which there are several liquid filled chambers, some of which contain heating elements (inputs) and others to be held at certain specified temperature levels (outputs). Here the states might be the absolute temperatures of each chamber.
3. Aircraft control: A familiar example of a multiple-input, multiple-output system is an aircraft with control variables (inputs) consisting of the amount of thrust, elevator and rudder deflections, and controlled variables (outputs), including air speed and altitude of the plane.

The reader can no doubt think of many other types of systems that naturally have a vector of inputs and outputs. For our example we choose a simple third-order system with two inputs and two outputs.

### EXAMPLE 8-10 (Multivariable Feedback Control)
Consider a plant with the following state-variable description:

$$\dot{\mathbf{x}}(t) = \begin{bmatrix} 0 & 0 & 0 \\ 0 & -1 & 0 \\ 0 & 0 & -2 \end{bmatrix} \mathbf{x}(t) + \begin{bmatrix} 1 & 0 \\ 1 & 1 \\ 0 & 2 \end{bmatrix} \mathbf{u}(t)$$

$$\mathbf{y}(t) = \begin{bmatrix} 1 & -1 & 0 \\ 1 & 0 & 1 \end{bmatrix} \mathbf{x}(t)$$

It is clear that the system is both controllable and observable (since it is in modal form without a zero row in $B$ or a zero column in $C$).

The plant is to be (digitally) controlled by a reduced-order estimator and state feedback so that a step input from either $u_1$ or $u_2$ will result in settled outputs after 2 sec.

**SOLUTION:** The ZOH equivalent with $T = 0.1$ sec is given by

$$\mathbf{x}(k + 1) = \begin{bmatrix} 1 & 0 & 0 \\ 0 & 0.9048 & 0 \\ 0 & 0 & 0.8187 \end{bmatrix} \mathbf{x}(k) + \begin{bmatrix} 0.1000 & 0 \\ 0.0952 & 0.0952 \\ 0 & 0.1813 \end{bmatrix} \mathbf{u}(k)$$

$$\mathbf{y}(k) = \begin{bmatrix} 1 & -1 & 0 \\ 1 & 0 & 1 \end{bmatrix} \mathbf{x}(k)$$

Since we want to use a reduced-order estimator, we need to transform the state $\mathbf{x}$ to a new state $\mathbf{v}$ so that $v_1 = y_1$ and $v_2 = y_2$. From the output matrix we write that

$$\mathbf{v}(k) = \begin{bmatrix} 1 & -1 & 0 \\ 1 & 0 & 1 \\ 0 & 0 & 1 \end{bmatrix} \mathbf{x}(k) = P^{-1}\mathbf{x}(k)$$

where $v_3$ was taken to be $x_3$. With this transformation of state the system is described by

$$\mathbf{v}(k + 1) = \begin{bmatrix} 0.9048 & 0.0952 & -0.0952 \\ 0 & 1 & -0.1813 \\ 0 & 0 & 0.8187 \end{bmatrix} \mathbf{v}(k) + \begin{bmatrix} 0.0048 & -0.0952 \\ 0.1000 & 0.1813 \\ 0 & 0.1813 \end{bmatrix} \mathbf{u}(k)$$

$$\mathbf{y}(k) = \begin{bmatrix} 1 & 0 & 0 \\ 0 & 1 & 0 \end{bmatrix} \mathbf{v}(k)$$

Referring to Eq. (8-47), we can write that

$$A_{22} - KA_{12} = [0.8187 + 0.1813(K_2 + 0.0952K_1)]$$

If we anticipate closed-loop poles with magnitude about 0.7 to meet the settling-time requirement, we can set the (single) estimator pole to 0.1, to be sufficiently faster than the system response. With this in mind let us choose the estimator gains as

$$K = [-7.549 \quad 0]$$

Introducing these gains into Eqs. (8-47) and (8-48) and reducing the expressions, we arrive at

$$w(k + 1) = 0.1w(k) + [0.0362 \quad -0.5374] \mathbf{u}(k)$$

$$+ [6.0758 \quad 0.7187] \mathbf{y}(k)$$

$$\hat{v}_3(k) = w(k) - 7.549y_1(k)$$

Translating back to the $\mathbf{x}$ state using the transformation matrix $P$,

$$\hat{\mathbf{x}}(k) = \begin{bmatrix} 0 & 1 & -1 \\ -1 & 1 & -1 \\ 0 & 0 & 1 \end{bmatrix} \begin{bmatrix} y_1(k) \\ y_2(k) \\ \hat{v}_3(k) \end{bmatrix}$$

and the complete state equations for the first-order estimator are

$$w(k + 1) = 0.1w(k) + [0.0362 \quad -0.5374 \quad 6.0758 \quad 0.7187]\begin{bmatrix} \mathbf{u}(k) \\ \mathbf{y}(k) \end{bmatrix}$$

$$\hat{\mathbf{x}}(k) = \begin{bmatrix} -1 \\ -1 \\ 1 \end{bmatrix} w(k) + \begin{bmatrix} 0 & 0 & 7.549 & 1 \\ 0 & 0 & 6.549 & 1 \\ 0 & 0 & -7.549 & 0 \end{bmatrix}\begin{bmatrix} \mathbf{u}(k) \\ \mathbf{y}(k) \end{bmatrix}$$

where the estimator input consists of both plant inputs and outputs.

The closed-loop pole locations are chosen at $z = 0$, 0.7, and 0.7, which gives us a desired characteristic equation:

$$p_d(z) = z^3 - 1.4z^2 + 0.49z = 0$$

The separation principle allows us to assume that the state $\mathbf{x}$ is accessible for the purpose of calculating the feedback matrix $F$. Recalling the method presented in Section 7-7.2, let us set

$$\boldsymbol{\alpha} = [1 \quad 1]^T$$

that is,

$$\mathbf{u}(k) = \begin{bmatrix} 1 \\ 1 \end{bmatrix} u_s(k)$$

Thus, the effective single-input plant becomes

$$\mathbf{x}(k + 1) = \begin{bmatrix} 1 & 0 & 0 \\ 0 & 0.9048 & 0 \\ 0 & 0 & 0.8187 \end{bmatrix}\mathbf{x}(k) + \begin{bmatrix} 0.1000 \\ 0.1904 \\ 0.1813 \end{bmatrix} u_s(k)$$

Matching coefficients with $p_d(z)$ above and

$$p(z) = \det [zI - (A + B_s F_s)]$$

(See Example 7-11 for details), we determine

$$\mathbf{u}(k) = F\hat{\mathbf{x}}(k) + Gr(k)$$

where

$$F = \begin{bmatrix} -53.34 & 25.62 & -4.79 \\ -53.34 & 25.62 & -4.79 \end{bmatrix}, \quad G = \begin{bmatrix} a & b \\ c & d \end{bmatrix}$$

To summarize, our key equations are of the form

$$\left.\begin{array}{l} \mathbf{x}(k + 1) = A\mathbf{x}(k) + B\mathbf{u}(k) \\ \mathbf{y}(k) = C\mathbf{x}(k) \end{array}\right\} \text{ Plant}$$

$$\left.\begin{array}{l} w(k + 1) = Dw(k) + E\mathbf{u}(k) + L\mathbf{y}(k) \\ \hat{\mathbf{x}}(k) = Hw(k) + J\mathbf{y}(k) \end{array}\right\} \text{ Estimator}$$

$$\mathbf{u}(k) = F\hat{\mathbf{x}}(k) + Gr(k) \quad \text{Feedback Law}$$

Using the composite state of $\mathbf{x}$ and $w$ and eliminating intermediate variables $\mathbf{u}$ and $\hat{\mathbf{x}}$, we have (after some algebraic manipulation)

$$\begin{bmatrix} \mathbf{x}(k+1) \\ w(k+1) \end{bmatrix} = \begin{bmatrix} A + BFJC & BFH \\ EFJC + LC & D + EFH \end{bmatrix} \begin{bmatrix} \mathbf{x}(k) \\ w(k) \end{bmatrix} + \begin{bmatrix} BG \\ EG \end{bmatrix} \mathbf{r}(k)$$

$$\mathbf{y}(k) = [C \quad 0] \begin{bmatrix} \mathbf{x}(k) \\ w(k) \end{bmatrix}$$

Substituting in our previous numerical results, we can write

$$\begin{bmatrix} \mathbf{x}(k+1) \\ w(k+1) \end{bmatrix} = \begin{bmatrix} -21.64 & 19.87 & -2.77 & 2.29 \\ -43.12 & 38.74 & -5.28 & 4.37 \\ -41.06 & 36.03 & -4.21 & 4.16 \\ 120.27 & -105.66 & 14.61 & -11.39 \end{bmatrix} \begin{bmatrix} \mathbf{x}(k) \\ w(k) \end{bmatrix}$$

$$+ \begin{bmatrix} 0.1a & 0.1b \\ 0.0952(a+c) & 0.0952(b+d) \\ 0.1813c & 0.1813d \\ 0.0362a - 0.5374c & 0.0362b - 0.5374d \end{bmatrix} \mathbf{r}(k)$$

$$y(k) = \begin{bmatrix} 1 & -1 & 0 & 0 \\ 1 & 0 & 1 & 0 \end{bmatrix} \begin{bmatrix} \mathbf{x}(k) \\ w(k) \end{bmatrix}$$

where the parameters $a$, $b$, $c$, and $d$ are the entries in the $G$ matrix which has not been determined. We will show that the $G$ matrix can be used to specify the steady state behavior of the two-output variables. ∎

Since the matrix gain $G$ in the above example acts on the input signals first, we can think of the closed-loop transfer matrix as the product

$$T(z)G = \begin{bmatrix} T_1(z) & T_2(z) \\ T_3(z) & T_4(z) \end{bmatrix} \begin{bmatrix} a & b \\ c & d \end{bmatrix} = \begin{bmatrix} aT_1 + cT_2, & bT_1 + dT_2 \\ aT_3 + cT_4, & bT_3 + dT_4 \end{bmatrix} \quad (8\text{-}62)$$

where the first factor $T(z)$ is the transfer matrix between $\mathbf{r}$ and $\mathbf{y}$ with $G = I$, an identity matrix.

We are assuming that $G$ is a constant matrix, so that if the steady state (dc) values of $T$ can be obtained, namely, $T(1)$, then we can, for example, set

$$T(1)G = \begin{bmatrix} 1 & p \\ q & 1 \end{bmatrix} \quad (8\text{-}63)$$

If Eq. (8-63) can be satisfied with $p = q = 0$ for some $G$ matrix, the system would be "statically decoupled" in that the first input $r_1$ would influence only the first output $y_1$ and $r_2$ would affect only $y_2$. Also, both decoupled parts would behave individually as a Type 1 system. Writing Eq. (8-63) out as if to solve for the vector of $G$ components $[a \quad b \quad c \quad d]^T$,

$$\begin{bmatrix} T_1 & 0 & T_2 & 0 \\ T_3 & 0 & T_4 & 0 \\ 0 & T_1 & 0 & T_2 \\ 0 & T_3 & 0 & T_4 \end{bmatrix} \begin{bmatrix} a \\ b \\ c \\ d \end{bmatrix} = \begin{bmatrix} 1 \\ q \\ p \\ 1 \end{bmatrix} \quad (8\text{-}64)$$

where the $T_i$ elements are evaluated at $z = 1$ for $i = 1, 2, 3, 4$. As we know, several possibilities exist concerning solution(s) of Eq. (8-64). For one, if the coefficient matrix is nonsingular, then there is a unique solution for $G$ to satisfy Eq. (8-63). However, how does one determine the elements of the coefficient matrix in Eq. (8-64)?

In answer to this question the analytic calculation of $T(z)$ would be too tedious. An alternative method is to initially set $G = I(a = d = 1, b = c = 0)$ and by simulation run both outputs to steady state for each of the two cases ($r_1 = 1, r_2 = 0$) and $r_1 = 0, r_2 = 1$). In the first case $y_1 = T_1$ and $y_2 = T_3$, and in the second case $y_1 = T_2$ and $y_2 = T_4$ (where these outputs are the steady state values obtained).

From the fourth-order composite system above we can write (since **y** does not depend on $w$) that

$$\mathbf{y}_{\text{steady state}} = C(I - A - BFJC)^{-1}B\mathbf{r}_{\text{steady state}} \qquad (8\text{-}65)$$

Using the two conditions stated above and Eq. (8-65), we find that

$$T(1) = \begin{bmatrix} 0.22 & -0.22 \\ -1.59 & 1.59 \end{bmatrix}$$

However, Eq. (8-64) does not have a solution if $p = q = 0$; and the only solution requires that

$$p = -0.14, \quad q = -7.23$$

Thus, the system cannot be statically decoupled by the $G$ matrix, but the transfer functions from $r_1$ to $y_1$ and from $r_2$ to $y_2$ can be made to behave in a Type 1 manner.

## 8-7.3 Ackermann's Formula

In Section 7-6 we discussed the design of state feedback for closed-loop pole placement. This method involved a transformation to controllable canonical form. As we will see below, there is a formula for feedback gain that is, perhaps, more suitable for computer-aided design. From the open-loop system description,

$$\mathbf{x}(k + 1) = A\mathbf{x}(k) + Bu(k) \qquad (8\text{-}66)$$
$$y(k) = C\mathbf{x}(k)$$

which is assumed to be controllable, but not in controllable form, we know from Eq. (7-35) that there exists a transformation

$$P_c = \mathscr{C}\mathscr{C}_c^{-1} \qquad (8\text{-}67)$$

which, under the change of variables,

$$\mathbf{x}(k) = P_c\mathbf{x}_c(k)$$

will transform the state model of Eq. (8-66) into an equivalent state model in controllable form. Also, if we define

$$F_c = [f_1 \quad f_2 \quad \cdots \quad f_n] \tag{8-68}$$

$$\mathbf{a} = [a_1 \quad a_2 \quad \cdots \quad a_n] \tag{8-69}$$

$$\boldsymbol{\alpha} = [\alpha_1 \quad \alpha_2 \quad \cdots \quad \alpha_n] \tag{8-70}$$

where $\{a_i\}$ and $\{\alpha_i\}$ $i = 1, 2, \ldots, n$ are, respectively, the (negative of the) coefficients in the characteristic polynomial, Eq. (7-37), and the corresponding coefficients of the desired closed-loop polynomial as in Eq. (7-46), then it is clear from Eq. (7-46), that

$$F_c = \boldsymbol{\alpha} - \mathbf{a} \tag{8-71}$$

Expanding the right-hand side into its components,

$$-F_c = \mathbf{a} - \boldsymbol{\alpha} = (a_1 - \alpha_1)\mathbf{e}_1^T + (a_2 - \alpha_2)\mathbf{e}_2^T + \cdots + (a_n - \alpha_n)\mathbf{e}_n^T \tag{8-72}$$

where $\mathbf{e}_j$ is the $j$th unit vector, specifically,

$$\mathbf{e}_j = [0 \quad 0 \quad \cdots \quad 0 \quad 1 \quad 0 \quad \cdots \quad 0]^T \tag{8-73}$$

where the unit occurs in the $j$th position.

The characteristic equation for $A$ or $A_c = P_c^{-1}AP_c$ is given by

$$p_{\text{OL}}(z) = z^n - a_n z^{n-1} - \cdots - a_2 z - a_1 = 0 \tag{8-74}$$

We also know by the Cayley–Hamilton Theorem (Appendix B) that a matrix satisfies its characteristic equation. Thus, substituting $A_c$ into Eq. (8-74) in place of the parameter $z$, we can solve for $A_c^n$:

$$A_c^n = a_1 I + a_2 A_c + \cdots + a_n A_c^{n-1} \tag{8-75}$$

To complete the development of Ackermann's formula, let us establish the matrix expression

$$p_{\text{CL}}(A_c) = A_c^n - \alpha_n A_c^{n-1} - \cdots - \alpha_2 A_c - \alpha_1 I \tag{8-76}$$

Although this expression does not equal zero, we may substitute for $A_c^n$ from Eq. (8-75) and collect terms to obtain

$$P_{\text{CL}}(A_c) = (a_1 - \alpha_1)I + (a_2 - \alpha_2)A_c + \cdots + (a_n - \alpha_n)A_c^{n-1} \tag{8-77}$$

Premultiplying Eq. (8-77) by $\mathbf{e}_1^T = [1 \quad 0 \quad 0 \quad \cdots \quad 0]$,

$$\mathbf{e}_1^T P_{\text{CL}}(A_c) = (a_1 - \alpha_1)\mathbf{e}_1^T + (a_2 - \alpha_2)\mathbf{e}_2^T + \cdots + (a_n - \alpha_n)\mathbf{e}_{n-1}^T \tag{8-78}$$

The right-hand side has taken into account that for the special "companion" form of the $A_c$ matrix,

$$\mathbf{e}_1^T A_c = \mathbf{e}_2^T, \ \mathbf{e}_2^T A_c = \mathbf{e}_3^T, \ \ldots, \ \mathbf{e}_{n-1}^T A_c = \mathbf{e}_n^T \tag{8-79}$$

The reader should verify Eq. (8-79).

We can now pull some pieces together. Comparing Eqs. (8-78) and (8-72),

$$-F_c = \mathbf{e}_1^T P_{CL}(A_c) = \mathbf{e}_1^T P_{CL}(P_c^{-1}AP_c) \qquad (8\text{-}80)$$

Factoring out the $P_c$ factors,

$$-F_c = \mathbf{e}_1^T P_c^{-1} p_{CL}(A)P_c \qquad (8\text{-}81)$$

From Eq. (7-48)

$$F = F_c P_c^{-1} = -\mathbf{e}_1^T P_c^{-1} p_{CL}(A) \qquad (8\text{-}82)$$

Finally, recalling Eq. (8-67)

$$-F = (\mathbf{e}_1^T \mathscr{C}_c)\mathscr{C}^{-1} p_{CL}(A) \qquad (8\text{-}83)$$

from which we write *Ackermann's formula for SVF:*

$$-F = [0 \;\; \cdots \;\; 0 \;\; 0 \;\; 1][B \quad AB \quad \cdots \quad A^{n-1}B]^{-1} p_{CL}(A) \qquad (8\text{-}84)$$

Again, it is the special structure of $\mathscr{C}_c$ (see Example 7-6) that gives us the result that

$$\mathbf{e}_1^T \mathscr{C}_c = \mathbf{e}_n^T$$

which was used in deriving Eq. (8-84) from Eq. (8-83).

**Remarks:** From Eq. (8-84) the state-variable feedback gains can be calculated using only matrix operations from a given (controllable) system model and knowledge of the desired pole positions $\{p_i\}$ $i = 1, 2, \ldots, n$ so that the polynomial

$$p_{CL}(z) = \prod_{i=1}^{n} (z - p_i) \qquad (8\text{-}85)$$

is available. This formula eliminates the necessity to transform the system into controllable form, thereby simplifying the calculations. Program 5 in Appendix D implements Ackermann's formula.

***The Estimator Gain Formula.*** A development similar to that just presented provides us with a gain formula for the estimator (or observer) gain matrix $K$:

$$K^T = \mathbf{e}_n p_o(A)\mathbb{O}^{-1} \qquad (8\text{-}86)$$

where $p_0(z)$ is the desired characteristic polynomial for the estimator system. To illustrate the use of these formulas, we will rederive the gain matrices $F$ and $K$ of Examples 7-8 and 8-4, respectively.

## EXAMPLE 8-11 (Ackermann's Formulas)
State-variable feedback gain: From Example 7-8

$$A = \begin{bmatrix} 1 & 2 & 0 \\ 3 & -1 & 1 \\ 0 & 2 & 0 \end{bmatrix}, \quad B = \begin{bmatrix} 2 \\ 1 \\ 1 \end{bmatrix}$$

$$C = [0 \quad 0 \quad 1]$$

The controllability matrix and its inverse are

$$\mathcal{C} = \begin{bmatrix} 2 & 4 & 16 \\ 1 & 6 & 8 \\ 1 & 2 & 12 \end{bmatrix}, \quad \mathcal{C}^{-1} = \begin{bmatrix} x & x & x \\ x & x & x \\ -0.125 & 0 & 0.250 \end{bmatrix}$$

Only the evaluated elements of $\mathcal{C}^{-1}$ are required in Ackermann's formula. Using the desired characteristic polynomial from Example 7-8,

$$p_d(A) = A^3 - 1.5A^2 + A - 0.25I$$

$$p_d(A) = \begin{bmatrix} -2.75 & 20 & -3 \\ 30 & -25.75 & 11.5 \\ -9 & 23 & -5.25 \end{bmatrix}$$

Thus, according to Eq. (8-84),

$$-F = [0 \quad \cdots \quad 0 \quad 0 \quad 1]\mathcal{C}^{-1}p_d(A) = [-1.9063 \quad 3.2500 \quad -0.9375]$$

which checks the results of Example 7-8.

Estimator gain: From Example 8-4 the same system matrices $A$, $B$, and $C$ are specified as given above. Without rederiving the results of Example 8-2, the system observability matrix and its inverse are given by

$$\mathcal{O} = \begin{bmatrix} 0 & 0 & 1 \\ 0 & 2 & 0 \\ 6 & -2 & 2 \end{bmatrix}, \quad \mathcal{O}^{-1} = \frac{1}{6}\begin{bmatrix} -2 & 1 & 1 \\ 0 & 3 & 0 \\ 6 & 0 & 0 \end{bmatrix}$$

The desired characteristic polynomial for the estimator system is given in Example 8-4 as $p_0(z)$. Evaluating the matrix polynomial,

$$p_0(A) = A^3 + 0.5A^2 + 0.25A + 0.125I$$

$$p_0(A) = \begin{bmatrix} 10.875 & 18.5 & 1 \\ 27.75 & -6.625 & 8.75 \\ 3 & 17.5 & -0.875 \end{bmatrix}$$

and from Eq. (8-86),

$$K^T = [-1.875 \quad 9.250 \quad 0.500]$$

which checks the results of Example 8-4.  ∎

*Remarks:*  The compact procedure of Ackermann's formulas provide a convenient approach to the calculation of either SVF gains or estimator gains. Unfortunately, the formulas only work for single-input, single-output systems.

**8-8**

## SUMMARY

In this chapter the concept of observability was presented. This concept provides an analytic method of determining if more sensors are required, and where they are needed for proper control of a system. Similar to the development of Chapter

7 on controllability, techniques were developed by which systems can be transformed into the observable canonical form for the purpose of designing estimators, systems that through appropriate signal processing can regenerate the states of a known system. Reduced-order estimators serve the same purpose with a minimum of dynamic calculations; this might be important, for instance, if the control is implemented on a small (slow) computer.

Certain aspects of Chapters 7 and 8 were tied together. The separation principle is an important development that shows that the SVF design and the estimator system can be linked to provide state feedback from the available system measurements. The concept of duality, although only a mathematical system relationship, nevertheless yields a useful computation tool, that of using a SVF algorithm to design estimator gains (or the other way around). Examples illustrating the complete output feedback as well as the individual calculations were presented in Section 8-7.

In the next chapter we will investigate the methods of designing SVF and estimators "optimally." The pole location information needed for calculating the SVF matrix, for example, will be implicitly available through a functional "performance index." The burden of the design, instead of specifying pole positions, is to provide the correct weighting matrices in the performance index.

## REFERENCES

**Section 8-1**  *Digital Control Systems;* B. C. Kuo; Holt, Rinehart and Winston, 1980.
**Section 8-2**  *Introduction to Linear System Theory;* C. T. Chen; Holt, Rinehart and Winston, 1970.

**Sections 8-3**
**to 8-7**  *Introduction to Dynamic Systems;* D. G. Luenberger; John Wiley and Sons, 1979.
*Linear Systems;* T. Kailath; Prentice-Hall, 1980.
*Modern Control Theory;* W. L. Brogan; Prentice-Hall (Quantum), 1974.
*Digital Control Systems;* B. C. Kuo; Holt, Rinehart and Winston, 1980.
*Digital Control System Analysis and Design;* C. L. Phillips and H. T. Nagle, Jr.; Prentice-Hall, 1984.
*Linear Optimal Control Systems;* H. Kwakernaak and R. Sivan; Wiley-Interscience, 1972.

## PROBLEMS

**8-1**    (a) Diagram the system

$$\mathbf{x}(k + 1) = \begin{bmatrix} 1 & 0 & 0 \\ 0 & 2 & 0 \\ 0 & 0 & 3 \end{bmatrix} \mathbf{x}(k) + \begin{bmatrix} 1 \\ 0 \\ 1 \end{bmatrix} u(k)$$

$$y(k) = [0 \quad 1 \quad 1] \, \mathbf{x}(k)$$

(b) Which states are controllable and which are observable?
(c) Calculate the pulse-transfer function $Y(z)/U(z)$. Explain your result.

**8-2** Determine if the following systems are observable.

**(a)** $\mathbf{x}(k + 1) = \begin{bmatrix} -1 & 1 \\ 0 & 2 \end{bmatrix} \mathbf{x}(k) + \begin{bmatrix} 0 \\ 1 \end{bmatrix} u(k)$

$y(k) = \begin{bmatrix} 1 & 0 \end{bmatrix} \mathbf{x}(k)$

**(b)** $\mathbf{x}(k + 1) = \begin{bmatrix} 1 & 0 & 1 \\ 0 & 2 & -1 \\ -1 & 1 & 0 \end{bmatrix} \mathbf{x}(k) + \begin{bmatrix} 1 \\ 1 \\ 0 \end{bmatrix} u(k)$

$y(k) = \begin{bmatrix} 1 & 1 & 0 \\ 1 & 0 & -1 \end{bmatrix} \mathbf{x}(k)$

**8-3** For the system described in Problem 8-2b, determine if the system is observable from each individual output.

**8-4** For the system described in Fig. P8-4:
**(a)** Calculate the transfer function $Y(z)/U(z)$.
**(b)** Write also a state model for the system.
**(c)** For what values of the parameter $\alpha$ does the system become unobservable? How does this show up in the transfer function description?

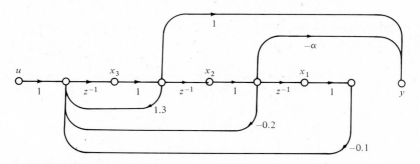

**FIGURE P8-4.**

**8-5** Write the observable form state model for the following systems.

**(a)** $\mathbf{x}(k + 1) = \begin{bmatrix} 0 & 1 & 0 \\ 0 & 0 & 1 \\ 1 & 2 & 3 \end{bmatrix} \mathbf{x}(k) + \begin{bmatrix} 0 \\ 0 \\ 1 \end{bmatrix} u(k)$

$y(k) = \begin{bmatrix} 2 & 1 & 1 \end{bmatrix} \mathbf{x}(k) + \begin{bmatrix} 2 \end{bmatrix} u(k)$

**(b)** $\mathbf{x}(k + 1) = \begin{bmatrix} 1 & 0 & -1 \\ 0 & 2 & 1 \\ 1 & -1 & 0 \end{bmatrix} \mathbf{x}(k) + \begin{bmatrix} 1 & 1 \\ 1 & 0 \\ 0 & -1 \end{bmatrix} \mathbf{u}(k)$

$y(k) = \begin{bmatrix} 1 & 1 & 0 \end{bmatrix} \mathbf{x}(k)$

**8-6** If the following system is observable, design a full-order estimator system with poles at $z = 0.1, 0.2, 0.3$.

$$\mathbf{x}(k + 1) = \begin{bmatrix} 0 & 1 & 0 \\ -1 & 1 & 0 \\ 2 & 1 & -3 \end{bmatrix} \mathbf{x}(k) + \begin{bmatrix} 1 \\ 0 \\ 0 \end{bmatrix} u(k)$$

$$y(k) = [\ 0 \quad 0 \quad 1]\ \mathbf{x}(k)$$

8-7   For the sampled and clamped continuous-time system shown in Fig. P8-7:
(a) Calculate a ZOH equivalent discrete-time system for arbitrary $T$.
(b) Is the system observable for all $T$?

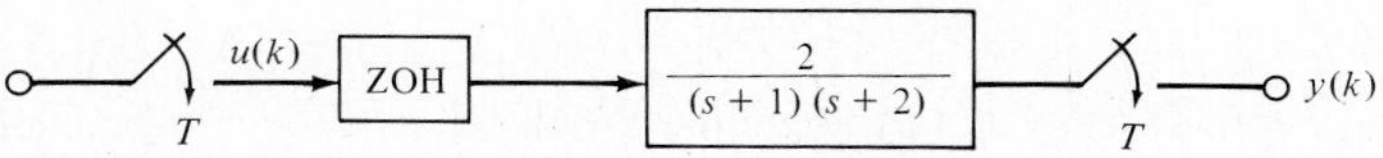

**FIGURE P8-7.**

8-8   A continuous-time plant is given by

$$\mathbf{x}(t) = \begin{bmatrix} 0 & 1 \\ -1 & 0 \end{bmatrix} \mathbf{x}(t) + \begin{bmatrix} 0 \\ 1 \end{bmatrix} u(t)$$

$$y(t) = [\ 1 \quad 1]\ \mathbf{x}(t)$$

(a) Determine the ZOH equivalent discrete-time model for arbitrary sample period $T$.
(b) Investigate the observability of both the original continuous-time system and the resulting discrete-time model. Specify any values of $T$ that make the latter unobservable.

8-9   Given the system

$$\mathbf{x}(k + 1) = A\mathbf{x}(k) + B\mathbf{u}(k)$$

$$\mathbf{y}(k) = C\mathbf{x}(k)$$

and its estimator system

$$\hat{\mathbf{x}}(k + 1) = (A - KC)\hat{\mathbf{x}}(k) + B\mathbf{u}(k) + K\mathbf{y}(k)$$

Assume the original system is observable and investigate the controllability and observability of the closed-loop system consisting of the original system, estimator, and feedback

$$\mathbf{u}(k) = F\hat{\mathbf{x}}(k) + \mathbf{r}(k)$$

*Hint:* Form the composite system with state

$$\begin{bmatrix} \mathbf{x}(k) \\ \hat{\mathbf{x}}(k) \end{bmatrix}$$

8-10   For the estimator designed in Example 8-4 suppose $u(k) = 0$ and $\mathbf{x}(0) = [1 \quad 0 \quad 0]^T$. Calculate both $\mathbf{x}(k)$ and $\hat{\mathbf{x}}(k)$ for $k = 1, 2, 3, 4$ if $\hat{\mathbf{x}}(0) = \mathbf{0}$.

**8-11**    As suggested in Example 8-4, translate the resulting design back to the original **x** formulation so that the estimator is given by

$$\hat{\mathbf{x}}(k + 1) = A\hat{\mathbf{x}}(k) + Bu(k) + K[y(k) - C\hat{\mathbf{x}}(k)]$$

where $A$, $B$, and $C$ are the matrices of the original system.

**8-12**    Repeat the exercise of Problem 8-10 using the estimator of Problem 8-11.

**8-13**    Design a reduced-order estimator for the following systems. In each case use a pole value of 0.2.

(a) $\mathbf{x}(k + 1) = \begin{bmatrix} 1 & 1 \\ 0 & 1 \end{bmatrix} \mathbf{x}(k) + \begin{bmatrix} 0 \\ 1 \end{bmatrix} u(k)$

$y(k) = [1 \quad 0] \, \mathbf{x}(k)$

(b) $\mathbf{x}(k + 1) = \begin{bmatrix} 0 & 1 \\ 0 & 1 \end{bmatrix} \mathbf{x}(k) + \begin{bmatrix} 0 \\ 1 \end{bmatrix} u(k)$

$y(k) = [-2 \quad 3] \, \mathbf{x}(k) + [1] \, u(k)$

**8-14**    (a) Construct a reduced-order estimator for a system with the transfer function

$$\frac{Y(z)}{U(z)} = \frac{z^3 + 3z + 4}{z^3 + 3z^2 + 2z + 1}$$

In order to make the estimator respond as fast as possible, place the poles at the origin. This is called a "deadbeat" estimator.

(b) For your design take $\mathbf{x}(0) = [1 \quad 1 \quad 1]^T$, the initial states of the estimator equal to zero and calculate the error sequence $\mathbf{e}(k) = \mathbf{x}(k) - \hat{\mathbf{x}}(k)$ for at least three steps.

**8-15**    (a) For the system of Problem 8-13a design a state feedback matrix $F$ so that $(A + BF)$ will have a double pole at $z = 0.5$.

(b) With the design results of Problem 8-13a, simulate the closed-loop zero-input response using $\mathbf{x}(0) = [1 \quad 0]^T$ and zero initial estimator state.

**8-16**    Repeat the exercises of Problem 8-15 for the system of Problem 8-13b.

**8-17**    Use the concept of duality and Ackermann's formula to determine the estimator gain matrix for the design requested in Problem 8-6.

**8-18**    (a) Repeat the exercise of Problem 8-17 to obtain a full-order estimator design for the system described in Problem 8-14.

(b) Write the two-input/three-output transfer matrix for the estimator.

**8-19**    (a) Repeat the exercise of Problem 8-13a with an estimator pole at zero.

(b) Design a feedback matrix to obtain closed-loop poles at zero.

(c) Simulate the (zero-input) closed-loop system with $\mathbf{x}(0) = [1 \quad 1]^T$ and a zero initial estimator state.

**8-20** Repeat the steps outlined in Problem 8-19, but using the system described in Problem 8-13b.

**8-21** For the system

$$\mathbf{x}(k + 1) = \begin{bmatrix} 0 & 0 & 0 \\ 0 & -1 & 0 \\ 0 & 0 & 1 \end{bmatrix} \mathbf{x}(k) + \begin{bmatrix} 1 & 0 \\ 1 & 1 \\ 0 & 2 \end{bmatrix} \mathbf{u}(k)$$

$$\mathbf{y}(k) = \begin{bmatrix} 1 & -1 & 0 \\ 1 & 0 & 1 \end{bmatrix} \mathbf{x}(k)$$

use the concept of duality and any appropriate method from Chapter 7 to design the estimator gain matrix for a full-order estimator having all its poles at the origin, (deadbeat estimator).

**8-22** Given the system $S_1$ and its estimator system $S_2$ as shown in Fig. P8-22:

$$S_1 \quad \begin{aligned} \mathbf{x}(k + 1) &= A\mathbf{x}(k) + B\mathbf{u}(k) \\ \mathbf{y}(k) &= C\mathbf{x}(k) \end{aligned}$$

$$S_2 \quad \hat{\mathbf{x}}(k + 1) = (A - KC)\hat{\mathbf{x}}(k) + B\mathbf{u}(k) + KC\mathbf{x}(k)$$

Show that the composite system with state $\begin{bmatrix} \mathbf{x} \\ \hat{\mathbf{x}} \end{bmatrix}$ is uncontrollable even if $S_1$ is

controllable.

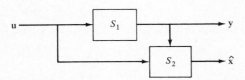

**FIGURE P8-22.**

**8-23** The *condition number* of a square nonsingular matrix $M$ is defined as

$$k(M) = |\lambda_{max}/\lambda_{min}|$$

where $\lambda_{max}(\lambda_{min})$ is the largest (smallest) magnitude eigenvalue of $M$. As a measure of *near unobservability* calculate the condition number of the observability matrix of the system given in Problem 8-13a for several positive values of the parameter $a$ when the output is taken to be

$$y(k) = [a \quad 1] \mathbf{x}(k)$$

Discuss what happens as $a \to 0$.

## CHAPTER 9

# Introduction to Optimal Control

Over the past several chapters we have seen different approaches to the design of feedback controllers; for instance, the root-locus technique to match an established ideal model transfer function and estimator-based state-variable feedback. In either case some information is required, an ideal transfer function in the first case and desired closed-loop pole locations in the second case. Other controller designs such as PID or deadbeat control rely on a fixed structure with emphasis on adjusting the parameters to achieve acceptable system behavior to certain types of inputs. In contrast, optimal control represents a distinct approach that requires the establishment of a "performance measuring function" at the outset of the problem. As we will see, a well-defined procedure then arrives at the required (state) feedback gains that are "optimal" in the sense that they are best for that particular performance indicator.

## 9-1

## QUADRATIC COST FUNCTIONALS

The basis for an optimal control system is the "cost functional" or the *performance index;* all responses are compared through this single criterion. A general performance index, $J$, will be written in the form

$$J = \sum_{k=0}^{N-1} g[\mathbf{x}(k), \mathbf{u}(k)] + h[\mathbf{x}(N)] \tag{9-1}$$

where the integrand $g$ is a non-negative scalar-valued function of the instantaneous states and inputs. For present purposes we will specify that

$$g(\mathbf{x}, \mathbf{u}) = \frac{1}{2}(\mathbf{x}^T Q \mathbf{x} + \mathbf{u}^T R \mathbf{u}) \tag{9-2}$$

where $Q$ and $R$ are constant (symmetric), positive semidefinite and positive definite matrices, respectively. Similarly, we will consider that

$$h(\mathbf{x}) = \frac{1}{2}\mathbf{x}^T H \mathbf{x} \tag{9-3}$$

where $H$ is positive semidefinite.

The simplest optimal control problem can be stated as follows.

**The Linear, Quadratic Regulator (LQR) Problem:** Given the plant model

$$\mathbf{x}(k + 1) = A\mathbf{x}(k) + B\mathbf{u}(k) \tag{9-4}$$

$$\mathbf{y}(k) = C\mathbf{x}(k) \tag{9-5}$$

and performance index

$$J = \frac{1}{2}\sum_{k=0}^{N-1} [\mathbf{x}^T(k)Q\mathbf{x}(k) + \mathbf{u}^T(k)R\mathbf{u}(k)] + \frac{1}{2}\mathbf{x}^T(N)H\mathbf{x}(N) \tag{9-6}$$

The above LQR problem is an $N$-stage problem. For many practical control problems $N \to \infty$. For a "finite time" problem $h$ is referred to as the *terminal cost* and the remaining part of $J$ is the *running cost*.

**Remarks:** Before deriving the solution to the LQR problem, let us consider the performance index more closely. As designers, we must specify $Q$, $R$, and $H$. Once they are established we will be able to calculate a feedback control law

$$\mathbf{u}(k) = F(k)\mathbf{x}(k) \tag{9-7}$$

that provides the optimal input as state feedback. Since this method is new to us, it will require some experience to know how to modify $Q$, $R$, and $H$ if we are not satisfied with the first design. For now, let us simply recognize that minimizing $J$ requires a compromise between driving $\mathbf{x}$ to zero rapidly (the $Q$ term) and keeping the input amplitudes low (the $R$ term). This tells us generally that with $Q$ large relative to $R$, nonzero $\mathbf{x}$ values are penalized more than $\mathbf{u}$ values so that the system response will be fast (with large actuation levels). Similarly, with $R$ large relative to $Q$ the system will tend to be sluggish, but the input amplitudes will be small.

## OPTIMAL REGULATION

In this section we will derive a solution to the LQR problem stated in the previous section. To accomplish this, we work backwards in a step-by-step fashion.

Starting with the terminal cost $J_{N,N}$, we define the matrix $D(N - 1)$ as the matrix $H$. Thus,

$$J_{N,N} = \frac{1}{2}\mathbf{x}^T(N)H\mathbf{x}(N) = \frac{1}{2}\mathbf{x}^T(N)D(N - 1)\mathbf{x}(N) \qquad (9\text{-}8)$$

where the double subscript notation on $J$ will serve to indicate the cost from a given stage to the terminal stage.

***Minimizing the Cost Over the Final Interval.*** The cost over the final interval can be written from Eq. (9-6) as

$$J_{N-1,N} = \frac{1}{2}\mathbf{x}^T(N - 1)Q\mathbf{x}(N - 1) + \frac{1}{2}\mathbf{u}^T(N - 1)R\mathbf{u}(N - 1)$$

$$+ \frac{1}{2}\mathbf{x}^T(N)D(N - 1)\mathbf{x}(N)$$

Substituting for $\mathbf{x}(N) = A\mathbf{x}(N - 1) + B\mathbf{u}(N - 1)$,

$$J_{N-1,N}(\mathbf{x},\ \mathbf{u}) = \frac{1}{2}\mathbf{x}^T Q\mathbf{x} + \frac{1}{2}\mathbf{u}^T R\mathbf{u} + \frac{1}{2}(A\mathbf{x} + B\mathbf{u})^T D(A\mathbf{x} + B\mathbf{u}) \quad (9\text{-}9)$$

where each nonconstant function has the argument $(N - 1)$, which was omitted for simplicity of notation. Rearranging the terms, we obtain

$$J_{N-1,N}(\mathbf{x},\ \mathbf{u}) = \frac{1}{2}[\mathbf{x}^T(Q + A^T DA)\mathbf{x} + \mathbf{x}^T(A^T DB)\mathbf{u}$$
$$+ \mathbf{u}^T(B^T DA)\mathbf{x} + \mathbf{u}^T(R + B^T DB)\mathbf{u}] \qquad (9\text{-}10)$$

We will denote $J$ with a single argument $\mathbf{x}$ as the *optimal* cost

$$J_{N-1,N}(\mathbf{x}) = \min_{\mathbf{u}} J_{N-1,N}(\mathbf{x},\ \mathbf{u}) \qquad (9\text{-}11)$$

where $\mathbf{x}$ is considered to be fixed for the minimization. For the actual minimization (since $\mathbf{u}$ is unconstrained) we will set

$$\frac{\partial}{\partial \mathbf{u}} J_{N-1,N}(\mathbf{x},\ \mathbf{u}) \overset{\text{set}}{=} 0 \qquad (9\text{-}12)$$

To review the process of taking a derivative of a scalar function with respect to a vector argument, the readers are referred to Appendix B. Differentiating Eq. (9-10) with respect to $\mathbf{u}$, we obtain

$$(B^T DA)\mathbf{x} + (R + B^T DB)\mathbf{u} = 0 \qquad (9\text{-}13)$$

Solving for **u**,

$$\mathbf{u}(N - 1) = F(N - 1)\mathbf{x}(N - 1) \qquad (9\text{-}14)$$

where

$$F(N - 1) = -[R + B^T D(N - 1)B]^{-1}[B^T D(N - 1)A]$$

is the feedback gain.

*Remarks:*
- The inverse in the calculation of $F$ exists because $R$ is required to be nonsingular (positive definite).
- The optimal input **u** in Eq. (9-14) minimizes $J_{N-1,N}$ because the second derivative of $J_{N-1,N}$ with respect to **u** is a positive definite (Hessian) matrix.
- This minimum is a global minimum because $J$ is a convex function (quadratic in **u**).

Introducing $\mathbf{u}(N - 1)$ of Eq. (9-14) back into Eq. (9-10) and simplifying the expression gives us

$$J_{N-1,N}[\mathbf{x}(N - 1)] = \frac{1}{2}\mathbf{x}^T(N - 1)D(N - 2)\mathbf{x}(N - 1) \qquad (9\text{-}15)$$

where

$$D(N - 2) = (A + BF)^T D(A + BF) + F^T RF + Q \qquad (9\text{-}16)$$

with all matrices on the right-hand side evaluated at $(N - 1)$.

**Summary of Single Stage Minimization.**   The minimum cost over the final interval is given by Eq. (9-15) with $D(N - 2)$ described in Eq. (9-16). $F(N - 1)$, in turn, is expressed in Eq. (9-14) with $D(N - 1) = H$. Thus, given $H$, $Q$, $R$, $A$, and $B$, we can calculate $F(N - 1)$, the feedback gain and $J_{N-1,N}[\mathbf{x}(N - 1)]$, the optimal (minimum) cost.

**Minimizing the Cost Over the Final Two Intervals.**   We are now in a position to extend the development to an arbitrary number of intervals as we shall see by considering a two-stage problem. The logic of minimizing a sequential process allows us to state that the minimum over two steps is the sum of the minima over the two individual steps, or, in other words, any portion of an optimal trajectory is also optimal. This idea is referred to as the *Principle of Optimality*.

In our case we can write that

$$J_{N-2,N}(\mathbf{x}, \mathbf{u}) = \frac{1}{2}\mathbf{x}^T Q\mathbf{x} + \frac{1}{2}\mathbf{u}^T R\mathbf{u} + J_{N-1,N}[\mathbf{x}(N - 1)] \qquad (9\text{-}17)$$

where **x** and **u** denote $\mathbf{x}(N - 2)$ and $\mathbf{u}(N - 2)$, respectively. Equation (9-17) is merely a statement that the cost over the final two steps is the explicit running cost over the next-to-last stage from Eq. (9-6) plus the optimal (minimal) cost over the last interval.

Substituting for $J_{N-1,N}$ from Eq. (9-15) into Eq. (9-17), we have

$$J_{N-2,N}(\mathbf{x}, \mathbf{u}) = \frac{1}{2}[\mathbf{x}^T Q\mathbf{x} + \mathbf{u}^T R\mathbf{u} + (A\mathbf{x} + B\mathbf{u})^T D(A\mathbf{x} + B\mathbf{u})] \quad (9\text{-}18)$$

where all variables now have the time argument $(N - 2)$. However, this is the same form as previously used in Eq. (9-9) for the single-stage minimization problem. Consequently, the solution will be of the same form with the arguments appropriately updated. In particular, the optimal input at time-step $(N - 2)$ is given by the state-variable feedback expression [see Eq. (9-14)]

$$\mathbf{u}(N - 2) = F(N - 2)\mathbf{x}(N - 2) \quad (9\text{-}19)$$

where

$$F(N - 2) = -[R + B^T D(N - 2)B]^{-1}[B^T D(N - 2)A] \quad (9\text{-}20)$$

Furthermore, we have in a similar fashion to Eqs. (9-15) and (9-16) the link to the "next stage":

$$J_{N-2,N}[\mathbf{x}(N - 2)] = \frac{1}{2}\mathbf{x}^T(N - 2)D(N - 3)\mathbf{x}(N - 2) \quad (9\text{-}21)$$

which implicitly defines $D(N - 3)$ as

$$D(N - 3) = (A + BF)^T D(A + BF) + F^T RF + Q \quad (9\text{-}22)$$

in terms of $D$ and $F$ values at $k = N - 2$. Recognizing that the solution at each stage will be of the same form, we can state the general recursive solution.

**9-3**

## SOLUTION BY DYNAMIC PROGRAMMING

The procedure of the previous section is an application of the method of dynamic programming. Our final solution is adaptable to the following recursive computation of the optimal feedback control law.

### 9-3.1 Minimization Over $N$ Stages

At any stage $K$ for $K < N$

$$\mathbf{u}(N - K) = F(N - K)\mathbf{x}(N - K) \quad (9\text{-}23)$$

where

$$F(N - K) = -[R + B^T D(N - K)B]^{-1}[B^T D(N - K)A] \quad (9\text{-}24)$$

The optimal (minimal) cost over the final $K$ stages is given by

$$J_{N-K,N}[\mathbf{x}(N - K)] = \frac{1}{2}\mathbf{x}^T(N - K)D(N - K - 1)\mathbf{x}(N - K) \quad (9\text{-}25)$$

where

$$D(N - K - 1) = (A + BF)^T D(A + BF) + F^T RF + Q \quad (9\text{-}26)$$

with the right-hand side variables taken at $(N - K)$.

***Computation of D and F.*** The development of optimal gains $F$ is accomplished in a backwards-in-time calculation that also requires the intermediate variable $D$ as follows (see Fig. 9-5):

1. $D(N - 1) = H$ (a given matrix).
2. $F(N - 1)$, from Eq. (9-24), $K = 1$.
3. $D(N - 2)$, from Eq. (9-26), $K = 1$.
4. $F(N - 2)$, from Eq. (9-24), $K = 2$.

This procedure continues between Eq. (9-26) and Eq. (9-24) until

$(2N)$.  $\quad D(N - N) = D(0)$

$(2N + 1)$.  $\quad F(N - N) = F(0)$

$(2N + 2)$.  $\quad D(-1)$, (Final step)

From these calculations the optimal input sequence is

$$\mathbf{u}(N - K) = F(N - K)\mathbf{x}(N - K) \quad (9\text{-}27)$$

for $K = 1, 2, \ldots, N$.
The *minimal cost* over the $N$-stage process is

$$J_{0,N}[\mathbf{x}(0)] = \frac{1}{2}\mathbf{x}^T(0)D(-1)\mathbf{x}(0) \quad (9\text{-}28)$$

Program 6 in Appendix D implements the above computations.

## 9-3.2 Alternate Expressions in Terms of the Forward Time Index

Often it is more convenient to refer to the optimality equations in terms of the forward time index $k = N - K$. For this purpose we rewrite the equations as

$$\mathbf{u}(k) = F(k)\mathbf{x}(k) \quad (9\text{-}29)$$

$$F(k) = -[R + B^T P(k + 1)B]^{-1}[B^T P(k + 1)A] \quad (9\text{-}30)$$

where $P(k + 1) = D(k)$, and

$$P(k) = [A + BF(k)]^T P(k + 1)[A + BF(k)] \\ + F^T(k)RF(k) + Q, \quad P(N) = H \quad (9\text{-}31)$$

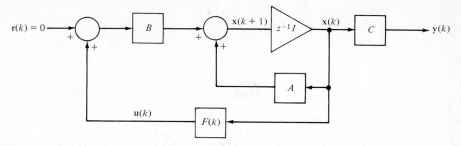

**FIGURE 9-1. Structure of the optimal feedback regulator.**

Equations (9-29) to (9-31) are alternate versions of Eqs. (9-23), (9-24), and (9-26).

The total (minimal) cost, which measures the optimal performance, is given by [alternate for Eq. (9-28)]

$$J_{0,N}[\mathbf{x}(0)] = \frac{1}{2}\mathbf{x}^T(0)P(0)\mathbf{x}(0) \tag{9-32}$$

A simpler, but equivalent, expression for $P(k)$ is

$$P(k) = Q + A^T P(k + 1)[A + BF(k)], \quad P(N) = H \tag{9-33}$$

Figure 9-1 shows the optimal closed-loop regulator with the precomputed gains $F(k)$. An example will help to explain the computations.

### EXAMPLE 9-1 (Linear-Quadratic Regulator, LQR)
For the plant

$$x(k + 1) = x(k) + 2u(k), \quad x(0) = 10$$

with performance index

$$J = \frac{1}{2} \sum_{k=0}^{10} [4x^2(k) + u^2(k)]$$

we wish to determine the input sequence that will drive any nonzero initial state to the origin (regulation) in such a way as to minimize $J$.

**SOLUTION:** Following the computational steps listed previously,

| | |
|---|---|
| $D(10) = 0$ | $F(10) = 0$ |
| $D(9) = 4$ | $F(9) = -2D/(1 + 4D) = -0.4706$ |
| $D(8) = 4.2353$ | $F(8) = -0.4721$ |
| $D(k) = 4.2361$ | $F(k) = -0.4721$ |
| $k = 7, 6, \ldots, -1$ | $k = 7, 6, \ldots, 0$ |

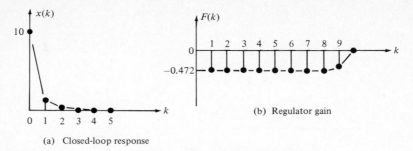

(a)  Closed-loop response

(b)  Regulator gain

**FIGURE 9-2.  Regulator gain and response for Example 9.1.**

These calculations show that a steady condition is reached very quickly. Figure 9-2 illustrates both the time-dependent feedback gains $F(k)$ and the response of the closed-loop system to an initial state $x(0) = 10$ (See the calculation below). Note that these plots are on the same time axis and that over the first six or seven time intervals $F(k)$ is essentially constant at a value of $-0.472$. Consequently, the time variation of $F$ is not used because the system state settles to zero long before $F$ begins to vary. ∎

To calculate the state trajectory, we return to the plant description in the example above and write that

$$x(k + 1) = x(k) + 2[-0.472x(k)]$$

$$x(k + 1) = 0.056x(k), \quad x(0) = 10$$

Thus,

$$x(k) = (0.056)^k 10$$

which is plotted in Fig. 9-2a.

The results seen in the previous problem are indicative of a general constant-parameter problem.

- If the plant is linear and the performance index is quadratic, then the optimal control results in a linear state feedback law. The feedback matrix will be generally time varying, but may be taken as constant if the control interval is large.

- In particular, if $A$, $B$, $R$, and $Q$ are constant matrices, $H = 0$; the pair $(A, B)$ is controllable and $N$ is large; then as $k$ becomes large, $F(N - k)$ approaches a constant matrix $F$. In this situation the closed-loop poles are implicitly specified by $R$ and $Q$. For instance, the closed-loop pole for the previous example was $z = 0.056$.

Let us consider further the case of steady state feedback gains. With the assumptions of controllability and constant matrices mentioned above, the constant gains become optimal for all time when the control interval $N$ becomes infinite; this is called an *infinite (control) horizon* problem.

INTRODUCTION TO OPTIMAL CONTROL

## 9-3.3 An Equivalent Two-Point Boundary-Value Problem

To evaluate the steady state feedback gains in more detail, we will first establish the following two equations:

$$\mathbf{x}(k + 1) = A\mathbf{x}(k) - BR^{-1}B^T\mathbf{p}(k) \qquad (9\text{-}34)$$

$$\mathbf{p}(k) = Q\mathbf{x}(k + 1) + A^T\mathbf{p}(k + 1) \qquad (9\text{-}35)$$

which represent the LQR problem as a simultaneous set of difference equations with "boundary values" at $\mathbf{x}(0)$ and $\mathbf{p}(N)$.

First, we define the vector $\mathbf{p}(k)$ as

$$\mathbf{p}(k) = P(k + 1)\mathbf{x}(k + 1) \qquad (9\text{-}36)$$

Utilizing Eq. (9-33) (advanced one step),

$$\mathbf{p}(k) = Q\mathbf{x}(k + 1) + A^TP(k + 2)[A + BF(k + 1)]\mathbf{x}(k + 1) \qquad (9\text{-}37)$$

Recognizing the last two factors of Eq. (9-37) as $\mathbf{x}(k + 2)$ and using Eq. (9-36), we arrive at

$$\mathbf{p}(k) = Q\mathbf{x}(k + 1) + A^T\mathbf{p}(k + 1)$$

which is Eq. (9-35)

To establish Eq. (9-34), note from Eq. (9-30) that

$$[R + B^TP(k + 1)B]F(k) = -[B^TP(k + 1)A] \qquad (9\text{-}38)$$

Next, we claim that the optimal input $\mathbf{u}(k)$ is

$$\mathbf{u}(k) = -R^{-1}B^T\mathbf{p}(k) \qquad (9\text{-}39)$$

To show this, we manipulate the right-hand side as follows:

$$R^{-1}B^T\mathbf{p}(k) = R^{-1}B^TP(k + 1)\mathbf{x}(k + 1)$$

$$R^{-1}B^T\mathbf{p}(k) = R^{-1}B^TP(k + 1)[A\mathbf{x}(k) + B\mathbf{u}(k)]$$

$$R^{-1}B^T\mathbf{p}(k) = R^{-1}B^TP(k + 1)A\mathbf{x}(k) + R^{-1}B^TP(k + 1)B\mathbf{u}(k)] \qquad (9\text{-}40)$$

In the first term on the right side of Eq. (9-40) we introduce the equivalence from Eq. (9-38) to obtain

$$R^{-1}B^T\mathbf{p}(k) = R^{-1}[-R - B^TP(k + 1)B]F(k)\mathbf{x}(k) + R^{-1}B^TP(k + 1)B\mathbf{u}(k) \qquad (9\text{-}41)$$

Since $\mathbf{u}(k) = F(k)\mathbf{x}(k)$, the right side of Eq. (9-41) reduces to $-\mathbf{u}(k)$ as claimed in Eq. (9-39).

Having validated Eqs. (9-34) and (9-35), let us take $z$-transforms:

$$z\tilde{\mathbf{x}}(z) - z\mathbf{x}(0) = A\tilde{\mathbf{x}}(z) - BR^{-1}B^T\tilde{\mathbf{p}}(z) \qquad (9\text{-}42)$$

$$\tilde{\mathbf{p}}(z) = zQ\tilde{\mathbf{x}}(z) - zQ\mathbf{x}(0) + zA^T\tilde{\mathbf{p}}(z) - zA^T\mathbf{p}(0) \qquad (9\text{-}43)$$

where $\tilde{\mathbf{x}}$ and $\tilde{\mathbf{p}}$ denote $z$-transforms of $\mathbf{x}$ and $\mathbf{p}$, respectively. Organizing Eqs. (9-42) and (9-43) into a partitioned matrix form, we find that

$$\begin{bmatrix} zI - A & BR^{-1}B^T \\ -Q & z^{-1}I - A^T \end{bmatrix} \begin{bmatrix} \tilde{\mathbf{x}}(z) \\ \tilde{\mathbf{p}}(z) \end{bmatrix} = \begin{bmatrix} z\mathbf{x}(0) \\ -Q\mathbf{x}(0) - A^T\mathbf{p}(0) \end{bmatrix} \quad (9\text{-}44)$$

A detailed study of the coefficient matrix in Eq. (9-44) reveals that its determinant is zero at points (eigenvalues) that are "circle images." That is to say, if $z_1$ is a root, then $z_1^{-1}$ is also a root. Furthermore, all roots are nonzero. We will work with this determinant in the following section.

## 9-4

## ROOT-SQUARE LOCUS

To relate Eq. (9-44) to the LQR problem, we first recognize that a finite value of the performance index $J$ for $N = \infty$ implies that the closed-loop system is stable (all closed-loop eigenvalues (poles) lie inside the unit circle in the $z$ plane). Thus, the state $\mathbf{x}(k)$ must decay to zero. Also, the solutions $\mathbf{x}(k)$ and $\mathbf{p}(k)$ represent natural responses from "initial" conditions and therefore must be linear combinations of terms involving powers of the eigenvalues of the coefficient matrix of Eq. (9-44).

A logical consequence of this reasoning is that $\mathbf{x}(k)$ contains only those eigenvalues that are "stable." And if there are less than $n$ stable eigenvalues, then the remaining closed-loop poles show up at the origin (as we will see shortly).

To simplify the next development, we will assume that the system has a single input $u$, and a single output $y$.

### *Regulator Problem*
Plant:

$$\mathbf{x}(k + 1) = A\mathbf{x}(k) + Bu(k) \quad (9\text{-}45)$$

$$y(k) = C\mathbf{x}(k) \quad (9\text{-}46)$$

Performance Index:

$$J = \frac{1}{2} \sum_{k=0}^{\infty} [qy^2(k) + u^2(k)] \quad (9\text{-}47)$$

From Eq. (9-44) (and some determinant relations of Appendix B)

$$\det \begin{bmatrix} zI - A & BB^T \\ -qC^TC & z^{-1}I - A^T \end{bmatrix} = \det M = 0 \quad (9\text{-}48)$$

(See Eq. B-32.)

$$\det M = \det (zI - A) \det [z^{-1}I - A^T + qC^TC(zI - A)^{-1}BB^T]$$

Factoring out $(z^{-1}I - A^T)$,

$$\det M = \det (zI - A) \det (z^{-1}I - A^T)$$

$$\det [I + qC^TC(zI - A)^{-1}BB^T(z^{-1}I - A^T)^{-1}]$$

(See Eq. B-19.)

$$\det M = \det (zI - A) \det (z^{-1}I - A^T)$$

$$\det [I + qB^T(z^{-1}I - A)^{-1}C^TC(zI - A)^{-1}B]$$

Finally,

$$\det M = D(z)D(z^{-1}) \det [I + qT(z^{-1})T(z)] = 0 \qquad (9\text{-}49)$$

where $T(z) = C(zI - A)^{-1}B$ is the transfer function between $u$ and $y$ and $T(z) = N(z)/D(z)$ as a ratio of polynomials. Equation (9-49) is in a "root-locus" form (with the parameter $q$ as the variable gain) because the argument of the determinant operation is scalar. Therefore,

$$1 + qT(z^{-1})T(z) = 0 \qquad (9\text{-}50)$$

is the locus of optimal closed-loop roots (those roots inside the unit circle). An example will certainly help to clarify the results of this tedious development.


### EXAMPLE 9-2 (Root-Square Locus)
Consider the optimal control problem

$$\mathbf{x}(k + 1) = \begin{bmatrix} 1 & 0.6321 \\ 0 & 0.3679 \end{bmatrix} \mathbf{x}(k) + \begin{bmatrix} 0.3679 \\ 0.6321 \end{bmatrix} u(k)$$

$$y(k) = [1 \quad 0] \mathbf{x}(k)$$

$$J = \frac{1}{2} \sum_{k=0}^{\infty} [qy^2(k) + u^2(k)]$$

Sketch the optimal closed-loop root locations as a function of the parameter $q$.

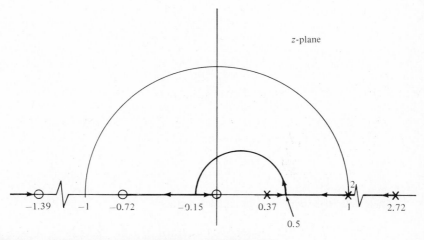

**FIGURE 9-3.** Root-square locus plot for Example 9-2.

**SOLUTION:** The transfer function $T(z) = C(zI - A)^{-1}B$ is

$$T(z) = \frac{0.3671(z + 0.7181)}{(z - 1)(z - 0.3679)}$$

Consequently, the root-locus function [from Eq. (9-50)]

$$qT(z^{-1})T(z) = 0.2642q \frac{z(z + 0.7181)(z + 1.3926)}{(z - 1)^2(z - 0.3679)(z - 2.7181)}$$

The root locus is presented in Fig. 9-3. ∎

**Remarks:**
- Only the upper-half plane loci inside the unit circle needs to be plotted since the locus is symmetric with respect to the real axis and also circle symmetric in the sense that a locus point $p$ inside the circle will correspond to a locus point $p^{-1}$ outside the circle.
- The (two) optimal poles exhibit a wide variation from the scalar parameter $q$, which, in essence, merely specifies the degree of emphasis on minimizing the closed-loop response time ($q > 1$) versus minimizing the control effort ($q < 1$).

A second example on this topic illustrates how the root-square locus method can be used to derive the optimal control sequence and corresponding optimal state trajectory.

### EXAMPLE 9-3 (Optimal Regulation/Root-Square Locus)

We wish to use the root-locus method to derive the optimal input sequence $u(k)$ for the following LQR problem:

Plant:

$$\mathbf{x}(k + 1) = \begin{bmatrix} 0 & 1 \\ -1 & 1 \end{bmatrix} \mathbf{x}(k) + \begin{bmatrix} 0 \\ 1 \end{bmatrix} u(k)$$

$$\mathbf{x}(0) = \begin{bmatrix} 1 & 1 \end{bmatrix}^T$$

Cost Functional:

$$J = \frac{1}{2} \sum_{k=0}^{\infty} [x_1^2(k) + u^2(k)]$$

**SOLUTION:** As before we will assume a variable $q$ multiplying the $x_1$ term in $J$ (and subsequently evaluate the result for $q = 1$):

$$T(z) = X_1(z)/U(z) = \frac{1}{(z - 1/2)^2 + (3/2)^2}$$

Therefore, the root-locus function becomes

$$qT(z^{-1})T(z) = \frac{qz^2}{[(z - 0.5)^2 + (0.866)^2]^2}$$

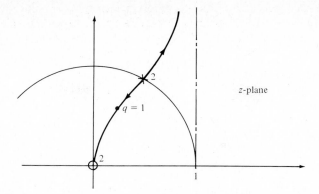

**FIGURE 9-4.  Root-square locus plot for Example 9-3.**

The root-locus plot is given in Fig. 9-4. For $q = 1$ the (stable) closed-loop poles are $(0.257 \pm j0.529)$ as indicated in the figure.

Thus, working from the calculated optimal pole locations, the (desired) characteristic equation is

$$p_{\text{CL}}(z) = z^2 - 0.514z + 0.346 = 0$$

Since the given system is in controllable form, it is a simple matter to use the method of Section 7-6 to arrive at the required feedback matrix:

$$F = [0.654 \quad -0.486]$$

With $u(k) = F\mathbf{x}(k)$, the optimal state trajectory and input can be found sequentially using the original system equation, starting with the specified initial state:

| $k$ | 0 | 1 | 2 | $\cdots$ |
|-----|-----|-------|--------|----------|
| $x_1$ | 1 | 1 | 0.168 | |
| $x_2$ | 1 | 0.168 | $-0.260$ | $\cdots$ |
| $u$ | 0.168 | 0.572 | 0.236 | |

■

In the next section we will build onto the LQR problem.

**9-5**

## SET-POINT CONTROL

Although the LQR problem can be useful in its own right, it is more often used as part of a more comprehensive problem. Perhaps the most useful of these is the set-point problem where a nonzero reference signal is used to "command" the controlled variable between different values, or "set-points."

The main distinction between a regulation problem and a set-point problem is that an independent input $\mathbf{r}$ is present to provide the reference commands. Set-points are generally held for long periods of time compared with the system response time.

**Development:**  Given the open-loop system

$$\mathbf{x}(k + 1) = A\mathbf{x}(k) + B\mathbf{u}(k) \qquad (9\text{-}51)$$

$$\mathbf{y}(k) = C\mathbf{x}(k) \qquad (9\text{-}52)$$

we will assume an input of the form

$$\mathbf{u}(k) = F\mathbf{x}(k) + G\mathbf{r}(k) \qquad (9\text{-}53)$$

Therefore, the closed-loop system is described by either the state model

$$\mathbf{x}(k + 1) = (A + BF)\mathbf{x}(k) + BG\mathbf{r}(k) \qquad (9\text{-}54)$$
$$\mathbf{y}(k) = C\mathbf{x}(k)$$

or the transfer matrix

$$H(z) = C[zI - (A + BF)]^{-1}BG \qquad (9\text{-}55)$$

To simplify the development, we assume that $H(z)$ is a square matrix (an equal number of inputs and outputs) and that the dc gain $H(1)$ is nonsingular.

Thus, if $\mathbf{y}$ is to be controlled to the set-point $\mathbf{y}_o$, then

$$\mathbf{x}_o = A\mathbf{x}_o + B\mathbf{u}_o \qquad (9\text{-}56)$$

$$\mathbf{y}_o = C\mathbf{x}_o \qquad (9\text{-}57)$$

Assuming that $\mathbf{u}_o$ can be determined to satisfy Eq. (9-56), we add Eqs. (9-51) and (9-52) to the negative of Eqs. (9-56) and (9-57), respectively, to obtain

$$\mathbf{x}(k + 1) - \mathbf{x}_o = A[\mathbf{x}(k) - \mathbf{x}_o] + B[\mathbf{u}(k) - \mathbf{u}_o] \qquad (9\text{-}58)$$

$$\mathbf{y}(k) - \mathbf{y}_o = C[\mathbf{x}(k) - \mathbf{x}_o] \qquad (9\text{-}59)$$

Defining

$$\Delta\mathbf{x}(k) = \mathbf{x}(k) - \mathbf{x}_o, \quad \Delta\mathbf{u}(k) = \mathbf{u}(k) - \mathbf{u}_o, \quad \Delta\mathbf{y}(k) = \mathbf{y}(k) - \mathbf{y}_o \quad (9\text{-}60)$$

Eqs. (9-58) and (9-59) reduce to

$$\Delta\mathbf{x}(k + 1) = A\Delta\mathbf{x}(k) + 3\Delta\mathbf{u}(k) \qquad (9\text{-}61)$$

$$\Delta\mathbf{y}(k) = C\Delta\mathbf{x}(k) \qquad (9\text{-}62)$$

as expected.

The problem of changing from one set-point to another in an optimal manner can now be formulated. We must determine $\Delta\mathbf{u}(k)$ to minimize the cost functional

$$J = \frac{1}{2} \sum_{k=0}^{\infty} [\Delta\mathbf{x}^T Q \Delta\mathbf{x} + \Delta\mathbf{u}^T R \Delta\mathbf{u}] \qquad (9\text{-}63)$$

where $\Delta\mathbf{x}$ and $\Delta\mathbf{u}$ represent $\Delta\mathbf{x}(k)$ and $\Delta\mathbf{u}(k)$, respectively. The usual conditions that $Q \geq 0$ and $R > 0$ are also assumed.

As in the standard regulator problem, the optimal $\Delta\dot{\mathbf{u}}$ is

$$\Delta\mathbf{u}(k) = F\Delta\mathbf{x}(k) \qquad (9\text{-}64)$$

which reduces to

$$\mathbf{u}(k) = F\mathbf{x}(k) + (\mathbf{u}_o - F\mathbf{x}_o) \qquad (9\text{-}65)$$

The last term in Eq. (9-65) is $G\mathbf{r}_o$,

$$G\mathbf{r}_o = \mathbf{u}_o - F\mathbf{x}_o \qquad (9\text{-}66)$$

To meet the steady state requirement,

$$\mathbf{r}_o = H^{-1}(1)\mathbf{y}_o \qquad (9\text{-}67)$$

where $H(1)$ is the dc-gain matrix for the closed-loop system. The $G$ matrix is available to allow $\mathbf{r}_o$ to be scaled to match $\mathbf{y}_o$ more closely. Let us illustrate the above ideas with a second-order discrete-time system.

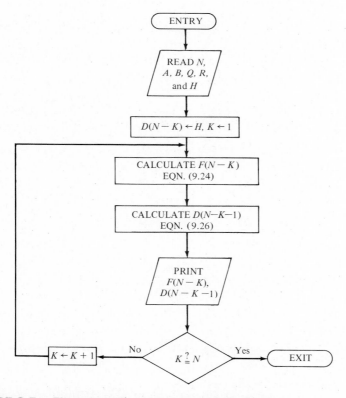

**FIGURE 9-5.  Flow chart for optimal feedback gains.**

### EXAMPLE 9-4 (Set-Point Control)

Given the plant and measurement model

$$\mathbf{x}(k + 1) = \begin{bmatrix} 1 & 0 \\ 0 & 0.9 \end{bmatrix} \mathbf{x}(k) + \begin{bmatrix} 1 \\ 1 \end{bmatrix} u(k)$$

$$y(k) = [\,1 \quad -1\,]\, \mathbf{x}(k)$$

and the cost functional expressed on the incremental signals $\Delta\mathbf{x}$ and $\Delta u$ by Eq. (9-63) with

$$Q = \begin{bmatrix} 4 & 0 \\ 0 & 1 \end{bmatrix}, \quad R = 1$$

We wish to determine $F$ and $G$ as in Eq. (9-53), $F$ to minimize $J$ and $G$ so that a unit reference corresponds to a unit set-point.

***SOLUTION:*** Since this is an infinite-horizon ($N = \infty$) problem, we can work with the steady state optimal gain values. For this purpose Eqs. (9-30) and (9-33) are run to steady state starting with $P(N) = 0$. Alternately, Eqs. (9-24) and (9-26) may be used. Using a program based on the flowchart of Fig. 9-5, the steady state feedback gains are

$$F = [-0.762 \quad -0.083]$$

The dc gain $H(1) = C[I - (A + BF)]^{-1}B$ must equal the reciprocal of $G$ from

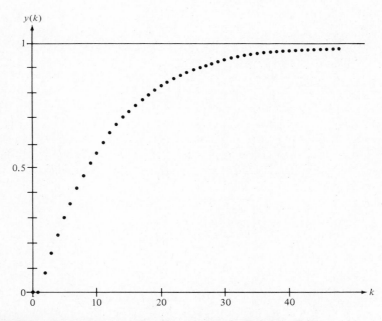

**FIGURE 9-6.  Step response for the system in Example 9-4.**

Eq. (9-67); thus with $H(1) = 1.313$,

$$G = 0.762$$

Let us now calculate the unit-step response to verify our design. With $u(k) = Fx(k) + Gr(k)$, the closed-loop system is given by

$$\mathbf{x}(k + 1) = (A + BF)\mathbf{x}(k) + BGr(k)$$

$$y(k) = C\mathbf{x}(k)$$

where

$$A + BF = \begin{bmatrix} 0.238 & -0.083 \\ -0.762 & 0.817 \end{bmatrix}, \quad BG = \begin{bmatrix} 0.762 \\ 0.762 \end{bmatrix}$$

Figure 9-6 presents the unit-step response for this system (with zero initial state). The 2% settling time is 40 time steps for this optimal response. For a faster response the parameter $R$ could be decreased relative to $Q$. To illustrate this effect, if the above example is resolved with $R = 0.2$, the step-response results are similar to that shown in Fig. 9-6, but having a settling time of just under 30 time steps. ■

## 9-6

# OPTIMAL STOCHASTIC CONTROL

Stochastic control attempts to deal with systems that have a significant amount of random noise in the system. The measurement process to obtain the system outputs is a major source of random errors or noise. Another source that can arise is that of random disturbances affecting the system such as the wind-gust effects on a large radar dish or the random irregularities of a road surface affecting the motion of a moving vehicle.

We are familiar with some modeling techniques that permit us to reduce a continuous-time system to a discrete-time system. There are also similar procedures for reducing a continuous-time random signal to an effective discrete-time model. Keep in mind that for purposes of linear control, only the mean value and the covariance information of the random signal is used; see Appendix C.

## 9-6.1  Stochastic Plant Model

In the previous chapters the plants were generally assumed to be completely known without error. Because of variations in parameters, or errors in some identification process, the matrices $A$, $B$, and $C$ will not, of course, be known exactly. To a moderate extent plant uncertainties can be masked by inserting a (typically) small amplitude white noise signal as an additional input to the plant.

As mentioned above, the input noise can also model a physical effect on the system. We will define the form of the "stochastic plant model" as follows:

$$\mathbf{x}(k + 1) = A\mathbf{x}(k) + B_1\mathbf{u}(k) + B_2\mathbf{w}(k) \tag{9-68}$$

where $\mathbf{w}(k)$ is a white noise sequence (not correlated from one time step to another). Without loss of generality we can take the average value of $\mathbf{w}(k)$ to be zero for all $k$; that is,

$$E[\mathbf{w}(k)] = \mathbf{0} \tag{9-69}$$

where $E[\ ]$ is the expected-value operation (Appendix C). [Any nonzero average value of $\mathbf{w}(k)$ can be included with the deterministic input $\mathbf{u}(k)$.]

For present purposes we may think of $\mathbf{w}(k)$ as a stationary Gaussian random vector. The covariance matrix is given by [see Eq. (9-74)]

$$E[\mathbf{w}(j)\mathbf{w}^T(k)] = Q\delta_{jk} \tag{9-70}$$

where $\delta_{jk}$ is the Kronnecker delta (equals 1 if $j = k$, zero otherwise) and $Q$ is a constant matrix. (Here we restrict $Q$ to be constant for simplicity.) Equation (9-70) is equivalent to specifying the variance for a scalar random variable. For notational convenience we will refer to the distribution of $\mathbf{w}(k)$ as *Normal* with mean $\mathbf{0}$ from Eq. (9-69) and covariance $Q$ from Eq. (9-70), denoted by

$$\mathbf{w}(k) \sim N[\mathbf{0}, Q] \tag{9-71}$$

to be read "$\mathbf{w}$ is Normally distributed with mean $\mathbf{0}$ and covariance $Q$."

The *stochastic plant model*, in summary, is given by

$$\mathbf{x}(k + 1) = A\mathbf{x}(k) + B_1\mathbf{u}(k) + B_2\mathbf{w}(k) \tag{9-68'}$$

with $\mathbf{x}(0) \sim N[\mathbf{m}, P_0]$ and $\mathbf{w}(k) \sim N[\mathbf{0}, Q]$. Since the system is being driven by a noise process, the state $\mathbf{x}(k)$ itself becomes a noise process, and, just as with $\mathbf{w}(k)$, we would like to describe the mean of $\mathbf{x}(k)$ and the covariance matrix of $\mathbf{x}(k)$.

## 9-6.2  Describing the State Gauss–Markov Process

A random process is said to be *Gauss–Markov* if it has both the property of possessing a Gaussian distribution and the property of being statistically dependent only on its previous time value (and not on its entire previous history). Our state $\mathbf{x}(k)$ is a Gauss–Markov process: (1) It is Gaussian since it is a linear combination of Gaussian (or Normal) vectors; recall Eq. (3-45)

$$\mathbf{x}(k) = A^k\mathbf{x}(0) + \sum_{i=0}^{k-1} A^{k-i-1}[B_1\mathbf{u}(i) + B_2\mathbf{w}(i)] \tag{9-72}$$

(2) It is Markov due to the intrinsic property of the state of a system.

To describe the process $\mathbf{x}(k)$, let us first look at the mean (or average) value of $\mathbf{x}(k)$. If we apply the (linear) expected-value operator $E$ to Eq. (9-68), we obtain

$$\overline{\mathbf{x}}(k + 1) = A\overline{\mathbf{x}}(k) + B_1\mathbf{u}(k), \quad \overline{\mathbf{x}}(0) = \mathbf{m} \tag{9-73}$$

where $\overline{\mathbf{x}}(k) = E[\mathbf{x}(k)]$ is a deterministic (nonrandom) signal. Note that taking the expected value of the nonrandom input $\mathbf{u}(k)$ leaves it unchanged. Equation (9-73) allows us to propagate (or calculate) the mean value of $\mathbf{x}(k)$ to any time step by simple recursion.

In a similar manner we can derive an equation that will allow us to propagate the covariance of $\mathbf{x}(k)$. The *covariance matrix* of $\mathbf{x}(k)$ is defined as

$$P(k) = E\{[\mathbf{x}(k) - \overline{\mathbf{x}}(k)][\mathbf{x}(k) - \overline{\mathbf{x}}(k)]^T\} \tag{9-74}$$

Using the corresponding expression for $P(k + 1)$, and introducing Eqs. (9-68) and (9-73), we have

$$P(k + 1) = E\{[A[\mathbf{x}(k) - \overline{\mathbf{x}}(k)] + B_2\mathbf{w}(k)][\ ]^T\} \tag{9-75}$$

where the expression under the transpose operation is identical to the first factor inside the braces, similar to Eq. (9-74).

By expanding the indicated multiplication in Eq. (9-75), we find that

$$\begin{aligned} P(k+1) = E\{A\tilde{\mathbf{x}}(k)\tilde{\mathbf{x}}^T(k)A^T &+ A\tilde{\mathbf{x}}(k)\mathbf{w}^T(k)B_2^T \\ &+ B_2\mathbf{w}(k)\tilde{\mathbf{x}}^T(k)A^T + B_2\mathbf{w}(k)\mathbf{w}^T(k)B_2^T\} \end{aligned} \tag{9-76}$$

where

$$\tilde{\mathbf{x}}(k) = \mathbf{x}(k) - \overline{\mathbf{x}}(k) \tag{9-77}$$

is the deviation of the state from its mean value. Fortunately, Eq. (9-76) simplifies. For one thing, the two middle terms vanish. We can see this by considering the dynamics of $\tilde{\mathbf{x}}(k)$.

Subtracting Eq. (9-73) from Eq. (9-68),

$$\tilde{\mathbf{x}}(k + 1) = A\tilde{\mathbf{x}}(k) + B_2\mathbf{w}(k) \tag{9-78}$$

Consequently,

$$\tilde{\mathbf{x}}(k) = A^k\tilde{\mathbf{x}}(0) + \sum_{i=0}^{k-1} A^{k-i-1}B_2\mathbf{w}(i) \tag{9-79}$$

Consider now that (using the linearity of $E$)

$$E[\tilde{\mathbf{x}}(k)\mathbf{w}^T(k)] = A^kE[\tilde{\mathbf{x}}(0)\mathbf{w}^T(k)] + \sum_{i=0}^{k-1} A^{k-i-1}B_2E[\mathbf{w}(i)\mathbf{w}^T(k)] \tag{9-80}$$

However, the first expected value on the right is zero because $\mathbf{x}(0)$ and $\mathbf{w}(k)$ are (assumed) to be statistically independent. (If $x$ and $y$ are statistically independent, $E[xy] = E[x]E[y]$.) The second expected value on the right is zero because $\mathbf{w}(k)$ was assumed to be white, Eq. (9-70). Thus, the right side of Eq. (9-80) is zero. Finally, taking the $E$ operator inside the braces in Eq. (9-76), we obtain

$$P(k + 1) = AP(k)A^T + B_2QB_2^T, \quad P(0) = P_0 \tag{9-81}$$

which is the propagation equation for the covariance matrix of the state $\mathbf{x}(k)$.

In summary, the key equations for describing $\mathbf{x}(k)$ are Eqs. (9-73) and (9-81). From these we can determine the mean and covariance of $\mathbf{x}(k)$ at any time step.

*Remark:* We could think of $\mathbf{u}(k)$ as the mean value of $\mathbf{w}(k)$ in Eq. (9-68), in which case Eqs. (9-68) and (9-69) can be written as

$$\mathbf{x}(k + 1) = A\mathbf{x}(k) + B\mathbf{w}(k)$$

$$E[\mathbf{w}(k)] = \mathbf{u}(k)$$

### EXAMPLE 9-5 (Working with the Stochastic State)
Given the discrete-time model

$$\mathbf{x}(k + 1) = \begin{bmatrix} 1 & 2 \\ 0 & 1 \end{bmatrix} \mathbf{x}(k) + \begin{bmatrix} 2 \\ 2 \end{bmatrix} w(k)$$

where $w(k) \sim N(0, 4)$, $E[w(k)w(j)] = Q\delta_{jk}$, and $\mathbf{x}(0) = \mathbf{0}$, calculate $E[(x_1(2) - 3)^2]$.

*SOLUTION:* As a first step, we will expand the desired quantity $e$:

$$e = E[(x_1(2) - 3)^2] = E[x_1^2(2) - 6x_1(2) + 9]$$

Using the linearity of $E$,

$$e = E[x_1^2(2)] - 6E[x_1(2)] + 9$$

where we have used the fact that the expected value of a deterministic quantity is itself, $E[9] = 9$.

To develop the terms of $e$, let us begin with the propagation equation for the mean of $\mathbf{x}(k)$:

$$\overline{\mathbf{x}}(k + 1) = \begin{bmatrix} 1 & 2 \\ 0 & 1 \end{bmatrix} \overline{\mathbf{x}}(k), \quad \overline{\mathbf{x}}(k) = \mathbf{0}$$

There is no input since $E[w(k)] = 0$, and therefore $\overline{\mathbf{x}}(k) = \mathbf{0}$ for all $k = 0, 1, 2, \ldots$; that is, the mean state is identically zero. (So that, in particular, $E[x_1(2)] = 0$.)

Next, let us recall the propagation equation for the covariance matrix of $\mathbf{x}(k)$, Eq. (9-81). Since $Q = 4$ was given,

$$P(k + 1) = \begin{bmatrix} 1 & 2 \\ 0 & 1 \end{bmatrix} P(k) \begin{bmatrix} 1 & 0 \\ 2 & 1 \end{bmatrix} + \begin{bmatrix} 2 \\ 2 \end{bmatrix} 4[2 \quad 2]$$

with

$$P(0) = \begin{bmatrix} 0 & 0 \\ 0 & 0 \end{bmatrix}$$

since $\mathbf{x}(0)$ was not random. Using recursion for two steps,

$$P(1) = 16 \begin{bmatrix} 1 & 1 \\ 1 & 1 \end{bmatrix}, \quad P(2) = 32 \begin{bmatrix} 5 & 2 \\ 2 & 1 \end{bmatrix}$$

Therefore, $E[x_1^2(2)] = p_{11}(2) = 160$ (since $E[x_1(2)] = 0$). Finally,

$$e = 169$$

is the desired result. ∎

In the next section we will derive the optimal estimator for a Gauss–Markov system model.

## 9-6.3  Optimal State Estimation—The Basic Kalman Filter

The following will be taken as our complete stochastic plant model:

$$\mathbf{x}(k + 1) = A\mathbf{x}(k) + B_1\mathbf{u}(k) + B_2\mathbf{w}_1(k)$$
$$\mathbf{y}(k) = C\mathbf{x}(k) + D\mathbf{u}(k) + \mathbf{w}_2(k)$$

(9-82)

where $E[\mathbf{w}(k)] = \mathbf{0}$ with

$$\mathbf{w}(k) = \begin{bmatrix} \mathbf{w}_1(k) \\ \mathbf{w}_2(k) \end{bmatrix}$$

$$E[\mathbf{w}(k)\mathbf{w}^T(k)] = \begin{bmatrix} Q_1 & Q_{12} \\ Q_{12}^T & Q_2 \end{bmatrix}, \quad Q_2 > 0$$

The initial state $\mathbf{x}(0)$ is assumed to be a $N(\mathbf{m}, P_0)$ vector.

The notation used in the following development is slightly cumbersome. The estimate of $\mathbf{x}(k)$ based on measurements up to (and including) time-step $k$ will be written as $\hat{\mathbf{x}}(k|k)$ or simply $\hat{\mathbf{x}}(k)$ for short. This distinguishes the "current estimate" from the "one-step predicted estimate" $\hat{\mathbf{x}}(k + 1|k)$, which is the estimate of $\mathbf{x}(k + 1)$ based on measurements up to (and including) time-step $k$.

In the previous chapter we designed a (full-order) estimator system with the form [see Eq. (8-25)]

$$\hat{\mathbf{x}}(k + 1) = A\hat{\mathbf{x}}(k) + B\mathbf{u}(k) + K[\mathbf{v}(k) - C\hat{\mathbf{x}}(k)]$$

(9-83)

where $\mathbf{v}(k) = \mathbf{y}(k) - D\mathbf{u}(k)$ was used as "output" to simplify the expression.

The gain $K$ was previously used to establish certain estimator pole locations that influenced the rate of decay of the estimation error. With a stochastic system we want to make the appropriate compromise between slow and rapid estimator response. If the response is too fast, the estimator will follow the noise superimposed on the state; too slow, and the estimate will not follow the signal fluctuations. Analytically, this means that there is an optimal value for $K$ which depends on the system model.

The choice of $K$ will now be based on minimizing the mean-squared error

$$\varepsilon = E[\mathbf{e}^T(k)\mathbf{e}(k)]$$

(9-84)

where

$$\mathbf{e}(k) = \mathbf{x}(k) - \hat{\mathbf{x}}(k)$$

Recognizing that without any (new) measurement, the estimates of $\mathbf{x}(k)$ and its covariance matrix would be given by the propagation equations, we have

$$\hat{\mathbf{x}}(k + 1|k) = A\hat{\mathbf{x}}(k|k) + B_1\mathbf{u}(k), \quad \hat{\mathbf{x}}(0|0) = \mathbf{m} \tag{9-85}$$

where $\mathbf{u}(k)$ is the deterministic (control) input and $\hat{\mathbf{x}}(k + 1|k)$ is the "estimate of $\mathbf{x}(k)$ based on the measurements up to time-step $k$," and

$$M(k + 1) = AP(k)A^T + B_2QB_2^T, \quad P(0) = P_0 \tag{9-86}$$

for $P(k)$ the covariance of $\mathbf{e}(k)$ and $M(k + 1)$ is the covariance of $\mathbf{e}(k + 1|k)$, the one-step predicted estimation error. Equations (9-85) and (9-86) will be referred to as the *extrapolation equations*.

From the definition of $\mathbf{e}(k)$, the model of Eq. (9-82), and the form of the estimator in Eq. (9-83), we can write the error dynamics as follows:

$$\mathbf{e}(k + 1) = \mathbf{x}(k + 1) - \hat{\mathbf{x}}(k + 1)$$

Substituting for the right-hand side,

$$\mathbf{e}(k + 1) = A\mathbf{x}(k) + B_1\mathbf{u}(k) + B_2\mathbf{w}_1(k) - A\hat{\mathbf{x}}(k) - B_1\mathbf{u}(k)$$

$$- K[\mathbf{v}(k) + \mathbf{w}_2(k) - C\hat{\mathbf{x}}(k)]$$

This last expression may be reduced to

$$\mathbf{e}(k + 1) = (A - KC)\mathbf{e}(k) + B_2\mathbf{w}_1(k) - K\mathbf{w}_2(k) \tag{9-87}$$

with $\mathbf{e}(0) = \mathbf{x}(0) - \hat{\mathbf{x}}(0)$. The mean-value of $\mathbf{e}(k)$ will be zero if $\hat{\mathbf{x}}(0) = E[\mathbf{x}(0)] = \mathbf{m}$. Then, the covariance matrix of $\mathbf{e}(k)$, $P(k)$, can be shown to satisfy

$$P(k + 1) = (A - KC)P(k)(A - KC)^T + B_2Q_1B_2^T$$
$$- B_2Q_{12}K^T - KQ_{12}^TB_2^T + KQ_2K^T, \quad P(0) = P_0 \tag{9-88}$$

in a manner similar to the development of Eq. (9-81).

***Remark:*** The gain matrix $K$ has generally been considered to be constant up to this point. Now, we must recognize that the optimal gains may, in fact, vary with time, and write $K(k)$.

Since the mean-squared $\varepsilon$ in Eq. (9-84) can be written as

$$\varepsilon = \text{tr } P(k) \tag{9-89}$$

(The trace of a matrix is the sum of its diagonal elements.), we can determine the optimal gains $K(k)$ from

$$\frac{\partial \text{ tr } [P(k + 1)]}{\partial K(k)} \overset{\text{set}}{=} 0 \tag{9-90}$$

where $P(k + 1)$ is expressed in Eq. (9-88). From Appendix B we use the result that

$$\frac{\partial}{\partial A} [\text{tr } ABA^T] = 2AB \tag{9-91}$$

for $B$ symmetric; therefore, applying Eq. (9-91) to Eq. (9-90),

$$-2(A - KC)P(k)C^T - 2B_2Q_{12} + 2K(k)Q_2 = 0$$

See Eqs. (B-39), (B-40), and (B-41). Solving for $K$,

$$K(k) = [AP(k)C^T + B_2Q_{12}][CP(k)C^T + Q_2]^{-1} \qquad (9\text{-}92)$$

To summarize, the optimal estimator (in the sense of the minimum mean-squared error) for the stochastic system described in Eqs. (9-82) is given by

$$\hat{\mathbf{x}}(k + 1) = A\hat{\mathbf{x}}(k) + B_1\mathbf{u}(k) + K(k)[\mathbf{y}(k) - D\mathbf{u}(k) - C\hat{\mathbf{x}}(k)] \qquad (9\text{-}93)$$

where $K(k)$ is the optimal sequence of gains determined from Eq. (9-92) and Eq. (9-88). Equations (9-93), (9-92), and (9-88) are called the *update equations*. These equations form the *discrete-time Kalman filter algorithm*. In a later development we will consider how the algorithm may be interpreted as a "filter."

**Duality:** It is interesting to reconsider the concept of duality and dual systems as applied to our more complete stochastic model. For simplicity we will take $Q_{12} = 0$ in Eq. (9-82); it is not unusual to have independent plant and measurement noise (which would satisfy this assumption).

The critical matrices of the model used for optimal control were

$$\{A, B, Q, R\} \rightarrow \{D, F\} \qquad (9\text{-}94)$$

For optimal estimation the corresponding matrices are

$$\{A, C, B_2Q_1B_2^T, Q_2\} \rightarrow \{P, K\} \qquad (9\text{-}95)$$

By comparing the optimal regulator equations, Eqs. (9-24) and (9-26), with the optimal estimator equations, Eqs. (9-92) and (9-88), we can state that solving for the estimator-gain matrix $K$ given the stochastic model consisting of the matrices $\{A, C, B_2Q_1B_2^T, Q_2\}$ is equivalent to solving for the SVF gain matrix $F$ given the model parameters $\{A^T, C^T, B_2Q_1B_2^T, Q_2\}$ corresponding to the set specified in expression (9-94). Once $F$ is thus determined, $K = -F^T$ is the desired estimator gain matrix.

*Remarks:*
- The only new dual parameters were $B_2Q_1B_2^T \sim Q$ and $Q_2 \sim R$ and the dependent variables $P \sim D$ and $K \sim -F^T$.
- If steady state gains are used, there is no problem; but, in the time-varying case the $F(k)$ values are calculated backwards in time from the final time, whereas $K(k)$ values are used in forward time [starting with $K(0)$].
- The $H$ matrix in Eq. (9-6) is dual to the covariance matrix of the initial state $\mathbf{x}(0)$.

Let us consider an example that discusses the design of an optimal estimator as well as illustrating some of the modeling involved.

### EXAMPLE 9-6 (Optimal Estimation)
A unit, point mass reacting to a (one-dimensional) random force $w_1(t)$ can be described by

$$\ddot{y}(t) = w_1(t)$$

where $y(t)$ is the position measured from some reference point. For this system we can write the state model (with $x_1 = y$ and $x_2 = \dot{y}$) as

$$\dot{\mathbf{x}}(t) = \begin{bmatrix} 0 & 1 \\ 0 & 0 \end{bmatrix} \mathbf{x}(t) + \begin{bmatrix} 0 \\ 1 \end{bmatrix} w_1(t)$$

As part of the model, we will assume that $\mathbf{x}(0)$ is distributed as a $N(\mathbf{m}, P_0)$ variable, where

$$\mathbf{m} = \mathbf{0}, \quad P_0 = \begin{bmatrix} 100 & 0 \\ 0 & 100 \end{bmatrix}$$

indicating a large uncertainty about the initial state. To reduce the problem to a discrete-time model, assume that

$$w_1(t) = w_1(kT) \quad \text{for} \quad kT \le t < kT + T$$

with $T = 0.5$ sec. This tells us that $w_1(t)$ is a random "staircase" function. [If this is an approximation, it can be made to describe $u(t)$ as accurately as needed by taking $T$ sufficiently small.] We also assume a position measurement given by

$$z(kT) = [1 \quad 0]\mathbf{x}(kT) + w_2(kT)$$

The noise statistics are given to be

$$E[w_1(kT)] = 0, \quad E[w_1^2(kT)] = 16$$

$$E[w_2(kT)] = 0, \quad E[w_2^2(kT)] = 1$$

with the assumption that $w_1$ and $w_2$ are uncorrelated Gaussian random signals.

**Problem:** To obtain the discrete-time Gauss–Markov model of the system and the optimal estimator for the system.

**SOLUTION:** The ZOH equivalent is easily obtained, leading us to the system model:

$$\mathbf{x}(k + 1) = \begin{bmatrix} 1 & 0.5 \\ 0 & 1 \end{bmatrix} \mathbf{x}(k) + \begin{bmatrix} 0.125 \\ 0.500 \end{bmatrix} w_1(k)$$

with measurement model

$$z(k) = [1 \quad 0]\mathbf{x}(k) + w_2(k)$$

The matrices $B_2 Q_1 B_2^T$ and $Q_2$ are

$$B_2 Q_1 B_2^T = \begin{bmatrix} 0.25 & 1 \\ 1 & 4 \end{bmatrix}, \quad Q_2 = 1$$

The estimator system, from Eq. (9-93), has the form

$$\hat{\mathbf{x}}(k + 1) = \begin{bmatrix} 1 & 0.5 \\ 0 & 1 \end{bmatrix} \hat{\mathbf{x}}(k) + \begin{bmatrix} K_1 \\ K_2 \end{bmatrix} \{z(k) - [1 \quad 0]\hat{\mathbf{x}}(k)\}$$

with $\hat{\mathbf{x}}(0) = \mathbf{m} = \mathbf{0}$. The gains $K_1$ and $K_2$ are "off-line" calculations based on

Eqs. (9-88) and (9-92); that is to say, the gains may be calculated in advance of "running" the estimator with incoming data $\{z(k); k = 0, 1, 2, \ldots\}$. The results of the calculations are given below:

| $k$ | 0 | 1 | 2 | 3 | 4 | 5 | 10 |
|---|---|---|---|---|---|---|---|
| $K_1(k)$ | 0.9901 | 1.8994 | 1.4128 | 1.2679 | 1.2500 | 1.2509 | 1.2500 |
| $K_2(k)$ | 0 | 1.8722 | 1.1473 | 0.9988 | 0.9970 | 1.0013 | 1.0000 |

■

*Remark:* For most applications of estimators in a control system the steady state gains are adequate. Note that the estimator poles are determined by the noise covariance matrices.

## SOLVED PROBLEMS

In this section we will look at three applications and extensions of the previous developments. The first application simply ties the optimal estimation and the optimal control together as a single controller design. The second and third problems involve some interesting extensions and interpretations of the material presented previously in this chapter.

### 9-7.1 An Optimal Stochastic Control Example

In Chapter 8 we studied the combination of SVF (pole placement) and (deterministic) estimator system design to achieve an output feedback dynamic controller. Underlying this design was the separation property which permitted us to design the feedback and estimator gain matrices independently. At this point in our studies we are considering linear systems with Gaussian noise that must be optimum with respect to a quadratic performance index. This class of problems is referred to as *LQG problems* (for the Linear, Quadratic, Gaussian assumptions on the model). The separation property fortunately extends to this class of problems, and we will work the following simple example to illustrate a complete optimal, stochastic controller design.

#### EXAMPLE 9-7 (Optimal Stochastic Control)
For the following stochastic system, design an optimal estimator-based feedback controller:

*Plant model* $\mathbf{x}(k + 1) = \begin{bmatrix} 1 & 0.5 \\ 0 & 1 \end{bmatrix} \mathbf{x}(k) + \begin{bmatrix} 0.125 \\ 0.50 \end{bmatrix} [u(k) + w_1(k)]$

*Measurement model* $y(k) = \begin{bmatrix} 1 & 0 \end{bmatrix} \mathbf{x}(k) + w_2(k)$

*Statistical assumptions* $E[\mathbf{w}(k)] = \mathbf{0}, \quad \mathbf{w}(k) = \begin{bmatrix} w_1(k) \\ w_2(k) \end{bmatrix}$

$$E[\mathbf{w}(k)\mathbf{w}^T(k)] = \begin{bmatrix} 16 & 0 \\ 0 & 1 \end{bmatrix}$$

$$E[\mathbf{x}(0)] = \mathbf{0}, \quad E[\mathbf{x}^2(0)] = \begin{bmatrix} 100 & 0 \\ 0 & 100 \end{bmatrix}$$

We assume also that

- $\mathbf{x}(0)$, $w_1(k)$, and $w_2(k)$ are mutually uncorrelated Gaussian random variables for each $k = 0, 1, 2, \ldots$ .
- $w_1$ and $w_2$ are white noise processes (uncorrelated from one time step to another).

*Performance index* $J = \dfrac{1}{2} \displaystyle\sum_{k=0}^{\infty} \{\mathbf{x}^T(k) \begin{bmatrix} 4 & 0 \\ 0 & 0 \end{bmatrix} \mathbf{x}(k) + u^2(k)\}$

**SOLUTION:** We begin with the optimal (deterministic) state variable feedback gain matrix $F$. Using Eqs. (9-24) and (9-26), we run the calculations (with $N$ a large number) until we arrive at the steady state solution

$$F = [-1.219 \quad -1.562]$$

The next step is to design the optimal estimator. For this we use Eqs. (9-88) and (9-92); however, this part of the design has been carried out in Example 9-6, the result of which is the steady state estimator gain matrix:

$$K = \begin{bmatrix} 1.250 \\ 1.000 \end{bmatrix}$$

Thus, the controller design is described by the following equations:

$$\hat{\mathbf{x}}(k + 1) = \begin{bmatrix} 1 & 0.5 \\ 0 & 1 \end{bmatrix} \mathbf{x}(k) + \begin{bmatrix} 0.125 \\ 0.5 \end{bmatrix} u(k) + K\{y(k) - \hat{x}_1(k)\}$$

$$u(k) = F\hat{\mathbf{x}}(k) + Gr(k), \quad \hat{\mathbf{x}}(0) = \mathbf{0}$$

where $r(k)$ is an independent reference input and $G$ is the reference gain. From these equations it is obvious that the controller accepts $r(k)$ and $y(k)$ as inputs and provides $u(k)$ as the output.

To complete the example, we will simulate the closed-loop response with $r(k) = 0$ and $\mathbf{x}(0) = [1 \quad 1]^T$. In order to implement a realistic simulation, we must make use of the pseudorandom number generation capabilities of digital computers. We need two scalar random numbers for each time step: one with a variance of 16, the other with a variance of 1. The vector $Bw_1(k)$ then becomes part of the input to the plant model. The second, $w_2(k)$, is suitable as the measurement error since $Q_2 = 1$ in the problem.

The random noise sequences were constructed from pseudorandom numbers distributed uniformly from 0 to 1. In particular, numbers that are approximately $N(0, \frac{1}{2})$ were derived by adding six uniform (0, 1) numbers and subtracting the mean of 3. Finally, these numbers can be multiplied by $\sqrt{2}$ or $\sqrt{32}$ to achieve, respectively, $N(0, 1)$ and $N(0, 16)$ variables.

The simulation equations appear as follows:

$$\mathbf{x}(k + 1) = A\mathbf{x}(k) + BF\hat{\mathbf{x}}(k) + Bw_1(k), \quad \mathbf{x}(0) = \begin{bmatrix} 1 \\ 1 \end{bmatrix}$$

$$\hat{\mathbf{x}}(k + 1) = (A + BF - KC)\hat{\mathbf{x}}(k) + KC\mathbf{x}(k) + Kw_2(k), \quad \hat{\mathbf{x}}(0) = \mathbf{0}$$

In terms of $\mathbf{x}(k)$ and $\mathbf{e}(k) = \mathbf{x}(k) - \hat{\mathbf{x}}(k)$, as in Eq. (8-55), the above equations are

$$\begin{bmatrix} \mathbf{x}(k + 1) \\ \mathbf{e}(k + 1) \end{bmatrix} = \begin{bmatrix} A + BF & -BF \\ 0 & A - KC \end{bmatrix} \begin{bmatrix} \mathbf{x}(k) \\ \mathbf{e}(k) \end{bmatrix} + \begin{bmatrix} Bw_1(k) \\ Bw_1(k) - Kw_2(k) \end{bmatrix}$$

where $[\mathbf{x}^T(0) \quad \mathbf{e}^T(0)] = [1 \quad 1 \quad 1 \quad 1]$, $w_1(k)$ and $w_2(k)$ are uncorrelated random inputs with variances 16 and 1, respectively. Figure 9-7 illustrates the simulation results; showing in (a), the derived random number sequences; in (b), the estimation error components; and in (c), the resulting state trajectory. With this design the closed-loop poles are $(0.533 \pm j0.295)$ and the estimator poles are $(0.375 \pm j0.331)$. ∎

### Remarks:

- With the high noise levels the estimation errors and system states are only slightly less noisy than the actual white noise processes $w_1$ and $w_2$ driving the system.
- For many control system designs it would be worthwhile to stimulate some (perhaps small) noise in the system (even if the design were not based on a stochastic model) as being more representative of a physical environment.

In the next section we will show how the root-locus method can be used to obtain the locus of optimal estimator poles.


## 9-7.2  Root-Square Locus for Estimation

By calling on the concept of duality, we can utilize the development of Section 9-4 in the design of optimal estimators. Equation (9-50) states the "root-locus equation" with $T(z^{-1})T(z)$ playing the role of the "loop transfer function," where $T(z)$ is the transfer function between input $u$ and output $y$. In terms of the dual problem, the corresponding transfer function relates the output $y$ from the plant noise input $w_1$. Thus, using the notation of Eq. (9-82), the locus of estimator poles will be the stable roots of

$$1 + KT_0(z^{-1})T_0(z) = 0 \tag{9-96}$$

where

$$T_0(z) = C(zI - A)^{-1}B_2$$

$$K = Q_1/Q_2$$

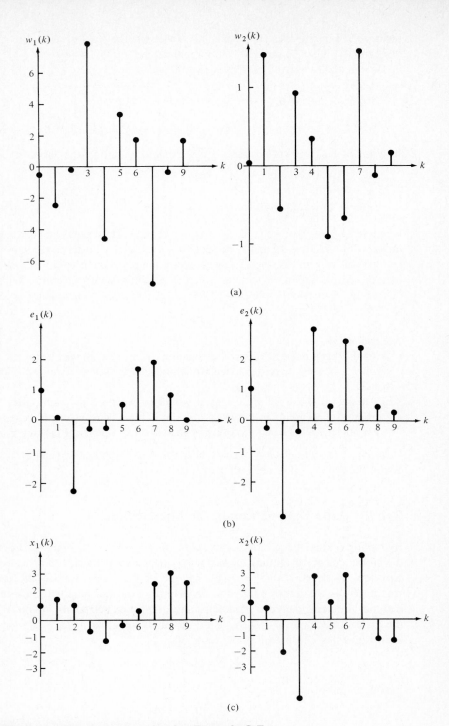

FIGURE 9-7.   Simulation results for Example 9-7.

(assuming that $w_1$ and $y$ are both scalar signals and that $Q_{12} = 0$). Let us illustrate the use of Eq. (9-96) with the following problem.

### EXAMPLE 9-8 (Locus of Optimal Estimator Poles)

Let us reconsider the problem of Example 9-6:

$$\mathbf{x}(k + 1) = \begin{bmatrix} 1 & 0.5 \\ 0 & 1 \end{bmatrix} \mathbf{x}(k) + \begin{bmatrix} 0.125 \\ 0.5 \end{bmatrix} w_1(k)$$

$$y(k) = \begin{bmatrix} 1 & 0 \end{bmatrix} \mathbf{x}(k) + w_2(k)$$

with the variance of $w_1(k)$ and $w_2(k)$ equal to 16 and 1, respectively. We wish to design a steady state gain estimator for the system (therefore, we do not need any statistical assumptions on the initial state).

**SOLUTION:** Applying Eq. (9-96), the transfer function,

$$T_0(z) = \begin{bmatrix} 1 & 0 \end{bmatrix} \begin{bmatrix} z - 1 & -0.5 \\ 0 & z - 1 \end{bmatrix}^{-1} \begin{bmatrix} 0.125 \\ 0.5 \end{bmatrix}$$

$$T_0(z) = \frac{0.125(z + 1)}{(z - 1)^2}$$

and the root-locus equation is

$$1 + \frac{Kz(z + 1)^2}{64(z - 1)^4} = 0$$

The root-locus plot is presented in Figure 9-8, showing the branches that lie in the unit circle (corresponding to the stable roots). The value of $K$ is 16 for this problem and the estimator pole locations are therefore specified for a gain of $(16/64)$ along the locus; these locations are indicated on the plot. Note that these pole locations check with the previous estimator design in Example 9-7. ∎

In the next section we will consider the estimator from the point of view of signal filtering.

### 9-7.3  Design of an Optimal Signal Filter

The $z$-domain functions that occur in the root-square locus, as we have seen in the previous section and in Section 9-4, have the property of being in "circle symmetry" [for every pole (or zero) located inside the unit circle, say, at $r\underline{/\theta}$, there is a corresponding pole (or zero) outside the unit circle at $(1/r)\underline{/-\theta}$]. This same property shows up in the $z$-domain description of a stationary random signal's spectral density. [See Eq. (C-21) in Appendix C.] To restate a fundamental result proved in Section C-3:

- A linear discrete-time system with transfer function $H(z)$ which is excited by a random input signal $u(k)$ with a spectral density $S_u(z)$ will have a random

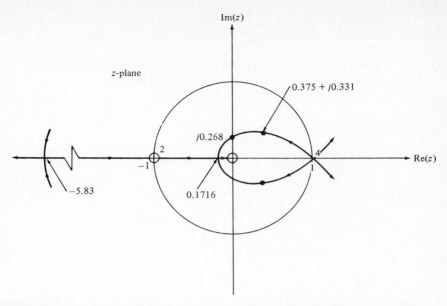

**FIGURE 9-8.** **Locus of estimator poles as a function of $Q_1/Q_2$ for Example 9-8.**

output signal $y(k)$ with spectral density given by

$$S_y(z) = H(z)H(z^{-1})S_u(z) \qquad (9\text{-}97)$$

*Modeling Stochastic Signals.* Equation (9-97) provides a method of "generating" random signals with prescribed spectral densities. For example, we might let $u(k)$ be a white noise signal with a spectral density of unity (constant) in which case by selecting $H(z)$ properly, we could obtain a signal $y(k)$ with some desired spectral density $S_y(z)$. One way $S_y(z)$ might be specified is by its real frequency variation $S_y(e^{j\omega})$.

### EXAMPLE 9-9 (Modeling a Random Signal)

It is desired to obain a mathematical model of a random signal whose (power) spectral density function is given by

$$S_y(\omega) = \frac{1.04 + 0.4\cos\omega}{1.25 + \cos\omega}$$

*SOLUTION:* By breaking the cosine terms into their exponential forms, we can factor $S_y(\omega)$ as follows:

$$S_y(\omega) = \frac{(e^{j\omega} + 0.2)(e^{-j\omega} + 0.2)}{(e^{j\omega} + 0.5)(e^{-j\omega} + 0.5)}$$

Introducing

$$z = e^{j\omega}$$

we see that

$$\hat{S}_y(z) = H(z)H(z^{-1})$$

where

$$H(z) = \frac{z + 0.2}{z + 0.5}$$

Consequently, our noise model is, as shown in Fig. 9-9, the output of a linear system with transfer function $H(z)$ in response to a white noise input sequence with unity spectral density. It is also noted in the figure that the inverse $z$-transform of $S_u(z)$ is the autocorrelation sequence $R_u(n)$. Refer to Appendix C for additional details.

The state model is also an acceptable representation for the signal model. Thus, from Fig. 9-9b,

$$x(k + 1) = -0.5x(k) + w(k)$$

$$y(k) = -0.3x(k) + w(k)$$

is the required signal model. ∎

A more general signal model is given by a deterministic part superimposed with a random part. Using the state-variable form, we can write our general random signal model as follows:

*Random Signal Model*

$$y(k) = s(k) + w_2(k) \tag{9-98}$$

where

$$\mathbf{x}_n(k + 1) = A_n\mathbf{x}_n(k) + B_n w_1(k)$$
$$w_2(k) = C_n\mathbf{x}_n(k) + D_n w_1(k) \tag{9-99}$$

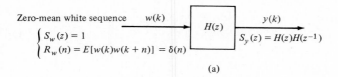

(a)

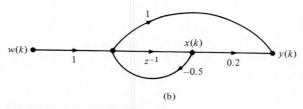

(b)

**FIGURE 9-9. Modeling a stochastic signal.**

is the noise model with the signal $w_1(k)$ taken to be a zero-mean, unit-variance, white sequence. The matrices $A_n$, $B_n$, $C_n$, and $D_n$ determine the desired spectral density of $w_2(k)$. The deterministic signal model given by

$$\mathbf{x}_s(k + 1) = A_s \mathbf{x}_s(k) + B_s u(k) \tag{9-100}$$

$$s(k) = C_s \mathbf{x}_s(k) + D_s u(k)$$

is deterministic with a known input $u(k)$.

It should be clear that once a signal is modeled as $y(k)$ is in Eq. (9-98), an optimal estimator can be derived that will accept $y(k)$ as an input and provide a "best estimate" for the underlying signal $s(k)$. The problem is seen to be the same as our previous estimation problems once the proper interpretation is made. The combined signal and noise states $\mathbf{x}_n(k)$ and $\mathbf{x}_s(k)$ provide the total state information. Combining them as a single vector we have

$$\mathbf{x}(k) = \begin{bmatrix} \mathbf{x}_n(k) \\ \mathbf{x}_s(k) \end{bmatrix} \tag{9-101}$$

and

$$\mathbf{x}(k + 1) = \begin{bmatrix} A_n & 0 \\ 0 & A_s \end{bmatrix} \mathbf{x}(k) + \begin{bmatrix} 0 \\ B_s \end{bmatrix} u(k) + \begin{bmatrix} B_n \\ 0 \end{bmatrix} w_1(k) \tag{9-102}$$

$$y(k) = [C_n \quad C_s] \, \mathbf{x}(k) + D_s u(k) + D_n w_1(k)$$

which is of the form of Eq. (9-82), the model of a stochastic "plant." Following Eq. (9-82) we were interested in estimating the (entire) state $\mathbf{x}(t)$, but here we need only an estimate of $s(k)$, namely,

$$\hat{s}(k) = [0 \quad C_s] \, \hat{\mathbf{x}}(k) + D_s u(k) \tag{9-103}$$

Since the vector $\mathbf{w}(k)$ of Eq. (9-82) would correspond to

$$\mathbf{w}(k) = \begin{bmatrix} w_1(k) \\ D_n w_1(k) \end{bmatrix} \tag{9-104}$$

we have with $w_1$ and $y$ both scalar valued that

$$E[\mathbf{w}(k)\mathbf{w}^T(k)] = \begin{bmatrix} 1 & D_n \\ D_n & D_n^2 \end{bmatrix} \tag{9-105}$$

since the variance of $w_1(k)$ was assumed to be unity.

**Remark:** The signal $s(k)$ could itself be stochastic in nature if $u(k)$ is assumed to have a random part; this would make the previous introductory development more general.

The next example is included to illustrate the interpretation of optimal signal filtering as well as the calculation of signal power.

### EXAMPLE 9-10 (Optimal Signal Filtering)

Consider the following stochastic system as a model of a communication channel with which a noisy constant signal is applied and out of which a noisy measurement is made:

$$\mathbf{x}(k + 1) = \begin{bmatrix} 1 & 1 \\ 0 & 1 \end{bmatrix} \mathbf{x}(k) + \begin{bmatrix} 0.5 \\ 1 \end{bmatrix} w(k), \quad \mathbf{x}(0) = \mathbf{x}_0$$

$$z(k) = [1 \quad 0] \mathbf{x}(k) + v(k)$$

where $\mathbf{x}_0 \sim N[\mathbf{0}, I]$, $w(k) \sim N[1, 1]$, and $v(k) \sim N[0, 1]$ are all mutually independent with $w(k)$ and $v(k)$ specified as white noise sequences. The output signal is $s(k) = E[z(k)]$ and the input signal is $w(k)$, which has a constant deterministic part (since $E[w(k)] = 1$). Calculate:

(a) the input signal-to-noise power ratio $(P_s/P_n)_{\text{in}}$, where $P_n$ = variance of the noise.
(b) the output signal-to-noise power ratio $(P_s/P_n)_{\text{out}}$ for $k = 1, 2$.
(c) Design an optimal filter to estimate the output signal.

**SOLUTION:** (a) Since the deterministic (average) of $w(k)$ is taken to be the signal input,

$$(P_s)_{\text{in}} = (E[w(k)])^2 = 1$$

The noise input is left as $w(k) - E[w(k)]$ or $w(k) - 1$, the (normalized) power of which is defined to be its variance, given as unity

$$(P_n)_{\text{in}} = \text{Var}[w(k)] = 1$$

Therefore, the input signal-to-noise power ratio is 1.

(b) To determine the output signal (which will change with time), we use the method of propagating the mean values:

$$\bar{\mathbf{x}}(k + 1) = \begin{bmatrix} 1 & 1 \\ 0 & 1 \end{bmatrix} \bar{\mathbf{x}}(k) + \begin{bmatrix} 0.5 \\ 1 \end{bmatrix} 1$$

$$\bar{z}(k) = [1 \quad 0] \bar{\mathbf{x}}(k)$$

For $k = 1$: $\bar{\mathbf{x}}(1) = [0.5 \quad 1]^T$

$$\bar{z}(1) = 0.5, \quad \text{signal out } (k = 1)$$

For $k = 2$: $\bar{\mathbf{x}}(2) = [2 \quad 2]^T$

$$\bar{z}(2) = 2, \quad \text{signal out } (k = 2)$$

Equation (9-81) can be used to obtain the propagation of the covariance matrix of the state:

$$P(k + 1) = \begin{bmatrix} 1 & 1 \\ 0 & 1 \end{bmatrix} P(k) \begin{bmatrix} 1 & 0 \\ 1 & 1 \end{bmatrix} + \begin{bmatrix} 0.5 \\ 1 \end{bmatrix} 1[0.5 \quad 1], \quad P(0) = I$$

$$P(1) = \frac{1}{4} \begin{bmatrix} 9 & 6 \\ 6 & 8 \end{bmatrix}, \quad P(2) = \frac{1}{2} \begin{bmatrix} 15 & 8 \\ 8 & 6 \end{bmatrix}$$

Having the state covariance matrix for $k = 1$ and $k = 2$, we can determine the variance of $z(k)$, which is interpreted to be the output noise power:

$$\text{Var } [z(k)] = E[z^2(k)] - \bar{z}^2(k)$$

$$\text{Var } [z(k)] = E\{[x_1(k) + v(k)]^2\} - \bar{x}_1^2(k)$$

$$\text{Var } [z(k)] = \{E[x_1^2(k)] - \bar{x}_1^2(k)\} + 2E[x_1(k)v(k)] + E[v^2(k)]$$

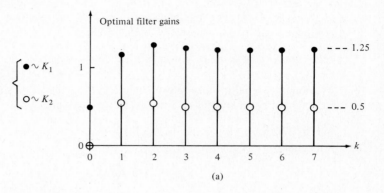

(a)

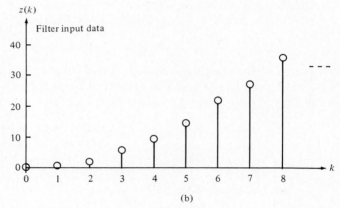

(b)

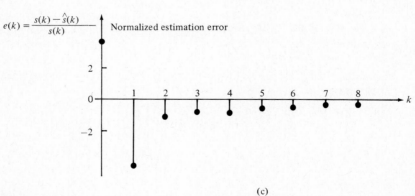

(c)

**FIGURE 9-10.** Simulation results for the optimal filter in Example 9-10.

**INTRODUCTION TO OPTIMAL CONTROL**

$$\text{Var}[z(k)] = P_{11}(k) + 0 + 1$$

$$\text{Var}[z(1)] = \frac{13}{4}, \quad \text{Var}[z(2)] = \frac{17}{2}$$

Therefore, the output signal-to-noise power ratio is

$$(P_s/P_n)_{\text{out}} = \frac{(1/2)^2}{13/4} = \frac{1}{13} \ (k = 1)$$

$$(P_s/P_n)_{\text{out}} = \frac{(2)^2}{17} = \frac{8}{17} \ (k = 2)$$

(c) The optimal filter algorithm is the optimal estimator, based on the given model with the additional equation that the signal estimate is

$$\hat{s}(k) = [1 \quad 0] \, \hat{\mathbf{x}}(k)$$

The filter algorithm is the set of equations given by Eqs. (9-93), (9-92), and (9-88).

The matrices involved are

$$A = \begin{bmatrix} 1 & 1 \\ 0 & 1 \end{bmatrix}, \quad B_1 = \begin{bmatrix} 0.5 \\ 1 \end{bmatrix}, \quad u(k) = E[w(k)] = 1$$

$$C = [1 \quad 0], \quad D = 0, \quad \hat{\mathbf{x}}(0) = \mathbf{0}$$

$$Q_{12} = 0, \quad Q_2 = 1, \quad P(0) = I$$

The simulation of the system is presented in Fig. 9-10. First, the data must be simulated by generating a sequence of pseudorandom numbers to approximate samples of a $N(0, 1)$ distribution. These elements are used for $x_1(0)$, $x_2(0)$, $w(k) - 1$ and $v(k)$ for $k = 0, 1, 2, \ldots$ . From these numbers and the original model, the data $\{z(k); k = 0, 1, 2, \ldots\}$ are generated and plotted in Fig. 9-10b. These data points are, in turn, used in the filter equation whose optimal gains are plotted in Fig. 9-10a. The filter equation, corresponding to Eq. (9-93), provides $\hat{\mathbf{x}}(k)$ for $k = 0, 1, 2, \ldots$ , and, finally, the signal estimate $\hat{\mathbf{x}}(k)$ is the first component $\hat{x}_1(k)$. The normalized estimation error $e(k) = [s(k) - \hat{s}(k)]/s(k)$ is plotted in Fig. 9-10c, where the "true" signal $s(k)$ was calculated directly from the model without its noise inputs and an initial state of $[-0.20, \quad 0.15]^T$. ∎

*Remarks:*
- In this problem the optimal filter gains reach steady state values within a few iterations. The gains will always settle to steady state values if all matrices (including those of the noise statistics) are constant.
- The "true" signal $s(k)$ as well as the data $z(k)$ are increasing rapidly with time. In this situation it is difficult for the estimator to follow the signal, but even so we can see that the normalized estimation error is generally getting smaller. The fact that the signal is becoming larger (with stationary noise), increases the signal-to-noise ratio permitting the estimator to perform better.

## SUMMARY

In this final chapter of the book we have been introduced to several advanced topics, all in some way concerned with optimizing the performance of a system.

Optimal control provides a packaged method for designing state-variable feedback for a system that requires the ability to use a computer, ideally in an interactive mode. In this way the designer can input the $Q$ and $R$ matrices, solve the optimal control problem, and simulate the system response at one sitting. If, then, the response is not satisfactory this procedure may be repeated (using different $Q$ and $R$ matrices) as many times as necessary. Such a design by hand would clearly be unreasonable however.

The previous notion of pole placement is reflected in the choice of $Q$ and $R$ matrices (for steady state gains); thus, the "design" problem is still there. Since steady state gains are sufficient for most control problems, the root-square locus technique is useful to provide some insight into the relation between pole locations and parameters in the performance index.

Section 9-5 presents an introduction to the practical problem of set-point control. The development emphasizes its relation to the design of regulators (the basic optimal control problem).

By duality, the developments of optimal state-variable feedback design carry over to the problem of designing optimal estimator gains for a stochastic (Gauss–Markov) model. In deriving these results we have had to discuss some of the probabilistic methods of modeling signals (based on the material of Appendix C). Stochastic control discussed in Section 9-6 is the combination of the two optimization problems: optimal feedback design and optimal estimator design.

In Section 9-7 several techniques were presented in the context of particular example problems. They include

- An illustration of optimal stochastic control design and simulation (using pseudorandom numbers).
- The use of root-square locus to determine how the optimal estimator poles vary with the ratio of plant noise power to measurement noise power.
- The design of an optimal filter for estimating a signal imbedded in noise.

This chapter is meant only to serve as an introduction to these more advanced topics and does not pretend to provide adequate coverage of them. The interested student will find further developments of these topics in the reference list.

## REFERENCES

**Sections 9-1–9-3**   *Optimal Control Theory;* D. E. Kirk; Prentice-Hall, 1970.
*Optimal Control;* A. Athans and P. L. Falb; McGraw-Hill Book Co., 1966.

**Sections 9-4, 9-5**   *Linear Optimal Control Systems;* H. Kwakernaak and R. Sivan; Wiley-Interscience, 1972.
*Linear Optimal Control;* B. D. O. Anderson and J. B. Moore; Prentice-Hall, 1971.

**Section 9-6, 9-7**   *Probability and Stochastic Processes for Engineers;* C. W. Helstrom; Macmillan, 1984.
*Stochastic Optimal Linear Estimation and Control;* J. S. Meditch; McGraw-Hill Book Co., 1969.
*Optimal Filtering;* B. D. O. Anderson and J. B. Moore; Prentice-Hall, 1979.

## PROBLEMS

**9-1**   Discuss qualitatively whether the $Q$ or the $R$ matrix in Eq. (9-6) should dominate the performance index when
(a) speed of response is desired.
(b) fuel economy is of greater importance.

**9-2**   Describe a control problem in which the terminal cost term would serve an important role.

**9-3**   Occasionally it becomes necessary to deal with a performance index that has the form

$$J = \frac{1}{2} \sum_{k=0}^{\infty} [\mathbf{x}^T(k)Q\mathbf{x}(k) + 2\mathbf{x}^T(k)M\mathbf{u}(k) + \mathbf{u}^T(k)R\mathbf{u}(k)]$$

Show that a preliminary feedback corresponding to

$$\mathbf{u}(k) = -R^{-1}M^T\mathbf{x}(k) + \mathbf{v}(k)$$

will reduce the problem to a standard performance index with no cross-product terms.

**9-4**   Given the scalar discrete-time system

$$x(k + 1) = x(k) + u(k), \quad x(0) = 1$$

and performance index

$$J = \frac{1}{2} x^2(N) + \frac{1}{2} \sum_{k=0}^{N-1} [x^2(k) + u^2(k)]$$

(a) Calculate and plot the optimal feedback gain sequence $F(k)$ for a three-stage process ($N = 3$). Three-place accuracy will suffice.
(b) Calculate and plot the optimal trajectory and control history. Find the control cost using the expression for $J$ and check your result by using Eq. (9-28).
(c) Determine the optimal steady state feedback gain (infinite horizon gain, $N = \infty$) $F$ to three-place accuracy.
(d) Estimate the restriction on the control interval such that $F$ of part (c) could be used on this system without significant degradation from optimal control.

**9-5** Repeat the exercises of Problem 9-4 for the following system.

$$x(k + 1) = x(k) + u(k), \quad x(0) = 10$$

$$J = \frac{1}{2} \sum_{k=0}^{7} [x^2(k) + 4u^2(k)]$$

**9-6** For the following scalar system and cost functional

$$x(k + 1) = x(k) + u(k)$$

$$J = 0.1x^2(N) + \sum_{k=0}^{N-1} [0.1x^2(k) + u^2(k)]$$

**(a)** Use recursion to establish the steady state feedback gain $F$ to three-place accuracy.

**(b)** Check the result of part (a) by assuming a steady state condition for $F$ and $D$ in Eqs. (9-24) and (9-26).

**9-7** Repeat the exercise of Problem 9-6 for the system

$$\mathbf{x}(k + 1) = \begin{bmatrix} -1 & 1 \\ 0 & -1 \end{bmatrix} \mathbf{x}(k) + \begin{bmatrix} 0 \\ 1 \end{bmatrix} u(k)$$

$$J = \frac{1}{2} \sum_{k=0}^{\infty} \left\{ \mathbf{x}^T(k) \begin{bmatrix} 1 & 0 \\ 0 & 4 \end{bmatrix} \mathbf{x}(k) + u^2(k) \right\}$$

**9-8** Use the system described in Problem 9-7 to repeat the exercise of Problem 9-4.

**9-9** For the sampled-data system shown in Fig. P9-9
**(a)** Write the discrete-time state model using the states labeled in the figure.
**(b)** Develop the SVF control using the performance index of Problem 9-7.
**(c)** Calculate the closed-loop poles for the system.

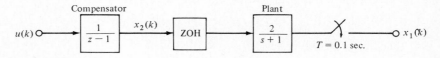

**FIGURE P9-9.**

**9-10** For the system described in Fig. P9-9:
**(a)** Find the locus of closed-loop system eigenvalues as a function of the parameter $q$ in the performance index

$$J = \frac{1}{2} \sum_{k=0}^{\infty} [qx_1^2(k) + u^2(k)]$$

**(b)** Determine the feedback gains for $q = 0.1$, 1, and 10.
**(c)** Plot the output $x_1(k)$ for $k = 0, 1, 2, \ldots, 10$ for each of the three sets of feedback gains found in part (b); use $\mathbf{x}(0) = [1, 0]^T$

**9-11**   For the discrete-time plant model

$$\mathbf{x}(k + 1) = \begin{bmatrix} 1 & 0.091 \\ 0 & 0.819 \end{bmatrix} \mathbf{x}(k) + \begin{bmatrix} 0.005 \\ 0.910 \end{bmatrix} u(k)$$

repeat the exercise of Problem 9-10.

**9-12**   Solve the optimal regulator problem

$$\mathbf{x}(k + 1) = \begin{bmatrix} -2 & 1 & 0 \\ 0 & -2 & 0 \\ 0 & 0 & 4 \end{bmatrix} \mathbf{x}(k) + \begin{bmatrix} 0 & 0 \\ 0 & 1 \\ 1 & 0 \end{bmatrix} u(k)$$

$$J = \frac{1}{2} \sum_{k=0}^{\infty} \left\{ \mathbf{x}^T(k) \begin{bmatrix} 1 & 0 & 0 \\ 0 & 0 & 0 \\ 0 & 0 & 4 \end{bmatrix} \mathbf{x}(k) + \mathbf{u}^T(k) \begin{bmatrix} 4 & 0 \\ 0 & 1 \end{bmatrix} \mathbf{u}(k) \right\}$$

**9-13**   Describe the locus of closed-loop poles for the system of Problem 9-12 with the cost functional

$$J = \frac{1}{2} \sum_{k=0}^{\infty} \{ q x_2^2(k) + [u_1(k) + u_2(k)]^2 \}$$

**9-14**   **(a)** Repeat the exercise of Problem 9-12 for the system

$$\mathbf{x}(k + 1) = \begin{bmatrix} -1 & 0.5 \\ 1 & -1 \end{bmatrix} \mathbf{x}(k) + \begin{bmatrix} 1 & 0 \\ 0 & 1 \end{bmatrix} \mathbf{u}(k), \quad \mathbf{x}(0) = \begin{bmatrix} 1 \\ 1 \end{bmatrix}$$

$$J = \frac{1}{2} \sum_{k=0}^{\infty} [\mathbf{x}^T(k)\mathbf{x}(k) + 0.5\mathbf{u}^T(k)\mathbf{u}(k)]$$

   **(b)** Find the closed-loop pole locations.
   **(c)** Plot the state trajectory: $x_1(k)$ and $x_2(k)$ versus $k$.
   **(d)** Plot the corresponding input history $u_1(k)$ and $u_2(k)$ versus $k$.

**9-15**   For the equivalent discrete-time system model

$$\mathbf{x}(k + 1) = \begin{bmatrix} -1 & 0.5 \\ 1 & -1 \end{bmatrix} \mathbf{x}(k) + \begin{bmatrix} 0 \\ 1 \end{bmatrix} u(k)$$

$$y(k) = [1 \quad 0] \mathbf{x}(k)$$

   **(a)** Develop the feedback and input gains $F$ and $G$ so that the system will respond to constant input commands in a Type 1 manner and that deviations from set-point condition recover by minimizing the performance index given in Eq. (9-63) with $Q = I$, $R = 4$
   **(b)** Plot the zero-state unit-step input response.

**9-16**   Repeat the exercise of Problem 9-15 using the same system, but with a change in $R$ to $R = 1$.

**9-17**    Consider the continuous-time plant described by the state model with associated cost functional given by

$$\dot{\mathbf{x}}(t) = \begin{bmatrix} 1 & 0 \\ 0 & -2 \end{bmatrix} \mathbf{x}(t) + \begin{bmatrix} 1 \\ 1 \end{bmatrix} u(t)$$

$$y(t) = [1 \quad 0] \mathbf{x}(t)$$

$$J = \int_0^\infty [y^2(t) + u^2(t)] \, dt$$

Suppose now that the actuation instants are $0, T, 2T, \ldots$ for $T = 0.5$ sec and that the output is measured at the same sample rate, but *not* at the same instants. Figure P9-17 illustrates the configuration of synchronized, but not time coincident, samplers. We can refer to the time interval of $\Delta = 0.2$ sec just prior to each actuation instant as the *control processing interval*. The fact that the output $y(t)$ is sampled at different instants of time from the actuation instants causes some modification in the ZOH model.

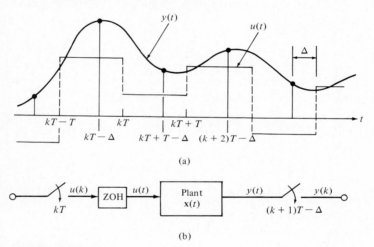

**FIGURE P9-17.**

**(a)** Develop the ZOH discrete-time model from the basic principles of Section 3-4. Your result should involve an output equation of the form

$$y(kT + T - \Delta) = C\Phi(T - \Delta)\mathbf{x}(kT) + C\Gamma(T - \Delta)u(kT)$$

where $\Phi$ and $\Gamma$ are as defined in Eq. (3-34).

**(b)** Discretize the continuous-time cost functional by first recognizing that

$$J = \int_0^\infty [\mathbf{x}^T(t)Q\mathbf{x}(t) + Ru^2(t)] \, dt$$

where

$$Q = \begin{bmatrix} 1 & 0 \\ 0 & 0 \end{bmatrix}, \quad R = 1$$

Second, write the integral as the sum of integrals over each actuation (sample) interval of $T$ seconds and show that

$$J = \sum_{k=0}^{\infty} [\mathbf{x}^T(k)\hat{Q}\mathbf{x}(k) + 2\mathbf{x}^T(k)\hat{M}u(k) + \hat{R}u^2(k)]$$

where

$$\hat{Q} = \int_0^T \Phi^T(t)Q\Phi(t)\, dt$$

$$\hat{M} = \int_0^T \Phi^T(t)Q\Gamma(t)\, dt$$

$$\hat{R} = \int_0^T [R + \Gamma^T(t)Q\Gamma(t)]\, dt$$

(c) Make an initial state variable feedback (as stated in Problem 9-3) to eliminate the cross-product term in $J$ from part (b).
(d) Calculate the optimal SVF gains $F$ such that $J$ is minimized subject to the sampled-data configuration of Fig. P9-17.
(e) Introduce the appropriate input gain $G$ for the closed-loop system to exhibit Type 1 behavior.
(f) Simulate the system's zero-state unit-step response for the completed design.

9-18    Draw the locus of closed-loop poles for the following system as a function of $q$.

$$\mathbf{x}(k + 1) = \begin{bmatrix} 1 & 0.632 \\ 0 & 0.368 \end{bmatrix} \mathbf{x}(k) + \begin{bmatrix} 0.368 \\ 0.632 \end{bmatrix} u(k)$$

$$y(k) = [1 \quad 0]\, \mathbf{x}(k)$$

$$J = \frac{1}{2} \sum_{k=0}^{\infty} [qy^2(k) + u^2(k)]$$

9-19    Discuss the dual statements that would correspond to the feedback statements made in Problem 9-3.

9-20    A uniform sampler and clamp (zero-order hold) is applied to a continuous-time input $u(t)$. The resulting staircase signal $w(t)$ drives a continuous-time system whose transfer function is $(s + 1)^{-1}$. The error $e(t) = u(t) - w(t)$ is to be considered as input noise. The system output is sampled in synchrony with the input sampler and is measured with a device whose error at any sample is an uncorrelated $N(0, 1)$ variable.
(a) Formulate a complete discrete-time Gauss–Markov model for the system. State any assumptions on $T$, $u(t)$, and/or $e(t)$.
(b) Design an optimal steady state estimator for the system. What is disturbing about the estimator gains?

**9-21** The input signal $v(k)$ shown in Fig. P9-21 is a white noise sequence with power spectral density $S_v(z) = N_o$. The figure illustrates how a nonwhite sequence can be modeled from a white sequence. If $|p| < 1$,
  **(a)** write an expression for the spectral density of the output $y(k)$ in terms of $z$ and the given parameters.
  **(b)** plot the input and output spectral density functions versus $\omega$ for $\omega < \pi$.
  **(c)** invert $S_v(z)$ and $S_y(z)$ to obtain the autocorrelation sequences associated with the signals $v(k)$ and $y(k)$, respectively.

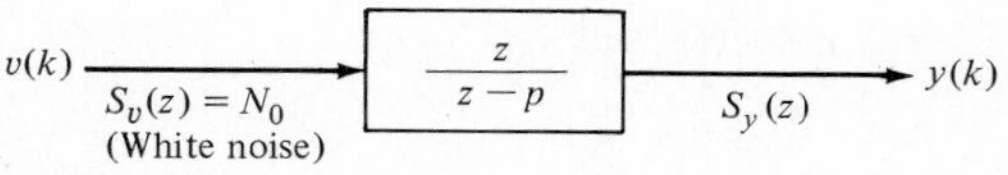

$$v(k) \longrightarrow \boxed{\dfrac{z}{z - p}} \longrightarrow y(k)$$
$$S_v(z) = N_0 \qquad\qquad S_y(z)$$
$$\text{(White noise)}$$

**FIGURE P9-21.**

**9-22** A discrete-time system is defined through the difference equation

$$y(k) + ay(k - 1) = x(k) + bx(k - 1)$$

with $|a| < 1$, $|b| < 1$, $a \ne b$, and $y(0) = 0$.
  **(a)** Write the transfer function $H(z) = Y(z)/X(z)$.
  **(b)** If $x(k) \sim N(0, 1)$ and is a white random sequence, calculate $S_y(z)$, the output power spectral density, and $R_y(n)$, the corresponding autocorrelation sequence.
  **(c)** Describe the equations that represent the propagation of the mean of $y(k)$ and the propagation of the variance of $y(k)$. Solve for the steady state value of the variance of $y(k)$ in terms of $a$ and $b$. Was this value previously known from $R_y(n)$?

**9-23** The frequency representation of the spectral density of the signal $x(k)$ is given by

$$S_x(e^{j\omega}) = \frac{2 + 2 \cos \omega}{5 + 4 \cos \omega}$$

Model this signal as the output of a unit-variance white sequence driving a (stable) linear system $H(z)$. Specify $H(z)$.

**9-24** The signal $y(k)$ is the output of the system

$$H(z) = \frac{z(z - 0.2)}{(z + 0.8)(z + 0.5)}$$

when the input is an independent random sequence each element of which is distributed as a $N(1, 1)$ variable.
  **(a)** Write an equation for the mean value of $y(k)$ if $y(0) = y(1) = 0$.
  **(b)** Find the steady state variance of $y(k)$.

**9-25**   Describe how one might model a zero-mean, random signal $s(k)$ whose spectral density is provided, not analytically, but as a specific plot versus frequency.

**9-26**   Draw the locus of estimator poles for a system whose transfer function between plant noise input and measured output is

$$H(z) = \frac{0.01(z + 0.8)}{(z - 1)(z - 0.6)}$$

as a function of the ratio of plant noise variance to measurement noise variance $Q_1/Q_2$.

**9-27**   A random signal $w(k)$ is distributed as $N(0, 4)$ for $k = 0, 1, 2, \ldots$. Determine a signal model for $w(k)$ if $w(k)$ is time-correlated from sample to sample with a correlation coefficient of 0.5.
*Hint:* Set up a model $w(k + 1) = aw(k) + v(k)$ and determine the parameter $a$ so that $E[w^2(k)] = 4$ and the variance of $v(k)$ so that the correlation coefficient

$$\rho = \frac{E[w(k + 1)w(k)]}{\text{Var } [w(k)]} = 0.5$$

**9-28**   A nonwhite random disturbance is modeled by the first-order system

$$w_1(k + 1) = 0.5w_1(k) + v(k)$$

where $v(k) \sim N[0, 3]$ is a white noise sequence. The plant model is given by

$$x(k + 1) = 0.5x(k) + w_1(k), \quad x(0) = 0$$

$$y(k) = x(k) + w_2(k)$$

Design an optimal estimator for $x(k)$ based on the measurements $y(k)$, $k = 0$, 1, 2, . . . , where $w_2(k) \sim N[0, 1]$ is a white noise process.
*Hint:* You will need to use the composite state $[x(k) \; w_1(k)]^T$

**9-29**   Describe how to obtain pairs of random numbers (to simulate a two-dimensional white sequence) having a mean $[1 \quad 3]^T$ and covariance matrix

$$\begin{bmatrix} 4 & 1 \\ 1 & 4 \end{bmatrix}$$

from independent $N[0,1]$ sample numbers.
*Hint:* If $\mathbf{x} \sim N[\mathbf{0}, P_x]$, and $\mathbf{y} = M\mathbf{x}$, then $\mathbf{y} \sim N[\mathbf{0}, MP_xM^T]$. Consider letting $M = D^{-1/2}V$, where $D = \text{diag } \{\lambda_1, \lambda_2, \ldots, \lambda_n\}$, the diagonal matrix of the eigenvalues of $P_x$ and $V$ is the normalized modal matrix of $P_x$ ($V^T = V^{-1}$).

**9-30**   Given the plant and measurement models [corresponding to $\ddot{y}(t) = u(t) = g$ and $y(t)$ measured every second as illustrated in Fig. P9-30]

$$\mathbf{x}(k + 1) = \begin{bmatrix} 1 & 1 \\ 0 & 1 \end{bmatrix} \mathbf{x}(k) \begin{bmatrix} 0.5 \\ 1 \end{bmatrix} u(k)$$

$$z(k) = [\, 1 \quad 0\,] \; \mathbf{x}(k) + v(k)$$

where

$$\mathbf{x}(0) \sim N[\mathbf{0}, \text{diag} \{0, 100\}], \quad v(k) \sim N[0, 1]$$

and

$$u(k) = 32.2 \text{ (constant) for } k \geq 0$$

with $v(k)$ white and uncorrelated with $\mathbf{x}(0)$:
**(a)** Develop the optimal estimator for $\mathbf{x}(k)$.
**(b)** Run the estimator given that

$$z(k) = \{25.3, 85.7, 174.3, \ldots\}, \text{ (three cycles)}$$

**(c)** What are the steady state gains for the optimal estimator?

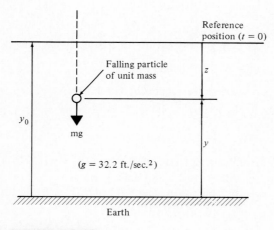

**FIGURE P9-30.**

**9-31**  For the discrete-time system shown in Fig. P9-31:
**(a)** Establish a state model using the indicated state variables $x_1$ and $x_2$. Assume that $w_1$ and $w_2$ are zero-mean, uncorrelated, white noise inputs having variances of 1.0 and 0.09, respectively, and that $\mathbf{x}(0) = \mathbf{0}$. The measured variable is $y$.
**(b)** Design a SVF matrix $F$ to minimize the cost functional

$$J = \frac{1}{2} \sum_{k=0}^{\infty} [\mathbf{x}^T(k)Q\mathbf{x}(k) + Ru^2(k)]$$

where

$$Q = \begin{bmatrix} 4 & 0 \\ 0 & 1 \end{bmatrix}, \quad R = 1$$

**(c)** Design an optimal steady state estimator so that the control input is $u(k) = F\hat{\mathbf{x}}(k) + Gr(k)$, where $\hat{\mathbf{x}}(k)$ is the estimator state.

**(d)** Draw the overall closed-loop system diagram.

**(e)** Simulate the unit-step response $[r(k) = 1(k)]$ of the stochastic control system and plot the state trajectory: $x_1(k)$ and $x_2(k)$ versus $k$ and the control history $u(k)$ versus $k$.

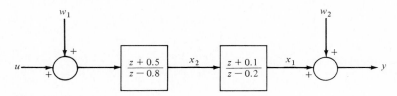

**FIGURE P9-31.**

# Laplace Transforms

The Laplace Transform provides a unique relationship between real-valued functions of time and functions of a complex variable $s$.

## A-1

## BACKGROUND

A complex number $z$ will be represented by a combination of two real numbers $x$ and $y$ with the following *rectangular form* notation

$$z = x + jy, \qquad \text{(A-1)}$$

where $j = \sqrt{-1}$ is the *imaginary unit*, $x$ is the *real part of z* and $y$ is the *imaginary part of z*. An alternate form called the *polar form* is given by

$$z = r\underline{/\theta} \qquad \text{(A-2)}$$

where $r$ is the *magnitude of z* and $\theta$ is the *angle of z*. The parameters of the two forms are related by

$$r^2 = x^2 + y^2, \quad \tan \theta = y/x \qquad \text{(A-3)}$$

Two complex numbers $z_1 = x_1 + y_1$ and $z_2 = x_2 + y_2$:

(i)   Add to form a new complex number of $z_3$

$$z_3 = z_1 + z_2 = (x_1 + x_2) + j(y_1 + y_2) \tag{A-4}$$

(ii)   Multiply to form a new complex number $z_4$:

$$z_4 = z_1 z_2 = (x_1 x_2 - y_1 y_2) + j(x_1 y_2 + x_2 y_1) \tag{A-5}$$

Euler's formula states that if $\theta$ is real,

$$\exp(j\theta) = \cos\theta + j\sin\theta \tag{A-6}$$

It follows that

$$r \exp(j\theta) = r\cos\theta + jr\sin\theta = r\underline{/\theta} \tag{A-7}$$

In other words, $\exp(j\theta)$ is simply a rotation of $\theta$ (radians) in the standard counter clockwise direction.

### Remarks:
- A real number is a special case of a complex number with zero imaginary part.
- Since $j = \sqrt{-1}, j^2 = -1, j^3 = -j, j^4 = +1$, and so on.
- The polar form is generally more convenient for multiplication:

$$z_4 = z_1 z_2 = r_1 e^{j\theta_1} r_2 e^{j\theta_2} = r_1 r_2 e^{j(\theta_1 + \theta_2)} \tag{A-8}$$

where the property of exponential functions has been used.

The *complex conjugate* of $z = x + jy = re^{j\theta}$ is $\bar{z} = x - jy = re^{-j\theta}$. Therefore, the magnitude of $z$ is $\sqrt{z\bar{z}}$.

### Functions of Complex Variables.
A mapping from one complex number plane to another can be described by a complex function, $z = f(s)$. Thus, given a "point" $s_o$ in the $s$ plane, the image point in the $z$ plane is $z_o = f(s_o)$.

Since complex numbers are points in a plane, there are special considerations concerning continuity and derivatives of complex functions. For instance, in taking the limit of $\Delta z$ as it approaches zero, one must specify the path of the approach. Fortunately, there is a large class of well-behaved functions, called *analytic functions,* whose derivatives exist (without regard to the path of the defining limit operation) in their region of definition. If

$$z = f(x + jy) = u(x, y) + jv(x, y) \tag{A-9}$$

then the *Cauchy–Riemann conditions,*

$$\frac{\partial u}{\partial x} = \frac{\partial v}{\partial y}, \quad \frac{\partial v}{\partial x} = -\frac{\partial u}{\partial y} \tag{A-10}$$

provide the defining relations for $f(\ )$ to be analytic.

*Complex Integration.*    The integral

$$I = \int_{z_1}^{z_2} f(z)\, dz \qquad (A\text{-}11)$$

is generally dependent on the particular path connecting $z_1$ and $z_2$; however, if $f(\ )$ is analytic, $I$ is independent of the path.

In our work we often come across complex functions that are analytic except at isolated singularities (poles). For this situation there is a particularly simple method of evaluating integrals in the complex plane known as the *Residue Theorem.*

The residue theorem deals with closed-path integrals, denoted by

$$\oint_C F(z)\, dz = I_C \qquad (A\text{-}12)$$

where $C$ is a simple closed path in the plane. Instead of evaluating the integral directly, the method of residues states that $I_C$ of Eq. (A-12) is given by

$$I_C = 2\pi j \sum_{i=1}^{n} [\text{residues of } F(z) \text{ at } z_i] \qquad (A\text{-}13)$$

where $z_i$ represent the poles of $F$ inside $C$.

### EXAMPLE A-1

We wish to evaluate $I_C$ in Eq. (A-12) given that $C$ is the unit circle (centered at the origin) and that

$$F(z) = \frac{z + 1}{z(z - 2)(z - 0.5)}$$

**SOLUTION:** There are two poles inside $C$: $z = 0$, $z = 0.5$. Calculating the residues (see Section 1-3.1):

$$\text{Res}\,[F(z), z = 0] = zF(z)|_{z=0} = 1$$

$$\text{Res}\,[F(z), z = 0.5] = (z - 0.5)F(z)|_{z=0.5} = -2$$

Therefore,

$$I_C = 2\pi j[1 - 2] = -2\pi j \qquad \blacksquare$$

### A-2

## THE LAPLACE TRANSFORM

Given a real-valued time function $f(t)$ defined for $t \geq 0$ satisfying that for some $\sigma > 0$

$$\int_{0^-}^{\infty} f(t)e^{-\sigma t} < \infty \qquad (A\text{-}14)$$

then, the *Laplace transform* of $f(t)$ is defined by

$$\mathcal{L}[f(t)] = F(s) = \int_{0^-}^{\infty} f(t)e^{-st}\, dt \qquad \text{(A-15)}$$

where $F$ is a complex function of the complex variable $s$. $F(s)$ is defined for all $s$ in the region Re $[s] > \sigma$.

### EXAMPLE A-2

We wish to calculate the Laplace transform $F(s)$ of $f(t) = \exp\,(-at)$, $t \geq 0,\ a > 0$.

### *SOLUTION:*

$$F(s) = \int_{0^-}^{\infty} e^{-at}e^{-st}\, dt = \int_{0}^{\infty} e^{-(s+a)t}\, dt$$

$$F(s) = \frac{1}{s + a}\left[e^{-(s+a)}\right]_{t=\infty}^{t=0}$$

$$F(s) = \frac{1}{s + a} \text{ for Re } [s] > -a \qquad \text{(A-16)}$$

since the term in the brackets approaches zero for large $t$ whenever Re $[s] > -a$. ∎

*Remark:* Normally the region of convergence can be omitted. If all functions $f(t)$ are transformable and single-sided, then the region of definition is always a right-half plane similar to that specified in Eq. (A-16).

Table A-1 presents a useful collection of transform pairs. This table can be used effectively to invert $F(s)$ to obtain $f(t)$ by first expanding $F(s)$ into partial fractions as discussed in Section 2-3.3 with the exception that $F(s)$ and not $F(z)/z$ is used for the expansion.

### EXAMPLE A-3

We wish to find $f(t)$, $t \geq 0$, which corresponds to the Laplace domain function

$$F(s) = \frac{2}{s(s + 2)}$$

*SOLUTION:* Expanding $F$ into partial fractions,

$$F(s) = \frac{A}{s} + \frac{B}{s + 2}$$

where $A = \text{Res }[F(s),\ s = 0] = 1.$ and $B = \text{Res }[F(s),\ s = -2] = -1.$ Therefore (from Table A-1), $f(t) = 1 - e^{-2t}$, $t \geq 0$ ∎

**TABLE A-1   Selected Laplace Transform Pairs**

| Time Domain $f(t),\ t \geq 0$ | Laplace Domain $F(s)$ |
|---|---|
| 1. Unit impulse, $\delta(t)$ | 1 |
| 2. Unit step, $1(t)$ | $s^{-1}$ |
| 3. Unit ramp, $t$ | $s^{-2}$ |
| 4. $t^k/k!$ | $s^{-(k+1)}$ |
| 5. $e^{-at}$ | $(s+a)^{-1}$ |
| 6. $te^{-at}$ | $(s+a)^{-2}$ |
| 7. $\sin bt$ | $b/(s^2 + b^2)$ |
| 8. $\cos bt$ | $s/(s^2 + b^2)$ |
| 9. $e^{-at}\sin bt$ | $b/[(s+a)^2 + b^2]$ |
| 10. $e^{-at}\cos bt$ | $(s+a)/[(s+a)^2 + b^2]$ |

Laplace transforms are particularly useful for solving constant coefficient, linear differential systems. The transform of time derivatives and other properties are listed in Table A-2.

**TABLE A-2   Selected Laplace Transform Properties**

| Time Domain | Laplace Domain |
|---|---|
| *Linearity* | |
| 1. $af(t) + bg(t)$ | $aF(s) + bG(s)$ |
| *Time Derivatives* | |
| 2. $\dot{f}(t)$ | $sF(s) - f(0^-)$ |
| 3. $\ddot{f}(t)$ | $s^2F(s) - sf(0^-) - \dot{f}(0^-)$ |
| *Integration* | |
| 4. $\int_0^t f(t)\,dt$ | $F(s)/s$ |
| *Time Shift (Delay)* | |
| 5. $f(t-a)\,1(t-a)$ | $e^{-as}F(s)$ |
| *Frequency Shift* | |
| 6. $e^{-at}f(t)$ | $F(s+a)$ |
| *Frequency Derivative* | |
| 7. $-tf(t)$ | $dF(s)/ds$ |
| *Final Value Theorem* | |
| 8. $f(\infty) = \lim\limits_{t\to\infty} f(t) = \lim\limits_{s\to 0} sF(s)$ providing that $sF(s)$ has | |

only left-half plane poles.

## EXAMPLE A-4 (Solution of a Differential Equation)

To solve for $y(t)$, $t \geq 0$ if $r(t) =$ unit-step input, $y(0^-) = 0$,

$$\dot{y}(0^-) = 4, \text{ and } \ddot{y}(0^-) = -2$$

$$\dddot{y}(t) + 2\ddot{y}(t) = 4r(t)$$

**SOLUTION:** Transforming,

$$[s^3Y(s) - s^2y(0) - s\dot{y}(0) - \ddot{y}(0)] + 2[s^2Y(s) - sy(0) - \dot{y}(0)] = 4/s$$

$$(s^3 + 2s^2)Y(s) - 4s + 2 - 8 = 4s^{-1}$$

$$Y(s) = \frac{4s^2 + 6s + 4}{s^3(s + 2)}$$

Inverting,

$$Y(s) = \frac{A}{s^3} + \frac{B}{s^2} + \frac{C}{s} + \frac{D}{s + 2}$$

$$A = s^3Y(s)\big|_{s=0} = 2$$

$$B = \frac{d}{ds}[s^3Y(s)]\big|_{s=0} = 2 \quad \text{(See Section 2-3.3.)}$$

$$C = \frac{1}{2}\frac{d^2}{ds^2}[s^3Y(s)]\big|_{s=0} = 1$$

$$D = (s + 2)Y(s)\big|_{s=-2} = -1$$

Therefore (from Table A-1),

$$y(t) = t^2 + 2t + 1 - e^{-2t}, \quad t \geq 0 \qquad \blacksquare$$

## A-3

## DERIVATION OF THE z-TRANSFORM

In Eq. (2-3) the Laplace transform of an ideally (impulse) sampled continuous-time function was given as a means for motivating the definition of the z-transform and thereby establishing the relation between the s and z variables, namely,

$$z = e^{sT} \tag{A-17}$$

where $T$ is the uniform sample period. We will now develop the z-transform in a different way that can help our understanding of the periodic nature of the discrete-time signal spectrum and signal reconstruction.

We know that in Laplace transform theory the product of two time-domain functions corresponds to a convolution of the associated transform pair functions in the s domain. This can be written as

$$\mathscr{L}\{f(t)g(t)\} = \frac{1}{2\pi j}\int_{\sigma_o-j\infty}^{\sigma_o+j\infty} F(p)G(s - p)\,dp \tag{A-18}$$

where $\sigma_o$ is chosen in the appropriate convergence region. Assuming that $f(t)$ is a causal signal [$F(s)$ converges for Re $[s] > \sigma_1$], the integration path must be taken so that

$$\sigma_1 < \sigma_o < \text{Re } [s] - \sigma_2 \tag{A-19}$$

where $G(s)$ is defined for Re $[s] > \sigma_2$ since the right-hand side of Eq. (A-18) converges for Re $[s] > \sigma_1 + \sigma_2$.

When we represent the impulse-sampled signal as

$$f^*(t) = f(t) \sum_{n=0}^{\infty} \delta(t - nT) \tag{A-20}$$

we recognize that it is a product of two time-domain signals. Thus, we apply Eq. (A-18) with

$$G(s) = \sum_{n=0}^{\infty} e^{-nTs} = \frac{1}{1 - e^{-sT}} \tag{A-21}$$

This combination gives us the transform of $f^*(t)$ as

$$F^*(s) = \frac{1}{2\pi j} \int_{\sigma_o - j\infty}^{\sigma_o + j\infty} \left[ \frac{F(p)\, dp}{1 - e^{-(s-p)T}} \right] \tag{A-22}$$

Figure A-1 shows typical pole placements using the fact that the zeros of the denominator expression in the integrand of Eq. (A-22) are the roots of

$$e^{-(s-p)T} = 1 \tag{A-23}$$

or

$$e^{-(\sigma-u)T} e^{-j(\omega-v)T + j2\pi k} = 1 \tag{A-24}$$

for $k = 0, \pm 1, \pm 2, \ldots$, where $s = \sigma + j\omega$ and $p = u + jv$. This implies

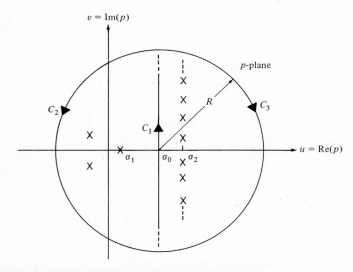

**FIGURE A-1.  Integration path for Equation A-18.**

(from the magnitude and angle) that

$$\sigma - u = 0, \quad \omega - v + \frac{2\pi k}{T} = 0 \tag{A-25}$$

Combining these results, the roots are

$$q_k = s + j2\pi k/T \text{ for } k = 0, \pm 1, \pm 2, \ldots \tag{A-26}$$

The key to evaluating Eq. (A-18) is to use the Residue Theorem. [See Eqs. (A-12) and (A-13).] Two results are forthcoming depending on whether we close to the left along $C_2$ or to the right along $C_3$. Closing a path to the left, as shown in Fig. A-1, along a circular path where

$$p = \sigma_o + Re^{j\theta} \tag{A-27}$$

for $\theta$ varying from $\pi/2$ through $\pi$ to $3\pi/2$, we obtain an integral of the form shown in Eq. (A-12). However, before using the result of Eq. (A-13), we must determine the integral contribution along the semicircular path. For this we require $F(s)$ to be strictly proper, that is, have at least one excess pole:

$$\lim_{s \to \infty} F(s) = 0 \tag{A-28}$$

In fact, from the differentiation property,

$$\lim_{s \to \infty} \int_{0^-}^{\infty} \dot{f}(t)e^{-st} \, dt = \lim_{s \to \infty} [sF(s) - f(0^-)] \tag{A-29}$$

The limit operation on the left may be taken inside the integral since the integration is independent of $s$. In this case the left-hand side of Eq. (A-29) is zero (in the region of Re $[s]$ greater than the abscissa of convergence), and we have the result that

$$\lim_{s \to \infty} sF(s) = f(0^-) \tag{A-30}$$

This is referred to as the *Initial-Value Theorem*.

Since $R$ will be taken to be very large, we approximate $p$ from Eq. (A-27) as $p = Re^{j\theta}$ and write

$$I_2 = \lim_{R \to \infty} \frac{1}{2\pi j} \int_{\pi/2}^{3\pi/2} \frac{f(0^-)}{Re^{j\theta}} jRe^{j\theta} \, d\theta = \frac{f(0^-)}{2} \tag{A-31}$$

where $F(p)$ has been replaced with $f(0^-)/p$ from Eq. (A-30) for large $p$ and the $G(s - p)$ factor is unity since the exponential term goes to zero:

$$\lim_{R \to \infty} e^{-(s-p)T} \Big|_{p=Re^{j\theta}} = \lim_{R \to \infty} e^{RT(\cos\theta + j\sin\theta)} = 0 \tag{A-32}$$

for $\pi/2 \le \theta \le 3\pi/2$ (since the cosine is negative).

Now, recalling Eq. (A-13), we can write Eq. (A-22) as

$$F^*(s) = \sum_k \text{Res} \left[ \frac{F(p)}{1 - e^{(p-s)T}}, p_k \right] - \frac{f(0^-)}{2} \tag{A-33}$$

where $\{p_k\}$ are the poles of $F(p)$. With $z = e^{sT}$ we have an alternate means of obtaining $z$-transforms, namely,

$$\hat{F}(z) = \sum_k \text{Res} \left[ \frac{F(p)}{1 - e^{pT}z^{-1}}, p_k \right] - \frac{1}{2} f(0^-) \tag{A-34}$$

### EXAMPLE A-5 (z-Transform Using Residues)

Obtain the $z$-transform of a unit-step function using Eq. (A-34).

**SOLUTION:** For a unit step $F(s) = 1/s$ has only one pole at the origin ($p_1 = 0$), so that

$$\hat{F}(z) = \text{Res} \left[ \frac{1}{p(1 - e^{pT}z^{-1})}, 0 \right]$$

Therefore

$$\hat{F}(z) = \left. \frac{1}{1 - e^{pT}z^{-1}} \right|_{p=0} = \frac{1}{1 - z^{-1}}$$

as expected. ∎

*Remark:* The initial-value term in Eq. (A-34) may also be interpreted as $f(0)$ instead of $f(0^-)$. In this case there is a difference between the $z$-transform pairs used in Chapter 2 and those obtained from Eq. (A-34) when the time-domain function $f(t)$ has a discontinuity at $t = 0$. With these functions the $z$-transform is modified to have the midpoint of the initial discontinuity. For consistency we will use Eq. (A-34) as stated [with $f(0^-) = 0$].

An alternate method for determining residues is sometimes useful when the denominator of $F(s)$ is not factorable. For a function $F(s)$ with simple poles at $p_1, p_2, \ldots, p_n$

$$\text{Res} [F(s), p_k] = (s - p_k)F(s)|_{s=p_k} \tag{A-35}$$

for $k = 1, 2, \ldots, n$. If we assume that $F(s) = N(s)/D(s)$, then

$$\text{Res} [F(s), p_k] = \left. (s - p_k) \frac{N(s)}{D(s)} \right|_{s=p_k} \tag{A-36}$$

where $p_k$ is a root of $D(s) = 0$. Thus,

$$(p_k - p_k) \frac{N(p_k)}{D(p_k)} = \frac{0}{0} \quad \text{(indeterminate)}$$

However, using L'Hospital's rule:

$$\text{Res } [F(s), p_k] = \left. \frac{(s - p_k)N'(s) + N(s)}{D'(s)} \right|_{s = p_k}$$

which reduces to

$$\text{Res } [F(s), p_k] = \frac{N(p_k)}{D'(p_k)} \qquad (A\text{-}37)$$

where $D'(s) = dD/ds$.

### EXAMPLE A-6

We wish to recalculate the result of Example A-5 using Eq. (A-37).

### SOLUTION:

$$\hat{F}(z) = 1/[p(-z^{-1}e^{pT}T) + (1 - e^{pT}z^{-1})]\big|_{p=0}$$

$$\hat{F}(z) = \frac{1}{1 - z^{-1}} \qquad \blacksquare$$

The second form for $F^*(s)$ in Eq. (A-22) mentioned earlier can be obtained by closing the contour to the right. The development follows along similar lines leading to the result that

$$F^*(s) = -\sum_{k=-\infty}^{\infty} \text{Res} \left[ \frac{F(p)}{1 - e^{(p-s)T}}, q_k \right] + \frac{f(0)}{2} \qquad (A\text{-}38)$$

where $q_k = s + j2\pi k/T$ for $k = 0, \pm 1, \pm 2, \ldots$ as developed in Eq. (A-26). The negative sign in Eq. (A-38) is the result of a clockwise, rather than a counterclockwise, contour in the $p$ plane in Fig. A-1.

Introducing Eq. (A-37) into Eq. (A-38), we obtain

$$F^*(s) = -\sum_{k=-\infty}^{\infty} \left. \frac{F(p)}{\dfrac{d}{dp} [1 - e^{(p-s)T}]} \right|_{p=q_k} + \frac{f(0)}{2} \qquad (A\text{-}39)$$

with $q_k$ as given in Eq. (A-38).

Carrying out the indicated operations in Eq. (A-39) gives us

$$F^*(s) = \frac{1}{T} \sum_{k=-\infty}^{\infty} F\left( s + j\frac{2\pi k}{T} \right) + \frac{f(0)}{2} \qquad (A\text{-}40)$$

Again, the $z$-transform of $f(t)$ may be written as

$$\hat{F}(z) = F^*(s)\big|_{s=\frac{1}{T} \ln z \, (z = e^{sT})} \qquad (A\text{-}41)$$

***Signal Reconstruction.*** Perhaps the most useful aspect of Eq. (A-41) is that of the frequency-domain representation of a $z$-domain function. If the orig-

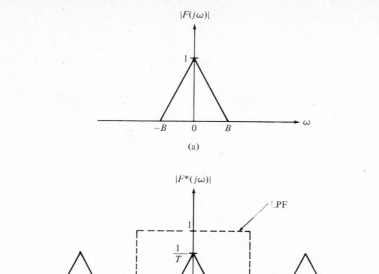

**FIGURE A-2.** (a) band limited continuous-time signal; (b) spectrum of the ideally sampled signal.

inal signal $f(t)$ is *band-limited,* then

$$F(s)|_{s=j\omega} = 0 \text{ for } |\omega| > B \tag{A-42}$$

and $B$ is the *bandwidth.* For example, $F(j\omega)$ may have a magnitude versus frequency plot as shown in Fig. A-2a. The frequency plot of the ideally sampled signal is given by Eq. (A-40) with $s = j\omega$:

$$F^*(j\omega) = \frac{1}{T} \sum_{k=-\infty}^{\infty} F[j(\omega + k\omega_s)] + \frac{f(0)}{2} \tag{A-43}$$

where $\omega_s = 2\pi/T$ is the sampling frequency in rad/sec. Working from the $z$-domain, the frequency response is given as

$$\hat{F}(z)|_{z=e^{j\omega T}} = F^*(j\omega) \tag{A-44}$$

That is to say, the frequency plot of $\hat{F}(z)$ is the same as that of $F^*(s)$. Figure A-2b illustrates the repetitive nature of the discrete-time signal spectrum.

**The Sampling Theorem:**   If a band-limited signal $f(t)$ with $F(j\omega) = 0$ for $|\omega| > B$ is sampled at a rate of $\omega_s = 2\pi/T$ rad/sec to obtain the discrete-time signal $f(kT)$, then $f(t)$ can be reconstructed as accurately as required from its samples if and only if

$$\omega_s > 2B \qquad \text{(A-45)}$$

One means of reconstructing $f(t)$ is to low-pass filter the sampled signal $f^*(t)$ with a filter whose frequency response approximates the dashed lines in Fig. A-2b. Since the filter response cannot achieve an abrupt cutoff as shown, the practical design is eased if $\omega_s \gg 2B$. Thus, one generally samples at 5 to 10 times the minimum rate of $2B$ (which is known as the *Nyquist* rate). See also Section 1-3.1.

# Matrix Algebra

## LINEAR EQUATIONS

We may represent the set of linear equations

$$a_{11}x_1 + a_{12}x_2 + \cdots + a_{1n}x_n = b_1$$
$$a_{21}x_1 + a_{22}x_2 + \cdots + a_{2n}x_n = b_2$$
$$\cdots$$
$$a_{n1}x_1 + a_{n2}x_2 + \cdots + a_{nn}x_n = b_n$$

(B-1)

in the matrix-vector form

$$A\mathbf{x} = \mathbf{b}$$

(B-2)

where $A$ is the array (matrix) of coefficients

$$A = \begin{bmatrix} a_{11} \ a_{12} \cdot \cdot \cdot a_{1n} \\ a_{21} \ a_{22} \cdot \cdot \cdot a_{2n} \\ \cdot \cdot \cdot \\ a_{n1} \ a_{n2} \cdot \cdot \cdot a_{nn} \end{bmatrix}$$

(B-3)

and both $\mathbf{x}$ and $\mathbf{b}$ are $n$-vectors

$$\mathbf{x} = \begin{bmatrix} x_1 \\ x_2 \\ \cdot \\ \cdot \\ \cdot \\ x_n \end{bmatrix}, \qquad \mathbf{b} = \begin{bmatrix} b_1 \\ b_2 \\ \cdot \\ \cdot \\ \cdot \\ b_n \end{bmatrix} \qquad \text{(B-4)}$$

Typically, $A$ and $\mathbf{b}$ are known and $\mathbf{x}$ is to be found.

An interpretation of Eq. (B-2) is to think of the matrix $A$ as an operator that transfers (or maps) the vector $\mathbf{x}$ into the vector $\mathbf{b}$. As such, then, for a solution $\mathbf{x}$ to exist, $\mathbf{b}$ must be in the *range of* $A$ (the set of vectors that are images of some vector under the operation $A$). Then any vector $\mathbf{y}$ in the range of $A$ can be written as a *linear combination* of the columns of $A$; that is,

$$\mathbf{y} = c_1 \mathbf{a}_1 + c_2 \mathbf{a}_2 + \cdots + c_n \mathbf{a}_n \qquad \text{(B-5)}$$

where

$$A = [\mathbf{a}_1 \ \mathbf{a}_2 \ \ldots \ \mathbf{a}_n] \text{ and the } c_k \text{ for } k = 1, 2, \ldots, n$$

are appropriate (constant) coefficients.

**Definition:**   A set of vectors is *linearly independent* if no vector in the set can be written as a linear combination of the others.

### EXAMPLE B-1 (Linear Independence)

Consider the set of vectors $\mathbf{x}$, $\mathbf{y}$, and $\mathbf{z}$ defined by

$$\mathbf{x} = \begin{bmatrix} 1 \\ 0 \\ 0 \end{bmatrix}, \quad \mathbf{y} = \begin{bmatrix} 0 \\ 1 \\ 0 \end{bmatrix}, \quad \mathbf{z} = \begin{bmatrix} 0 \\ 0 \\ 1 \end{bmatrix}$$

It is straightforward to show that there are no constants $c_1$ and $c_2$ such that

$$\mathbf{x} = c_1 \mathbf{y} + c_2 \mathbf{z}$$

or

$$\mathbf{y} = c_1 \mathbf{x} + c_2 \mathbf{z}$$

or

$$\mathbf{z} = c_1 \mathbf{x} + c_2 \mathbf{y}$$

Consequently, the vectors $\mathbf{x}$, $\mathbf{y}$, and $\mathbf{z}$ form a linearly independent set of vectors.

Returning to Eq. (B-2), we can say that a solution $\mathbf{x}$ exists if and only if $\mathbf{b}$ is not linearly independent of the columns of $A$. In fact, we already know that

$$\mathbf{x} = A^{-1}\mathbf{b} \qquad \text{(B-6)}$$

whenever the columns of $A$ are linearly independent (so that $A$ is invertible).  ■

For the cases where there are more or less equations than unknowns, the reader is referred to Section 7-2

**MATRIX ALGEBRA**

## EIGENSYSTEMS

The eigenvalues $\lambda$ and eigenvectors $\mathbf{e}$ of a matrix $A$ must satisfy that

$$A\mathbf{e} = \lambda\mathbf{e} \tag{B-7}$$

Equation (B-7) may be written as

$$(A - \lambda I)\mathbf{e} = \mathbf{0} \tag{B-8}$$

In order that a nontrivial solution ($\mathbf{e} \neq \mathbf{0}$) exist, $(A - \lambda I)$ must be singular; that is, det $(A - \lambda I) = 0$. However, if $A$ is an $n \times n$ matrix, then there are $n$ (possibly some repeated) roots of this $n$th-order polynomial equation. These roots are called the *eigenvalues* of $A$. Corresponding to each distinct eigenvalue there is at least a one-dimensional solution $\mathbf{e}$ to Eq. (B-8) called an *eigenvector*. The collection of eigenvalues and corresponding eigenvectors is called the *eigensystem* of $A$.

Whenever there are $n$ distinct eigenvalues for an $n \times n$ matrix, there will be $n$ linearly independent eigenvectors. By collecting these eigenvectors to form an $n \times n$ matrix $E$, we can write from Eq. (B-7) that

$$AE = E\Lambda, \qquad E^{-1}AE = \Lambda \tag{B-9}$$

where $E = [\mathbf{e}_1 \ \mathbf{e}_2 \ \ldots \ \mathbf{e}_n]$ is called the *modal* matrix of $A$ and $\Lambda = $ diag $\{\lambda_1, \lambda_2, \ldots, \lambda_n\}$ is a diagonalized version of $A$. The relation between $A$ and $\Lambda$ through the matrix $E$ is known as a *similarity transformation*.

### Special Cases
- If $A$ is a symmetric matrix, there will always exist $n$ linearly independent eigenvectors, even with repeated eigenvalues.
- The eigenvectors of a symmetric matrix $A$ are mutually orthogonal:

$$\mathbf{e}_i^T\mathbf{e}_j = 0 \quad \text{for } i = j \tag{B-10}$$

- Generally, when $A$ has repeated eigenvalues, there will not be $n$ linearly independent eigenvectors and $A$ cannot be diagonalized. A generalization is the Jordan canonical form, which is block diagonal as mentioned in Section 3-6.3.

## QUADRATIC FORMS

A quadratic expression in the variables $x_1, x_2, \ldots, x_n$ may be written as the scalar-valued function

$$Q(\mathbf{x}) = \mathbf{x}^T A\mathbf{x} \tag{B-11}$$

for some symmetric matrix $A$. Since $A$ is diagonalizable, we can write from Eq. (B-9) that

$$A = E\Lambda E^{-1} \tag{B-12}$$

Furthermore, we can normalize the columns of $E$ to have unit lengths so that $E^{-1} = E^T$. With the change of variables

$$\mathbf{x} = E\mathbf{y} \tag{B-13}$$

the quadratic function becomes

$$Q(\mathbf{y}) = \mathbf{y}^T E^T A E \mathbf{y} = \mathbf{y}^T \Lambda \mathbf{y} \tag{B-14}$$

Alternately,

$$Q(\mathbf{y}) = \lambda_1 y_1^2 + \lambda_2 y_2^2 + \cdots + \lambda_n y_n^2 \tag{B-15}$$

The matrix $A$ is said to be *positive definite* (denoted $A > 0$) if $Q = \mathbf{x}^T A \mathbf{x} \geq 0$ for all $\mathbf{x}$ and $Q = 0$ only for $\mathbf{x} = \mathbf{0}$. Removing the latter requirement, $A$ is *non-negative definite* (or positive semidefinite) if $Q = \mathbf{x}^T A \mathbf{x} > 0$ for all $x$. Reversing the inequality, one can similarly define *negative definite* and *non-positive definite* (negative semidefinite).

**Remarks:**
- The symmetric matrix $A$ is positive definite (nonnegative definite) if and only if its eigenvalues are all strictly positive (non-negative).
- A matrix is positive definite if and only if all of its principal minor determinants are positive.
- Elementary row operations may be used to triangularize a matrix and thereby determine if the matrix is positive definite.

### EXAMPLE B-2
We wish to determine if $A$ (below) is positive definite:

$$A = \begin{bmatrix} 16 & -2 & 8 \\ -2 & 10 & 2 \\ 8 & 2 & 16 \end{bmatrix}$$

***SOLUTIONS:*** (1) Solving $\det(A - \lambda I) = 0$ we find that the eigenvalues of $A$ are 2, 4, and 8. These are all positive, so tht $A > 0$.
(2) Principal Minor Determinants

$$16 > 0, \quad \begin{vmatrix} 16 & -2 \\ -2 & 10 \end{vmatrix} = 156 > 0$$

$$\det A = 1728 > 0$$

These are all positive, therefore $A > 0$. ∎

## B-4

## SOME USEFUL RESULTS WITH DETERMINANTS

Consider first the two matrices

$$C = I + AB, \quad D = I + BA \tag{B-16}$$

where $C$ is $n \times n$ and $D$ is $m \times m$ dimension. It follows from Eq. (B-8) that there is a one-to-one correspondence between eigenvalues of $C$ and those of $AB$. Thus, if $\lambda$ is an eigenvalue of $AB$, then $(1 + \lambda)$ is an eigenvalue of $C$. Similarly, for $D$ and $BA$. Note also that the eigenvectors are the same.

If we assume that $n > m$, then a nonzero eigenvalue $\lambda$ of $BA$ satisfies

$$BA\mathbf{x} = \lambda\mathbf{x} \tag{B-17}$$

for some corresponding (nonzero) eigenvector $\mathbf{x}$. Premultiplying by $A$

$$AB(A\mathbf{x}) = \lambda(A\mathbf{x}) \tag{B-18}$$

which shows that $\lambda$ is automatically an eigenvalue of $AB$ (with corresponding eigenvector $A\mathbf{x}$). Consequently, the $m$ eigenvalues of $BA$ are also eigenvalues of $AB$, and vice versa, so that the remaining $(n - m)$ eigenvalues of $AB$ must be zero.

Applying this result to $C$ and $D$ of Eq. (B-16), the $m$ eigenvalues of $D$ are also eigenvalues of $C$, and the remaining eigenvalues of $C$ are unity. Therefore, the product of the eigenvalues of $C$ equals the product of the eigenvalues of $D$; or, in other words, the determinants are equal:

$$\det (I + AB) = \det (I + BA) \tag{B-19}$$

***Partitioned Matrices.*** Using the Laplace expansion of a determinant, it is readily shown that

$$\det (AB) = (\det A)(\det B) \tag{B-20}$$

$$\det (A) = \det (A^T) \tag{B-21}$$

$$\det \begin{bmatrix} A & 0 \\ B & C \end{bmatrix} = \det (A) \det (C) \tag{B-22}$$

The fact that partitioned matrices obey the same rules as ordinary matrices with respect to multiplication and addition permits us to generate some interesting expressions for inverse matrices. Suppose $B$ is $A^{-1}$, then (with compatible partitions)

$$\begin{bmatrix} A_1 & A_2 \\ A_3 & A_4 \end{bmatrix} \begin{bmatrix} B_1 & B_2 \\ B_3 & B_4 \end{bmatrix} = \begin{bmatrix} I & 0 \\ 0 & I \end{bmatrix} \tag{B-23}$$

Thus,

$$A_1 B_1 + A_2 B_3 = I \tag{B-24}$$

and

$$A_3 B_1 + A_4 B_3 = 0$$

are the $(1, 1)$ and $(2, 1)$ terms of the product. Solving for $B_1$ and $B_3$,

$$B_1 = (A_1 - A_2 A_4^{-1} A_3)^{-1} \tag{B-25}$$

and

$$B_3 = -A_4^{-1} A_3 (A_1 - A_2 A_4^{-1} A_3)^{-1} \tag{B-26}$$

Similarly, the remaining equations permit solving for $B_2$ and $B_4$:

$$B_2 = -A_1^{-1}A_2(A_4 - A_3A_1^{-1}A_2)^{-1} \qquad \text{(B-27)}$$

and

$$B_4 = (A_4 - A_3A_1^{-1}A_2)^{-1} \qquad \text{(B-28)}$$

completing $B = A^{-1}$.

Many matrix identities can be developed by repeating the above process with a reversed product order, $BA = I$, and equating the two expressions for $B$ (since $A^{-1}$ is unique for any nonsingular matrix $A$). In particular, the *matrix inversion lemma* is

$$(A^{-1} + C^TBH)^{-1} = A - AC^T(CAC^T + B^{-1})^{-1}CA \qquad \text{(B-29)}$$

A final result can be realized using the fact that

$$\det \begin{bmatrix} I & 0 \\ M & I \end{bmatrix} = 1 \qquad \text{(B-30)}$$

for any matrix $M$. Therefore,

$$\det \begin{bmatrix} A & B \\ C & D \end{bmatrix} = \det \begin{bmatrix} I & 0 \\ -CA^{-1} & I \end{bmatrix}\begin{bmatrix} A & B \\ C & D \end{bmatrix} \qquad \text{(B-31)}$$

assuming that $A$ is nonsingular. Multiplying out,

$$\det \begin{bmatrix} A & B \\ C & D \end{bmatrix} = \det \begin{bmatrix} A & B \\ 0 & D - CA^{-1}B \end{bmatrix}$$

$$\det \begin{bmatrix} A & B \\ C & D \end{bmatrix} = \det(A)\det(D - CA^{-1}B) \qquad \text{(B-32)}$$

**B-5**

## MATRIX DIFFERENTIATION

If a scalar-valued function $q$ of an $n$-vector $\mathbf{x}$ is smooth enough for its first partial derivatives to exist, one may define the *gradient* of $q$ with respect to $\mathbf{x}$ as

$$\frac{\partial q}{\partial \mathbf{x}}(\mathbf{x}) = \left[\frac{\partial q}{\partial x_1}, \frac{\partial q}{\partial x_2}, \cdots, \frac{\partial q}{\partial x_n}\right]^T \qquad \text{(B-33)}$$

Note that the derivative of a scalar with respect to a vector is a vector.

### EXAMPLE B-3 (Gradient of a Quadratic Form)
Consider

$$Q(\mathbf{x}) = \mathbf{x}^TA\mathbf{x}$$

Thus, by the product rule of differentiation

$$\frac{\partial}{\partial \mathbf{x}} (\mathbf{x}^T A \mathbf{x}) = \frac{\partial}{\partial \mathbf{x}} (\mathbf{x}^T \mathbf{y}) + \frac{\partial}{\partial \mathbf{x}} (\mathbf{z}^T \mathbf{x}) \qquad \text{(B-34)}$$

where $\mathbf{y} = A\mathbf{x}$ and $\mathbf{z} = A^T \mathbf{x}$ are taken as constants. Transposing the scalar $(\mathbf{z}^T \mathbf{x})$ gives us

$$\frac{\partial Q}{\partial \mathbf{x}} = \frac{\partial}{\partial \mathbf{x}} (\mathbf{x}^T \mathbf{y} + \mathbf{x}^T \mathbf{z}) \qquad \text{(B-35)}$$

and applying Eq. (B-33),

$$\frac{\partial Q}{\partial \mathbf{x}} = \mathbf{y} + \mathbf{z} = A\mathbf{x} + A^T \mathbf{x} = 2A\mathbf{x} \qquad \text{(B-36)}$$

In a similar manner the derivative of a vector with respect to a vector is defined as follows. If $\mathbf{f}$ is a smooth $(m \times 1)$ vector-valued function of the $(n \times 1)$ vector $\mathbf{x}$, then

$$\frac{\partial \mathbf{f}}{\partial \mathbf{x}} = \begin{bmatrix} \partial f_1/\partial x_1 & \partial f_1/\partial x_2 & \cdots & \partial f_1/\partial x_n \\ \partial f_2/\partial x_1 & \partial f_2/\partial x_2 & \cdots & \\ & & \cdots & \\ \partial f_m/\partial x_1 & & \cdots & \partial f_m/\partial x_n \end{bmatrix} \qquad \text{(B-37)}$$

is an $(m \times n)$ matrix. ∎

## EXAMPLE B-4

The second derivative of $Q(\mathbf{x})$ from Example B-3 with respect to $\mathbf{x}$ is

$$\frac{\partial^2 Q}{\partial \mathbf{x}^2} = \frac{\partial}{\partial \mathbf{x}} (2A\mathbf{x}) = 2A \qquad \text{(B-38)}$$

Some additional matrix identities will be proved using a tensor, or elemental notation. For instance, the result of Eq. (B-36) can be proved as follows:

$$\frac{\partial}{\partial \mathbf{x}} (\mathbf{x}^T A \mathbf{x}) = \frac{\partial}{\partial x_i} (x_j a_{jk} x_k)$$

$$= \delta_{ij} a_{jk} x_k + x_j a_{jk} \delta_{ik}$$

$$= a_{ik} x_k + x_j a_{ji}$$

$$= a_{ik} x_k + a_{ji} x_j$$

$$= A\mathbf{x} + A^T \mathbf{x}$$

Any repeated subscript implies a summation and the $\delta_{mn}$ is the Kronecker delta (1 for $m = n$, 0 otherwise.) The trace of a matrix is the sum of its diagonal elements. Thus, the trace of the product $AB^T$ would be represented as

$$\text{tr } AB^T = \delta_{ik} a_{ij} b_{kj}$$

and

$$\frac{\partial(\text{tr }AB^T)}{\partial B} = \frac{\partial}{\partial b_{mn}}(\delta_{ik}a_{ij}b_{kj})$$

$$= \delta_{ik}a_{ij}\delta_{mk}\delta_{nj} = a_{mn}$$

$$\frac{\partial(\text{tr }AB^T)}{\partial B} = A \qquad (\text{B-39})$$

Consider the following with $B$ a symmetric matrix:

$$\frac{\partial}{\partial A}(\text{tr }ABA^T) = \frac{\partial}{\partial a_{mn}}(\delta_{ip}a_{ij}b_{jk}a_{pk})$$

$$= (\delta_{ip}a_{ij})(b_{jk}\delta_{mp}\delta_{nk}) + (\delta_{ip}\delta_{mi}\delta_{nj})(b_{jk}a_{pk})$$

$$= a_{mj}b_{jn} + b_{nk}a_{mk} = a_{mj}b_{jn} + a_{mk}b_{kn}$$

$$= 2a_{mj}b_{jn} = 2AB$$

$$\frac{\partial(\text{tr }ABA^T)}{\partial A} = 2AB \qquad (\text{B-40})$$

Similarly,

$$\frac{\partial \text{ tr }(AB)}{\partial A} = B^T \qquad (\text{B-41})$$

The reader should be able to develop a proof for this last relation. ∎

## B-6

## THE CAYLEY-HAMILTON THEOREM

We know from Section B-2 that a matrix $A$ with distinct eigenvalues is similar to a diagonal matrix. Recall Eq. (B-9)

$$\Lambda = \text{diag. }\{\lambda_1, \lambda_2, \ldots, \lambda_n\} = E^{-1} A E \qquad (\text{B-42})$$

where $\{\lambda_i\}$, $i = 1, 2, \ldots, n$ are the (assumed distinct) eigenvalues of the $n \times n$ matrix $A$, and $E$ is the modal matrix of $A$ whose columns are the eigenvectors corresponding to the eigenvalues in $\Lambda$.

Note that an integer power of $\Lambda$ takes the form

$$\Lambda^m = (E^{-1} A E)_1(E^{-1} A E)_2 \ldots (E^{-1} A E)_m = E^{-1} A^m E \qquad (\text{B-43})$$

It follows that for a polynomial $p(\lambda)$, the corresponding matrix polynomial

$$p(A) = E\, p(\Lambda)\, E^{-1} \qquad (\text{B-44})$$

And since $\Lambda$ is diagonal,

$$p(\Lambda) = \text{diag.} \{p(\lambda_1), p(\lambda_2), \ldots, p(\lambda_n)\} \tag{B-45}$$

For the particular polynomial which is the characteristic polynomial of $A$, we have that

$$p_{\text{char}}(A) = E \, p_{\text{char}}(\Lambda) \, E^{-1} = 0 \tag{B-46}$$

since $p_{\text{char}}(\lambda_1) = 0$ for $i = 1, 2, \ldots, n$ by definition of the eigenvalues. This result may be summarized in the statement that "the matrix $A$ satisfies its own characteristic equation."

**Cayley-Hamilton Theorem:** If $p(\lambda) = \det[\lambda I - A]$ is the characteristic polynomial of the (square) matrix $A$, then $p(A)$ is the zero matrix.

Our development assumed distinct eigenvalues for $A$, but it can be shown that the Cayley-Hamilton Theorem is valid for any square matrix.

# Discrete-Time Random Signals

Random variables and random signals are used to model the natural randomness and inaccuracies that occur in physical systems. For example, any measurement will have errors due to its internal processing; this is an inescapable phenomenon. In addition, modeling with random variables may be used to cover an undue amount of complexity. For instance, a particular design parameter may vary naturally from one unit to another; and to model the variational effects over the collection of units, a random parameter may be used that exhibits a statistical variation similar to that measured from the devices.

## C-1

### RANDOM VARIABLES

A random variable can be thought of as, not a single physical quantity, but a (possibly large) collection of related quantities such as a box of resistors instead of a single resistor. Whereas a single resistor has a specific value that can be measured with some precision, the collection of resistors must be described by aggregating or grouping the effects of the individual elements to avoid bewildering numerical complexity. As an example, the random variable $R$, representing this collection of resistors, may be determined to have certain statistical averages. To encompass all the information that may be obtained by measurements, we will assume a distribution of random variable values similar to a bar chart with very small quantizations. This distribution will be indexed to the random variable and essentially used to define the random variable.

### The Probability Density Function.

For a given random variable $X$, there is a non-negative function $f_X(x)$ that is called the (*probability*) *density function* (pdf) for $X$. Density functions are useful theoretical models of the actual distribution of the associated random variables. As such they all have the following properties.

If $f_X(x)$ is the density function for the random variable $X$, then

$$f_X(x) \geq 0 \quad \text{for all } x \qquad \text{(C-1)}$$

and

$$\int_{-\infty}^{\infty} f_X(x) \, dx = 1 \qquad \text{(C-2)}$$

The usefulness of a pdf is in formulating probabilities that the random variable takes on specific values. Formally,

$$Pr\{x_1 < X \leq x_2\} = \int_{x_1^+}^{x_2^+} f_X(x) \, dx \qquad \text{(C-3)}$$

where, by including or excluding the end points, we allow for possible Dirac delta (impulse) functions as part of $f_X$. Some examples will help to explain.

### EXAMPLE C-1 (A Binary Distribution)

A binary variable has two states such as a coin toss experiment or the state of a flip-flop. In such a case the variable can take on only two distinct values. For this example we will take these values to be 0 and 1. Thus,

$$f_X(x) = p\delta(x) + (1 - p)\delta(x - 1) \qquad \text{(C-4)}$$

where $p$ is the probability that $X$ takes on the value $x = 0$ and $(1 - p)$ is the probability that $X$ takes on the value $x = 1$. Note that properties (C-1) and (C-2) are satisfied. The graph of this distribution is shown in Fig. C-1a. ∎

### EXAMPLE C-2 (A Uniform Distribution)

If the value of a random variable $X$ is equally likely to occur in an interval $a \leq x \leq b$, the random variable is said to be *uniformly* distributed on $[a, b]$. For such a variable,

$$f_X(x) = \begin{cases} \dfrac{1}{b - a}, & a \leq x \leq b \\ 0, & \text{other } x \end{cases} \qquad \text{(C-5)}$$

This pdf is presented in Fig. C-1b. ∎

## EXAMPLE C-3 (A Gaussian Distribution)

Clearly there are infinitely many distributions that could be defined, but there is one distribution that occurs with great frequency in nature—the Gaussian distribution. The primary reason for this is that it is a limiting distribution representing the accumulated effect of many contributing factors; for instance, the distribution of height for a large population of men is approximately Gaussian. The density function for a *Gaussian* random variable, $X$ is

$$f_X(x) = (2\pi\sigma^2)^{-1/2} \exp \{-(x - m)^2/2\sigma^2\} \tag{C-6}$$

where $m$ and $\sigma$ are two parameters that define the particular distribution out of the class of Gaussian distributions. Another name given for this distribution is a *normal* distribution and a common notation for the function of Eq. (C-6) is

$$X \sim N[m,\sigma^2] \tag{C-7}$$

which is read: $X$ is a normal random variable with mean $m$ and variance $\sigma^2$. The pdf of Eq. (C-6) is sketched in Fig. C-1c. ◼

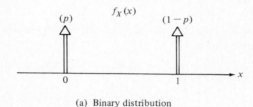

(a) Binary distribution

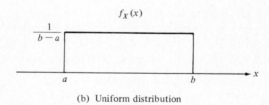

(b) Uniform distribution

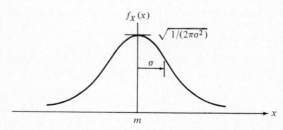

(c) Gaussian (Normal, $N(m, \sigma^2)$) distribution

**FIGURE C-1. Example probability density functions for some common distributions.**

## EXPECTED VALUES

The process of taking statistical averages of a random variable is well known. For instance, if $X$ is a particular random variable, the *average* of $X$ is defined as

$$\bar{x} = \frac{1}{N} \sum_{i=1}^{N} x_i \tag{C-8}$$

where $x_i$ are samples of $X$ and $N$ is taken to be a large value. The corresponding theoretical value is called the *expected value* (or the *mean*) of $X$, denoted $E[X]$, and defined in terms of the pdf of $X$ as

$$E[X] = \int_{-\infty}^{\infty} x f_X(x) \, dx \tag{C-9}$$

The expected value is interpreted as the "true average" of $X$, which is only approximated by Eq. (C-8) for any $N$. The reader may verify that the mean values of the distributions of Examples C-1, C-2, and C-3 are as listed below.

$$E[X] = (1 - p), \quad (a + b)/2, \qquad m \tag{C-10}$$
$$\text{(Binary)} \quad \text{(Uniform)} \quad \text{(Gaussian)}$$

Another useful "average" of a probability distribution is the *variance,* or dispersion about the mean:

$$\text{Var } [X] = E[X - E(X)]^2 = E[X^2] - (E[X])^2 \tag{C-11}$$

In terms of the pdf,

$$\text{Var } [X] = \int_{-\infty}^{\infty} [x - E(X)]^2 f_X(x) \, dx \tag{C-12}$$

For our three example distributions,

$$\text{Var } [X] = p(1 - p), \quad (b - a)^2/12, \qquad \sigma^2 \tag{C-13}$$
$$\text{(Binary)} \quad \text{(Uniform)} \quad \text{(Gaussian)}$$

## RANDOM SIGNALS

Perhaps the most common random effect with which control engineers are concerned is the effect of random signals such as the "noise" of signal measurement. A random signal may be thought of as a time-varying random variable. The fact that time is a parameter means that the "random variable's" distribution may be changing with time and, more importantly, the distributions may be related from one time instant to another.

The simplest discrete-time random signal is a sequence of "uncorrelated" variables with identical distributions. "Uncorrelated" is taken to mean that each variable in the sequence is statistically unrelated to any other. More formally, if $X$ and $Y$ are two random variables, they are said to be *uncorrelated* if

$$E[XY] = E[X]E[Y] \tag{C-14}$$

Note that if either $X$ or $Y$ has a zero mean, Eq. (C-14) simplifies to $E[XY] = 0$. A discrete-time signal is uncorrelated (also called *white noise*) if each pair of its sequence values are uncorrelated as in Eq. (C-14).

## C-4

## SYSTEM RESPONSE TO RANDOM SIGNALS

Let us characterize a general discrete-time linear system by the linear operator $L$. Thus if $x(k)$ is an input sequence, the response sequence $y(k)$ is given by

$$y(k) = L[x(k)] \tag{C-15}$$

In addition, we define the *autocorrelation* function for a (scalar) discrete-time random signal $x(k)$ to be

$$R_x(k_1, k_2) = E[x^*(k_1)x(k_2)] \tag{C-16}$$

where $*$ represents complex conjugate if $x$ is complex valued. Knowing the mean and autocorrelation function of a random input sequence, we now show how to calculate the mean and autocorrelation of the response sequence.

***Output Mean.*** Since the expected-value operator $E$ is also a linear operation,

$$E[y(k)] = EL[x(k)] \tag{C-17}$$

A fundamental theorem in statistical analysis permits the interchange of linear operations in Eq. (C-17), thereby obtaining

$$E[y(k)] = LE[x(k)] \tag{C-18}$$

that is, the output mean is simply the response of the system to the (deterministic) input mean.

***Output Autocorrelation.*** A similar approach may be taken to calculate the output autocorrelation function from Eq. (C-16):

$$R_y(k_1, k_2) = E[y^*(k_1)y(k_2)]$$

$$R_y(k_1, k_2) = EL_{k1}[x^*(k_1)]L_{k2}[x(k_2)]$$

where the linear operator operates "partially" with respect to its subscript (as in partial differentiation). Interchanging the order of operations,

$$R_y(k_1, k_2) = L_{k1} \circ L_{k2}E[x^*(k_1)x(k_2)]$$
$$R_y(k_1, k_2) = L_{k1} \circ L_{k2}[R_x(k_1, k_2)]$$

(C-19)

Equation (C-19) indicates that the linear operation must be applied *twice* to the autocorrelation of the input to get the autocorrelation of the output.

**Stationarity.**  We will concern ourselves only with modeling *stationary* signals (or processes), one whose statistical description does not change with time. Fortunately, stationary signals offer some simplification in that

- The mean of a stationary process is constant.
- The autocorrelation function depends only on the difference of the arguments $(k_2 - k_1)$; See Eq. (C-16).

**Spectral Density.**  The power present in a random signal may be represented as a function of radian frequency $\omega$ through the *power spectral density function $S_x(e^{j\omega T})$* of a stationary signal, $x(kT)$, where

$$S_x(z) = Z\{R_x(k)\}$$

(C-20)

that is, the (double-sided) $z$-transform of the autocorrelation function of $x(k)$ [which is a function of $k = k_2 - k_1$ in Eq. (C-16) for a stationary signal].

If the linear system with random input signal $x(k)$ has a pulse transfer function $H(z)$, then the output spectral density is

$$S_y(z) = H(z)H(z^{-1})S_x(z)$$

(C-21)

**Proof:**  From first principles (Section 1-5) the response sequence is

$$y(k) = \sum_{n=0}^{\infty} h(n)x(k - n)$$

(C-22)

The autocorrelation sequence for $y$ is then

$$R_y(p - q) = E[y^*(q)y(p)]$$

(C-23)

Expanding

$$R_y(p - q) = E\left[\sum_{m=0}^{\infty} h^*(m)x^*(q - m) \sum_{n=0}^{\infty} h(n)x(p - n)\right]$$

(C-24)

Taking the expected value operation of the $x$ factors,

$$R_y(p - q) = \sum_{m=0}^{\infty} h^*(m) \sum_{n=0}^{\infty} h(n)E[x^*(q - m)x(p - n)]$$

(C-25)

Recognizing the autocorrelation function of $x$ on the right side,

$$R_x(p - q + m - n) = E[x^*(q - m)x(p - n)]$$

(C-26)

Introducing $r = p - q$ and taking $z$-transforms,

$$\sum_{r=0}^{\infty} R_y(r)z^{-r} = \sum_{r=0}^{\infty} \sum_{m=0}^{\infty} h^*(m) \sum_{n=0}^{\infty} h(n)R_x(r + m - n)z^{-r} \quad \text{(C-27)}$$

With the final change of variables $v = r + m - n$, we have

$$S_y(z) = \sum_{m=0}^{\infty} h^*(m)z^m \sum_{n=0}^{\infty} h(n)z^{-n} \sum_{v=0}^{\infty} R_x(v)z^{-v} \quad \text{(C-28)}$$

which may be written as Eq. (C-21), thereby completing the proof.

A useful special case is that when $S_x(z) = 1$ [for $x(k)$ a white noise sequence with zero mean and unit variance], the variance of the output sequence is given by $R_y(0)$, which may be calculated either directly by inversion of Eq. (C-21) or by the expression

$$R_y(0) = \frac{1}{2\pi j} \oint_C H(z)H(z^{-1})z^{-1} \, dz \quad \text{(C-29)}$$

where $C$ is the unit circle.

# Basic Language Programs

## PROGRAM 1

### STATE VARIABLE MODEL

This program generates the solution of a linear discrete-time state model by recursion.

**Model**

$$\mathbf{x}(k + 1) = A\mathbf{x}(k) + B\mathbf{u}(k), \quad \mathbf{x}(0) = \mathbf{x}_0$$

$$\mathbf{y}(k) = C\mathbf{x}(k) + D\mathbf{u}(k)$$

The program requires entering the order of the system, the number of inputs, the number of outputs, the constant matrices $A$, $B$, $C$ and $D$ individually by rows, the initial state $\mathbf{x}_0$, and an analytic expression for each component of $\mathbf{u}(k)$, the number of recursion steps and the number of recursions per printout.

The $M$ components ($M \leq 9$) of the input vector may be any defined (or intrinsic) function available in BASIC. If no user supplied input functions are defined, the program defaults to a unit-step input for the first component with all other inputs zero.

To enter a function of $k$ for the $i$th component of $u$, the user must enter a defining function on line number 5$i$00. Any component not specified will revert to the default assignment. For example if

$$\mathbf{u}(k) = \begin{bmatrix} 0.8^k \\ \cos 2k \end{bmatrix}, \quad (M = 2),$$

then before running the program the user would enter

```
5100 DEF FNU1(X) = 0.8^X
5200 DEF FNU2(X) = COS(2*X)
```

The program output is a listing of the system matrices, initial state and input and output vectors at each printout step beginning with $k = 0$.

```
100    OPTION BASE 1
110    INPUT "order of the system = ",N
120    INPUT "number of inputs = ",M
130    INPUT "number of outputs = ",P
140    INPUT "number of time steps = ",NT
150    INPUT "number of steps per printout = ",P1
160    DIM A(N,N), B(N,M), C(P,N), D(P,M)
170    DIM X(N), Y(P), U(M), W(N)
180    FOR I=1 TO N
190    FOR J=1 TO N
200    PRINT "a(";I;",";J;") = ";
210    INPUT A(I,J)
220    NEXT J
230    NEXT I
240    FOR I=1 TO N
250    FOR J=1 TO M
260    PRINT "b(";I;",";J;") = ";
270    INPUT B(I,J)
280    NEXT J
290    NEXT I
300    FOR I=1 TO P
310    FOR J=1 TO N
320    PRINT "c(";I;",";J;") = ";
330    INPUT C(I,J)
340    NEXT J
350    NEXT I
360    FOR I=1 TO P
370    FOR J=1 TO M
380    PRINT "d(";I;",";J;") = ";
390    INPUT D(I,J)
400    NEXT J
410    NEXT I
```

```
420    PRINT "INPUT THE INITIAL STATE"
430    FOR I=1 TO N
440    PRINT "x(";I;") = ";
450    INPUT X(I)
460    NEXT I
470    PRINT "ARE THERE USER DEFINED INPUT FUNCTIONS?"
480    PRINT "ANSWER 1 FOR YES AND 0 FOR NO."
485    INPUT "answer = ",F
490    FOR I=1 TO M
500    U(I) = 0
510    NEXT I
520    LET U(1) = 1
530    LPRINT
540    LPRINT "THE A MATRIX IS"
550    FOR I=1 TO N
560    FOR J=1 TO N
570    LPRINT A(I,J),
580    NEXT J
590    LPRINT
600    NEXT I
610    LPRINT
620    LPRINT "THE B MATRIX IS"
630    FOR I=1 TO N
640    FOR J=1 TO M
650    LPRINT B(I,J),
660    NEXT J
670    LPRINT
680    NEXT I
690    LPRINT
700    LPRINT "THE C MATRIX IS"
710    FOR I=1 TO P
720    FOR J=1 TO N
730    LPRINT C(I,J),
740    NEXT J
750    LPRINT
760    NEXT I
770    LPRINT
780    LPRINT "THE D MATRIX IS"
790    FOR I=1 TO P
800    FOR J=1 TO M
810    LPRINT D(I,J),
820    NEXT J
830    LPRINT
840    NEXT I
850    LPRINT
860    LPRINT "THE INITIAL STATE IS"
```

```
870    FOR I=1 TO N
880    LPRINT X(I),
890    NEXT I
900    LPRINT
910    FOR K=0 TO NT
920    IF F = 0 THEN 960
930    FOR Q=1 TO M
940    ON Q GOSUB 5100, 5200, 5300, 5400, 5500, 5600,
       5700, 5800, 5900
950    NEXT Q
960    FOR I=1 TO P
970    Y(I) = 0
980    FOR L=1 TO M
990    Y(I) = Y(I) + D(I,L)*U(L)
1000   NEXT L
1010   NEXT I
1020   FOR I=1 TO P
1030   FOR L=1 TO N
1040   Y(I) = Y(I) + C(I,L)*X(L)
1050   NEXT L
1060   NEXT I
1070   IF K=0 GOTO 1100
1080   IF (INT(K/P1)*P1) = K THEN 1100
1090   GOTO 1230
1100   LPRINT
1110   LPRINT
1120   LPRINT "TIME STEP = ",K
1130   LPRINT "THE INPUT VECTOR IS"
1140   FOR I=1 TO M
1150   LPRINT U(I),
1160   NEXT I
1170   LPRINT
1180   LPRINT "THE OUTPUT VECTOR IS"
1190   FOR I=1 TO P
1200   LPRINT Y(I),
1210   NEXT I
1220   LPRINT
1230   FOR I=1 TO N
1240   W(I) = 0
1250   FOR L=1 TO N
1260   W(I) = W(I) + A(I,L)*X(L)
1270   NEXT L
1280   NEXT I
1290   FOR I=1 TO N
1300   X(I) = 0
1310   FOR L=1 TO M
```

```
1320  X(I) = X(I) + W(I) + B(I,L)*U(L)
1330  NEXT L
1340  NEXT I
1350  NEXT K
1360  END
5000  REM THIS SECTION IS FOR USER DEFINED INPUT
      FUNCTIONS
5100  GOTO 5990
5110  U(1) = FNU1(K)
5120  RETURN
5200  GOTO 5990
5210  U(2) = FNU2(K)
5220  RETURN
5300  GOTO 5990
5310  U(3) = FNU3(K)
5320  RETURN
5400  GOTO 5990
5410  U(4) = FNU4(K)
5420  RETURN
5500  GOTO 5990
5510  U(5) = FNU5(K)
5520  RETURN
5600  GOTO 5990
5610  U(6) = FNU6(K)
5620  RETURN
5700  GOTO 5990
5710  U(7) = FNU7(K)
5720  RETURN
5800  GOTO 5990
5810  U(8) = FNU8(K)
5820  RETURN
5900  GOTO 5990
5910  U(9) = FNU9(K)
5990  RETURN
6000  END
```

### EXAMPLE D-1

For this example we first establish the input functions. To do this, we write two statements as follows:

```
5100    DEF FNU1(X) = .5^X          and
5200    DEF FNU2(X) = 1
```

The program is told to do 4 time steps with a printout every 2 steps.

### SOLUTION:

```
THE   A   MATRIX IS
 0                 1              0
 0                 0              1
 .25             -.3             1

THE   B   MATRIX IS
 1                 0
 0                 1
 1                 1

THE   C   MATRIX IS
 1                 0              1
 0                -1              1

THE   D   MATRIX IS
 0                 0
 0                 1

THE INITIAL STATE IS
 1                 1              1

TIME STEP =     0
THE INPUT VECTOR IS
 1                 1
THE OUTPUT VECTOR IS
 2                 1

TIME STEP =     2
THE INPUT VECTOR IS
 .25               1
THE OUTPUT VECTOR IS
 15.5             1.2

TIME STEP =     4
THE INPUT VECTOR IS
 .0625             1
THE OUTPUT VECTOR IS
 71.215          -1.350
```

# PROGRAM 2

## RESOLVENT MATRIX

This program calculates the resolvent matrix, $(zI - A)^{-1}$, for a given constant $(N \times N)$ $A$ matrix using Leverrier's Algorithm. The resolvent matrix is closely related to the transfer matrix for a state model with the corresponding $A$ matrix as well as the transition matrix for the system.

The program requires entering the dimension $N$ of the $A$ matrix and the elements of $A$ by rows.

The output is a printout of matrix $A$, the coefficients of the characteristic polynomial, $p(z)$, as well as the (matrix) coefficients $\{R_i$ for $i = 1, 2, \ldots, N\}$ for the expression:

$$(zI - A)^{-1} = \frac{1}{p(z)} [R_1 z^{N-1} + R_2 z^{N-2} + \cdots + R_N]$$

Eq. (3-99) may be used as a check on the numerical accuracy.

```
100  OPTION BASE 1
110  INPUT "order of the system (dimension of A) = ",N
120  DIM A(N,N), R(N,N), W(N,N)
130  FOR I=1 TO N
140  FOR J=1 TO N
150  R(I,J) = 0
160  NEXT J
170  NEXT I
180  FOR I=1 TO N
190  R(I,I) = R(I,I) + 1
200  NEXT I
210  FOR I=1 TO N
220  FOR J=1 TO N
230  PRINT "a(";I;",";J;") = ";
240  INPUT A(I,J)
250  NEXT J
260  NEXT I
270  LET C = 0
280  FOR L=1 TO N
290  C = C + A(L,L)
300  NEXT L
310  FOR I=1 TO N
320  FOR J=1 TO N
330  W(I,J) = 0
340  FOR L=1 TO N
350  W(I,J) = W(I,J) + R(I,L)*A(L,J)
360  NEXT L
370  NEXT J
380  NEXT I
390  LPRINT
400  LPRINT "MATRIX A IS"
410  FOR I=1 TO N
420  FOR J=1 TO N
430  LPRINT A(I,J),
```

```
440  NEXT J
450  LPRINT
460  NEXT I
470  LPRINT
480  FOR K=1 TO N
490  LPRINT
500  LPRINT "COEFFICIENT ALPHA(";K;") = ";C
510  LPRINT
520  LPRINT "MATRIX R(";K;") IS"
530  FOR I=1 TO N
540  FOR J=1 TO N
550  LPRINT R(I,J),
560  NEXT J
570  LPRINT
580  NEXT I
590  FOR I=1 TO N
600  W(I,I) = W(I,I) - C
610  NEXT I
620  FOR I=1 TO N
630  FOR J=1 TO N
640  R(I,J) = W(I,J)
650  NEXT J
660  NEXT I
670  FOR I=1 TO N
680  FOR J=1 TO N
690  W(I,J) = 0
700  FOR L=1 TO N
710  W(I,J) = W(I,J) + R(I,L)*A(L,J)
720  NEXT L
730  NEXT J
740  NEXT I
750  LET C=0
760  FOR L=1 TO N
770  C = C + W(L,L)
780  NEXT L
790  C = C/(K+1)
800  NEXT K
810  END
```

## EXAMPLE D-2

```
MATRIX  A  IS
 1              0
 0              2


COEFFICIENT ALPHA( 1 ) =   3
```

```
MATRIX  R( 1 )  IS
  1                 0
  0                 1

COEFFICIENT ALPHA( 2 ) = -2

MATRIX  R( 2 )  IS
 -2                 0
  0                -1
```

■

# PROGRAM 3

## STATE TRANSITION MATRIX

This program calculates the state transition matrix for a given constant $(N \times N)$ matrix $A$ and a time interval $T$.

**Model:**

$$\dot{\mathbf{x}}(t) = A\mathbf{x}(t), \quad \mathbf{x}(0) = \mathbf{x}_0$$

$$\mathbf{x}(T) = \Phi(T)\, \mathbf{x}_0 \text{ where}$$

$$\Phi(T) = e^{AT} \text{ is the state transition matrix.}$$

The program requires entering the order of the system (dimension of $A$)$N$, the matrix $A$ by rows, the time interval $T$ and the number of terms in the series expansion $M$. (Typically, $M$ is taken as 15 for a first run. Additional terms are required, $M = 16, 17, \ldots$, until no further change takes place in the state transition matrix. For more detail see the discussion in Section 4-1).

The output is a print-out of $A$, $T$ and $e^{AT}$.

```
100   OPTION BASE 1
110   INPUT "order of the system (dimension of A) = ",N
120   INPUT "sample time interval = ",T
130   INPUT "number of terms to be used in series
      expansion = ",M
140   DIM A(N,N), P(N,N), W(N,N)
150   FOR I=1 TO N
160   FOR J=1 TO N
170   PRINT "a(";I;",";J;") = ";
180   INPUT A(I,J)
190   NEXT J
200   NEXT I
210   FOR I=1 TO N
```

```
220  FOR J=1 TO N
230  P(I,J) = 0
240  NEXT J
250  NEXT I
260  FOR I=1 TO N
270  P(I,I) = P(I,I) + 1
280  NEXT I
290  LET K=M
300  FOR I=1 TO N
310  FOR J=1 TO N
320  W(I,J) = 0
330  FOR L=1 TO N
340  W(I,J) = W(I,J) + A(I,L)*P(L,J)*T
350  NEXT L
360  NEXT J
370  NEXT I
380  FOR I=1 TO N
390  FOR J=1 TO N
400  W(I,J) = W(I,J)/K
410  NEXT J
420  NEXT I
430  FOR I = 1 TO N
440  W(I,I) = W(I,I) + 1
450  NEXT I
460  FOR I=1 TO N
470  FOR J=1 TO N
480  P(I,J) = W(I,J)
490  NEXT J
500  NEXT I
510  K = K-1
520  IF K <> 0 THEN 300
530  LPRINT
540  LPRINT "THE SAMPLE TIME INTERVAL IS";T
550  LPRINT
560  LPRINT "MATRIX A IS"
570  FOR I=1 TO N
580  FOR J=1 TO N
590  LPRINT A(I,J),
600  NEXT J
610  LPRINT
620  NEXT I
630  LPRINT
640  LPRINT "THE STATE TRANSITION MATRIX IS"
650  FOR I=1 TO N
660  FOR J=1 TO N
670  LPRINT P(I,J),
```

```
680  NEXT J
690  LPRINT
700  NEXT I
710  END
```

### EXAMPLE D-3
This example uses 5 terms in the series.

```
THE SAMPLE TIME INTERVAL IS .5

MATRIX   A   IS
-1                0
 0               -2

THE STATE TRANSITION MATRIX IS
 .6065104        0
 0               .3666667
```

This example uses 15 terms in the series.

```
THE SAMPLE TIME INTERVAL IS .5

MATRIX   A   IS
-1                0
 0               -2

THE STATE TRANSITION MATRIX IS
 .6065307        0
 0               .3678795
```

## PROGRAM 4

### FREQUENCY RESPONSE

This program calculates the magnitude and phase of a discrete-time transfer function as a function of $\omega T$ on the interval 0 to $\pi$.

**Model:**

$$F(z) = \frac{a_M z^M + a_{M-1} z^{M-1} + \cdots + a_1 z + a_0}{b_N z^N + b_{N-1} z^{N-1} + \cdots + b_1 z + b_0}$$

The program requires entering the order of the numerator polynomial $M$, the order of the denominator polynomial $N$, the numerator coefficients $a_0$ to $a_M$, the denominator coefficients $b_0$ to $b_N$ and the number of values to be calculated over the interval 0 to $\pi$.

The output is a listing of the magnitude $|F(\omega T)|$ and phase (in degrees) $\underline{/F(\omega T)}$ versus $\omega T$.

```
100    INPUT "order of numerator polynomial = ",M
110    INPUT "order of denominator polynomial = ",N
120    DIM A(M),B(N)
130    PRINT "ENTER NUMERATOR COEFFICIENTS STARTING
       WITH CONSTANT TERM"
140    FOR I=1 TO M+1
150    PRINT "numerator coefficient a(";I-1;") = ";
160    INPUT A(I-1)
170    NEXT I
180    PRINT "ENTER DENOMINATOR COEFFICIENTS STARTING
       WITH CONSTANT TERM"
190    FOR I=1 TO N+1
200    PRINT "denominator coefficient b(";I-1;") = ";
210    INPUT B(I-1)
220    NEXT I
230    PRINT "SPECIFY HOW MANY POINTS TO BE CALCULATED
       IN THE RANGE 0 TO PI"
240    INPUT "number of frequency points = ",NPOINT
250    DIM F(NPOINT+1),PH(NPOINT+1)
260    PI = 3.141593
270    DEL=PI/NPOINT
280    WT=0
290    FOR I=1 TO NPOINT+1
300    RNUM=0
310    GNUM=0
320    RDEN=0
330    GDEN=0
340    FOR J=1 TO M+1
350    WKT=WT*(J-1)
360    C=COS(WKT)
370    S=SIN(WKT)
380    RNUM=RNUM+A(J-1)*C
390    GNUM=GNUM+A(J-1)*S
400    NEXT J
410    FOR J=1 TO N+1
420    WKT = WT*(J-1)
430    C=COS(WKT)
440    S=SIN(WKT)
450    RDEN=RDEN+B(J-1)*C
```

```
460    GDEN=GDEN+B(J-1)*S
470    NEXT J
480    MAGNUM=SQR(RNUM^2 +GNUM^2)
490    ARG1=ABS(RNUM)
500    ARG2=ABS(GNUM)
510    REAL=RNUM
520    IMAG=GNUM
530    GOSUB 670
540    PHASEN=ANGLE
550    MAGDEN=SQR(RDEN^2 + GDEN^2)
560    ARG1=ABS(RDEN)
570    ARG2=ABS(GDEN)
580    REAL=RDEN
590    IMAG=GDEN
600    GOSUB 670
610    PHASED=ANGLE
620    F(I)=MAGNUM/MAGDEN
630    PH(I)=(PHASEN-PHASED)*57.29578
640    WT=WT+DEL
650    NEXT I
660    GOTO 940
670    REM SUBROUTINE TO COMPUTE ARC TANGENT IN THE
       CORRECT QUADRANT
680    IF (SGN(REAL)=1 AND SGN(IMAG)=1 ) THEN 780
690    IF (SGN(REAL)=1 AND SGN(IMAG)=-1) THEN 800
700    IF (SGN(REAL)=-1 AND SGN(IMAG)=-1) THEN 820
710    IF (SGN(REAL)=-1 AND SGN(IMAG)=1) THEN 840
720    IF (SGN(REAL)=0 AND SGN(IMAG)=1) THEN 860
730    IF (SGN(REAL)=0 AND SGN(IMAG)=-1) THEN 880
740    IF (SGN(REAL)=1 AND SGN(IMAG)=0) THEN 900
750    IF (SGN(REAL)=-1 AND SGN(IMAG)=0) THEN 920
760    PRINT "ERROR IN ARCTANGENT COMPUTATION, BOTH
       ARGUMENTS ZERO"
770    GOTO 1000
780    ANGLE=ATN(ARG2/ARG1)
790    GOTO 930
800    ANGLE= - ATN(ARG2/ARG1)
810    GOTO 930
820    ANGLE=PI + ATN(ARG2/ARG1)
830    GOTO 930
840    ANGLE=PI - ATN(ARG2/ARG1)
850    GOTO 930
860    ANGLE=PI/2
870    GOTO 930
880    ANGLE=-PI/2
890    GOTO 930
```

```
900    ANGLE=0
910    GOTO 930
920    ANGLE=PI
930    RETURN
940    LPRINT "wT",":F(wT):",",/_F(wT)"
950    LPRINT "_____"
960    FOR I=1 TO NPOINT+1
970    WT=(I-1)*DEL
980    LPRINT WT,F(I),PH(I)
990    NEXT I
1000   END
```

## EXAMPLE D-4

We wish to determine the frequency response of

$$F(z) = \frac{z^2}{z^2 - 0.7z + 0.1}$$

at increments of $\omega T = 22.5°(\pi/8)$.

### *SOLUTION:*

| wT | :F(wT): | /_F(wT) |
|---|---|---|
| 0 | 2.5 | 0 |
| .3926991 | 2.138594 | -24.93955 |
| .7853983 | 1.559731 | -38.02857 |
| 1.178097 | 1.140164 | -41.05172 |
| 1.570797 | .8770579 | -37.87499 |
| 1.963496 | .7164987 | -30.933 |
| 2.356195 | .6214964 | -21.70172 |
| 2.748894 | .5712704 | -11.15278 |
| 3.141593 | .5555556 | 9.334668E-06 |

## PROGRAM 5

### POLE PLACEMENT

This program assumes a controllable single-input system and calculates the constant feedback gains of Eq. (8-84) for which the closed-loop system will have specified pole locations, $\{p_i, i = 1, 2, \ldots, N\}$.

**Model**

$$F = -[0 \ \ldots \ 0 \ 0 \ 1][B \ \ AB \ \ \ldots \ \ A^{N-1}B]^{-1}P_{CL}(A)$$

$$P_{CL}(z) = \sum_{i=1}^{N} (z - p_i) = z^N - \alpha_N z^{N-1} - \cdots - \alpha_2 z - \alpha_1$$

The program requires entering the order of the system $N$, the constant $(N \times N)$ matrix $A$, the constant $(N \times 1)$ matrix $B$ and the coefficients of the desired polynomial $P_{CL}(z)$ in the form shown above.

The output is a listing of the $A$, $B$ and $F$ matrices along with the desired characteristic polynomial coefficients.

```
1000    OPTION BASE 1
1010    INPUT "order of the system = ",N
1020    DIM A(N,N), B(N), P(N,N), C(N,N), W(N)
1030    DIM X(N), W3(N,N), W4(N,N), AUG(N,N+1), BI(N)
1040    FOR I=1 TO N
1050    FOR J=1 TO N
1060    PRINT "a(";I;",";J;") = ";
1070    INPUT A(I,J)
1080    NEXT J
1090    NEXT I
1100    FOR I=1 TO N
1110    PRINT "b(";I;") = ";
1120    INPUT B(I)
1130    NEXT I
1140    FOR I=1 TO N
1150    PRINT "coefficient alpha(";I;") = ";
1160    INPUT ALPHA(I)
1170    NEXT I
1180    FOR I=1 TO N
1190    W(I) = B(I)
1200    NEXT I
1210    FOR J=1 TO N
1220    FOR I=1 TO N
1230    C(I,J) = W(I)
1240    NEXT I
1250    FOR I=1 TO N
1260    W(I) = 0
1270    FOR L=1 TO N
1280    W(I) = W(I) + A(I,L)*C(L,J)
1290    NEXT L
1300    NEXT I
1310    NEXT J
1320    LET M=N
1330    FOR I=1 TO M
1340    FOR J=1 TO M
1350    W3(I,J) = C(I,J)
1360    NEXT J
1370    NEXT I
1380    GOSUB 5000 : REM C INVERSE = W4
1390    FOR I=1 TO N
```

```
1400  FOR J=1 TO N
1410  P(I,J) = 0
1420  C(I,J) = 0
1430  W3(I,J) = 0
1440  NEXT J
1450  NEXT I
1460  FOR I=1 TO N
1470  C(I,I) = C(I,I) + 1
1480  W3(I,I)=W3(I,I) + 1
1490  NEXT I
1500  FOR K=1 TO N
1510  FOR I=1 TO N
1520  FOR J=1 TO N
1530  P(I,J) = P(I,J) - ALPHA(K)*C(I,J)
1540  NEXT J
1550  NEXT I
1560  FOR I=1 TO N
1570  FOR J=1 TO N
1580  C(I,J) = 0
1590  FOR L=1 TO N
1600  C(I,J) = C(I,J) + A(I,L)*W3(L,J)
1610  NEXT L
1620  NEXT J
1630  NEXT I
1640  FOR I=1 TO N
1650  FOR J=1 TO N
1660  W3(I,J) = C(I,J)
1670  NEXT J
1680  NEXT I
1690  NEXT K
1700  FOR I=1 TO N
1710  FOR J=1 TO N
1720  P(I,J) = P(I,J) + C(I,J)
1730  NEXT J
1740  NEXT I
1750  FOR J=1 TO N
1760  F(J) = 0
1770  FOR L=1 TO N
1780  F(J) = F(J) - W4(N,L)*P(L,J)
1790  NEXT L
1800  NEXT J
1810  LPRINT
1820  LPRINT "THE A MATRIX IS"
1830  FOR I=1 TO N
1840  FOR J=1 TO N
1850  LPRINT A(I,J),
```

```
1860  NEXT J
1870  LPRINT
1880  NEXT I
1890  LPRINT
1900  LPRINT "THE B (TRANSPOSE) MATRIX IS"
1910  FOR I=1 TO N
1920  LPRINT B(I),
1930  NEXT I
1940  LPRINT
1950  LPRINT
1960  LPRINT "THE SVF MATRIX F IS"
1970  FOR I=1 TO N
1980  LPRINT F(I),
1990  NEXT I
2000  LPRINT
2010  LPRINT
2020  LPRINT "THE (CLOSED LOOP) CHARACTERISTIC
      POLYNOMIAL COEFFICIENTS ARE"
2030  FOR I=1 TO N
2040  LPRINT ALPHA(I),
2050  NEXT I
2060  LPRINT
2070  END
5000  REM SUBROUTINE MAT.INV
5010  FOR K=1 TO M
5020  FOR L=1 TO M
5030  AUG(K,L)=W3(K,L)
5040  NEXT L
5050  NEXT K
5060  FOR I=1 TO M
5070  FOR J=1 TO M
5080  IF J=I THEN 5110
5090  BI(J)=0
5100  GOTO 5120
5110  BI(J)=1
5120  NEXT J
5130  FOR N1=1 TO M
5140  AUG(N1,M+1)=BI(N1)
5150  NEXT N1
5160  FOR K=1 TO M-1
5170  PIVOT =0
5180  FOR L=K TO M
5190  TEMP=ABS(AUG(L,K))
5200  IF PIVOT >= TEMP THEN 5230
5210  PIVOT =TEMP
5220  IPIVOT=L
```

```
5230   NEXT L
5240   IF IPIVOT =0 THEN 5540
5250   IF IPIVOT =K THEN 5310
5260   FOR K1=K TO M+1
5270   TEMP=AUG(K,K1)
5280   AUG(K,K1)=AUG(IPIVOT,K1)
5290   AUG(IPIVOT,K1)=TEMP
5300   NEXT K1
5310   IP1=K+1
5320   FOR K2=IP1 TO M
5330   Q1=-AUG(K2,K)/AUG(K,K)
5340   AUG(K2,K)=0
5350   FOR K3=IP1 TO M+1
5360   AUG(K2,K3)=Q1*AUG(K,K3)+AUG(K2,K3)
5370   NEXT K3
5380   NEXT K2
5390   NEXT K
5400   IF AUG(M,M)=0 THEN 5540
5410   X(M)=AUG(M,M+1)/AUG(M,M)
5420   FOR K4=1 TO M-1
5430   Q1=0
5440   FOR K5=1 TO K4
5450   Q1=Q1+AUG(M-K4,M+1-K5)*X(M+1-K5)
5460   NEXT K5
5470   X(M-K4)=(AUG(M-K4,M+1)-Q1)/AUG(M-K4,M-K4)
5480   NEXT K4
5490   FOR K6=1 TO M
5500   W4(K6,I)=X(K6)
5510   NEXT K6
5520   NEXT I
5530   RETURN
5540   LPRINT"ERROR IN GAUSS SUBROUTINE"
5550   END
```

### EXAMPLE D-5

We want the matrix $F$ such that the closed-loop poles are both at $z = 0.5$.

### *SOLUTION:*

```
THE  A  MATRIX IS
 1            0
 0            2


THE  B  (TRANSPOSE) MATRIX IS
 1            1
```

```
THE SVF MATRIX  F  IS
 .25            -2.25

THE (CLOSED LOOP) CHARACTERISTIC POLYNOMIAL
COEFFICIENTS ARE
-.25             1
```

■

## PROGRAM 6

### OPTIMAL FEEDBACK GAINS

This program calculates the optimal state variable feedback gains for the discrete-time linear regulator.

**Model**

$$\mathbf{x}(k + 1) = A\mathbf{x}(k) + B\mathbf{u}(k)$$

$$J = \frac{1}{2} \mathbf{x}^T(N)H\mathbf{x}(N) + \frac{1}{2} \sum_{k=0}^{N-1} [\mathbf{x}^T(k)Q\mathbf{x}(k) + \mathbf{u}^T(k)R\mathbf{u}(k)]$$

The program requires entering the order of the system, the number of inputs, the number of stages (time periods) $N$, the constant matrices $A$, $B$, $H$, $Q$ and $R$ individually by rows and the number of stages per printout, $P$.

The output is a printout of the matrices $A$, $B$, $Q$, $R$ and $H$ as well as the calculated feedback gains $F(N - K)$ and the running cost matrix $D(N - K)$ at the print intervals $N - KP$ for $K = 1, 2, 3, \ldots, N/P$.

```
100    OPTION BASE 1
110    INPUT "order of the system = ",N
120    INPUT "number of inputs = ",M
130    INPUT "number of time periods = ",NT
140    DIM A(N,N),B(N,M),R(M,M),H(N,N),Q(N,N),PK(N,N)
150    DIM F(M,N),W1(M,N),W2(M,M),W3(M,M),W4(M,M),
       W6(N,N)
160    DIM W7(N,N),W8(N,N),X(M),AUG(M,M+1),BI(M),
       PK1(N,N)
170    INPUT "number of stages per printout = ", P
180    FOR I=1 TO N
190    FOR J=1 TO N
200    PRINT "a(";I;",";J;") = ";
210    INPUT A(I,J)
220    NEXT J
230    NEXT I
240    FOR I=1 TO N
250    FOR J=1 TO M
```

```
260     PRINT "b(";I;",";J;") = ";
270     INPUT B(I,J)
280     NEXT J
290     NEXT I
300     FOR I=1 TO N
310     FOR J=1 TO N
320     PRINT "h(";I;",";J;") = ";
330     INPUT H(I,J)
340     NEXT J
350     NEXT I
360     FOR I=1 TO N
370     FOR J=1 TO N
380     PRINT "q(";I;",";J;") = ";
390     INPUT Q(I,J)
400     NEXT J
410     NEXT I
420     FOR I=1 TO M
430     FOR J=1 TO M
440     PRINT "r(";I;",";J;") = ";
450     INPUT R(I,J)
460     NEXT J
470     NEXT I
480     LPRINT
490     LPRINT "THE A MATRIX IS"
500     FOR I=1 TO N
510     FOR J=1 TO N
520     LPRINT A(I,J),
530     NEXT J
540     LPRINT
550     NEXT I
560     LPRINT
570     LPRINT "THE B MATRIX IS"
580     FOR I=1 TO N
590     FOR J=1 TO M
600     LPRINT B(I,J),
610     NEXT J
620     LPRINT
630     NEXT I
640     LPRINT
650     LPRINT "THE Q MATRIX IS"
660     FOR I=1 TO N
670     FOR J=1 TO N
680     LPRINT Q(I,J),
690     NEXT J
700     LPRINT
710     NEXT I
```

```
720    LPRINT
730    LPRINT "THE R MATRIX IS"
740    FOR I=1 TO M
750    FOR J=1 TO M
760    LPRINT R(I,J),
770    NEXT J
780    LPRINT
790    NEXT I
800    FOR I=1 TO N
810    FOR J=1 TO N
820    PK(I,J)=H(I,J)
830    NEXT J
840    NEXT I
850    LPRINT
860    LPRINT "THE H MATRIX IS"
870    FOR I=1 TO N
880    FOR J=1 TO N
890    LPRINT H(I,J),
900    NEXT J
910    LPRINT
920    NEXT I
930    FOR J3=1 TO NT
940    FOR I=1 TO M
950    FOR J=1 TO N
960    W1(I,J)=0
970    FOR K=1 TO N
980    W1(I,J)=W1(I,J) + B(K,I)*PK(K,J)
990    NEXT K
1000   NEXT J
1010   NEXT I
1020   FOR I=1 TO M
1030   FOR J=1 TO M
1040   W2(I,J)=0
1050   FOR K=1 TO N
1060   W2(I,J)=W2(I,J) + W1(I,K)*B(K,J)
1070   NEXT K
1080   NEXT J
1090   NEXT I
1100   FOR I=1 TO M
1110   FOR J=1 TO M
1120   W3(I,J)=W2(I,J)+ R(I,J)
1130   NEXT J
1140   NEXT I
1150   GOSUB 5000 :REM RETURNS WITH INVERSE OF W3
1160   FOR I=1 TO M
1170   FOR J=1 TO M
```

```
1180  W4(I,J)=-W4(I,J)
1190  NEXT J
1200  NEXT I
1210  FOR I=1 TO M
1220  FOR J=1 TO N
1230  W5(I,J)= 0
1240  FOR K=1 TO M
1250  W5(I,J)=W5(I,J) +W4(I,K)*W1(K,J)
1260  NEXT K
1270  NEXT J
1280  NEXT I
1290  FOR I=1 TO M
1300  FOR J=1 TO N
1310  F(I,J)=0
1320  FOR K=1 TO N
1330  F(I,J)=F(I,J) +W5(I,K)*A(K,J)
1340  NEXT K
1350  NEXT J
1360  NEXT I
1370  FOR I=1 TO N
1380  FOR J=1 TO N
1390  W6(I,J)=0
1400  FOR K=1 TO M
1410  W6(I,J)=W6(I,J) +B(I,K)*F(K,J)
1420  NEXT K
1430  NEXT J
1440  NEXT I
1450  FOR I=1 TO N
1460  FOR J=1 TO N
1470  W6(I,J)=W6(I,J) + A(I,J)
1480  NEXT J
1490  NEXT I
1500  FOR I=1 TO N
1510  FOR J=1 TO N
1520  W7(I,J)= W6(J,I)
1530  NEXT J
1540  NEXT I
1550  FOR I=1 TO N
1560  FOR J=1 TO N
1570  W8(I,J)=0
1580  FOR K=1 TO N
1590  W8(I,J)=W8(I,J) + W7(I,K)*PK(K,J)
1600  NEXT K
1610  NEXT J
1620  NEXT I
1630  FOR I=1 TO N
```

```
1640  FOR J=1 TO N
1650  PK1(I,J)=0
1660  K=1 TO N
1670  PK1(I,J)=PK1(I,J) + W8(I,K)*W6(K,J)
1680  NEXT K
1690  NEXT J
1700  NEXT I
1710  FOR I=1 TO M
1720  FOR J=1 TO N
1730  W5(I,J)=0
1740  FOR K=1 TO M
1750  W5(I,J) = W5(I,J) + R(I,K)*F(K,J)
1760  NEXT K
1770  NEXT J
1780  NEXT I
1790  FOR I=1 TO N
1800  FOR J=1 TO N
1810  W6(I,J)=0
1820  FOR K=1 TO M
1830  W6(I,J)=W6(I,J) + F(K,I)*W5(K,J)
1840  NEXT K
1850  NEXT J
1860  NEXT I
1870  FOR I=1 TO N
1880  FOR J=1 TO N
1890  PK(I,J)=PK1(I,J)+W6(I,J)+Q(I,J)
1900  NEXT J
1910  NEXT I
1920  IF (INT(J3/P)*P) = J3 THEN 1940
1930  GOTO 2120
1940  LPRINT
1950  LPRINT
1960  LPRINT "TIME INTERVAL =",NT-J3
1970  LPRINT "THE FEEDBACK MATRIX F IS"
1980  FOR I=1 TO M
1990  FOR J=1 TO N
2000  LPRINT F(I,J),
2010  NEXT J
2020  LPRINT
2030  NEXT I
2040  LPRINT
2050  LPRINT "THE RUNNING COST MATRIX D IS"
2060  FOR I=1 TO N
2070  FOR J=1 TO N
2080  LPRINT PK(I,J),
2090  NEXT J
```

```
2100  LPRINT
2110  NEXT I
2120  NEXT J3
2130  END
5000  FOR K=1 TO M
5010  FOR L=1 TO M
5020  AUG(K,L)=W3(K,L)
5030  NEXT L
5040  NEXT K
5050  FOR I=1 TO M
5060  FOR J=1 TO M
5070  IF J=I THEN 5100
5080  BI(J)=0
5090  GOTO 5110
5100  BI(J)=1
5110  NEXT J
5120  FOR N1=1 TO M
5130  AUG(N1,M+1)=BI(N1)
5140  NEXT N1
5150  FOR K=1 TO M-1
5160  PIVOT =0
5170  FOR L=K TO M
5180  TEMP=ABS(AUG(L,K))
5190  IF PIVOT >= TEMP THEN 5220
5200  PIVOT =TEMP
5210  IPIVOT=L
5220  NEXT L
5230  IF IPIVOT =0 THEN 5530
5240  IF IPIVOT = K THEN 5300
5250  FOR K1=K TO M+1
5260  TEMP=AUG(K,K1)
5270  AUG(K,K1)=AUG(IPIVOT,K1)
5280  AUG(IPIVOT,K1)=TEMP
5290  NEXT K1
5300  IP1=K+1
5310  FOR K2=IP1 TO M
5320  Q1=-AUG(K2,K)/AUG(K,K)
5330  AUG(K2,K)=0
5340  FOR K3=IP1 TO M+1
5350  AUG(K2,K3)=Q1*AUG(K,K3)+AUG(K2,K3)
5360  NEXT K3
5370  NEXT K2
5380  NEXT K
5390  IF AUG(M,M)=0 THEN 5530
5400  X(M)=AUG(M,M+1)/AUG(M,M)
5410  FOR K4=1 TO M-1
```

```
5420  Q1=0
5430  FOR K5=1 TO K4
5440  Q1=Q1+AUG(M-K4,M+1-K5)*X(M+1-K5)
5450  NEXT K5
5460  X(M-K4)=(AUG(M-K4,M+1)-Q1)/AUG(M-K4,M-K4)
5470  NEXT K4
5480  FOR K6=1 TO M
5490  W4(K6,I)=X(K6)
5500  NEXT K6
5510  NEXT I
5520  RETURN
5530  LPRINT"ERROR IN GAUSS SUBROUTINE"
5540  END
```

## EXAMPLE D-6

This is a three ($N = 3$) stage problem with matrices as printed below along with the calculated F and D matrices.

```
THE   A   MATRIX IS
 1                 0
 1                 1


THE   B   MATRIX IS
 1
 0


THE   Q   MATRIX IS
 1                 0
 0                 4


THE   R   MATRIX IS
 1


THE   H   MATRIX IS
 0                 0
 0                 0


TIME INTERVAL =                 2
THE FEEDBACK MATRIX  F  IS
 0                 0


THE RUNNING COST MATRIX  D  IS
 1                 0
 0                 4
```

```
TIME INTERVAL =                    1
THE FEEDBACK MATRIX   F   IS
-.5              0


THE RUNNING COST MATRIX   D   IS
 5.5            4
 4              8


TIME INTERVAL =                    0
THE FEEDBACK MATRIX   F   IS
-1.461538      -.6153846


THE RUNNING COST MATRIX   D   IS
 8.615385       6.153847
 6.153847       9.538462
```

# Answers to Selected Problems

## CHAPTER 1

**1-1**    **(a)** L,    **(b)** NL,    **(c)** L,    **(d)** NL

**1-2**    **(a)** S,    **(b)** S,    **(c)** NS,    **(d)** NS

**1-3**    $z(x, t)$ = line voltage, $c = (LC)^{-1/2}$,
$L$ = Inductance per unit length
$C$ = Capacitance per unit length

**1-4**    $v(k) = e(0) + e(1) + \cdots + e(k) \approx \int_0^{kT} e(t)\, dt$

**1-5**    $X(j\omega) = 0$ for $|\omega| > 10$; $(T^{-1})_{\min} = 10/\pi$   $s^{-1}$

**1-6**    $x(k) = \{3.00, 1.82, -0.86, -2.41, -1.24, 1.69, 3.81\}$

**1-8**    $200\pi$ rad/$s$

**1-12**    **(a)** 6.136%,    **(b)** 6.168%

**1-13**    $c(k) = 2 - (0.5)^k, \quad k \geq 0$

**1-14**    **(a)** $z(k) = \{1, 1, 1, 2, -5, 1, 1, -2\}$

**1-15**  $332.14

**1-16**  $\{4, 7, 9, 10, 10, \ldots\}$

**1-18**  **(a)** $y(k) = [1 - 4(-2)^k]/3, \quad k \geq 0$

## CHAPTER 2

**2-2**  $X(z) = \dfrac{z^2 + z + 1}{z^2(z - 1)}$

**2-3**  **(a)** $c(k) = \{1, 3, 4, 4, 4, \ldots\}$
**(b)** $c(k) = \{0, 1, 1, 2, 1, 2, 1, 2, \ldots\}$

**2-4**  **(a)** $y(k) = \{0, -2, 4, -8, 16, \ldots\} = (-2)^k, \quad k \geq 0.$

**2-5**  $h(k) = \dfrac{1}{2} \delta(k) + \dfrac{17}{2} (-2)^k - 4(-1)^k, \quad k \geq 0.$

**2-6**  **(a)** $\Delta^2 = (1 - 2z^{-1} + z^{-2})$

**2-7**  $D(z) = \dfrac{3.8z^2 - 2.6z - 0.2}{z^2 - 0.4z - 0.6}$

**2-8**  $h(k) = [1, 0, 2, -1, -2\}$

**2-9**  $\dfrac{z(6z - 2)}{(z - 2)(z + 1)}$

**2-10**  **(a)** IIF,  **(b)** FIR,  **(c)** FIR.

**2-11**  $(1 - 2z^{-10} + z^{-20})$

**2-13**  $D(z) = z/(z - 0.5)$

**2-14**  $y(k) = 6 - 3(0.5)^k, \quad k \geq 0$

**2-15**  **(a)** $\dfrac{1}{d(z)}, \quad d(z) = z^3 + 2.9z^2 + 1.2z + 0.4$
**(b)** $(z + 0.4)/d(z)$

**2-17**  **(a)** $y_a(k) = 6 - 5\delta(k) + k^2 - 8k, \quad k \geq 0$

**2-18**  $x(k) = (2 + 3k)(-1)^k, \quad k \geq 0$

**2-19**  $4^7$ dollars

**2-22**  **(a)** $G_a(z) = \dfrac{T^2(z + 1)}{2(z - 1)^2}$

**2-25**  **(a)** $-0.5 < \alpha < 0.25$

**2-29**  No (positive) $T$ for a stable system.

## CHAPTER 3

**3-1**  **(a)** $x_1(k) = 0\ 3\ -2\ 5\ -4\ 7\ -6\ 9 \ldots$
$x_2(k) = 2\ 0\quad 2\ 0\quad 2\ 0\quad 2\ 0 \ldots$

**3-3** (a) $\dot{T}_1 = -4T_1 + 3T_2 + 0.5p + T_0$

$\dot{T}_2 = T_1 - 2T_2 + T_0$

(b) 400 W

**3-4** (a) $\dot{x}_1 = x_2$

$\dot{x}_2 = -4x_1 + f$

(b) $x_1(k + 1) = (\cos 2T)x_1(k) + 0.5 (\sin 2T)x_2(k) + \dfrac{1}{4}(1 - \cos 2T)f(k)$

$x_2(k + 1) = -2 (\sin 2T)x_1(k) + (\cos 2T)x_2(k) + \dfrac{1}{2}(\sin 2T)f(k)$

**3-6** (a) $x_1(t) = t^2/2, \quad t \geq 0$

$x_2(t) = t, \quad t \geq 0$

**3-8** (a) $\hat{G}_a(z) = \dfrac{T^2(z + 1)}{2(z - 1)^2}$

**3-9** Open-loop plant: $\mathbf{x}(k + 1) = A\mathbf{x}(k) + Bu(k)$

$y(k) = [1 \quad 0]\mathbf{x}(k)$

$A = \begin{bmatrix} (2e^{-T} - e^{-2T}) & (e^{-T} - e^{-2T}) \\ (-2e^{-T} + 2e^{-2T}) & (-e^{-T} + 2e^{-2T}) \end{bmatrix}$,

$B = \begin{bmatrix} (\frac{1}{2} - e^{-T} + \frac{1}{2}e^{-2T}) \\ (e^{-T} - e^{-2T}) \end{bmatrix}$

**3-11** (a) $\dot{x}_1(t) = x_2(t)$    (b) $x_1(k + 1) = x_1(k) + Tx_2(k) + \dfrac{T^2}{2}u(k)$

$\dot{x}_2(t) = u(t)$            $x_2(k + 1) = x_2(k) + Tu(k)$

$y(t) = x_1(t)$           $y(k) = x_1(k)$

(c) $y(k) = \{0, T^2/2, 2T^2, 9T^2/2, \ldots\}$

**3-12** $h(k) = \dfrac{T^2}{2}\left[\delta(k) - 1 + \dfrac{2}{T}k\right], \quad k \geq 0$

**3-16** (a) $x_1(k + 1) = x_2(k)$

$x_2(k + 1) = -4x_1(k) - x_2(k) + u_1(k)$

$x_3(k + 1) = x_4(k)$

$x_4(k + 1) = 2x_4(k) + 2u_2(k)$

$y_1(k) = 5x_1(k) + 2x_4(k) + 2u_2(k)$

$y_2(k) = x_3(k) + u_1(k)$

**3-17** (a) Jordan form:

$\dot{\mathbf{x}}(t) = \begin{bmatrix} 0 & 0 & 0 \\ 0 & -1 & 0 \\ 0 & 0 & -2 \end{bmatrix} \mathbf{x}(t) + \begin{bmatrix} 1 \\ 1 \\ 1 \end{bmatrix} u(t)$

$y(t) = [1 \quad 2 \quad -3]\,\mathbf{x}(t)$

**(b)** $\mathbf{x}(k + 1) = \begin{bmatrix} 1 & 0 & 0 \\ 0 & e^{-T} & 0 \\ 0 & 0 & e^{-2T} \end{bmatrix} \mathbf{x}(k) + \begin{bmatrix} T \\ (1 - e^{-T}) \\ \frac{1}{2}(1 - e^{-2T}) \end{bmatrix} u(k)$

$y(k) = \begin{bmatrix} 1 & 2 & -3 \end{bmatrix} \mathbf{x}(k)$

**3-20** **(a)** $G(z) = \dfrac{1.2z - 0.95}{z^2 - 2z + 0.9}$

## CHAPTER 4

**4-1**   1 term   1.8 E-1   4 terms $-6.4$ E-5 $= -6.4 \times 10^{-5}$
2 terms $-1.9$ E-2   5 terms   2.6 E-6
3 terms   1.3 E-3   6 terms $-8.6$ E-8

**4-3** **(a)** $\mathbf{x}(k + 1) = \begin{bmatrix} 1 & a \\ 0 & b \end{bmatrix} \mathbf{x}(k) + \begin{bmatrix} c \\ a \end{bmatrix} u(k)$

$a = \dfrac{1}{2}(1 - e^{-2T}), \quad b = e^{-2T}, \quad c = \dfrac{1}{4}(2T - 1 + e^{-2T})$

For $T = 0.1\ s$; $\quad a = 0.0906, \quad b = 0.8187, \quad c = 0.0047$

**4-6** **(a)** $H(z) = \dfrac{3z\,e^{-3}}{(z - e^{-3})^2} = \dfrac{0.1494z}{(z - 0.0498)^2}$

**4-9** **(a)** $16/\pi = 5.0930$

**(b)** $I_0 = 5.0274, \quad I_1 = 5.0274, \quad I_2 = 5.0937$

**4-16** **(a)** $\hat{H}(z) = \dfrac{0.1488(z + 1)^2}{(z - 0.5488)(z - 0.6703)}$

**4-18** **(a)** $\hat{G}_a(z) = \dfrac{0.61(z + 1)}{z + 0.22}$

**4-22** **(c)** $m(k) = \dfrac{1}{3}[10(2)^k + 2(-1)^k - 3], \quad k \geq 0$

**4-25** **(a)** $d(k) = \{0, 1, -1/2, 0, 1/4, \ldots\}$

**4-28** **(a)** $z^2 + (ac + bd - adef)z + abcd = 0$

## CHAPTER 5

**5-1** **(a)** Precise:   0, 0.588, 0.951, 0.951, 0.588, 0, . . .
Quantized:   0, 0.6, 1.0, 1.0, 0.6, 0, . . .

**5-3** **(a)** Sampled output

0, 0, 0.06, 0.16, 0.26, 0.32, 0.32, . . .

The continuous-time output (in this case) is formed by connecting the samples by straight lines.

**5-5**    **(a)** Magnitude at $\omega T = k\pi/32$ for $k = 0, 1, \ldots, 6$

Precise:   0.914, 0.892, 0.833, 0.757, 0.680, 0.609, 0.548

Quantized:   1.000, 0.947, 0.827, 0.701, 0.595, 0.511, 0.445

                    Angle at same frequencies (in degrees)

Precise:   0.0, $-10.2$, $-19.3$, $-26.5$, $-31.9$, $-35.7$, $-38.2$

Quantized:   0.0, $-16.2$, $-29.0$, $-37.6$, $-43.1$, $-46.2$, $-47.9$

**5-6**    **(a)** Open loop $G(z) = \dfrac{0.0906K\,z}{(z - p)(z - 0.8187)}$

      **(b)** $S_K^T = K/(1 + G) = \dfrac{0.2z^2 - 0.3437z + 0.1474}{z^2 - 1.7006z + 0.7368}$

**5-9**    **(b)** Controllable form:

Output variance $= 0.079\ W$

## CHAPTER 6

**6-1**    **(a)** $\sqrt{K}$    **(b)** $1/(2\sqrt{K})$

**6-3**    **(a)** $a = 0.410$,   $b = 0.676$

**6-4**    **(a)** poles: $0.620 \pm j0.269$

zero: 0.429, gain $= 0.380$

**6-8**    $G_a$ and $G_c$

**6-14**    **(a)** Open-loop gain $G(z) = \dfrac{T(z - 0.4)}{z(z - 1)}$

      **(b)** $T = 1.429s$

**6-15**    **(a)** 0.1961

## CHAPTER 7

**7-1**    **(a)** Yes

**7-3**    Depends on model, but for $p = -1, -2,$ or $-3$ the system may not be controllable.

**7-4**    $R_1 = $ span of $[1 \quad 0 \quad 0 \quad 0]^T$

$R_2 = $ span of $[1 \quad 0 \quad 0 \quad 0]^T$ and $[1 \quad 1 \quad 0 \quad 0]^T$

**7-5**    $T = k\pi,\ k = 0, 1, 2, \ldots$

**7-7**    **(a)** $p = -1$

**7-8**    $\hat{p}_1 = -0.8, \hat{p}_2 = 3.7$

**7-9**    $u(0) = a\,c(0)/(1 - e^{aT})$

**7-10**    **(a)** $u(0) = 2x_1(0) + x_2(0)$

$u(1) = 2x_2(0)$

**7-11**    **(a)** $E_u = 13$

**7-14**   (a) $D(z) = \dfrac{236.6z - 167.4}{z + 0.4855}$

**7-15**   $F = [-0.5 \quad -1]$

**7-16**   (a) yes

**7-17**   $F = \dfrac{1}{32} \begin{bmatrix} -4 & 8 & 5 \\ -4 & 8 & 5 \end{bmatrix}$

**7-19**   (a) $\mathbf{x}(k + 1) = \begin{bmatrix} 0 & 1 \\ 1 & 0 \end{bmatrix} \mathbf{x}(k) + \begin{bmatrix} 0 \\ 1 \end{bmatrix} u(k)$

$y(k) = [1 \quad 2] \, \mathbf{x}(k)$

$F = [-1.4225 \quad 1.1974]$

**7-22**   (a) $A = \begin{bmatrix} 0.5 & 6 & 6 \\ 0 & 2 & 2 \\ 0 & 0 & 1 \end{bmatrix}, \quad B = \begin{bmatrix} 30 \\ 10 \\ 5 \end{bmatrix}$

(b) $F = [0.002067, 0.1086, 0.2]$

**7-23**   $G = 0.625$

**7-24**   $G = \begin{bmatrix} 0.169 & 0.508 \\ -0.203 & 0.141 \end{bmatrix}$

**7-25**   $\xi_1(k + 1) = \xi_1(k) - q_1(k)$

$\xi_2(k + 1) = 3\xi_2(k) + q_2(k)$

**7-27**   $\xi(k + 1) = \begin{bmatrix} 1 & 0 & 0 \\ 0 & 2 & 0 \\ 0 & 0 & 0.5 \end{bmatrix} \xi(k) + \begin{bmatrix} 1 \\ 1 \\ 1 \end{bmatrix} u(k)$

$y(k) = [-60 \quad 80 \quad 10] \, \xi(k)$

**7-28**   $[1 \quad -1], \quad [0 \quad 1]$

**7-29**   $F = [-0.05 \quad 0.80 \quad -1.35]$

## CHAPTER 8

**8-1**   (b) $x_2$ is not controllable, $x_1$ is not observable

**8-2**   (a) yes     (b) yes

**8-4**   (a) $\dfrac{z^2 - \alpha z}{z^3 - 1.3z^2 + 0.2z + 0.1}$

**8-6**   $K = [0.058, \, -0.070, \, -12.556]^T$

**8-8**   (b) $T = k\pi, \quad k = 0, 1, 2, \ldots$

**8-9**   Not controllable

**8-13** (a) $w(k + 1) = 0.8w(k) + u(k) - 0.64y(k)$
$\hat{x}_2(k) = w(k) + 0.8y(k)$

**8-15** (a) $F = [-0.25 \quad -1]$

**8-18** (a) From the controllable form,
$K = [-0.379 \quad 0.768 \quad -1.730]^T$

**8-21** $K = \begin{bmatrix} 0 & 0 & 0.5 \\ 0 & 0 & 0.5 \end{bmatrix}^T$

## CHAPTER 9

**9-1** (a) $Q$,    (b) $R$

**9-4** (a) $F(k) = \{-0.615, -0.6, -0.5\}, \quad k = 0, 1, 2.$
(c) $-0.618$

**9-5** (a) $F(k) = \{-0.390, -0.389, -0.386, -0.379, -0.359, -0.310, -0.200,$
$0\}, \quad k = 0, 1, \ldots, 7.$
(c) $-0.390$

**9-6** (a) $-0.270$

**9-7** (a) $F_{ss} = [0.329 \quad 1.221]$

**9-9** (a) $A = \begin{bmatrix} 0.905 & 0.095 \\ 0 & 1 \end{bmatrix}, B = \begin{bmatrix} 0 \\ 1 \end{bmatrix}$

(b) $F_{ss} = [-0.082 \quad -0.839]$

**9-12** $F = \begin{bmatrix} 0 & 0 & -3.766 \\ -2.441 & 3.113 & 0 \end{bmatrix}$

**9-14** (a) $F = \begin{bmatrix} 0.837 & -0.454 \\ -0.799 & 0.763 \end{bmatrix}$

**9-15** (a) $F = [-1.611 \quad 1.156]$
$G = 3.986$

**9-21** (a) $S_y(z) = \dfrac{N_o z}{(z - p)(1 - pz)}$

**9-22** (a) $H(z) = \dfrac{z + b}{z + a}$

(b) $S_y(z) = \dfrac{(z + b)(1 + bz)}{(z + a)(1 + az)}$

$R_y(k) = \dfrac{b}{a} \delta(k) + c[(-a)^k - (-a)^{-k}]$

where $c = \dfrac{(b - a)(1 - ab)}{a(a^2 - 1)}$

**9-23**  $H(z) = \dfrac{z + 1}{z + 0.5}$

**9-24**  (a) $M_y(z) = H(z)\dfrac{z}{z - 1},\ M_y(z) = Z\{m_y(k)\}$

   (b) 12.2

# INDEX

## E

Eigenvalues (*see also* Pole placement), 138, 407
Eigenvector assignment (*see* Pole placement)
Eigenvectors, 287, 407
Equilibrium state, 125, 128
Error constants, 229
Estimator, 313
  -based state feedback, 331
  deterministic design, 313, 316
  optimal (stochastic) design, 367
  reduced-order estimator, 319
Euler's identity, 394
Exponential matrix (*see* State transition matrix)

## F

Feedback control, 10, 224, 273, 280, 325
Feedforward control, 222
Fibonacci numbers, 76
Filtering, 15, 186, 245, 367, 375
  low-pass, 15
Final value theorem
  of Laplace transform, 397
  of $z$-transform, 49
FIR filter, 90
First-order hold, 184, 190
Forward rectangular rule, 156
Frequency domain (*see also* Root-locus design), 13, 152, 356
Frequency folding (*see* Aliasing)
Frequency response, 152
  computer program, 431

## G

Gain formula, 68
Gauss-Markov process, 364
Geometric series, 43, 44
Golden ratio, 77
Gradient, 410
Group property, 103

## H

Hold equivalence, 63, 104
Homogeneous equivalent systems, 166

## I

Ideal low-pass filter, 13
Ideal (impulse) sampling, 16, 41, 60
IIR filter, 90
Impulse response, 22, 61
Input gain, 284, 333
Interest calculation, 5, 23, 30
Interpolation formula, 15
Intersample response (*see also* Simulation), 170, 254
Inverse $z$-transform methods, 51
  inversion (residue) formula, 58
  partial fraction expansion, 55
  power series expansion, 53

## J

Jacobian (*see* Linearization)
Jordan canonical form, 114, 200
Jury stability test, 78, 87

## K

$K_a$, acceleration error constant, 229
$K_p$, position error constant, 229
$K_v$, velocity error constant, 229
Kalman filter, 245, 367
Kalman form for estimator, 315
Kronecker delta, 21

## L

Laplace transform, 43, 393
  table of properties, 397
  table of transform pairs, 397
Lead compensator, 187
Least-squares solution, 268
Leverrier's algorithm, 135, 426

Pulse amplitude modulation, 12
Pulse transfer function, 60
Pulsewidth modulation, 176

## Q

Quadratic form, 407
  derivative of, 411
Quadratic performance index, 347
Quantization, 18, 191
  effects of, 194, 206, 207
  noise, 193
  roundoff, 192
  truncation, 192
Quantizer, 209

## R

Random access memory, 204
Random signals, 417
Random variable, 414
  expected value of, 417
  Gaussian (Normal), 416
  roundoff error, 193
  uniform, 415
Reachability, 109, 264
Read-only memory, 204
Realizations, 199
Real time control, 76, 168, 386
Recurrence formula (*see* Difference equations)
Recursive solution, 107
Region of convergence
  for Laplace transforms, 396
  for *z*-transforms, 44
Registers, 203
Regulation, 270
Regulator (optimal), 351, 356
Residues, 52
  theorem, 58
Resolvent matrix, 106, 426
Rise time, 221
Robust control, 243
Root-locus design, 231, 252, 256
  construction rules, 234, 239, 241
Root-square locus, 356, 373
  optimal state variable feedback, 356
  optimal estimator, 373

Roundoff (*see* Quantization)
Routh (-Hurwitz) criterion, 124

## S

Sample and hold (*see also* Zero-order hold), 20
Sampled-data system, 62, 86, 104
  simulation, 173, 209
Sample period, 21
  selection criteria, 255
Sampler, ideal model, 41
Sampling (*see also* Ideal), 12
  theorem (*see also* Interpolation formula), 403
SCR control, 177
Second-order system, 220
Sensitivity, 194, 243
  parameter, 194, 243
  pole, 244
Separation principle, 324
Set-point control, 359
Settling time, 221
Shift operator, 26
Signal conversion, 16, 19
Signal-flow graphs, 66, 76, 85
  Mason's gain formula, 68
Signal quantization (*see* Quantization)
Signal reconstruction, 15, 402
Similarity transformation, 407
Simpson's rule, 93, 157, 188
Simulation
  of continuous-time systems, 167
  of digital/sampled-data systems, 170, 209
  of discrete-time systems, 168
  of nonlinear elements, 180
  of sampled-data systems, 173
Sinc function, 15
Specifications for design, 222
Spectral density, 419
Stability (*see also* Jury stability test)
  BIBO, 78, 122
  boundary, 73
  Liapunov, 125
Stabilizable system, 286
Star product (*see* Convolution)
State of a system, 97